Transcultural Research – Heidelberg Studies
on Asia and Europe in a Global Context

Series Editors

Madeleine Herren
Axel Michaels
Rudolf G. Wagner

For further volumes:
http://www.springer.com/series/8753

Hans Harder • Barbara Mittler
Editors

Asian Punches

A Transcultural Affair

 Springer

Editors
Hans Harder
Department of Modern South Asian
 Languages and Literatures
South Asia Institute
Heidelberg University
Heidelberg, Germany

Barbara Mittler
Institute of Chinese Studies
Heidelberg University
Heidelberg, Germany

ISSN 2191-656X   ISSN 2191-6578 (electronic)
ISBN 978-3-642-28606-3   ISBN 978-3-642-28607-0 (eBook)
DOI 10.1007/978-3-642-28607-0
Springer Heidelberg New York Dordrecht London

Library of Congress Control Number: 2013939976

© Springer-Verlag Berlin Heidelberg 2013
This work is subject to copyright. All rights are reserved by the Publisher, whether the whole or part of the material is concerned, specifically the rights of translation, reprinting, reuse of illustrations, recitation, broadcasting, reproduction on microfilms or in any other physical way, and transmission or information storage and retrieval, electronic adaptation, computer software, or by similar or dissimilar methodology now known or hereafter developed. Exempted from this legal reservation are brief excerpts in connection with reviews or scholarly analysis or material supplied specifically for the purpose of being entered and executed on a computer system, for exclusive use by the purchaser of the work. Duplication of this publication or parts thereof is permitted only under the provisions of the Copyright Law of the Publisher's location, in its current version, and permission for use must always be obtained from Springer. Permissions for use may be obtained through RightsLink at the Copyright Clearance Center. Violations are liable to prosecution under the respective Copyright Law.
The use of general descriptive names, registered names, trademarks, service marks, etc. in this publication does not imply, even in the absence of a specific statement, that such names are exempt from the relevant protective laws and regulations and therefore free for general use.
While the advice and information in this book are believed to be true and accurate at the date of publication, neither the authors nor the editors nor the publisher can accept any legal responsibility for any errors or omissions that may be made. The publisher makes no warranty, express or implied, with respect to the material contained herein.

Printed on acid-free paper

Springer is part of Springer Science+Business Media (www.springer.com)

We shall always play PUNCH, for we consider it best to be merry and wise— "And laugh at all things, for we wish to know, What, after all, are all things but a show!"—Byron.

"The Moral of Punch," inaugural editorial, Punch, 17 July 1841.

Preface

This book is the outcome of a conference on the transcultural aspects of *Punch* magazine, held in November 2009 at Heidelberg University. The event was convened by a research group called 'Gauging Cultural Asymmetries: Asian Satire and the Search for Identity in the Era of Colonialism and Imperialism', working under the auspices of the Heidelberg Cluster of Excellence 'Asia and Europe in a Global Context: Shifting Asymmetries in Cultural Flows'. *Asian Punches* attempts to bring together for the first time research on late-nineteenth- and early-twentieth-century versions of the *Punch*, and similar satirical journals from various parts of Asia (including Cairo, which is, of course, North Africa, and Istanbul on the border between Asia and Europe). Many satirical periodicals of the time were directly inspired by the British *Punch* magazine and often even adopted the name *Punch*. It is hoped that this overview of Ottoman, Egyptian, South Asian, Chinese and Japanese *Punch* versions and other *Punch*-inspired satirical periodicals will add a new dimension to research on *Punch*, and 'Victorian' satirical journalism generally. We also hope to show the necessity of adopting a transcultural perspective when dealing with such phenomena, as well as making some headway towards providing clues for what such a perspective might entail.

Assembling materials from a number of different Asian languages, this book uses their respective conventions for the transcription of terms, quoted passages or bibliographic references. The transliteration of Ottoman Turkish is based primarily on that found in the Redhouse dictionaries: James W. Redhouse, *A Turkish and English Lexicon*, and *Redhouse Yeni Türkçe-İngilizce Sözlük*.[1] For Arabic, transliteration is restricted to the indication of long vowels, hamza and ʿayn. For the South Asian languages, conventional diacritics are used, with some additions suggested

---

[1] James W. Redhouse, *Redhouse Yeni Türkçe-İngilizce Sözlük* (Istanbul: Redhouse Press, 1986); James W. Redhouse, *A Turkish and English Lexicon* (Istanbul: Çağrı Yayınları, 2001).

by Rahul Peter Das.[2] Chinese is rendered into Latin script in accordance with the *Hanyu Pinyin* system and Japanese is transcribed into *Rōmaji*.

We are grateful, first of all, to the Cluster and its sponsor, the German Research Foundation, for funding this project. We would like to thank all contributors for sharing our enthusiasm for this endeavour by writing and rewriting chapters for this book. Some of them agreed at very short notice to compose additional chapters: Ritu Khanduri, who rewrote an article on Indian versions of *Punch* for us, and Marilyn Booth, who contributed an additional article on *The Cairo Punch*.

Last but not least, we would also like to thank those without whose help it would hardly have been possible to put this book together: Verena Vöckel, who did an excellent job organising the conference; Jessica Fischer for very prompt copy-editing; Emily Mae Graf and Anne Moßner for producing the typescript, the latter especially for coordinating unified transliterations and assembling the images; Judit Árokay for her support with the Japanese titles; Eliane Ettmueller for the transliteration of the Arabic citation in Marilyn Booth's first chapter; Nasir Abbas Nayyar for his help with the transliteration of several Urdu titles, Richard Littler for graphics restoration of the illustrations; and Andrea Hacker for supervising the publication on behalf of the Cluster of Excellence and Springer-Verlag.

Hans Harder
Barbara Mittler

---

[2] See Rahul Peter Das, "Review of Dušan Zbavitel, *Bengali Literature* (Wiesbaden: Harrassowitz, 1976)," *Indo-Iranian Journal 27* (1984): 51–69; 66, n. 2. In the following chapters, there are, however, a few deviations from this system. For example, the vocalic -r- is written as ṛ, the retroflex -r- as ṛ, and -b- as the last part of a Bengali conjunction is written as -v- wherever Sanskrit-derived words are concerned.

Contents

Prologue: Late Nineteenth and Twentieth Century Asian *Punch* Versions
and Related Satirical Journals..................................... 1
Hans Harder

Part I *Punch*, the Template

The Presence of *Punch* in the Nineteenth Century................. 15
Brian Maidment

Part II *Punch* in South Asia

Punch and Indian Cartoons: The Reception of a Transnational
Phenomenon.. 47
Partha Mitter

The Possibility of Satire: Reading Pratap Narain Misra's *Brāhmaṇ*,
1883–1890... 65
Alok Rai

From *Punch* to *Mat'vālā*: Transcultural Lives of a Literary Format... 75
Prabhat Kumar

The *Punch* Tradition in Late Nineteenth Century Bengal:
From Pulcinella to Basantak and Pãcu.............................. 111
Chaiti Basu

Crossing Boundaries: *Punch* and the Marathi Weekly *Hindu Pañca*
(1870–1909)... 151
Swarali Paranjape

Punch in India: Another History of Colonial Politics? 165
Ritu Gairola Khanduri

Part III *Punch* in the Middle East

Insistent Localism in a Satiric World: Shaykh Naggār's 'Reed-Pipe'
in the 1890s Cairene Press. 187
Marilyn Booth

Abū Nazzāra's Journey from Victorious Egypt to Splendorous Paris:
The Making of an Arabic *Punch*. 219
Eliane Ursula Ettmueller

Teodor Kassab's Adaption of the Ottoman Shadow
Theatre *Karagöz*. 245
Elif Elmas

What's in a Name? Branding *Punch* in Cairo, 1908. 271
Marilyn Booth

Part IV *Punch* in East Asia

'Punch Pictures': Localising Punch in Meiji Japan. 307
Peter Duus

'*Punch*'s Heirs' Between the (Battle) Lines: Satirical Journalism in the
Age of the Russo-Japanese War of 1904–1905. 337
Sonja Hotwagner

Participating in Global Affairs: The Chinese Cartoon Monthly *Shanghai
Puck*. 365
I-Wei Wu

'He'll Roast All Subjects That May Need the Roasting': Puck and
Mr Punch in Nineteenth-Century China. 389
Christopher G. Rea

Epilogue: Ten Thousand *Pucks* and *Punches*—Satirical Themes and
Variations Seen Transculturally. 423
Barbara Mittler

Prologue: Late Nineteenth and Twentieth Century Asian *Punch* Versions and Related Satirical Journals

Hans Harder

The *Punch* magazine is in itself quite a landmark in the history of newspaper and magazine publishing. In terms of the duration of its publication, it is certainly one of the top 100 newspapers and magazines worldwide. Apart from some interruptions during its last years, *Punch* was published over a period of more than 160 years (1841–2002).[1] When limiting this list to satirical magazines, *Punch* easily qualifies as the longest-published journal to date. More importantly for the present context, the history of *Punch* is intrinsically connected with that of the British Empire; the Empire, in a way, provided for its distribution beyond Great Britain. In many parts of the world *Punch* was, and probably still is, the most popular 'brand name' for a satirical magazine—its conscious, skilful branding being a major key to *Punch*'s success, as Brian Maidment shows. It was first and foremost the combination of textual and graphic satire that was the characteristic trait of *Punch*, and the visual attraction of its cartoons made *Punch*'s name famous.[2]

This volume deals with the presence of *Punch* in Asia. But the story this book attempts to tell is more than simply an appendix to the story of the London-based *Punch*. Its point of departure is the somewhat striking fact that *Punch* had a second and little-acknowledged life outside Britain, in places as far away from each other as Cairo and Calcutta, Shanghai, Istanbul, and Tokyo. This is not simply because the British magazine was distributed to all those places, resulting in an international reception

---

[1] According to the World Association of Newspapers (WAN): "Oldest Newspapers Still in Circulation," accessed 20 January 2011, http://www.wan-press.org/article2823.html.

[2] For a comprehensive account of *Punch*'s first decade, see Richard D. Altick, *Punch: The Lively Youth of a British Institution 1841–1851* (Columbus: Ohio State University Press, 1997). There is, by the way, a proper history of writing about the development of *Punch*, as evidenced by the late nineteenth century publication by Marion H. Spielmann, *The History of 'Punch'* (London: Cassell & Co. Ltd, 1895).

H. Harder (✉)
Department of Modern South Asian Languages and Literatures, Heidelberg University, Im Neuenheimer Feld 330, Heidelberg 69120, Germany
e-mail: h.harder@uni-heidelberg.de

history. It is because its format and name were adapted for satirical ventures, some in English, but more so in various other languages, in places like Egypt, the Ottoman Empire, British India, China and Japan. And the versions of *Punch* brought out there were more than a few: dozens of satirical journals from various parts of Asia, some of them subjects of this volume, were published under the name of *Punch* or under other names but with a reference to *Punch*, and counting all those that could not be covered here, we would probably arrive at a three-digit number.[3]

How did this wave of *Punch* versions come about? When did they start publishing, and what made them disappear? While questions such as these are covered by individual contributions to this volume and deserve individual treatment, a rough time frame should be delineated here. The first Asian versions of *Punch* began to surface in 1860, but particularly after 1870. The high tide of such journals seems to have been in the last decades of the nineteenth and the first three of the twentieth century. After that, most of these enterprises dwindled, and it appears that the wave came to an end before World War II. The first non-British *Punch* was apparently Armenian, published in Istanbul and was followed by *Punch*-inspired ventures such as the Turkish *Diyogen* in 1870 (see Elif Elmas's chapter, Teodor Kasab's Ottoman Adaptation of the Ottoman Shadow Theatre *Karagöz*, in this volume). Also in the 1870s, a number of English-language publications from South Asia or erstwhile British India, such as the *Gujarati Punch* and *Hindi Punch*, first saw the light of day. These were complemented by satirical magazines in regional South Asian languages, some of them explicitly named *Punch*, while others acknowledged *Punch* as a model or inspiration. The earliest of these seems to be the Marathi-language *Hindu pañca*, which was published from 1870 until 1909 (see Swarali Paranjape in this volume)—a long-lasting presence compared to short-lived satirical magazines in other regional languages of South Asia. In Bengali, for example, two illustrated satirical magazines called *Basantak* and *Har'bolā bhā̃r*, both starting in 1874 and dwindling soon thereafter, spearheaded a whole series of rather short-lived attempts to publish satirical weeklies (see Chaiti Basu's contribution).[4] Also in Urdu and, geographically speaking, in the North-Western and United Provinces of British India, the *Avadh Punch* began publication in 1878 and was followed by others, which, after the 1890s, resulted in a real rivalry between a number of *Punch* versions.[5] In Hindi, the *Hindū Pañc* came out in Calcutta in 1926, but *Punch*'s presence had often been evoked before (see Alok Rai and Prabhat Kumar in this volume).

---

[3] Mushirul Hasan estimates that there were more than 70 versions of *Punch* by the 1890s in India alone. See Mushirul Hasan, *Wit and Humour in Colonial North India* (Delhi: Niyogi Books, 2007), 12.

[4] For a good survey, see the Bengali article by Svapan Basu, "Uniś śataker byaṅgapatrikā," *Sāhitya-pariṣat--patrikā* 113, no. 4, (1413/2006–2007): 101–140, whose list of nineteenth century Bengali satirical magazines contains dozens of names. On *Basantak* and *Pañcā-nanda*, see Chaiti Basu, chapter The *Punch* Tradition in Late Nineteenth Century Bengal: From Pulcinella to Basantak and Pãcu in this volume.

[5] See Ritu Khanduri in this volume; the *Avadh Punch* is the subject of Mushirul Hasan's above-quoted *Wit and Humour*.

In the Arabian literary sphere, *The Cairo Punch* began publication in 1907 (see Marilyn Booth, this volume) and was preceded by other satirical journals: *Abu Nazzara* began to appear in 1878, and *Al-Arghul* was published between 1894 and 1901. Here, however, the *Punch* connection is not as clear as it is in the examples mentioned earlier (see Eliane Ettmueller and Marilyn Booth, this volume).

East Asia, too, had a number of *Punch* versions or *Punch*-inspired magazines: In China, the series started off with English-language magazines published in foreign enclaves such as *The China Punch* (1867–1868, 1872–1876) and *Puck, or the Shanghai Charivari* (April 1871-November 1872) (see Christopher Rea, I-Wei Wu and Barbara Mittler in this volume); the first Chinese-language satirical journal with cartoons was the 'Shanghai Puck' (上海潑克) which began publication in 1918 (see I-Wei Wu in this volume); in Japan, the most noteworthy *Punch* version was the *Nipponchi* 日ポン地 (see Peter Duus' and Sonja Hotwagner's contributions).

If we then state that between the 1870s and the early twentieth century *Punch* had an Asia-wide presence and inspired various offshoots, it is, however, important not to gloss over their very unequal geographical distribution. In South Asia, i.e. the earstwhile British India, the *Punch* versions were particularly numerous, which might be due to the comparatively strong impact that British cultural production had on its colony. In the Near East, the *Punch* legacy appears to have been considerably weaker, and in East Asia, too, *Punch*'s influence in a concrete sense was not so pronounced, remaining mostly confined to publications of the British colonial diaspora and one single Japanese journal.

One striking feature of most of the *Punch* accounts in this volume is the 'discontinuity of the loan'. In contact linguistics, one can encounter cases in which loan words from other languages become old-fashioned and get replaced by fresh loans of the same original words. The Bengali term *āpis* is a good illustration: apparently an early nineteenth century loan representing the English 'office', *āpis* falls out of use in the twentieth century and is replaced by a phonetically more accurate *aphis*/'office' in educated colloquial speech and sometimes even in writing, in a move of retrospective purification and perceived cosmopolitanism. In a similar manner, latter-day historians of literature and satirists would make it a point to refer to the original *Punch* and disavow the interim period of imperfect 'imitation'. The general neglect of the *Punch* versions which are investigated in this volume demonstrates the failure, in South Asia and elsewhere, to stabilise their historical status and give them a durable presence. In particular, literary historians do not seem to have taken the *Punch* versions very seriously. Apart from a few laudable and recent exceptions such as Mushirul Hasan's book on the *Avadh Punch*,[6] the Bengali *Basantak* reprint[7] and the

---

[6] Hasan, *Wit and Humour*.

[7] Caṇḍī Lāhiṛī, ed., *Basantak: 1m barṣa-2ẏa barṣa* (Kal'kātā, Niu Ej Pāb'liśārs, n.d. [first published around 2008]).

Japanese Manga editions by Shimizu Isao,[8] the *Punch* versions by and large seem to have been relegated to oblivion.

The question of how to conceptualise the *Punch* versions vis-à-vis *Punch*, the original, is, in part, also a question of intertextuality. The biologistic models that come to mind most readily—a genealogical table, a tree diagram—would favour the idea of an organic, familial relationship, and imply the usual hierarchies of precedence and causality that such models contain. It is telling that in one of the few explicit intertextual references, *Punch* (2 March 1904) refers to the *Hindi Punch* as 'family' and 'Indian cousin'. However, the limitations of such organic metaphors become clear through a mere comparison of the timelines of the 161-year-old British *Punch* and its short-lived Asian counterparts. Apart from explicit naming and referencing, there are of course many other dimensions to this issue. Tobias Heinzelmann, for instance, in the context of a discussion of Ottoman *Punch* loans, suggests a loan scheme and distinguishes between avowed loans, unavowed ones and modifications.[9] In most cases, however, direct links to the British *Punch* are in fact the exception, and the loan is merely that of a format put to very different uses.

An attempt to make sense of the Asian *Punch* versions has to be sensitive to a certain centre-periphery relationship between *Punch* and *Punch* versions, then, and start by suspending that perspective in order to refocus these phenomena. Otherwise one runs the risk of creating just another centre-oriented narrative, which ultimately affirms the superiority of the original English *Punch* magazine in terms of sheer size, originality, unsurpassed durability, lasting impact, etc., which accordingly relegates the Asian *Punch* versions to the margins. In this way, one would reassert the usual centre-periphery constellations and completely miss the momentum of the individual *Punch* versions under scrutiny. Even if such a centre-periphery relation is found to govern the then contemporary and later perceptions in the respective literary cultures, this volume insists on the basic differences between the various local Asian enunciations in the name of *Punch*. Although there may be a point in showing the British *Punch*'s superiority on a number of counts, such evaluations are not the aim of this volume—because reading those *Punch* versions simply in terms of *Punch* would gloss over the gist of this account, which is one not just of creative translation but more of fundamental re-contextualisation.

Still, one might wonder whether *Punch*—the British *Punch* magazine—is not the very centre of such an attempt to address the *Punch* versions, and whether such manoeuvres are nothing but mere exercises in goodwill, but ultimately condescending political correctness. If this volume were not about a transcultural

---

[8] Shimizu Isao, *Manga-zasshi hakubutsukan*: Meiji jidai-hen (Manga-Magazine Museum: Meiji Period Edition). (Tōkyō: Kokusho Kankōkai, 1986).

[9] Tobias Heinzelmann, *Die Balkankrise in der Osmanischen Karikatur* (Stuttgart: Franz Steiner Verlag, 1999), 254, for his discussion of a 'modified loan' from *Punch*; the loan scheme was broached in personal communication during a lecture for the research group at the Heidelberg Cluster of Excellence in 2009.

reading of *Punch* and *Punch* versions but, say, about Coca Cola and other colas, questions would indeed have to be posed differently. For even without going into the intricacies and 'identity politics' of drinks such as Pepsi, the Indian Thums Up, the Chinese Wahaha, Afri and Club Cola (West and East German respectively), or the latest German avatar, Fritz Cola, it seems certain that in these cases difference is nothing to be aspired to; rather, utmost similarity with the perceived original has to be achieved. Not so in the case of *Punch*: even though one of the meanings of 'punch' is a mixed drink with a recipe, and one may suppose that some kind of recipe also underlay the *Punch* magazine and triggered attempts of copying, a magazine belongs to a different category of artifact than copying a drink. The cultural transaction of such an entity would have to make sense beyond the immediate senses; it would have to involve a very complex translation of the way a society and the world are perceived. A better analogy would therefore be a literary form or media format such as the daily newspaper, TV news, talk and game shows.

Positing *Punch* as a kind of archetypal model would also miss that *Punch* itself was an imitation—namely, of the French satirical journal *Charivari*, as *Punch*'s subtitle, *The London Charivari*, made clear. Monika Lehner has reminded us that *Punch* was only one of a great variety of nineteenth century satirical periodicals in Europe.[10] Some of the following chapters show that other periodicals, such as *Puck*, also had their Asian versions and that a good number of Asian periodicals were neither called *Punch* nor did they attempt to be a version of *Punch*.

But these matters are not always perceived this way. The tendency to appreciate the model and not the imitations—assuming that the model is better, more original, and the imitation merely derivative—is what Matthew Potolsky has qualified as a particular (and a very modern) moment in the history of mimesis.[11] And while the cultures from which the *Punch*-inspired satirical journals treated in this volume emerged cannot be expected to unanimously share such notions, their tacit or outspoken *déclassement* of the *Punch* versions in retrospect seems to obey a very similar logic, defining the *Punch* makers as imitators and not as inventors.[12] The pertinence of such evaluative policies is obvious, for this point could easily be extended from a literary format to the evaluation of entire historical epochs (most virulently of modernity) and lead to much-debated issues such as the claim of precedence of the European Enlightenment and the alleged derivativeness of other, 'second-hand' modernities that are mere results of colonialism, imperialism, or simply of contacts with more advanced cultures. In any case, it is not our intention

---

[10] Monica Lehner gave an important paper at the *Punch* conference in Heidelberg "Form(at) Follows Function: *Punch* as a Model for the Transcultural Adaptability of a Medium", parts of which will be published elsewhere, see Monika Lehner, *Der Chinadiskurs in der satirisch-humoristischen Publizistik Österreich-Ungarns 1894–1917* (forthcoming).

[11] Matthew Potolski, *Mimesis* (London: Routledge, 2006). (A book on the changing evaluations of mimesis and the hype around originality); see Prabhat Kumar, chapter From *Punch* to *Mat'vālā*: Transcultural Lives of a Literary Format in this volume.

[12] For an outspoken *déclassement*, see cartoonist Rasipuram Laxman (cited in Khanduri).

to take up such ambitious issues here, though we will be attentive to them; the intention of this volume is not to advocate the superiority of the original over its imitations, but rather to trigger an open-minded curiosity about what made the *Punch* format so attractive in very diverse parts of the world, and how the name of *Punch* was employed in these contexts.

One important feature here is the fact that it was not only *Punch* that travelled: in East Asia, for example, the American *Puck* appears to have been equally, or perhaps even more of a role model (see I-Wei Wu in this volume). This somewhat complicates genealogies and makes it possible to conjecture that what was at the root was not always necessarily connected with *Punch, or The London Charivari*, but rather some common feature of the satirical periodical format. It needs to be taken into account that the 'satirical format' was, of course, not the only to be copied, but one of the various commercial print formats that dispersed into all kinds of environments at that time, perhaps not having undergone such a special development after all (see Ritu Khanduri in this volume). And from a European perspective, Punch was also just one among a huge number of satirical magazines. Journals such as the French *La Caricature* and *Charivari*, the Austrian *Figaro* and *Floh*, the German *Simplicissimus*, etc., might claim similar importance for their respective language-cultures. But the comparative assessment of European satire magazines is clearly beyond the scope of this book. Still, these notes of caution, some of which will be further elaborated below, cannot diminish the spectacular propensity of *Punch* to inspire adaptations over such a variety of cultures.

Another astonishing feature of the history of these Asian *Punch* versions is that they all perished around the same time before the Second World War. Strictly in terms of their life-span, the *Punch* versions therefore seem to belong to what one may term the age of colonialism and imperialism; and it may seem reasonable to seek an intrinsic link between them and that age. The British Empire, as both a giant potential space for distribution and an intercultural semantic framework that held despite being highly fragmented, might account for some of this linkage. In her contribution, Ritu Khanduri shows that *Punch* served as a useful format to address specific issues of colonialism, and implicitly one might extend this argument and claim that such a format was bound to become outdated once colonialism ceased to exist.

However, some basic thoughts about affinities between colonialism/imperialism and satire are in order if this line of argument is to be substantiated. A general answer to the question of why the *Punch* versions were such a distinctively colonial phenomenon, has to refer to the role of satire as a literary mode. Satire may be characterised as an oblique type of literary communication. It relies on the distortion and/or dislocation of its subject in order to achieve a mock description of it. It can indeed be destructive, as Pirandello has famously claimed,[13] albeit usually not

---

[13] Luigi Pirandello, *L'umorismo* (Milano: Mondadori, 1986), 39.

in the form of direct attack, but through indirect reference which needs to be decoded before its critical potential is revealed. Many definitions of satire hold that its most basic feature is the incongruity between object and account, or content and form;[14] and in fact, satirical accounts are characterised by a fundamental asymmetry of representation. Satire highlights and exaggerates the tensions between norm and reality, aspiration and actual failure, *Schein* and *Sein*,[15] and thereby reveals asymmetries inherent in its chosen targets.

The point is that asymmetry is also an apt term for describing relations between colonisers and colonised. Since the end of the nineteenth century, much has been written about the asymmetry of economic relations, with the colonial production sites of raw products that cater to the newly emerging industries of the imperial metropolis, bringing about, for example, drain of wealth theories by Indian nationalists.[16] Cultural encounters in colonial settings produced empowered notions of the coloniser's superiority—a superiority imposing itself as undeniable on the colonised—and triggered moves of emulation perceived as both a necessity and a curse. More importantly, these encounters brought about a bifurcation of cultural norms that shook traditional social structures in the colonies, created new interfaces and reshuffled relations of class, gender, etc.

In such an environment, it can be conveniently argued that satire came in handy as an expressive faculty in that it bestowed an overarching symmetry between the asymmetries of living conditions and those of their (satirical) depiction. Satire could tackle such topsy-turvy realities from an aesthetical distance that allowed to cast a mocking glance at the world without having to define any all-too-precise standpoint of its own. Satire also had an element of camouflage that was necessary to avoid censorship. It thus created a virtual space for venting irritation about contemporary injustices, incongruities and aberrations especially within the respective colonised societies—a remarkable feature of the satirical production in the countries concerned as such internal criticism by far outweighed the rare instances in which the coloniser/imperialist was made the target of satire.

But why did the momentum of the Asian versions of *Punch* in particular, and presumably of satirical text production in general, abate towards the middle of the twentieth century? Sudipta Kaviraj refers to the perceived decay of satirical expression in Bengali literature towards the middle of the twentieth century and advances the thesis that growing nationalism in the period took over and favoured serious

---

[14] For a recent example, e.g. Brian A. Connery and Kirk Combe, eds, *Theorizing Satire: Essays in Literary Criticism* (New York: St. Martin's Press, 1995); Brian A. Connery and Kirk Combe, "Theorizing Satire: A Retrospective and an Introduction," in Connery and Combe, eds, 1–15; 5.

[15] Or the contradiction between reality and the ideal, famously elaborated in Friedrich Schiller, *Über naive und sentimentalische Dichtung* (originally published Tübingen: Cotta, 1795) (Stuttgart: Philipp Reclam Jun., 1986), 37.

[16] Dadabhai Naoroji, *Poverty and Un-British Rule in India* (London: Sonnenschein, 1901); Romesh Chunder Dutt, *The Economic History of India* (London: Kegan Paul, Trench, Trubner, 1902 and 1906).

idioms of reform, accusation, action, etc., that ultimately brought about the end of humour in post-independence India.[17] The validity of Kaviraj's reasoning for other South Asian contexts finds support in Markus Daechsel's work.[18] However tempting it may be, though, to generalise such contentions, our judgment at present will have to stop at the *Punch* versions and avoid statements about satire in general. South Asian colonial settings are too distinct from the various other areas covered in this volume to make such contentions anything more than hazardous.

If, then, the role of satire in colonial and imperial settings may be described as an asymmetrical literary mode that addresses asymmetrical cultural and social processes, it remains somewhat puzzling, in our case, that while other (more or less indigenous) formats existed, it was the metropolitan *Punch* that served as such a prominent medium for this type of satirical communication. Authors and journalists critical of colonial and imperialist developments could have been expected to choose other satirical formats and names, and to avoid the one most clearly connoted with the imperial centre. One reason for why they didn't was very probably a certain compliance with *Punch* as a perceived counter-voice of that centre. But the adaptation of *Punch* can also be interpreted as giving expression to the very ambivalent attitude towards the coloniser or imperial master: a widespread fascination with their cultural outlook uneasily existed side by side with a (mutual) repulsion especially since the second half of the nineteenth century. While general statements appear as yet impossible at this initial stage, to probe into these issues is in fact part of the endeavour at hand.

Our transcultural approach to the Asian versions of *Punch* involves the suspension of judgment on the issue of original and copy. This means, at least to a certain extent, naturalising imitation and cultural loans as an integral part of such processes. Secondly, such an approach demands a special sensibility towards changes, framings, redefinitions and reapplications that occur when objects, ideas or formats travel, and consequently requires a new openness towards such hybrid products, or cross-cultural expressions.

Having said all this, we may now turn to the reasons for *Punch*'s astonishing connectivity. This connectivity appears to have been most pronounced in the case of South Asia. The question of why the South Asian *Punch* versions are so numerous—Mushirul Hasan speaks of more than seventy[19]—and *Punch*'s impact

---

[17] Sudipta Kaviraj, "Laughter and Subjectivity: The Self-Ironical Tradition in Bengali Literature," *Modern Asian Studies* 34, no. 2 (May 2000): 379–406.

[18] Markus Daechsel, *The Politics of Self-Expression: the Urdu middle-class milieu in mid-twentieth century in India and Pakistan* (London: Routledge, 2006). He follows Kaviraj in his basic contention and gives evidence for such a decrease of satirical literature in Urdu of the same period. See also Sonja Hotwagner's contribution, chapter '*Punch*'s Heirs' Between the (Battle) Lines: Satirical Journalism in the Age of the Russo-Japanese War of 1904–1905 in this volume, on war-time Japanese periodicals and the radically changed role of satire in them.

[19] Hasan, *Wit and Humour*, 12 as referred to above: 'By the end of the nineteenth century, 70 *Punch* papers/magazines appeared, quite remarkably, from more than a dozen cities'. Unfortunately, he does not give any references.

is so dominant, can be answered quite easily by the long-lasting presence of British colonialism. But beyond this, there must have been a specific propensity to take up *Punch* as a model. Firstly, there were various assonances and possible uses of the word/motif 'punch' in East Asia (see the articles in the East Asian section) and particularly South Asia.[20] *Punch*, in fact, connects particularly well with many of South Asian languages and creates numerous assonances. Sanskrit *pañca*, which is common in most modern Indo-Aryan languages along with derivatives such as *pãc/ pāc* and similar words, means 'five', a number with manifold cultural and sacred connotations.[21] Moreover, there is the headman of the village council or judge (*sar'pañc/pañc*) in a number of languages,[22] and the word also figures in 'mixture' (*prapañc* in Hindi)—a term that actually comes quite close to the colourful bowl or *satura lanx* that is the most widely accepted etymology of 'satire', and, of course, to the 'punch' as a mixed drink. So the appellation 'punch' covered a rich semantic field and didn't even have to be translated. In such circumstances, it is little wonder that it was so widely appropriated.

Secondly, what also must have appealed to Asian satirists in the *Punch* model was the narrator figure Mr Punch, a kind of trickster, who maintained the outsider position facilitating a satirical view of surrounding realities and who had starred in a popular puppet show. Punch, the satirical journal was, in a way, a translation of a traditional performance into the format of a printed weekly periodical. This demonstrated how to put to use such existing patterns, and that it could easily be transferred into local traditions: if Punch could make it from the marketplace puppet performance into print, *Karagöz* (Ottoman shadow theatre) or the *bhãṛ* (Bengali jester) could move into periodicals, too. This template—a common feature of European periodicals of the time—provided for smooth adaptations and promoted, at least in South Asia, the indigenisation of *Punch*. Punch or Punch-like characters were connected with earlier cultural expressions—which was a precondition for them to be 'fun'. Significantly, in almost all cases, the traditional puppet-like iconography of the trickster was retained.

Thirdly, but of equal importance, was the cartoon as a means of visual satire. *Punch* brought with it a specific relationship between text and picture, with a pun often arising out of the particular combination of the two. This again provided ample opportunities for taking up local traditions of visual representation; and a comparative look at the visuals in this volume would aptly demonstrate the cultural diversity at work here. Generally speaking, then, there were previous satirical traditions in all the cultures represented here, for which the *Punch* format permitted integration. Thus this seems to be a common feature in all the various versions of *Punch* under discussion. An analysis would, in these circumstances, have to steer clear of any indigenism that would claim such satirical expressions to be entirely

---

[20] See Kumar, Basu and Swarali Paranjape in this volume.

[21] Pratap Narayan Mishra/Prabhat Kumar; see Basu, this volume, on Bengali connotations.

[22] The Marathi *Hindū pañca* introduced such a *sar'pañc* as its principal narrator; see Paranjape in this volume.

native or national (which is a hypothetical suggestion, since this does not seem to have been attempted yet; as stated above, these productions have as of yet remained largely ignored). It would rather have to focus on an effect of transcultural synergy in which a foreign format allows indigenous elements to resurface.[23]

Actual knowledge of *Punch* magazine on the part of the Asian satirists, however, varied greatly. Its great name and high visibility did not necessarily translate into market success, as Ritu Khanduri argues in the case of India in this volume, and there is reason to doubt that its fame included actual availability. Some of the South Asian examples suggest that *Punch*'s undeniable presence was a distant one. This seems to be the case, for example, when the *Dvija patrikā* from Patna features a humorous section entitled *Pañc-prapañc* (see Prabhat Kumar's contribution in this volume): such usage shows that *Punch* was not coterminous with any actual weekly that could be bought and read, but had become a generic term for a particular type of humour. In a second, more concrete case, *Punch* was still not perceived as the actual periodical, but simply as a journal-cum-cartoon that was not even necessarily satirical.[24] This is borne out by the fact that a number of *Punch*es were not particularly satirical (e.g., the Marathi *Hindu pañca*; see Paranjape in this volume). Only in some cases do we get the impression that *Punch* was a well-known, constant presence beyond its basic idea and template as a weekly magazine.[25] Moreover, hardly any of the Asian versions of *Punch* displayed the British *Punch*'s emphasis placed on visuals, in either quality or quantity.

Another issue to be tackled in the individual contributions is the question of targeted readerships of the various Asian *Punch*es. For the British *Punch*, Brian Maidment (in this volume) defines the author-audience relationship, broadly speaking, as one of jobbing journalists and artists rather indeterminate in terms of class affiliation, catering to the newly formed middle classes of Britain. How did this relationship get reconfigured in Asian societies under the sway of colonialism and imperialism, where such middle classes at the time were often rudimentary? Alok Rai (in this volume) explores the (limited) possibilities of satire for the emergent Hindi literary sphere in Northern India, where such a middle-class audience had not yet crystallised. In general, this touches upon the issue of nineteenth century journalistic and literary production in general, which had to depend on a very small audience that, in some cases, quite literally had to be talked into existence.

More specifically, and mostly with regard to South Asia, the question is how *Punch* as an expression of a distinctly middle-class sensibility in mild opposition to the working classes translated into emerging colonial middle-class idioms. This is complicated by the position of colonial elites in an imperial set-up: while they could

---

[23] See Kumar in this volume.

[24] See A.R. Venkatachalapathy, "Chap. 3: Caricaturing the Political: The Cartoon in Pre-Independence Tamil Journalism," in *In Those Days There Was No Coffee*, A.R Venkatachalapathy (New Delhi: Yoda Press, 2006), 42–58.

[25] E.g., in the Bengali *Basantak* and *Pañcā-nanda*; see Basu's contribution in this volume.

comply with the British middle class in the context of their own societies, the imperial framework simultaneously reduced them to subalterns. Could *Punch*-type satire undergo a reversal and express anti-colonial and emancipating visions? While this cannot be answered summarily, it appears that although the functional equation between British and colonial audiences did not exist, neat reversals, such as satire turning anti-British, were the exception rather than the rule.

This leads to another question regarding the nature of laughter and the standpoints of the Asian satirists who produced the *Punch* versions and related periodicals. What, in short, are the politics of laughter in an age of colonialism and imperialism? In recent debates, there has been a certain infatuation with the idea of a liberating, carnivalesque nature of laughter, initiated mostly by the work of Mikhail Bakhtin.[26] It would, however, be wishful thinking to expect satire, as institutionalised in the Asian *Punch* versions under discussion, to warrant such cathartic humour. If, for the British *Punch*, laughter can be linked to a class habitus and is a means to rid oneself of disliked aspects in one's own society, it is part of the exercise of this volume to find out what kind of bias is at work in its Asian versions, and to seriously investigate the pejorative and cruel sides of laughter and satire, too. It needs to be stressed that not all the Asian satirists belonged to the reformist strands of their respective societies.[27] In quite a number of cases, the satirists behind the Asian versions of *Punch* appear to have been highly conservative and even reactionary—as far as these terms can be applied to a colonial setting in which turning to a tradition may be inherently anti-colonial or anti-imperial and take on a 'progressive' aspect as well. It is necessary, in any case, to reflect on the attitudinal and social consensus that a satirist needed to be understood.

These are some of the issues this volume attempts to address. The contributions are divided into four parts geographically, and even if the usual centralities are to be shaken, it obviously makes sense in terms of historical precedence to start with an essay on the British Punch and then to move to South Asia, West Asia/North Africa and finally East Asia in separate sections. As editors, we—Barbara Mittler and Hans Harder—are privileged to frame the other authors in this volume; and while this introduction raises some of the questions guiding this endeavour, Barbara Mittler's epilogue takes stock of the answers given.

---

[26] Mikhail M. Bakhtin, *Rabelais and his World* (Bloomington: Indiana University Press, 1984).

[27] As, in fact, could also be said about the British *Punch*'s satirists.

Part I
Punch, the Template

The Presence of *Punch* in the Nineteenth Century

Brian Maidment

The central project of this book is to consider the ways in which the London based weekly journal *Punch* (1842–2002) served the nineteenth century world as a model for, an influence on, or a legitimating force for satirical magazines published outside Britain, often in societies both geographically and culturally remote from British Victorian metropolitan culture. In this context, it is important to begin by reconsidering those characteristics of *Punch* that established and maintained its transcultural public presence throughout the latter half of the nineteenth century. Defining such characteristics clearly requires discussion both of the wide range of genres and humorous modes through which *Punch*'s 'content' was constructed and of the variety of self-conscious business practices through which the magazine sustained its early celebrity. Many cultural historians, most notably R. D. Altick, have mined *Punch* for its views, expressed both verbally and visually, on contemporary events,[1] and the magazine remains, along with the *Illustrated London News*, a frequently cited illustrative resource for thinking about Victorian politics, manners and public events. The pure and uninterrupted fecundity of *Punch* has made it irresistible to historians, who have quarried its thousands of pages and images in pursuit of its expressed attitudes towards even the most trivial of subjects. Such fecundity clearly makes the task of writing a general overview of the magazine here an impossible task. Altick took over 500 pages to discuss merely what *Punch* thought about the world between 1841 and 1851, the first 10 years and 20 half yearly volumes of its existence.[2] There were, to cite one unexpected minor

---

[1] Richard D. Altick, *Punch: The Lively Youth of a British Institution 1841–1851*. (Columbus: Ohio State University Press, 1997).

[2] A useful bibliography of secondary commentary on *Punch* up to 1994 can be found in J. Don Vann and Rosemary T. van Arsdel, eds., *Victorian Periodicals and Victorian Society* (Toronto: Scolar Press, 1994), 281–283.

B. Maidment (✉)
University of Salford, Salford, UK
e-mail: B.E.Maidment@salford.ac.uk

Punch obsession, over 50 images of dustmen in the first 20 volumes. But given the particular focus of this book, it seems necessary to approach *Punch* via a slightly different route, beginning with a brief overview of its history, then moving on to consider the generic complexity of its content, with complex shifts between satire, invective, travesty, burlesque and whimsy, before concentrating on its physical manifestations, or perhaps its 'aura' (to use a term borrowed from Walter Benjamin[3]). The aim is to suggest how *Punch* constructed itself, or was constructed as, a hugely powerful and widespread 'presence' in Victorian culture.

A Brief History of *Punch*

Punch was published weekly right through the nineteenth century from its first issue of 17 July 1841, and remains one of the key sources for elucidating the opinions of nineteenth century middle England.[4] The 12 page double column issues, each costing 3d. in the first instance, comprised text, full page wood engraved cartoons, a variety of wood engraved vignette comic illustrations dropped into the text, and a range of visual embellishments, including elaborate capital letters and tiny silhouettes, which ran over from the weekly parts into the index of the reprinted volumes and the yearly supplementary *Almanack*. In its early days, there was no good reason why *Punch* should have been any more successful than the many short lived satirical journals of the time that failed. *Punch* assembled a number of requisite elements for success: the tradition of wood-engraved, politically radical illustration derived from the Hone/Cruikshank pamphlets of 20 years before,[5] Seymour's images for *Figaro in London* from the 1830s,[6] the use of a highly evolved persona drawn from popular culture to serve as a satirical presiding spirit (as well as 'Figaro', 'Punch' had already been used in such a role by Douglas Jerrold for the short-lived 1832 *Punch in London*), and the example of French satirical periodicals (Phillipon's Paris based magazine *Charivari* gave *Punch* its sub-title 'The London Charivari').

Not least of these was the versatile squarish, double-columned page, which was especially well adapted to the kind of interplay between visual and textual elements

---

[3] Walter Benjamin, "The Work of Art in the Age of Mechanical Reproduction," in *Illuminations*, ed. Hannah Arendt (New York: Schoken Books, 1969).

[4] This section of the chapter is based on my entry on *Punch* in Laurel Brake and Marysa Demoor, eds., *The Dictionary of Nineteenth Century Journalism* (London: British Library, 2008) and is republished by permission.

[5] For Hone and Cruikshank's political pamphlets see Edgell Rickword, *Radical Squibs and Loyal Ripostes* (Bath: Adams and Dart, 1971); Marcus Wood, *Radical Satire and Print Culture 1790–1822* (Oxford: Oxford University Press, 1994). There is no room here to consider *Punch* in relation to more explicitly political and oppositional illustrated satirical journals like *The Penny Satirist*. In such journals the simple vernacular woodcut was often preferred to the more sophisticated wood engravings used by *Punch*.

[6] *Figaro in London* ran from 1831 until 1839.

that *Punch* required. To such prerequisites were added an experienced and well-connected staff, and an ability to both sustain the traditions of Regency mockery, while also developing a newer, whimsical mode of comedy that focused on the trials and aspirations of the still emergent middle classes. The little financial backing that the nascent *Punch* had was supplied largely by the engraver Ebenezer Landells,[7] and the printer James Last who underwrote Mark Lemon and Henry Mayhew's uncertain editorial venture. Early sales, while they reached the substantial level of 6,000 copies, could not sustain *Punch* for long, but more permanent support was supplied by the firm of Bradbury and Evans who were able not only to capitalise the new magazine properly but also supplied both its printing and publishing needs.

Bradbury and Evans's decision to invest heavily in *Punch* may well have been prompted by the spectacular sales of the annual supplementary *Almanack*, which for many years outsold the weekly numbers by a huge margin.[8] As the page shown as Fig. 1 suggests, considerable attention was given to constructing the complex page used by the *Punch Almanack*, a level of concern that contributed hugely to its success.

Largely the brain child of Henry Mayhew, who had also worked on the *Comic Almanack*, the *Punch Almanack* became one of the most characteristic and popular elements of the *Punch* brand, and is discussed in more detail below. If its early years were somewhat chaotic, *Punch* nonetheless rapidly developed some remarkably stable characteristics over the following 60 years. It had very few editors, several of whom enjoyed lengthy tenancies—Henry Mayhew was joint editor with Mark Lemon from 1841 to 1842, but then Lemon became sole editor until 1870, to be followed by Shirley Brooks (1870–1874), Tom Taylor (1874–1880) and Sir Francis Burnand (1880–1906).[9] After Ebenezer Landells, one of the founding figures of the magazine, was sacked in 1843, Joseph Swain took over the crucial role of overseeing the engraving of the many illustrations and, building his business on his agreement with *Punch*, remained in that role until 1900. His promptness and efficiency formed a crucial element in *Punch*'s subsequent development.[10] The coterie of slightly

---

[7] For Landells see Marion H. Spielmann, *The History of 'Punch'* (London: Cassell & Co. Ltd., 1895), 15–19; Rodney K. Engen, *Dictionary of Victorian Wood Engravers* (Cambridge: Chadwyck-Healey, 1985), 149–150; Simon Houfe, *The Dictionary of British Book Illustrators and Caricaturists 1800–1914*, revised ed. (Woodbridge: Antique Collectors Club, revised ed. 1981), 364; Laurel Brake and Marysa Demoor, eds., *Dictionary of Nineteenth Century Journalism* (British Library and Academia Press 2008), 345.

[8] I am extremely grateful for this information (and much else) to Patrick Leary. His work on the *Punch* ledgers suggests a sales figure of 90,000 for the 1842 *Almanack* and over the next 20 years sales figures of 40,000–60,000 were the annual norm.

[9] See Sir Francis C. Burnand, *Records and Reminiscences Personal and General*, 2 vols. (London: Methuen, 1904). Burnand, as well as his long spell as editor, was invaluable to *Punch* as a contributor for many years before he took over as editor.

[10] For Swain see Spielmann, *History of Punch*, 247–253; Engen, *Victorian Wood Engravers*, 251–253. See also entries in the *Oxford Dictionary of National Biography* and the *Dictionary of Nineteenth Century Journalism*.

Fig. 1 *Punch Almanack* 1843 'February'

bohemian and sometimes politically radical journalists, authors and writers who formed the inner circle of early contributors, and included Douglas Jerrold,[11] Gilbert a Beckett, Horace Mayhew, Thomas Hood and William Makepeace

---

[11] For Jerrold see Michael Slater, *Douglas Jerrold 1803–1857* (London: Duckworth, 2002).

Thackeray[12] among its writers, and John Leech,[13] Richard Doyle,[14] John Tenniel,[15] and Charles Keene[16] among its artists, remained, apart from occasional rows and defections, coherent and famously sociable. Renowned in its early years for outspoken criticism of various social ills, notably the exploitation of women in the sweatshops of the clothing industries, *Punch* lost much of its radical energy in its later history, but remained a broad-based repository of social and political commentary. It continued to attract artists of the calibre of George du Maurier,[17] Phil May and Linley Sambourne to draw its cartoons, artists who brought a complex notion of social realism and reportage to humorous illustration, and a range of now relatively little known humorous writers including Shirley Brooks, Percival Leigh, Francis Burnand, George and Weedon Grossmith and Andrew Lang. Long outliving the nineteenth century, there were several attempts to sustain the magazine into the twenty-first, but it finally expired in 2002.

A Page of *Punch*

As a means of contemplating both the comic modes used by *Punch*, and as a way to suggest its distinctive engagement with contemporary attitudes I want to look in some detail at a page published as 'February' in the first issue of the *Punch Almanack* dated 1842 (Fig. 2).

In discussing this page I want to consider a number of issues: the physical appearance of the *Punch* page, the centrality that wood engraved illustration plays here, the nature of its humour, and its representation of central socio-political issues, in this instance its attitude to social class. The first point to make concerns

---

[12] Thackeray also drew for *Punch*. See John Buchanan-Brown, *The Illustrations of William Makepeace Thackeray* (Newton Abbot: David and Charles, 1979); Marion H. Spielmann, *The Hitherto Unidentified Contributions of W. M. Thackeray to 'Punch'* (London: Harper & Brothers, 1899); Richard Pearson, *W. M. Thackeray and the Mediated Text: Writing for Periodicals in the Mid-Nineteenth Century* (Aldershot: Ashgate, 2000).

[13] For Leech see William P. Frith, *John Leech: His Life and Works*, 2 vols. (London: Bentley & Son, 1891).

[14] For Doyle see Daria Hambourg, *Richard Doyle—His Life and Works* (London: Art and Technics, 1948); Rodney K. Engen, *Richard Doyle* (Stroud: Catalpa Press, 1983).

[15] For Tenniel see Roger Simpson, *Sir John Tenniel: Aspects of his Work* (London: Associated University Presses, 1994).

[16] For Keene see George Somes Layard, *Life and Letters of Charles Keene* (London: S. Low, Marston & Company, 1892); and Joseph Pennell, *The Work of Charles Keene: With an Introduction and Comments on the Drawings Illustrating the Artist's Methods* (London: T. Fisher Unwin and Brandbury, 1897).

[17] For Du Maurier see Derek P. Whiteley, *George du Maurier—His Life and Work* (London: Art and Technics, 1948); Leonee Ormond, *George Du Maurier* (London: Routledge and Kegan Paul, 1969).

Fig. 2 *Punch Almanack* 1842 'February'

the nature of the *Punch* page—double columned, squarish in shape, big enough to accommodate an assembly of small images dropped into the text or a large single image (the 'pencilling' or cartoon which I will discuss later), and capable of the elaboration of rules, borders and devices of the kind shown in Fig. 3, a page drawn from a slightly later volume of *Punch*.

As these two examples suggest, the *Punch* page is a very particular one.

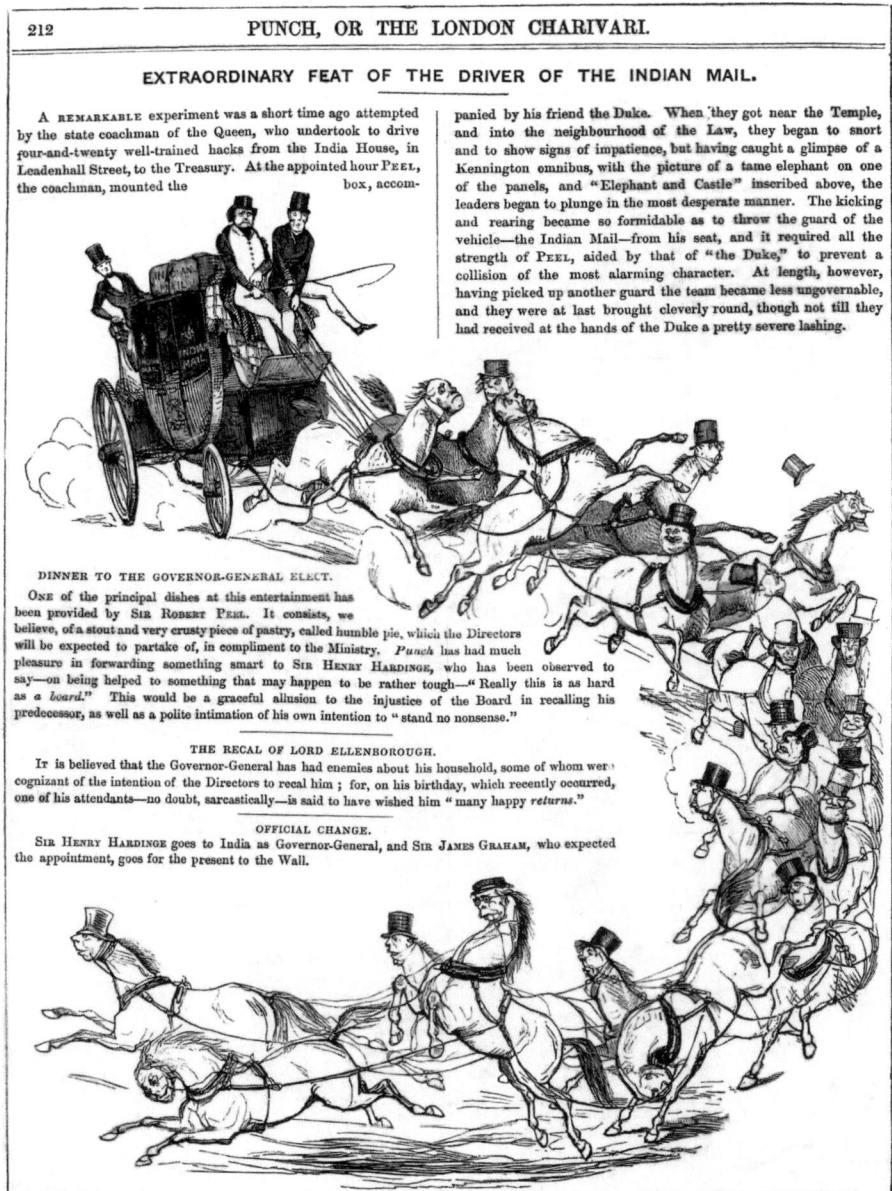

Fig. 3 *Punch*, vol. 6 (1844), p. 212

There were precedents for such a shape and size of page, and for the kind of organisation of text and image on the page—most obviously the radical/progressive satirical journal *Figaro in London*, edited by Gilbert à Beckett (who was to become a major contributor to *Punch*) which ran successfully through much of the 1830s

Fig. 4 George Cruikshank et al., *Gallery of comicalities, embracing humorous sketches by the brothers Robert and George Cruikshank, Robert Seymour, and others, part IV* (London: Charles Hindley, 1891). This publication reprinted articles and illustrations from *Bell's life in London* using the same broadsheet page format as the magazine

and was illustrated with vignette wood engravings by Robert Seymour. But *Punch*, which maintained this distinctive page size throughout the nineteenth century (partly to facilitate stereotype reprinting and stock cloth bindings), steered a careful course between the self-conscious gigantism of illustrated broadside magazines like *Bell's Life in London, The Illustrated London News* or *Cassell's Illustrated Family Magazine* and the 'pocket' octavo formats derived from the 'information' magazines of the 1820s. The distinctively 'square' shape of the *Punch* page became a key element of its identity (Fig. 4).

A second obvious feature of the *Punch* page, which is clear from both Figs. 2 and 3, is that it could only be conceived and constructed through the medium of wood engraving. There isn't time here to rehearse the complex history of the wood engraving from its revival by Thomas Bewick at the end of the eighteenth century who used end-grain blocks as both a medium of scrupulous scientific accuracy and as a new form of miniaturised aesthetic expressiveness in mass circulation educative journals such as *The Penny Magazine,* to becoming the dominant medium of Victorian self-representation associated with unproblematic naturalism in journals like *The Illustrated London News*. But this *Punch* page offers an immediate insight into the key advantages that wood engraving offered over expensive copper plate, steel engraved or etched reprographic media—it could be combined with type so that dropping images into the text became the norm; it was a cheap and speedy method to execute, so that images could proliferate on the page; it had, by 1842, an increasingly significant history as a comic mode of image making, already having largely replaced the satirical mode of etched and engraved single plate caricature with a more whimsical, diverse and accessible comic vocabulary; and it could range from the tiny (implicit in the box wood blocks and exploited in the unframed vignette image) to the immense (through the use of multiple blocks, which could be drawn by different artists locked together to form a full page or even a fold out image). The page shown in Fig. 2 celebrates all these qualities. The traditional type set elements are formally laid out in the almanac style shown in Fig. 5 complete with rules and tables.

But these traditional elements are assaulted by a mass of circumambient imagery that deconstructs the centrality of the word in carnivalesque profusion. The images, as a casual glance suggests, are drawn from different graphic traditions that include the silhouette visual/verbal jokes in the 'Remarks' column, which derive from the annuals and comic gift books of the 1820s and 1830s,[18] the tiny, simplified silhouettes that run riotously down either side of the page, again referring back to Regency obsessions with body shape, and the more elaborately drawn images at the top of the page which combine urban observation with whimsical humour.

As well as these issues about the visual modes used by *Punch* it is important to say something about the artists the magazine gathered on to its staff. *Punch* was founded exactly at that moment when, as the British caricature tradition faded, those artists trained in its uninhibited traditions of satire, invective and

---

[18] William Newman was the jobbing artist most often used by *Punch* for these kinds of images, in which he specialised. See Spielmann, *History of Punch*, 413–414.

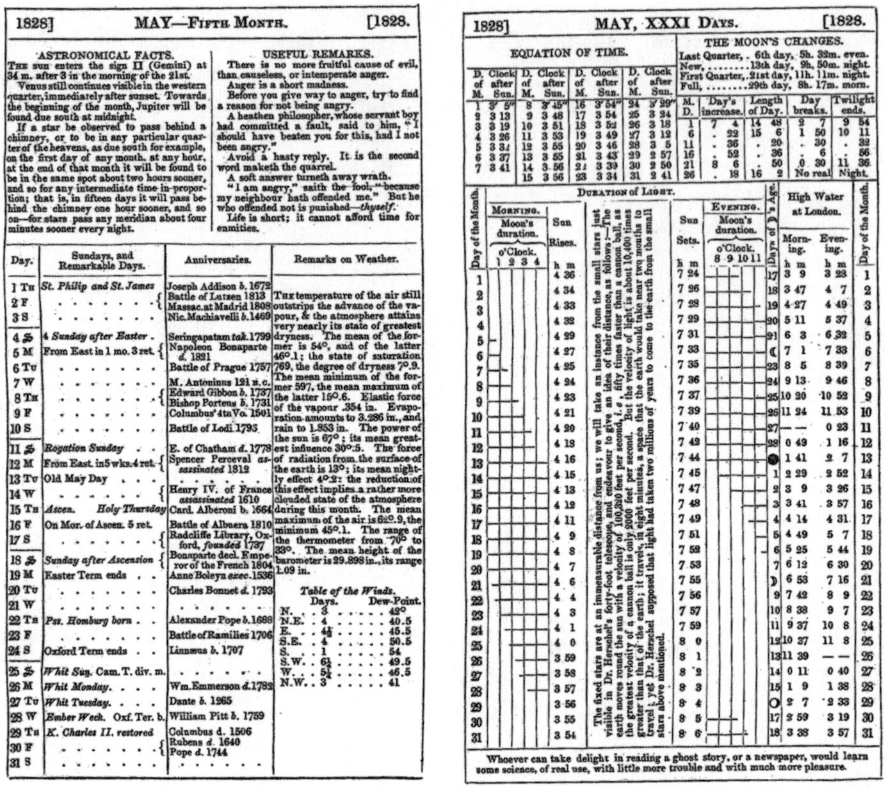
1828] MAY—FIFTH MONTH. [1828.

ASTRONOMICAL FACTS.

THE sun enters the sign II (Gemini) at 34 m. after 3 in the morning of the 21st.

Venus still continues visible in the western quarter, immediately after sunset. Towards the beginning of the month, Jupiter will be found due south at midnight.

If a star be observed to pass behind a chimney, or to be in any particular quarter of the heavens, as due south for example, on the first day of any month, at any hour, at the end of that month it will be found to be in the same spot about two hours sooner, and so for any intermediate time in proportion; that is, in fifteen days it will pass behind the chimney one hour sooner, and so on—for stars pass any meridian about four minutes sooner every night.

USEFUL REMARKS.

There is no more fruitful cause of evil, than causeless, or intemperate anger.

Anger is a short madness.

Before you give way to anger, try to find a reason for not being angry.

A heathen philosopher, whose servant boy had committed a fault, said to him, "I should have beaten you for this, had I not been angry."

Avoid a hasty reply. It is the second word maketh the quarrel.

A soft answer turneth away wrath.

"I am angry," saith the fool, "because my neighbour hath offended me." But he who offended not is punished—*thyself*.

Life is short; it cannot afford time for enmities.

1828] MAY, XXXI DAYS. [1828.

EQUATION OF TIME. THE MOON'S CHANGES. DURATION of LIGHT.

Whoever can take delight in reading a ghost story, or a newspaper, would learn some science, of real use, with little more trouble and with much more pleasure.

Fig. 5 A double page spread from the *British Almanac for 1828* published by the society for the diffusion of useful knowledge that shows the characteristic layout used for each month's entry

denunciation, were forced to turn from etching and engraving to the linear and tonal simplifications of wood engraving in order to survive. As Newman's silhouettes here demonstrate, such images belonged to a Regency idiom that was fast becoming outmoded. But *Punch* in its early years at least was keen to maintain the carnivalesque abundance and energy of Regency graphic humour alongside its very particular development of the wood engraving, with its more naturalistic, even documentary, aspirations. Whatever their training, the artists *Punch* hired as 'house' artists—John Leech, Richard Doyle, John Tenniel and Charles Keene—in the first decades of its existence, were essentially a new generation of 'black and white' artists central to the wider development of monochrome book and periodical illustration, and eager to exploit the potential of the wood engraved page. They were, by both training and inclination, not only, perhaps not even primarily, political caricaturists as much as wry observers of the manners, tastes, fashions and pretensions of urban life, and, if not enthusiastic about, then at least reconciled to their rapid drawings being translated into printable images by jobbing engravers.

Thirdly, this *Punch* page offers a humorous commentary on the almanac form, built up out of a variety of comic modes, most obviously pastiche, travesty and satire.[19] The travesty of a range of print genres is absolutely central to *Punch*'s satirical project. The literature of advice and self-improvement, in the form of conduct books, children's books, history textbooks and letter writing manuals, proved an especially rich source for *Punch*'s scorn, but the theatre and theatrical people, literature, the public documents produced by self-important societies and organisations and, of course, politics and politicians were also open to the magazine's derision. Several series of *Punch* parodies, published as serials or occasional pieces in the magazine, were later re-issued in book form. Douglas Jerrold's Mrs *Caudle's Curtain Lectures,* a series of bedtime tirades by a nagging wife, and Gilbert a Beckett's and Richard Doyle's much-reprinted *Comic History of England,* for example, both brought parodic elements in *Punch* to a wider audience.[20]

The particular social history of the almanac made it a sitting target for *Punch.* Throughout the eighteenth and early nineteenth century, the almanac had been a contested form of print culture. As a source of useful information especially for those engaged in agriculture, an almanac could be found in almost every household. But equally easily available were almanacs built round superstitious prognostications and pseudo-scientific predictions that, for the forces of rational social improvement, catered to ignorance and credulity rather than social utility.[21] The first half of the nineteenth century saw a pitched battle between these two modes. The enforcement of Government legislation (including taxation), licensing rules and the granting of monopoly status to the Stationers' Company slowly gave power to the rationalist camp, led by the Whig progressives of the Society for the Diffusion of Useful Knowledge, whose publisher, Charles Knight, issued the po-faced and painfully utilitarian *British Almanack* as well as leading the attack on superstition and apocalyptic prognostication that characterised many of the most popular almanacs. The satirical opportunities offered by both the prognosticating and the rationalist almanacs had been quickly recognised by the irreverent new breed of metropolitan journalists and graphic satirists of the 1830s like Gilbert a Beckett, Henry Mayhew

---

[19] Satirical versions of established literary and pedagogic genres formed a staple of early Victorian caricature and comic art. Obvious examples include Percival Leigh's *Comic Latin Grammar* (London: Charles Tilt, 1839), which parodies school textbooks, and Robert Seymour's *New Readings of Old Authors, Shakespeare* (London: E. Wilson, 1833–1834), in which Shakespearean quotations are subverted by acting as captions for mundane contemporary events.

[20] One of *Punch*'s most prolific contributors, Gilbert a Beckett, produced a sequence of extremely popular travesties, including comic histories of Rome and Britain and a parody of the legal textbook Blackstone. His *Quizzology of the British Drama,* which lampooned a number of contemporary dramatists and their works, was published by the Punch Office in 1846.

[21] There is no room here to consider various other, potentially highly subversive, kinds of almanacs that gained substantial circulations in the 1840s. There were, for example, several Chartist almanacs that memorialised a year that comprised radical or progressive socio-political events rather than the standard anniversaries of monarchs, saints and historical figures that featured in most almanacs.

Fig. 6 Title page for the 1838 volume of *the comic Almanack*

The Presence of *Punch* in the Nineteenth Century   27

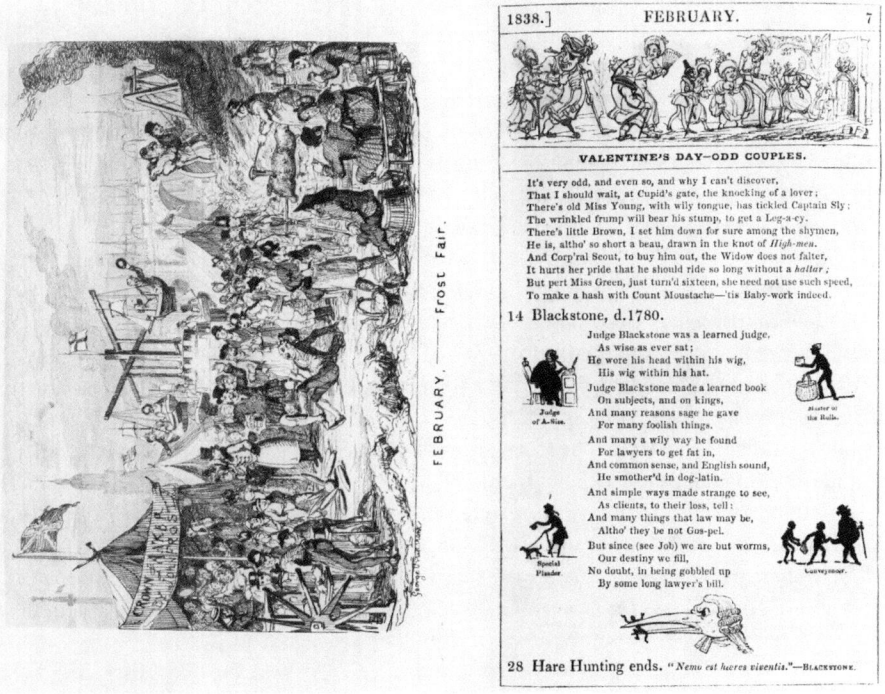

Fig. 7 Double page spread for February from *the comic Almanack* (1838) showing the combination of full page etchings, wood engraved vignettes and silhouettes used to construct the double page

and George Cruikshank, who pooled their satirical experience to produce the long running *Comic Almanack* (1835–1853) (Fig. 6).[22]

The *Comic Almanack* used a small page structured as a parody of the traditional almanac page and combined full page etchings by Cruikshank with many small wood engraved images dropped into the text (Fig. 7).

Punch built many spreads from a similar combination of illustrative components, though instead used wood engraving rather than etching for the full page images. Several contributors later worked for *Punch*, although Cruikshank, almost alone among gifted comic artists of the 1840s, never contributed to the magazine. By the time *Punch* began to produce its own highly subversive almanac in 1842, the almanac style had become available for satire in two different ways. On the one hand, as the 1842 page demonstrates (see Fig. 2), *Punch* satirised the ignorant and misleading advice and apocalyptic if generalised predictions offered

---

[22] For the *Comic Almanack* see Richard A. Vogler, *Graphic Works of George Cruikshank* (New York: Dover Publications, 1979); Robert L. Patten, *George Cruikshank's Life Times and Art*, 2 vols. (Cambridge: Lutterworth Press, 1996), vol. 2; 8–10, 79–80, 189–190, 198–200.

in the down-market popular almanacs—the burlesque 'Prophetic' paragraph at the bottom of the right hand column offers an immediate example of the delight *Punch* took in irrationality and mumbo-jumbo, rounded off in true Regency style with a visual/verbal pun. In the tiny accompanying silhouette the cosmic pseudo-insights of the predictive almanac are bathetically translated into early Victorian street culture—a milkmaid on her street rounds is tripped by a frantic pig that is being chased by a tiny dog and is thus, punningly, 'in the milky way'. But on the other hand, this *Almanack* offers a varied satirical commentary on 'officialese'—that is, the linguistic modes of instruction and regulation through which normative social order is constructed and managed. Thus at the bottom of the page the supposedly regulated activities of London cabmen, as laid out in their official scale of charges, are deconstructed by an account of their actual practices, which depend on highly subjective criteria derived from the willingness of their customers to being swindled through naivety, drunkenness or the urgency of their journey. In the right hand column under 'Domestic' the conventions of the recipe are applied satirically to human rather than comestible subjects. Thus we learn how to make 'a disagreeable young man' out of a menu of grotesque physical characteristics and absurd clothes. Further up the right hand column, 'Directions to Medical Students' offers the students not the expected rules for how to behave in the dissecting room but rather advice on how to carry out seasonal practical jokes on their fellows and teachers, thus confirming the popular view of medical students as riotous, time wasting ne'er-do-wells. This whole page of the *Punch Almanack* pokes fun at a wide range of 'official' print culture in great detail. Such boisterous disrespect for the dominant culture and its use of print culture to maintain social order and respectability was central to *Punch*'s popularity. Worst of all in *Punch*'s view was the widespread attempt to regulate and repress 'fun', whether such fun was to be derived from mocking the ignorance and tastes of the labouring classes or from satirising the pretensions and anxieties of the middling classes in their quest for respectability. The visual and verbal profusion of this *Almanack* page which was barely contained within the rules, the typographical structures and generic conventions of the almanac form, represents precisely the yearning for a disorderly 'other' to middle class respectability that is central to *Punch*'s conceptualisation of the function of humour. The proponents of 'respectable', informative and socially cohesive literature who sought to eradicate the superstitious and predictive elements in many almanacs and replace them with socially and politically neutral information were precisely the kinds of people *Punch* liked to mock. But quite aside from the cultural critique here, *Punch* was also keen to ridicule the formal almanac pages which laid out information in visually dull and rigidly tabular ways (see Fig. 5). The carnivalesque profusion of the *Punch Almanack* was as much a typographical travesty as a social satire. Such *Punch* humour was largely the product of the bohemian/radical, unaffiliated and socially indeterminate class occupied by the jobbing journalists and artists who became its inner circle of contributors. The magazine encouraged its essentially respectable readers to fantasise out an alternative society based on whimsy, travesty and satire and thus construct a carnivalesque mental world in which conformity was equated with dullness, and where civil public discourse entered the realms of the absurd and the ridiculous.

Another visual moment in this crowded page works through ideas about inversion, otherness and a world turned upside down in a more grotesque, albeit entirely literal way (Fig. 8).

Fig. 8 Detail of Fig. 2

In the top left hand corner of the page is a vigorous drawn image of a skating accident. The ice around a notice board has given way, causing one skater to cling desperately to the pole supporting the notice. A second skater, shown in a cut away diagram, has been upended with his feet sticking up vertically through the hole in the ice, his head submerged. The reversal is so absolute that the skater suddenly finds himself discoursing with fish rather than people, while his legs wave comically in the air. This visual trope of sudden reversal is given added force by the verbal content of the image, where a crack in the notice-board has startlingly turned the noun 'notice' into the self-evident but nonetheless disconcerting pronouncement 'not ice'. A second way of reading the fractured notice-board offers another unequivocal pronouncement—'not safe'. Such elaborately wrought if simply drawn puns formed the basis of popular Regency comic literature, and here the way in which a commonplace substantive could be robbed of its normal meaning and turned into a humorous commentary on the graphic content of the image it accompanies reinforces dramatically ideas of misrecognition, misinterpretation and elusive signification—in short, a world turned upside down where language, both graphic and verbal, is 'not safe'.

This complex page is thus constructed out of a variety of humorous modes. First, the modes of public utterance are subjected to sustained travesty and pastiche. Second, the forms of formal documents are satirised and ridiculed. Third, the page uses with evident delight the central element of Regency visual humour—the verbal/visual pun in which words and image offer differing meanings, and thus a comically de-stabilised universe. However, the page's headpiece, organised around the banner headline 'February', operates in a rather different humorous mode. Taking St. Valentine's Day to characterise February, the image shows a street scene that is noticeably both more naturalistic and more whimsical than the rest of the page. A group of winged cherubs mischievously stir up amorous activity. In the background, one cherub affixes the cuckold's ass's ears to a strutting gentleman. A rotund man chases after a slim young woman, who throws up her arms in alarm. In the foreground an elderly and rather shrivelled genteel woman walking her dog is distressed to be reminded of the excesses of love by a capering cherub. But the key to the image is the couple depicted at either edge. On the left a yearning amorous dustman, holding a picture of his beloved, has the embers of his lust fanned into flame by an obliging cherub with a pair of bellows. His beloved, a plump but extremely ragged, dirty cinder sifter, is pictured on the right, also holding an image of her beloved, and she is pierced through by an arrow of desire. The choice of these two characters to exemplify the mysterious ways of love is hardly accidental. Both the dustman and the cinder sifter were representatives of one of the most degraded trades in the spectrum of urban employment. For both, contact with dirt was a daily event, and their presence on the urban scene reminded all respectable people of something they wished above all to conceal—their dependence on the removal of their waste products.

Both dustman and cinder sifter are represented satirically but not entirely unsympathetically. Even the low and contaminated are comically shown to be moved by the same sentimental amorousness as the rest of society. Thus, for all their vulgarity, they participate in a universal social ritual, so that the mockery here is directed at the foolish sentimentality of society at large rather than specifically at the pretensions of the vulgar. This acknowledgement of common humanity, prone to universal vanities, self delusions and weaknesses, comes at precisely the moment when perceptions of class and the nature of the workforce to be found on the streets were rapidly changing. The few existing late eighteenth and early nineteenth century caricatures of the urban labouring classes show working people as degraded, animalistic, and driven by appetite and sensuality. They appear on streets that are depicted predominantly as theatrical spectacles where often grotesque but always vivid groups of passers-by mix and mingle, locked together by an often irritating but usually visually amusing contiguity. But by the 1840s, early Victorian society had come to perceive the urban street as predominantly a site of potential danger, a gathering place for the disorderly, the dispossessed and those without useful employment. Dustmen, who were employed on a franchise system by parishes, were startlingly free of regulation, and could chose to work to their own timetable. Consequently they were often to be found cluttering up the streets with their burly, aggressive and potentially contaminating (even blackening) presence.[23] Given their reputation—they were generally believed to be idle (or at least easily diverted), drunken, lecherous, disputatious, and, most challenging of all, often wealthy—dustmen represented everything that the respectably genteel feared most (Fig. 9).

---

[23] For the representational history of dustmen see Brian E. Maidment, *Dusty Bob: A Cultural History of Dustmen* (Manchester: Manchester University Press, 2007).

VALENTINE'S DAY—CUPID'S HOLIDAY.

Fig. 9 Detail of Fig. 2

This *Punch Almanack* image, however, rather than acknowledging the social and cultural anxiety that the figure of dustman represented for its readers, chooses to stress the harmlessness and humanity of the dustman and his cinder sifter sweetheart by depicting their sentimental attachment as a comic pastiche of polite Valentines. Indeed, the potentially threatening burly masculinity of the dustman has been nullified by his descent into a soppy form of adoration. He has been in effect 'unmanned' by his affections. While dustman and cinder sifter are mocked for their pretensions, the comedy is defensive, laughing away the possibility that the rise of the dustman to wealth and civility could upset the social order. Such a strategy of good humoured mockery of the labouring classes, regardless of how brutalised their jobs and socially challenging their street presence may have been, is a crucial element in the ideological construction of *Punch* humour. At the centre of *Punch* is a determination to depict, and hence situate and accommodate, the labouring classes as comical and largely unsuccessful in their strife to acquire the manners, habits of mind, and respectability of exactly those emergent middle classes who bought *Punch* and regarded it as the voice of their own opinions. *Punch*'s sustained account of the labouring classes over the nineteenth century saw them as unlikely but highly motivated claimants to bourgeois respectability. Thus, tacitly, *Punch* constantly re-asserted bourgeois respectability (which was itself, of course, subject to constant *Punch* mockery) as the norm to which the whole of society aspired. However satirical it became of the absurdities and compulsions of genteel conduct, *Punch* nonetheless maintained a firm alliance with its readers in its defence.

Punch the Brand

If the nature of its humour and its congruence with the concerns of emergent middle-class culture proved the dominant reason for its sustained success, a further key way in which *Punch* maintained and expanded its public presence throughout the nineteenth century was through the sustained exploitation of its brand image. Central to this process was a constant re-issuing of back numbers, which were already available as part of weekly, monthly and half-yearly issues. They could also be obtained in cheaper formats which saw up to four volumes' worth of issues in one bulky tome that was bound in blind-stamped publishers' red cloth.

While many periodicals astutely reformulated their issues into monthly and yearly volumes as they were published, few sustained a back run of every issue from the date of first publication or persistently republished early issues for so long after their first appearance. Thus, throughout the century you could buy, even if you had not been a subscriber to the journal as issued, all issues of *Punch* from 1841 in a durable and relatively affordable form produced to look good on the shelves of the aspiring bourgeoisie. *Punch* accordingly attempted to transcend topicality—an obvious characteristic of a magazine, especially a weekly one—and thus sustained interest: it made itself exist in a continuing present tense. Such an implicit denial of topicality as a key rationale of a satirical magazine raises some interesting questions about the interests and tastes of its readers, even allowing for the fact that a massed row of *Punch* volumes, however little read, might form part of the cultural capital of ambitious domesticity. While much of *Punch*'s political satire did no doubt date, possibly beyond the comprehension of later readers, its perspectives on a range of socio-cultural issues—the presumption of the working classes, for example, or the absurdity of the aspirations of women to public life, or the effete posturing of the fin de siecle intellectuals—remained nonetheless as accessible as it was popular. The trans-historical elements of some of *Punch*'s sources of humour may well have been a reason it sustained its international appeal. Additionally, the stereotype graphic versions of public figures that its artists had evolved became a source of amusement and pleasure in their own right regardless of their association with particular political issues. This notion of the ever available, continuously reprinting *Punch* goes a long way towards explaining its dominance of the comic and satirical element in the popular consciousness, and was certainly something that no other satirical magazine could match. The relatively short life and limited circulation of *Punch*'s rivals, as well as the lack of resources provided by its printer/publisher Bradbury and Evans, seems to have precluded journals like *Judy* and *Fun* from using a similarly ambitious reprinting policy. But there were many other ways in which the name and the idea of *Punch* were sustained in public awareness. The brilliantly inventive early *Punch Almanacks*, which we have already glimpsed, were republished in volume form by the Punch Office as *Punch's Twenty Almanacks 1842–1861* thus linking *Punch* back to its initial Regency exuberance even for readers 20 years later. What we would now call 'branded memorabilia' was widely available, including the *Punch Pocket Book*, a combination of a diary, almanac and comic magazine in a leather folding case that was issued for many years.[24] The *Pocket Book,* with its aspirations to gentility, further reinforced the idea of *Punch* as a constant helpmate to the middle-class urban man. The Punch Office, along with Bradbury and Evans, *Punch*'s printers and publishers,

---

[24] The first *Punch Pocket Book* appeared in 1845, and boasted 'ruled pages for cash accounts and memoranda for every day of the year, an almanack, and a variety of useful and valuable business information'. The format, a folded leather binding held together by a flap, suggested that utility was the dominant characteristic of the *Pocket Book*, but the hand-coloured folding frontispiece by Leech and a variety of other illustrations offered more traditional *Punch* pleasures.

Fig. 10 Opening page of the first volume of *Almanack of the month* (January 1846)

became substantial publishing businesses, launching many works by key *Punch* contributors, most obviously Gilbert a Beckett and G. A. Sala. Some of these volumes became extremely popular, most notably a Beckett's two volume *Comic History of England*, which appeared under the Punch Office imprint in 1847 with etched full page plates and wood engraved vignettes dropped into the text, all by *Punch*'s most celebrated artist John Leech. A number of these volumes were directly drawn from the pages of *Punch*.[25] The Punch Office also issued important periodicals, including the seven half yearly volumes of *Douglas Jerrold's Shilling Magazine* (1845–1848) aimed at aspiring lower middle class and artisan readers, one of a number of progressive journals from the 1840s aimed at broadening public awareness of socio-political issues. More startling still, the Punch Office launched an apparent rival to its own popularity in Gilbert a Beckett's *Almanack of the Month* in 1846, which reduplicated many of the characteristic features of *Punch,* but also offered an original take on the almanac idea (Fig. 10).

---

[25] *Punch's Letters to his Son* and *Punch's Complete Letter Writer* were actually reprinted by Bradbury and Evans from 1853 in many editions.

Fig. 11 Opening page of issue 11 (vol. 2) of *The Man in the Moon* (1847)

In its use of a smaller format with a preponderance of text, however, the *Almanack of the Month* might be read rather as a mark of confidence by the *Punch* team rather than a rival to its popularity—perhaps a Beckett and his colleagues wanted to try to match the continuing success of the long running *Comic Almanack,* which had been launched in 1835 using the presence of the best known comic artist of the day, George Cruikshank, as its major attraction. Cruikshank never drew for *Punch* and his popularity outstripped even than of the *Punch* artists.[26] Even those writers who had dropped out of the *Punch* circle, like Albert Smith, ingenuously used the *Punch* name to sell his Christmas publication *A Bowl of Punch*, which was published in 1848, several years after Smith had left the magazine. At this time, Smith was co-editing a rival to *Punch* called *Man in the Moon*, a journal that spent a lot of energy in scornful accounts of its rival—'Ay, now we rise; but whence thy wild amaze?/Why, Punch, we are but rising

---

[26] A number of *Punch* writers and artists had worked for *The Comic Almanack* since its launch in 1835, and its sustained and eloquent pastiche of the almanac format, as well as its perpetual delight in, and parodying of, officialese, must have influenced *Punch*.

as thou didst in other days' runs one couplet from a provokingly scornful poem published in the second volume of *Man in the Moon* (Fig. 11).[27]

A Bowl of Punch,[28] a paper-bound shilling pamphlet of 126 pages crammed with little joking wood engravings (including the tiny silhouettes and punning visual/verbal jokes so characteristic of comic visual culture in the 1830s and 1840s), comic poems, parodies of official documents and plays, and anecdotes, appeared to be an entirely characteristic *Punch* publication, but in fact used the *Punch* name in an entirely cynical, perhaps even hostile, way.

Punch's visual self-memorialising, almost the creation of an instant archive, began with similar vigour with regard to its graphic content. Barely had the first few issues been published when the magazine announced, in a full page advertisement at the end of the monthly issues, the publication of *Punch's Pencillings, containing eight of the larger caricatures of Punch*. This 'first portfolio' was the first of a long series of reprints. It is significant that at this moment in 1841 *Punch* was still marketing its full page cartoons as 'caricatures' and publishing them in the paper covered 'portfolio' format used for the etchings and engravings of the artists still working in the eighteenth century satirical mode.[29] But under this marketing ploy, the *Punch* staff knew full well that the whole page comic political wood engravings that made up the *Pencillings* were innovative in both format and mode. Within a few years the new generation of *Punch* artists like Leech, Tenniel and Richard Doyle, all trained in the new wood engraved comic idiom rather than the traditional etched or metal engraved caricature, had become widely known and celebrated. As a result they were able to reprint their many *Punch* cartoons in often quite elaborate volumes—John Leech's four oblong folio volumes of *Pictures of Life and Character* proved especially popular and were extensively reprinted in the 1860s. Although they were issued in fragile paper boards, they can often be found in quite elaborate library bindings, suggesting that they were much valued by their owners.[30] Late in the century, Phil May proved to be another *Punch* artist successful enough to be able to print off his contributions in a series of volumes, although he did far less than his predecessors to link his work to the magazine, perhaps in the hope that he would attract more lower class purchasers for his images of street life among the working populace.[31] It is important to note that such volumes shied away from the political, perhaps largely because of the ephemerality of political controversy, in favour of an exploration of class and manners that focused particularly on the pretensions of pseudo-genteel middle class behaviour and the comic clamorousness of public manifestations of working class life (Fig. 12).

---

[27] "Our Flight With Punch," in *The Man in the Moon*, ed. Albert Smith and Angus B. Reach *Man in the Moon*, vol. 2 (London: Periodical Publications 1847); no. 11, 242.

[28] Albert R. Smith, *A Bowl of Punch* (London: David Bogue, 1848).

[29] For example, Henry Heath, William Heath, Henry Alken and George Cruikshank who were all maintaining this mode of publication as the last remnant of the single plate etched or engraved caricature tradition of Gillray, Rowlandson, Newton and Bunbury.

[30] John Leech, *Pictures of Life and Character*, 4 vols. (London: Bradbury and Evans, 1854–1869).

[31] Phil May's *Sketches from Punch* was published by the Punch Office in 1903 in the wake of *Phil May's Sketchbook* which had proved a popular success after first publication by Chatto & Windus in 1895.

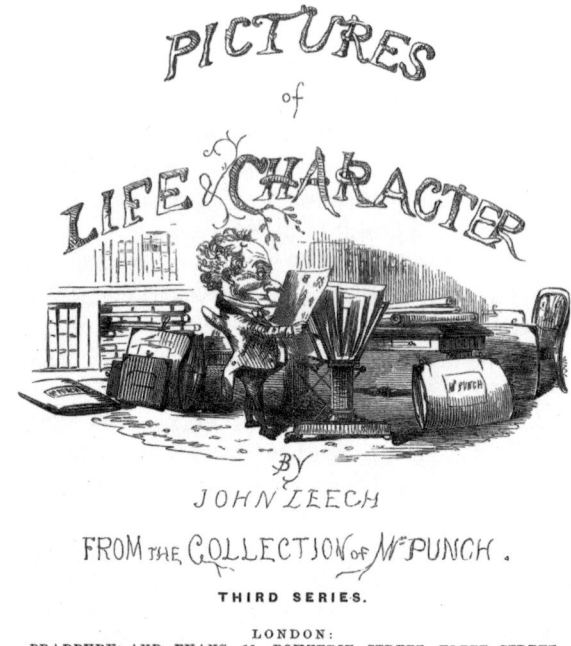

Fig. 12 Title page of the third series of John Leech's *Pictures of Life and Character* (London: Bradbury and Evans, 1860)

Other volumes of collected *Punch* articles, like Douglas Jerrold's *Punch's Letters to his Son*[32] or the many retrospective volumes of Thackeray's comic contributions to the magazine,[33] maintained *Punch* in their title despite being issued by other publishers, who were no doubt glad to make use of the cachet given by the association. Such use of the *Punch* title was particularly associated with Christmas annuals and gift books, suggesting how precisely the magazine had become identified with, and willing to exploit, the cult of seasonal domestic celebrations. *Punch's Snapdragons,* another comic miscellany, was published in 1845 with illustrations by Leech, Hine and Henning, all *Punch* regulars.[34] An earlier example of a similar publication is provided by the 1842 *A Shilling's Worth of Nonsense,*

---

[32] A long-lived favourite of mid-Victorian readers *Punch's Letters to his Son* was first issued by W. S. Orr in 1843 with many illustrations by Kenny Meadows which included a gold stamped image of Punch on the front cloth cover and a satirical image of Punch reading the book's dedication as a frontispiece. The book was frequently issued subsequently by Bradbury and Evans as part of a cheap collected edition of Jerrold's work.

[33] Although not all of Thackeray's contributions were attributed until Spielmann's more or less comprehensive *The Hitherto Unacknowledged Contributions of W. M. Thackeray to 'Punch'* published in 1899, most collected editions of his works devoted a volume to his work for *Punch*.

[34] Anon., *Punch's Snapdragons* (London: Punch Office, 1845).

Fig. 13 Title page of *A Shilling's Worth of Nonsense* (1842)

printed by Bradbury and Evans and written by 'the editors of Punch or the London Charivari' (Fig. 13).[35]

With its highly decorative, whimsical printed paper board covers, full page wood engravings on tinted paper, as well as vignettes and miscellaneous 'essays' offering a pastiche of serious magazines, this little book (which in fact cost half a crown) operates in the ground between the expensive gift book annual and the ephemeral humour of *Punch*, perhaps because of its place in the early days of the magazine. Another publication from this period, *The Comic Album—A Book for Every Table* while not obviously linked to *Punch* through any editorial commentary or allusion and edited anonymously, nonetheless alluded to the layout of the magazine in its design, and contained several contributions written by named *Punch* regulars.[36] All these publications served another useful purpose in giving the *Punch* writers and artists a named identity that unequivocally associated them with the magazine— *Punch* contributions were published anonymously, and even though the authorship of many articles and images was a "common secret", it can have done the magazine and its authors no harm to remind the public of the names of its staff writers in this way, especially as the covers of some *Punch* carried advertisements for many of its contributors' other publications.

In all these ways *Punch* built its own conception of time through the construction of a comic year, which was essentially derived from weekly encounters with the magazine, but then both memorialised and foretold in the *Almanack*, and locked in to the celebratory occasions of comfortable Victorian family life, especially Christmas. *Punch* accordingly transcended its serial nature, and became a fixture within the popular consciousness in a way that superseded the topical and occasional nature of its contents. *Punch*'s advanced brand consciousness inevitably compromised its potential radicalism. In reprinting his cartoons, Leech, ever deferential to the reading occasions and sensibilities of his public and undoubtedly seeking the best financial returns, anthologised only his social satire, omitting political images which, in any case, became quickly detached from their precise context. While the stereotyped reprints of *Punch* volumes of course retained all of their original content, they suffered similarly from the short span of public memory for political detail, and thus it was likely to have been the comic analysis of class habits, personality quirks and social mores that proved the main attraction for most readers. The volume *Punch* spin-offs, like *Punch's Pocket Book*, were largely offered as gift books devoid of political commentary. That the *Almanacks*, which were seemingly ineluctably tied to a particular temporal moment, were successfully reprinted in volume form, suggests how far the decorative and apolitically comical elements of *Punch* outweighed political and social satire—this is not to say, of course, that there are not outspoken or controversial images in the *Almanack*.

---

[35] The Editors of "Punch, or the London Charivari", *A Shilling's Worth of Nonsense* (London: Bradbury and Evans, 1842).

[36] Anon., *The Comic Album—A Book for Every Table* (London: W.S.Orr, 1843).

Punch and Its Late Victorian Imitators

Punch famously served in various ways as the model for the many generally short-lived illustrated satirical and comic journals that punctuated the period between 1850 and 1900.[37] But several were successful. One of the longest lived of these, and the closest in format to *Punch*, was *Judy* (1867–1910) (Fig. 14).

Fig. 14 Title page of *Judy*, vol. 4 (1868)

---

[37] A helpful overview of Victorian comic periodicals with a good bibliography is provided by Vann and van Arsdel, *Victorian Periodicals*, 279–290.

So close was *Judy* to *Punch* that its first issue described the latter magazine as a 'caitiff husband', although the success of the journal was largely due to the fact that the sophistication of *Punch* had left behind its lower middle class readers, and was perhaps too male in its address and interests to attract women readers in any numbers.[38] While generally a successful venture with many spectacular double page cartoons, *Judy* lacked a well-known and easily identifiable lead artist, which may well have contributed to its secondary position behind *Punch*. One similar venture perhaps did rather better in developing its artists and their illustrations into distinctive and memorable features of its production. *Fun* (1861–1901) found in James Frank Sullivan an artist who, as well as producing accomplished large scale cartoons, was a pioneer in Britain of the comic strip format, chronicling over many years the small-scale trials and triumphs of the 'British Working Man', and thus making one of *Punch's* perennial themes into a continuing graphic narrative (Fig. 15).[39]

Fun was also successful in turning itself into a 'brand', and followed *Punch* in issuing volumes of cartoons drawn from its pages. Again like *Punch*, *Fun* used the travesty of public discourses as a central element in its humour, and offered its readers a broad range of political, burlesque and visual commentary and parody that required considerable sophistication from its readers to be understood. The similarity of its appearance, address and content to *Punch,* as well as its long life, has led one commentator to described *Fun* as 'perhaps the second most important comic periodical in the Victorian period'.[40] Other journals like the *Tomahawk* (1867–1870), which espoused a radical brand of conservatism, the more orthodoxly conservative *Moonshine* (1879–1902) and *Will O' The Wisp* (1867–1871) were explicitly more sectarian in their views than *Punch* or *Fun*, and combined satire with a range of serious commentary or, in the case of *Moonshine*, extensive theatre reviews.

Despite their differences over point of view and the balance of content, all these magazines drew two central characteristics from *Punch*. First, they all recognised the centrality of spectacular large-scale topical cartoons to their success, and continually drew on caricature figures of well-known politicians like Gladstone and Disraeli as subjects. As already noted, James Sullivan significantly developed a new kind of comic strip in *Fun* as a form of sympathetic if amused engagement with working class culture and the origins of the hugely influential comic graphic persona of Aly Sloper can be found in embryonic form in *Judy*. The *Tomahawk* had in Matt Morgan's ground-breaking two colour folding caricatures perhaps the most outstanding graphic achievement to be found anywhere in British nineteenth century comic journalism, although John Proctor's work for *Will O' The Wisp*, again on a huge scale, is also extremely impressive. The fact that these artists were

---

[38] Brake and Demoor, *Nineteenth Century Journalism*, 327–328.

[39] Ibid.

[40] Vann and van Arsdel, *Victorian Periodicals*, 287. Thackeray is rumoured to have referred to the magazine as *Funch* so closely did it resemble its old established rival.

Fig. 15 Title page of *Fun* new series, vol. 14 (1872)

prominently named in their respective magazines suggests their importance to the success of their respective journals.

The second central strategy these magazines derived from *Punch* was the necessity of developing a branded satirical persona to serve as the 'voice' or collective identity of the periodical and its contributors. In doing this, of course,

FIGARO IN LONDON.

Satire should, like a polish'd razor keen,
Wound with a touch that's scarcely felt or seen.—LADY MONTAGUE.

"Political Pasquinades and Political Caricatures are parts (though humble ones) of Political history. They supply information as to the personal habits, and often as to the motives and objects of public men, which cannot be found elsewhere."—CROKER'S NEW WHIG GUIDE.

No. 17.]   SATURDAY, MARCH 31, 1832.   [Price One Penny.

HORRORS OF LIMBO.   **THE POLICE FORCE ON DUTY.**

FIGARO V. THE BLUE DEVILS.

It will be seen by recent police reports, that a very unpopular attempt has been made by a perjured Blue Devil, in the shape of a policeman, to put a stop to the progress of the ever-welcome *Figaro*. The liberality of the Government, and the enlightened taste of the London Magistrates has, however, nipped in the bud this malicious and mercenary attempt to curtail England of her amusements: and a release has been granted to a poor devil who would otherwise have been made by three week's imprisonment a victim to the avaricious rapacity of a falsely swearing policeman. The above caricature represents our unfortunate vender undergoing for three days, during which he was remanded, the horrors of *limbo*. What a miserable picture does he present compared with his appearance, when offering in Leicester Square, the new number of Figaro for sale, to the innumerable relishers of cheap wit, who perambulate the metropolis. Were government to show a disposition to oppose Figaro, we could scarcely answer for its security; for how could the 50,000 of our countrymen, who look for it with the regular appetite of true *gourmands*, forego their weekly dish of *piquant* entertainment. Even the worthy Magistrates

N. B. We have taken the liberty of changing the names of the above caricatures, which are in the *Comic Magazine*, (by no means a political publication) called " *Strong Room for Improvement*," and " *Staff at Head Quarters*."

Fig. 16 A page from the first volume of *Figaro in London* (1832) with wood engravings by Robert Seymour

journals were following a long tradition of the figuration of public voices through the mechanisms of semi-mythical individuals—early in the nineteenth century, British identity was often figured through John Bull. But highly politicised radical periodicals from the 1830s and early 1840s like *The Black Dwarf*, *Asmodeus in*

The Presence of *Punch* in the Nineteenth Century

London and *Figaro in London* had shown the value (and perhaps also the political prudence) of cloaking a magazine's identity in a ventriloquising persona (Fig. 16).

Mr Punch, as constructed in the popular consciousness, drew brilliantly on this tradition by combining the qualities of the clown, the outsider, the lord of misrule, and the friend of the oppressed or misunderstood. Brash, outspoken, irrepressible, disruptive and certainly capable of violence, Mr Punch also presented himself as an incorruptible defender of moral standards, and thus able to offer the non-partisan objectivity of the outsider in his views. The magazines that imitated *Punch* tried extremely hard to construct such a complexly sympathetic if troubling figure that would speak their texts and draw their images. The last issue of a satirical journal called *Echoes*, published on 2 October 1869 as the magazine changed its name and format to become *The Period*, published a double page cartoon in which the modish 'Miss Echo' introduces the highly fashionable couple who are to speak for *The Period*, watched by the assembled graphic personae of the four leading satirical magazines of the time. *Punch* is represented by a benign Mr Punch wearing a rather rakish boater (Fig. 17).

Fig. 17 Part of a cartoon from *Echoes* (2 October 1869) showing the graphic personae used by four comic journals, *Judy, Punch, Fun* and the *Tomahawk,* to represent their titles

To his right is *Judy* in the guise of what looks like a rural schoolmistress complete with black cat. A rather bemused and insipid looking jester forms *Fun* and a glaring, tense Native American brave characterises the *Tomahawk*. *Echoes*, soon to be *The Period*, was perhaps somewhat rash in invoking this array of well-established competitors, for neither version of the magazine has entered historical consciousness to the extent of *Punch* or even *Tomahawk*. Yet, for all its lack of success with its own figureheads, *Echoes* was all too easily able to identify that for the success of a satirical journal it was important to develop a readily identifiable, sympathetic editorial persona, something that several of the Asian comic journals, which form the topic of this book, also recognized.

Why Was *Punch* So Influential?

The above essay, while forming a highly abbreviated overview, has suggested a number of largely material reasons for *Punch*'s dominance of the comic periodical market throughout the Victorian period. The most obvious of these, all discussed above, are the magazine's early backing by a financially stable printer/publisher, its brilliance at self-promotion supported by a canniness about exploiting the marketplace through the development of the *Punch* brand, its appointment and retention of a succession of brilliant illustrators and cartoonists who built on the page format, technical support and stable long-term finances of the magazine, and its development of Mr Punch as its chosen collective editorial voice. But the central reasons for *Punch*'s sustained success concern its content and ideological position. *Punch*'s sustained interest in central and immediate political topics of the day—the nature of the monarchy, the Irish question, or the 'condition of England' question—was offset by its continued pleasure in the comedy of manners provided by the aspirations and eccentricities of the British class system. Its initial radicalism was replaced by a less adventurous amusement at almost every major issue which could occasionally harden into a bluff conservatism on such matters as the emancipation of women.

Yet, the content of *Punch*, as suggested above, was not simply 'humorous' or 'satirical' but was rather constructed out of sustained interplay between satire, travesty, invective and whimsy. These disparate qualities nonetheless formed a compelling whole, offsetting the political engagement of the satirical and denunciatory elements against the gentler fantasies of whimsy and parody. *Punch*, after an early interest in inherited elements of Regency caricature, replaced the grotesquerie of eighteenth and early nineteenth satire with a more fanciful kind of humour that delighted in parodying the pomposity and overstatement of public discourses of all kinds. While it could be outspoken in its denunciation of social evils or political chicanery, *Punch*'s satire was perhaps more defensive than confrontational. Humour in *Punch* both recognised and cathartically laughed away the fears and anxieties of its readers, reducing perceived dangers and threats to manageable proportions through the construction of a comic world turned upside down. As with the upside-down drowning skater in the 1842 *Almanack,* the view from a place of crisis using the comic inversions of the *Punch* world view was not so much threatening as unexpected and wondrous.

Part II
Punch in South Asia

Punch and Indian Cartoons: The Reception of a Transnational Phenomenon

Partha Mitter

When proposing to look at the relationship between the Punch and Indian cartoon, the thrust of my argument relates to colonial India, which is my own particular field of study. I take up the story of Punch's progress and spread throughout the subcontinent. *Punch* was turned into an effective weapon of political resistance and social criticism by the Indian followers of the English magazine in a way not envisaged by its creators. Yet this is not the entire story. *Punch* exemplifies the wider question of how a concept or technology originating in one culture undergoes transformations of meaning and inflection subsequent to its introduction in a culturally different society. This perennial question assumes special urgency during the high tide of imperialism, which represents the first great phase of globalisation. Therefore, in order to pose general questions about the nature and mechanism of transfers of ideas and technologies across cultures, and their impact on those who receive them, one needs to shift the discussion over to the debate on globalisation. The urgency of this debate is underscored by the concern of this publication to discuss *Punch* as a transcultural phenomenon. Within this remit, my own analysis is informed by the fact that while post-colonial studies have led the field in uncovering the Western agenda in its analysis of the world colonial order, recent critics have recognised the need for greater nuances in studies of the period of high imperialism. As a new publication puts it in its study of the period 1880s–1940s, a period that includes the career of *Punch*:

> [A] new look at the possibilities and ultimate failures of this period that is considered to have witnessed the first wave of globalization, may provide some insight for the dynamics of our own time. This may prove quite significant for the current attempts to hold the balance of an arguably more modern but less Western, more interconnected, and yet more multipolar international system.[1]

---

[1] Sebastian Conrad and Dominic Sachsenmaier, "Introduction: Competing Visions of World Order: Global Moments and Movements, 1880s–1930s," in *Competing Visions of World Order:*

P. Mitter (✉)
Emeritus Professor of Art History at the University of Sussex, United Kingdom
e-mail: parthamitter@btinternet.com

The comic magazine *Punch, or The London Charivari*, founded in 1841, was the main inspiration behind political and social cartoons and humorous magazines in India. What was the reason behind the enduring success of *Punch* while others existed only briefly? For us today its cartoons do not seem particularly funny. The earlier English cartoonists James Gillray, Thomas Rowlandson, and George Cruikshank displayed brilliant savagery in their caricature that is absent from this Victorian publication. Drawings in *Punch* seldom compared with the cartoons of the great Honoré Daumier or the Expressionist graphic artists who illustrated the German magazine, *Simplicissimus*. By comparison they seem rather tame and respectably middle class. And yet the name *Punch* is synonymous with comic magazines the world over. It redefined the word 'cartoon' in the English language to stand for satirical drawings, shedding its original sense of a preparatory drawing.[2] Its staying power has been phenomenal, its reputation surviving even after its demise in 2002.

What makes it especially fascinating for the historian of empire is that the comic magazine's influence was not confined solely to colonial India simply as one of a series of artefacts exported from the metropolis to the empire as part of the westernising process. It successfully travelled in the nineteenth century from London all the way to Hong Kong, Tokyo and Melbourne, with diversions into in Arab countries and India. Not only did it enjoy an enviable worldwide circulation in its heyday, it also provided the model for numerous similar publications in far corners of the globe, including regions that were not directly colonised. Brian Maidment offers us persuasive reasons for the phenomenal success and unusual longevity of this quintessentially English product. The comic magazine replaced the grotesqueries of the previous political and social caricaturists with a hybrid genre that combined whimsy, travesty, invective, burlesque and satire, introducing the interplay of text and image in its square double-columned page format and layout. These technical aspects were supported by stable editorship, astute branding and the business nous of a financially secure publisher.[3]

But its very success in being transplanted to regions culturally alien to the British provides us with the ideal means to understand the nature of transcultural transmission of ideas, images and motifs as they cross national boundaries in our contemporary world. Of course, this sort of cultural migration is in itself nothing new. Since antiquity tangible goods and intangible commodities, such as ideas and technologies, have travelled great distances to foreign lands, where they were reinterpreted, reassembled, transformed and occasionally assimilated. The newness lies in the sheer scale and self-conscious manner in which these transmissions took

---

Global Moments and Movements, 1880s–1930s, eds. Sebastian Conrad and Dominic Sachsenmaier (New York: Palgrave, 2007), 1–9; 3.

[2] Maurice Horn, "Caricature and Cartoon: An overview," in *The World Encyclopedia of Cartoons*, ed. Maurice Horn (New York & London 1980), 15–34.

[3] I have learnt a great deal from Brian Maidment's deeply researched paper "The Presence of *Punch* in the Nineteenth Century," Chap. 2 in this volume.

place in the nineteenth century. This was the apex of the Empire that saw large population movements and intense cultural exchanges. The comic magazine became one of the major Western 'commodities' of international consumption in these fluid times.

Therefore the question that I would reiterate is this: what are the wider reasons for such a phenomenal spread of *Punch* around the world, or to put it differently, what were the forces that contributed to its enormous distribution network and international consumption? The Victorian era was a great watershed in world history. It witnessed an unprecedented expansion of travel as steam trains and steamships spanned great distances nationally and internationally. British venture capital and the Indian colonial government's need for internal security over the vast territory joined hands in the laying down of what was to be the largest rail network in Asia. Apart from territorial control, commercial considerations such as moving goods rapidly throughout India played an important part in the success of the rail network; an unexpected consequence was the popularity of train travel among Indians of all classes who took to travelling for pleasure, pilgrimage, and various other family reasons. On the high seas, the Indian Raj was able to secure fast and direct links with the Home Government as steamships drastically cut the travel time between England to India. The English magazine printed in London was able to reach Indian ports within the month and receive India-wide distribution while the topics were still fresh. Unlike a book, the time factor is of course particularly important in the case of monthly magazines.

However, even if it was possible for *Punch* to be widely distributed in India, the language barrier could have restricted it to the expatriate English. One may deduce the enthusiastic reception of the English monthly among the English-speaking élite from the fact that they eagerly emulated its format and the style of its cartoons, as can be witnessed by the enormous number of Indian versions of *Punch*. This only became possible with the introduction of the English language and print technology in colonial India.[4] Colonial rule had introduced literacy in English primarily for political reasons. The Law Member of the Governor-General's Council,

---

[4] Recently, Ritu G. Khanduri, "Vernacular Punches: Cartoons and Politics in Colonial India," *History and Anthropology* 20, no. 4 (December 2009): 459–486, and again in this volume (chapter *Punch* in India: Another History of Colonial Politics?) has investigated the reasons as to why vernacular versions of *Punch*, which were very popular, had been neglected until now. In this connection she argues that *Punch* failed to establish a market in India, conjecturing that the regional versions posed a challenge to the English magazine. Her argument is based on two points: (a) the correspondence of the owners of *Punch*, who were unsure about its clientele in India, and (b) the profusion of vernacular *Punch* magazines. While she makes a strong case for the importance of vernacular *Punch* versions, there seems to be little concrete evidence, such as sales figures, to draw any firm conclusion about the failure of the market for *Punch*. Of course, no English publication could have large sales in India, if only because of language restrictions. On the other hand, each vernacular version of *Punch* taken individually had a limited sale within the region because there was no lingua franca in India, except perhaps English. However, the very fact that is was widely known and provided a model for vernacular cartoons suggests *Punch*'s renown in India, though it was necessarily confined to the English-speaking elite.

Thomas Babington Macaulay, expressed with his usual candour that the English literate élite in India would be

> interpreters between us and the millions we govern [...] [to] that class we leave it to refine the vernacular dialects...with terms of science borrowed from the [West] [...] and render them [...] fit vehicles for conveying knowledge to the great mass of the population.[5]

To take the example of Bengal, the *bhadralok* took full advantage of the opportunities offered by this new learning. It gave them access to world literature and Enlightenment values. Bengali, the vernacular language of the region, benefited from colonial culture as it underwent modernisation at this time, with the development of a new simplified script and a unified language, which could be disseminated by means of print technology. *Punch*, which became available in Bengal soon after its inception, could thus be ensured of a ready market in this bilingual milieu.

The second and in some ways perhaps even more momentous development in India was the far-reaching information revolution. Arriving in the colonial period, print technology was initially used by Christian missionaries for conversion purposes.[6] Global print culture began with the invention of the moveable type in China in the eleventh century, followed by Johannes Gutenberg's printing press in the fifteenth, when the easy replication, multiplication and transmission of data became possible.[7] The great advantage of the new technology was its ability to print large quantities of material quickly and at a modest cost, which allowed for wide diffusion of information. Modernity has come to be associated with the endless 'repeatability' of information, and the technology to replicate infinitely, about which Walter Benjamin wrote so eloquently.[8] In short, in the colonial period, print culture and the English language overcame local and regional differences. They helped the Indian intelligentsia to forge a new unity among the Western literate, giving rise to organised and vocal opposition to the imperial government.

Of course, one cannot speak of universal literacy in colonial India, or for that matter anywhere in the nineteenth century, with some notable exceptions such as

---

[5] Thomas B. Macaulay. "Minute on Education," in *Sources of Indian Tradition*, vol. 2, ed. William T. DeBary (New York: Columbia University Press, 1963), 44–49; 49. Interestingly, Rammohun Roy also supported English education but for different reasons, see DeBary, *Sources of Indian Tradition*, vol. 2, 40–43.

[6] Christopher A. Bayly, *Empire and Information* (Cambridge: Cambridge University Press, 2000) discusses communication explosion in the colonial period. The Raj used revolutionary technology to maintain control over the subcontinent. The same technology was used by Indian nationalists to forge new 'communities' and norms.

[7] Douglas C. McMurtrie, *The Book: the Story of Printing and Bookmaking* (New York: Oxford University Press, 1943).

[8] Walter Benjamin, "The Work of Art in the Age of Mechanical Reproduction," in *Illuminations*, Walter Benjamin, ed. Hannah Arendt (Suffolk, 1982), 219–253.

Victorian Britain. But compared with pre-colonial India, where only a minority of men of the élite strata—Brahmins, Muslim divines, court officials, clerks and accountants—could read and write, colonial India saw a substantial widening of literacy among the urban élite in the metropolitan cities of India.[9] Flourishing vernacular newspapers in Bengali, Marathi, Tamil, Hindi, and other languages made linguistic groups conscious of their regions, while a growing India-wide English readership, created through British policy and the spread of English newspapers, magazines and books, helped forge a common political vocabulary. Print technology provided the impetus for national aspirations of the westernised élite, giving rise to an imagined community that sought to bypass castes, regions, religions and languages. Not surprisingly, in this articulate milieu there would be a ready market for such an innovative publication that could use humour to call into question government policy and ridicule high officials. Not only was *Punch* eagerly received but its format and style were also found to be relevant in the Indian context. In time there would be Indian versions of the English comic magazine in both English and regional languages. Astonishingly, there existed Indian entrepreneurs even in small towns in rural Bengal, who had taken to English education with alacrity, and were prepared to bring out local versions of *Punch*.[10]

As part of print culture that created a self-conscious, articulate élite who communicated across India through books, magazines and newspapers, colonial culture opened up the subcontinent to another new technology that would ultimately have far reaching consequences. In a nutshell, mechanical reproduction of images, which arrived in India as part of nascent modernity, was at the heart of the information and communication revolution that complemented the rise of printed newspapers, magazines and books. The new technology encouraged 'visual literacy', as replications of images on a mass scale made it possible to circulate pictorial information to a widely dispersed population throughout India as never before. The impact of print technology as well as printed images on modern Indian nationalism has received the attention of scholars.[11] There was an unprecedented availability of prints throughout India in the late nineteenth century which can be attributed to

---

[9] Aparna Basu, *The Growth of Education and Political Development in India, 1898–1920* (Delhi: Oxford University Press, 1974).

[10] Partha Mitter, *Art and Nationalism in Colonial India 1850–1922: Occidental Orientations* (Cambridge: Cambridge University Press, 1994), 138, on *Purneah Punch* which was published from a remote district of Bengal.

[11] Uma Dasgupta, *The Rise of an Indian Public: Impact of Official Policy, 1870–1880* (Calcutta: Rddhi, 1977); Anil Seal, *The Emergence of Indian Nationalism: Competition and Collaboration in the Later Nineteenth Century* (Cambridge: Cambridge University Press, 1968) on the impact of print technology on Indian nationalism. Mitter, *Art and Nationalism*, part two, section four (The Power of the Printed Image), 120–178, discusses the impact of mechanical reproduction on the creation of a visually alert society that contributed to the construction of national identity.

their easy reproducibility and to the new modes of transport. The railways were able to transport bulks of printed matter, such as newspapers and magazines across the subcontinent speedily, inexpensively and efficiently.[12] Here I would like to remind the readers that, while mechanically reproduced prints could reach a wide segment of the non-literate population and thus contribute to the growth of nationalist consciousness, one should not overlook the role of illustrated magazines in making the élite respond to the power of images.[13] Parallel to the introduction of illustrations in newspapers, especially cartoons, the rise of illustrated magazines greatly facilitated the reception of illustrated comic magazines such as *Punch*.

It is in connection with the emergence of an audience that could engage critically with pictorial information, that it would be interesting to examine more closely the way visual languages migrate to culturally different societies, and to examine the mechanism behind them. During the nineteenth century, the graphic arts gained prominence in the West because copies of original works became readily available to the poor who could not afford the originals, a process accelerated by the invention of mechanical reproduction. In a colonial society such as India, European originals were rare and hardly impinged on popular consciousness. Only aristocratic families were able to collect original European art, and not always of the highest quality. In this colonial environment, in the absence of originals, art reproductions became the standard reference point for artists. However, this phenomenon was by no means confined to colonial India but applied more generally to global modernity. Mechanical reproduction gained an overwhelming importance in modern times irrespective of whether originals existed or not. More importantly, in the case of mechanical replication, there is no question of authentic versus copy since it is meaningless to speak of an authentic print. Prints begat prints.[14]

Printed images created the visual world not only of Indian artists and illustrators but the population in general who were bombarded with material as diverse as prints, art plates of European masterpieces, illustrations in diverse books and journals, not to mention the plethora of pictorial imagery on imported goods from matchboxes to baby foods. By the middle of the century, as Victorian tastes took a firm hold in India, a lucrative market in European illustrated books, magazines and art reproductions flourished. The English-literate illustrator ransacked these sources for ideas, which radically altered his work methods, as well as the perception of art itself. The importance of Art Nouveau, Jugendstil and Art Deco graphic design for

---

[12] Bayly, *Empire and Information*, discusses the effect of modern technology in the quick and efficient dissemination of information during the colonial period.

[13] Partha Mitter, "Mechanical Reproduction and the World of the Colonial Artist," in *Beyond Appearances: Visual Practices and Ideologies in Modern India*, ed. Sumathi Ramaswamy (New Delhi: Sage Publications: 2003), 1–30; 23 on the impact of mass prints on the non-literate population.

[14] Benjamin, "Work of Art," 220–28.

Bengali illustrators of books and magazines cannot be gainsaid.[15] In this milieu, where printed images reigned supreme, *Punch* cartoons offered not only a most persuasive genre for political and social comment but also a model for a new kind of publication.

In view of the above discussion, it is easy to see why art historians dominate the field of visual culture and thus affect our study of the migration of images. For the art historian the transmission of styles, ideas, motifs, and the syntax of art forms has been a central problem. From earliest times, ideas and technology have crossed cultural borders with impunity, new forms being absorbed within the body fabric as they create fresh meanings in new cultural contexts. These exchanges of ideas and forms need not necessarily be interpreted through ideas of domination and dependence. However, today, 'influence' as a model of cultural transmission is felt to be far too simple to understand the complex process of the global circulation of ideas. This is largely because colonial art history has insisted on the derivative and passive nature of the reception of styles from the West to the rest of the world. During the period of Western ascendancy in the nineteenth century, the nature of stylistic influence became increasingly politicised as societies were ranked within a global hierarchy of race, hierarchy and evolution. The relationship between representation, power and authority has been thoroughly exposed by post-colonial scholars with considerable skill and insight. While acknowledging the contribution of discourse theory in challenging colonial perceptions, I feel the time has come to extend the debate on how ideas cross borders and migrate to new regions where they generate entirely new meanings commensurate with the imperatives of that society.[16]

In this era of obsession with globalisation, historians have begun to turn to this question, not least because they are forced to take on board the post-colonial critiques of Edward Said and other scholars who characterise colonial culture simply as one of imposing power and authority on the colonised.[17] They address the question: how are ideas transmitted across the global arena in the age of communication revolution that followed European expansion in Asia, Africa and the Americas? In a formulation proposed by Mary Louise Pratt, a leading proponent of discourse theory, 'contact zones' become 'social spaces where cultures meet, clash, and grapple with each other, often in contexts of highly asymmetrical relations of power'.[18] This nuanced reading of colonial encounters allows for the agency of the individual even though the role of power and authority is not ignored. What we cannot overlook is the fact that even though alternative visions of global

---

[15] For examples of the transformation of Art Nouveau motifs, see Mitter, *Art and Nationalism*, 126.

[16] Partha Mitter, "Decentering Modernism: Art History and Avant-Garde Art from the Periphery," *The Art Bulletin* 90, no. 4 (December 2008): 531–548.

[17] Edward W. Said, *Orientalism* (London: Routledge and Kegan Paul, 1978).

[18] Mary L. Pratt, *Imperial Eyes: Travel Writing and Transculturation* (London: Routledge, 1992), 6.

modernity have existed in the nineteenth and twentieth centuries, the recent debates have been dominated by the Western interpretations of global modernity as a reflection of the world colonial order, of which the art historical obsession with influence forms only a part.[19] The aim of our study of the worldwide transmission of the new genre of comic magazines as epitomised by *Punch* is to unpack the web of modern global interactions, realised during the high tide of imperialism. Because of the weight of scholarship on Western expansion, conceptually it becomes a tough assignment if one were to go beyond the model of Western domination for this period. The question that needs to be answered is whether the English magazine, belonging to the home of the largest empire, is yet another tool in perpetuating Western hegemony, or not. This would be true if the reception of *Punch* in India and other parts of the globe was a passive act, but we must ask whether artistic agency played a transformative role here. From this viewpoint, at the risk of sounding like a revisionist, the thrust of my argument has been that the story is more complex where an essentialist approach falls short of a proper explanation.

We may examine one area where the asymmetrical relations between centre and periphery play a less determining role—the global circulation of printed literature across the world. Benedict Anderson has made a major contribution to our understanding of what he terms print capitalism with his definition of nationhood as 'an imagined community', which is a product of literacy and print culture.[20] I would like to extend the scope of print culture in order to draw out its global implications, which Anderson is not primarily concerned with. In the high tide of colonialism, three languages are normally associated with international communication in terms of printed literature, namely English, French and Spanish. I would like to theorise this universe of printed text as a virtual community, where communication is indirect because it takes place through the print medium without the need for direct contact between individuals, and, indeed, rarely do individuals communicate directly in this context. I have described this phenomenon as 'virtual cosmopolitanism', simply because transactions take place entirely on the level of imagination and intellect.[21]

The notion of 'cosmopolitanism' is a useful tool here because it allows the agency of the individual to participate in a wider universal cultural exchange. However, one does come up against the problems inherent in cosmopolitanism because it cannot circumvent uneven power relations between centre and

---

[19] See Conrad and Sachsenmaier, "Introduction".

[20] See Benedict Anderson, *Imagined Communities: Reflections on the Origin and Spread of Nationalism* (London: Verso, 1983).

[21] See Partha Mitter, *The Triumph of Modernism: India's Artists and the Avant-Garde, 1922–1947* (London: Reaktion Books, 2007), 10–13 on virtual cosmopolitanism.

periphery.²² Even here, the metropolis has the authority to form canons and speak for the peripheries. For instance, in the colonial order of the nineteenth century, it would be unimaginable to expect *Punch* to originate in Calcutta, Cairo or Shanghai, rather than London. Nonetheless, power comes less into play in the virtual cosmopolis than in actual encounters. The Periphery shares a body of ideas on modernity and actively and fruitfully engages with global knowledge. The most important aspect of this virtual cosmopolis is that it engenders new ideas within the Periphery and occasionally in the Centre that are relevant in their own cultural contexts.²³

The process is of course complex and I will propose here another concept whose dynamics explain better the nature of transmission and reception of ideas within the transcultural framework. One of the most influential ideas in cross-cultural studies since the late 1970s has been the unravelling of the colonial discourse, which engaged in 'dominating, restructuring, and having authority over the Orient'.²⁴ While the truth of this assertion is not in doubt, Orientalism tends to foreclose any possibility of dialogue across cultures. Here, the particular definition of the text by the Russian literary critic Mikhail Bakhtin could take us further into cross-cultural studies by precisely stressing the possibility of dialogue, even while granting the asymmetry between centre and periphery. Bakhtin coins the term 'dialogic' as a form of intertextuality to describe a continuous dialogue between a text vis-à-vis other texts. Such a dialogic process appropriates the words of others and transforms them according to one's creative intention related to one's own context. This intertextual process is dynamic, relational, and engaged in endless re-descriptions of one's own world vision. Additionally, the particular merit of the dialogic method is that it allows for the co-existence of different approaches in a relativist way,

---

²² Anthony K. Appiah, *Cosmopolitanism: Ethics in a World of Strangers* (New York: W.W. Norton, 2006) views cosmopolitan values as bringing human beings together. He rejects both the politics of difference and nationalist fabrications of exclusive claims to cultural patrimony. While he makes some valuable points, his universalist view does not allow for the role of power and authority. James Clifford, "Mixed Feelings," in *Cosmopolitics: Thinking and Feeling Beyond the Nation*, eds. Pheng Cheah and Bruce Robbins (Minneapolis: University of Minneapolis Press, 1998): 362–370; 362–365, proposes 'discrepant cosmopolitanism' from the viewpoint of the poor and dispossessed that addresses the role of power. My own concern here is the relationship of Centre and Periphery in the global circulation of ideas. There is certainly the problem of power and authority, but my model takes into account the power relationship that does not prevent the generation of new ideas within the global colonial order.

²³ Two instances can be cited to counter the notion that ideas always flow from the West to other regions. A remarkable instance of the periphery striking back is the case of the great Indian poet and Nobel Laureate Rabindranath Tagore, who was one of the most famous individuals of the inter-bellum years. His reputation was created by the publication of *Gitanjali*, a book of poems, in English, and later in other languages, which was very much the product of the global print culture. Another example is the gradual spread of the knowledge of Indian philosophy and religious texts such as the *Upanishads* or the *Bhagavadgita* in the West. Of course, in both these cases English acted as a mediating language partly because India was part of the British Empire.

²⁴ Said, *Orientalism*, 3.

and does not set up an essentialist hierarchy of ideas and values, as in the case of discourse theory for instance.[25]

In the global outreach of English commodities during the Victorian era as part of the marketing strategy of the Empire, *Punch* soon captured a large segment of the market in imported literature. Against this perspective, the impact of *Punch* on its Indian versions in English and the vernacular languages can be studied in terms of the original idea and its constant re-interpretations or transformations in the light of specific Indian requirements. Expressed in another way, the essay seeks to unravel the dialogic relations between colonial hegemony, migration of ideas and nationalist resistance as expressed in the wide and diverse range of Indian *Punch*-inspired cartoons. Let me give an example of how the process works. Both the texts and the images in *Punch*, initially addressing the English expatriates in India and their social milieu, underwent unintended consequences and became the source material for entirely different publications.

If one were to take typical cartoons on the Indian Empire, including their captions in *Punch*, the impression formed is of the cartoonist mirroring imperial ideology, even if he disagreed with particular policies. This had the effect of bolstering the sense of superiority of the English in India by making them an essential part of the avowed imperial mission. In addition, the *Punch* cartoons on social topics satisfied their nostalgia for the life left behind at home in Britain. The enterprising among the British expatriates, who were delighted to discover *Punch*, brought out a number of local versions of the comic magazine. These tended to virtually reproduce the parent magazine's political views, also eagerly emulating the aura of Victorian respectability popularised by *Punch*. As Brian Maidment has shown, the English magazine initially expressed sympathy for the socially degraded, as it condemned the exploitation of women. Its radical energy soon lost steam. It took refuge in endorsing bourgeois values which helped boost sales figures.[26] The English periodicals in India used gentle humour to depict Anglo-Indian lifestyle, disclosing a lack of self-criticism that may be explained by the fact that the imperial bureaucracy had turned into benevolent despotism as the British community became racially exclusive. Thus they became an index of imperial aims and aspirations.

The Indian illustrators of comic magazines in English and the vernacular scrutinised *Punch* cartoons for their visual impact and Indianised them for their own specific ends, which substantially altered their original meaning and significance. These political and social cartoonists frequently reused and reinterpreted these images as a weapon of resistance against the colonial rulers, as we shall see with the Indian versions of *Punch*. In the process, the generally pro establishment

---

[25] Mikhail M. Bakhtin, *The Dialogic Imagination: Four Essays*, ed. Michael Holquist, trans. Caryl Emerson and Michael Holquist (Austin: University of Texas Press, 1981) and Michael Holquist, *Dialogism: Bakhtin and His World* (London: Routledge, 2002).

[26] Maidment, chapter The Presence of *Punch* in the Nineteenth Century in this volume, 11–13.

English magazine was miraculously transmuted in India into an organ of social satire and anti-colonial resistance that recalled Gillray and other radical early nineteenth century caricaturists. As other papers in the volume will illustrate, the multicultural reincarnations of *Punch* worldwide recreated new genres that spoke directly to the local population, which distanced them significantly from the original intentions of the publisher in London.

Caricature and parody in texts and images exist in all societies and one comes across caricature and the grotesque in Indian art from the ancient period, the earliest probably in the ancient Buddhist reliefs at Sanchi.[27] But caricature, parody, satire and travesty as modern weapons of social comment began in earnest in colonial Calcutta, strikingly in the 'low art' of Kalighat. Modern journalistic caricature on contemporary topics was introduced by the British in India. Ultimately however, no publication made a greater impact than *Punch*. The following were only a few of the publications directly inspired by the English comic magazine: *The Indian Charivari*; *Delhi Sketch Book*; *Momus*; *Basantak*; *The Avadh Punch*; *The Delhi Punch*; *The Punjab Punch*; *The Indian Punch*; *Urdu Punch*; *Gujarati Punch*; *Hindu Punch*; *Parsi Punch*, which was renamed *The Hindi Punch* in 1878.[28]

Of the comic magazines published by the English in India, none was more accomplished than *The Indian Charivari or The Indian Punch*, founded in 1872. It claimed to offer an illustrated paper that reviewed current political and social topics in a light, playful spirit. Its front cover paid homage to Richard Doyle's famous cover of *Punch*. In fairness, *The Indian Charivari* did not express a uniformly hostile view of Indians, routinely expressing approval of the landed gentry, but suspicions of social reformers. It made vociferous comments on government policy, and as representative of the Anglo-Indian lobby, applied conservative brakes to liberal measures. A plate from the magazine entitled, 'The Modern Krishna', shows its hostility to women's emancipation (Fig. 1). Education would lead innocent women astray since the god Krishna had seduced the *gopī*s or rustic maidens with his magic flute.[29]

In the final analysis, Indian peculiarities as examples of Oriental behaviour offered a bonus to the illustrator in the post-1857 era of mounting racism. Caricature thrives on collective representations and stereotypes of other groups. The essential humour of *The Indian Charivari* lay in its witty caricatures of the Bengali character, exploiting the existing view of the westernised Bengali as a buffoon with touching pretensions to rival the British in culture and intellect. British resentment of the competitive and politically conscious Hindus, especially the Bengali elite, was deep seated, as popularised in Kipling's short stories.[30]

---

[27] See Partha Mitter, *Indian Art* (Oxford: Oxford University Press, 2001), 19, Fig. 6.

[28] The first *Punch*-inspired magazine was *Delhi Sketchbook*, which the leading newspaper *The Englishman* brought out in 1850. After the Uprising of 1857 the magazine was relaunched by its owners as *The Indian Punch* which ended in 1862. *Momus* came out in the 1868. *Hindu Punch* was proscribed in 1909 for sedition.

[29] *The Indian Charivari*, 1 October 1875.

[30] See Mitter, *Art and Nationalism*, 150.

Fig. 1 The modern 'Krishna'. *The Indian Charivari*, 5 March 1875. Cited in: Partha Mitter, *Art and Nationalism in Colonial India: 1850–1922* (Cambridge: Cambridge University Press, 1997, 168)

By contrast, the Indian-owned media used this new device to highlight Indian grievances against real or perceived injustice. Inevitably they parted company with *Punch* very early on. The Indian-owned magazines naturally pay homage to *Punch* in their close adaptation of the English magazine's masthead, but they evolve creative designs with the letters of the Urdu or Bengali script, and even the English language monthly *Hindi Punch* mimics the Devanagari letters on its masthead. They duly recast the universally recognised figure of Mr Punch and reuse the format and caption of *Punch* cartoons. However, in terms of creating new meanings and nuances, they totally transform *Punch* on Indian soil, making its Indian offshoots more radical and oppositional in their response to British rule in India, a reflection of the growing nationalist resistance to imperialism. If *Punch* reaffirmed imperial values, then these new offshoots engaged in undermining these very same certainties.

I shall use a few examples here to illustrate the dialogic interactions between the received source, namely the format and motifs of *Punch*, and the local satirical tradition. The earliest version of *Punch* was *Basantak,* published in 1874 in Calcutta; a vitriolic Bengali periodical that used the innovative format to serve up a familiar satirical tradition, 'old wine in a new bottle', to paraphrase the old adage.[31] Calcutta inherited a thriving Bengali tradition of literary satire that employed wit, malice, innuendo and irony, to expose cant and pretension. Caricature became a prime weapon in this highly self-conscious and individualist milieu for parodying contemporary manners. Significantly, criticism of modern ideas did not emanate from traditional rural groups but from within the urban *bhadralok* population. Social satire exposed an ambiguous relationship that characterised the different strata of the westernised intelligentsia—a divided society where traditional signifiers of status, such as caste, no longer went unchallenged.

The cartoonists inherited an earlier tradition of literary parodies and this conjunction of the old and the new offers us an opportunity to study the intertextuality of literature and pictures in nineteenth century Calcutta. The classic text of this literary genre was *The Observant Owl* or *Hutom pyā̃cār nak'śā* (1862), a brilliant set of satirical sketches on early colonial Calcutta and its various Bengali stakeholders.[32] *The Observant Owl*'s anonymous author was a wealthy man of letters and philanthropist, Kali Prasanna Sinha, who staked his considerable fortune in aiding Reverend James Long's campaigns against the oppression of peasants by the white indigo planters. *Hutom* is written in a robust and colloquial style, making use of a vulgar street argot that often verged on what was later deemed indecency by the social reformers. Before the 'cleansing' of Bengali literature under the impact of the reforming Hindus, led by the Brahmos, nineteenth century writers had been accustomed to employing crude and sexual imagery that was not

---

[31] *Har'bolā bhā̃ṛ* and *Basantak*, both published in 1874 and soon on the heels of *The Indian Charivari*, were the first illustrated Bengali versions of Punch, which included a paraphrase of the English magazine's famous masthead.

[32] Aruṇ Nāg, ed, *Saṭīk hutom pā̃cār nak'śā* (Kal'kātā: Subarṇarekhā, 1991).

considered indecorous. Prose writers such as Sinha nonetheless continued to mix colloquialisms often for effect in their writings, even in this period of transition. The deliberate use of the coarse, bawdy language invests *Hutom* with a vivid immediacy, which brings to life the Rabelaisian atmosphere of the age.[33]

The earliest successful Bengali comic magazine *Basantak* belongs to this tradition, complementing the urban image portrayed by *Hutom*. Even the title of the magazine is a play on different meanings, namely, the spring season, the court jester and the dreaded smallpox. Appearing almost immediately after *The Indian Charivari*, the Bengali magazine may have adapted its format from the English magazine, but it is more likely that the editor and the illustrator went straight to the source of *Punch*. The anonymous paper lasted barely a few years. The editor Prananath Datta belonged to an aristocratic *bhadralok* family of North Calcutta, who opted to work independently rather than join the colonial service. His barbed invectives exposed social mores with savage candour. Datta's nephew, who provided the cartoons, Indianised the *Punch* masthead that paid homage to the English monthly by inventing a Bengali incarnation of *Punch*, a leering, obscenely fat Brahmin court jester, surrounded by scenes of utter depravity to which westernised Calcutta had sunk. *Hutom*'s essays had already described the social scene in graphic detail. Here is a small passage from the *Hutom* to give you a flavour of the work:

> The city wears a festive look on Saturday nights [. . .] The *pān* [spicy betel nut] shops were hung with beautiful cut-glass lanterns. The city was heady with the scent of jasmine [. . .] *Khem'ṭā* nautches were being rehearsed in some houses on either side of the road. [*Khem'ṭā* was a popular form of suggestive public dance performed by the demi-monde.] Hearing the sound of *ghuṅgur* [ankle bells] [. . .] passers-by stood transfixed on the road savouring a whiff of heaven. A brawl was going on somewhere, and somewhere a constable was dragging a small-time rogue to the station.[34]

It only needed a cartoonist to flesh out these literary descriptions in his drawings, as we see in *Basantak*. Its main targets were English officials and their Bengali collaborators. There was a coarse immediacy to the wiry drawings, furnished by Datta's nephew, that ideally suited his savage attacks. Hard-hitting satires included the crushing of Indian handlooms by Manchester textiles, corrupt city fathers, and the mismanagement of official famine relief. The cartoon depicts English officials forcing food down the throats of the overfed and obese, while the rest of the population starves to death. *Basantak* reserved its most biting satire for the westernised élite in many ways reminiscent of Kalighat paintings. Datta's victims included the great social reformer Ishvarchandra Vidyasagar and his 'Society for the Prevention of Obscenity'. In a mock celebration of the new social reforms, the cartoon dresses the conventionally naked goddess Kali in European blouse and skirt, while her consort Shiva sports a pair of tweed trousers. The satirist was attacking both the new Puritanism of the westernised élite that accepted the

---

[33] Nāg, *Saṭīk hutom pãcār nak'śā*, 1–12.

[34] Kali Prasanna Sinha, *The Observant Owl*, trans. Swarup Roy (Delhi: Black Kite, 2008), 8.

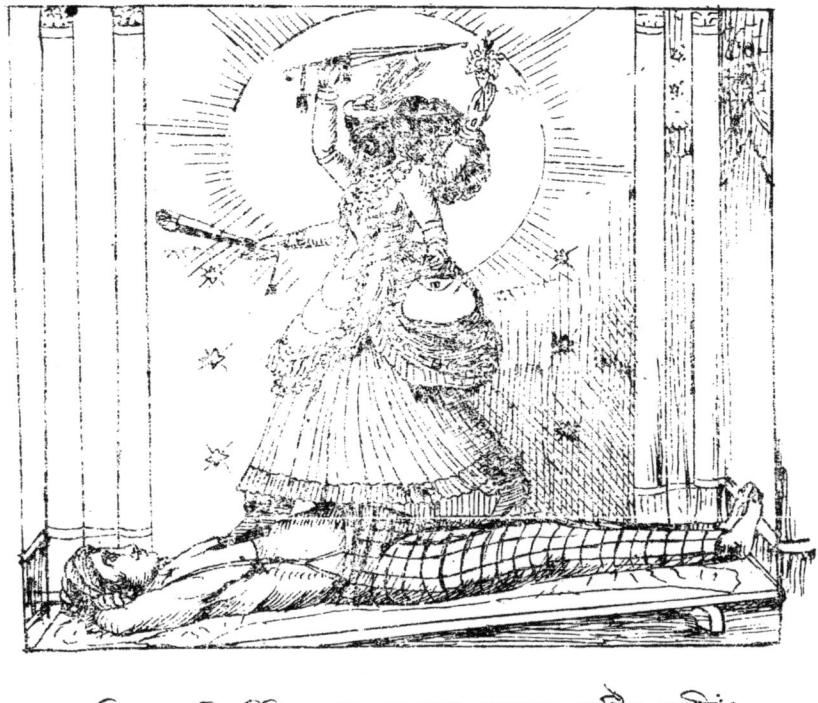

Fig. 2 'What changes are taking place after the establishment of the Society for the Prevention of Obscenity' (Goddess Kali in the house of a member of the Society for the Prevention of Obscenity). *Basantak*, vol. 1, issue 3 (1874) (Source: Savifa, Virtual Library South Asia, Heidelberg)

condemnation of Hinduism by Christian missionaries and the Victorian clothes fashion adopted by the upper strata (Fig. 2).[35]

The movement for women's education and the removal of their social disadvantages gathered force in the nineteenth century. *Satī*, or immolation of widows, was abolished in 1829/30, but there remained other disabilities, such as low literacy rate and infant marriage. The first women to be emancipated became the butt of the conservative cartoonist's pen in *Basantak*. There was fear among the orthodox sections of the community that educated women would desert hearth and home for the glamour of the outside world. The nationalist support for women's education was tempered by the expectation that the emancipated woman would not demand equal rights with men as in the West, but in a true Indian tradition, she would be an inspiring mother and wife, the *gṛhalakṣmī* (goddess of hearth and home). A widespread anxiety pervaded a society where reforms had only scratched

---

[35] Mitter, *Art and Nationalism*, 160–66.

Fig. 3 The wife: 'Can't you close the door while blowing the fire?' *Basantak*, vol. 2, issue 9 (1875) (Cited in: Caṇḍī Lāhiṛī, ed., *Basantak: 1m barṣa-2ẏa barṣa* (Basantak: First to second years) (Kal'kātā, Niu Ej Pāb'liśārs, n.d. [first published around 2008]), *2ẏa barṣa*, 149)

the surface, where child marriage and dowry were still part of everyday life. The socially backward *Basantak* made clear the pitfalls of marrying an educated woman. A cartoon published in *Basantak* shows the wife relaxing with a romantic novel while the poor husband tries to light the coal fire oven in the kitchen. As smoke enters the room, the wife, engrossed in the book, says in irritation, 'Can't you close the kitchen door while lighting the fire?' (Fig. 3)[36]

In North India, Muhammad Sajjad Husain of Lucknow edited an early comic magazine in Urdu, *The Avadh Punch*, from 1877. Many of its lithographic cartoons copied or recycled images from *Punch*, *Fun* and other English magazines, in order to criticise imperial policy. For example, it made an effective use of a *Punch* cartoon about the West Indian Rebellion of 1865, drawing an analogy between the rebellion and nationalist unrest in India. The cartoon alludes to student unrest in Bengal, portraying the DPI (Director of Public Instruction) of Bengal as John Bull, who sent down student leaders after a political demonstration.[37] In South India, the

---

[36] *Basantak* 2, no. 9, 1875, 109–110.

[37] Archibald Constable, ed., *A Selection From the Illustrations Which Have Appeared in the Oudh Punch From 1877 to 1881* (Lucknow: Oudh Punch Office, 1881), Pl. 15; *Punch*, 16 December 1865; Mushirul Hasan, *Wit and Humour in Colonial North India* (New Delhi: Niyogi Books 2007).

leading Tamil literary figure, Subramania Bharati published cartoons regularly in the Tamil language weekly, *India*, between 1906 and 1910. As a supporter of the Maharashtrian Extremist leader Bal Gangadhar Tilak, he launched regular attacks on government policy.[38]

I want to end with possibly the best-known and longest lasting version of *Punch* in India, *The Hindi Punch*. The founding editor, the Parsi entrepreneur Barjorji Naoroji, supported the Moderates in the newly founded Indian National Congress. Between 1878 and 1930 the magazine remained the chief mouthpiece of the liberal nationalists who agitated for constitutional reforms to gain greater representation in the governance of India. In many ways, its moderate tone accorded well with its extensive use of the artistic vocabulary of the *Punch* cartoons, its tame drawing style often emulating the English magazine. *The Hindi Punch* created Panchoba, a memorable Indian incarnation of Mr Punch, who presided over the burning political issues of the day in an avuncular fashion. One is tempted to speculate that Panchoba was a cartoon version of liberal Indian nationalists such as Dadabhai Naoroji or Surendranath Banerjea.

Naoroji cleverly reused widely known oleographs of the celebrated Indian painter, Raja Ravi Varma to make political points. One of its cartoons depicts the Viceroy, Lord Curzon, the *bête noir* of the nationalists, as Sarasvati, the Hindu goddess of learning (after a Varma print). Several cartoons parodied his high-handed treatment of Indian academics at the Simla Education Conference. Curzon was largely responsible for the Partition of Bengal in 1905, which earned him universal unpopularity among the intelligentsia. This was duly voiced by the *The Hindi Punch*. However, as the nationalist movement gathered force that led to widespread unrest, revolutionary terrorism, and the split between the Moderates and the Extremists, *The Hindi Punch* increasingly fell out of step with mainstream politics. Failing to draw inspiration from Mahatma Gandhi's *satyāgraha* movement, it remained a relic of the past political era as late as the 1930s, and eventually died a natural death.

I will conclude with a few reflections on the afterlife of Indian versions of *Punch* and the lasting legacy of the English comic magazine in the subcontinent, a legacy that was by necessity an ambivalent one with its attendant tensions. In many ways, the rich crop of Indian comic magazines that adapted the general format and occasionally the layout of the *Punch* during the period 1870s–1930s were a spent force by the 1930s, as the image of imperial benevolence could no longer be sustained in a period of mounting unrest. The presence of the English magazine however continued not in comic magazines, which virtually ceased to exist by now, but in individual cartoons. The wiry linear woodcuts that were a predominant and easily recognisable feature of *Punch* throughout its history filtered down to cartoons in newspapers and literary magazines, whose influence can be seen even in the

---

[38] See A.R. Venkatachalapathy, "Caricaturing the Political: A Brief History of the Cartoon in Tamil Journalism," *Art India* 8, no. 4 (2003): quarter 4; and Partha Mitter, "Cartoons of the Raj," *History Today* 47, no. 9 (September 1997): 18.

works of recent cartoonists such as R. K. Laxman.[39] We have seen the reasons for the all-encompassing spread of *Punch* across continents. But to reiterate one particular aspect of its existence in India, and by analogy over the whole domain of British dominance: *Punch* dominated over all other traditions, almost to their exclusion. This safe, gentle middle-class attitude may have inhibited Indian cartoonists, with a few notable exceptions, from adopting a more grotesque, outré, sexualised and visceral drawing technique, as seen in the art of German Expressionists such as Dix and Grosz, and Mexican illustrators such as Posada. The notable exception was the artist Gaganendranath Tagore whose ferocious drawings were turned by a street lithographer into brilliant coloured lithographs that combined bold lines with large, flat, coloured surfaces of grey or beige. Tagore preferred the illustrators of the German comic magazine *Simplicissimus* to the better-known cartoons in *Punch*. His three original volumes of cartoons produced circa 1917 contain a rich storehouse of stock characters, such as the wealthy Bengali *bhadralok* visiting the whorehouse, the westernised Bengali or the venal Brahmin who pretends to uphold sacred rites while secretly scoffing alcohol and forbidden flesh. The prose essayist Nirad C. Chaudhuri describes this brief memorable chapter in the history of cartoons of nationalist resistance as follows: 'the only expression in art ever given to Hindu liberalism [was] a set of lithographs by Gaganendranath Tagore'.[40]

---

[39] Khanduri, "Vernacular Punches": 460; chapter *Punch* in India: Another History of Colonial Politics? in this volume.

[40] Nirad C. Chaudhuri, *The Autobiography of an Unknown Indian* (London: Macmillan & Co., 1951), 454.

The Possibility of Satire: Reading Pratap Narain Misra's *Brāhmaṇ*, 1883–1890

Alok Rai

Issues of community, audience and address are crucial to the possibility and performance of satire. They both depend upon a delicate and fluctuating relationship between the objects of satire—the targets, so to speak—and the intended audiences. Too close an identification between the two and the performance veers towards sermonising or ranting. On the other hand, too little identification, too great a perceived distance, so that the audience of satire does not feel at all implicated in the critique, produces relatively crude satire, a mere mockery. James Sutherland described this kind of satire, a propos Ben Jonson and Samuel Butler, thus:

> [they] [...] have little subtlety, and only a limited awareness of what lies beneath the surface of life; they can bring down the obvious follies with both barrels—but the birds have to be large, and preferably of ponderous flight. In stable periods, too, when moral standards are more or less fixed and a code of social behaviour is generally accepted, many lesser men will acquire the confidence which comes from conformity, and will satirise those who straggle from the herd.[1]

Then again, the possible variety of satire may be distinguished on the basis of the implicit position of the satirist, the subject position. Thus, the satirist may speak from the perspective of commonsense and mock deviations from that commonsense. Or, contrariwise, it may be the conventional commonsense that is mocked from some other position—in Frye's terms mere 'fossilised dogma'.[2] In *A History of English Laughter*, Manfred Pfister addresses this issue in a slightly different way: 'Laughter is always caught up in the kinds of distinctions between centre and margins every society employs to establish and stabilise its identity: in one society, the predominant form of laughter can be that which aims from the site of the ideological or power centre at what is to be marginalised or excluded

---

[1] James Sutherland, *English Satire* (Cambridge: Cambridge University Press, 1958), 18.
[2] Alvin Kernan, *The Plot of Satire* (New Haven: Yale University Press, 1965), 15.

A. Rai (✉)
Emeritus Professor of English Literature at Delhi University
e-mail: alokrai1@gmail.com

altogether; in another, the most significant form of laughter can arise from the margins, challenging and subverting the established orthodoxies, authorities and hierarchies'.[3] However, whereas a certain disparity or incongruity is crucial to satire, in extending his initial perception to the colonial situation, Pfister points out that not all incongruities enable humour or laughter: 'The relationship between the former coloniser and the former colonised is [...] an example of a non-humorous disparity. Here the matrices of power and powerlessness, centre and margin, ruler and ruled, meet in a relationship that is fundamentally inequitable'.[4] This fundamental fact does not, of course, rule out the possibility of satire per se: satire is often the revenge of the victims, a weapon of the weak. But it is the variability of the origin/location of the satire's voice which is directly germane to the problem of the possibility of satire in the colonial situation—where the hierarchies of the colonised world are themselves subject to the powerfully distorting magnetic fields of colonial association. Who laughs, at what, and where? All of this is crucial to understanding the functioning of satire, especially in a literary sphere yet under construction, as in the case of the Avadh region and Pratap Narain Misra's *Brāhmaṇ*, which is the subject of this present chapter.

Satire in a Colonial Context

Beyond the inequalities of power and incongruent hierarchies, there is more at play in colonial contexts. This can be observed in an instance that is described vividly in a study of English satire in the turbulent period before the First Reform Bill of 1832. (This is the tradition of which *Punch* is, in some sense, an inheritor, though clearly *Punch*'s trajectory from radicalism to respectability is determined by its location in the relatively quiescent high-Victorian context.) The satire, by Thomas Wooler, who edited a radical journal called *Black Dwarf* in the deeply hostile climate of the Regency, relates an incident in which something was thrown at the Prince Regent's carriage, breaking a window. Wooler published a satirical account of an imaginary trial following the incident. The cobblestones are acquitted of the offence, since 'they might have been lying there in their honest avocation of making a firm footing for the carriage of royalty'.[5] But the potatoes that were found at the site had no such alibi: 'In the emphatic language, however, of Mr Magistrate Hicks,—"the POTATOES *speak for themselves. It is not the practice to pave streets with potatoes. Ergo,* the potatoes must have been there with some treasonable design. They could have no

---

[3] Manfred Pfister, *A History of English Laughter: Laughter From Beowulf to Beckett and Beyond* (Amsterdam: Rodopi, 2002), cited in Susanne Reichl and Mark Stein, eds., *Cheeky Fictions: Laughter and the Postcolonial* (Amsterdam: Rodopi, 2005), 9.

[4] Ibid.

[5] *Black Dwarf* 4 (1817), 59–62, cited in Marcus Wood, *Radical Satire and Print Culture 1790–1822* (Oxford: Clarendon Press, 1994), 1.

lawful business outside the kitchen or the market place"'.⁶ Wooler's potatoes are an ideal of dumb passivity that Wooler's Magistrate then proceeds to condemn through cold-blooded legal sophistry:

> When questioned, the poor potatoes *said nothing*, they had not even an excuse to offer. They were as mute as death [...] The worthy Magistrate then proceeded to substantiate his charge.—'The Potatoes', my lords and gentlemen, '*speak for themselves!* I do not mean that they express themselves in the common forms of language. But there is my lords and gentlemen, as we all know, a *dumb sort of eloquence* that speaks louder than words and silences of the most noisy advocates [...]. Their language is a silent confession of their evil intentions, which as I said before is palpable from the very presence of the potatoes at such a place.⁷

Marcus Wood's comment on this reveals, by way of contrast, the colonial difference that I am trying to establish:

> Where does this satire come from? A self-educated working-class radical takes on a tone of satiric hauteur to upbraid those without power for their passivity. He speaks [...] in a language of urbane irony which is equally appropriate for another audience, those with power. Where does this work stand in relation to a fixed notion of a language of class? What are its formal and linguistic sources? What is the basis for its knowing confidence?⁸

Thus, while hierarchies of power are relevant, they are by no means disabling. Nevertheless, a further aspect needs to be taken into account: the availability of an adequate language in which *both* the victims and their oppressors might be addressed.

The classic statement on the matter of urbane irony comes from Dryden's *Essay on Satire*: 'there is still a vast difference betwixt the slovenly butchering of a man, and the fineness of a stroke that separates the head from the body, and leaves it standing in its place.'⁹ But the fastidious indirectness and subtlety of irony, its capacity to address more than one audience at different levels, depends on questions of language and of literacy and especially on existing traditions of urbane, witty discourse[s]. 'When a satirist writes a parody which closely and delicately reproduces the manner of his victim, or when he depends strongly on the device of irony, or when his smile is subtle and his humour mild, or when he pretends rather convincingly to be telling the truth, then he may easily be mistaken for a dispassionate commentator, an amiable comedian, a frank forthright fellow, a genuine admirer of the stuff he parodies, or even one of its adepts'.¹⁰ Gilbert Highet recounts a Swift anecdote, apparently told to Pope, about an Irish bishop who read *Gulliver's Travels* and declared that he didn't believe a word of it! Writing about the English *Punch*, Richard Altick observed: 'By its very nature, the voice of irony requires ears that can detect the tell-tale pitch that distinguishes it from the C

---

⁶ *Black Dwarf* 4,, 60, cited in Wood, *Radical Satire*, 1.
⁷ Ibid., 61, cited in Wood, *Radical Satire*, 1–2.
⁸ Wood, *Radical* Satire, 2.
⁹ Cited in Kernan, *Plot of Satire*, 8.
¹⁰ Gilbert Highet, *The Anatomy of Satire* (Princeton: Princeton University Press, 1962), 15.

major of plain statement. The ironist in any age has to contend with the tone-deaf readers against whom his inflections beat in vain'.[11]

However, these general remarks on satire cannot simply be extended or mapped onto the writings that are my subject. The colonial context of their production and consumption must be an integral part of any account: thus, on the one hand, we have to factor in the low levels of literacy and the role of censorship; on the other hand, there is the existence of vernacular, and frequently vulgar, oral traditions of mockery and burlesque. Here one might have expected a reference to the vast body of postcolonial critical writing and theory. However, as Reichl and Stein remark in their introduction to *Cheeky Fictions: Laughter and the Postcolonial*, postcolonialism in general has been relatively indifferent to the matter of laughter, of satire and humour.[12] Its attention has been reserved for 'serious' issues, for the monstrous catalogue of colonial infamy, both in its visibility in *and* its exclusion from the record. This is no doubt a worthy project—I say this *without* irony—but it is of little help in this case. So, while I believe that the colonial situation is critical to reading the possibility and performance of satire *in* the colony, I use 'postcolonial' infrequently and only to signal the relevance of colony-specific factors in reading this material.

The Case of Avadh

Obviously there are significant regional variations of satire. For example, the much-studied region of Bengal has a profusion of satire, not only in English but also in the vernacular, in verbal as well as in visual forms.[13] Also, satire in Bengal encompasses both the babus and the sahibs, natives and gentlemen, so to speak. Partha Mitter remarks in his study of *Art and Nationalism in Colonial India 1850–1922*, that 'Indian cartoonists, being insiders, especially in Bengal, offer us a penetrating self-parody of the elite in the period of nationalist politics. In Bengali cartoons the exposure of social mores attained the ruthless candour of Gillray and Rowlandson'.[14]

The reference to the specificity of Bengal is both salutary and timely: generalising from Bengal to India is a risky enterprise. The cultural dynamics in the North Western Provinces of British India (hereafter NWP)—the state of Avadh in the late nineteenth century—are different from the rest of the country in certain

---

[11] Richard Altick, *Punch: The Lively Youth of a British Institution, 1841–1851* (Columbus: Ohio State University Press, 1997), xx.

[12] Reichl and Stein, *Cheeky Fictions*, 2.

[13] Partha Mitter, *Art and Nationalism in Colonial India 1850–1922: Occidental Orientations* (Cambridge: Cambridge University Press, 1994); also see Hans Harder, "The Modern Babu and the Metropolis: Reassessing Early Bengali Narrative Prose," in *India's Literary History: Essays on the 19th century*, eds. Stuart Blackburn and Vasudha Dalmia (Delhi: Permanent Black, 2002).

[14] Mitter, *Art and Nationalism*, 139.

respects. Mitter's Bengal elite evidently possessed sufficient cultural confidence to turn their satirical gaze on both the colonial rulers and themselves. In the NWP at this time, however, what was being played out was a long and deeply consequential struggle between the culturally hegemonic Avadh elite, comprising both the landowning gentry and the official classes, and a proto-elite consisting of the mofussil (up-country) commercial classes, as well as the new products of reformed colonial education in the period after 1857. Language and script were the basis on which *both* these elites defined themselves: Urdu written in the Persian script in the case of the former, Hindi written in Devanagari in the case of the latter. This is a long and complicated story, but it is sufficient for present purposes to note that neither the beleaguered Avadh elite, nor the aspirant Hindi proto-elite were in a position to deploy satire with the confidence that the Bengal elite of the same period obviously had. Thus, the periodical *Avadh Punch*, in Urdu, was the conservative voice of the Avadh elite and sought to articulate their opinions, particularly in respect to current political matters.[15] This paper, however, is particularly concerned with one prominent member of the Hindi proto-elite, the ideologue, poet and prose satirist Pratap Narain Misra. Misra's journal *Brāhmaṇ*, in turn, carries references to many other *Punches*—thus, there is an exchange concerning the much-alleged inadequacies of the Urdu script with someone in the *Fatehgarh Punch*,[16] as well as a reference to a Hindi *Rasik Punch* which had to close down quickly due to unsustainable losses.[17] Elsewhere, an association called the *Punch Club* is mentioned, which consisted mainly of Muslims—though it had two Brahmins also—and apparently contributed to Hindu-Muslim amity.[18] However, I have been unable to trace any record of these colonial incarnations of *Punch* in archives, and so can do little more than register the remarkable resonance that was achieved by the London periodical—a resonance that is rendered all the more remarkable when one reflects on the inhibitions, difficulties and distortions that afflict the actual practice of satire in the colony.

Pratap Narain Misra's *Brāhmaṇ* in Context

Pratap Narain Misra (1856–1894) was a younger contemporary of one of the founding fathers of modern Hindi, Bharatendu Harischandra, and a member of the literary circle, known as the Bharatendu Mandal, associated with him. Other members include Balmukund Gupta and Balkrishna Bhatt. For about 7 years, from 1883 to 1890, Misra brought out a Hindi journal called *Brāhmaṇ* from his native Kanpur. It is unlikely that the journal ever attained a large circulation. Issue after issue is littered with appeals in

---

[15] Mushirul Hasan, *Wit and Humour in Colonial North India* (Delhi: Niyogi Books, 2007).

[16] Pratāp'nārāyaṇ Miśra, *Pratāp'nārāyaṇ granthāvalī*, ed. Vijay'śaṃkar Mall (Vārāṇasī: Nāgarī Pracāriṇī Sabhā, 1992), 82–83.

[17] Ibid., 122.

[18] Ibid., 126.

various modes—pleading, demanding, reproaching—appeals made to absent and desperately needed subscribers who were, by definition, *not* reading them.

> All the [affluent-seeming ones] in their flamboyant yellow turbans, with their red cheeks and well-fed paunches, are not always honest. People who are sincere in their conduct do not [need to] put up appearances. But what do I care, [I have suffered some small loss but at least] I have learnt a valuable lesson [about such people]—who have revealed themselves, [like the] dog which broke the utensil in trying to steal the food.[19]

The journal closes with a declaration by Misra that he could not personally sustain any further costs, and expresses the (forlorn) hope that if ever in the future there should be sufficient funds, he would resume publication. In an essay on publishing in North India at around this time, Francesca Orsini writes: 'commercial publishing [...] faced two daunting challenges: the challenge of low literacy, and the widespread habit of pursuing cultural pleasures orally and visually'.[20] The situation is further complicated by the fact that the oral cultures of mockery and burlesque—as well as other pleasures—existed in a 'linguistic repertoire'[21] that was under particular attack from language ideologues like Pratap Narayan Misra. As we shall see, however, his ideological imperative was often subverted by his own linguistic practice.

To a significant extent, it is nationalism that in one form or another drives most cultural production during this period—certainly high-cultural production, though this statement might well be circular in reasoning. But before we turn to the fraught workings of satire in Misra's vernacular nationalism, it might be interesting to look briefly at what was happening in the so-called *Hindi Punch* at roughly the same time. I should clarify that *Hindi Punch* was not a Hindi paper. The language of this paper was English, and I have only been able to access a selection of the cartoons published therein. This is clearly an ultra loyal Parsee paper, and announces its publication '[u]nder the Patronage of H.E. Lord Curzon of Kedleston, Viceroy and Governor-General of India'. The very first cartoon depicts four Parsee-looking ladies, identified as the Congress, 'Gently knocking at Mother Empress' door' and below the caption is a quotation from *Matthew* vii, 7: 'Ask, and it shall be given; seek, and ye shall find; knock, and it shall be opened to you'. Another cartoon, captioned 'Maternal Love', shows the Congress represented as a sari-clad woman, kneeling at the feet of the Empress, but the British lion beside her looks distinctly bewildered. The ground that is being ploughed by the Congress in another cartoon is littered with 'broken promises', clearly associated with the Anglo-Indian bureaucracy—but the two bulls that pull the plough of the Congress are still

---

[19] *Pīlī pīlī pag'ṛī, lāl lāl gāl, moṭe moṭe toṃd'vāle sabhī īmān'dār nahīṃ hote. jo vyavahār ke sacce hote haiṃ veh jhūṭī banāvat nahīṃ rakh'te. Yahāṃ kyā hai, ham'ne samajh liyā, dam'ṛī kī hāṛiyā phūṭī, kutte ki jāt pah'cānī.* This complaint pertained to those people who subscribed to the journal but refused to pay up when the time came. Ibid., 35 (my translation).

[20] Francesca Orsini, *Print and Pleasure: Popular Literature and Entertaining Fictions in Colonial North India* (Delhi: Permanent Black, 2010), 274. Also see pp. 168–169.

[21] Orsini credits David Lelyveld with the formulation, ibid., 275.

identified as Loyalty and Constitutional Agitation. The innocence is breathtaking. The cartoons, for example, depict polite petitioners, images of the dawn, the Indian tiger licking the British lion affectionately and respectfully.[22]

Vernacular nationalism, similarly subject to colonial censorship, was just as prone to loyal genuflection, as the polite Anglophone nationalism of *Hindi Punch*. (Examples abound, somewhat to the embarrassment of the ideologues who would like to put Hindi into a larger, and later, story of anti-colonial nationalism.) There is a difference nonetheless: As a function of language and social position, and even of the social position of his particular language, Misra had to speak, perforce, from outside the sphere of power. Thus, the 'nationalism' expresses itself primarily in the register of reform. Though this is never articulated in so many words, the project is one of 'reforming'—actually, forming—a community that might become worthy of power, worthy of being a nation before even staking a claim to power, howsoever modest. Hindi, script and language, is a crucial part of this project, both as instrument and symbol. Throughout this period, community and language were caught up in a dizzying dialectic of reciprocal formation. Neither modern 'Sanskritised' Hindi nor its Hindu nationalist community had existed before the inception of this process. But there was a powerful and mutually-reinforcing complementarity between the two when the process got under way.[23]

Social Critique in Unstable Settings

Social critique is inevitably one of the registers in which this reforming agenda manifests itself. Misra's social vision was that of a satirist, someone who saw the society of his time as riddled with practices—both traditional and Western modern—that filled him with rage and a desire to mock them out of existence. But the issues of audience and address referred to at the outset had a direct bearing on the performance and even on the possibility of satire.

Given that the vehicle was fabricated in historical transition, it is not surprising that there is an inherent instability in Misra's language. There is of course the reaching out towards the gravity and resonance, the authority of Sanskrit, which would become much more marked as modern 'Hindi' evolved. But there is also the distinct and enlivening presence of a linguistic repertoire drawing freely upon Urdu and Persian, as well as Arabic, which the language movements of the late nineteenth and early twentieth century in the NWP were determined to erase— with limited success. Furthermore, there is an interesting admixture of dialect forms, including entire passages in dialect. This occasional deployment of dialect works at one level to establish the 'authenticity', the localness, of the writer, but

---

[22] Barjorjee Nowrosjee, ed. *The Indian National Congress Cartoons from The Hindi Punch (from 1886 to 1901) with a selection of the Indian Social Conference Cartoons* (Bombay, circa 1902).

[23] Alok Rai, *Hindi Nationalism* (Delhi: Orient Longman, 2000).

it also gives his prose a vivacity that it would lack if expressed exclusively in a formal Sanskritic register.

For example, in 1884–1885, in several issues of his journal, Misra published a series of fake etymologies, reminiscent of Ambrose Bierce's *Devil's Dictionary*.[24] The 'wit' and bite of these etymologies and glosses derives from combining elements derived from different languages. Thus, the proposed etymology for '*brāhmaṇ*', rendered here in its popular pronunciation as '*bāṃbhan*'—which names both Misra's journal and his own caste—is fake Sanskrit: '*bā iti bhanati sa bāṃbhanaḥ*' [that animal whose call is 'bā' is a '*bāmbhan*'] i.e., a bullock, which is again glossed in a Sanskrit phrase: '*vidyāvihīnaḥ paśuḥ*', i.e., a brainless animal.[25] But '*ij'lās*', i.e., a court of law might be a reference to the colonial legal apparatus, etymologised with recourse to English—so it becomes 'is loss', with the 'z' sound of 'is' rendered as the vulgar 'j'.[26] The proposed etymology for '*mahātmā*' combines elements from Sanskrit and Persian. The Sanskrit '*mahā*', meaning 'great', is added to the Persian '*ṭamā"*', meaning 'greed', and thus becomes 'greatly greedy'.[27] Examples are manifold, but the range already indicated suggests that Misra's imaginary audience could only be a small group of highly literate Hindu men, rather like himself, who are familiar with Persian, Arabic and Sanskrit, who can also dip into a range of dialects, deriving pleasure from witty if fictitious conjunctions.

The occasional deployment of dialect helps, I have suggested, to establish the 'authenticity', the localness of the writer. The authenticity of dialect speech—of the mainly illiterate folk—is used to mock the pretensions of the literate, particularly the westernised literate. But at the same time, the use of dialect becomes a parody itself and implicates both the targeted literati and the people who are ventriloquised in dialect: In a piece severely critical of Western-educated 'superfools' ('*bajramūrkh*'), Misra expresses the attitude of ordinary folk towards this westernised class in dialect: '*bahut paṛh'ne se man'ī bailāy jāt hai. Paṛhe likhe te laṛikā meh'rā ho jāt hai*' [with too much education one loses one's mind, and a boy becomes a eunuch]. But clearly, the wit is directed against the superfools, as well as their illiterate critics.[28]

This linguistic vivacity—the taste for linguistic play—is directly related to the satire: The English 'honorary magistrate' is rendered as '*andherī magistrate*'. The '*andher*' here recalls the '*andher*' of his mentor Bharatendu's famous satire of contemporary governance—*andher nag'rī caupaṭ rājā* [*Andher* is flagrant wrongdoing]. Similarly, the colonial decoration CSI, Commander Star of India, awarded to loyal natives, is mocked as '*śrī īsāī*'—Mr Christian, I suppose.

---

[24] Ambrose Bierce, *The Devil's Dictionary* (New York: Neale Publishing Company, 1911).
[25] Miśra, *Pratāp'narāyaṇ grathāvalī*, 51.
[26] Ibid., 54.
[27] Ibid., 51–55.
[28] Ibid., 316 (my translation).

Corresponding to the vivacious instability of Misra's language—trampolining up and down the linguistic registers—there is an analogous instability with regard to the community being addressed. Irony, which is critical to the possibility and performance of satire, depends on the indiscernible movement from sincerity to insincerity, the barely discernible slippage from meaning what one says to meaning something other than, or even the opposite of what one's words appear to be saying. This playing with linguistic codes and registers depends, in turn, on the confidence that one's audience will, in the main, enjoy the play and, simultaneously, grasp the serious polemical intent that must, for historically variable reasons, express itself in the camouflage of irony and satire. Thus, irony presumes the existence of a community, at the very least, a community of reception. But the 'instability' at the level of community, unlike that of language, has a largely negative impact on Misra's satire.

As I suggested earlier, Misra's audience could easily have been people like himself, multi-lingual, poly-vocal, at home in the linguistic repertoire of North India. However, his reforming project involves the invention of a community that can be identified with the Hindi that is in the process of being invented. It is something of a shock to find Misra, with his linguistic range, fulminating about the use of the Arabic-derived word '*bagīcī*' in the title of a book.[29] It doesn't take very much for the felt hostility towards a language and a script, explicitly identified as '*śatru*', i.e., an enemy, to slip into hostility against the community that was identified with the script and the language, i.e., Muslims.

The fraught nature of the project of reform has a direct bearing on the possible communities to which the social critique/satire can either relate or refer. While Misra is critical of sectarian squabbling in a piece entitled '*Deśonnati*', the possible community that could be the beneficiary of such reform turns out to be Hindu and is asked to unite against the '*duṣṭa yavanas*', i.e. 'cruel Muslims'.

So, while Misra was critical of sectarian traditionalists and saw himself, after Bharatendu, as a kind of indigenous moderniser, he, from time to time, expressed allegiance to unreconstructed traditional values. For example, he counselled the so-called lower castes to shed their 'progressive' desire to become like their 'betters'—i.e., babus—and to stay loyal instead to their traditional caste roles of rendering service to the upper castes. After all, one can have too much equality, as he expressed it in a local metaphor, '*unnati kā lakṣan hi yah hai ki nāī kī barāt meṃ sab ṭhākur hī ṭhākur!*'[30] [it is entirely typical of 'progress' that (everyone claims to be high caste)—in the barber's wedding procession, everyone claims to be a *thakur!*].

The difficulty of Misra's social position finds plaintive expression in a piece entitled '*Kyā likhaiṃ?*' [What should I write?] Everything he wrote, whether about political matters or social practices, about public morals or about heedless

---

[29] Ibid., 76.
[30] Ibid., 341.

westernisation, merely caused offence to some group or other, traditional or modern, and earned him the opprobrium: 'old fool!'[31]

The one steady target in the rants of the 'old fool' was, in fact, the westernised, oriental gentleman—a.k.a. wog and, of course, 'babu'—who was the universal butt of ridicule. Examples abound. The piece entitled '*bajramūrkh*', cited earlier, mocks colonial education, and the dietary and sartorial habits that the beneficiaries of this colonial education acquire, along with their diplomas and degrees—'their small or big tails of the letters A, B, C, D, E . . .'[32] But there is a curious sense of irony that attends this otherwise assured, confident performance—a sense of ineffectuality, as if Swift were to write 'A Modest Proposal' in a language unknown to the English oppressor, in Hindi, exiled from the corridors of power. Finally, overcome by a sense of his own futility, the satirist becomes the butt of his own satire. Thus, Misra visualises a situation in which he might, at last, acquire some influence: 'if I were to apply some white paint and started calling myself Reverend Mister P. Naroyegem Messur A.B..C.D.E...'[33]

I'll close with one last, possibly significant, illustration—a brilliant lampoon published in *Harishchandra Magazine* in 15 May 1874. The target here, once again, is the 'wog', who introduces himself: 'I am/Poora gentilman'. The language here is a pitch-perfect parody of 'Babu English', the patter of the semi-literate, which is interspersed with vernacular elements:

> I have no prejudice Sahab, I drink
>   Soda-water, wine;
>   Though beef buri chiz[34] for a Hindoo
>   But I eat for sake of thine...
>   [...]
>   Put head on foot, and I say true,
>   You are all my, I have none;
>   Save me father! Save me father!
>   I am your sipharsi[35] son.
>   I introduce myself to you Sir
>   I am poora gentilman
>   Take my salam, give me chair,
>   Honour me very much, if you can.[36]

It is easy to enjoy the vivacity and wit of this mockery of the brown sahib. But it is difficult to miss the contrast with Misra's own conflicted, self-lacerating mockery.

---

[31] Ibid., 381.

[32] Ibid., 317.

[33] Ibid., 422.

[34] *burī cīz* (Urdu/Hindi): 'bad thing'.

[35] *sifāriśī* (Urdu/Hindi): 'depending on recommendations'.

[36] Facsimile edition of *Harishchandra Magazine*, ed. Satyaprakash Misra (Allahabad: Hindi Sahitya Sammelan, 2002): 214–215.

From *Punch* to *Mat¹vālā*: Transcultural Lives of a Literary Format

Prabhat Kumar

Punch, or the London Charivari was a popular nineteenth-century English satirical periodical not only in Britain but also outside its national territory. While much has been written about the history of the periodical in Britain, *Punch*'s transcultural lives as a literary format beyond Britain are yet to be documented.[1] This chapter attempts to map its transcultural journey in the late nineteenth and early twentieth century Hindi literary sphere.[2] I will begin by delineating the characteristic features of *Punch*. At the risk of simplification it can be summarised as follows:[3]

1. It publicised the carefully cultivated personalised self of Mr Punch in the role of an irreverent iconoclast and a slayer of privileges, corruption and deceit.
2. It also constituted a parody of newspapers in its own right. It had all the features of a typical periodical and consisted of editorials and other news columns and

---

[1] I use the plural form 'lives' because *Punch* inspired any number of periodicals in the nineteenth century, cutting across literary cultures in South Asia, China, Japan, Egypt, and Turkey, not to mention Europe. In South Asia its reverberations were felt not only in English-language periodicals owned by Europeans, as well as Indians, but in Marathi, Bengali, Gujarati, Urdu, Hindi, etc., as well. For an elementary survey in South Asia see Partha Mitter, "Cartoon and the Raj," *History Today*, 47, no. 9 (1997). For a general survey see Bellary Shamanna Kesavan, *History of Indian Journalism* (Delhi: Publication Division, 1955).
[2] For the general understanding of Hindi literary sphere see Francesca Orsini, *The Hindi Public Sphere: Language and Literature in the Age of nationalism 1920–1940* (Delhi: Oxford University Press, 2002) and also Vasudha Dalmia, *The Nationalization of Hindu Traditions: Bhāratendu Hariśchandra and Nineteenth-Century Banaras* (Delhi: Oxford University Press, 1997).
[3] Richard D. Altick, *Punch: The Lively Youth of a British Institution 1841–1851* (Columbus: Ohio State University Press, 1997).

I am grateful to Benjamin Zachariah, Barbara Mittler, Hans Harder, and Gita Dharampal-Frick, for their helpful comments.

P. Kumar (✉)
Assistant Professor at the Department of History of Presidency University, Kolkata
e-mail: kumar@asia-europe.uni-heidelberg.de

reports on subjects such as politics, society, art and literature. But unlike typical newspapers, it expected its readers to have an active sense of participation in public life and an a priori knowledge of news and events, which were selected and commented upon using the tool of satiric deformation and presented in the familiar forms of lampoon, joke, hoax, gossip, etc.

3. It exploited the flexibility of language by employing puns, conundrums, and by playing with the multiple meanings of individual words.
4. Its verbal and comic art had a remarkable penchant for uncovering connections—not only in figurative/metaphoric forms but also through parallels, analogies and echoes, wherever likeness or contrast could be used for what amounted to a kind of continuous performance on the printed page, either for its own sake or to convey a message. Where resemblances did not exist they were manufactured in the form of parodies of literary texts and graphic burlesques of high and popular art.
5. It combined two representational registers of comic distortion: literary parody and visual caricature in the form of cartoons.
6. It dipped into streams of popular and elite culture and indulged in street slang, as well as sophisticated canonical vocabulary.
7. Politically, it remained bourgeois and patriarchal. It poked fun at the culture of the English middle class, but its humour ultimately reasserted bourgeois patriarchal ethos.

After delineating *Punch*'s salient literary features to map its transcultural life in the Hindi literary sphere, it is important to introduce a note of caution here. Writing a history of the transcultural flow of an idea or a cultural commodity—in this case a literary form—involves serious risks: there is, on the one hand, the chance of falling prey to the simplistic 'derivative discourse',[4] thereby pre-judging *Punch*'s colonial avatar as originating from, but falling short of, or deviating from the original;[5] on the other hand, there is the danger of succumbing to the telos of nationalist 'indigenism', which holds that all such ideas had pre-colonial indigenous, and more often 'classical', roots.[6] To avoid both of these traps we need to ask a few

---

[4] See Partha Chatterjee, *Nationalist Thought and the Colonial World: A Derivative Discourse?* (London: Zed Books, 1986).

[5] For a critique of this approach in the context of early novels in India see Meenakshi Mukherjee, "Epic and Novel in India," in *The Novel*, vol. 1, *History, Geography and Culture*, ed. Franco Moretti (Princeton: Princeton University Press, 2006) 596–631.

[6] This has been the problem of nationalist literary historiography, as well as of left historiography informed by anti-imperialist position. See Vasudha Dalmia, *Poetics, Plays, and Performance: The Politics of Modern Indian Theatre* (Delhi: Oxford University Press, 2004) and also Chap. 5 of Dalmia, *Nationalization of Hindu Traditions*, 222–324. For a general overview of the politics of entanglement between nationalist ideology and literary historiography in South Asian literary cultures see Hans Harder, ed., *Literature and Nationalist Ideology: Writing Histories of Modern Indian Languages* (Delhi: Social Science Press, 2010). For a critique of residual nationalist frame in modern Indian historiography see the Introduction of Benjamin Zachariah, *Nation Game* (Delhi: Yoda Press, 2012).

questions, such as: How popular was *Punch* or satirical journalism within the Hindi literary sphere? How did the contemporary Hindi litterateurs receive *Punch* and/or its literary format? What kind of deflections did it undergo as a result of its interaction with the local literary repertoire? Was it informed by and re-inscribed with new social meaning in the Hindi literary sphere? And if so, how? What kind of political and cultural mediation did it perform to be relevant in the new context?[7]

The existing scholarship on the history of Hindi journalism[8] suggests that a full-fledged satirical periodical with some significance was *Mat'vālā* (the intoxicated), which was published in Calcutta in 1923. *Mat'vālā*, indeed, had most of the aforementioned characteristics of *Punch*. Its circulation figures were fairly high.[9] In order to assign novelty to *Mat'vālā*, however, scholars underplay the richness of the early satirical œuvre of nineteenth century Hindi literary culture. So as to understand the broader currents and to contextualise our prime concern, then, this chapter is divided into two parts. In the first section the circulation and popularity of *Punch* in the late nineteenth century is gauged by foregrounding the reproduction of its content, as well as internal literary references and acknowledgements. The contemporary reception and adaptation of Mr Punch as a satiric narrator is elucidated by unravelling the rich semantics of the word *punch*. The communicative mechanisms and political function of the satirical mode, which appeared in a number of periodicals as *Punch* or *Punch*-like columns, and in a variety of other literary forms, is examined in the wider context of the nascent but vibrant Hindi public sphere before 1920. In the second section the distinction of *Mat'vālā* is made salient and is contextualised in the changed historical circumstances of the post-1920 Hindi public sphere. The literary format of *Mat'vālā* is mapped in relation to the characteristic features of *Punch* as outlined at the beginning. An analysis of the magazine's cultivated self persona and consolidated public identity is followed by the examination of the structure, communicative mechanisms and political functions of literary and visual satire. It ends with a note on mutations of *Punch* and the indiscernible trajectory of its transcultural genealogy in the twentieth century.

---

[7] Borrowing from Michael McKeon's idea of 'generic instability' from his work *The Origins of the English Novel: 1600–1740* (Baltimore: John Hopkins University Press, 1987), Francesca Orsini makes a very important point in the context of the analysis of early Hindi-Urdu novels. She argues that the idea of some pure or authentic model of a genre (such as the novel), which was available in Europe and then imported into the colony, is deeply flawed and redundant. A genre should be examined so as to explain the particular social and cultural functions it performs and the dialectical relationship it has with other genres at any given point in history. Francesca Orsini, *Print and Pleasure: Popular Literature and Entertaining Fictions in Colonial North India* (Delhi: Permanent Black, 2009), 164.

[8] Ram Ratan Bhatnagar, *The Rise and Growth of Hindi Journalism* (Varanasi: Vishwavidyalay Prakashan, 2003); Kṛṣṇa Bihārī Miśra, *Hindī patrakāritā*. (Dillī: Bhār'tīya Jñān'pīṭh, 1985).

[9] This is discussed in the next section.

Circulation of *Punch*

Punch, or The London Charivari not only struck the imagination of the English-reading public in Europe and North America,[10] but also the Indian.[11] It was accessible to the Indian intelligentsia, which was always eager to know about metropolitan culture and politics, and was also in search of new idioms and forms of self-articulation and assertion within the emerging colonial public sphere.[12] *Punch* acquired a legendary status as a periodical amongst the contemporary editor-journalists.

One of the earliest references to its popularity can be found in Bharatendu Harishchandra's satirical composition *Muśāy'rā*[13] (Assembly of Poets). In one of the paragraphs of the *Muśāy'rā* a nouveau-riche merchant, who pretends to be a poet, mentions the superiority and popularity of the *Punch* in India:[14]

> No paper so far could supersede the *Pañc*
> That it has established its dominance is a matter of fact.[15]

In another paragraph the socially-aspiring wife of this rich merchant, who is educated by a white tutor-governess, wishes to get her poem published in *Punch*.

> I pray to you my mischievous husband
> Why don't you get it published in the *Pañc*?[16]

Interestingly, we find mutual acknowledgement of their individual existences within the pages of the British *Punch* and one of the Indian versions of *Punch*,

---

[10] Altick, *Punch*.

[11] *Punch* had individual subscribers in India. An Indian cartoonist, born in 1924, when recalling his young days, mentions that his father had a collection of old volumes of *Punch*. Rasipuram K.I. Laxman, *The Tunnel of Time: An Autobiography* (Delhi: Penguin India, 1998), 8–9. Ritu Khanduri has highlighted not only the availability and popularity of British *Punch* in India, but also noted that its commercial potential was clear to its owners as well, who were seriously considering bringing out overseas editions of the periodical, including an edition from India. See chapter *Punch* in India: Another History of Colonial Politics? in this volume, as well as Ritu Khanduri, "Vernacular Punches: Cartoon and Politics in Colonial India," *History and Anthropology*, 20, no. 4 (2009): 459–486.

[12] For the best conceptualisation of the nature of colonial public sphere in India see Neeladri Bhattacharya, "Notes Towards a Conception of the Colonial Public," in *Civil society, Public Sphere, and Citizenship: Dialogues and Perceptions*, ed. Rajeev Bhargava (Delhi: Sage Publications, 2005), 130–156.

[13] Bharatendu Harishchandra is popularly known as the 'Father of Modern Hindi'. He wrote *Muśāy'rā* in the early 1870s. All translations are mine. See Bābū Rām'dīn Siṃh, ed., *Śrīhariś candrakalā ath'vā golok'vāsī bhārat'bhūṣaṇ bhār'tendu hariścandra kā jīvan sarvasva*, vol. 6, part 1 (Baṅkīpur: Khaḍgavilās Press, 1889), 62.

[14] In all probability, according to the compilers of Harishchandra's work, this poem was published in the early years of the 1870s, which means before the beginning of *Avadh Punch*, an Urdu satirical periodical published from Lucknow, in January 1877. Even if this speculation is untrue, it nevertheless makes the point of the popularity of *Punch*, albeit via *Awadh Punch*.

[15] All translations unless otherwise cited are mine. I use the spelling Pañc rather than Punch when it is used in Hindi. Siṃh, *Śrīhariścandrakalā*, 62.

[16] Ibid.

namely the *Hindi Punch* (1878), which was published in Bombay. A selection of cartoons from the year 1903 was, for example, published in the form of a handbook with Gujarati and English subtitles by the owner of the *Hindi Punch*. In its fourth edition the handbook carried a reprint of press reviews of its previous edition. One of the reviews in this handbook, dated 2 March 1903, was from the British *Punch*, and contained *Punch*'s wishes to the *Hindi Punch* in a somewhat patronising tone.[17]

The 15 November 1873 issue of *Harischandra's Magazine*, which started as a bilingual literary supplement to *Kavivacan'sudhā* (1868),[18] reprinted an article from the British *Punch*. The title of the article was 'From "Punch"—The Mussulman Platform'.[19] This was an article that made a nuanced satirical attack on the Permissive Prohibitory Bill (PPB). *Punch*, in consonance with the Victorian middle-class mores,[20] appeared to be in no disagreement with the prohibition of the sale of liquor, which apparently caused social crime and loss of economic and moral wealth. However, it strongly opposed the indiscriminate ban on the sale of 'infernal drug[s]' including wine 'which intoxicates those who abuse it, and does those who use it good [*sic*]'. It made caustic comments on the members of the British House of Commons representing an organisation for the temperance movement called United Kingdom Alliance.[21] For, according to *Punch*, they spoke in evangelical language in favour of the PPB, as if they were in a religious council. *Punch* argued that the orthodox idea of a blanket prohibition, which calls wine an infernal drug, fell short of the liberal British ideal and could not be but inspired by an ideal of its *other*, i.e., the 'Turk/Muslim'.[22] For, according to the tacit premise of this argument, which played upon the stereotype of authoritarian Islam, it was only a state governed by Islamic ideology that could go for such a law. The platform hosting such discussion was, thus, of 'Mussulman'.

This example adds to the evidence of *Punch*'s familiarity and popularity amongst the avant-garde of Hindi intelligentsia, like Bharatendu Harishchandra who was experimenting with the format of a literary periodical for a projected national language and its community of readers.[23] It would be pertinent to examine the contemporary relevance of the reproduction of this particular piece. Considering *Harischandra's Magazine*'s format along with a larger intellectual, political engagement of contemporary intelligentsia as reflected within its pages, some plausible explanation can be offered. Firstly, it was part of a larger editorial agenda

---

[17] For a full quote of this review, see Swarali Paranjape, chapter Crossing Boundaries: *Punch* and the Marathi Weekly *Hindu Pañca* (1870–1909) in this volume.

[18] It was Harishchandra's first journal.

[19] See the Facsimile edition *Harischandra's Magazine*, ed. Satyaprakash Misra (Allahabad: Hindi Sahitya Sammelan, 2002), 70–71.

[20] Brian Maidment's chapter, The presence of Punch in the Nineteenth Century, on *Punch* in this volume deals with the periodical's class character.

[21] Brian Harrison, "The British Prohibitionists 1853–1872: A Biographical Study," *International Review of Social History* 15, no. 3 (1970): 375–467.

[22] The denomination Turk and Muslim is used interchangeably.

[23] Dalmia, *Nationalization of Hindu Traditions*, 222–324.

of attracting and making its bilingual readers—emerging middle classes who were still a primarily English and Urdu reading public—familiar with the topical issues of Britain and engagements of the empire along with the issues in British India. The humorous political items added to its catholicity. Secondly, this piece highlighted the problem of alcoholism and differing opinions on how to deal with it. This was synchronous with the literary engagement with this issue, especially within contemporary Hindi satirical literature.[24] The alcohol-drinking practice was perceived as a menacing social vice brought about by colonial culture. The very next issue of *Harischandra's Magazine*, for instance, carried the satirical piece '*Pāc'veṃ paigambar*' (the fifth prophet).[25] The subject matter of this satire was very complex. Suffice it to say that alcohol was identified as the favourite drink of the first person satiric narrator, namely, the Fifth, or Sucking Prophet, who was the embodiment of colonialism in its various political and cultural forms.[26] Finally, this stereotype of Muslims/Islam was in consonance with the dominant attitude of the contemporary Hindu intelligentsia.[27]

Punch as *Pañc*: Problematising the Transculturality of *Punch* in the Hindi Literary Sphere

Punch as *Pañc*, by which I mean its transmuted life in the Hindi literary sphere, subsumed all connotations available in the existing linguistic register. Yet within the formats of Hindi periodicals the presence of the British weekly *Punch* remains

---

[24] Although the temperance movement in India is said to have begun in the late 1880s and acquired some prominence in the 1890s, its expression in Hindi literature preceded it by at least a decade. For a general overview of the temperance movement in colonial India and its British linkages see Lucy Carroll, "The Temperance Movement in India: Politics and Social Reform," *Modern Asian Studies* 10, no. 3 (1976): 417–447, and Lucy Carroll, "Origins of the Kayastha Temperance Movement," *Indian Economic Social History Review* 11 (1974): 432–447.

[25] Bhār'tendu Hariścandra, "Pāc'veṃ paigambar," *Harischandra's Magazine*, 15 December 1873. *Facsimile Edition*, ed. Satyaprakash Misra (Allahabad: Hindi Sahitya Sammelan, 2002), 84–86. Examples can be multiplied. *Kalirāj kī sabhā* (assembly of the Lord of Fallen Times) was serialised between 15 October (one issue before the publication of *Mussulman Platform*) and February, 1874. Ibid., 38–39 and 138–142.

[26] In the farce and skits we also find negative depictions of characters, for instance, English-educated, westernised and zealous 'anti-Hindu' social reformers, often Bengalis, who are fond of alcohol. In some cases the corrupt king, an allegorical representation of the colonial ruling elite, and his collaborators, like debauched priests, are represented as eating meat and being intoxicated with alcohol. See, for example, "Vaidikī hiṃsā hiṃsā na bhavati" (Vedic violence is no violence), first published in *Kavivacan'sudhā*, June 21, 1872. It was also published as an independent booklet from Medical Hall Press in 1873. Hemant Śarmā, ed. *Bhār'tendu samagra* (Vārāṇasī: Hindī Pracārak Saṃsthān, 1989), 309–318.

[27] For instance, "Pāc'veṃ paigambar", mentioned above, can also be cited as one of the many examples. For greater detail see Sudhir Chandra, *The Oppressive Present: Literature and Social Consciousness in Colonial India* (Delhi: Oxford University Press, 1992).

discernible in the overarching literary usage of the term. From *Kavivacan'sudhā* onwards the term *Pañc* within the format of literary periodicals stood for satire.

In its early years *Kavivacan'sudhā* carried a column entitled *Pañc kā prapañc* (the tangles [or gossip-mongering] of *Pañc*). In its usual form the column consisted of a dialogue, which was prompted by contemporary discussions on modes of gossip between *Pañc* and one or two other characters about town.[28] Following the example of *Kavivacan'sudhā*, we can find similar characters and columns in periodicals like *Hindī pradīp* (light of Hindi, [Allahabad, 1877]), *Brāhmaṇ* (Brahmin [Kanpur, 1883]) and *Bhārat jīvan* (life of India [Benares, 1888]). Interestingly, periodicals with an avowedly Brahmanic agenda like *Dvija patrikā* (twice-born's magazine [Patna, 1890]) also had a section for humour and satire titled *Pañc prapañc*. Its cover page advertised that it aims at reforming Brahmins, Kshatriyas and Vaishyas,[29] and would be publishing

> [...]on Knowledge, Religion [*dharma*], Morality, Manners, Duty, History, Ancient System, Translation, Poetry, Drama, Satire, Literature, Philosophy, Women's Education, *Pañc prapañc* [my italics], Letters to the Editor and miscellanea.[30]

The literary periodical *Sarasvatī* (goddess of learning [Allahabad, 1900]) started under the aegis of the *Nāgarī Pracāriṇī Sabhā* (society for the propagation of Hindi) advertised in its first issue:

> And what topics will this journal cover—one should guess this from the very fact that its title is *Sarasvatī*. It will include prose, verse, poetry, plays, novels, [...] history, biographies, *pañc*, *hāsya*, *parihās* [my italics], jest, ancient history, science, handicrafts, arts, and as many other topics of literature as space permits, and it will review, as appropriate, forthcoming books.[31]

The usage of the term *hāsya* and *parihās*, which can be translated as humour and satire, alongside *Pañc* is suggestive of the popularity and establishment of satirical skits as a distinct literary style which had been initiated by Bharatendu Harishchandra with overt inspiration from the British *Punch*.

How did *Punch* mutate into *Pañc*? What did the term mean? Tracing the literary genealogy of *Pañc* columns in *Kavivacan'sudhā*, Vasudha Dalmia points out that the British *Punch* has a lineage that goes far back to the European tradition of *commedia dell'arte*'s Pulcinella, which was to be reproduced in England in the

---

[28] In some cases it could be gossip between characters with different names but still carried out in the same style. For instance, see "Do mitroṃ kā vārtālāp: kul'pālak aur viśvabandhu kā samāgam" (Dialogue between two Friends: Rendezvous of a Noble Patron and a Universal Brother), *Harischandra Magazine*, October 1873. *Facsimile Edition* ed. Satyaprakash Misra (Allahabad: Hindi Sahitya Sammelan, 2002), 19–22.

[29] According to the classical, textual Hindu social stratification system, these three classes of priests, warriors and merchants are twice-born, while the fourth class of Shudras, or labouring class, is not twice-born and hence impure. This is a very simplified explanation of a terribly complex concept of the Hindu social system.

[30] See the cover page of *Dvija patrikā* 1, no. 1, Phālgun (February–March) 1890.

[31] *Sarasvatī* would become the most influential literary periodical in Hindi.

form of the rowdy Mr Punch in the Punch-and-Judy puppet show.[32] In the Indian context, *Punch* was fused yet again with the *vidūṣaka* (clown) tradition of Sanskrit drama and, by virtue of the similarity of names in many Indian languages, with *pañc*—the arbiter of the village judiciary, whose authority is legitimised by his folkloric juxtaposition with God as Pañc Parameśvar.[33] This *pañc*, then, had both the irreverence of the clown and the sacred authority of the village judge.[34]

According to Syamsundar Das, a leading Hindi activist, intellectual, linguist and lexicographer, *pañc* stood for a collective of people, common folk and a pioneer simultaneously.[35] The best exposition of contemporary elaborations of the contextual meaning of *pañc* can be gleaned from the essay *Pañc parameśvar* by Pratap Narayan Misra.[36] The essay was written to establish the moral legitimacy of the educated middle class as the cultural vanguard of the Indian nation. What is useful to us is that Misra develops his point by using the concept of *pañc* in north India. He plays with the semantics of this word, underlines its polysemy, delves deeper into its etymology and then assigns a contemporary relevance to it. This essay illuminates the semantic richness of the term.

> With *pañc'tattva* [five elements] the Parameśvar [Highest God] creates the cosmos; [...] Control over the lord of *pañcendriya* [five senses] facilitates proximity with Parameśvar; given the centrality of *pañc'saṃskār* [five moral-religious rituals] in *dharma*, of *pañc'gaṅgā* [another name for river Ganges at the holy city of Benaras] amongst pilgrimage sites, of *pañc'pavitrātmā* [five holy spirits] in Islam, one has reasons to believe that *pañc* is intimately associated with Parameśvar.
>
> On this basis our learned forefathers made those proverbs popular in which ordinary, humble, this-worldly folks (if they have faith in Parameśvar) accept Pañc, meaning a collective of people, a representative of Parameśvar. He is shapeless and spotless, hence not visible to anyone with external eyes, nor has anyone ever seen him doing any work; therefore it is the proposition of many thinking men that whatever Pañc [a collective of people] decides or does is in many ways the truth.

---

[32] Dalmia, *Nationalization of Hindu Traditions*, 252–53.

[33] *Parameśvar*: the highest god.

[34] Besides the satirical columns containing the figure of Pañc and other homologous narrators, there are many satirical pieces like "Pāc'veṃ paigambar" by Bharatendu, *Yam'lok kī yātrā* by Radhacharan Gosvami, etc., where the satirical narrator is created by the author as a literary strategy. This fictional narrator and his narrative style are invested with the attributes of a quasi-divine, liminal outsider who could state the unstated, visualise the concealed and potentially break what Sudipta Kaviraj calls, the 'grammar of reality'. Sudipta Kaviraj, *The Unhappy Consciousness: Bankimchandra Chattopadhyay and the Formation of Nationalist Discourse in India* (Delhi: Oxford University Press, 1995), 29. In the case of satirical journalism, this is quite clear also from at least two examples of the twentieth century. For instance, a column titled *Siv'śambhu ke ciṭṭhe* (Letters from Lord Shiva) the narrator of which has the name and attributes of Lord Shiva, and also in the character of Mat'vālā who saw himself as god personified, or at least as an emissary and reporter of Lord Shiva on earth.

[35] Śyām'sundar Dās, *Hindī śabd'sāgar* (Kāśī: Nāgarī Pracāriṇī Sabhā, 1929, 2729).

[36] Pratap Narayan Misra was one of the leading Hindi intellectuals of the late nineteenth century and a member of the Hindi literary circle named *Bhāratendu maṇḍal*. He was the editor of *Brāhmaṇ* (Kanpur) and coined the emblematic slogan 'Hindi-Hindu-Hindustan', which summarised the dominant political agenda of Hindi nationalism.

That is why '*5 pañc mil kije kāj hare jite hoe na lāj*' [action taken in unison by people is beyond victory and defeat], [...] and other similar proverbs are expounded by the learned and it is often noted by commoners that '*5 pañc ki bhāṣā amit hotī hai*' [statement of a collective is incontestable]. No matter how powerful, rich, or learned you are, if you go against Pañc's opinion, [...] it would be very difficult, if not impossible, for you to survive in this world [...].

Going against the majority practice [even for a very noble cause] is tantamount to making your life hell. Those who are determined to sacrifice everything to redeem others are hailed, but when? Only if they are accepted by the Pañc! However, as long as they live, they are unable to even breathe conveniently, because going against the *pañc* is like going against the Parameśvar, for which there is no escape from penalisation. Greatness hardly comes to your defence [...].

O readers! By the grace of Parameśvar and your forefathers you do not lack knowledge. Therefore open your eyes wide and look at the direction in which the educated Pañc are moving and see how bravely, firmly and naturally they are marching without being discouraged from fear of abuse, threat and the might of small but strong opposition; they are ready to be an example by forsaking not only their wives, sons, wealth and family but by sacrificing themselves.[37]

In the first paragraph, Pañc's semantic identity with the sacred numerology of Hinduism and Islam is established by emphasising its centrality in the overall relationship with God so that its quasi-divine status is underlined. In the second paragraph, through mobilisation of the semantic resources of popular idiomatic expressions and by extension popular opinion, Pañc is explicated as the collective of people. The acts of Pañc then are legitimised and made unassailable as the will of the divine by a virtual negation of God's interventionist presence in the everyday life of the society. In the next paragraphs, the Pañc, as a collective of people, is described as the representative of majority opinion, and consequently as the embodiment of the public at large. Once Pañc is designated as the embodiment of a public with quasi-divine status, his authority is made unassailable. Finally, in the concluding paragraph, Pañc is equated with the contemporary, educated middle class that is dedicated to social and moral reform. In other words, Pañc is the metaphor of the educated urban middle class speaking in the register of reform on behalf of the Indian nation, and hence, to be followed by the people.

Pañc: Literary Forms and Political Contents

Skits

Let us examine the literary form and political content of skits with some examples. They were light, lively, biting and sparkling. The Pañc of these columns is a fascinating mixture of characters who are raucous, impious and clowning

---

[37] It needs to be emphasised here that the *pañc* and/or Parameśvar are quintessentially male. This essay was first published in *Brāhmaṇ* vol. 6, no. 12, 15 July, 1888. The citation is from Candrikā Prasād Śarmā, ed., *Pratāp'nārāyaṇ miśra rac'nāvalī*, vol. 2 (Dillī: Bhār'tīya Prakāśan Saṃsthān, 2001), 114–116.

men-about-town usually at odds with authority. On the one hand, he stands outside events; on the other hand, he, as a judge, is involved in events. Pañc, time and again, goes into the messy world, becomes a participant observer, and then retreats. For example, a skit appeared in the June 1873 issue of *Kavivacan'sudhā*,[38] wherein Pañc turns his sharp wit on much more personal, and for all their apparent slightness, heavily symbolic topics, such as the controversy over British judges stopping Indians from entering law courts with their shoes on. This was contrary to a law which had been passed in the previous decade legalising wearing shoes while attending court proceedings.[39] The setting of the skit is the city of Benaras. The periodical noted that:

> We are in the year 1872, and Pañc is listening to the conversation of two friends, Munshi Bhairoprasad, a *kāyastha*, and a *mahājan*, Babu Ramnath, who makes gentle fun of his bookish friend, the Munshi. The Munshi has been perusing the papers earnestly as usual and has come across a significant piece of news. The news has to do with an object whose identity he does not disclose, apart from the fact that it goes in pairs, has to do with leather and is expensive, for millions have been affected by ventures connected with it. Babu Ramnath is unable to guess what this is.
> Babu: What does it look like?
> Munshi: It's rather long in appearance. In effect it looks like the country it comes from.
> Babu: Hmm, the *vilāyat*[40] of the English. What does the thing look like there?
> Munshi: In the *vilāyat* of the English the thing is smooth and greasy and often of black colour and it is considered most pure amongst them. They carry it with them wherever they go.
> Babu: Brother mine, I haven't really understood what it is. What does it look like in Hindustan?
> Munshi: Here it has a sort of beak.
> Babu: Is it some fantastic pair of birds?
> Munshi: Oh no, it is a very useful thing, it protects from the sun, from dirt and slime, from heat and cold, from all these things.
> Babu: Quick tell me its name, I'm getting quite agitated.
> Munshi: It is called the shoe.
> Babu: Come, what weighty matter have you touched on there. What on earth does the shoe have to do with the newspaper?
> Munshi: No, really, of late the Honourable Shoe has been hot news.
> Babu: Well, what new news of it?
> Munshi: There is an order saying you have to take off your shoes before you enter court.
> Babu: And why this?
> Munshi: How do I know?
> Babu: And who could bear to part with his shoes?
> Pañc (coming forward): This isn't true. It's years ago, since Lord Lawrence's day, that it was decided that anyone could enter government offices and courts or other public places in English shoes (though they had to be polished to shine like a mirror). Then why all this ado?

---

[38] *Kavivacan'sudhā*, June 1873. Cited from Dalmia, *Nationalization of Hindu Traditions*, 254–255.

[39] For an interesting insight into cultural politics behind the shoe controversy see Kandiyur N. Panikkar, "The Great Shoe Question: Legitimacy and Power in Colonial India," *Studies in History* 14, no. 1 (1998): 21–36.

[40] *vilāyat* (Urdu/Hindi): lit. 'province', 'foreign country'; common appellation of England in colonial times.

Munshi: Well sirs, your thinking is simple-minded. I agree that there was an order once, but there are so many who pay no heed to it. Didn't you go to Mughal Sarai to see the new Governor General? Even if the world obeys the order, in Benaras it was never heeded to nor will it ever be.
Pañc: What, you mean that even the Government Gazette won't be obeyed?
Munshi: Yes, it won't be obeyed. What do you think you can do about it?

Pañc responds by making the most impotent of gestures. He runs to the concerned authorities and asks them what they mean by all this. Yet Pañc's insistence on the letter of the law is double-edged. If, on the one hand, it makes mockery of the bureaucracy that thinks that such matters can be dealt with by passing laws and regulations, it also seeks to make these very authorities abide by their own laws. After all, it was humiliating forms of social interaction with the 'ruling race' that injured the ego of the Indian middle classes the most. This skit, like many others, was based on widely-circulated news items already known to potential readers. There is an interesting historical background to the plot of this skit: After the sensational case of defiance of this racist custom in 1862 by a certain Manockjee Cowasjee Entee in a criminal court in Surat, the colonial government passed a law that Indians could enter the court room with their shoes on. But British judges continued to insist on the custom in lower courts, thereby causing uproar in the newspapers.[41]

The Pañc skits are also consistently directed against the debauched practices of the rich, who include the native chiefs, the rich *mahajans* (merchants), the priestly class,[42] in short, the socially privileged. In one of the columns titled '*Melā-thelā*' (marketplace), Pañc watches the activities of these social types in a marketplace and assumes the role of a judge in disguise.[43] In another column entitled '*Pañc kā nyāy*' (the justice of Pañc), he is actually a judge and makes a mockery of himself; while acting as the presiding officer of a meeting of an association of lower castes called *kurmī*, he mocks the entire state of affairs. This association of newly educated, lower caste youths is apparently trying to resist their traditional place in the Hindu social hierarchy by claiming higher social status. They bolster their claim by tracing a pseudo-historical lineage to a mythical Hindu god called *Kurmāvatāra*, the turtle incarnation among Lord Vishnu's ten *avatāra*s, building on the phonetic similarity with their caste name.[44]

'*Pañc kā nyāy*' is a satire on the growing process of Sanskritisation amongst lower castes[45] in the colonial context. As a result of the economic and social change

---

[41] This incidence was first reported in the *Pioneer*. For a detailed report of this incident, see the appendix of Panikkar, "The Great Shoe Question".

[42] *Hindī pradīp*, February–March 1892.

[43] *Hindī pradīp*, April 1906.

[44] *Hindī pradīp*, June–July 1899. Also see "Pañc kā ek prapañc," *Hindī pradīp*, July–August 1903.

[45] Mysore N. Shrinivas, *Social Change in Modern India* (Berkely: University of California Press, 1966).

under the new colonial dispensation, the social groups that earned upward economic mobility, but had a lower status in the Hindu social hierarchy, started redefining their social positions in the wake of the colonial census operation and the consequent objectification of caste. The census department, under the influence of H. H. Risley's theory of social precedence, had started classifying all social and occupational groups under the broader textual Hindu Brahmanic schema of the *varṇa* system.[46] By adopting and consequently subverting social rituals and customs of the upper caste Hindus these social groups began to rewrite their mytho-historical origin.[47] On these bases they put forth their claims to the high ritual and social status in a new forum—the census department of the colonial government. They argued that they should be accorded a higher place in the Hindu social hierarchy. The satire mocks not only the assertion of a lower caste from a Brahmanic perspective, but also the absurdity of the modern institution of caste associations.

Pañc did not always play the judge; he could be raucous and turbulent, could chase after young and comely women with a thirst for education, and make a thorough nuisance of himself. His opinions, however, for all the tomfoolery, carried the weight of public opinion. One of the *Punch* columns dealt precisely with this theme. When a young and beautiful *meh'tarānī* (sweeper-woman), set out to reach for the sky through education, Pañc not only sought to make indecent advances towards her, thus demeaning her moral standing and subverting her claims to a higher status, but also reprimanded her severely for entertaining false ambitions.[48]

---

[46] Bernard Cohn, "The Census, Social Structure and Objectification in South Asia," in *The Bernard Cohn Omnibus* (Delhi: Oxford University Press, 2008), 224–254.

[47] In this process of sanskritisation, the role of Arya Samaj, a Hindu reformist organisation which questioned the prevalent notion of birth based social status and advocated its determination on the basis of one's present vocation and moral standing, was very crucial. M.S.A. Rao's study of the Shri Narayan Dharmapala movement in Kerala and the Yadava movement in north India is a good early work of historical sociology on the social and political transformation with a focus on lower caste associations, See Madhugiri S.A. Rao, *Social Movements and Social Transformation: A Study of two Backward Classes Movements in India* (Delhi: MacMillan, 1979). For an overview of the role of caste associations amongst the Kayasthas of Bihar Bengal and the United Province and their claim to a higher social status, see Lucy Carroll, "Colonial Perceptions of Indian Society and the Emergence of Caste(s) Associations," *Journal of Asian* Studies 37, no. 2 (1978): 233–250. For an overview of Indian nationalists taking on the question of caste, see also Susan Bayly, "Hindu Modernisers and the Public Arena: Indigenous Critiques of Caste in Colonial India," in *Swami Vivekananda and the Modernisation of Hinduism*, ed. William Radice (Delhi: Oxford University Press, 1998), 93–137. For an overview of the role of lower caste associations in accumulating political power in Bihar and north India from the late nineteenth to the late twentieth century see Prasanna Kumār Caudharī and Śrīkānt, *Bihār meṃ sāmājik parivartan ke kuch āyam* (Dillī: Vāṇī Prakāśan, 2001).

[48] *Kavivacan'sudhā*, 17 August 1872. Cited from Dalmia, *Nationalization of Hindu Traditions*, 259–260.

Jokes and Conundrums

In some of the issues of *Kavivacan'sudhā*, under the title *Pañc kā prapañc*, we find a poem written with light but piercing satire in the pre-modern *lavanī* or *dohā* form. Occasionally this space was filled with jokes and conundrums which had a politico-ethnic subtext. For example, there was a joke titled 'Very Well', targeting the foolishness of the cuckolded English official who is unaware of the adulterous relationship between his wife and the domestic:

> A domestic became very intimate with the wife of a British Officer. Once it so happened that when he was smooching the Memsahib, the Sahib[49] saw him. Memsahib also saw the Sahib coming and anxiously told the servant in her accented Hindi that her husband had seen them kissing, and that she was in trouble now. The domestic asked her calmly not to worry, and when the Sahib came he put his turban at the Sahib's feet and said: I am going to quit my job; Memsahib has accused me of stealing ghee [purified butter] and has gone so far as to smell my mouth! Hearing this, the Sahib turned to his wife and said—Yes I saw you smelling his mouth, but he is very honest and can never indulge in such an act. Then he turned to the domestic and said dear chef I'll double your pay, but please don't leave this job; to which the latter replied—Very well Sir![50]

The joke cited above has a striking structural resemblance with the pre-modern misogynistic jokes on cuckoldry and female adultery.[51] In fact, this joke on a husband unable to control his hypersexual wife in liaison with the domestic is slightly modified by replacing generic characters with contemporary racial identities: white master, his wife and an Indian domestic. In the colonial context, then, the joke becomes politically charged for a Hindi reading public. It plays on the stereotype of the sexually licentious white woman. It underlines the patriarchal anxiety about the dangers of a nuclear family, without family elders keeping vigil over potentially licentious household women, who are exposed to the proximity of other sexually threatening males, such as domestics. Finally, it establishes the supremacy of an Indian male subaltern who wittingly dupes his colonial master and wins money and the body of a white woman.

Nearly all periodicals mentioned so far published columns variously titled '*Hāsī-dillagī kī bātem*' (wit and humor), '*Cuṭ'kule*' (jokes), '*Bujhavval*' (conundrum) at regular intervals that contained racy popular jokes with a direct or indirect political subtext. For example, a joke published in *Kṣatriya patrikā* (warrior-caste's

---

[49] 'Sahib' and 'Memsahib' were the Indian terms for 'white master' and his 'wife'.

[50] This is a literal translation of a nineteenth century Hindi joke which has been made at the cost of the rules of English grammar in order to be faithful to the original. See Siṃh, *Śrīhariścandrakalā*, 34.

[51] Jokes about cuckoldry were already in circulation through oral and their printed versions. *Pañcatantra*, for instance, has many similar stories. See Franklin Edgerston, *The Panchatantra Reconsidered*, vol. 2, *Introduction and Translation* (New Heavens Connecticut: American Oriental Society, 1924), 289–91, 378–79. Lee Siegel also cites many jokes from the *Pañcatantra*, *Kathāsaritsāgara, Śukasaptati* and other folktales. Lee Siegel, *Laughing Matters: Comic Tradition in India* (Chicago: University of Chicago Press, 1987), 62–63, 126–36, 197–98, 204, 206.

magazine, 1884) touched upon issues, such as child marriage, which were at the centre of public controversy. The joke went something like this:

> Once, a priest was married to a child bride. With his child bride on his shoulder he was crossing a marketplace. A rowdy *jaj'mān* [religious client] quipped—is it your daughter Chaubeju? The priest replied: both my son and daughter are into her only.[52]

Significantly, many of these jokes as the one cited above on cuckoldry, which were part of the north Indian oral repertoire, were reprinted without any changes or with only minor contextual changes, while retaining the original structure of the plot. To cite just one example, a joke on caste-based favouritism of the *kāyasthas*[53] appeared in *Kavivacan'sudhā* and *Kṣatriya patrikā* bearing the title of '*Jātīya pakṣapāt*' in the 1880s. It had already been published without a title in Lallujilal's *Latīfa-i Hind* in 1810 under the aegis of the Calcutta Fort William College. The joke was as follows:

> Once, a Kaith [*kāyastha*] of high administrative rank was going somewhere. On his way there he found a Kaith tree [*acacia catechu*]. Pointing towards the tree he asked his servants, who is it? They replied: Lala Sahib, this is Kaith. Listening to this he joyously said, Oho, he is my caste-fellow! Ask him why he is standing in my way. The servants wittily replied: it is saying I am unclothed and suffering from cold. Upon hearing this the *kāyastha* ordered his servants to grant 25 bundles of silk from his storehouse to his caste-fellow.[54]

The text of this joke is complex. It adopts the genealogy of caste myths as a rhetorical form. It draws from the structure of a traditional story of a social group's totemic genealogy and the consequent justification of kinship ties. The narrator of this joke mocks the partisan behaviour of a caste group member and, simultaneously, the textual form of the myth. A purely semantic similarity between two completely unrelated objects, a botanic and human entity, and the consequent favouritism underline the absurdity of caste-based sociality. Given the context of its print when hitherto dispersed and socially unconnected *kāyastha*s of different regions—Bengal, Bihar and the United Province—were uniting under one caste association,[55] the absurdity of an unrelated and coincidental similarity of terms referred to in the joke acquires a contemporaneous allegorical referentiality. Jokes on *kāyastha*s may have been in circulation for a long time but acquired new meanings in the time of their reproduction. Jokes and satires targeting them with clear references to late nineteenth century historical processes can be found aplenty. A joke book carried an epigrammatic comment on the inability of a *kāyastha* to ride

---

[52] The priest meant to say that both his son and daughter would come out of his child-bride's womb. This joke is in Braj dialect and hence very difficult to render into English. I have provided an approximate rendition here. *Kṣatriya patrikā*, Jyeṣṭha-Āṣāṛh 1939/June–July 1882.

[53] A traditional clerical caste with administrative clout since pre-colonial times.

[54] *Kṣatriya patrikā*, Kārtik (October) 1890, Siṃh, *Śrīhariścandrakalā*, 38, Lallujilal, *Latifa-e-Hind* Or *The New Encyclopedia Hindoostanica of Wit* (Calcutta: Indian Gazette Press, 1810), 13.

[55] Carrol, "Colonial Perceptions of Indian Society".

a horse around the same time when, erstwhile considered as shudras, the *kāyasthas* started claiming themselves to be kshatriyas (warriors).[56]

> A novice *kāyath*, awkwardly sitting on horseback, was going to the marketplace, a cavalier saw him sitting behind the saddle and asked, O brother, sit a little ahead. The *kāyath* asked, why? He clarified, your saddle is empty. The *kāyath* replied, why should I follow you? I sit in a position in which my horse keeper put me.[57]

Essays

Like the British *Punch*, satirical essays, not uncommon in Pratap Narayan Misra's *Brāhmaṇ*, endlessly played with words, made false linguistic connections and teased new meanings out of them. In 1888 an editorial titled "Ṭ" was published.[58] It questioned the British imperialist character through a mock exercise in social linguistics obliquely communicating the pressing political anger of a Hindi intellectual crushed under the asymmetries of colonialism:

> This letter neither has the loveliness of L, nor the difficulty of D, nor the motherly touch of M. Think a little: you will find it filled with selfishness. If observed minutely, Arabs and Persians are not unalloyed forms of deceit and cunning—they know how to kill or get killed, how to oppress the weak being the mightier, and how to help against all odds when pleased. And where calculation doesn't work, they simply fawn; but taking care of their public image and greasing others to further self-interest, which is indeed so essential, are absolutely alien to them. Look into the characters of all the Kings in history. You won't find a single one whose good or bad character could remain undercover for long. That's why they don't have Ṭ in their alphabet! Ask a Persian to pronounce *ṭaṭṭī*, he will make more than 20 attempts but ultimately utter *tattī*! Never ever hunted from behind a *ṭaṭṭī* [veil], how could they have this word? On the other hand see our White-lord, *haiṭ* (hat) on his head, *pyeṃṭ* (pant) and *būṭ* on his legs. The name of the God, *ālmāiṭī* (almighty);[59] the name of the Preceptor *ṭiuṭar* [<tutor>] or *māsṭar* [<master>], [...] or *ṭīcar* [<teacher>]; the title of the beloved, *misṭres*; the name of work, *ṭreḍ* [<trade>]; word for profit, *benīphiṭ*; the word for the poet, *poyaṭ*; the word for idiot, *sṭupiḍ*; they eat on a *ṭebil* and earn by *ṭeks*. How far should I stretch this *ṭiṭil ṭeṭil* (chattering); take any of the big dictionaries, you'll hardly find a word without Ṭ. [...] He is the crown of the world because of this Ṭ. Leave aside the issue of comprehending his policy, common educated people can't articulate the meaning of a single word of this policy [...] Your selfishness is great! Came here as a merchant but became king of the kings! Why not, with whom everything is full of Ṭ, is it at all surprising that he should digesṬ anything and everything of others?[60] This is called morality.

---

[56] Ibid.

[57] Anon., *Manohar kahānī* (Lakhʹnaū: Navalʹkiśor Press, 1880), 6. Horse riding is traditionally associated with military prowess.

[58] First published in *Brāhmaṇ* 4, no. 11, June 15, 1888. Cited from Candrikā Prasād Śarmā, ed., *Pratāpʹnārāyaṇ Miśra racʹnāvalī* (2001), 59–61. In South Asian languages, the English *t* sound is usually realised as a retroflex *ṭ*, and this rule underlies this whole passage.

[59] The terms in brackets are the Hindi equivalents of the respective English terms in Devanagari script.

[60] Ṭ is given as *ṭakār*, and the rhyming word to that is *ḍakār* from *ḍakārʹnā*, literally not 'to digest' but 'to burp'.

The author assigns essential wickedness to the letter *Ṭ* and offers a historical assessment of the moral character of the ruling classes of India by illustrating the lack or preponderance of this letter in their languages. A deficiency of this letter in Persian, the official language of the state in pre-British India, serves as evidence of a better state of affairs in medieval times. Likewise, preponderance of this letter in English is turned into an explanation for the political reality and nature of the British colonial rule.

Another good example of parody was the use of 'mock' lexicographies and dictionaries. *Punch* had this variety of satire aplenty.[61] It is difficult to assume a linear connection between this kind of satire published in *Punch* and that published in *Brāhmaṇ* or *Hindī pradīp*. In colonial Northern India it sought to describe the colonial cultural condition by using pseudo-lexicographical keywords of Indian society and politics. This was achieved with a deliberate (mis)application of grammatical methods to elaborate on contemporary cultural meaning of everyday social and political parlance. And, by extension, it turns out to be a compressed articulation of multiple asymmetries in a colonial society perceived as, in Sudhir Chandra's words, the 'oppressive present' of colonialism.[62] For instance, Misra's *Kalikoś* (encyclopaedia of fallen times) describes the following groups:

> *Brāhmaṇ*—'*Bāmbhan*', one who sounds *bā*, meaning an ox—an animal without education.
> *Gurū*—Shameless, scoundrel, crazy, etc., evident by the [living] encyclopedia of Benares.
> [...]
> *Paṃḍit*—P for *pāpī* [sinner], Ḍ for *ḍākū* [robber], T for *taskar* [smuggler].
> [...]
> *Chatrī* [Warrior]—One who does not even walk to the urinal without a *chat'rī* [umbrella], in other words the embodiment of feminine delicateness.
> [...]
> *Vaiśya* [Trader]—Seems to be the masculine counterpart of *veśyā* [prostitute] because 'for the sake of money (s)he is ready to forsake self-esteem and be a slave'. But they are so envious that 'this prostitute is expert in stealing others' wealth and conscience' and they earn for the Englishmen.

---

[61] Altick, *Punch* cites such examples. A parody of Olivian Lore was serialised in the year 1843. Written by Percival Leigh and illustrated by H. G. Haine, it cast Hercules as Punch's surrogate who deals with his numerous antagonists until 1843:
The Nemean Lion = war
The Hydra = the law ('the offspring of necessity by wickedness')
The Buck of the Brazen Countenance = swindlers typified by 'Jew bill-discounters'
The Great Boer = quackery (in medicine)
The Augean Stables = parliament, bureaucracy, and courts to be cleaned by the force of public opinion
The Harpies = vultures 'of a certain "persuasion"' who batten on debtors
(Altick, *Punch*, 100).
[62] Cf. Chandra, *Oppressive Present*.

[...]
Agnihotra [Fire sacrifice]—One who spoils the atmosphere by spending thousands of rupees on firecrackers for a marriage celebration.
Hospitality—Serving food to the British, honouring sacred thread, *coṭī* and *tilak* with eggs and chicken.
Dharma—Abusing followers of another sect.
Veda—Seed of division between Ārya Samāj and Dharma Sabhā.
[...]
Śivālay [Temple of Lord Shiva]—The place of *śivā* or the jackal [...]
[...]
Nāstik [Atheist]—One who follows the dicta of each and every sect except our own [...].
Kacah'rī [Law court]—*kac* means hair and *harī* means remover [...]
Darbār—*darb* means wealth, *ari* means enemy [...]
Hākim [Government officer]—The oppressed says *hā* [shouts in pain] and his highness says *kim*, meaning why the hell are you shouting?
Bakīl (Advocate)—*buḥ* + *kil*, one who nails your heart, or in another language, *voḥ* + *kī*, What (is with you)? Give it to me [...]
[...]
Mard [Man]—One who has been trampled [...].
[...]
Santān [Son]—One who is born after the visit of a *sant* or characterless monk![63]

From the title onwards this piece can be read symptomatically. The author uses the trope of the Age of *kali*[64]—an age of all-pervasive moral and cultural downfall. As a parodying encyclopaedia of colonial ethnography[65] and scholarly register of Sanskrit lexicography, the content of this essay satirises the general socio-cultural condition under colonialism. The Brahmans, a traditional social group with scholarly pursuits, are no more than the proverbial ignorant oxen, the spiritual preceptors are thugs, the warrior or ruling class is wallowed in pleasure and is emasculated, the merchant class is unethical and collaborates with the colonial masters, the epitome of the educated service class, *agnihotrī*, are far from being austere. The culture of hospitality is deeply colonised, the philosophical tradition of religious debate has been debased, the philosophers of atheism have become deeply opportunistic and superficial, and finally the colonial institutions of justice and welfare are misnomers and exploitative to their core.

---

[63] It was first serialised in *Brahman* between 1884 and 1886. The citation is from Miśra, *Pratāp'nārāyaṇ Miśra rac'nāvalī*, 27–31. Similar writings by Radhacharan Gosvami can be found in *Hindī pradīp*, July 1882.

[64] The Kali age is the last and worst temporal phase in the circular time of Hindu cosmology. See Romila Thapar, *Time as a Metaphor of History*, Krishna Bhardwaj Memorial Lecture, (Delhi: Oxford University Press, 1996). For the cultural politics of the invocation of the Kali age in the colonial period, see Sumit Sarkar, "'Kaliyuga', 'Chakri' and 'Bhakti': Ramakrishna and His Times," *Economic and Political Weekly* 27, no. 29 (1992): 1543–1566.

[65] Gosvami suggestively entitled his piece as 'Mimicry of a new encyclopedia by Mr W'. Here Mr. W stands for none other than the orientalist scholar/administrator H. H. Wilson.

Cartoon

Another significant development in late nineteenth century Hindi periodicals was the incorporation of illustrations. In this context, what is significant is the beginning of illustrations in satirical columns. Cartoons in the sense of the British *Punch* were very much in vogue in Urdu, Bengali, Gujarati, and Marathi language periodicals from the second half of the 1870s. In Hindi they made their presence felt a little later. Beginning in the 1880s, a few attempts by the writer-editors themselves could be observed. For instance, Radhacharan Gosvami drew and published a cartoon titled '*Unnati kī gāṛī*' (the cart of progress). It showed the cart of progress driven by a whip-carrying Englishman named *śāsan* (governance) and *anuśāsan* (discipline). This cart is pushed forward by Bengali, Marathi and Punjabi gentlemen, while a Hindustani (north Indian) is left behind, ensnared by *avidyā* (ignorance) and *ālasya* (idleness).[66] Mahavir Prasad Dvivedi, who was the editor of the influential literary monthly *Sarasvatī* for 17 years and regarded as a moderniser of Hindi language, made cartoons a regular feature in the initial years of *Sarasvatī*.[67] They were usually drawn by commissioned artists and their subject remained limited to literary polemics.[68] *Sarasvatī*, for instance, published a cartoon titled '*Kharī bolī kā padya*' (Khari Boli poetry) in September 1902[69] (see Fig. 1). The cartoon targeted Ayodhya Prasad Khatri, who had been leading a literary movement for Khari Boli[70] to replace Brajbhasha[71] as the language of modern Hindi poetry.[72] He wrote a book, *Kharī bolī kā padya*, to highlight the variety of poetic compositions in the language to justify its potential viability to convey poetic sensibility. The cartoon mocked Khatri's linguistic and ethnographic classification of Khari Boli poetry as ridiculous and, borrowing from the imagery of Hindu mythology, graphically represented it as a man with five heads: (1) Court or clerk style, (2) Muslim style, (3) Brahmin style, (4) Eurasian style and (5) European style. Interestingly, the head representing a Brahmin style is in the middle and hence the chief amongst them. An epigrammatic comment below this illustration says:

---

[66] See Rām'nirañjan Parimalendu, *Mohan'lāl mah'to viyogī* (Dillī: Sāhitya Akādemī, 2007), 21.

[67] Dvivedi was its editor between 1903 and 1920.

[68] It cannot be established whether Dvivedi himself drew these cartoons. What can be argued with conviction is that he conceptualised the themes of the cartoons, which were largely on literary polemics, and gave detailed instruction to draw accordingly.

[69] This cartoon is reprinted in Śiv'pūjan Sahāy, ed., *Ayodhyā prasād khatrī smārak granth* (Paṭ'nā: Bihār Rāṣṭrabhāṣā Pariṣad, 1960), 101.

[70] Khari Boli was a dialect spoken in the Delhi-Agra region, and language of communication in the north Indian cities. It was made the principal base of modern standard Hindi.

[71] Brajbhasa was also a dialect in the Mathura area and had been the language of poetry since early medieval times.

[72] Ayodhya Prasad Khatri was a Hindi nationalist who was of the opinion that if Khari Boli Hindi wished to be a language of literature its poetic œuvre should not be in Brajbhasa but in Khari Boli. See Alok Rai, *Hindi Nationalism* Tracts For the Times, 13 (Delhi: Orient Longman, 2001).

Fig. 1 '*Kharī bolī kā padya*' (Khari Boli poetry). *Sarasvatī*, September 1902

> A torso on two legs with stunning five heads over them,
> Lo behold the beautiful symmetry of my penta-colour poetry.

Dvivedi's cartoon did not oppose the necessity of poetic composition in Khari Boli but, through graphic exaggeration, he underlined the absurdity of the internal diversity of Khari Boli as strange and demonic. It gave a clear hint at his future agenda of purging Khari Boli of its diversity, which he would do as the editor of *Sarasvatī* after a few months.[73]

Bhārat'jīvan published a skit titled '*Pañcānan kī peśī*' (the court of Panchanan). The pictures of an owl and a donkey are inserted in the satirical column.[74] At the court of Panchanan, two 'strange species' enter—an owl named 'Ocean of

---

[73] Exercising the authority of the editor of the monthly, which was affiliated with the powerful cultural institution Nāgarī Pracāriṇī Sabhā (society for the propagation of Hindi), Dvivedi shaped a homogenous and standard style of literary prose and poetry in Khari Boli, borrowing heavily from Sanskrit register and simultaneously discouraging use of 'dialects' or rustic Hindi and words of Perso-Arabic roots.

[74] '*Pañcānan kī peśī*' (the court of Panchanan). *Bhārat'jīvan*, 16 March 1903.

Wisdom' and an ass that is afraid of education. The first introduces himself as a representative of a literary critic. He writes favourable or damning reviews and commentaries on monetary considerations.[75] The second introduces himself as a young man from the class of newly-rich merchants with no interest in modern education. They then leave. We need to recall the tradition of popular Indian fables, *Pañcatantra*, to trace one genealogical line of the usage of visual imagery: animals type-cast with human attributes of a social class. Significantly, this example also displays the initial attempts by the editors to incorporate illustrations in satirical columns. However, after 1920, with the proliferation in print and readership, the cartoon became an essential feature of most of the periodicals, and professional artists and cartoonists started to be employed.

Characteristic Features of Late Nineteenth Century Satirical Journalism
Using several examples, I have shown that there existed a literary space and style of satirical journalism of the *Punch* variety within the Hindi literary sphere prior to 1920. This tradition of satirical journalism was informed as much by the British *Punch* as by the existing literary and oral traditions of satire. The literary format of the periodical experimented with familiar but disparate literary and oral cultural repertoires of humour. It contributed towards attracting and training a readership with diverse tastes, new to the world of Hindi print, and in the process of self-constitution. Satirical columns using parody, farce, jokes, etc., were structurally familiar to readers from their lives before and beyond the printed word.[76] Their inclusion in literary periodicals added entertainment and pleasure value to their otherwise morally overloaded, dry nationalist messages.[77] In the introduction to his *Nāpit'stotra*,[78] Radhacharan Gosvami,

---

[75] The figure of a corrupt literary critic under satiric attack is an interesting case which points towards a broader development in the Hindi literary sphere. In 1900, what Alok Rai calls 'The MacDonnell Moment', the battle to establish Nagari/Hindi as the court language, was won (Rai, *Hindi Nationalism*, 17–49). With this, the process to reorganise, institutionalise, standardise and expand the literary world of Hindi was intensified further. Consequently, the question of moral and institutional authority as an arbiter in the literary field also becomes prominent.

[76] For the interface between oral and printed literature of entertainment in Hindi and Urdu, see Francesca Orsini, "Barahmasas in Hindi and Urdu," in *Before the Divide: Hindi and Urdu Literary Cultures*, ed. Francesca Orsini (Delhi: Permanent Black, 2010), 142–177.

[77] Orsini makes a very important point about the publication of cheap tracts of entertainment literature in connection with the success of commercial printing in Hindi and Urdu. The success of the printer lay in tapping the proto-literate readership, which was trained to read already familiar modes of entertainment such as popular song and theatre. Drawing from the work on children's literature by the Italian scholar Ermanno Detti, she argues that, though often frowned upon by educationists, a deeply pleasurable experience of, what Detti calls, 'sensuous reading' is necessary to develop a habit of reading, which is an essential pre-requisite for the development of a reading practice in general. These texts of pleasure, in which we can also include printed jokes, conundrums, skits, epigrammatic comments on politics and society, etc., can be seen as absolutely necessary in order to win people over to the printed page. Orsini, *Print and Pleasure*, 22–23.

[78] Rādhācaraṇ Gosvāmī, *Nāpit'stotra* (Baṃkīpur: Khaḍgavilās Press, 1882). Also published in *Kṣatriya patrikā*, July 1881. It depicts the Brahmanic anxiety and consequent attacks on the rising

one of the key Hindi literary figures of the time, clearly underlined the entertainment aspect of satire and its prospective role in attracting a greater readership:

> Although the *Nāpit'stotra* is primarily humorous, yet it will be fruitful [...] Humour should increase interest in reading Hindi books and hence shall be a national service.

Compared to other articles written by the same set of people in the same periodicals on the same question of colonialism and its wider politico-cultural implications in Indian society, the examples above show another stark peculiarity of the satirical mode of writing. The general ambivalence of the intelligentsia towards colonial rule[79] is less apparent in satirical modes. Instead, the satirical attack is full-fledged and hardly spares any aspect of colonialism. The colonial intelligentsia—a product of the colonial encounter—uses satire as a potent means to tackle the perceived cultural asymmetries which colonialism produced through the general political subordination of the country. It consequently paved the way for what was considered to be a destabilisation of the Indian/Hindu social equilibrium visible in the assertions of the lower castes and women.

The Context of the *Mat'vālā* Moment

Mat'vālā carries forward the late nineteenth century literary experiments with its own novelty in the changed historical circumstances of the 1920s. With the rise of anti-colonial mobilisation under middle-class leadership[80] in the aftermath of the First World War, the publication and circulation of periodicals rose substantially in each and every district town, targeting and shaping the literate and semi-literate, potentially nationalistic, Hindi reading public.[81] Hindi language had been deemed to be the most appropriate language of nationalist politics by none other than the 'Father of Indian Nation' Mahatma Gandhi himself.[82] Hindu–Muslim identity politics had acquired a new dimension. In the nineteenth century community identity was articulated by the Hindi intelligentsia largely within the dominant nationalist logic as a different but constituent part of one Indian body politic. This

---

social power and liberty of the *nāpit* or barber caste which, according to the text, is reflected in their 'cunning' and assertive activities, particularly in the cities in colonial times.

[79] See Chandra, *Oppressive Present*; K.N. Panikkar, *Culture, Ideology, Hegemony: Intellectuals and Social Consciousness in Colonial India* (Delhi: Tulika, 1998).

[80] Gyanendra Pandey, *The Ascendancy of the Congress in Uttar Pradesh 1926–1934: A Study in Imperfect Mobilization* (Delhi: Oxford University Press, 1978).

[81] Its background had been set in the late nineteenth century. The programmatic political attempts of the pioneers of Hindi nationalism of the late nineteenth century and the consequent politics of Hindi-Hindu-Hindustan have been largely successful in transforming the linguistic choice of north India, and consequently, in winning over a large number of Hindu readers from Urdu to Nagari/Hindi.

[82] Orsini, *Hindi Public Sphere*.

articulation was progressively giving way to violent and mutually hostile communal identity formations during this period.[83]

In literary gossip, as well as factual accounts in the memoirs of the Hindi literati, or in books on the history of Hindi journalism in general, the story of the publication of *Mat'vālā* from Calcutta is described as a momentous event.[84] The *Annual Report on Newspaper and Periodical published from Bengal* shows that it had 200 annual subscribers and a circulation of approximately 2,000.[85] A leading member of its editorial team, however, wrote in his memoirs that it reached the unprecedented mark of 10,000 within a year.[86] There were many articles and cartoons on *Mat'vālā* in contemporary periodicals, which can also be taken as an index of its popularity.[87] It was a self-proclaimed humorous weekly with a judicious mixture of heterodoxy and commercialism. The press and the paper were owned by a young nationalist literary connoisseur and essayist, Mahadev Prasad Seth, who belonged to a rich merchant family of Mirzapur.[88] He successfully channelled the unrestrained, youthful literary talents of diverse, unique and path-breaking individuals like Suryakant Tripathi 'Nirala' and Pandey Bechan Sharma 'Ugra' on the one hand, and dedicated and disciplined ones like Munshi Navjadiklal Shrivastav and Shivpujan Sahay on the other.[89] In the moralist-rationalist Hindi world, dominated by hegemonic figures such

---

[83] Pradip Kumar Datta, *Carving Blocs: Communal Ideology in the Early Twentieth Century Bengal* (Delhi: Oxford University Press, 1999); William Gould, *Hindu Nationalism and Language of Politics in Late Colonial India* (Cambridge: Cambridge University Press, 2004).

[84] Usually downplayed in the history of Bengal/Calcutta since the inception of the printing industry, it has been one of the major centres of Hindi printing. Apart from the first Hindi periodical *Uddaṇḍ mārtaṇḍ*, Calcutta always had more than one long lasting Hindi periodical, like *Sār'sudhānidhi*, *Bhārat'mitra*, *Ucit'vaktā*, which had circulation figures between 500 and 1,500. See, for instance, 'Report on Newspaper and Periodical in Bengal for the Week Ending 22 December 1882 in *Indian Newspaper Reports, c1868–1942, from the British Library, London [microform]*, part 1: *Bengal, 1874–1903* (Marlborough: Adam Matthew Publications Ltd., 2005). Besides a sizable Hindi readership in Bara Bazar area, entire Bihar, north of the river Ganges, was a potential sphere of circulation. Calcutta was better connected than Allahabad, Benaras or even Patna.

[85] *Statement of Newspapers and Periodicals Published or Printed in Bengal—Revised Upto 31st December 1925* (Calcutta: Bengal Government Press, 1926).

[86] Śiv'pūjan Sahāy, *Merā jīvan* (Paṭ'nā: Parijāt Prakāśan, 1985), 101.

[87] To cite just one example here, see a cartoon on *Mat'vālā* in the monthly *Bhār'tendu* (Allahabad), December 1928. While publishing each other's appreciation and reviews was common in the fraternity of the periodical, *Mat'vālā*'s case was different. *Mat'vālā* attracted extra attention of the literary public as well as the government for its bold and provocative moral, political and literary stance. Finally, it succumbed to the dual pressure of the dominant, modernist, patriarchal moral orthodoxy of Hindi public sphere for promoting low-brow literature, and the colonial clampdown for writing inflammatory political articles within 6 years of its inauguration.

[88] *Statement of Newspapers and Periodicals Published or Printed in Bengal—Revised Upto 31st December 1925*.

[89] For general information on the story of the first year of *Mat'vālā maṇḍal* or *Mat'vālā* literary circle, there exist some (hagiographic) accounts. Sahāy, *Merā jīvan*; Karmendu Śiśir, "Mat'vālā maṇḍal: sāhityik patrakāritā kā ek anūṭhā adhyāy," *Pahal*, Special Issue (1988). For a more critical account of its early period until the great Poet Nirala was associated with it, see Śarmā, Rām'bilās, *Nirālā kī sāhitya sādhanā*, vol. 1 (Dillī: Rāj'kamal Prakāśan, 1972).

as Mahavir Prasad Dvivedi,[90] this weekly produced a refreshing change. Its scathing attacks on the orthodoxies of the Hindi literary sphere can be gleaned from its appearance.[91] The name of the weekly itself celebrates liquor, which was in marked contrast with other publications: *Sarasvatī* (goddess of learning), *Abhyuday* (dawn), *Maryādā* (dignity), *Bhārat'mitra* (friend of India), *Cā̃d* (moon), *Viśāl bhārat* (sublime India), which symbolised lofty moralism. The image of an intoxicated Shiva dancing on the front page is accompanied by a couplet celebrating the theme of intoxication as a symbol of pleasure and detachment, and it continues in this vein stating its price: 'One anna per cup, three rupies in advance for an annual bottle.' The periodical and its writers were either loved or hated, but could not be ignored. They remained at the centre of public controversy whether for Nirala's experiments in Hindi poetry and his acerbic criticism of orthodoxy in Hindi literary culture,[92] or for Ugra's bold and realist short stories on homosexual and cross-community love affairs.[93]

Mat'vālā: The Satiric Narrator

In the closing years of the nineteenth and the early years of the twentieth century an interesting phenomenon occurs: Apart from *Punch* columns, the most famous and popular satirical columns begin to appear under the title of *Śiv'śambhu ke citthe* (letters from Śiv'śambhu), which became famous for their biting attacks on government policies in the *Bhārat'mitra* (friend of India) of Calcutta. In a way, we can observe a process of gradual transformation in the self-image of the satiric narrator—irreverent, quasi-divine and an articulator of public opinion—from Pañc's heterogeneous lineages to his Hindu origins, perhaps culminating in Mat'vālā.[94]

---

[90] Śarmā, Rām'bilās, *Mahāvīr prasād dvivedī aur hindī nav'jāgaran* (Dillī: Rāj'kamal Prakāśan, 1989).

[91] Cf., e.g., the cover page of *Mat'vālā* 32, 1 Caitra śukla (March–April) 1925.

[92] Śarmā, *Nirālā kī sāhitya sādhanā*, vol. 1; David Rubin, "Nirala and the Renaissance of Hindi Poetry," *The Journal of Asian Studies* 31, no. 1 (1971): 111–126; Heidi Pauwels, "Diptych in Verse: Gender Hybridity, Language Consciousness, and National Identity in Nirālā's 'Jāgo Phir Ek Bār'," *Journal of the American Oriental Society* 121, no. 3 (2001): 449–481.

[93] Pandeya Bechan Sharma 'Ugra', *Chocolate, and Other Writings on Male–Male Desire*, trans., intr. Ruth Vanita (Delhi: Oxford University Press, 2006). Also, see Francesca Orsini, "Reading a Social Romance: 'Chand hasino ke khatoot'," in *Narrative Strategies: Essays on South Asian Literature and Films*, ed. Vasudha Dalmia and Theo Damsteegt (Delhi: Oxford University Press, 1998): 185–210.

[94] According to Shivpujan Sahay, *Mat'vālā* took its immediate inspiration from a Bengali satirical weekly, *Abatār*, which had been started just a couple of months before in 1923. Sahāy, *Merā jīvan*, 99. *Abatār* was a cheap, full-scape weekly. Its title page carried an illustration of an Indian youth simultaneously clad in a *dhotī* (a long piece of cotton clothing to be tied around the waist, worn by traditional Hindus) and trousers, with a hat on his head. It was edited by Amulyacharan Sen of Dakshineshvar. Its language was racy, rustic and contained a ruthlessly critical editorial. I am thankful to Chaiti Basu for this information on *Abatār*. This *Abatār* issue raises some significant questions. Can we map *Punch*'s influence on *Mat'vālā*? Given the evidence that the nineteenth century traditions of Bengali satirical journalism (*Basantak*, *Pañcā-nanda*, *Har'bolā bhā̃r*, etc.) were very much modelled on *Punch*, as the essays by Partha Mitter and especially Chaiti Basu in

The first issue of *Mat'vālā* talked about the self-image of the periodical in a long satirical essay.[95] The persona of Mat'vālā is described as the opium, weed-smoking henchman of Lord Shiva, named Vīr'bhadra (noble-brave). On the insistence of his consort, Parvati, who had overheard some hue and cry coming from the direction of *Bhārat'varṣ* (India), he was sent to earth by the Lord himself to observe political and social affairs. The Lord asked him to throw his trident with full force and follow its direction to its landing place. In a state of intoxication, he heard a loud echo of a human cry coming from the east and confused this with the roar of a demon. He threw his trident to kill him, but the demon was nowhere to be seen. Looking for his trident in order to decide the location of his headquarter[96] as per his master's instruction, he arrived in the land of the Goddess Kali, *Kali-kāntā* (Calcutta), and finally chose to stay in the street named after his master, i.e., Shankar Ghosh Lane. Yet he kept wondering about his inability to find the demon (colonialism) at whom he had thrown his trident. He could clearly see the demon's *māyā* (vicious effects) but not the *māyāvī* (demon). In other words, the reporter Mat'vālā is God's emissary, hence invested with quasi-divine authority and answerable to his Lord. He is an impartial outsider, but stays inside society. He is a celestial being and therefore not bound by any social norms. He is always intoxicated and, in this state of drunkenness, is not restricted by reason, hence has the liberty to see beyond reality. He can articulate the unarticulated and can feel the mood of people being crushed by harsh reality.[97]

Mat'vālā as a Brand

Like the British *Punch*, the satirical weekly *Mat'vālā* not only cultivated a self persona, but also functioned as an internally cohesive editorial team leading to the consolidation of a strong literary identity amongst the reading public.[98] Most of the columns were titled accordingly and signed by the kind of pseudonyms that went well with the overall aura of *Mat'vālā* as aggressive, virile, irreverent, and iconoclastic. One of the characteristic features of *Mat'vālā*, for instance, was the short epigrammatic satirical comments in columns like '*Cal'tī cakkī*' (the unstoppable grinder), or '*Cābuk*' (the whip) (see Fig. 2).

---

this volume suggest, *Punch*'s formative influence can be linked to *Abatār* and then to *Mat'vālā*. After all, in the literary cultures of South Asia, many Western literary forms travelled indirectly via another, neighbouring literary culture, in this case in Hindi via Bengali or Urdu. Early historical, social or detective novels were introduced via Bengali. Orsini mentions, for instance, the circulation and translation of detective novels from English to Bengali and then to Hindi. Francesca Orsini, "Detective Novels: A Commercial Genre in Nineteenth-century North India," in *India's Literary History: Essays on the Nineteenth Century*, eds. Stuart Blackburn and Vasudha Dalmia (Delhi: Permanent Black, 2004), 435–482.

[95] It was written by Shivpujan Sahay after his discussion with other members of the team. Sahāy, *Merā jīvan*, 100.

[96] '*heḍ'kvārṭar*' in the Hindi original.

[97] *Mat'vālā*, August 26, 1923.

[98] For the case of *Punch*, see "Chap. 2: Mr Punch and His Men" in Altick, *Punch*, 41–66.

Fig. 2 '*Cābuk*' (the whip). *Mat'vālā*, undated

'*Cābuk*' commented on literary affairs. It was written under the pseudonym of Śrīmān Gar'gaj'siṃh Varmā Sāhitya-Śārdūl or Mr Great Lion Armoured Literary Roc.[99] The illustration in the column depicts two north Indians fearfully running away from a giant with a whip. The caption below is a poem by Urdu poet Insha. It appealed to the audience/reader to listen to his affectionate plea to stop trembling in anger. Likewise '*Cal'tī cakkī*', a column on political affairs, portrayed Mat'vālā as a devil who grinds a man in his grinder[100] and the verse below explains that he is determined to indiscriminately grind everything beneath the sky.

The young members of the *Mat'vālā* literary circle stayed as bachelors in one house working and indulging in leisure together. In the case of a public debate over literary or political issues, which often arose from the pages of *Mat'vālā* and involved other periodicals and litterateurs, the responses were written under the collective moderation of the team, at least in the early years.[101] Litterateurs of

---

[99] A young litterateur born in the Unnav district of the present day Uttar Pradesh and brought up in Bengal Suryakant Tripathi, who wrote poems in a new style under the penname *Nirala*, was the main contributor to this column.

[100] This imagery of *Mat'vālā* puts him closer to the proverbial henchman of the death god, who is entrusted with dispensing justice in the hell of Hindu mythology. Cf. the cover of '*Cal'tī cakkī*' (the unstoppable grinder). *Mat'vālā*, undated.

[101] See Śarmā, *Nirālā kī sāhitya sādhanā*, especially the chapter on *Mat'vālā maṇḍal*, which discusses the controversy over the originality of Nirala's poetry and Nirala's arrogant comments on the language of the periodical *Sarasvatī* and the consequent polemics.

Mat'vālā maintained an everlasting friendship. Even when they left for different periodicals later, they defended each other's writings from the attacks of opponents.

A Variety of Literary Forms in the Service of Political Satire

Epigrammatic Political Comments
Short epigrammatic satirical comments in columns like '*Cal'tī cakkī*' (unstoppable grinder), '*Mat'vāle kī bahak*' (intoxicant's fluttering), '*Cābuk*' (whip), '*Āṃyeṃ bāṃyeṃ sāṃyeṃ*' (nonsense), '*Caṇḍūkhāne kī gapp*' (gossips of the opium tavern) contained burning social, political, and literary issues, real or imagined, and remarked on public figures at the helm of affairs. These epigrammatic comments, like those of *Punch*, required a prior knowledge of their core issues, which were already in the centre of public discourse either through newspapers and/or other oral sources. These comments were opinions, often had biting effects, and used literary strategies of satire such as incongruity, deformation or decontextualisation. I hereby quote a few of them to illustrate my points:

> It seems the ghost of Lenin is ruling over Kemal Pasha's head. Muhammad Ali [Indian leader of the pro-caliphate movement] should look for an exorcist to cure him.[102]

A strong similarity with *Punch*'s penchant for hoaxing and rumour mongering can be noticed here.[103] In the first sentence, two forms of communication, news and rumour are intermeshed.[104] News and rumour are both acts of communication from one source to another. While the original source of news is theoretically verifiable, the source of rumour is not.[105] 'Lenin has died' is news, his turning out to be a ghost is a deformation of news into rumour. 'A ghost has entered Kemal Pasha's body' is a statement. This statement, then, either makes a conjectural connection between Lenin's death and Pasha's decision to abolish the caliphate, thus insinuating that Pasha is occupied by a spirit who is not able to make rational decisions. Or, it is an allegorical statement about an overlap between the two leaders' ideologies, at least for those who knew that Lenin had welcomed Atatürk's revolution and that Lenin and revolutionary Russia were anti-religious. The first sentence reproduces news in the form of an allegory and/or rumour. Thus, it brings down the seriousness of

---

[102] *Mat'vālā*, 15 March 1924.

[103] Altick, *Punch*, 71–72.

[104] I have shown the tradition of printing jokes and gossip in the periodicals. Reporting political rumour also has strong roots in the Hindi newspapers, at least during the anti-colonial mass movement in the twentieth century. See appendix of Shahid Amin, "Gandhi as Mahatma: Gorakhpur District, Eastern UP, 1921–1922," in *Subaltern Studies*, vol. 3, ed. Ranajit Guha (Delhi: Oxford University Press, 1984), 1–61.

[105] See Chap. 6 "Transmission" in Ranajit Guha, *Elementary Aspects of Peasant Insurgency in Colonial India* (Delhi: Oxford University Press, 1983), 220–277.

major political events. It was juxtaposed with the second statement prescribing magical treatment for the political dilemma the Indian Muslim leader faces, and thus decontextualises it from its local dynamics.

> At a recently held convention in Allahabad priests of Hindu pilgrimage centres have taken a vow to do away with the custom of *dakṣiṇā* [offering to the priest], provided young and comely women of their Hindu clientele visit the shrines in a libertarian way [*svacchandatā pūrvak*].[106]

This statement invokes two malpractices associated with the priestly class of Hindus, which are widely criticised by the male Hindi middle class: first, monetary exploitation of the believers by the clergy and, second, sexual exploitation of women, who move outside their patriarchal households to visit holy shrines. The satiric grotesqueness is achieved by making the culprits bargain, in a mock democratic forum of a convention, for the sanction of the second and more serious malpractice to quit the first.

> The *māsik* [meaning both 'monthly' and 'menstruation cycle'] of Jabalpur's *Śrīśāradā* [a monthly periodical with irregular issues] has gone awry! What else could be the result of being *anek'patigāminī* or going around with so many men [editors].[107]

Here is the case of a gendered description of literary news in which two seemingly incongruous objects are paralleled—an unfortunate literary periodical with a woman. It derives pleasure from invoking the hidden sexual meaning of words.

> It is heard that few *meh'tar*s [scavenger caste] also read newspapers. Therefore upper caste Hindus should quit this practice; after all, caste Hindus must refrain from following untouchables.[108]

Here we see the satiric inversion of the logic of Brahmanic social ideology. The (ir)rationality of Brahmanic ideology is extended to the point of absurdity through the logic of mathematical rationality. It is a Brahmanic axiom that caste Hindus should not do what untouchables do. Hence, they should not read newspapers.

> Some low-caste Hindus eat pork, therefore they are considered impure by Muslims. Muslims eat beef, so they are considered impure by Hindus. Englishmen eat both; hence they are considered pious and are worshipped by both.[109]

Here, the rationale of dietary regime and its mutual social manifestation amongst (upper caste) Hindus and Muslims is made incongruous by juxtaposing it with their contradictory behaviour vis-à-vis the ruling elite.

Editorial Essays
The periodical always carried an editorial. It moved between satire and lampoon and was, at times, invective. It appropriated each and every spectacular public event like Hindu festivals, such as Holī, Dīvālī, or Vijayādaśamī, and even communal

---

[106] *Mat'vālā*, 7 March 1925.
[107] *Mat'vālā*, 15 March 1924.
[108] *Mat'vālā*, 22 April 1923.
[109] *Mat'vālā*, 10 May 1924.

riots,[110] as an occasion to satirise 'dormant' and 'emasculated' Indian/Hindus suffering under British oppression. The language of the acerbic prose was highly aggressive, virile and masculinist. One example is this excerpt from an editorial titled '*Cūṛī sāṛī kī jay bolo*' (victory to bangle and petticoat).

> The distance between an eye and an ear is four fingers, but the difference between the acts of seeing and listening is like that between the sky and earth. I am sick of hearing repeatedly that Lord Ramchandra had his great victory march on the day of *Vijayādaśamī*, [...] that the entire *Bhārat'varṣ* [India] gets bedazzled every year by the shine and sound of arms and ammunitions on the day of *Vijayādaśamī* [...] But my eyes are not willing to accept the truth of these words that fall upon my ears. These poor eyes can see that Lord Rām is no more, that the victory march, arms worship, warrior's instinct and the sound of armoury are to be found no more; that the breast of the nation is pulverised, the forehead of bravery is smashed and that self-pride is demolished. What then is the use of *Vijayādaśamī* and its sacred memory? That's why I say 'Victory to Bangle and Petticoat' [...] Instead of the musical sound of arms, the cry for councils is there; instead of justice, unbearable oppression, instead of peace, great hue and cry. See the joys of Vijayā? Well, close your eyes now or you'll be blinded; keep your mouth shut, or your tongue will be plucked out; don't pen down your feelings, or your heart will be squeezed [...]. Beware! Tolerate the shower of abuse, listen to the sound of arms, and even fall prey to arms; but never utter a word, lower your gaze, if mother earth gives you refuge, bury yourself[...] When all directions approach you with sympathy, shout at your loudest the immortal words: Victory to Bangle and Petticoat [...] When they ask: Who are you? Reply immediately and boldly: I am Indian. They'll ask: Why this new slogan of victory? Then, out of ten directions, speak pointing towards the white-complexioned, blood eyed, 'Westward direction', in a dim shy voice: Please ask this possessor of sword and skull, garlanded with human head, the great White goddess![111]

This quotation is typical of *Mat'vālā*'s masculinist invocations of a glorious mythical Hindu past and its juxtaposition with the emasculated colonial present to

---

[110] Spectacular public events, such as communal riots in Calcutta in 1926, provided another occasion for publishing sensational articles and satirical comments with gory details of real or imagined violence. A government report said that: 'The Hindi papers underwent marked deterioration during the year under review. They devoted much of their energies towards promoting communal antagonism [...] Sanction was given in May 1926 to the prosecution of the editor, printer and publisher (Mahadeb Prasad Seth) of the '*Mat'vālā*' newspaper for the publication of objectionable articles entitled (1) "Lalkar svikar", (2) "Tumdar Darhom Patpat" and (3) "Upvas cikitsa" [*lal'kār svīkār, tum dār dār ham pāṭ pāṭ, up'vās cikitsā*] in its issues of the 27, 28 and 29 April 1926 respectively. The editor was convicted and sentenced to 4 months' "simple imprisonment".' *Annual Report on Indian Papers Printed or Published in the Bengal Presidency for the Year 1926* (Calcutta: Bengal Government Press, 1927). Interestingly, even when the editor of the paper underwent prosecution and the trial was going on in court, the publication of such articles continued. The judgment on the prosecution of *Mat'vālā* under section 153 A of the Indian Penal Code for publishing objectionable article inciting communal riots noted: 'They are the most dangerous and poisonous description [...] There was clearly a malicious intension on the part of the writer and he had no shred of an honest view to remove matters which were causing ill-feeling between the communities [...] The learned Public Prosecutor draws my attention to the facts that the accused has continued to write in the similar strain.' Interestingly, in the annual assessment of the press and its role during communal riots the government noted that the popularity and circulation of communal papers went up. File no. 236, Political Department (Political), West Bengal State Archive, Calcutta.

[111] *Mat'vālā*, 20 October 1923.

awaken the 'dormant' members of the Hindu nation. The narration of valour and chivalry of Hindu gods and goddesses and their acts of violent subjugation of the treacherous ruling authorities of the mythical past is debased by contrasting that narration's continuum with the oppressive present of their emasculated and enslaved descendants under colonialism. This literary strategy of satirical debasement creates a self-irony for the Hindu present.

Cartoons in the Twentieth Century: The Case of *Mat'vālā*

Mat'vālā was one of the earliest Hindi periodicals that published cartoons on a large scale. Before *Mat'vālā*, *Prabhā* (Kanpur, 1920) published cartoons regularly.[112] They were usually independent in themselves, but sometimes functioned as illustrations of juxtaposed written columns. These cartoons were equally direct and blatant in their attack and multiplied the journal's aggressive approach. Cartoons exemplify *Mat'vālā*'s endeavour to grapple with multiple asymmetries of contemporary colonial India, from a Hindu nationalist vantage point.[113] This is reflected in the cartoons about the question of forms of anti-colonial politics, caste, gender and community relations.

Mat'vālā was a staunch admirer of Gandhi because he was anti-British. Cartoons like '*Paśubal kā ullās*' (the joy of brute power) highlighted the asymmetries of power between the colonial state and the nationalist opposition by depicting the government's brute suppression of the Gandhian movement.[114] The picture shows a laughing fat man in Western apparel, named *Brute Force*, jumping on the flattened *dhotī*-clad human bodies named *Non-violence* with full force. Clearly, the jumping man in coat, trousers and boots with a stick in his hands is emblematic of the colonial power. The flattened human bodies are the faceless masses of India, who are following Mahatma Gandhi's principle of non-violence during the non-cooperation movement against the colonial government at that time. However, Mat'vālā did not hesitate to poke fun at Gandhi's conservative views on female sexuality.[115]

---

[112] *Annual Report on Indian Papers*, noted in its report on the Hindi press that the appearance of the few illustrated magazines (*Mat'vālā* and then *Hindu Punch*) with improved sales was noteworthy in this section of the Press. *Annual Report on Indian Papers Printed or Published in the Bengal Presidency for the Year 1925* (Bengal Government Press: Calcutta, 1926).

[113] With a belief in the foundation myth of India as a Hindu civilisation at its core, Hindu nationalism could take the form of an exclusivist and supremacist to moderately assimilative stance. See Gould, *Hindu Nationalism*.

[114] See '*Paśubal kā ullās*' (the joy of brute power). *Mat'vālā*, 29 September 1923.

[115] 'According to Mahātmājī [Gandhi], those widows should be remarried who hardly encountered their husband. But what to do with those child widows, who died two-four months after consummating with their husbands? It would be better if the Mahatma articulates the internal logic of widow remarriage!' This epigrammatic comment is published after Gandhi subscribed to the patriarchal idea of limited social reform allowing only those widows to be remarried who did not have sexual intercourse with their husbands and hence had their virginity intact. The last

It virulently attacked liberal constitutionalists that showed faith in colonial political institutions. The cartoon entitled '*Adbhut unnati*' (unprecedented progress) can be cited as representing Mat'vālā's strong opposition to them.[116] In the aftermath of the non-cooperation movement, the Indian National Congress was divided over the approach to the colonial government's limited political reforms, aiming at sharing some legislative power with the Indian political parties. The Swarajists or 'Pro-changers' in the Congress argued that the Indians should enter into the legislative council and oppose and expose the government from within. The 'No-changers' rejected this idea as a measure to co-opt Indians by the government. In this picture, the Swarajists favouring the entry of the Congress into the legislative councils are shown as pushing the boulder of the Congress into a gorge. The gorge is symbolic of

Fig. 3 '*Hindū-mus'lim ek'tā*' (unity of *Hindus* and Muslims). *Mat'vālā*, 15 March 1924

---

sentence of the comment is directed at the absurdity of this patriarchal logic. For a general positive idea, see Madhu Kishwar, "Gandhi on Women," *Race and Class* 28, no. 43 (1986).

[116] Cf. '*Adbhut unnati*' (unprecedented progress). *Mat'vālā*, 5 January 1924.

the deep and dangerous entrapment of colonial political institutions. The 'No-changers' try to save the party by stopping the boulder of Congress from falling down.

It belaboured the Congress for turning a deaf ear to the question of the Hindu victims of communal riots and the insecurity of women. This is quite well illustrated in another cartoon entitled '*Anveṣaṇ!*' (discovery).[117] At the door of a makeshift tent of the 1925 Annual Conference of the Indian National Congress, malnourished Hindu poor, recognisable by their braided hair,[118] and *dhotī*, are waiting with young Hindu women clad in sari. The leaders of the Congress are apparently inside, busy 'discovering' the solution through futile deliberation.

The next cartoon, entitled '*Hindū-mus'lim ek'tā*' (unity of Hindus and Muslims), can be viewed in conjunction with the cartoon '*Anveṣaṇ!*'. It ridiculed the attempt to unite Hindus and Muslims after the spate of communal violence in the 1920s. It showed the inconvenience of the 'forced' cooperation between the traditional leaders of the two communities. A Brahman priest's *coṭī* (hair lock) is tied to the beard of his Muslim counterpart (see Fig. 3). *Mat'vālā*, simultaneously, underlined the irony of a superficial unity in the wake of communal conflicts. For instance, the cartoons entitled '*Bhrātṛprem*' (brotherhood) showed that the beneficiary of their mutual antagonism (which is always instigated by Muslims!) was the colonial government. It portrayed an aggressive Muslim attacking a Hindu monk, who was passing by a mosque singing an innocent religious song. The dragon of colonial bureaucracy ensnares both[119] (see Fig. 4).

Mat'vālā's cartoons and editorials derived from and contributed to the Hindu nationalist discourse on communitarian and communal politics.

It spat fire at the imagined Muslim tyranny against the Hindus. It echoed the idea of a dying Hindu race—a result of the abduction and conversion of Hindu women by the Muslim (and British/Christian) goons,[120] and the conversion of untouchables by the *Tablīġī Jamāʿat* and Christian missionaries. But it also found faults with the negligent attitude of the orthodox custodians of Hinduism and the 'dormant' Hindu middle class. Hence, it brazenly ridiculed the *Sanātanī Hindu* organisations opposing the anti-untouchability movement. Sometimes, *Mat'vālā* gave space to writers with a proto-feminist and socialist agenda speaking in the language of human

---

[117] Cf. '*Anveṣaṇ!*' (discovery). *Mat'vālā*, 16 January 1926.

[118] A tuft of never-cut hair kept on the back of the head by caste Hindus.

[119] The spectre of communal violence in the public arena of South Asia over the often repeated issues of music in front of the mosque, and the role of colonial state in this communal discourse, has been studied by Sandria Freitag and Gyan Pandey. Sandria Freitag, *Collective Action and Community: Public Arenas and the Emergence of Communalism in India* (Berkeley: University of California Press, 1989); Gyanendra Pandey, *The Construction of Communalism in Colonial North India* (Delhi: Oxford University Press, 1992).

[120] *Mat'vālā* along with two other Hindi periodicals published from Calcutta, *Hindū Pañc* and *Viś vāmitra* were classified as fiercely communal by the colonial government. They drew from the Hindu nationalist discourse of the 'dying Hindu race,' which was widespread especially in Calcutta. See Datta, *Carving Blocs*.

Fig. 4 *'Bhrātṛprem'* (brotherhood). *Mat'vālā*, 9 August 1924

rights.[121] They can be read as an attempt to include the dissenting voices—providing space to radical opinions within the periodical, but not engaging with their political agenda.

The cartoon entitled *'Dharm-sāṛ'* (bull of religion) shows a creature with the torso of a Brahman priest and the head of a bull making advancements towards a young Hindu woman, who is frightened and runs away.[122] *'Hā hindū!'* (o Hindu, shame on you)

---

[121] "Aurat 'mard' kā jhag'ṛā yā rām'nareś satyavādī saṃvād," *Mat'vālā*, November 29, 1924. This was an excerpt from a polemic over the question of women's rights between a patriarch, Pandit Ramnaresh Tripathi, and a rights-conscious woman, Satyavati Arya, published in *Strī darpaṇ* (women's mirror) of Kanpur. Veer Bharat Talwar discusses the political-ideological significance of articles which started appearing in Hindi in the 1910s and 1920s in periodicals like *Strī darpaṇ*. Veer Bharat Talwar, "Feminist Consciousness in Hindi Journals," in *Recasting Women*, eds. Kumkum Sangari and Sudesh Vaid (Delhi: Kali for Woman, 1990), 204–32.

[122] Cf. *'Dharm-sāṛ'* (the bull of religion). *Mat'vālā*, 20 February 1926.

पद-विच्छेद !
(चित्रकार—'वक्षी')

हिन्दू-धर्म खड़ा है स्थिर, चरण-शूद्र कटते तुरफ़न ।
'मियाँ' 'पादरी' चेत रहे हैं, बाबाजी करते हैं चैन !

Fig. 5 '*Pad-vicched*' (the cutting of feet). *Mat'vālā*, 7 March 1925

portrays sari-clad (Hindu) women being abducted by Muslim and British goons, while the Hindu gentleman, like a fool (symbolised by an owl) stands still in the centre.[123] And another cartoon entitled '*Tiraskār aur satkār*' (insult and respect) shows how an untouchable is kicked by a Brahman. In the background, he is caressed by a Muslim priest who points towards the mosque, and by extension, towards Islam.[124]

Likewise, the cartoon '*Pad-vicched*' (the cutting of feet) depicts Muslim and Christian missionaries cutting the feet of a Hindu monk with a rat on his body (Fig. 5). The monk eaten by a rat symbolises decomposing Hinduism. His feet symbolise the Shudras, as per the mythology of the traditional body-politic of the

---

[123] Cf. '*Hā hindū!!!*' (o Hindu, shame on you). *Mat'vālā*, 29 November 1924.

[124] '*Tiraskār aur satkār*' (insult and respect). *Mat'vālā*, February 16, 1924.

Hindu social hierarchy. The chopping of the monk's feet symbolises further disintegration of Hinduism hastened by the conversion of untouchable castes into the folds of Christianity and Islam.

All the cartoons cited here feed on widely known themes and draw from the dominant rhetorical forms of modern and pre-modern registers of representation.[125] The iconography of social groups is based on their essentialised social markers with a satiric deflection achieved through caricatured exaggeration. The first stage in the production of a cartoon is the discovery and/or creation of subject matter. The analysis of the *Mat'vālā* cartoons reveals some major, innovative *topoi*: topicality, literary/cultural allusions, essentialised character traits of social groups. Topicality, like literary satire, forms the raison d'être of political cartoons in the sense that one cannot create a political cartoon without attracting readers' attention, at least momentarily, by some agreed-upon component of politics. A second source of cartoon image making is the literary/cultural allusion: any fictive or mythical character, any narrative or form, drawn from legend, folklore, literature, etc. The meaning of the image derives not solely from the topicality it employs but also from the interaction of the topical events with an allusion to an identifiable fiction. To decipher the cartoon, it is presumed that the reader is already familiar with the literary or cultural source to which it refers.

A third innovative source draws upon popular perceptions of the dominant stereotypes of the represented community, social class, political institution, etc. Such essentialised cultural traits as 'aggressive Muslims' or 'dormant Hindus' can be transformed into a combination of imagery and caption. No trait can be *totally* invented by the cartoonist. The trait must exist to some extent in popular consciousness or dominant public discourse before it can be amplified and caricatured by the artist.

Topicality, literary/cultural allusions and essentialised character traits of social groups form the creative storehouse from which cartoonists draw and construct first-order enthymemes that invite the reader to respond with certain values, perceptions, prejudices and predispositions. The targeted audience, (male) Hindu middle-class readers, fills in the missing premise as it reads the cartoon.

Mat'vālā: A Summary

The satirical weekly *Mat'vālā* was a discursive, literary-visual space that spoke in the political language of Hindu nationalism, with an occasional incorporation of contending voices on a variety of issues, in the contemporary Hindi public sphere of the 1920s. It was simultaneously a supporter of Gandhi, sympathetic to

---

[125] The following analysis draws heavily from Martin J. Medhurst and Michael A. DeSousa, "Political Cartoons as Rhetorical Form: A Taxonomy of Graphic Discourse," *Communication Monographs* 48, no. 3 (1981): 197–236; 204.

From *Punch* to *Mat'vālā*: Transcultural Lives of a Literary Format 109

Fig. 6 Cover page of the *Hindū Pañc*, 19 June 1917

revolutionary terrorists, and virulently anti-Muslim. It dared to raise taboo questions by publishing stories on homosexuality and Hindu–Muslim love affairs in a titillating language, but mutilated its radical potential by arriving at conservative resolutions asserting heteronormative Hindu patriarchal values. It gave space to proto-feminists and women's reform initiatives, yet the language is sexist and gendered,[126] and the patriarchal idea of woman as a repository of the community's honour was asserted. It supported the 'uplift' of 'untouchable' castes, but was guided by concerns of the perceived weakening of the majoritarian power of the Hindu community. Politically, the magazine remained Hindu nationalist despite its multiple contradictions.

Inheriting the legacy of its nineteenth century predecessors, *Mat'vālā* transformed the older style to such an extent that the elements of transcultural influences, which were visible until the beginning of the twentieth century, become difficult to grasp. Only a broader similarity in the characteristic features of satirical journalism remains. Three years after the publication of *Mat'vālā*, a weekly named *Hindū Pañc* was started in Calcutta under the editorship of Pandit Ishvari Prasad Sharma, and published and printed by Babu Ramlal Varma. Unlike *Mat'vālā*, which was registered as a satirical weekly and politically pro-Congress and anti-Muslim, the *Statement of Newspapers and Periodicals Published or Printed in Bengal for the year 1927* classified *Hindu Pañc* as an illustrated weekly with an overtly 'anti-

---

[126] Interestingly, the linguistic and visual space of *Punch* were also gendered and remained almost misogynist. See Julie Codell, "Imperial Differences and Culture Clashes in Victorian Periodicals' Visuals: The Case of Punch," *Victorian Periodical Review* 39, no. 4 (2006): 410–428.

Muslim', politically 'extremist' attitude.[127] The cover page of the periodical (see Fig. 6) had an illustration depicting five types of male Hindus: an elderly Brahmin priest in his traditional apparel, and a topless young man with modern hairstyle, without any overt marker of community on the left; and a probable *Ārya Samājī* preacher in action, along with an educated Hindu gentleman with anointed forehead on the right, while the clumsy-looking *Pañc* is shouting in the middle, stretching his hands over the shoulders of the young man and the preacher. The motto of the paper, printed below the illustration, made its political agenda very clear.[128]

> To protect the honour of Hindus, to save the fame of Hindus;
> *Hindū Pañc* has appeared in *Hind*, in order to awaken the Hindus.

Hindu Pañc for all practical purposes remains an illustrated political weekly with only two elements of *Punch*'s literary format cited in the beginning, namely cartoons and short epigrammatic comments on news in columns like '*Pañc'rāj kī kacah'rī*' (the court of *Pañc'rāj*). The latter become less satirical and oblique and more blunt and direct in their condemning. The term *pañc* itself had been loaded with local meanings, obscuring its transcultural genealogy, and cartoons no longer remained a monopoly of satirical periodicals but spread to all varieties of journals. So, ironically, it is a *pañc* that is seen to bring the immediate *Punch* legacy in Hindi satirical periodicals to an end.

---

[127] *Statement of Newspapers and Periodicals Published or Printed in Bengal—Revised up to 31st December 1927* (Bengal Government Press: Calcutta, 1928).

[128] It was an unapologetically militant Hindu nationalist/communalist paper with equal antagonism towards the Muslims and the British. Its selected articles and cartoons targeting Muslims, and special issues like *Balidān aṅk* (martyr special), were proscribed many times. 'Martyr Special' celebrated death for the cause of the nation and included short biographies of Indian heroes, ranging from early medieval Hindu icons to the then *Ārya Samājī* Hindus apparently killed by Muslims.

The *Punch* Tradition in Late Nineteenth Century Bengal: From Pulcinella to Basantak and Pãcu

Chaiti Basu

The English satirical magazine *Punch, or the London Charivari* (1841–1992) was the source of inspiration and imitation for many vernacular magazines and periodicals in colonial India. Late nineteenth century Bengal experienced a particularly intense flourishing in the production of satirical magazines, two of which will be the focus of this paper's investigation: *Basantak* (1874–1875) and *Pañcānanda* (1878–1883).

After brief expositions of their backgrounds, this paper looks at the origins and characteristics of the narrator figures of these periodicals, both of which can be traced further back than *Punch*'s nineteenth-century England in the character of Pulcinella of sixteenth-century Italian *commedia dell'arte* and also in the figure of the *kathak*[1] from either indigenous oral and classical literary traditions of South Asia. It also confirms how satiric journalism helped to reflect on the formation of a self-image of the colonial subjects in their colonial contexts. Encompassing the innate incoherencies and inconsistencies, satiric journalism directed an introspective gaze to themselves. It began mainly with obliquely criticising the existing pattern of the asymmetrical relations in a colonial society and the functional organs of the colonial Government. Simultaneously, the paper tries to ascertain the nature of reception of satire by 'mainstream' Bengali literati by gauging their reactions to these two periodicals.

---

[1] The word *kathak* means a speaker, or a professional narrator of scriptural and mythological stories (Subhas Bhattacharya, *Saṁsad Bengali English Dictionary*, third edition (Kolkata: Sahitya Samsad, 2008), 172). The word originates from the Bengali noun *kathā*, which means words spoken or mode of speaking (ibid.).

C. Basu (✉)
Doctoral Candidate at the South Asia Institute, Heidelberg University, Heidelberg, Germany
e-mail: chaitibasu@hotmail.com

Why *Punch*?

Besides gaining popularity in Europe,[2] the satirical magazine *Punch* (1841–1992) also inspired adaptations all over the world in the nineteenth and twentieth century, from the Ottoman Empire to Japan. The secret of its popularity rests in the successful employment of satire, both written and visual, especially in the use of cartoons and caricatures. Recognising its scope and reach, Indian intelligentsia engaged themselves in exploiting this particular literary format. At the same time they experimented with appropriate modes from the classical and oral tradition of Indian satire. All these culminated in the publication of various satirical periodicals in vernacular languages from the middle of the nineteenth century.

The presence of *Punch* was felt quite strongly in the literary field of satirical magazines. In their quest to establish themselves as the 'original' progenies of *Punch* in India, there seemed to be almost a fierce competition amongst the early Bengali satirical periodicals. This particular scenario will be explained later in this paper. But more interesting is the rivalry which made this unique mode of literary production a locus of intellectual antagonism. Taking clues from the existing scholarship on *Punch*,[3] we see that although some characteristics of the original journal[4] were maintained in their Indian manifestations, many of these attributes were relocated and reinterpreted in their new contexts.

In the Bengali literary sphere in particular, this presence was clearly visible in the attempts to exploit the popularity of the English *Punch* in Bengal. Acquaintance with Western education resulted in an increasing curiosity and consciousness about the European cultures in nineteenth century Bengal. In the wake of the so-called boom of the printing press, new types of readership also started to emerge. Sometime around the mid-nineteenth century, educated Bengalis became acquainted with *Punch*.

Locating Bengali *Punch* Versions in Their Socio-Political Context

The socio-political background of the time was mostly marked by the immediate aftermath of the Indian Sepoy[5] Mutiny of 1857. This alarming experience for both the British and the Indians, and the consequent transfer of power from the East India Company to the British Crown played a significant role in the political history of the

---

[2] See Richard D. Altick, *Punch: The Lively Youth Of A British Institution 1841–1851* (Columbus: Ohio State University Press, 1997), 17.

[3] See Marion H. Spielmann, *The History of 'Punch'* (London: Cassel & Co. Ltd., (1895)) (e-book by Project Gutenberg, 2007) and Altick, *Punch*.

[4] See Brian Maidment's article "The Presence of Punch in the Nineteenth Century," Chap. 2 in this volume.

[5] In the nineteenth century Sepoy (from the Hindustani word *sipāhī*) was a designation given to an Indian soldier engaged in the service of a European power. In the national armies of many countries in modern South Asia, it denotes the rank of private soldier.

Indian subcontinent. The memory of the turbulent years of the mutiny was still fresh in the mind of the British government. It resulted in a major shift in the administrative attitude[6] of the government towards a more conservative stance with regard to religion and education. Also, on the political level, a new 'white collar' Indian elite was surfacing with the spread of university education, and with the Viceroy's policy of integrating more Indians, especially from the upper castes, into various Governmental offices as civil servants. Such measures, mostly accessible to the upper class, were given to Indians to prevent the chance of another 'mutiny' taking place in the near future. This indigenous participation as administrative functionaries of the government, especially in the municipal corporations and the election process of its members, increased the chance for Indians to be taken seriously in their roles in the field of colonial politics.

Early Bengali Satirical Journals

Towards the end of the century, municipal politics in Kolkata featured in numerous Bengali magazines. The most prolific critique came from the satirical magazines that employed cartoons and caricatures as their main contrivances. It was most likely *Brāhman'sebadhī* (worshipper of Brahmins, 1821) that initiated the trend of satiric periodicals that mainly dealt with debates on current topics, in particular on controversial social and political issues. They were infused with a touch of irony and sarcasm, ridicule and mockery, scorn and derision. The most prolific among these periodicals and magazines were *Dal'bṛttānta* (tale of factionalism, 1832) *Saṃbād rasarāj* (king of juicy news, 1835–1839), *Pāṣaṇḍa pīṛan* (chastisement of rogues, 1840–1857), *Bhairab'daṇḍa* (the staff of Bhairaba [the henchman of the god of death Yama], 1847), *Prakṛta mud'gar* (the veritable mace, 1854), *Durjjan'daman mahānabamī* (the wicked quelling monthly, 1847), *Yeman karma temni phal* (as you sow, so you reap, 1861), *Har'bolā bhāṛ* (the ventriloquist/mimicking jest, 1874), *Hutom* (the hooting owl, 1875), *Baṅgīya bhāṛ* (the bengali jest, 1875). A clear tone of aggressive violence (the staff, mace, quelling, etc.) is detectable in many of the above-mentioned titles. Most of these magazines engaged in undiscriminating mud-slugging and slanderous scandal-mongering and relied mainly on gossip,

---

[6] Victoria's proclamation of November 1858 stated that 'We hold ourselves bound to the natives of our Indian territories by the same obligations of duty which bind us to all our other subjects [...] We declare it to be our royal will and pleasure that none be in any wise favoured, none molested or disquieted, by reason of their religious faith or observances, but that all shall alike enjoy the equal and impartial protection of the law; and we do strictly charge and enjoin all those who may be in authority under it that they abstain from all interference with the religious belief or worship of any of our subjects on pain of our highest displeasure. And it is our further will that, so far as maybe, our subjects, of whatever race or creed, be freely and impartially admitted to office in our service, the duties of which they may be qualified by their education, ability, and integrity duly to discharge'. In I. Arthur B. Keith, ed., *Speeches and Documents on Indian Policy, 1750–1921*, vol. 1 (London: Humphrey Milford, 1922), 382–386.

Fig. 1 Cover page of *Basantak*, first year, issue 2, 1874. (Caṇḍī Lāhiṛī, ed., Basantak: 1m barṣa-2ẏa barṣa (Basantak: First to second years) (Kal'kātā, Niu Ej Pāb'liśārs, n.d. [first published around 2008]), 1m barṣa, 2)

personal attacks, and sensationalised reporting on controversial topics of the time, all of which were received well by the readers. Citing this specific trend of literary factionalism, or *dalādali*, a recent scholar, Yuthika Basu, in her research on nineteenth-century Bengali satire, mentions a comment from Soumendranath Basu's book titled *Kācher mānuṣ baṅkim'candra*: 'if ridicule and mockery and similar compositions are not very *original—smart,—to the point*, they could not be *effective*. Then these are only abuses.'[7] Both of them ascribe the comment to Bankimchandra Chattopadhyay (1838–1894), the so-called father of modern Bengali and the author of the first novel proper in Bengali.

The first *Punch*-inspired Bengali journal seems to be *Bidūṣak* (1870),[8] though it is devoid of any cartoon or illustration and the format is different from that of *Punch*. Modern Bengali historiographers, however, endow the status of the first

---

[7] "[…] byaṅga, bidrūp esab racanā khub *Original—smart—to the point* nā haïle *effective* haẏ nā. Eṭā śudhu gālāgāli baṭe." In Saumendranāth Basu, *Kācher mānuṣ baṅkim'candra* (s.l., n.d.), 141–145. Quoted by Yuthikā Basu, *Bāṃlā sāhitye byaṅga racanā (uniś śatak)* (Bardhamān: Bardhamān Biśvabidyālaẏ, 1982), 44 (my translation, italics for original English words used in the book).

[8] It has been self-introduced as 'an imitation of *Punch* in England'. Cf. Svapan Basu, *Sāhitya-pariṣat·-patrikā*, *113 barṣa* (113rd year), *4tha saṃkhyā* (4th issue) (Kal'kātā: Baṅgīẏa Sāhitya Pariṣat. Māgh-Caitra 1413/2006), 102.

Bengali *Punch* to another periodical called *Har'bolā bhāṛ* (January 1874), whose cover page exhibits an instantly recognisable similarity to the illustration on the cover page of *Punch* and also carries the subtitle 'The Indian Punch'.[9] Thus, the trend of satiric magazines began in Bengal and escalated to greatness within a few years as we will see in the next section. These early periodicals, along with the new socio-political consciousness of the Bengali intelligentsia, characterise the publication of satirical journals such as *Basantak* and *Pañcā-nanda*.

Publishing Details Basantak

Basantak (1874–1875) was published on January 31, 1874, in Chitpur, Kolkata (Figs. 1–3). The editor was Prananath Datta but on the paper itself, one of Prananath's employees' names, Hari Sing, was credited as the editor. He was the caretaker and sweeper (*zamādār*). This choice indicated the journal's intention to criticise contemporary socio-political evils, including personal attacks, and making it necessary to take shelter in anonymity. In the 23 and 24th issues, the name of another of Prananath's employees, Ramdas Bandyopadhyay, appeared as the editor.[10]

Six cartoons were published in the very first issue and were well-praised for their artistic quality by other contemporary journals, but at the same time the periodical had been advised to improve its quality.[11] Gradually it came to be so well-received that from the third issue they had to print more copies than usual. *Basantak* did not last long though; it stopped publication in 1875 after just 12 issues. Modern scholars cite irregular payments and even non-payments by subscribers as the main reasons for this.[12]

Pañcā-nanda

On 26 October 1878, Indranath Bandyopadhyay (1850–1911) edited and published the satiric periodical *Pañcā-nanda* in Chunchura (Chinsura), Hugli, due to the persuasion of his friends and mainly of his mentor, Akshaychandra Sarkar, (1846–1917) the editor of *Sādhāraṇī* (1873),[13] a semi-conservative Bengali weekly. Its main agenda can be gleaned from the early proclamations in the form of editorial notes, advertisements and from Indranath's own accounts. After the

---

[9] Ibid., 102–103.

[10] '*pratham bāiś'ti saṃkhyā hari siṃher sampādanāẏ prakāśita haleo teiś o cabbiś naṃ saṃkhyā'duṭir sampādak hisābe "beṅgal lāibreri kyāṭālage" rām'dās bandyopādhyāẏer nām pāi. Inio chilen prāṇanāther betan'bhogī karmī*' (Though the first 20 issues were published under the editorship of Hari Sinha, in 'Bengali Library Catalogue' we get the name of Ramdas Bandyopadhyay as the editor. He was also a paid employee of Prananath). Basu, *Sāhitya-pariṣat--patrikā*, 111.

[11] Ibid., 107.

[12] Ibid., 111 and Lāhiṛī, *Basantak, 1m barṣa*, 234–136; *2ẏa barṣa*, 177–178.

[13] Besides Indranath, many of the 'conservative' leaders of the 'neo-Hindu' faction of Bengali literati such as the proprietor of *Baṅgabāsī*, Yogendra Chandra Basu (1854–1905), Shashadhar Tarkacurmani (1851–1928), and editor Krishna Candra Mitra (1851–1911), began their literary journey in *Sādhāraṇi*.

বসন্তক।

মাসিক পত্র।

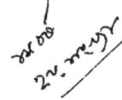

নবপরিণয়যোগাৎ স্ত্রীয়ু হাস্যাভিযুক্তঃ, মদবিলসিত-নেত্রং চাঞ্চচন্দ্রার্দ্ধ-মৌলিং ।
বিগলিত-ফণি-বন্ধং মুক্তবেশং শিবেশং, প্রণমতি দিনহীনঃ কালকূটাভকণ্ঠং ॥

| ডাকমাস্কুল সমেত বাৎ-সরিক মূল্য ৩/০ নগরের অগ্রিম মূল্য ৩ টাকা, প্রতি খণ্ডের মূল্য ০ আনা। | এই পত্র সম্বন্ধীয় পত্রাদি কলিকাতার চিৎপুর রাস্তার ৩২৬ নং ভবনে শ্রীকিশোরীমোহন ঘোষের নিকট প্রেরিত হইবে। | অগ্রিম মূল্য না পাঠাইলে ডাকযোগে পত্র পাঠান হইবে না। |

সভ্যগণ, জয়স্ত! আজ আর আপনাদের বিজাতীয় ভাষায় অভিবাদন না কোরে পুরাণ ধরণই রাখলেম। প্রথমটা আপনাদের রকম সকম দেখে বোধ হয়েছিল যে গঙ্গাস্নানের চেয়ে জড়ডান জলে স্নান কোরে এলে ভাল হোতো; আর মনে ভয় হয়েছিল, পাছে ওল্ড ইষ্টুপিডিটী বোলে গোট্‌হেল কোরে দেন। কিন্তু আমার সেকেলে ধরণ দেখে যখন অসন্তুষ্ট হন নাই, তখন বোঝা গেছে যে যদিও জড়ডান জলে তোমাদের ভক্তি আছে, তথাপি গঙ্গাজল দেখলে হাইড্রোফোবিয়া রোগীর মত জ্বলো না। বোধ হয়, মুসলমানী কুত্তার মতন বিলাতী ডগের বিষ নাই। যা হোক, ভাল হইয়াছে, আমাকে আর শেষদশায় পিঠে কুলা বাঁধতে হবে না, তবে দুই এক জন যাঁরা নামকাটা স্যা-

ষ্টটা গোরা হয়েছেন, তাঁদের কাছে থেকে মাঝে মাঝে ছুঁইপের ভয়টা রইলো, তা কি কত্তে পারি, জগতের রীতি এই রকম, কখন সুখ্‌ কখন দুখ্‌! কিন্তু সকলে তা বোঝে না, সুখের বেলা মজা করে বেড়ায়, আর দুঃখের বেলা বাবারে মারে ডাক্‌ছেড়ে দেশ গাবায়ে ফেলে। আমরা সে দলের লোক নই বোলেই পূর্ব্বের কথাটা বলেছি। পণ্ডিতেরা লিখিয়াছেন "সুখ-দুঃখ-ভেদ জ্ঞানাভাবকেই মুক্তি বলে" তা আমার এত দিন এত দর্শন শাস্ত্র অধ্যয়ন ও অধ্যাপনা করিয়াও যদি না হবে তো হবে কার ? আর বিশেষ বেল্লীকতন্ত্রসংহিতায় এ বিষয়ের উৎকৃষ্টতর মীমাংসা থাকাতে আমার সুবিধা ঘটেছে, কেন না চতুর্ব্বেদে যেরূপ ব্রাহ্মণ ভিন্ন অপর জাতির সম্পূর্ণ অধিকার নাই, সেইরূপ সাক্ষাৎ শঙ্কর-

Fig. 2 First page of *Basantak*, first year, issue 2, 1874

Fig. 3 Back cover page of *Basantak*, first year, issue 2, 1874

very first issue, further editions of the periodical were published from Bhabanipur, Kolkata from 29 January onwards, and then from Burdwan (Bardhamān) from January 1881 till June 1881.

One of the earliest advertisements published in *Sādhāraṇī*, which announces the arrival of *Pañcā-nanda*, proclaims that it will be 'a periodical with humour and critique'[14] and boasts that it is 'to be edited by the very humorous writer of Bengal and adorned with articles penned by the most important humorous author, Pañca'.[15] The periodical highlights itself as the 'source of precious advice, witty satire, harsh sarcasm and pure fun'.[16] In a distinctive way, the first issue comes with a unique suggestion: as none of the Bengali periodicals maintains the promise of

---

[14] '*rasapradhān patra o samālocanā*'. (Basu, *Sāhitya-pariṣat-patrikā*, 115).
[15] Ibid.
[16] Ibid., 116.

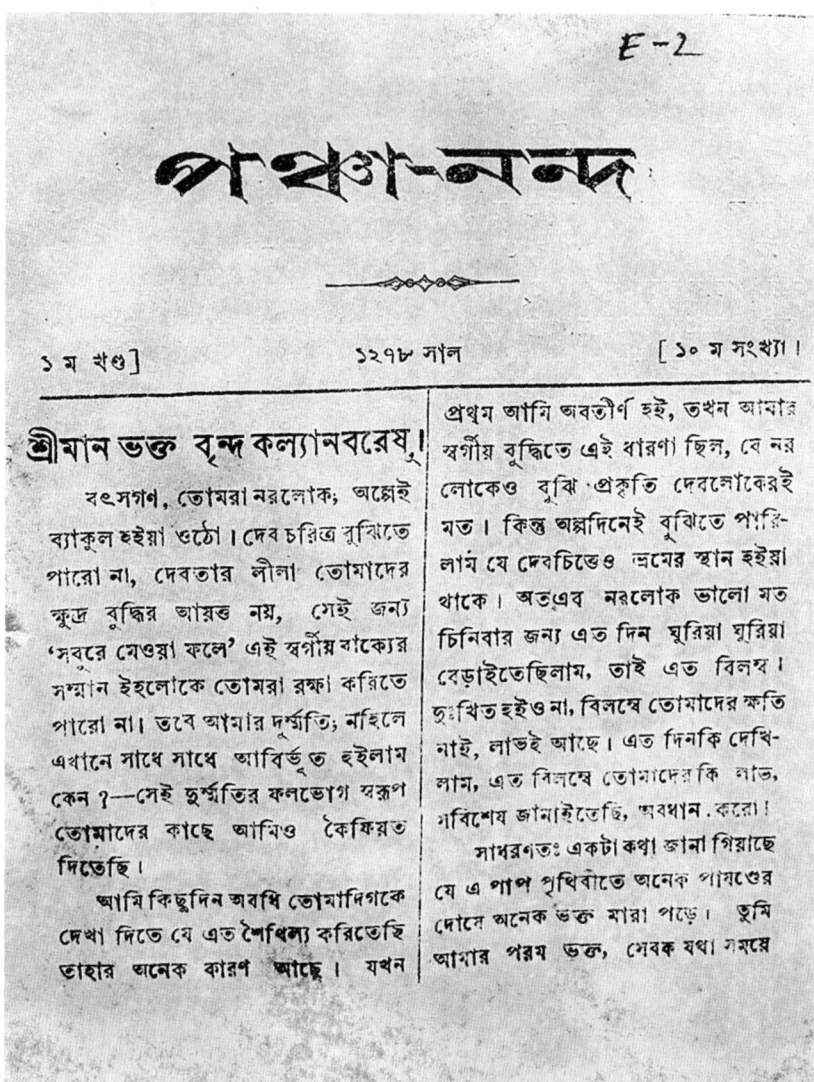

Fig. 4 First page of *Pañcā-nanda*, vol. 1, issue 10, 1880

publishing on a regular basis, *Pañcā-nanda,* as a rule, will be only published irregularly (Fig. 4).

It was printed from the Sadharani Printing Press and the price of the first issue was four paisa. In the second issue the yearly price was set at five rupees. The price had to be paid in advance to ensure its publication.[17]

---

[17] Ibid.

Table 1 Circulation chart of contemporary popular Bengali periodicals in comparison with *Baṅgabāsī*. (Svapan Basu and Mun'tāsīr Māmun, eds., *Dui śataker bāṃla sambād sāmaẏikpatra* (Kal'kātā: Pustak Bipaṇi, 2005), 20)

Yearly subscriptions

Periodical's name	Year			
	1884	1894	1898	1900
Baṅgabāsī	12,000	12,000	20,000	26,000
Sañjībanī	4,000	4,000	4,000	3,000
Basumatī	–	–	–	15,000
Hitabādī	–	3,000	6,000	35,000

Indranath discontinued *Pañcā-nanda*'s publication after the first volume as he moved to various places in Bengal. In early 1880, its publication resumed from Kolkata as a fortnightly periodical. In the coming years, *Pañcā-nanda*'s publication became rather erratic as Indranath shifted his residence from Kolkata to Bardhaman in order to pursue his career as a lawyer.[18] In 1880, *Pañcā-nanda* was published in Bhabanipur, Kolkata; in 1881 from Burdwan, before it finally merged with *Baṅgabāsī* in 1883.

The satirical columns of Indranath, written under the pseudonym Pãcu Ṭhākur or Pañcānanda in *Baṅgabāsī*, were well received by the readers and contributed to the periodical's increased popularity. Although a recent scholar mentions that the circulation of *Pañcā-nanda* was never more than 500,[19] the scenario changed after the merger. In terms of circulation, *Baṅgabāsī* sold considerably well in comparison to the 'mainstream' periodicals of the time, as becomes clear from Table 1 below:

Indranath's affiliation with the popular *Baṅgabāsī* helped both Pãcu and the columns of *Pañcā-nanda* to reach out to a larger readership. Simultaneously, *Baṅgabāsī*'s more regular dates of publication ensured that Pãcu Ṭhākur's columns would print more frequently than in *Pañcā-nanda*.

As Indranath joined *Baṅgabāsī*, he continued to write his columns under the pen-name Pañcānanda. His first article in *Baṅgabāsī* is '*Surendrāẏan*'. The proprietor of *Baṅgabāsī*, Jogendra Chandra Basu, published a collection of Indranath's previous articles which he had written for *Pañcā-nanda* in two volumes under the title *Pãcu ṭhākur*.[20] The collections of Indranath's later articles, written for *Baṅgabāsī* as Pañcānanda, were also published in three more volumes of *Pãcu ṭhākur*.

---

[18] Brajendranāth Bandyopādhyāẏ, *Sāhitya sādhak carit'mālā*, vol. 34, *Indranāth bandyopādhyāẏ* (Kalikātā: Baṅgīẏa Sāhitya Pariṣat·, 1386/1980), 14.

[19] Basu, *Sāhitya pariṣat· patrikā*, 121. Also see Indranāth's own account on its circulation in Rañjan Bandyopādhyāẏ, ed., *Indranāth granthābalī*, vol. 2 (Kal'kātā: Dīp Prakāśan, 2007), 373.

[20] "Prakāśaker nibedan," [publisher's note], in *Indranāth granthābalī* (Kal'kātā: Baṅgabāsī Press, 1925); 33–34.

Objectives of the Periodicals

Basantak

Most of *Basantak*'s attacks are directed towards the inner politics in the municipal board in Kolkata. A little biographical detail about its editor will make this particular rationale more comprehensible. Prananath Datta (1840–1888) was born in a wealthy upper-caste Hindu family of North Kolkata. His father had also been an artist,[21] and his mentor, Rajendralal Mitra[22] (1823–1891), was actively associated with the municipal politics of Kolkata. Mitra became a 'Justice of the Peace' of the Calcutta municipality from 1863 to 1876, and in 1876 was elected as a member of its executive committee. His influence was replicated in Prananath's support for the native tax-payers' demands for active participation in the Municipal election.[23]

Perhaps his venturing into the field of satirical journalism was mostly aimed at vilifying the British high officials, and at the same time, maligning his Bengali opponents in municipal politics. Besides the aforementioned associations, the famous Bengali poet Michael Madhusudan Datta (1824–1873) is also believed to have been one of the patrons of the Dattas.[24]

There is a twofold reason behind his interest in publishing *Basantak*. Firstly, the presence of the English *Punch* began to be felt in Kolkata, not only among the Europeans of the so-called white town,[25] but also among the educated babus[26] and

---

[21] "Basantaker paricaẏ," in Lāhiṛī, *Basantak*, ṅa-ca; ṅa.

[22] Besides being one of the key figures of Bengal's 'Revival', Rajendralal Mitra was the first Indian to become a modern Indologist. He was associated with the Asiatic Society from 1847 until his death and became its first Indian president in 1885. In different phases of his life he was associated with the leading educative journals of his times, *Tattvabodhinī patrikā* (1848/1850), *Bibidhārtha saṃgraha* (editor 1852–1859) and *Rahasya sandarbha* (editor from 1863 to 1869). Incidentally, Prananath himself was a sub-editor of *Bibidhārtha saṃgraha* and later became the editor when Rajendralal retired.

[23] In 1847 the electoral system was introduced for the first time in the Municipal Corporation of Kolkata and the Justices of the Peace, who had shouldered the administrative responsibility until then, were replaced by a board of seven paid members, four of whom were elected by the taxpayers. After several new experimental systems, in 1876, a new Corporation (the current Municipal Corporation of Kolkata) was set up with 72 Commissioners; 48 of them were elected by the taxpayers and 24 were appointed by the government. See Parmanand N. Parashar, *History and Problems of Municipal Administration in India*, vol. 2, *Comparative Perspectives on Municipal Administration* (New Delhi: Sarup & Sons, 2003), 37–39.

[24] Basu and Māmun, *Dui śataker bāṃlā sambād sāmaẏikpatra*, 237.

[25] This widely used term denotes the part of the city of Kolkata where mostly European foreigners used to live.

[26] Babu is generally an address for Bengali males. A suffix is added to a person's name to show respect. In the nineteenth century it became synonymous with the emerging middle class in Bengal and became the butt of ridicule in literature, especially in social satires depicting their immorality, debauchery, hypocrisy and other vices. Hans Harder describes him as 'the lecherous, alcoholic, imitative, pompous, pretentious and anti-traditionalist Babu, a cultural stereotype of nineteenth-century Bengal that had already been codified to a certain extent. He had therefore arguably

bhadralok (gentle folk). Many of them were well-versed in English and other European literatures and cultures, and they saw in *Punch* the ablest means of self-criticism and self-mockery. They tried to employ this very mechanism to expose the hypocrisy and corruption in their own society. On the other hand, it had also enabled the babus and *bhadralok* to exercise indirect criticism of British colonial power without entering into any direct open conflict, as was witnessed some years later in 1891 with the defamation suit against the neo-Hindu *Baṅgabāsī* by the British Government.[27]

Secondly, Prananath ably utilised the artistic skill of his cousin-brother Girindranath Datta,[28] whose illustrations were believed to have earned the paper much the fame and popularity amongst its readers. Girindranath studied the art of wood-engraving, figure-sketching and lithography in Kolkata's School for Industrial Art from Mr. Rigo, a European arts teacher. Modern scholars, such as Svapan Basu, claim in contemporary journals that it is Girindranath's special ability in figure drawing along with his own sense of humour that is the main reason for the effectiveness in conveying through his cartoons the message of the periodical.[29] His art explores 'political commonplaces, literary/cultural allusions, personal character traits, and situational factors'.[30] Girindranath employs an active communicative method with his readers depending on the 'audience's ability and participation',[31] as he 'invite[s] the readers to respond in accord with certain values, beliefs, and predispositions'.[32]

On the other hand, *Basantak*'s cartoons, despite being accused of 'a coarse immediacy',[33] are seen by today's art historians like Partha Mitter as quite suitable to Prananath's 'savage invective'.[34] His book elaborates on *Basantak* extensively, mentioning that the periodical became actively 'involved in political factionalism

---

become a piece of exaggerated literary imagination which was perceived as such, rather than any kind of description of any concrete human being' (Hans Harder, *Bankimchandra Chattopadhyay's* 'Śrīmadbhagabadgītā' (New Delhi: Manohar, 2001), 210).

[27] The State Prosecution of the *Baṅgabāsī* in 1891 was highlighted not only in *Baṅgabāsī*, but in all the contemporary newspapers. For a detailed account of this case, see Mahendra Kumār Basu, "Yogendra smaraṇī," part 2, in *Yogendra candra basu racanābalī*, vol. 2 (Kalikātā: Granthamelā, 1976), 25–37 and J. Ghosal, *Celebrated Trials in India*, vol. 1 (Bhowanipore: M. Banerjee, 1902), 165–233.

[28] According to Caṇḍī Lāhiṛī, Girindranath is also the illustrator of the first two books of Michal Madhusudan Datta. Lāhiṛī, "Raṅgaraser patrikā," in Basu and Māmun, *Dui śataker bāṃlā saṃbād sāmaẏikpatra*, 237.

[29] Basu, *Sāhitya pariṣat· patrikā*, 107, 110.

[30] Martin J. Medhurst, "Political Cartoons as Rhetorical Form: A Taxonomy of Graphic Discourse," *Communication Monographs* 48, no. 3 (September 1981): 197–236; 204–205.

[31] Ibid.

[32] In the same article as above, Medhurst justifies this specific mechanism: 'The artist must know and utilize the beliefs, values, and attitudes of his audience if he or she is to be an effective persuader' (ibid.)

[33] Partha Mitter, *Art and Nationalism in Colonial India 1850–1922* (Cambridge: Cambridge University Press, 1994), 161.

[34] Ibid.

around 1875'[35] and 'claimed to defend the interests of the ordinary citizens of Calcutta [Kolkata] against the officials, the landed magnates and their mouthpiece, the *Hindoo Patriot*, edited by Krishto Das Pal'.[36] This particular outlook, which *Basantak* voiced in this issue, prompted some scholars to opine that *Basantak* is only a periodical of the factional politics (*dalādali*) of the Bengali upper-middle class *kāẏasthas*[37] of Kolkata (Dattas of Hatkhola), which only 'hurls raillery and obscene vilification' at their opponents.[38]

But this can also be seen as an attempt to play down somewhat the periodical's significance to visual illustration in the history of Bengali visual print media. Most of Basantak's cartoons and caricatures portray the malfunction of colonial politics; the favourite targets of the city-bred literati's attack are the municipality, the demoralised government officials, their corrupt Bengali consorts, Hindu-reformists, the Brahmo Samaj (Brāhma Samāj), and radical modernists. It reprobates excess of any kind, especially in the controversies surrounding these issues. More prominent was the criticism of Anglophile Bengalis, emancipation of women, and the issue of obscenity as observed by puritan Brahmos. Most of the cartoons are accompanied by a short text or refer to an article published in the same issue, maintaining the same mood of ludicrous distortion. The raw and blatant mood is captured quite well in the usage of linear sketches with rough edges.

Basantak was a self-proclaimed[39] progeny of *Punch* and also the self-professed 'pioneer' in this particular field. This claim is supported by the later Bengali historiographers of both art history and literature.[40] In the quest to establish itself as the first simulator of *Punch*, *Basantak* attacked other periodicals and newspapers, which also aspired to publish *Punch*-like journals or periodicals. The well-known accusation made by *Basantak* against the *Indian Mirror* and *Amṛta bājār patrikā* in the foreword of its very first issue denounced the latter's claim of publishing a Bengali version of *Punch* in another contemporary periodical only as a hoax, because they had already published *Basantak*, the *Punch* in Bengali. At the same time, it attacked and even threatened the former journals with legal consequences for publishing such a false claim.[41] From another viewpoint, the

---

[35] Ibid., 162.

[36] Ibid., 163.

[37] The second highest caste in the traditional Hindu hierarchy of castes in Bengal; second to the priest caste of Brahmins. In the nineteenth century the most flourishing economic class in Bengal belonged to this caste. They received modern education, thereby securing well-paid jobs in the colonial offices or in mercantile ventures in association with the Europeans.

[38] Sukumār Sen labeled Basantak as '*Kal'kātār kāẏet'der gālāgāli ār kısti-kheuṛer kāgaj*' ("Basantaker paricaẏ", ca).

[39] '*Pyañc-ām'rā prakāś kariba*' (Lāhiṛī, *Basantak*, 27).

[40] As by Canḍī Lāhiṛī, Svapan Basu and Partha Mitter in their respective books mentioned earlier in this paper.

[41] '*Āmār āgaman bārtā peẏei "mirar" tār dastur-matābek ek'bār cak'makiẏe uṭhe likhe phelecen, ye, amṛta bājār patrikā sampādak ek'khani pyañc bāhir kariben; kintu yena jel bāc'ẏe karen!*' (Receiving the news of my arrival, *The Mirror*, as per rule, wrote that the editor of *Amṛta bājār*

Bengali intelligentsia's competitive struggle for launching the first Bengali version of the *Punch* can also be interpreted as a purely mercantile enterprise. Many rich Bengalis tried their hand in the literary field during this time. The genre of satirical literature, made more effective with visual representation, was a yet unexplored territory, and proved a lucrative commercial option for literary entrepreneurs.

Pañcā-nanda

Pañcā-nanda, on the other hand, was published quite reluctantly by satiric author Indranath Bandyopadhayay (1850–1911). It was the persuasive insistence of his friends in the literary circle[42] to which he succumbed. The dates and places of its publication were quite irregular[43] until it merged with *Baṅgabāsī* in 1883, as mentioned before. Although the trend of cartoons started before *Pañcā-nanda*, Indranath, in his obituaries, has often been called the man who 'introduced' the art of cartoon in Bengal.[44] One of the earliest cartoons published under the caption *Reception* shows a man in traditional attire named as 'fortune' (*saubhāgya*) shaking hands with the westernised monkey named as 'civilisation' (*sabhyatā*) in *Pañcā-nanda* (Fig. 5).

In the foreword of the second volume, published in 1880, *Pañcā-nanda* voiced its purpose of publishing the periodical:

> There is no doubt that Bengal needs Pañcānanda. But Pañcānanda would be here not only for making fun and frolic—that is the job of a jester, a clown. [...] Pañcānanda is needed for graver purposes, such as to show the distorted image of illusion, to expose falsity, to nourish the Bengali language, to encourage genuine welfare of the country; Pañcānanda is needed for these.[45]

In this respect, mention must be made of what Indranath himself thought about satire and humour. In the foreword to *Pañcā-nanda,* he clearly reflects that he has

---

patrikā will publish a *Punch*; but he must do it by avoiding the jail.) and again '*Mirar [...]* *likhiẏācen ye "amṛta bājār patrikā sampādak ek khāni pyañc prakāś kariben"*. *Pyañc—āmrā prakāś kariba! Amṛta bājār patrikā sampādaker sāthe uhār kono sambandha nāi'*. (The Mirror [...] wrote that *Amṛta bājār patrikā* will publish a *Punch*. Punch—we will publish! It has nothing to do with the editor of *Amṛta bājār patrikā*) (Lāhiṛī, *Basantak, 1 m barṣa*, 3, 17).

[42] Akshaychandra Sarkar (*Sādhāraṇī*, 1873), Kaliprasanna Kabyabisharad etc.

[43] Vol. 1, issue 1 from *Cūcuṛā*, 26 October 1878; republished from Bhabanipur (Kolkata), 29 January 1880. Until vol. 1, issue 10, (31 October 1880), were published from here. Vol. 1, issue 11 (19 January 1881) and issue 12 (8 February 1881), vol. 2, issue 1 (April 1881), issue 4 (30 August 1881) and issues 5 and 6 together (20 June 1881) were published from Bardhaman before the merger with '*Baṅgabāsī*' in 1883. Bandyopādhyāẏ, *Sāhitya sādhak charit'mālā*, no. 34.

[44] For details of its publication, see *Baṅgabāsī* edition of *Indranāth granthābalī*, 1925, reprinted in *Indranāth granthābalī*, vol. 2, ed. Rañjan Bandyopādhyāẏ, (Kal'kātā: Dīp Prakāśan, 2007), 318–28; 328.

[45] Basu, *Sāhitya-pariṣat--patrikā*, 116.

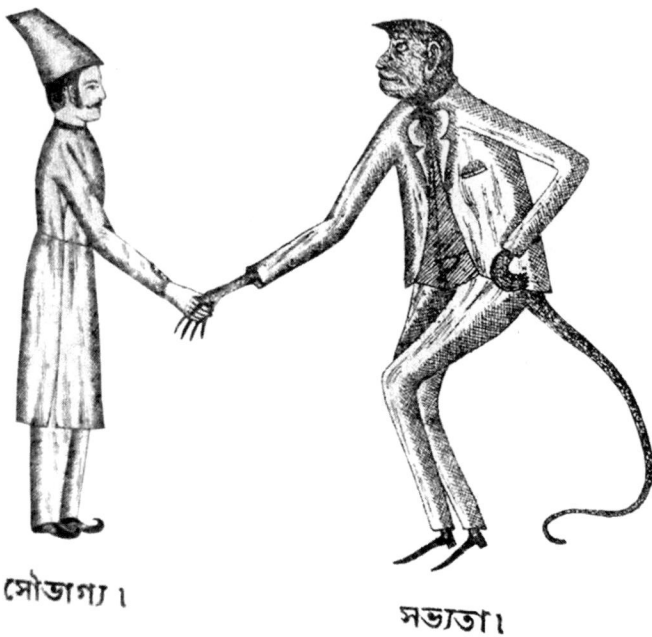

Fig. 5 *'Abhyarthanā'* (reception). *Pañcā-nanda*, vol. 1, issue 10, 1880

never written only for the sake of fun because 'the day of only laughing and making others laugh has not yet arrived in Bengal'.[46] Indranath laments in one of his letters that although he felt inspired to make satire enjoyable for the Bengali readers after reading the works of French satirists,[47] this particular literary format had unfortunately not yet been properly deployed by contemporary writers. Neither could they make satire popular among the masses.[48] Pure satire, in his opinion, must be toned down with glimpses of the incongruities and discrepancies of the real world.[49]

The periodical *Pañcā-nanda* usually carries an introduction followed by various articles, short essays, treatises, etc. Not all the articles were written by Indranath;

---

[46] Bandyopādhyāẏ, *Indranāth granthābalī*, vol. 2, 134.

[47] Bandyopādhyāy, *Sāhitya sādhak charit'mālā*, vol. 34, 23–24.

[48] Ibid, and Bandyopādhẏ, *Indranāth granthābalī*, vol. 1, xx.

[49] Ibid.

Fig. 6 *'Siṃha, nek'ṛe bāgh o meṣ'pāl'* (lion, wolf and the flock of sheep). Published in *Pañcā-nanda*, vol. 2, issue 1. 1880

some were by his associates, but their names are now very difficult to trace. In 1880, it also flaunted some cartoons in its pages.[50] They often portray humans either directly as animals, i.e., a monkey, lion, wolf, sheep, or with some animal-like physical features. Not much has been written about *Pañcā-nanda*'s cartoons; from both a quantitative and qualitative viewpoint, they do not demonstrate any special modes or unique norms, but rather follow the convention of *Har'bolā bhāṛ*. Below is an example of such a cartoon (Fig. 6):

(Quoted from Vishnu Sharma's *Hitopadeśa*).[51]

> Lion: (tears the stomach of the first sheep, as the wolf enters). "Who are you?"
> Wolf: 'My lord, I am a small landlord [*jamidār*] (looking at the sheep) Are these my lord's own subjects?'
> Lion: 'Yes. They are my subjects from Midnapur [Medinīpur]. What do you want?'
> Wolf: 'Oh! Incarnation of moral duty [*dharma*], I came to learn how to rule subjects.'

---

[50] Basu, *Sāhitya-pariṣat--patrikā*, 116.

[51] The *Hitopadeśa* is a classical Sanskrit compilation of fables. The present lines are of course a fake quote, and such fake quoting from scriptures and classics was a common practice for many satirists of the time.

Language

The language of *Basantak* is sober and controlled and its tone constrained compared to some of other contemporary satirical journals, which were more vocal and aggressive in their attacks. But *Basantak* does not lack its own bite and sarcasm. The periodical, however, did face the problem of choosing the right language. Although modern Bengali already arrived with Bankimchandra, Bengali was yet to come to terms with a standard and/or a popular form. The more sanskritised *sādhu bhāṣā* (a high form of Bengali, mostly used in writing) of Vidyasagar (1820–1891),[52] was not very suited to the tongue of the common people or the target readers of satire, cartoons, caricatures or parodies. But even the dialect of the 'popular' culture, which was mostly oral,[53] was not particularly suitable for literary rendition. *Basantak* tried, quite successfully, to combine the colloquial with the elite written language, which also conferred literary credibility to the former.

Both *Basantak* and *Pañcā-nanda* employ *vyājastuti* (mock-praise), *vakrokti* (oblique comment), *upahāsa* (ridicule), and *śleṣa* (irony), all the prime instruments of early Bengali satire, mainly of Sanskrit origin, with some modifications. Along with latter day colloquial cockney and rural slangs, they constitute the social dialect of late nineteenth-century Kolkata urban city life. This is perhaps the most suitable medium for capturing the innate cynicism of the satirists that Prananath and Indranath exhibited through the language of the skits, which are full of new word plays in the form of puns, double entendres, quips, repartees, parodies, spoofs, lampoons, allegories, metaphors, hyperboles, etc., which are difficult to understand for today's readers. These specific linguistic modes, as well as cartoons, fulfilled their communicative function fairly successfully in their immediate social contexts. But for today's readers, especially the sociological and the communicative modes often pose a problem. As they mostly 'contained a timely message [...] [having] little salience beyond their immediate context. It is this truism which makes so many historical cartoons [and satirical articles] incomprehensible to modern readers'.[54]

The periodicals observe the contemporary events and modes of daily entertainments closely and ridicule and examine them at the same time. Besides jokes[55] and short skits,[56] they also contain satiric depictions of national and

---

[52] Vidyasagar reconstructed the system of Bengali alphabets in his *Barṇa paricaẏ* as well as introduced the modern form of Bengali prose.

[53] The oral language of the popular forms of entertainment such as *kabiẏāl, pācālī, saṅ, kheur*, and *yātrā*, were much loved by common people both in rural areas and in the city.

[54] Medhurst, "Political Cartoons as Rhetorical Form," 202.

[55] "Cuṭki" and "Kautukbindu". (Lāhiṛī, *Basantak*, 131, 214); and various jokes in Bandyopādhyāẏ, *Indranāth granthābalī*, vol. 2, 200–203.

[56] "Brāhmikār bāhire gaman" (a Brahmo women goes out), "Rām'śaraṇ pāler jaẏ" (hail, Ramsharan Pal), and "Peṭuk brāhmaṇ" (gluttonous Brahmin) etc. (Lāhiṛī, *Basantak*, 1m barṣa, 36–37). "Praśnottar 1–4" (Bandyopādhyāẏ, *Indranāth granthābalī*, vol. 2, 199–200).

international socio-political events, dialogues, reportages of sensationalised news items, poems, and mock-praises.[57] As far as the visual language of the cartoon goes, the artist Girindranath tried to employ a clever strategy which kept in mind 'the interaction of the commonplace with an allusion to an identifiable fiction. To decode a cartoon, one must be somewhat familiar with the literary or cultural source to which it refers'.[58]

The Narrator Figures

Pulcinella
In *Basantak*, the physical features are very much similar to that of Mr Punch,[59] who in turn, is modelled on the dramatic character of Pulcinella. His full name is Pulcinella Cetrullo, which means 'stupid little chick'.[60]

The character of Pulcinella, according to Pierre Louis Ducharte, appeared for the first time on the Italian stage in 540 AD[61] and resurfaced again in the *commedia dell'arte* of seventeenth-century Italy. John Rudin, in his book *Commedia dell'Arte: An Actor's Handbook*, also cites an ancient origin of the narrator-figure by using a quote of George Sand,[62] who firmly believed in the classical origin of the *commedia dell'arte*. The quote, made in 1852, has originally been used by her son Maurice Sand in his book *The History of the Harlequinade*:

> The most ancient of all the types is the Neapolitan Polichinelle. He descends in direct line from Maccus[63] of the Campagna, or, rather, he is the same character. The ancient Maccus did not appear in regular comedy but in that very ancient kind of satirical drama called Atellanse, from the name of the city of Atella, which had given it birth. A bronze statue, discovered in Rome in 1727, can leave no doubt on the score of the identity of Maccus and Polichinelle [...] I am confirmed in this opinion by the fact that in the Neapolitan farces two Pulcinellas are to be found: one is base and doltish, the veritable son of Maccus

---

[57] The columns are titled "Saṃbād" (Lāhiṛī, *Basantak*, *1m barṣa*, 17, 27, 109–113), "Ṭīkā ṭippani", and "Khabar" (in Bandyopādhyāŷ, *Indranāth Granthābalī*, vol. 2, 270–271, 274.276).

[58] Medhurst, "Political Cartoons as Rhetorical Form," 202.

[59] For the origin of Mr Punch, see D.S. Maurice et al., *Punch and Judy, With Illustration Designed and Engraved by George Cruikshank, Accompanied by the Dialogue of the Puppet-Show, an Account of Its Origin, and of Puppet-Plays in England*. (London: Printed for S. Prowett, 1828).

[60] Pulcino (day-old chick); citrulo (half-wit, stupid).

[61] Pierre Loius Ducharte, *The Italian Comedy* (New York: Dover Publication, 1966), 210.

[62] George Sand, quoted by John Rudin in: John Rudin, *Commedia dell'Arte: An Actor's Handbook*. (London: Routledge, 1994), 13.

[63] Maccus, a character of the Atellan farce of Campagna, is believed to be the predecessor of Pulcinella. The character reached the Roman stage around the fourth century BC. Maurice Sand says 'Pulcinella had never ceased to exist from the days of the Atellanae, in which he went by the name of Maccus, the mimus albus' (Maurice Sand, *The History of the Harlequinade* (London: Martin Secker, 1959), 26).

[Pulcinello]: the other is daring, thieving, quarrelsome, Bohemian and more of a modern creation [Pulcinella].[64]

There are several theories for the origin of this particular name. One theory suggests that the name had been bestowed upon him for his peculiar movement of 'hen step' and a high-pitched chicken-like voice.[65] Another theory traces the long nose which looks almost like a beak, which may have inspired the name.

Pulcinella is humpbacked and potbellied, loud, pretentious, self-centred and has no respect for anything or anyone. As already mentioned before, there are two characteristic sides of Pulcinella: one is 'intelligent, sensual, sly, keen', while the other is 'a dull and coarse bumpkin'.[66] Still, to some extent, they demonstrate similar traits: both are endowed with a superb prowess of agility and mobility, and are never bound by any particular responsibility—familial or professional.

In his theatrical version Pulcinella is always dressed in white and wears a black mask, hence conciliating the opposites of life and death. His main defensive strategy lies in his pretentious stupidity about the immediate happenings. As props, he usually carries a cudgel or a stick and has been associated with different animals such as a cockerel, chick or a toad.

Mr Punch

In the first years of *Punch*, Mr Punch is often portrayed on the cover pages as the puppet of Punch and Judy theatre of seventeenth-century England. Still, many of the physical features of Pulcinella, mentioned above, are also present in Mr Punch, albeit with some localised cultural divergences. In *Punch* he is similarly pot-bellied but the head-gear changes its forms according to occasions with culture-specific associations. His nose is still a long crooked one, almost like a beak, and he now has very clear and prominent jaw-line. In some sketches he resembles a vulture rather than a chicken, as in his Italian origin. Mr Punch is often found in the company of a dog or other animals, in particular a lion, with which British colonial power has often been identified. Mr Punch appears frequently with his wife, Judina, the Judy of Punch and Judy. They also have a daughter named Julia. These familial bonds meet the nineteenth-century English middle-class social values perfectly. Although Mr Punch is described as 'a teacher of no mean pretensions',[67] 'moderate and gentlemanly in tone',[68] and is sympathetic towards 'the poor, the starving, the ill-housed, and the oppressed; [...] the ill-paid curate and the worse-paid clerk; [...] the sempstress, the governess, the shop-girl',[69] he also displays 'rude and boisterous

---

[64] Ibid. 111–112.

[65] Ducharte, *The Italian Comedy*, 210–212.

[66] Ibid.

[67] Spielmann, *The History of 'Punch'*, 2.

[68] Ibid.

[69] Ibid., 3.

mirth'[70] and hurls 'abuses from the highest to the lowest'[71] and 'sham gentility, vulgar ostentation, crazes and fads, linked aestheticism long drawn out, foolish costume, silly affectations of fashion in compliment and language—all have been set up as targets for his shafts of ridicule or scorn' and he 'has been a moral reformer and a disinterested critic'.[72]

Basantak

Coming back to the late nineteenth-century colonial Bengal from the world of ancient Greece, of sixteenth-century Italy and nineteenth-century London, we see that the figure of the narrator of *Basantak* changes substantially with the socio-cultural context. Let us consider the visual and characteristic similarities, or deviations, which he has undergone in the process.

Basantak's image (Figs. 1 and 3) is printed on both the front and back cover pages. On the front cover page, his pot-bellied upper body is naked,[73] at his waist he is sporting a traditional Bengali clothing (*dhuti*), and headgear (*śirobandh*), a religious (more ritualistic, believed to have hailing power) ornament (*tābij*) on his left upper arm. He is observing the worldly matters from above the hills (most probably the Himalayas, abode of Gods) with half-closed eyes and a smirk on his face. Although he adorns the sacred thread of the Brahmans (*paitā*) and holds an old scripture (*pūthi*) in his hand, Basantak seems happier gossiping with his messenger, the crow, who is sitting on a nearby hill-top. This bird also plays a more important role, which can be traced back to Hindu mythology with the allusion of the utter chaos and destruction[74] that is taking over the world. The crow vaguely reminds us to some extent of the association of the chicken with Pulcinella. But clearly, the narrator in *Basantak* is situated in an exclusively Bengali socio-cultural sphere, completely different from that of Pulcinella or Mr Punch.

Partha Mitter describes Basantak's physical features and his surroundings as they appear on the cover page of the periodical in the following terms: 'an obscenely fat Brahmin—Punch transmogrified no less—leers out of its cover, while the scenes around are of the utter depravity to which Calcutta [Kolkata] sunk: 'bibendum', baboodom and courting English couples'.[75] The outer frame

---

[70] Ibid., 2.

[71] Ibid., 3.

[72] Ibid., 2.

[73] In the first editorial he apologises profusely for offending the sentiments, dictated by Victorian social, moral, and behavioural codes, of the 'enlightened' people and reflects on his appearance as that of an 'old fool'. He expresses his readiness to change into more 'civilised' clothes of 'half-socks, flannel shirt, glasses, double spring shoes and a walking stick' and cover the holy scriptures of Hinduism as a book and even cut off his *śikhā*, the tuft of hair at the back of the head, a symbol of Brahmanism (Lāhiṛī, *Basantak, 1m barṣa*, 2).

[74] A battle between crows and owls is said to have inspired the final bloody night of the *Mahābhārata* war. Also, Hindus believe that crows will take food and offerings to the dead.

[75] Mitter, *Art and Nationalism*, 159.

surrounding the figure of Basantak on the cover page contains a series of images. These enact a sense of anarchy and pandemonium prevailing in contemporary Kolkata, symbolising the impending doom, i.e., the *kaliyuga*. It depicts among others, a broken chariot, which embodies the present state of Hinduism; people indulging in drinking and smoking *gājā* (hemp, marijuana); broken music instruments, which indicate a 'fallen' Bengali moral and cultural world; and chaotic street scenes of Kolkata—all exposing the Bengali society in a state of rupture. The figure of Basantak, situated amidst all these, derives a sense of grotesque pleasure from the whole situation. The strong rough black lines make the asymmetrical depiction of the colonial city, as the site for destruction of all tradition-bound socio-cultural and religio-economic norms, more appealing and effective in the mind of the readers.

The meaning of the narrator's name, Basantak, is multi-layered. On the one hand, the word denotes a clown, similar to that of the *vidūṣaka*, or royal court-jester in Sanskrit. On the other hand, the word *basanta* denotes both the season of spring and the disease of pox,[76] which represents the narrator's dual characteristics of lively entertainer and dreaded critic at the same time. Lastly, in the very first issue, Basantak equates himself with an '*abatār*' (*avatāra,* incarnation of God) and claims to be a born scholar in all *śāstra*s like the great mythological sages and the narrators of the Indian epic *Mahābhārata*, Vyāsa and Śukadeva.[77]

Similar to Mr Punch, Basantak has a female counterpart, Bāsantikā. She does not play just a stereotyped role. Bāsantikā is Basantak's third wife, whom he married after the untimely demise of his first two wives.[78] A picture of Bāsantikā and Basantak is printed at the back cover of *Basantak*. There Bāsantikā is wearing a sari in a traditional way with old-fashioned jewellery. In the picture, she is covering her mouth with her right hand. There are various possible explanations for this gesture: she is hiding a smirk, saying something harsh and critical, or something utterly silly and nonsensical. Most significantly, it also conveys a contradictory message. It is a symbol of denial to assign women an active social voice in the visible public sphere such as a literary periodical. But we see from the texts that her role is not merely that of a passive female bystander but is much more significant.

Basantak scurrilously lashed out at his favourite targets through dialogues with his wife. Though sweet-natured and humorous, Bāsantikā does not hesitate to use harsh words in an enraged or irritated state, though her scorn is not lasting. We see her taking an active part in the discursive pieces. Basantak turns to her whenever in

---

[76] Ibid., 160.

[77] Lāhiṛī, *Basantak, 1m barṣa*, 3.

[78] Their names are significant. The first wife was Cirahāsinī ('One Who Always Laughs'). She epitomises humour, but proved to have a very short life-span. His second wife was Kaṭubhāṣiṇī ('One Who Talks Bitterly'), who symbolises harsh criticism. She died to save her husband, because her bitter tone evoked general wrath towards Basantak. Metaphorically, the narrator warns about the negative effects of these two modes of expression, i.e., humour and harsh criticism, and adopts a subdued but more effective one—the mirth of satire (Lāhiṛī, *Basantak, 1m barṣa*, 15).

need of advice or guidance, i.e., in determining his own role in the society[79] or what his exact function should be.[80] In the very first issue, she cautions Basantak about the serious function of satire and states how English satire, and more specifically *Punch*, works. She mentions that the English essayists Addison and Steele started the trend of exposing negative sides of society, its harmful customs and rituals, and that this was later adopted by *Punch*. Instead of practicing mere buffoonery, Bāsantikā encourages Basantak to do the same.[81] Furthermore, she tells him that he should only engage himself with those topics that are interesting and associated with the welfare of common people. Bāsantikā also criticises the contemporary trend of hurling abuses at individuals for no apparent purpose, and prefers to point out only the condemnable social practices through satire to make people conscious of the prevailing corruption in contemporary society.

Unlike Pulcinella and Mr Punch, Basantak has other relatives. He also has a twin brother, Niśāntak; the literary meaning of his name is 'one who ends the darkness of night'.[82] Niśāntak appears in the very first issue to declare his main objective—to destroy the clouds and darkness in the minds of the people by mental warfare, which is quite similar to that of his brother.

Pañcānanda/Pãcu Ṭhākur

Besides being the name of the periodical, Pãcu Ṭhākur/Pañcānanda is the name of the narrator Indranath devises for his periodical. Unlike Pulcinella, Mr Punch or Basantak, in *Pañcā-nanda*, we do not get any precise visual depiction of the narrator, as such. But we do get some general biographical information written by the Pãcu himself in a mock-autobiographic tone, which is sometimes misleading. It presents different personas of the narrator from different perspectives and in different times.

Barring some fleeting references about his persona, which remain at the level of vague generalisations because of their light-hearted and unserious tone, we hardly know who Pãcu really is. The texts describe him as God's chosen messenger who, in a quite detached way, observes the world and earthly happenings, and portrays them obliquely, quite similar to the pictorial representation of the figure of Basantak. He poses as a commoner but this is actually his disguise. The texts

---

[79] Ibid., 144.
[80] Ibid., 13–16.
[81] '*bilāte ādisan, iṣṭil prabhṛti lekhak'gaṇ deśīya rītyādir dūṣaṇīya bhāg sakal'ke byaṅga pūrbbak barṇan karite ārambha karen ebaṃ pare pyañc haiÿā sei sakal kārya karitece; tā tomāro seirūp karā karttabya; ho ho kare bhaṇḍāmi nā kare deśer rīti nītir nakal dekhāÿo*' (in England, authors like Addison and Steele had started showing people the evil sides of unjust social rituals and customs and *Punch* later took that over; it is your duty also; reflect the social realty instead of making light-hearted fun) (Ibid., 15).
[82] '*āmi basantaker yamaj bhrātā; āmār kārya timir parihār karā*' (I am Basantak's twin brother; my duty is to destroy the darkness [of mind]) (Ibid., 5).

explicitly celebrate his ability to denounce this world at anytime and transcend its realms. He often goes to the heavenly sphere to communicate with gods and goddesses and is even shown manipulating them.[83] This divine association brings Pãcu closer to his predecessor, the narrative figure of Basantak because of the latter's self-claim to be in the ranks of the great sage Vyāsa, and have the demi-god status of an *avatāra*.

Pãcu distorts the sense of historical and mythical time and space in his interpretation of the ten *avatāra*s of the God Vishnu in the prose piece *Daś abatār*[84] (ten incarnations) in visible colonial terms. They are the police, court-officers, magistrate and judge in the first age (*satyayuga*), lawyer, landlord and tax-free land holder in the second age (*tretāyuga*), Bengali newspapers and Bengali people in the third age (*dvāparayuga*) while, the last *avatāra*, Kalki, is Pãcu himself, shouldering the responsibility of mixing up everything, thereby creating the corresponding chaos. This idea of Pãcu's divine aspect returns again and again in many articles in *Pañcānanda*.

Indigenous Influences on Basantak and Pãcu

Basantak and Pãcu, despite their obvious and willing indebtedness to Mr Punch, cannot ignore the influences of the indigenous narrative traditions entirely. The resemblance which these narrators share with the character of the *vidūṣaka*[85] of Sanskrit dramatic tradition has been mentioned earlier. The *vidūṣaka*, despite being perceived as a comical character, is intelligent, ironical, cunning and very much socially aware. He comments satirically on various themes, e.g., on religious institutions, political authorities, social customs, contemporary realities, and common problems.

Also, the influence of the character of the *kathak* in both written and oral traditions of India cannot be ignored. A *kathak*, popularly called '*kathak ṭhākur*', is the one who chants religious texts in the oral traditions, putting himself into the position of 'god's messenger'; Basantak and Pãcu claim the same status.

Like Basantak, Pãcu constantly asserts his status as a demi-god, but distances himself from his predecessor by remaining flexible in his claim to sacred eminence.

---

[83] "Pãcu-puraṇe śib-nāiad sambād," (Bandyopādhyāẏ, *Indranāth granthābalī*, vol. 2, 111–118).

[84] Bandyopādhyāẏ, *Indranāth granthābalī*, vol. 2, 243–246.

[85] The *vidūṣaka* holds a major place in Sanskrit theatre, especially in *prakaraṇa*, *prahasana*, and *bhāṇa*. Although he shows mirth by allowing himself to be made the butt of ridicule, he is not a buffoon or fool. In spite of his clownish nature, he is intelligent and poses as the social critic. He frequently sounds a note of caution whenever he notices something wrong. In many of such dramas there appears a similar character who is also sometimes named Basantak *(Vasantaka)*, as in Śrī Harṣa's (606–647 AD) *Ratnāvalī*. This role of a social critic is also asserted in *Basantak* when Basantak tries to determine his role and in this respect, Bāsantikā speaks the function of a *bidūṣak* as a fearless critic and moral guide. (Lāhiṛī, *Basantak, 1 m barṣa*, 144).

His status oscillates between the rank of an *avatāra*[86] and a *ṭhākur*[87]—the former denoting a more elitist divine order, while the latter represents a more localised divinity. This gradual decline in the status of the narrator's name from the initial Pañcānanda to Pãcu Ṭhākur is significant for understanding his relationship with his readers. While the former personifies an elite divinity in the Brahmanic order, the latter one brings him nearer to a more local Bengali socio-religious culture, where we find many such local gods (*ṭhākur*) as Śani, Śītalā and Manasā. This change in the name makes the narrator more easily accessible to the readers. It is an effort to bridge the gap between the readers of the 'elite' Brahmanic order and those belonging to the 'lesser' folk and 'popular' traditions. Indranath consciously uses the name Pãcu Ṭhākur to make his columns more popular among the readers residing in the outskirts of the city of Kolkata and in semi-rural Bengal. Thus, despite being a champion of the cause to restore the Brahmanic order[88] (he belonged to the caste of the Brahmins), Indranath consciously created a dialogical level where the readers would relate to the Pãcu as someone from their own localised tradition, rather than from a distant 'elite'. Still, the subtle references to these influences seem insignificant when pitted against the more pronounced and prominent claims which eagerly sought to establish the narrator as the progeny of the English *Punch*.

Such an overt self-identification with the narrator of the famous English journal was, on the one hand, strategic to raise the sales for Bengali periodicals by propagating this claim. On the other hand, this proclaimed affinity to the European model was a consciously chosen strategy of the Bengali middle class, the *bhadralok* or babus, to assert themselves as respectable'[89] by distancing themselves from the above-mentioned 'popular' oral indigenous traditions, although not quite successfully.

Self-Image of the Bengalis

Satire in nineteenth-century Bengal articulated the most significant rupture in the self-representation of Bengali colonial consciousness. It also touched upon the question of identity in a coloniser-colonised and master-subject orientated hierarchical social order. Satirical magazines, with their subversive potential, were the main purveyors of these types of colonial representation.

---

[86] Bandyopādhyāẏ, *Indranāth Granthābalī*, vol. 2, 243–246.

[87] Ibid., 361.

[88] 'The root of social philosophy in respect of the Bangabasi writers especially so in the case of Jogendra Chandra Basu and Indranath lies in their unflinching belief in the rigid, hierarchical ordering of Hindu society in which obviously the supremacy of the Brahman assumes a pivotal importance'. (Amiya P. Sen, *Hindu Revivalism in Bengal 1872–1905: Some Essays in Interpretation* (Delhi: Oxford University Press, 1993), 257).

[89] Altick, *Punch*, 4.

While expressing their almost panic-stricken concern over the various socio-political and religio-economic developments taking place in Bengal, journals such as *Basantak* and *Pañcā-nanda* both voiced a conservative Hindu hegemonic order. Both reflected the syncretism between the theory and practice of the 'development' and 'reform' by underlining the futility of the whole corpus of colonial institutions.

Basantak intrudes into the psyche of the *bhadralok*s by expressing the hypocrisy of the middle-class Bengalis. The short poem '*Yakhan yeman takhan teman*' (opportunism), maps their opportunist mentality. He describes the 'modern' man as success-oriented, cunning and as manipulative:

> If one wants to be everyone's favourite,
> He must understand the need of the hour,
> The wish of the people and serve them accordingly.
> One who makes a range of people of varying interests happy,
> Who can equate him?
> He, who discards his natural character,
> To follow others' orders, is great.
> He who understands the mind of others,
> Is the cleverest in this world.
> The quality of flattery with figurative speeches is necessary for him
> Who could satisfy others' wishes.
> There are no other means in the world
> Better than this, in order to manipulate others.
> No one can secure comfort without slyness.
> Cunning in talk, sly in mind,
> Cunning in action, sly in behaviour.
> These are the main assets of a shrewd person.

And then the author laments towards the end that old tradition-bound people like him are branded as 'superstitious' and are becoming unfit for the 'civilised' world:

> Forget prejudices and superstitions, they are the root of all troubles,
> Like a thorn in the mind, hated in society.
> The new 'civilised' communities, especially,
> Blame prejudiced people for various reasons.
> If you want to retain your prejudice,
> Then leave the city and lurk alone in the jungle.[90]

Being one of the main parties in the socio-political schism which moved the Bengali public sphere[91] in late nineteenth century, *Basantak* explored the factional

---

[90] From "Yakhan yeman takhan teman," in Lāhiṛī, *Basantak*, 2ẏa barṣa, 29–30 (my translation).

[91] This term is not used here in a typical Habermatian sense. Habermas uses the German term *Öffentlichkeit* (public sphere) in the context of eighteenth-century France and Great Britain. 'The bourgeois public sphere may be conceived above all as the sphere of private people coming together as a public; they soon claimed the public sphere regulated from above against the public authorities themselves, to engage them in a debate over the general rules governing relations in the basically privatized but publicly relevant sphere of commodity exchange and social labor. The medium of this political confrontation was peculiar and without historical precedent: people's public use of their reason (*öffentliches Räsonnement*)'. Jürgen Habermas, *The Structural Transformation of the Public Sphere: An Inquiry into a Category of Bourgeois Society*, originally titled *Der Strukturwandel der Öffentlichkeit. Untersuchungen zu einer Kategorie der bürgerlichen*

politics of the Kolkata intelligentsia. The narrator describes the constellation of the members of the reception committee for welcoming Prince Edward in 1875, according to their religious and caste categories.[92] In another text, published in the tenth issue of the second year, he highlights the different literary groups built around different journals by articulating their respective patrons,[93] the elite, rich landlords and businessmen of Kolkata. In the eleventh issue of the second year, a list of the invitees to a reunion of the Presidency College students[94] elaborates another type of social segmentation based on occupational criteria.

On the other hand, Indranath's most dominant characteristic is his notion of *khāṭi bāṅgāliẏānā* or 'pure Bengaliness', as reflected in the pages of *Pañcā-nanda*. This central principle occupies a major role in almost all his works, a term which remains problematic to date. One of the main literary goals of Indranath's was the (r) evoking of the lost 'Bengaliness' among fellow Bengalis.[95] Before going into any detailed discussion of the texts, the notion of this 'Bengaliness' should be made clear.

The notion of 'Bengaliness' is replete with a considerable amount of doubt and threat. It is mainly dictated by the '"Occidental Self" [which] was in command'[96] [upon the] 'Oriental Self', [which] 'had to be commanded'[97] in the colonial set-up of nineteenth century Bengal, as 'the official disparagement of Bengali male sexuality and its feminization within the construct of the "effeminate" Bengali was part of the ideological equipment of the empire'.[98] Especially the educated and modern Bengali elite, popularly termed as '*bābu*s', were never bestowed with the virility of the Marathas, Punjabis or Rajputs and 'were haunted by the unhappy awareness that they were creatures of colonial modernity'.[99] Indira Chowdhury mentions that this terminology insinuates that certain Bengalis possess the 'frailty of women and the powerless submissiveness of a slave'.[100]

On the other hand, it can be said that the construct of the 'manly Englishman' and the 'effeminate *bābu*' was 'substantially modified to respond to the political

---

Gesellschaft, trans. Thomas Burger (Cambridge: The MIT Press, 1989, 27). With regard to this view of a rather homogeneous European society and the presence of a rational public, I contest that it is mainly due to the heterogeneous character of the various public(s) and the public sphere formations in India, that his argument is not suitable here.

[92] Lāhiṛī, *Basantak*, *2ẏa barṣa*, 134.

[93] Ibid., 177.

[94] Ibid., 187–189.

[95] Ujjval Gaṅgopādhyāẏ, [foreword], in *Indranāth granthābalī*, vol. 2, ed. Rañjan Bandyopādhyāẏ, (Kal'kātā: Dīp Prakāśan, 2007), xi–xxi; xi.

[96] Indira Chowdhury, The Frail Hero, Virile History: *Gender and the Politics of Culture in Colonial Bengal* (Delhi: Oxford University Press, 1998), 2.

[97] Chowdhury, The Frail Hero, 2.

[98] Ibid. 67.

[99] Subho Basu and Sikata Banerjee, "The Quest For Manhood: Masculine Hinduism and Nation in Bengal," *Comparative Studies of South Asia, Africa and the Middle East* 26, no. 3: 476–490; 478.

[100] Chowdhury, *The Frail Hero*, 67.

and economic shifts of the last quarter of the nineteenth century'.[101] I show two alternate sides of Indranath's satire, which mirrors his critique on two presupposed premises, countering firstly the alleged effeminacy and, secondly, the hypocrisy of the educated Bengali middle class in defying this colonial accusation.[102]

In the 1880s, in capturing the panic-stricken white men's agitated and insecure state at the prospective initiation of the Ilbert Bill,[103] satire and parody were used abundantly. The satirists also tried to subvert the claim of 'effeminacy' towards the colonial power which until then had used this term for denoting their subjects. The response of the Bengali intelligentsia to the Ilbert Bill provided a suitable chance for striking back against the alleged 'effeminacy' of the colonial subjects, i.e., Bengalis and the 'virility' of the colonial power, the British. Thus, it tries to rearticulate the power relations in the colonial society.

In the poem titled '*Ilbārt bil*', Pãcu compares the whole process of the passing of the Bill with the plight of a pregnant woman, thus attributing feminine qualities to the colonial state. At the end, the pregnant woman, who is also represented by the allegory of a mountain because of her pregnant state, gives birth to a tiny mouse, infusing a sense of banality and insignificance to the whole controversy,[104] as, at the end, Lord Ripon bent to the demands of the anti-bill stance of the Anglo-Indians and the Bill was passed with adopted compromises known as the 'Concordat'.

Pãcu indiscriminately mocks and parodies the colonial 'Other' and, at the same time, mirrors a twisted image of the Bengalis. On one side he expresses his doubt about the moral righteousness of the Brahmin priest class (supposedly the beholder of *dharma*) and mercilessly criticises their debauchery, and on the other side he directs his unscrupulous criticisms both towards the 'modern' Bengali society and the Hindu reformists.

In '*Bholāntīyārī kābya*'[105] (Poem on Volunteers) Pãcu rips the veil of the so-called reform movement to shreds (*uddhār sabhā*s, which literally means associations for social elevation), exposing their hypocrisy. Pãcu succumbs, in a way, to the colonial claim of 'effeminacy' imposed upon the educated middle-class

---

[101] Mrinalini Sinha, *Colonial Masculinity: The 'Manly Englishman' and the 'Effeminate' Bengali in the Late Nineteenth Century* (Manchester: Manchester University Press, 1995), 14.

[102] This project was predominantly a metropolitan middle-class one, which defied the aggressive image of rustic Indian males. Citing John Rosselli's study, Subho Basu and Sikata Banerjee argue that 'by claiming the loss of manhood under colonial rule and by initiating a project to reclaim masculinity through political action, Bengali elites could distinguish their political project from the already existing rustic culture of violence and brute physical force exercised by landlords and their retainers. Such exclusive political focus actually transformed elites into sole actors losing and gaining manliness in Bengal divorced from a wider rustic but robust physical culture'. (Basu and Banerjee, "The Quest for Manhood," 477).

[103] The Ilbert Bill was introduced in 1883 for British India by Viceroy Ripon (1827–1909). It proposed an amendment to existing laws in the country that allowed Indian judges and magistrates the jurisdiction to try British offenders in criminal cases at the district level, something not allowed until that time.

[104] The Bengali proverb goes '*parbater mūṣik prasab*', quite similar to 'much ado about nothing'.

[105] Bandyopādhyāỵ, *Indranāth granthābalī*, vol. 2, 106–111.

Bengalis, who in the nineteenth century often fancy endeavours of 'reform', 'development' and 'modernisation', which are utterly amateurish and impractical. But he asserts the claim only in order to criticise it by exposing the true character of the people behind such 'trendy' hobbies.

The characters of '*Bholāntīyārī kābya*' are feminised firstly for their behavioural traits and secondly for their very names; i.e., Bipinkṛṣṇa, (one of the various names of the playful and mischievous Hindu god Kṛṣṇa) and his friends Nandamanī ('the jewel of Nanda'), Nanī (cream), and Phaṇī (snake), which hint at their 'feminine', opportunist and treacherous traits. These characters have a meeting to discuss how to fight the Russians attacking Afghanistan.[106] Their physical movements are actually a mockery of the labour that they are enduring. For example, a slight physical movement, such as sitting down after giving a short speech, is captured in minute detail in lines such as 'the emotion of bravery started oozing profusely in the form of sweat' (*bīr'ras gharmma rūpe dara dara dhāre/ lāgilā jharite*). The poem ends with the military training of Bipin who attempts to learn how to use the rifle. The absurdity between the wish to participate in the war and the actual reality of going to war is reflected in the training process. Bipin is surrounded by servants and friends, some fanning him, some holding umbrellas to protect him from the sun, one firmly holding his waist, one providing fire for the rifle; the servants are preparing brandy, soda and snacks (significantly, no typically Bengali food is served, but European 'dinner' foods, with cutlets and eggs are). The whole setting evokes laughter by revealing the sheer futility of such attempts. This shows the vain initiatives undertaken by Bengali *bhadralok* to overcome the label of being 'unmanly' and not belonging to a 'martial race' like the Punjabis or the Marathas.[107]

Pãcu also uncovers the Bengali babu's moral corruption in his futile, dishonest and amateurish attempts to 'reform' Hinduism and emancipate women. He criticises the debauchery of the babu who adopts the more liberal Brahmo discourse only to escape the Hindu conservative social structure. The real motive behind his observance of Brahmo ideals is only to mask lecherous escapades in the name of love, and 'licentious' practices such as drinking alcohol and eating meat. The babu covers these up by his outward extreme adherence to the Brahmo ideals of 'moral righteousness' and 'refined taste'.

This becomes evident as Pãcu offers a mock-course in the doctrines of Brahmo called *Brāhmakors*[108] (exposition on Brahmo ideals). The short text is very interesting as it exposes the actual motivations for joining the Brahmos: disregard for castes, free mixing of men and women, remarriage and widow remarriage, education for women (including the learning the arts of singing, dancing, having love affairs, novel reading), social elevation, drinking, smoking, etc. By means of

---

[106] The Second Anglo-Afghan War (1878–1880).

[107] The biggest argument supporting the claim of 'effeminacy' of Bengali males was their preference for clerical jobs in the colonial administration as, 'clerical pursuits implies a lack of heroism'. (Chowdhury, *The Frail Hero*, 53).

[108] Bandyopādhyāẏ, *Indranāth granthābalī*, vol. 2, 279.

exaggeration, it exposes the panic of the Bengali intelligentsia at 'modern' women making the readers aware of such dangers.

Thus, Basantak and Pãcu mirrored a distorted image of their targets in order to make them aware of the inaccuracies and discrepancies of the colonial system. Moreover, Pãcu turns the very idea of 'effeminacy', formulated by the British colonial machinery for justifying their hold on power, against itself by infusing the colonial state with the traits of frailty, vulnerability, insecurity and effeminacy by means of reformulation, recontextualisation and subversion. Instead of criticising the colonial power directly, he uses the method of 'self-flagellation'.[109] The butt of English ridicule of the 'native subject' was mostly the Bengalis' peculiar mannerisms and language, particularly the 'babu English' spoken by the middle class. In retaliation, both in *Basantak* and *Pañcā-nanda,* satire is used as a means to get rid of this sense of inferiority by criticising the broken Bengali spoken by the Englishmen.

Thus, these two Bengali satiric periodicals exhibit a self-image of the Bengalis in the colonial context by constructing a particular terminology.[110] In order to trounce the colonial charges, Bengali intelligentsia offered a new concept of masculinity, which 'move[s] beyond mere material concerns'[111] and, at the same time, blamed the colonial system for creating the dissolute babus and the emasculated middle class.

The 'Other' Selfhood

The nineteenth-century Bengali satirists produced an image of a homogenous counterpart of the self. As Chakravorty Spivak talks about the formation of the 'Other' that takes place 'in the persistent constitution of the Other in the Self's shadow,'[112] similarly the 'strategies of selfhood'[113] formation also resulted in the construction of the 'Other' in Bengal. This 'Other' manifested not only in the

---

[109] Sumanta Bandyopādhyāẏ, *Ūniś śataker kal'kātā ebaṃ sarasvatīr itar santān* (Kal'kātā: Anuṣṭup, 2008), 98.

[110] This supports Benita Parry's observation: 'Anticolonialist writings did challenge, subvert and undermine the ruling ideologies, and nowhere more so than in overthrowing the hierarchy of colonizer/colonized, the speech and stance of the colonized refusing a position of subjugation and dispensing with the terms of the coloniser's definitions'. (Benita Parry, "Resistance theory/ theorizing resistance, or two cheers for nativism," in *Colonial Discourse/Postcolonial Theory*, eds. Francis Barker and Peter Hulme and Margaret Iverson (Manchester: Manchester University Press, 1994), 172–196; 176).

[111] Chowdhury, *The Frail Hero,* 72.

[112] Gayatri Chakravorty Spivak, "Can the Subaltern Speak?" in *Marxism and the Interpretation of Culture,* eds. Cary Nelson and Larry Grossberg (Chicago: University of Illinois Press, 1988), 66–111; 75.

[113] Homi Bhabha, *The Location of Culture* (Cornwall: Routledge, 1994), 2.

character of the 'modern' babu and *bhadralok*, but also in their counterparts the *bhadramahilā* and *bibi*.

Nasirām melā[114] (The fair of Nasirām) in *Basantak* presents the problems of the modern system of education for women. Some young girls aged between 3 and 12 years, from the local girls' school, are interviewed by an examiner at the fair. The interviews provided an insight into anomalies in Bengali households caused by the introduction of female education. The girls display no signs of womanly shyness and deny doing any petty household work, i.e., cooking, washing, fetching water, serving the elders, etc. Rather, they expressed their wishes by taking pleasure in the 'modern' and 'developed' (*unnata*) habits of novel and journal reading.[115]

Similarly in *Basantak*, besides the active participation of Bāsantikā in the discourses with her husband, we find citations of various forms of public spheres, i.e., various meetings (*sabhā*), fairs (*melā*), theatres, marketplaces (*bājār*, *hāṭ*), etc., where both men and women are physically and vocally present. Although we see Bāsantikā mostly within the four walls of her house, she still queries about these public places to Basantak. Thus, middle-class women's yearning for information and knowledge about the outside world is constituted, but at the same time it also warns them about the possible dangers lurking there.

In *Kāsārīder sañ*[116] (jester of the braziers), the eagerness of the Brahmo women for witnessing the procession of the jesters is portrayed as immoral. It involves songs, gestures and the body movements of men disguised as women, all of which are considered as 'indecent' and 'obscene' in society, and therefore unfit for women to witness. The incongruity arises between the homogeneous standardisation of such norms of decency and obscenity in society, and the keen interest in such events by women (especially by the supposedly 'morally upright' Brahmo women) (Fig. 7).

> Which actions modern people (lit. those frequenting the steps of civilisation) are undertaking in the panic of the fair.
> The Brahmo leader will lock the door to protect the purity of his wife.
> The attraction to witness the clown of the braziers is great.
> Above — Basantak: 'Bāsantikā said, I want to go to the clown at the fair of the braziers. I was at my wit's end.'
> Below — The woman outside: 'Come. Let's go.'
> The wife: 'Shhh, shhh. You go first.'
> The husband: 'Let's lock the door before I leave.'

Similarly, in *Pañcā-nanda,* an image of a middle-class Bengali household in the prose piece *Strī-svādhīnatā*[117] (Women's Emancipation) reversed the entire male–female gender relation. Here the 'enlightened' wife, Kāminī Sundarī Basu,

---

[114] Lāhiṛī, *Basantak*, *2ẏa barṣa*, 145–152.

[115] See Fig. 3 in Partha Mitter, chapter *Punch* and Indian Cartoons: The Reception of a Transnational Phenomenon in this volume, 64. The wife: 'Can't you close the door while blowing the fire?' (*Basantak*, vol. 2, issue 9).

[116] Ibid., 167–171.

[117] Bandyopādhyāẏ, *Indranāth granthābalī*, vol. 2, 187–189.

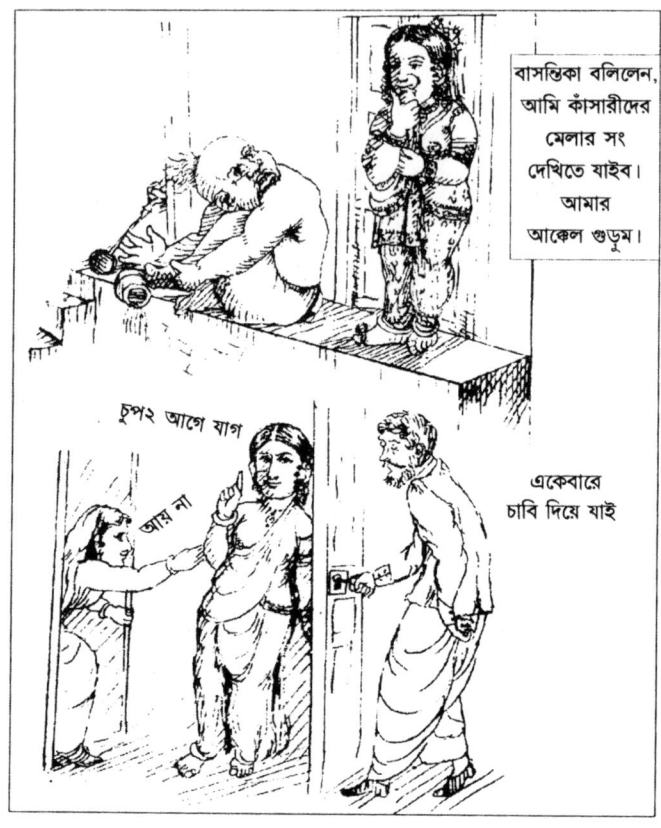

Fig. 7 *Kāsārīder melā* (fair of the braziers). *Basantak*, second year, issue 10, 1875. (Lāhiṛī, *Basantak, 2ẏa barṣa*, 168)

goes to work and earns money, while the shy and subdued husband Bhairab stays at home. Curiously enough the name carries a virile masculine connotation,[118] but the reality is just the opposite. Tame, delicate and feminised, he stays inside the confines of the home and takes care of the household chores. In the text he actually calls himself a *piñjarābaddha bihaṅga*, or a 'chained bird'. He is Kāminī's second husband. Kāminī also has a child from her previous marriage. Bhairab is at the mercy of his wife and must even ask permission to go and have small chit-chats with his neighbourhood friends, who are also caught in similar situations. But Bhairav is

---

[118] Bhairav means 'terrible' or 'tremendous'. (Bhattacharya, *Saṁsad Bengali English Dictionary*, 720).

happy and content to have his wife's love in the form of affection and gifts such as jewellery and dresses. But a possessive Kāminī jealously forbids Bhairab to go out with his friends, while she herself goes out and drinks alcohol in abundance, enjoying music and dances performed by men. All the vices of the middle-class babu are dislocated to impose them upon the body of the *bibi*.

A parallel plot runs with the same role reversal in the domain of the servants. The figure here is a maid, Menakā, and not a male-servant, who serves Kāminī. The male servants are shying away from Kāminī and stay mostly in the *andar'mahal* or the inner courtyard of the house. As Kāminī goes out to her friends, refusing her husband's tearful plea to visit his neighbourhood friend, the piece ends with a note of caution from the narrator: 'Come my dear [female] readers. Let us also go along with Kāminī Sundarī Basu—(to hell?)'.[119]

The conservative neo-Hindu part of the Bengali intelligentsia supported this attitude of *Basantak* and *Pañcā-nanda,* especially as regards the question of female education and emancipation. The attempt to streamline the unequal asymmetrical worlds of the coloniser and the colonised, especially in the marginal groups of the colonised, i.e., women, was therefore resisted. It was seen as an intrusion into the private sphere of the Hindu household, still untouched by the colonial gaze. Remaining within the position of subjugation in the colonial hierarchy, the last sphere where a Hindu man could still determine his power and reassure his exercise to control was slipping. Therefore, a monstrous vision of the crumbling social order was needed to alert people. By means of exaggeration, it made readers aware of the panic that the Bengali intelligentsia felt about 'modern' women. Being acutely conscious of how the mechanism of satire operates, Indranath emphasises the necessity of such exaggeration in another text, where he reviews Jogendra Chandra Basu's popular novel *Maḍel bhaginī* and defends the use of this kind of extreme exaggeration:

> Some do not understand why exaggeration takes place, why it is created. But for the sake of preventing our future from further damage and for ensuring the development and nourishment of the future, if the present is not depicted in exaggerations, if people are not warned of the disease by showing the prognosis, there is a chance that they will become negligent of it—if we remember this, then exaggeration will not seem to be such a huge problem.[120]

Critique of the Colonial Power

In the turbulent Bengali literary sphere of the late nineteenth century, ideas and identities became clouded with a sense of multiplicity because everyone was trying to carve a unique identity for themselves. In its quest to create a new identity, the

---

[119] Bandyopādhyāẏ, *Indranāth granthābalī*, vol. 2, 189 (my translation). For the original and a German translation, cf. also Hans Harder, *Verkehrte Welten: Bengalische Satiren aus dem kolonialen Kalkutta* (Heidelberg: Draupadi, 2011), 208–215.

[120] Ibid., 159 (my translation).

intelligentsia was constantly redefining and reshaping its positions in the colonial hierarchy. Both the narrators, Basantak and Pãcu, portray the prevailing social pattern(s) and expose the very areas of discomfort which had unsettled the moral world of the middle- and lower-middle class reading public and audience. They try to break the norms by reversing the traditional social rules and by mocking the new colonial order.

The criticism of the colonial power is more pronounced in the reportages, which are based on real events but then transformed into oblique representations. The readers were already aware of the real incidents but looked for another mode of interpretation, a new perspective set by a value system mediated by the author. For Prananath and Indranath this value system, irrevocably and obviously orthodox and conservative, is one to which their readers can easily connect in these reportages. So, on the one hand, this is a simultaneous subversion of both the modes of news writing and news reading. On the other hand, the mock tones provide the readers with a subtext to decipher. The capturing of the polyglot social structure and its inherent anomalies provides the readers with enough flexibility for their individual interpretations. Thereby these texts try to secure the strategies of selfhood-affinities with certain sections of the Bengali readership, while distancing themselves from the others. In particular, the authors mock Christian and Brahmo faiths and parody their ideals, especially the ritual of repenting and the principle of moral sin, which are almost the same in their view.

The events are mostly taken from the pages of contemporary newspapers and periodicals published in both vernacular and European languages, and then are modified into satirical sketches, which in turn take the forms of sensational contemporary news items and even gossip: the Anglo-Afghan war in Kabul (1878–1880), the appointment of Lord Ripon as the Viceroy of India (1880–1884), the victory of the Liberal Party in England in 1880, and the Vernacular Press Act of 1878 are just a few examples. In many of his articles he strongly insinuates doubt in the validity of colonialism itself. The correspondence letters and the war-correspondence also support Kevin G. Barnhurst and John Nerone in that: '[T]he newspaper was supposed to take part in the process of continually generating legitimate authority and help to sustain a sphere of rational public deliberation'.[121] At the same time, they satirise the very idea of the rational public. Pãcu locates himself within the realm of European Universalism as an educated *bhadralok* Bengali when he argues that,

> There are no more stupid people in the world than the Kabulis (people of Kabul). As stupid people do not realise their own good, the same can be said about the Kabulis; that is why I do not like to live amongst them. [...] The British is a civilised, educated and honest race, what immense good they have done by coming to Bengal, by coming to India—I'm not talking here about the benefits for the English, but the benefits they have given us—no one can forget as long as one is alive! But Kabulis do not listen to the words of such good deeds;

---

[121] Kevin G. Barnhurst and John Nerone, *The Form of News: A History* (New York: Guilford Press, 2001), 16.

they just say that they do not want any good deeds from a foreign race coming from a foreign land, and they wouldn't allow them to do any harm either. Ok, if you do not allow it—then die! [...] and what do they mean by foreign race, foreign nationals—I do not comprehend such words. The all-sympathetic lord created us all. Therefore all humans belong to the same race: what is it, a foreign race? Kabulis are so stupid that they have never heard of Cārupāṭh[122]; where the universality of human race is mentioned repeatedly. Besides this, the world is same, the soil is the same, the water is same—all are the same.[123]

Like Parashuram's[124] short story *Ulaṭ puraṇ*, (the epic of a world turned upside down) Indranath tries his hand at the subversion of colonial order in the series of letters titled *Bilāter saṁbād'dātār patra 1, 2* (letters of the England correspondent 1, 2),[125] where he challenges the 'concept of fixity in the construction of otherness'.[126] It also helps to break the perception of ambivalent stereotypes.

In the correspondent letters, Pãcu, standing in London, the very centre of the British Empire, unabashedly addresses the Englishman as the 'native' (*neṭib*),[127] a term infamously used by Europeans in India for Indians. Moreover, he made these English 'natives' more sensitive to being made into butts of ridicule than their Indian counterparts,[128] therefore making their position vulnerable and fragile. In the second letter in the series, the basic concepts of colonialism are elucidated by an Englishman in terms of a 'prey-hunter' (*khādya khādak*, literally 'food-consumer')[129] in relation to India and England. Figure 7, a cartoon published in *Pañcā-nanda*, also bitterly criticises this hierarchical relation. Using the mock-praise style again, Pãc describes the caste system in England as civilians, military, merchants, etc., all united to 'uplift' (*unnati karā*) India and the Indians.

Similarly, news was presented in the form of gossip or rumours about incidents or events of the recent past or in current times, with which the readers were more or less familiar. Two short jokes from *Basantak* illustrate this:

The discovery of nineteenth century[130]
Vidyasagar was denied entry into the Asiatic Society building. It has been reported that on his way back, he was chanting the following verse (albeit with slight changes of wordings) from a well-known Sanskrit verse:
Knowledge and shoes cannot be compared.
Knowledge is worshipped in its own sphere, but shoes are worshipped everywhere.

---

[122] Written by Akshay Kumar Datta (1820–1886) in 1855–1859, it was once the mandatory primary school text book in Bengal for almost three generations in the nineteenth century.
[123] From "Kābulastha saṁbād'dātār patra-3 (Letters of Kabul Correspondence-3)," in Bandyopādhyāẏ, *Indranāth granthābalī*, vol. 2, 154 (my translation).
[124] Pseudonym of Bengali satirist Rajsekhar Basu (1880–1960).
[125] Bandyopādhyāẏ, *Indranāth granthābalī*, vol. 2, 193–199.
[126] Bhabha, *Location of Culture*, 66.
[127] Ibid. 194.
[128] Ibid. 195.
[129] Ibid. 196.
[130] Lāhiṛī, *Basantak, 1m barṣa*, 105, 131 (my translation).

In order to completely understand the inherent meaning of the jokes, the innuendo conveyed by the subsequent replacement of certain words—in this case, the incongruous relation between knowledge and shoes—the reader must know what the original verse in Sanskrit is, who Vidyasagar is, what the Asiatic Society is and, lastly, why Vidyasagar is denied entry there. In the colonial world, where rationality rules everywhere, everything loses its value. It is exactly in the culmination of all the above criteria that the punch-line of this joke lies.

In the same vein there is a joke about the reformer Brahmos,

> The real steps of development[131]
> One emancipated Brahmo was giving advice to educated youths:
> My fellow brothers! Bring out the women. Bring out the women.

The joke mainly comes from the double entendre of the Bengali phrase '*bār karā*', which literally means to bring out. But here it means both emancipating, as well as eloping with, women. Again, one has to understand the dichotomy between the ideals of the Brahmo faith and the instable situation of the Brahmos in contemporary Bengali society, especially how the conservative faction view them. This piece demonstrates the hypocrisy behind this plea.

Another short skit in *Basantak* states:

> Twenty years ago, there was a dearth of books in Bengali language. Nowadays 'great' authors are more in number than the readers. I cannot decide how to maintain the balance. It has been heard that the members of the admirable Obscenity Prevention Committee are going on strike, demanding the burning of English books written by obscene and dirty authors such as Shakespeare, Fielding, Chaucer, Byron, etc., and thereby making the aforementioned balance work perfectly with the English readers. This is not at all a bad idea.[132]

To decipher the main point of conflict, this joke demands a prior knowledge of the literary situation in Bengal, as well as some information about the English authors mentioned in the joke. The newly-gained social consciousness of some of the Bengali intelligentsia, who tried to emerge as the moral authority, is mercilessly targeted here. Inspired by the Victorian Puritanism of Europe, similar associations, such as the Society for the Prevention of Obscenity (Vidyasagar, late nineteenth century) were established. Their obsessive concern with the issues of morality, righteousness and purity became the object of constant criticism among the conservative press.[133]

Pañcā-nanda concentrated primarily on various contemporary issues: social, economic, educational, and even, to some extent, political. Besides this, in the

---

[131] Ibid. (my translation).

[132] Ibid., 49 (my translation).

[133] See Fig. 2 in Partha Mitter, chapter *Punch* and Indian Cartoons: The Reception of a Transnational Phenomenon in this volume, 12; adjust page after typesetting 'What changes are taking place after the establishment of the Society for the Prevention of Obscenity' (Goddess Kālī in the house of a member of the Society for the Prevention of Obscenity) (*Basantak*, vol. 1, issue 3).

এস্তেহার

সর্বসাধারণকে জ্ঞাত করা যাইতেছে যে বহুকষ্টে একটি রাজা খেতাব খালি করা গিয়াছে।
গ্রহণেচ্ছুগণেরা শীঘ্র করিয়া দরখাস্ত করিবেন ও ফেমিনের জন্য কত টাকা সহি করিবেন স্পষ্টাক্ষরে লিখিবেন
ও সর্ব বিষয়ে কি সহি করিবেন লিখিবেন। নিজের গুণাগুণ লিখিবার আবশ্যকতা নাই।

Fig. 8 Notice. *Basantak*, first year, issue 6. (Lāhiṛī, *Basantak, 1m barṣa*, 112)

columns titled *Ṭīkā-ṭippanī*,[134] comments about contemporary magazines, periodicals and authors, albeit with satiric undertones, feature quite regularly. Pãcu's method is to mock, parody, and poke fun at his target, sometimes even with personal attacks, but mostly remaining within certain parameters. In its entire life-span there is probably only one instance where *Pañcā-nanda* hurled its vilification against Bankimchandra, but apologised profusely for the whole incident in the next issue.[135]

---

[134] Criticism of contemporary periodicals also find a place on *Pañcā-nanda*'s pages; first, it criticises itself, and then two other Bengali periodicals—*Sadānanda,* a periodical with satire and criticism, published in Dhaka, and *Rasik'rāj,* an illustrated satirical magazine published from Kolkata. *Pañcā-nanda*, vol. 2, issues 5, 6, 1288/1882, 97–10.

[135] For more detail about this incident see Basu, *Sāhitya-pariṣat-·patrikā*, 120–122.

Pañcā-nanda mirrors a distorted self-image of his targets in order to make the readers aware of the associative discrepancies. In his pedagogical task, Indranath belongs to the group of satirists who 'go even further in helping their readers recall the 'right' lessons, in channelling memory along predominant lines. [...] Like ancient bards who utilized rhythmic speech patterns to influence audience interpretation [...]'.[136] Although Medhurst made this comment in the context of political cartoons, it seems quite appropriate for *Pañcā-nanda* as well, considering the narrator's supposed position of a divine entity that helps people—via various literary genres such as skits, poems, songs, reportage, gossip, and columns of criticism— towards the 'righteous' path in a world where everything goes wrong.

The following cartoon, with the accompanying short note, and the next joke ridicule the British Government's system of bestowing honorary titles on their subjects (Fig. 8):

It is announced for the interest of all that after much effort one title of *Rājā* has been made available. Interested persons apply immediately and mention clearly how much they are going to sign [on the bank-cheque] for the famine [fund] and how much for all [other] issues. No need to write about their qualities.

The New Title of Vidyasagar[137]
Hearing that Vidyasagar had been endowed with another title by the British Government, a teacher of a village school came to meet him. He asked Vidyasagar: What is your new title?
Vid.: CIE
Teacher: What does that mean?
Vid.: *Chāi* [ash].
Teacher: Excellent! Excellent! Everything sounds beautiful when uttered by the royal mouth.

A prior knowledge of the colonial honours system and about Vidyasagar are needed here. To understand the punning word play, one must understand both English and Bengali. The first prose piece in the second issue of *Basantak*, second year, echoes similar attitudes towards such titles conferred on Indian elites.

In the next piece, the attack on colonialism is more direct and Pãcu uses another mock genre, mock dictionary:

Anglo-Bengali Dictionary (Ibid., 153 (my translation))

Word	Meaning
To fear Russians	To mistrust India
War	Draught
Enemy	Those who do everything for the sake of their country and duty
Treaty	Prisoner
Right to nationhood	To keep in possession only as much land as is needed for standing until one dies
To lead an army	Positioning army in such a way that in the time of need one group could not help another
Uncivilised race	

(continued)

---

[136] Medhurst, "Political Cartoons as Rhetorical Form," 223.

[137] Bandyopādhyāẏ, *Indranāth granthābalī*, vol. 2, 276 (my translation).

Word	Meaning
	[People] with whom there is no need to obey any civilised rules and religious regulations while interacting, and there is no stigma in destroying their palaces and houses, which are considered as the prime symbols of their culture and art.[138]

This text requires a twofold prior knowledge: linguistic understanding and a certain amount of political consciousness in order to see through the demarcating ideologies which work behind the reception of its subject-matter. At the same time it also underlines the differences between the words written and conveyed on both contextual and conceptual levels.

Many such short parodies are set in poetic forms, especially those with a touch of musical and rhythmic tones, and were once meticulously memorised by the readers and recited or sung publically. An abundance of various mock genres such as mock war reports, foreign correspondence, travelogues, reportage, jokes, histories, advice pieces, letters, advertisements, diaries, autobiographies and essays, and mock self-criticism are commonplace in both the periodicals. The points of demarcation between the two periodicals were mainly their individual objectives, treatments, styles, tones, and, obviously, the quality of the cartoons.

Response

Basantak was quite well-received in the nineteenth-century Bengali literary sphere. From the accounts of its criticism in contemporary journals we see that it is mostly praised for the cartoons. *Madhyastha* comments on its first issue: 'It contains six illustrations. All of these successfully fulfil their aims [...] but although its literary style is not bad, it is not up to the standard as was expected'.[139]

Sādhāraṇī goes into detail discussing the illustrations and the literary style and observes that it suffers from the overbearing influence of *Amṛta bājār patrikā*. It also expresses unhappiness about the language of the articles not being as spontaneous and humorous as the images. *Sādhāraṇī* also warns *Basantak* about exaggeration in depicting the political 'Other' in a negative manner, and threatens him with consequences which he will suffer from his wife, Bāsantikā.[140] *Hindoo Patriot* also praises *Basantak* in comparison to *Har'bolā bhāṛ*: 'Both are imitations, but the last [*Basantak*] is a decided improvement upon the first'.[141] Commenting on its cartoons, *Amṛta bājār patrikā* writes that 'the cartoons are excellent'.[142]

---

[138] Ibid. (my translation).
[139] Basu, *Sāhitya-pariṣat--patrikā*, 107 (my translation).
[140] Ibid., (my translation).
[141] Ibid., (my translation).
[142] Ibid., 110 (my translation).

Writing about the first issue of *Pañcā-nanda*, *Ārya darśan* expresses enthusiasm about the publication of this satiric periodical and stresses the need for such journals. It also meticulously lists all the articles published in the first issue. *Ārya darśan* comments further that 'all the articles are full of strong satiric undertones. Some satiric comments seem to be exaggerated. The result of exaggeration is often negative. *Pañcānanda* does not spare any faction of society'.[143] *Bāndhab* regards *Pañcā-nanda* as an 'old and trusted friend. In the last 2–3 years, *Pañcānanda* appeared on the Bengali literature's horizon, only to vanish again like a comet'.[144] In 1882, after the re-appearance of *Pañcā-nanda*, *Sādhāraṇī*, one of its prime supporters and associates, voiced, in superlatives, a sense of exalted joy: '[W]e are very happy to see *Pañcānanda* again after a long gap. It can really be said that his type of periodical cannot be found in Bengal, not in India, not anywhere in the world. *Pañcānanda* makes us proud [...] if any journal can take pride in its language only Pañcānanda can take this credit [...] *Pañcānanda* is really juicy in its language. In its critique, *Pañcānanda* is unique, and never shies away in speaking the right words [...] *Pañcānanda* does not even spare itself'.[145]

Conclusion

To conclude, I would like to highlight some points which become evident from the whole discussion: Firstly, roughly tracing the whole process of how the cultural phenomena of the narrator's various forms, i.e., Pulcinella, Mr Punch, Basantak and Pãcu, underline his journey through different cultures and time-periods. Furthermore, it reveals that, despite sharing some commonalities, the authors still introduced in their narrator figures some individualistic approaches. At the same time, this particular genre of satirical journalism with its associated transformation(s) in text and cartoon shows that they still successfully retained some of their original traditions.

Secondly, Basantak and Pãcu are not merely 'imitations' of the English *Punch*; they also show shifts in the portrayals of the narrator-figure, from Sanskrit drama and various local oral traditions in India and into colonial times.

Thirdly, satire helps establish a sense of the self in the colonial subjects. It works as self-critique by mirroring a distorted image of the Self, and the narrator supports this objective by highlighting social evils. Satire provides the narrator with a medium sufficiently explicit to be understood and enjoyed by its readership(s) but subtle enough not to enrage his targets.

---

[143] Ibid., 116 (my translation).
[144] Ibid., 117 (my translation).
[145] Ibid., (my translation).

Finally, colonial satire attacks and questions the validity of colonialism itself. It presents dissonant voices which question disjunctive ideologies of European colonialism. This particular function of satire united the various factions of the literary sphere in Bengal to some extent, which were otherwise quite hostile to each other.

With satiric journalism, satire, which had occupied a somewhat marginal position in Bengali literary history, came to be acknowledged as a mode of literary, as well as visual, expression in late nineteenth century. It started to receive its due recognition as one of the central loci of the Indian literary sphere by exposing the pretentious facades of colonial power.

Crossing Boundaries: *Punch* and the Marathi Weekly *Hindu Pañca* (1870–1909)

Swarali Paranjape

The brand name *Punch or The London Charivari* from imperial Britain marked its presence not only in the British literary sphere, but its legacy also travelled to other cultures and blended in with their respective literary traditions. This chapter focuses on the *Hindu pañca,* the first journal in the Marathi language resembling *Punch,* and also the first to mark the advent of Marathi satirical journalism, even if it was not entirely satirical. The chapter acknowledges the remarkable efforts made by the creator of the *Hindu pañca* in the late nineteenth century, which have been neglected by literary critics and historians. It also looks at the similarities between *Punch* and *Hindu pañca* and delves into the issue of trans cultural flows between the different literary cultures. The following is based upon the available issues of *Hindu pañca* from 1880 to 1887 and 1897, and on the only available critique by Marathi writer Sarojini Vaidya.

Introduction

Hindu pañca was founded in 1870 in Thane,[1] Maharashtra, by journalist Kashinath Vishnu Phadke, 30 years after the first publication of *Punch*. One of Phadke's fellow journalist, Vaman Balkrishna Ranade[2] and Phadke's son Krishnaji

---

I am thankful to Prof. Dr. Hans Harder and Prof. Dr. Harald Fischer-Tiné for their valuable comments and to Ms. Aparna Velankar for her help with the translations.

[1] Thane: a city in Maharashtra, India and part of the Mumbai conurbation.

[2] Ranade, Vaman Balakrishna (1854–1899): scribe for *Lokahitavādī* (see below) and editor of the journals *Hindu pañca, Sūryoday, Kalpataru* and *Jñānacakṣu.*

S. Paranjape (✉)
Department of Modern South Asian Languages and Literatures, South Asia Institute, Heidelberg University, Heidelberg, Germany
e-mail: swarali.paranjape@gmail.com

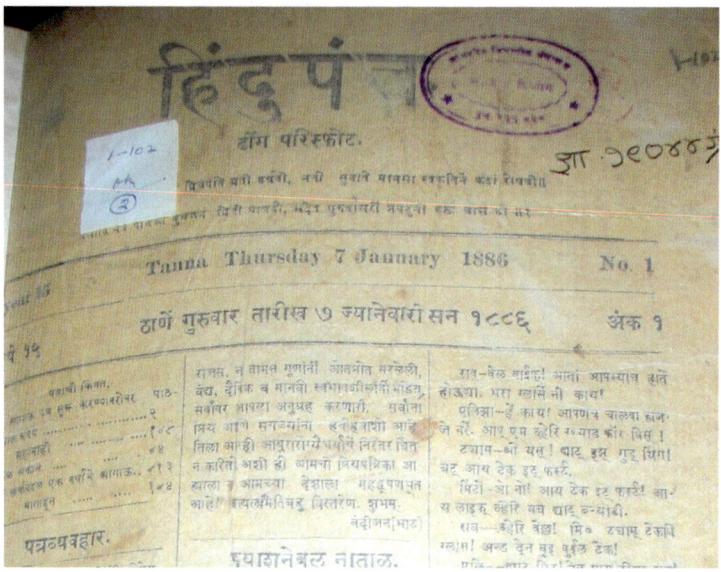

Fig. 1 *Hindu pañca* (lit. *hiṃdu paṃca*) written as a heading on the issue dated 7 January 1886

Kashinath Phadke[3] contributed to the writing and editing of this weekly. It was printed in Kashinath Phadke's own printing press, *Aruṇoday*.[4] The last issue of the *Hindu pañca* was printed in 1909. However, the weekly issues between the years 1880 and 1887 and of the year 1897 were the only bound files that could be traced and photographed in the periodical section of Pune's government library (Fig. 1). Although an encyclopedia of Marathi literature *Saṅkṣipta marāṭhī vāṅmay'koś* claims that it was popular among its readers, who belonged to different classes,[5] the 39 years of *Hindu pañca*'s remarkable presence is hardly mentioned in the Marathi literary histories. This encyclopedia also states that in 1909, *Hindu pañca* published provocative articles criticizing Gopal Krishna Gokhale[6] and the British government, holding them responsible for Lokamanya Tilak's[7] imprisonment. Gokhale filed and won the case against *Hindu pañca*. It was banned thereafter and Phadke was convicted for his misleading articles against Gokhale.

---

[3] Phadke, Krishnaji Kashinath (?-1920): journalist and writer; editor of *Hindu pañca*, *Vinod*, *Vikṣipta* and *Vidūṣak*.

[4] Phadke's first publication, launched in Thane in 1866, was also called *Aruṇoday*.

[5] Jayā Daḍ'kar et al., eds., *Saṅkṣipta marāṭhī vāṅmay'koś: Ārambhāpāsūn 1920 paryantacā kāl'khaṇḍa* (Mumbaī: G. Rā. Bhaṭakaḷ Foundation, 2003–2004), 357.

[6] Gokhale, Gopal Krishna (1866–1915): a senior leader of the Indian National Congress.

[7] (1856–1920) The most famous nationalist leader prior to the Gandhian era.

Phadke published a collection of 68 humorous anecdotes from *Hindu pañca* in the form of a booklet named *Tās'bhar Mauj*[8] (an hour of fun) in August 1886. On the cover page of this booklet he had the sentence 'the jesting, small jokes and funny incidents from *Hindu pañca* to entertain the public' printed. This 90 page booklet could be seen as Phadke's strategy to publicise his weekly.

Sarojini Vaidya discusses the narrator and the narrative style of *Hindu pañca* in her article *Pañcaājobā*[9] almost 70 years after the last issue was published. This is the only elaborate article on *Hindu pañca* that I could find. In the epilogue of her book *Saṃkramaṇ*,[10] she mentions a note published in *Marathi vṛttapatrāṃcā itihās*[11] in 1984 by R. K. Lele on *Hindu pañca*, which, according to her, is partially based upon her article *Pañcaājobā*. This note by Lele indicates that *Hindu pañca* was being translated in Hindi by Pandit Govindshastri Dugavekar from Kashi and was published by L. N. Garde. Lele also mentions that this translated edition was well received in the Hindi literary sphere.[12]

The Narrator *Pañcaājobā* and His *Pañcapatrikā Hindu pañca*

The title *Hindu pañca* is indeed a conscious loan from the title of the British satirical magazine *Punch* which, in turn, recalls Pulcinella of the *commedia dell' arte* and the popular British puppet show *Punch and Judy*.[13] The title itself can be read as outlining the targeted readership of the journal. *Hindu*, in this context, seems to be used for the Hindu religious community rather than for the natives of Hindustan. As for *Pañca,* apart from transliterating the English *Punch*, it means a referee or judge in Marathi. The governing body of a village is called *pañcāyat* and this committee of five people is led by a *pañca*, the administrative as well as judiciary head of the village. In addition to this, *pañca* also means 'five'. This number five is considered sacred and divine according to Hindu mythology as it refers to the ultimate power of *pañcamahābhūta*[14] and *pañcadevatā*.[15] And in fact the narrator of *Hindu pañca* is named *Pañcaājobā*, which furnishes him the

---

[8] Hindu pañca kartā [Kṛṣṇājī Kāśināth Phaḍke], ed., *Tāsbhar mauj* (Puṇe: Śri Śivajī Cāpkhānā, 1886).

[9] Sarojinī Vaidya, "Pañcaājobā," in *Saṃkramaṇ* (Puṇe: Śrividyā Prakāśan, ca. 1985) (originally published in *Lalit, divāḷī aṅk* (1978)).

[10] Ibid.,173.

[11] R.K. Lele, *Marathi vṛttapatrāṃcā itihās* (Pune: Continental Prakāśan, 1984), 180–189.

[12] Vaidya, *Saṃkramaṇ*, 174.

[13] Ritu G. Khanduri, "Vernacular Punches: Cartoons and Politics in Colonial India," *History and Anthropology* 20, no. 4: 459–486; 463. See also chapter *Punch* in India: Another History of Colonial Politics? in this volume.

[14] The five elements which created the universe.

[15] The gods Brahmā, Viṣṇu, Maheśa, Sureśa, Gaṇeśa.

convenient status position of the eldest person with the highest authority in a patriarchal family. He is dressed in traditional attire, wearing turban, *dhotī*, and a shawl around his neck, *puṇerī*[16] footwear, and sporting an untrimmed mustache. The combination of the words *pañca* and *ājobā* makes him the ultimate authority. He not only enjoys homely affairs and praises his grandchildren like a loving grandpa would, but also serves his duty as the highest authority-figure by judging and criticising the British government and evaluating local rituals and traditions. *Pañcaājobā*, with his age and social position, therefore appears well-suited for casting his vote on current events in society. The title may thus be interpreted as promising a predominantly Hindu readership *Punch*-like reading delights in terms not at all alien to rather traditional milieus.

The narrator *Pañcaājobā* has his own fantasy kingdom, called *Pañcarāṣṭra*,[17] and he is its *sarkār,* the governor of this kingdom. He has established imaginary administrative departments and a judiciary system similar to the colonial government. He deputes new members to different posts and transfers them from one department to another. His fictional citizens write him letters in which they complain about their problems, share their joy and sorrow, and thereby reflect various social issues. They even have advertisements published in the weekly.

Pañcobā refers to his journal as *Pañcapatrikā,* which is a supplement-size, four-page, black-and-white newspaper. The issues from 1880 to 1887 are printed in three columns and the 1897 issues have five columns. The year in which this change took place remains unknown due to the unavailability of the issues between 1887 and 1897. *Indian Newspaper Reports of Bombay*[18] between the years 1868 and 1942 state that the circulation figure of *Hindu pañca* for the years 1901–1921 was 500.

The Editor and His *Pañca*

Phadke's tremendous imaginative power and creativity, along with his command over different literary repertoires and colloquial Marathi in the journal, made him an exception amongst his contemporary writers and journalists. The imaginary kingdom in his narrations can be seen as a mockery of the British administration and judiciary system. As is evident from the various colonial South-Asian literatures, the confrontation with British rule, culture and ideology not only caused the formation of an anti-British front in India, but also provoked Indians to reflect upon their own culture, traditions and customs. Marathi writers were no exception. But while contemporaries

---

[16] Traditional footwear made in Pune.

[17] Kingdom of the Pañca.

[18] *Indian Newspaper Reports of Bombay* (Wiltshire, England: Adam Matthew Publication) digital guides, part 7.

of Phadke, such as Vishnushastri Chiplunkar[19] and Gopal Hari Deshmukh (1823–1893) alias *Lokahitavādī*,[20] were attempting to enlighten society with their serious reformative approach towards social, religious and political issues such as child marriage, widow remarriage, pros and cons of colonial rule and its policies, etc., Phadke chose a new and very different approach to handle these concerns.

What made Phadke choose humor and satire to articulate his views on the tension-ridden surroundings? On the occasion of completing 26 successful years of the publication, Phadke wrote an editorial on the narrator *Pañcaājobā* in the issue dated 13 January 1898. Phadke's *Pañcaājobā* thanks his readers for their support and looks forward to the next issues with enthusiasm and energy. In the following he comments on the narrator's, and by extension, magazine's stand:

> But what exactly is this haggard *Pañca*? Is he an orthodox[21] or a reformer?[22] The answer is not quite clear.
>
> Some would surely label this effort as the height of orthodoxy. But friends, let me tell you, this old funny chap is not that ardently orthodox. I welcome, accept and even appreciate a new approach. Orthodoxy despises novelty. I do not have the slightest hatred towards what is happening and changing around and would not ever want to wear blindfolds.
>
> A reformer is one who always embraces and appreciates new things. Reformers always support and encourage changes. They even think that morality is not bound by some medieval texts and should be considered flexible enough to be compatible with the changing times.
>
> Criticizing and at times even condemning reformers has become an obsession in some quarters.
>
> But if you ask this funny old chap, the very word 'reformer' should be applauded and accepted with a big heart. It is an honour to believe in all kinds of reform. *Pañcasar'kār* has always welcomed and never failed to embrace this new wave of reforms when their very thoughts were aligned with the basics of moral practices.
>
> Condemning pretence, attacking hypocrisy, criticizing all the wrongdoing, applauding everything that is right, praising reforms, supporting reformers and entertaining those overstressed guys who are buried under the huge responsibility of worshiping dear sister Victoria, are some of the main duties that we undertake.
>
> It is evident and our readers are very much aware of our journey so far.
> 13 January 1898[23]

It is of course not the reformist agenda that is remarkable in the *Hindu pañca*, but precisely the featured satire in the weekly and the attempts to mock the entire

---

[19] Marathi writer (1850–1882) who founded the newspapers *Kesarī* (Marathi) and *Maratha* (English) together with Gopal Ganesh Agarkar and Bal Gangadhar Tilak, and established two printing presses, namely *Āryabhuṣaṇ cāp'khānā* and *Citraśāḷā*.

[20] G. H. Deshmukh worked as a translator for the government under the British Raj. He wrote articles against child marriage, dowry system, polygamy in the newspapers under the pen name *Lokahitavādī*.

[21] Sarojinī Vaidya, *Saṃkramaṇ* (Śrividyā Prakāśan: Puṇe, 1985), 124. Phadke used the word 'orthodox' (written in Devanagari) in this editorial.

[22] Ibid.; '*riphormar*' (written in Devanagari).

[23] Ibid. (my translation).

literary format of the newspaper. As was the case with reformist journalism at that time, *Hindu pañca* also took notice of the socio-political happenings and did not hesitate to criticise them. At the same time, the innovation and courage of a Brahmin journalist of using satire, which was considered a trivial literary form, as a tool to handle highly inflammatory issues and to address forbidden subjects, such as sexual desire, must have been highly controversial.

Issues Addressed in *Hindu pañca*

Hindu pañca dealt with diverse subjects. They vary from domestic affairs, political remarks and social reality, to traditions and rituals. *Pañcaājobā* embodies the saying 'the pen is mightier than the sword' and attacks governmental and socio-political issues alike with the help of humor. For instance, *Pañcaājobā*'s daughters write him letters complaining about their husbands, who are staying in different cities due to their work or education and do not meet them often. *Pañcaājobā* routinely scolds his sons or son-in-laws enthusiastically. Apart from his imaginary children, he also does not hesitate to include some British officers in his fictional world, and even the prime minister of the United Kingdom, William Ewart Gladstone, who features as his good friend. He calls him '*ānandī dagaḍ*', which is a translation of the words 'glad (happy)' and 'stone' in Marathi, and mentions Lord Dufferin as his elder sibling and Lady Dufferin as his sister-in-law.[24] Another example is his reports on domestic affairs, rituals and traditional functions, which not only make his readers aware of their own traditions but also indicate and ridicule their shallowness at times.

Unlike other nationalist journals at that time, however, criticizing British rule was not the only motive driving this weekly. On the contrary, *Pañcaājobā* occasionally writes pleasant words about some officers he values, for example, the above-mentioned William Gladstone and Lord Dufferin. In most of his other articles and news items, he depicts the world around him with its values, traditions and social issues. He ridicules evil social practices and unveils harsh realities, e.g. child marriage, the pitiful condition of widows and forced pregnancies. Apart from this, he also publishes fictional letters, legal notices, advertisements and reports in order to point out the flaws in his own society.

As stated above, *Hindu pañca* cannot be entirely categorised as satirical, but a good number of articles from the journal are significant examples of social satire and thus furnish an early glimpse of modern Marathi satire. *Pañcaājobā* mocks different genres in his writings: from ancient traditions like *subhāṣita*,[25] *ukhāṇā*,[26]

---

[24] Ibid., 127.

[25] Moral preaching in prose and poetry composed in Sanskrit.

[26] In Hindu tradition husbands and wives are not supposed to call each other by their names. On the occasion of marriages and other ceremonies men and women compose their spouse's names in a short poetry.

and moral stories, to modern literary genres such as letters, legal notices, and advertisements. He hardly leaves any genre untouched. Apart from the daily news and reports, he specialises in mock reporting. *Pañcaājobā* invents peculiar characters that send him letters, advertisements and legal notices to publish in the weekly. Sarojini Vaidya therefore rightfully argues in her article that the creative and distinct effort of Phadke deserves an honorable mention in the literary history. She wonders whether Shripad Krishna Kolhatkar[27] could still be recognised as the 'Founder of Modern Marathi Humor'[28] if Phadke's work was taken into account.

Let us then look at some examples. In the issue dated 20 January 1881, Phadke published a legal notice signed by a 1 year-old son to his father, accusing the father of depriving him his childhood pleasures because of his mother's immediate pregnancy. He threatens to drag his father to the court of the honorable *Pañcasar'kār* if his demand for appropriate compensation is not fulfilled in the next two and a half days. Here is an excerpt from that notice:

To my Respected Father Nanasaheb,
It is hereby brought to your notice by the undersigned, that I am your one year old son. I have just completed thirteen months and my mother is already six months pregnant carrying your next child. I want to bring to your notice that it is becoming very difficult to suck milk from my mother's sagging breasts. I do not get enough milk that I am entitled by my birth right and even the small portion that is left for me has gone salty in taste. I do not like the taste. It has started pinching my belly. I am becoming malnourished because of starvation. [...] I have landed in this grim situation only because of you. You could not control your sexual urge and slept with my mother when I was just three months old.
[...]
For Gangaram Narayan,
M. V. Parkar. Atane and Solicitors
20 January 1881[29]

Forced pregnancies were a very delicate issue discussed by the reformers. Early and serial pregnancies affected women's as well as their newborns' health—as shown by the remarkable death rate of newborns and casualties during the birth.[30] Tarabai Shinde discusses this issue in her essay *Strīpuruṣ'tulanā* and holds women partly responsible for their low status in the family. She encourages women to raise their voice against injustice and suppression. This legal notice was published just 1 year before Tarabai's essay, which elaborates on the miserable state of women in patriarchy. In this difficult situation, *Pañcaājobā* creates a 13-month old narrator to explain his and his mother's horrifying state to the father. Gangaram, the son, blames his father for not controlling his sexual urge and impregnating his mother immediately after his

---

[27] Śrīpād Kṛṣṇa Kolhaṭ'kar (1871–1934), a prominent playwright, humorist and satirist.

[28] Bal Gadgil, "Modern Marathi Humor," in *A History of Modern Marathi Literature*, vol. 2, (*1800–2000*), eds. Rajendra Banahatti and G.N. Jogalekar (Pune: Maharashtra Sahitya Parishad, 2004).

[29] Vaidya, *Saṃkramaṇ*, 128 (my translation).

[30] Tārābāī Śinde, *Tārābāī Śinde-likhit strīpuruṣ'tulanā*, ed. Vilās Khole (Pune: Pratimā Prakāśan, 1997); 22.

birth. Suing the other party and sending legal notices to solve disputes is a practice related to the colonial legal system, and *Pañcaājobā* mocks this established style of writing. A legal action is ideally taken against illegal acts and the guilty person is prosecuted with an appropriate punishment. However, in the above mentioned example, the legal notice is of course not meant to prosecute the accused, but to intensify the issue. At the time of the publication of this text, discussing sexual relations in public was a taboo. It was considered obscene to speak about male and female sexual desires.[31] A 1-year-old boy writing about this to his father makes this piece satirical. The readers laugh and feel discomfort at the same time.

The next example is a letter published in the issue of *Hindu pañca* dated 20 April 1882. This letter is from a 60-year-old widow named *Saṭʰvābāī*[32] and addresses other young widows. Child marriage and widow remarriage were some of the most controversial social issues discussed by reformers, most of who were elaborating on the horrifying conditions of young widows and their miserable lives. In the letter, by contrast, *Saṭʰvābāī* tells young widows to stop mourning their husband's death and start living their lives to the fullest. She gives hints about how to fulfill their sexual desires without letting others know about it. Following is a longish excerpt from the letter:

> I lost my husband when I was just fifteen. [...] I became a widow. Not my fault. Why should I refrain from living life? I lived it to the fullest!
>
> I was young, untouched. Many were lusting after me. I dealt with them and had my secret pleasures. But nobody came to know, ever. I was that shrewd.
>
> I had to be.
>
> After my husband's death, I aborted eleven babies from my own body. Four survived in my womb. I disposed all of them near the river bank in our backyard. All this was done in the dark hours of midnight. Nobody knew, ever. If you do not want to believe me, I don't care. If you wish, come with me, I will dig up all four holes on the banks of the river and can show you the proof, the remains of my own children. They were born years after my husband's death.
>
> [...] Nobody knows about this. People respect me and seek my guidance.
>
> [...] Look, is there any point in wasting your life? [...] How can you stay away from sexual pleasures? And why should you? You are nothing but a mortal human being. You have a body and your body has its demands. There is nothing wrong with it. Things do happen. Let them happen.
>
> See, God is unfair to us women. He has burdened us with the ability of getting pregnant. Men are free. They just have their pleasure, and walk off. [...] Unfair, but unfortunately true!
>
> Don't ever forget, if you are going to warm the bed with a man, you have to act smartly here. Keep track of your menstrual cycle. If you miss it for two to three months, act then and act fast. [...] Don't be stupid again. If you go and consult a male doctor, the chances are clear; he will want to sleep with you first, forget abortion!
>
> These are secrets best kept among women. You should never share the news of your pregnancy with any man, even if you trust him. [...]
>
> Do not worry now. I will take good care of you and shall help you get rid of that bulging tummy.

---

[31] Charu Gupta: "'Dirty' Hindi Literature: Contests around Obscenity in Late Colonial North India," *South Asia Research* 20, no. 2 (2000): 89–118.

[32] The second woman, used as a bad word.

That's why I always insist on remarriage. That is the only way of keeping your head high, whatever the situation may be! So, listen to me and do not act foolishly, stupid!
—*Saṭ'vābāī*
20 April 1882[33]

As is evident in this fictional letter, Phadke creates a narrator, a widow named *Saṭ'vābāī*. A widow is considered to be an upright woman by society. It is clear from the letter that she is respected and that people seek her guidance and follow her suggestions, but her name *Saṭ'vābāī*, which means 'the other woman', negates the respect given to her. She reveals her secrets to a pregnant young widow who has come to her to get rid of her unborn child.

The pitiful condition of widows is evident from such contemporary accounts as Tarabai Shinde's. There were rules and regulations for a widow and she was left with no choice but to give away her aspirations and desires. Widows were made to shave off their hair, so that no men would look at them because of their ugliness.[34] In this social situation the letter conveys the need for widow remarriage by portraying the danger of forcing a miserable life on young widows. If a mature widow gives this advice to young widows, the 'morality' of the society according to the orthodoxy will be in danger.

This letter comes across as supporting widows who break the norms and go against societal rules set to fulfill their sexual needs. Similar to the previous example, this text also handles a taboo subject—the sexual needs of a widow. This letter aims to shock the reader. The imaginary situation here is not at all humorously narrated, but is rather crude.

If one reads more into it, however, there is another implicit layer to this text. This letter portrays a cruel, selfish, adulterous woman—a woman who kills her 11 babies and seeks sexual pleasure, a woman who definitely would not be respected. Generally, however, in spite of living under many strict social norms, the widows had a respectful status and authority in the patriarchal society. An elderly widow used to be the ultimate authority in the family. The newly emerged, educated middle class and university education gave women an opportunity to be literate, independent, and to take control of their own lives.[35] A growing insecurity about losing control over their sexuality and the consequent patriarchal anxiety in educated middle-class men is noticeable in many colonial satirical writings.[36] *Hindu pañca*'s letter of a widow could be read as an example of this anxiety. Degrading the picture of an 'ideal' woman could be considered as one of the strategies to overcome this anxiety.

Such provocative articles have also been labeled as indecent. A famous poet and reformer, Govind Vasudev Kanitkar,[37] wrote a review on the weekly, which was published in the issue dated 11 March 1886, pointing out only one flaw, namely

---

[33] Vaidya, *Saṃkramaṇ*, 136–137 (my translation).

[34] Śinde, *Strīpuruṣ'tulanā*, 1.

[35] Ibid., 26.

[36] Prahlād Keśav Atre, *Vinod gāthā* (Mumbaī: Parcure Prakāśan Mandir, 1970), 12.

[37] Kanitkar, Govind Vasudev (1854–1918): poet, lawyer in the high court, and reformer.

Fig. 2 *Hindu pañca* (lit. *hiṃdu paṃca*), dated 5 June 1907

indecency. Educated men and women should, however, not feel ashamed to read the articles, writes Kanitkar. He tells *Pañcaājobā* to follow the footsteps of Dickens in avoiding vulgarity, even when sketching characters with low moral values in his books, and, in fact, gives him an example of a humorous journal, named *London Charivari*,[38] to demonstrate how one could avoid vulgarity. He ends his review by saying that vulgar writings never achieve dignity.

Charu Gupta discusses obscenity and sexually coded representations that elaborate the case of Hindi literature in the United Province in her essay titled 'Dirty' Hindi Literature: Contests around Obscenity in Late Colonial North India'.[39] She argues that in spite of signed agreements, various rules and regulations for the suppression of obscene publications, the term 'obscene' has remained vague and has never been really defined. It was used not only in the context of 'pornography', but also in a broader sense, where the distinctions were often blurred. The issue of obscenity somehow always revolved around the chastity of the Hindu woman and this was apparently not different in the context of Marathi literature. The issues which were considered taboo were often related to the purity of women. The texts chosen above do not use vulgar language, but they discuss some volatile public issues, which leads to them being categorised as indecent.

The *Pañca* and the Punch

Phadke's parody of a newspaper and his mocking of different genres to address the most inflammable issues in society create an aggressive satire. Though *Hindu pañca* could not achieve the same success as British *Punch,* the old, sarcastic

---

[38] i.e., of course, the London *Punch* (1842–2002), referred to by its subtitle *'London Charivari'*.

[39] Gupta, "'Dirty' Hindi Literature".

Crossing Boundaries: *Punch* and the Marathi Weekly *Hindu Pañca* (1870–1909) 161

Fig. 3 Title page of *Punch*, vol. 16, 6 September 1849

Pañcaājobā's sincere efforts to reform society surely deserve an honorable mention in literary history. Although *Hindu pañca* and the narrator *Pañcobā* fit perfectly in the contemporary Marathi culture and society, and the *Hindu pañca* cannot be considered a mere adaptation of *Punch*, flows between these two counterparts are nevertheless evident. Apart from similarities in the agenda and motive of the journals, even a glance at the lay-out of the cover page of the later issues suggests that *Punch* was the model for *Pañca*. In the early issues of *Hindu pañca*, the title appeared in bold letters as a heading of the first page (Fig. 1).

An illustration later replaced it (Fig. 2). This illustration on *Hindu pañca* resembles the illustration on the front page of *Punch* (Fig. 3). A figure similar to the narrative figure, Mr Punch, is visible, standing on the table in clown-like attire, observing *Pañcobā* on the cover page of *Hindu pañca*. The floral ornaments framing the illustration appear on both journals. While elfish figures circle Mr Punch, small human figures appear at the bottom of the illustration on *Hindu pañca*.

The narrators of these journals share some similarities too. Both *Pañcobā* and Mr Punch have the privilege of travelling through different parts of the world and have the opportunity to witness various fictional incidents in society, which are similar to the plots in reality. Both narrators have the authority to state their opinions. However, unlike *Punch*, the issues of *Hindu pañca* from 1880 to 1887 do not contain any caricatures. The note by R. K. Lele suggests that after 1904 visuals were printed in *Hindu pañca*,[40] but given the unavailability of those issues, this claim cannot be verified.

Mr Punch, His Cousin 'Brahmin Punchoba' and the Marathi *Pañcaājobā*

The effort made to market *Punch* in colonial India did perhaps not lead to a commercial success, but it certainly helped establish a domestic market for humorous magazines.[41] Once the concept of humorous magazines had established itself, in some cases it produced its own legacies. An example of this is the periodical *Hindi Punch*. It was a bilingual weekly published in English and Gujarati from 1878 to 1930 in Mumbai by Burjorji Nowroji Apakhtyar.[42] The narrator of *Hindi Punch* carries the same name, Punchoba, as the narrator of the Marathi *Hindu pañca*, and just like the *Hindu pañca*'s *Pañcaājobā*/*Pañcobā,* this *Hindi Punch*'s 'Punchoba' puts himself in the position of a holy, sacred persona that is worshiped by others.

Interestingly, the bilingual journal *Hindi Punch* reprinted a review of its 'Fourth Publication of the Cartoons from The Hindi Punch', which was originally published in the British *Punch* on 2 March 1904, along with other reviews published in contemporary journals (Fig. 4). Mr Punch mentions in the review that he is delighted to know that his family is well represented and highly popular in India. He congratulates his cousin, the 'Brahmin Punchoba', and wishes him good luck with the reforms.

Missing links seem to be a part of the Indian *Punch* story. The Marathi *Hindu pañca* directly inspired the *Hindi Punch*, the evidence for which is apparent in the similar narrator figures. However, the *Hindu pañca*, which shares a closer relationship with its other Indian contemporaries, goes unacknowledged in this chain of events, whereas the remoter relationship with the London *Punch* is upheld with

---

[40] Vaidya, *Saṃkramaṇ*, 174.

[41] Khanduri, "Vernacular Punches," 463. See also her contribution, chapter *Punch* in India: Another History of Colonial Politics? in this volume.

[42] Ibid., 470.

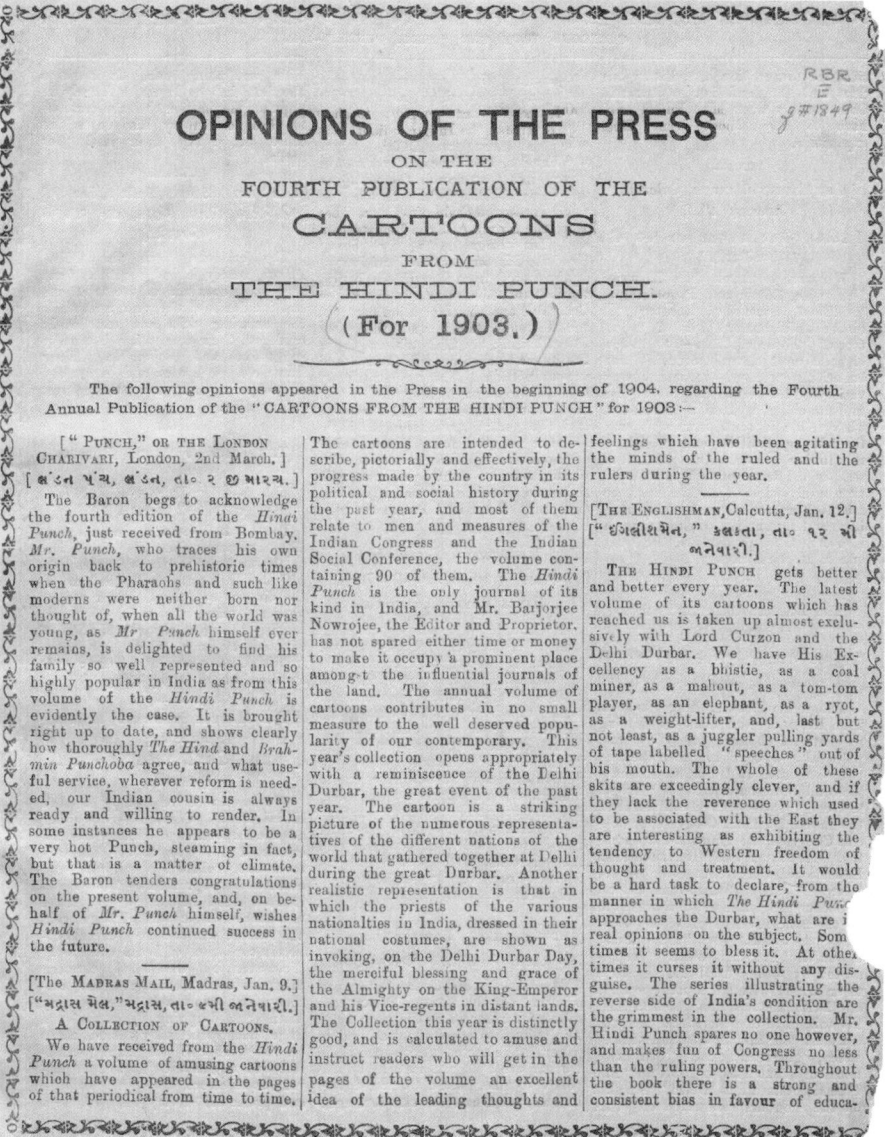

Fig. 4 Review of *Hindi Punch* in *Punch* or *The London Charivari*, London, dated 2 March 1904 (Cited in: *Cartoons from the Hindi Punch* (1904). [Bombay: Hindi Punch Office, 1905?], David M. Rubenstein Rare Book & Manuscript Library, Duke University)

pride. Such asymmetries have continued through the pages of Marathi literary histories, as shown above, and give a taste of the various biases and center-bound narratives that have to be dealt with when trying to newly contextualise a phenomenon like the *Hindu pañca*. The sheer size of this task and the lack of sources limit the scope of this chapter. However, I hope that it manages to shed some light on this long-forgotten trans-cultural literary format in Marathi.

Punch in India: Another History of Colonial Politics?

Ritu Gairola Khanduri

> Punch in India. The idea seems unpromising [...] As far as face and figure—that is to say, nose and hump are concerned, he bears a strong family likeness to his English brother; but the Indian Punch wears a turban, and has otherwise accommodated himself to 'the prejudices of the natives'. Instead of the dog Toby, his attendant is a monkey with a ring tail and a remarkably intelligent cast of countenance [...] As a general rule, I find that subjects popular in the London Punch are very punctually taken and adapted to Indian manners.
>
> Charles Dickens (1862)[1]

> Meanwhile, the London humorous weekly Punch arrived. Its comic drawings and jokes were almost our first exposure to this kind of art which distorted reality. The educated class of Indians who were in a minority and could read and write English became addicted to this magazine. Punch became a household name and a synonym for humor. Even those who couldn't understand the captions could enjoy looking at the drawings of characters with exaggerated ears and elongated noses, at obese women at seaside and bean-pole-like men. For the educated, humor in this visual form was an altogether new experience. They were so impressed with it that they came to believe that British humor was the best.
>
> Cartoonist R.K. Laxman (1984)[2]

Introduction

These two initial statements, one with its condescending tenor, the other its silence, conveniently outline the neglect the numerous Indian *Punch* versions have suffered at the hand of critics and posterity. This denial runs counter to the attention generally

---

[1] *All the Year Round. A Weekly Journal* 7, nos. 151–175 (1862), 462–469.
[2] Rasipuram K.I. Laxman, "Freedom to Cartoon, Freedom to Speak". *Daedalus* 118, no. 4 (1984): 68–91; 70.

This chapter draws on my book manuscript titled 'Caricaturing Culture'. The Social Science Research Council, Fulbright Foundation and the Institute for Historical Research-Mellon Foundation aided my research for this project. Parts of this chapter appeared in *History and Anthropology* 20, no. 4 (2009).

R.G. Khanduri (✉)
Assistant Professor in Anthropology at the University of Texas in Arlington, United States
e-mail: khanduri@uta.edu

paid to the press in accounts of colonial history.[3] Such attention to print media and official management of broadcasting colonial matters in the metropolis tends to focus on the prose of news while images, in particular cartoons, remain understudied. Whether it was the Sepoy Mutiny in 1857 or the Jalianwala Bagh massacare in 1919, cartoons picturing colonial events provoked for British readers an ambivalent distrust and empathy for the "natives" and a critique of imperial violence. Given the cartoons' sensory appeal and the transcultural flow of modern cultural artifacts, it should not surprise that with the growth of the press, late nineteenth-century colonial India also saw a profusion of comic newspapers. A large number of these vernacular comic papers were modeled around the popular British humor magazine *Punch*. The vernacular *Punch* versions appropriated the nomenclature "Punch" and portrayed their spokesman as an indigenized version of Mr Punch (Fig. 1). The local *Punch* versions varied in their production styles, in their regional reach and in their circulation figures. However, despite the popularity and wide circulation of the vernacular *Punch* versions, it is puzzling that *Punch* and not the vernacular publications became the vanishing point for historical narratives of Indian cartooning—all the more so since, despite the proprietors' sustained efforts, *Punch* failed to establish a market in colonial India.[4] To highlight this dual aspect of *Punch*'s history in colonial India—its enduring presence and failed market—is to acknowledge that imperial cultural artifacts had an uneven presence in the colony. Punch failed as a marketable product but lingered on as a form for imagining colonial politics. Thus, the history of cartooning in India poses an interesting dilemma about how to unravel the relationship between *Punch* and the vernacular versions of *Punch*.

Distinguishing between 'hard' and 'soft' cultural forms, Arjun Appadurai's analysis of cricket in contemporary India, as a unique example of the indigenization of a hard cultural form, serves as a fruitful starting point for situating cartoons in India.[5] Cartoons certainly nurtured a new disposition to politics and humour—a quality of hard cultural forms. But at the same time, cartoons also were malleable in new contexts—a quality of soft cultural forms. Casting indigenization as a 'product of collective and spectacular experiments with modernity, and not necessarily of the subsurface affinity of new cultural forms with existing patterns in the cultural repertoire' would mean that to understand the popularity of vernacular versions of *Punch* it is not sufficient to evoke colonial traditions of satire and their kinship with the British *Punch*.

Emphasizing the reception of cartoons and the practice of cartooning reveals that 'copying' was a key signifier for proximity and distance from modernity. Cartoons

---

[3] Chandrika Kaul, *Reporting the Raj. British Press and India, c. 1880–1922* (Manchester: Manchester University Press, 2003).

[4] This commercial disappointment for the *Punch* proprietors however should not be presumed to signal that *Punch* did not have a cultural impact in colonial India.

[5] Arjun Appadurai, *Modernity at Large. Cultural Dimensions of Globalization* (Minnesota: University of Minnesota Press, 2005), 90.

Punch in India: Another History of Colonial Politics? 167

Fig. 1 "Safe!" Hindi Punch, January 1904 (Cited in: *Cartoons from the Hindi Punch* (1904)). (Bombay: Hindi Punch Office, 1905?), David M. Rubenstein Rare Book & Manuscript Library, Duke University

in *Punch* and the vernacular *Punch* versions often poked fun at 'natives' and their attempts to copy British cultural practices. For example, *The Indian Charivari*, an Anglo comic newspaper in colonial India, in successive frames carefully dissected the babu's 'progress' into a failed copy of the modern British subject.[6] Caricaturing the babu's morality, his loyalty and acquisition of British sartorial taste, the full-page panel cast sophistication and progress as a cultural inheritance that the babu did not own. In turn, the Hindu *Punch*, ridiculed the accoutrements of modernity embodied by foreign-returned 'Saheb Babu'—a cigar, trousers and a jacket, a hat, a pet dog, and a white wife on his arm.[7] Although such representations flourished in newspaper cartoons, the copyable nature of the cultural form itself—the making of cartoons, and the ability of the natives to appreciate humor was hotly debated in colonial and postcolonial years. The indigenous proprietors' insistence on being imitators of *Punch* added a new dimension for understanding the place of cultural forms, such as the cartoon, which was neither absolutely hard nor soft. Appropriating *Punch*, whether in the newspaper's title or its cartoon style, implied a kinship that tested colonial officials' tools for critiquing a persuasive copy: It was a close call.

The history of *Punch* and the vernacular *Punch* versions in India offers an insight into the processes of everyday consumption and decolonization that we tend to see more easily in postcolonial contexts. Historians of empire observe that bringing the metropolis and the periphery into a "single analytical field" illuminates their mutually constitutive role.[8] Following this analytical trajectory, this chapter's analysis of *Punch* in Britain and in colonial India is also animated by current debates about the place of everyday commodities for writing history. At the center of this debate is the question whether everyday objects have a significant place in the history of empire. Erika Rappaport notes that imperial culture and its consumption has become one of the key terrains on which the disciplinary battle between different forms of historical practice is being pitched.[9] In fact the history of *Punch* and the vernacular *Punch* versions in India offers insight into the processes of consumption and decolonization that we tend to see more easily in postcolonial contexts. Beginning with a discussion of interpretations of *Punch*'s India cartoons, in the next three sections, this chapter will analyze the failure of *Punch* in India, the relationship between the vernacular versions of *Punch* and the British *Punch*, and the eclipsed history of Indian versions of *Punch*.

---

[6] "The Baboos Progress," *The Indian Charivari*, 3 August 1877.

[7] "Saheb Babu," *Hindu Punch*, 16 June 1927.

[8] Frederick Cooper and Ann Laura Stoler, *Tensions of Empire. Colonial Cultures in a Bourgeois World* (Berkeley: University of California Press, 1997), 4.

[9] Erika Rappaport, "Imperial Possessions, Cultural Histories, and the Material Turn. Response," *Victorian Studies* 50, no. 2 (2008): 289–296; 292. Rappaport elaborates why consumption of everyday objects has stirred historical debate: "This debate about commodities is about empire, but as I have said it is also about the politics of history, the uses of evidence, and the nature of interpretation (both by historians and by historical subjects). It carries with it unexplored and long-standing attitudes about the significance of material culture and its consumption."

India in *Punch*

In *Punch*, the hunch-backed and hook-nosed Mr Punch articulated the public perception and came to be the spokesman of the times. Encompassing topics that ranged from politics, review, arts, and social fashions, the magazine was a digest of happenings in imperial Britain and offered a platform to several cartoonists who have come to occupy an important place in the annals of British cartooning. Several editors in Britain and in the colonies requested permission to reproduce the magazine's cartoons. From the early twentieth century onwards, *Punch*, by then a brand name, and its ambassador Mr Punch, were effectively employed by the magazine's proprietors to market several consumer products and seasonal commodities such as biscuit tins, special cartoon editions, calendars, and Christmas cards. Mark Lemon, the founding editor of *Punch*, elaborated on the reason for his publication's popularity, which offers an insight into the enduring scholarly attention bestowed on the magazine as an important piece of British print history:

> *Punch* has made a strong impression upon the public. It was considered a wonder in current literature. Nothing so pretentious in form and material had ever been published at so low a price. It was quoted much by the press, and excited proportionate interest in society.[10]

Given its long publishing life, it has been possible to cast *Punch* as a pool of images that had an impact on the cultural imagination of satire in imperial Britain. This history of *Punch* has consistently been cast within a socio-political framework of British domestic politics with the caricatures of colonies figuring in the analysis as representation of popular attitudes and reception of the colonial others. Since its publication in 1841, *Punch* regularly pictured imperial politics and in particular, caricatured colonial India.[11] The lion, tiger, sepoys and Colonia offer visual tropes signaling how cartoons employ gender, animals and objects to formulate the human experience of colonial politics. This is not simply a process of anthropomorphism. Instead, through caricature, the *Punch* cartoons categorize human experience and produce colonial affect. This was particularly the case in John Tenniel's famous Cawnpore cartoons (Fig. 2) and his introduction of 'animal types' (Fig. 3). During the embattled months of the 1857 Sepoy Mutiny, Tenniel drew several cartoons that represented the unrest which was also termed the first battle of Indian independence. These often reproduced *Punch* cartoons from 1857 and their critical assessment exemplifies some of the sensory contours of this critique. It is possible to approximate some of this affective production when attending to readings of *Punch* cartoons. In a column titled 'Punch on India', the British newspaper *The Free Press* noted:

---

[10] Mark Lemon, *Mr Punch: His Origin and Career* (London: Jas Wade, 1870), 28–9.

[11] Fredeman discusses the neglected images of Queen Victoria in *Punch*. William E. Fredeman, "A Charivari for Queen Butterfly: 'Punch' on Queen Victoria," *Victorian Poetry* 25, no. 3-4 (1983): 47–73.

Fig. 2 John Tenniel, "Justice". *Punch*, vol. 63, 12 September 1857, 109

The last number of Punch presents us with a wonderful cartoon. Justice, in a Greek peplum, accompanied by British soldiers, mangling Hindu bodies, and with the features of revenge. In the distance there is a row of guns with Sepoys about to be blown from them. In the rear, disconsolate women and children of Hindus. The title of it is Justice. Leaving to the imagination of the reader to fill in the words 'of English CHRISTIANS IN THE YEAR 1857'.

THE BRITISH LION'S VENGEANCE ON THE BENGAL TIGER.

Fig. 3 John Tenniel, "The British Lion's Revenge on the Bengal Tiger". *Punch*, vol. 63, 22 August 1857, 76–77 (Source: The Punch Office, London)

Was the drawing designed to horrify Britons with the sight of themselves, or to brand upon them their new demon? The likelihood is that the latter was the purpose of fingers periodically manipulating Treasury Bank notes.[12]

The *New York Daily Times* also published an assessment of Tenniel's famous cartoon:

A recent number of *Punch* has a large picture, in which the state of feeling in England towards India is forcibly represented by a fierce lion springing upon a Bengal tiger, which is crouching upon a woman and her infant child. The lion is England, the tiger is rebel India, and the woman and child the Anglo-Indian subjects who have been sacrificed by the cruel sepoys. The temper of the British nation has been thoroughly aroused, and sooner or later a terrible retribution will be visited upon the heads of the rebel Indians who have shown a disposition to glut their revenge for a century of oppression and misgovernment. No one can doubt the final result of the contest in India; the power is on the side of Great Britain, and she will exert it with unfaltering resolution to regain her empire in the East, and to avenge the wrongs and indignities that have been heaped upon her by her rebel subjects. 'If any one is ambitious of making himself thoroughly unpopular', says a late English journal, 'let him by all means propose some scheme for mitigating the vengeance of the country towards the rebels in India, or attempt to interfere with the plans of the Government for their suppression and punishment'. We imagine that the most radical of the Manchester peace party will not have the temerity to raise a voice against the expenditure of money for

---

[12] *The Free Press*, September 16, 1857.

putting down the revolt in India. The roar of the British lion will soon strike terror into the heart of the Bengal tiger.[13]

The lion, tiger, sepoys and Colonia offer visual tropes signaling how cartoons employ gender, animals and objects to formulate the human experience of colonial politics. This is not simply a process of anthropomorphizing. Instead, through caricature, the Punch cartoons categorize human experience and produce colonial affect.

During the embattled months of the 1857 Sepoy Mutiny Tenniel drew several cartoons that represented the unrest, also termed the first battle of Indian independence. These often reproduced Punch cartoons from 1857 and its critical assessment exemplifies some of the sensory contours of imperial critique.

The significance and attention Tenniel's Cawnpore cartoons garnered cannot be overstated. The cartoons featured in Spielman's illustrated *History of the Punch* (1895), which aimed to narrate almost half a century of *Punch*:

> Once this fine drawing is seen, of the royal beast springing on its snarling foe, whose victims lie mangled under its paw, it can never be forgotten. It is a double spread cartoon splendidly wrought by the artist at the suggestion of Shirley Brooks; and while it responded and gave expression to the feelings of revenge which agitated England at the awful events that had passed at the time of the Indian Mutiny, and served as a banner when they had raised a cry of vengeance, it alarmed the authorities, who feared that they would thereby be forced on the road which policy and the gentler dictates of civilisation forbade.[14]

These readings of *Punch* cartoons persuasively suggest that cartoons evoked sense and sentiment: terror, horror, and fear constitute the vocabulary for translating a visual form. Thus, how cartoons were read offers insightful clues to the affective register of the imperial experience.

Colonial Markets and Imperial Wares

Several letters from the public to the *Punch* office requesting an evaluation of their inherited *Punch* paraphernalia attest to the tremendous popularity of *Punch* that circulated among the British public in many forms other than as a weekly magazine. Apart from its magazine, *Punch* also established a domestic market for cartoon digests with various themes. These digests were advertised as suitable gifts for Christmas. Its thematic focus on professions like doctors, sportsmen, and lawyers, among other professions, ensured that the cartoons would appear to be suitable personalized gifts with relevance to the professional life of the recipient. Thus *Punch* positioned its seasonal products as suitable corporate gifts. Apart from such cartoon based publications, the *Punch* logo was used for marketing commodities such as biscuit tins. Mark Lemon touches on this aspect of *Punch*'s marketing strategy:

---

[13] *New York Daily Times*, 9 September 1857, 4.

[14] Marion H. Spielman, *The History of 'Punch'* (London: Cassell & Co. Ltd., 1895).

Punch had become so popular that a strong personal interest was attached to him. A *Punch* writer at a festive assembly was a lion. Out -of- doors all kinds of things were named after *Punch*—restaurants, wine, snuff, pickles, and what not [. . .].[15]

Punch therefore became a licensed trademark that could be purchased for marketing a wide range of commodities. A cartoon aesthetic now spilled over to shape the consumption of edible products.

Letters, ledgers and records of the *Punch* archive also show that the colonies were an important business proposition for the magazine's proprietors. *Punch* got enquiries and requests for its magazine and subsidiary products from readers worldwide including the Indian subcontinent. The military personnel in the colonies formed a major constituency of *Punch*'s readers and consumers. The reply to a letter from Lieutenant G. M. Gordon of the Lahore division of the Indian contingent requesting *Punch* pictures for framing suggests not only that there was a sizeable readership in the empire but that the proprietors nurtured this relationship by responding to readers' letters and kept them informed of future prints and publications. The letter in 1914 to Lieutenant G. M. Gordon of the Lahore Division of the Indian contingent is indicative of the proprietors' interest in nurturing these enquiries and correspondences:

> In reply to your letter, the 'Alphabet' to which you refer will be reissued immediately after the end of this year as a small booklet, price 3d. The reproduction of the illustration will be considerably improved, and the pictures will have possibly a small amount of colour. In this form it would be particularly suitable for framing, as you suggest. For framing purposes, you will, of course, require two copies. If you will send us an order by the middle of January, we should be in a position to supply them.[16]

That these files of letters from readers in the colonies exist is more testimony that the proprietors tracked and recorded such requests and letters from their overseas patrons. The proprietors guarded their copyright and in most instances refused the use of their trademarks. However, permission for reproducing *Punch* drawings was forthcoming to the military during the war years in 1914. For example, the *Punch* granted Major R. J. Blackburn from Simla, India permission to reproduce its cartoons in the *Indian Ambulance Gazette*.[17] Such concessions to the military, especially during war time, were typical of *Punch*. The proprietors were keen to establish their patriotic identity and even provided free copies of their magazine for the soldiers overseas. Advertisements seeking donations of used copies of *Punch* for the enjoyment of troops overseas was often published in the magazine. It was in this spirit of patriotism that *Punch* relaxed its license fee for biscuit tins to be sent to the British soldiers overseas.

---

[15] Lemon, *Mr Punch*, 68–9.

[16] *Punch* archive, unpublished letter.

[17] The letter dated 18 December 1914 to Maj. R. J. Blackburn from The St. John Ambulance Association in Simla notes: "Replying to your letter of the 23rd ultimo, we shall be pleased to allow you to the *Punch* picture to which you refer in the 'The Indian Ambulance Gazette', provided you insert an acknowledgement at the head of it that it is being 'reproduced by the special permission of the proprietors of *Punch*'."

The *Punch* proprietor's eagerness to organize the magazine for its soldiers overseas, while being a patriotic gesture, also needs to be seen against its larger concern with the colonies as viable and potential markets. Toward the end of the nineteenth and the first decade of the twentieth century the British *Punch* proprietors in London, Evans and Agnew, recognized the colonies, in particular India, as a promising market for their publication. *Punch* proprietors had long noticed the profusion of *Punch* versions in several parts of the globe and in particular the British Empire. This perception of potential markets encompassing different parts of the British Empire spawned *Punch* proprietors' ambitious plans to produce multiple editions of *Punch* and reach a global market. These plans also emerged from the realization of dwindling profitability in Britain.

In its long publishing life, the ownership of *Punch* changed many hands. Even as he recalled the 'wonder' of *Punch* and its popularity, Mark Lemon also noted that the magazine was far from being a profitable publication in Britain:

> When the accounts were examined from week to week, it was found that the number of its supporters was not enough to support it [...]. But it was an unfortunate fact that the cash received by Mr. Bryant, the publisher, for the copies sold at the office (No. 3 Wellingdon—street, Strand) were insufficient to meet the expenses incurred. Still all concerned went manfully on. Some made sacrifices, in hopes of the day of success—which they knew would come sooner or later—being then at hand. But all expenses were necessarily large, and the profits, it must be remembered, were smaller than they are in these days of cheap paper, cheap advertising, and cheap circulation.[18]

It was such financial pressures in 1842 that compelled Joseph William Last to sell *Punch*'s proprietorship to Bradbury and Evans. An added perspective of the financial prospects of the magazine can be gauged from Lemon's comment that Bradbury and Evans were an enterprising firm, but were not prepared to make any extensive investment in the way of purchase-money. Last consented to "make over the 'property' to them, upon consideration of receiving the amount of the still outstanding liabilities."[19] Given Last's experience and successful career as a printer and proprietor, *Punch*'s financial crisis raises questions about its position in the publications market. Commenting on Last's exemplary success with other periodicals prior to *Punch*, Lemon also noted:

> Mr. Last had been the printer and proprietor of several publications, circulating their tens of thousands weekly, and enjoying a remarkable degree of success for those times, when the mass of the people were but beginning to read. Even at that early date he had the reputation of possessing as extensive a knowledge of the machinery and practical working of the printing business as any man.[20]

Last's reputation was such that even Ingram consulted him and his famous magazine, the *Illustrated News,* was launched shortly after *Punch.* Last reprinted

---

[18] Lemon, *Mr Punch*, 28–9.
[19] Ibid., 30.
[20] Ibid., 14.

the early numbers of the *Illustrated News* with the same machinery that he had erected for the printing of *Punch*.[21]

From the time Bradbury and Evans took over proprietorship of *Punch*, the colonies were a place the *Punch* proprietors were eager to reach, observe, and get a grip on. India was certainly a marked area for promoting the magazine and the proprietors had made arrangements for its circulation and marketing. By 1902 India was an important and much discussed market for *Punch*. It was with these hopes that on 20 February 1902 one of the proprietors, Lawrence Bradbury, set sail on a 6 month world tour with "the object chiefly of 'booming' *Punch* in distant lands."[22] During the course of this 6-month trip Lawrence and Agnew maintained frequent correspondence, exchanging their opinions and aspirations of the outcome of Lawrence's business visit to distant lands. I reproduce two letters from this lively exchange that offer insight into the business plans and working of the proprietors. While Lawrence initiated the process and established contacts in the colonies, Agnew took steps to set the process into motion. That the exercise would yield results over a season, not immediately, was well recognized by both partners. By 13 March 1902 Agnew had already received two letters from Lawrence, mailed from Cairo and Port Said. Agnew adds in response to one of the letters:

> From the information you give it seems to me that you have sown a certain amount of good seed which ought to bear fruit next season. I am making a careful digest of your letters for business purposes, picking out what is essential; Merrie has a copy of this which he enters into his book. The copies of 'Punch' have already gone out to the Firms recommended by you, and in each case a letter from us accompanies them. By the time this letter reaches you, you will, I suppose, have begun to realise what the world is! I sometimes cannot help envying you your trip, and I often think I should like to be with you for a brief time. For goodness' sake take every care of yourself—be careful of what you eat and drink in a hot climate! I am looking forward to having a very favourable report from you about India generally. I think this is the most likely market for our goods. Do not scruple to throw in winged words about our various publications, also about the 'Punch' sets.

Thus, even though the colonies were being tested for markets there was an abiding belief in the prospects of one of its colonies—India. Not only issues of the magazine, but the *Punch* sets of themed cartoons were among the 'goods' that the proprietors hoped to export and 'winged words' would ensure that these goods would impress the various local magazine agents whose confidence and support would be essential.

Private correspondences between the *Punch* proprietors show that their enduring conviction of the profitability of the colonial markets shaped the choice of the imagery in *Punch*'s cartoons. In their correspondences the proprietors were quick to acknowledge that the *Punch* images, which earlier were made for the British readers, needed to be changed if the magazine was to be popular and marketable

---

[21] Ibid, 15.
[22] Philip Agnew's letter to Garnon, dated 20 February 1902, "Mr. Bradbury has started on a journey round the world today with the object chiefly of booming 'Punch' in distant lands, and, as he will be away some six months [...]."

in the colonies of which India was deemed their most promising market. In anticipation of approaching these new markets, particularly India, and on the eve of Bradbury's journey, certain changes were introduced every week in *Punch* to "interest our Colonial brethren". It was with this idea in mind that the end of 1901 saw a 'charming' cartoon by Bernard Partridge in which Britannia is shown "dancing with Colonia" (Fig. 4).

Agnew's letter to Bradbury is explicit about how the interest in an Indian readership would shape images in *Punch*:

> I have often had talks with Owen Seaman about increasing the interest of the paper throughout the whole of the English Colonies and India, and, arising out of these conversations, I have discussed the matter frequently with Laurence and with our Publisher Merrie. Under our existing organization we send each week to an Export Merchant in the City perhaps a couple of hundred dozen copies of 'Punch' for distribution in various parts of the world—these being supplied by us to him according to the orders which he receives. He has no interest in pushing the Paper, and we have no opportunity of seeing where the copies go. It is quite obvious that our only chance of inducing people in the Colonies to take an interest in 'Punch' is to personally visit all those who are wholesale distributors of papers throughout the Colonies and India and endeavor to secure their interest by allowing them in future to have, for a period to be agreed upon, their copies of 'Punch' 'on sale'. This is the simplest and the most direct way of increasing our circulation, and the only risk we should run around would be a probable increase in the number of returned copies of 'Punch' for the period during which we grant this privilege. We feel very strongly that this scheme can be rendered successful only by the personal influence of a Representative of 'Punch'—and I suggest the firm should send out Lawrence for this purpose. I want you to thoroughly understand that it is impossible to make a cut and dried scheme: it is pure speculation whether the Colonies, in spite of this rapidly growing Imperialistic idea, can be made to take a substantial interest in 'Punch', but in any case a visit can do us no possible harm, and may do us a great deal of good. If you approve of the general idea, we will at once take steps to carry out such details as can be settled here before the journey begins. Directly Lawrence leaves England we should endeavor each week to introduce something into the paper which might interest our Colonial brethren; and it was really with this idea in view that we introduced at the end of the year a charming Cartoon by Bernard Partridge, in which Britannia is shown dancing with Colonia. I mentioned the matter to George yesterday, and he considered the scheme an excellent one, and the business risk one which was well worth running. I may mention that the scheme was suggested by me to Lawrence, who is, not unnaturally very keen to go: he is ambitious to run 'Punch' for all it is worth, and I am sure he can carry out this job successfully. It is possible that his visit might influence the sale of 'The First Fifty Years of Punch', and we should propose to ask the Clarke Company to make suggestions to us in reference to this.

This correspondence and others from the *Punch* archive offer a new perspective for the framing of the imagery and representations of the colonies in *Punch*. While the colonies were referred to as a cluster of markets, it was embodied specifically in terms of the market the proprietors thought would potentially yield more enthusiasm and profit—India. The *Punch* proprietors thus imagined a visual content that would be conducive to a readership in colonial India: *Britannia embracing Colonia* was one such composition. Such private discussions over the visual content of *Punch* brings to the fore the collective nature and politics of visual production. While the cartoon *Britannia embracing Colonia*, bears the style of Bernard Partridge, it has to be seen against the context of a strategic collaboration of business and artistic

Punch in India: Another History of Colonial Politics?

Fig. 4 Partners. Britannia: "After all, my dear, we needn't trouble ourselves about the others." Colonia: "No; We can always dance together, you and I!" Cartoon by Bernard Partridge, *Punch*, vol. 121, 25 December 1901, 453

interests in which the representation of colonies became a central marketing concern. *Britain embracing Colonia* was also a route for *Punch* to embrace and court the Indian readership.

The shift in *Punch* images of colonial India at this time is starkly apparent when compared to Tenniel's Cawnpore cartoons, such as the 'Wrath of the British Lion' (Fig. 2). Such depictions of the Indian colony, as well as of the 1857 revolt, in *Punch* need also to be seen against the context of the domestic market that *Punch* was addressing. The shift in imagery marks a shift in market. Toward the end of Bradbury's long overseas tour, what seemed in earlier exchanges a confidence in the Indian market was tempered when doubts of the salability of *Punch* seemed to surface. As Agnew's explicitly wrote in the above quote:

> [i]t is impossible to make a cut and dried scheme: it is pure speculation whether the Colonies, inspite of this rapidly growing Imperialistic idea, can be made to take a substantial interest in 'Punch'.

Why did the initial confidence in the 'cut and dried' scheme give way to a shaky confidence? A possible challenge to *Punch* in colonial India may have emerged from the popularity of the regional variety of vernacular *Punch* versions. Such variation in terms of linguistic and local politics addressed in the regional *Punch* versions may have posed an insurmountable challenge to the proprietors' plans for marketing a single English edition to the entire colony. The lingering doubts over the force of the 'imperialistic idea' in making *Punch* an essential part of the colonial milieu are an important indication and acknowledgement of the unevenness of the cultural force of imperialism. This unevenness in turn draws attention to the force of local politics that was central to the proliferation of *Punch* versions in colonial India. The power of imperialism as a cultural force thrived as a 'cut and dried idea', but it did not eventually convince the proprietors of *Punch* (and probably other businesses too) whose stakes in the Empire were calibrated through commodities, markets, financial gains and losses. However, despite their shaky prognosis, India was a business risk *Punch* was willing to attempt. Their ambivalence and weighed risk can be gauged from a final assessment that Lawrence's explorations would certainly 'not lead to a loss if not a gain'. Thereafter, with similar goals in mind, Agnew visited India in 1910, as well as in 1914. As an incentive for effective marketing, the proprietors promised a 'sale' price for the personal copies of *Punch* issues for the local agents—wholesale distributors who would market the magazine.

The Eclipsed History of the Indian Punches

As early as 1857 *Punch* proclaimed its exalted status by citing its influence and role as a model for political satire in Europe and elsewhere. This awareness was made public in a short article titled 'Progress of civilization':

> There is an imitation of *Punch* regularly published at Turin. There is to be a *Punch*, also, in St. Petersburgh. The latter at all events will be a novelty, though we can hardly understand 'Wit dancing a hornpipe in fetters'. Our vanity will not allow us to believe that *Punch* will be any the better for being 'bound in Russia', and for having clasps put by the Censorship to

each volume. However the two facts above are highly promising. As the world grows more civilized, we shall next hear of *Punch* appearing, as second *Pasquin* at Rome, or at Naples, perhaps; and who knows but we may yet see a *Punch* in Paris.[23]

Not yet anticipated by the *Punch* proprietors in the 1850s, the magazine was soon to make its appearance in colonial India in Urdu as the *Avadh Punch* (1877), followed by numerous versions in Urdu, Hindi and Gujarati. Ruminating on the impossibility of *Punch*, its local versions and the Anglo comic newspapers such as the *Delhi Sketch Book* and the *Indian Punch* that were already in circulation, Charles Dickens noted the cultural gap between the Asiatic and British sense of humor:

> A professed jester must surely be out of place among a people who have but little turn for comedy. The Asiatic temperament is solemn, and finds no enjoyment in fun for its own sake. A Bengalee or an Hindustanee can laugh at what is ridiculous; but his laughter is contemptuous, and it may be malignant.[24]

For Dickens, it was not just about a difference in the sense of humour that marked the colonizer and colonized but also 'incongruity': "Fancy *Punch* among palm-trees and palaces all domes and minarets, and going about in a palanquin." Dickens surely did not anticipate the proliferation of vernacular *Punch* versions merely a decade later. However, the impossibility of vernacular *Punch* cartoonists matching the British *Punch* that Dickens articulated in his long write-up was a recurring theme.

Colonial records of publications for the late nineteenth century reveal several vernacular newspapers with 'Punch' appended to their title. Titular similarities aside, a comparison of the imagery in these cartoons shows that Indian cartoonists appropriated and adapted *Punch* cartoons to articulate colonial politics. The hunchbacked, hook-nosed Mr Punch was the leitmotif of *Punch* versions in the colonies. The vernacular newspapers appropriated Mr Punch and presented him in their cartoons as 'Mian Punch' (*Miyān panč*) and 'Subedar Punch' (*Ṣūbedār panč*), among several other local incarnations, for example in the Hindi newspaper 'Hindu Punch' (*Hindū pañc*), published in Calcutta. Some *Punch* stereotypes that had a consistent presence and symbolized the British Empire—John Bull and Britannia—were also absorbed by the Indian journals in their depictions of the colonizing British. The image of *Britannia* was incorporated and reconstituted by *Punch* versions to picture *Bhārat mātā*. Regional in their distribution and produced by Indian proprietors, these vernacular versions in colonial India mark an important moment in which cartoons became integral to political critique in the public sphere.

Colonial surveillance records list a number of newspapers that indicate the local profusion of *Punch* versions. By 1890, there were intense rivalries among the various *Punch* versions and other vernacular newspapers, particularly in two

---

[23] *Punch*, 5 December 1857, 236.
[24] *All the Year Round. A Weekly Journal* 7, nos. 151–175 (1862), 462.

regions: the North-West Provinces and United Provinces. By 1910, a number of *Punch* titles were published in the North-West Provinces and Avadh. The variety of comic-based *Punch* versions within the North-West Provinces indicates that there was an immense volume of graphic satire being produced in Urdu at this time. The 'Kannauj Punch' (*Qanauj panč*), an Urdu weekly edited by Abdur Rahim Khan, had a circulation of 500 copies; the 'Rafiq Punch' (*Rafīq panč*), an Urdu weekly from Moradabad edited by Mahmud-ul-Hasan, had a circulation of 450 copies; and 'Etawah Punch' (*Iṭāvah panc*), another registered newspaper, did not have a record for its circulation figures. The 'Etawah Punch' (*Sarpanc*) from Shahjahanpur, an Urdu daily published by Saiyid Zehur Ahmad, had a circulation of 400 copies in 1914. The higher circulating Urdu newspapers of the region were 'Sadiq-ul-akhbar'(*Ṣādiqu'l akhbār*) from Bhawalpur which, in December 1877, registered 699 copies, and 'Avadh akhbar' (*Avadh akhbār*) from Lucknow which, in January 1858, registered 700 copies.

In the midst of many rivals, the *Avadh Punch* (see Fig. 5) had a circulation of 300 copies, comparable to Munshi Nawal Kishore's popular daily edition of the 'Avadh akhbar'. In January 1878, the *Avadh Punch* had a registered circulation of 230 copies, and by April 1878 there had been a considerable increase to 400 copies. The *Avadh Punch* and 'Avadh akhbar', both Urdu newspapers, belonged to different political factions, and this aspect of their relation to the colonial state led to intense rivalry. A weekly from Lucknow, the *Avadh Punch*, was owned and edited by Sheikh Sajjad Hussain, the son of Mansur Ali, a deputy collector in the Nizam's dominions. Within Lucknow, the *Avadh Punch* had additional rivals in the genre of 'comic papers', such as the weekly *Sir Punch-Hind*, which in December 1877 had a circulation of 150 copies. Two new comic papers, which started publication in 1878, added to the competition: the 'Akhbaron ka qiblagah' (*Akhbāroṇ kā qiblahgāh*)—that is, the 'father patron of newspapers'—at Lahore, and the other was a supplement to the Akhbar-e tamannai (*Akhbār-i tamannā'ī*) of Lucknow. The subscription and circulation of these newspapers was unstable. For example, by 1879, there was a reduction in the circulation of 'Avadh akhbar' to 714 copies and of *Avadh Punch* to 320 copies. Outside of the North-West Provinces, the statement records also have brief notes on comic newspapers in Gujarat, which included the *Gujarati Punch*, 'Gup shup' (*Gap'śap*) and the *Hindi Punch*.[25] Their circulation figures for 1910 far exceed those of the Urdu *Punch* versions listed above. The *Gujarati Punch* was an Anglo Gujarati weekly with a circulation of 3,400 copies and published in Ahmedabad. Owned and edited by 35 year old Somalal Mangaldas Shah, a 'Hindu Mesri Bania', the surveillance report noted that the newspaper contained tracts of local news, public topics and was moderate in tone and locally

---

[25] "Selections from the Vernacular Newspapers Published in the Punjab, North-Western Provinces, Oudh, and the Central Provinces" (1878, unpublished material held by the Lucknow State Archive). Spellings of the periodicals have been retained.

Fig. 5 Title cover of *Avadh Punch* (spelled "*Oudh Punch*" here) during the period January 1877 to January 1888 (Source: Lucknow State Archive)

influential. 'Gup shup' was a Gujarati comic journal published in Bombay, with a circulation of 1,400 copies. It was owned and edited by Shavaksha Jehangir B. Marzban, 'a Parsi aged twenty-five'. The 'Rewari Punch' from Rewri, Gurgaon was a comic supplement of 'Sadiq-ul-akhbar'. It had a circulation of 300 copies fortnightly. The proprietor was Siyid Maqbul Husain Sadiq, the son of Saiyid Motbil Husain, a resident of Rewari. Formerly a *hakīm*, he was at the time a petty contractor in Bakanir state, where his father was a 'camel sawar'. He was a man of 'very ordinary education'—in addition to being a contractor of the district he was practicing as a physician at Rewari. The editor was Saiyid Safdar Husain of Husainpur Konal, Gurgaon.[26]

Circulation of the vernacular Punch versions was shaped by government offices, library and individual subscriptions. Postal marks indicate, for example, that the *Avadh Punch* was also distributed to libraries in various universities such as the Allahabad University. Thus, the subscription figures of the newspapers are equivocal and there were several times more readers, both women and men. In its politics, the vernacular press in colonial India in the late nineteenth century could be broadly distinguished as supporters and critics of the British Empire. For example, the *Hindi Punch*, an Anglo Gujarati comic weekly published from Bombay, which had a circulation of 800 copies, was an organ of Sir Phirozshah Mehta and of the congress moderates. It was also a municipal critic. The publication's proprietor and editor was Burjorji Nowroji (Barjorji Naoroji) Apakhtyar. The *Hindi Punch*'s distribution overseas and its republication in journals such as the *Review of Reviews*, a popular news digest in Britain and America, placed Indian cartoons quite prominently on the map of political caricature.

The rich production of vernacular *Punch* versions is carefully recorded in colonial surveillance reports. The eclipsed history of vernacular *Punch* versions can be attributed to a general disinterest in the role of cartoons as historical sources, and their evaluation as a copy rather than an original; therefore, barely a sign of modern consciousness.[27] In his assessment of those decades of Indian cartooning, particularly in reference to the *Hindi Punch*, the popular contemporary cartoonist R. K. Laxman noted:

> Though they were called cartoons, the rudiments of cartoons as we know them were missing. They were rather jejune drawings of the academic type. The cartoonist of those days was basically a painter from the art schools trained to turn out portraits of kings and noblemen and other classical characters. For pecuniary reasons he became a cartoonist. But alas, he could not shake off the stiff academic training and allow his lines the free flow that is the soul of caricature and cartoon. To add to it the ubiquitous Punch magazine style, which he no doubt saw regularly for inspiration and sometimes for copying, when he desperately needed guidance in drawing a figure, stood in the way of flexibility of draftsmanship. Even in England in those days the popular cartoonists were Bernard Partridge and John Tenniel, who adhered to a classical style with no liberty taken in drawing human features or the human figure. So our cartoonist under the influence of the Punch artists and his own limitations continued to draw cartoons without any element of distortion or caricature in them.[28]

---

[26] "Selections from the Vernacular Newspapers Published in the Punjab, North-Western Provinces, Oudh and the Central Provinces" (1914, unpublished material held by the Lucknow State Archive). Spellings of the periodicals have been retained.

[27] Brummett, in her extensive study of cartoons, argues for an "Ottoman cartoons space" that was porous. For Brummett, *Punch* images were copied, but there were also several examples of indigenous styles that displayed a "memory for various traditions." Palmira J. Brummett, *Image and Imperialism in the Ottoman Revolutionary Press, 1908–1911* (Albany: State University of New York Press, 2000), 39.

[28] Laxman, "Freedom to Cartoon, Freedom to Speak," 76.

For Laxman, imitation is a limitation. This pronounced and shared perspective about the vernacular *Punch* versions, a broad academic disinterest in the cartoon as a cultural form and perhaps the vernacular comic papers' local circulation—all combined to result in the eclipsing of their history. It would seem that for Laxman's generation of cartoonists, it was difficult to craft a narrative about colonial modernity that was plotted by images of *Bhārat mātā* (Mother India) and animal types that echoed John Tenniel's cartoons. However, for colonial editors, imitation was a strategic claim to their British disposition and ability to caricature. The editor of the popular Urdu newspaper 'Agra akhbar' (*Āgrah akhbār*) conceded that the vernacular *Punch* cartoonists in colonial India had indeed learned the art of cartooning from *Punch*. This acknowledgment came in the form of a question: with their offensive taste and humor, were the vernacular cartoons 'imitators or inventors' of impertinence? In the pages of the 'Agra akhbar', this puzzle was followed by a condemnation of British sense of caricature and humor and contrasted with a more refined sensibility of the colonial cartoons. Through this appraisal the 'Agra akhbar' turned British taste on its head. Not only had the vernacular *Punch* versions learned cartooning from *Punch*, they had achieved a higher moral standard.

Conclusion

Scholars observed the impact of *Punch* in shaping the practice of cartooning outside of Britain, and a few studies have reflected on the colonial versions of *Punch* in Tokyo, India and Australia.[29] Because studies of *Punch* have focused mainly on the iconography, scholarly attention has tended to focus on representation and its appropriation by colonial cartoonists.[30] Contextualizing this appropriation in relation to *Punch*'s commercial failure in colonial India and consumption of cartoons, points to the role of language and locality in determining the endurance of specific media forms, such as comic newspapers and satire.

To situate *Punch*, colonial politics and the vernacular *Punch* versions relationally is to discuss a network of issues about historical production, the

---

[29] Peter Duus, "Presidential Address: Weapons of the Weak, Weapons of the Strong—the Development of the Japanese Political Cartoon," *Journal of Asian Studies* 60, no. 4 (2001): 965–998; Marguerite Mahood, *The Loaded Line. Australian Political Caricature 1788–1901* (Carlton: Melbourne University Press, 1973); Partha Mitter, *Art and Nationalism in Colonial India 1850–1922. Occidental Orientations* (Cambridge: Cambridge University Press, 1994).

[30] While in the case of the British *Punch* a complete print run is easily available in many American and British libraries, the same does not hold true for the colonial versions of *Punch*. The *Oudh Punch*, *Hindi Punch* and *Hindu Punch* are some of the journals that are available, though complete print runs for most titles are not available. This lack of archival sources creates an imbalance not particular to only the *Punch* versions. In some ways it suggests the idea of the British metropolis as a well maintained and available whole, while the colonies are fragmented, unaccountable and in a sense lost to the archive and record keeping.

interconnectedness of cultural spaces that are geographically distant, the sensory dimension of colonialism, the failure of specific colonial commodities, and indigenous claims of imitation and not invention. This illuminates not only the mutual movement of images between the metropolis and the colony but also affective registers of colonial politics generated by viewing the images. Since *Punch* circulated far and wide in the colonies and in America, its cartoons entailed commentary on India. Thus, a story of *Punch* needs to also account for its presence in other places, such as Turkey.[31] Furthermore, it is important to study the processes of the traffic in images as at least a two-way process: not only were the colonies appropriating *Punch* but they provided a pool of imagery and were a popular topic for *Punch* cartoons. Focusing on both the British *Punch* and the vernacular *Punch* versions shows how cartoons became a new form to reconfigure the colonial experience. It also demonstrates that imperial cultural products such as *Punch* were not necessarily marketable in the colony. However, when adapted to regional and vernacular contexts and produced by local proprietors, *Punch*-style comic newspapers did find a market in the colony. The proliferation of multiple *Punch* versions and their regional distribution shows that creative agency inhabits even a peripheral cultural space. This of course led to intense official surveillance of comic newspapers and created an administrative need to detect embedded insurgency in them. The vernacular cartoon became suspect; it still is as cultural historical material, hence its eclipsed history. While the British could appreciate *Punch* humor, the cartoons of the vernacular *Punch* versions did not seem to them a laughing matter.

---

[31] Brummett notes that in the Ottoman press, images of imperialism and the suffering of 'fellow' Muslims in India could generate rhetoric of unity and resistance that transcend national and ethnic lines (Brummett, *Image and Imperialism*, 111). Furthermore, the image of India served to show "how complete and how extensive Britain's imperial conquest could be" (ibid., 110–111).

Part III
Punch in the Middle East

Insistent Localism in a Satiric World: Shaykh Naggār's 'Reed-Pipe' in the 1890s Cairene Press

Marilyn Booth

> Al-gāmiʿ fī īūm al-gumʿa
> Fādī wa-l-khamāra gāmiʿa
> The mosque on Friday, day of gathering
> Stands empty while the bar collects all

This plaintive line appears in a colloquial Arabic poem in the Cairo-based journal *Al-Arghūl* (the reed-pipe) soon after its founding in September 1894. Entitled 'A Load of Poetry: The Reed-Pipe's Zajal on Fashion', the three-page poem attacks Egypt's *fin de siècle* youth as a 'good-for-nothing generation' (*gīl khāyib*).[1] It is a generation that drinks alcohol, sucks up Egypt's resources, gets pregnant before marriage, fears no father or mother, never suckled on the milk of good upbringing, and rides around Cairo, especially to the Rawda pleasure-garden area, in European-style phaetons, sporting tarbushes and *zikitta*s (jackets) and no beards. It is a generation of *mōda*, fashion; the label, a European loanword, verbally enacts the invasive presence that penetrates this satirical poem.

A long and narrativised verbal caricature, this poem, as aurally created image, offers visual exuberance in the persona of the young Egyptian dandy in the street. Animated by and through a familiar vernacular Arabic mode of verse composition, this aural image strategically incorporates European loanwords remoulded in local

---

[1] [Muhammad al-Najjār], "Al-qism al-adabī: himl zajal al-arghūl fī'l-mōda," *al-Arghūl* 1, no. 2, 15 Rabīʿ al-awwal 1312/15 September 1894, 41–43; 42. By convention, unsigned or unattributed works in the journal were authored by Naggār; when giving titles and authors, I transliterate according to standard (rather than colloquial) Arabic conventions. All translations in this essay are mine. The same conventions hold for *al-Hilāl*, where the editor, Jurjī Zaydān, likely wrote most of the unsigned copy but we cannot be absolutely certain. Similarly, in *Punch*, most articles are published without a by-line, and I simply give these references by item headline. Thus, I do not give author names when there is no by-line, but neither are these cases of 'anonymous' publication.

M. Booth (✉)
Professor of Arabic and Islamic Studies at the University of Edinburgh, United Kingdom
e-mail: M.Booth@ed.ac.uk

pronunciation (*zikitta, mōda, faytūn*). It is a precursor of the visual image of Masri Efendi, the more-or-less secularly and imperfectly educated, nightlife loving, gullible spendthrift; a city street-dawdling, upwardly mobile hopeful Cairene or Egyptian (Masri, in Egyptian colloquial Arabic) whose cartoon figure will parade through popular magazines of the 1920s.[2] These later images are a visual culmination of the verbally composed (and often aurally received) caricature portraits of *al-Arghūl* and a few other Arabic satirical-colloquial periodicals before the turn of the twentieth century.[3]

'A Load of Poetry [. . .] on Fashion' illustrates and elaborates the pun inherent in the line of poetry of the epigraph above. In Arabic, 'Friday' (*yawm al-jum'a;* colloq., *yom iggum'a*) and 'communal mosque' (*jāmi'; gāmi'*) are derived from the verb *jama'a* (*gama'*), 'to gather or collect'. Friday is the day of communal prayer. The time and place of this magazine's likely readership's most publicly visible and most important gathering (symbolically, spiritually, socially) are vacated here in favour of the bar—the mosque's social and moral antithesis. The bar stands in metaphorically (as institution and as English loanword) for the community's political and financial adversary, the British government, which had occupied Egypt just a dozen years before, in 1882, and the assorted European population that had been flocking to Egypt in search of profits. Juxtaposing these two radically opposed spaces offers a spatial trope of what the poet regards as Egypt's social and spiritual demise, engendered by capitulation to European-provenance habits of dress, behaviour and daily schedule. A familiar complaint in Egypt's public discourse of the 1890s, it is rendered here in concretely resonant terms—the punning space of Friday prayer (or bar) communal gathering time.

Privileging the Vernacular

Al-Arghūl was founded by al-Azhar University scholar-teacher (shaykh) and colloquial poet Muhammad al-Najjar (al-Najjār, colloquially, in-Naggār, 'the carpenter' or even more felicitously, 'the joiner'). Introducing his new magazine to readers, Naggār emphasised its dedication to preserving and reforming Egyptian society and the broader Muslim community (*umma*). This notion of community, though, implied Muslim-ness as a core marker of Egyptian-ness, a non-inclusive vision that silently relegated Egyptian Jews and Christians to the margins of the nation. All contributors to *al-Arghūl* bear identifiably Muslim names; in a sense,

---

[2] Lucie Ryzova has studied the Efendi as a social category. Lucy Ryzova, "*Efendification!* The Rise of Modern Middle Class Culture in Egypt" (Ph.D. diss., Faculty of Modern History, University of Oxford, 2008).

[3] On these see Marilyn Booth, "Colloquial Arabic Poetry, Politics, and the Press in Modern Egypt," *International Journal of Middle East Studies* 24, no. 3 (1992): 419–440.

Fig. 1 *Al-Arghūl* cover, 1:11 (15 Shaʿban 1312). Private collection, M. Booth, Pharoanic pipers

this journal was a counterweight, if a light one in its short life and no doubt limited circulation, to the strong editorial and contributors' presence in the *fin de siècle* Egyptian press of émigré Syrian Christian Arab intellectuals (Fig. 1).[4]

The journal's title—*al-Arghūl*, 'the reed-pipe'—enunciated this publication as 'verbal-aural' and 'vernacular', watchwords of its intervention in public discourse. Bearing the image of a homegrown musical instrument associated with popular song and poetry, and rural culture, the title accentuated the journal's Egyptian-ness (though the instrument was familiar elsewhere in the region). The title bypasses the contours of urban modernity that then defined the lives of many Egyptians. The journal's cover image—its sole visual—shifted halfway through the first year from an image of Pharaonic pipe-players to a young turbaned Egyptian peasant playing his instrument under a tree, next to the river, its bank lined with reeds.[5] Though the Pharaonic musicians graced the cover of the seventh issue (Fig. 2), as of the sixth issue, the peasant and the Nile—emerging national symbols of Egypt's authenticity and fecundity—began to appear on the masthead, whereas previously there had been no visual there. Subscribers, it seems, would have at least briefly had both images in front of them, but the contemporary (or 'timeless') Egyptian peasant boy won pride of place (Fig. 3). This idyllic portrait of a space alternative to the city (not to mention the reference to Pharaonic Egypt's political power and cultural richness) seems both nostalgic and assertive, and contrasts with the be-*zikitta*'d aspiring young urbanites that Naggār's poems castigate. Yet, the lack of visual clues to a historical moment in which the peasant plays means that it can also signal contemporaneity: a different road to the modern.

This image of the artist playing an instrument in a public but non-social and definitely non-urban space hints at the likely identity of its first consumers, as monolingual Egyptians. It also intimates al-Naggār's interpretation and indeed production of an audience he envisioned. The literate Arabic readership base of the time was restricted but we must keep in mind the power of such modes in contexts of oral communication. *Al-Arghūl* would have been shared aloud in public and private spaces, a consumption pattern to which its texts refer.[6]

---

[4] One poem that bears no signature is introduced by the journal as being by a poet from the group *rijal al-haridi*. This may refer to 'rag-tag' street poets. My colleague Tony Gorman suggests it might refer to the Haredim (Orthodox Jews) in Egypt—if so, this intercommunal participation would be intriguing in this journal. [Untitled *zajal*], *al-Arghūl* 1, no. 18, 15 Dhū al-hujja 1312/ 8 June 1895, 313–16; 313.

[5] While I have a full run of the first volume in my private collection, I have only seen two issues with covers. When such magazines were bound by owners or by the magazine editor for retrospective sale, they generally lacked the cheap coloured-paper front and back covers, alas for the researcher.

[6] Ettmueller, chapter Abū Nazzāra's Journey from Victorious Egypt to Splendorous Paris: The Making of an Arabic *Punch* in this volume, refers to the performance aspects of the earlier *Abū Nazzāra*.

Fig. 2 *Al-Arghūl* cover detail, 1:11 (15 Shaʿban 1312). Private collection, M. Booth, Pharoanic pipers

What relation does *al-Arghūl* have to circuitries of satire in a globalising nineteenth century, where the British *Punch* served as a touchstone, inspiration and perhaps target for journals throughout Asia, as well as closer to the imperial centre? As the figure of the lone piper in turban suggests, *al-Arghūl* is sited at a considerable cultural distance from the cosmopolitan figurations of cartoon and text that travelled from London along circuitous, unpredictable and uneven cultural and political paths—and that would at least be recognised, a mere 9 years later, in the title of another Arabic satirical journal, *al-Siyāsa al-musawwara/The Cairo Punch*.[7] *Al-Arghūl* partakes of a centuries-long local-regional tradition of vernacular satirical

---

[7] See Marilyn Booth, chapter "What's in a Name? Branding *Punch* in Cairo, 1908," in this volume.

Fig. 3 *Al-Arghūl* masthead and page 1, 1:21 (1 August 1895). Private collection, M. Booth. Contemporary Egyptian piper

verse and a newer practice in the Arabic press of colloquial didactic dialogue while showing no directly dialogic relationship to (or interest in) *Punch* or its varied offspring and parallels. There may be an indirect linkage through the earlier and short-lived (in Egypt) magazine *Abū Nazzāra Zarqā'*,[8] or through the Istanbul-based Turkish satirical press,[9] but even those possibilities are not attested. *Al-Arghūl*'s indigenous genealogy, its genres of satire and (other) critique, and its presumed audience seem a world away from *Punch*'s London (and indeed, from *Japan Punch*'s Yokohama or *Pañca*'s Maharashtra).[10] Yet, as representative of a local tradition of satiric intervention in public politics at a moment of imperial transcultural circuitry, *al-Arghūl* does in a sense speak back to the imagined, satiric world that *Punch*, in London, is enunciating in the same decade. By viewing the two journals stereoscopically, we can see that *Al-Arghūl* also underscores ways that *Punch* partook of its own imperial moment and its own localness. If this was a local product that was beginning to reach for audiences across the Empire, those audiences were likely envisioned as being from London, mostly as servants and pupils of The Empire. In creating my own dialogue between *al-Arghūl* and *Punch*, I suggest that we attend to each journal's provinciality while also noting the asymmetrical possibilities of travel for each.

But first, this chapter considers *al-Arghūl* in its genealogical framework, sketching the Egyptian press scene in the 1890s and the emergence of satirical journalism in Arabic. Next, I explicate genres through which the magazine shaped its message and the intertwined thematic discourses these forms articulated. Both *zajal* (colloquial strophic poetry) and prose colloquial dialogues posed didactic satire, reiterating points that also surface through more soberly toned editorial essays. *Al-Arghūl*'s texts—*zajal*, dialogue, expository prose—invoke a set of themes common to the time, not all of which can be elaborated in this chapter. First, they pose an internally focused critique of society within a nationalist, territorial framework but implicitly encompass the broader community of Muslims (*ummat al-Muslimīn*) and exclude non-Muslim Egyptians.[11] Second, they construct an Oriental-Occidental dichotomy as they critique imitation and acceptance of European lifeways, with a focus on generational difference. Third, they highlight the behaviour of girls and women in public spaces and offer running commentary

---

[8] See Ettmueller, chapter Abū Nazzāra's Journey from Victorious Egypt to Splendorous Paris: The Making of an Arabic *Punch* in this volume, on Ya'qūb Sannū''s (Jacob Sanua's) series of journals. I follow her spelling of his name in this chapter and in chapter What's in a Name? Branding *Punch* in Cairo, 1908.

[9] See Elif Elmas chapter Teodor Kasab's Ottoman Adaptation of the Ottoman Shadow Theatre *Karagöz* in this volume.

[10] See Chapters by Christopher G. Rea "'He'll Roast All Subjects That May Need the Roasting': Puck and Mr Punch in Nineteenth-Century China," and Swarali Paranjape "Crossing the Boundaries: 'Punch' and the Marathi Weekly *Hindu Pañca* (1870–1909)," in this volume.

[11] In his presentation of *al-Arghūl* to readers, Naggār defines himself first as a member of the Egyptian *umma*; thus the territorial definition as 'nation' seems predominant. But the magazine's emphasis on Muslims as targets of its critical voice suggests also *umma* as the collectivity of Muslims wherever they might live. [Muhammad al-Najjār], "Taqdīm al-jarīda li-dhuwiyy al-'ilm wa-arbāb al-ma'rifa wa-ashāb al-imāra," *al-Arghūl* 1, no. 1, 1 Rabī' al-awwal 1312/1 September 1894, 3–6; 3.

on the public and discursive politics of gender. Fourth, the texts in *al-Arghūl* mount a didactic-educational discussion of right practice for Muslims, leadership of the *umma* locally and the state of the *'ulamā'* (religious scholars, Azhar teachers). Finally, *al-Arghūl* sustains a meta-commentary on problems of language, communication and/as reform, and media: on newspapers, readership, circulation, the economy of the print sector, and the viability of a public sphere. To the extent that the journal enters a dialogue on the consumption of print media and the efficacy of satire, though, it is firmly based in indigenous practice: there is no sign of awareness of what we might call a *Punch* model. The beginnings of such awareness—with the possible exception of Sanua's journals—will occur more than a decade later, with the emergence of graphic satire that gestures to *Punch*'s visuality but does not overtly dialogue with it.

In discussing at least some of these themes, I consider the partial convergence of *al-Arghūl*'s satirical targets and its audience, asking how this encapsulates the position of Egyptians in the economy of imperial relations and juxtaposing it with *Punch*'s treatment of empire in the same decade. How are the two journals' stances on the imperial relations between Britain and Egypt indicative of their respective positions in the trans-culture of late nineteenth-century imperialism? This introduces discussion of the social locations of satiric voices and the presence of personae constructed in the journals: Shaykh Naggār versus Mr Punch. Is there any utility in comparing Naggār (as persona in the text, in a continuum with the named proprietor of the magazine) as participant in the *muhawara* (dialogue) within the journal, with Mr Punch as observer, lurking behind his satirical targets in the elaborate cartoons of 'his' journal, and as speaker of its jibes?

Finally, I note briefly *al-Arghūl*'s meta-commentary on local and transnational cultures of publishing and questions of consumption, linking caricature as text to its efficacy through circulation among social locations. Does the magazine work to construct a new Egyptian subject, resistant to the kinds of world-making power that *Punch* blithely if sardonically seems to assume? Is the magazine perhaps most effective as a satire of itself and of the local expressive public sphere as a whole? *Al-Arghūl* seems to question the possibility of finding (or rather making) an audience that would respond to social critique by instigating productive social and political change. At the same time, its nostalgia for a disappearing social world suggests a conservatism of view that would not brook such change. How efficacious, then, can its satire be as social and political activism? Does the plaintive tone of the reed-pipe carry any potential blast? In what register does Shaykh Naggār 'speak back' to Mr Punch—if indeed he does?

Print Cultures, the Press, and Satirical Journalism in Egypt

Al-Arghūl emerged not only out of an indigenous vernacular tradition of colloquial Arabic humour and satire but also out of the newer emergence on the Egyptian scene of satirical journals (such as *Abū Nazzāra*) that seem closer in form to

European-provenance satirical-visual periodicals. We do not know whether Naggār was familiar with satirical periodicals from elsewhere; it seems unlikely, though if there was any link, it likely came through Ottoman periodical publications, since cultural ties between the Egyptian and Ottoman elites were close and publications travelled from one to the other.[12]

The early 1890s press scene in Egypt was animated and buoyant, comprising a range of independent or quasi-independent dailies, bimonthlies and monthlies aimed at the growing though still small literate elite. Yet journalism was a tough career path; only a few publications managed to survive, as the editor of the monthly miscellany *al-Hilāl* (founded 1892) warned in 1901:

> For journalism is one of the roughest lines of work, especially in our country [...] with the divergence of readers' inclinations hindering writers' pens and the inconsistent and clashing morals and customs, which is not the case in the European countries. Therefore, journalism has been a most perilous project here. If we consider periodicals published during the past ten years and compare their numbers to those still in existence, we find a fatality rate of ninety per cent. Anywhere in the world, you will hardly find a trade or industry with such risk. Existing newspapers and magazines—they do not exceed twenty or thirty—are mere remnants of the hundreds of newspapers or more that did not live beyond a few months. Think about it.[13]

Naggār was one person who did think about it; his journal and narrative persona had rather acerbic things to say about founders of periodicals, as we shall see.

Locally produced Arabic periodicals had begun with government-produced newspapers—first, *al-Waqā'i' al-misriyya,* founded in Cairo (1828) at the behest of the viceroy, Muhammad 'Ali Pasha, emerged from an earlier practice of publishing news of central and provincial governments in Arabic and Turkish by a central bureau known as *al-jurnāl;* then the Ottoman-founded *Hadīqat al-akhbār* in Beirut (1858); and others in Iraq (possibly as early as 1816) and North Africa.[14] Shortly thereafter appeared periodicals produced by individuals: *al-Jawā'ib,* founded in Istanbul in 1861 by Ahmad Faris al-Shidyaq is regarded as the earliest.[15]

If Egypt's rulers were in general strongly able to define and control the early press, their support for it as a *de rigueur* emblem of modernity opened doors to press

---

[12] On satire and journalism in late Ottoman culture see Palmira Brummett, *Image and Imperialism in the Ottoman Revolutionary Press, 1908–1911* (Albany: State University of New York Press, 2000).

[13] "Al-Sihāfa wa-al-'ilm," *al-Hilāl* 9, no. 11, 1 March 1901, 324–26; 326.

[14] The Iraqi newspaper, *Jurnāl al-'iraq,* published in Arabic and Turkish in Baghdad, is mentioned by William Rugh, "Newspapers and Print Media: Arab Countries," in *Encyclopedia of the Modern Middle East and North Africa,* 2nd edition, vol. 3, eds. Reeva Simon and Philip Mattar and Richard Bulliet (Detroit: Thomson Gale, 2004), 1678.

[15] On *al-jurnāl,* see Ibrāhīm 'Abduh, *Tatawwur al-sihāfa al-misriyya 1798–1951,* 3rd ed. (Cairo: Maktabat al-adab bi'l-Jammāmiz, 1951), 27–29. Napoleon Bonaparte's administration founded a French-language newspaper during the French occupation of Egypt (1798–1801) and apparently planned an Arabic one.

entrepreneurs, leading to the uncontrolled exuberance that *al-Hilāl* bemoaned.[16] Egyptians and émigré Syrians manoeuvred amongst competing political forces so their works could survive in print. Intellectuals argued for and practiced an evolving 'language of the press' as a simplified yet educated (and educational) style that would, some believed, bring the masses—potential readers—to 'higher' cultural levels.[17] It was a remarkably fast progression to the plethora of periodicals that Egyptians (and Arabic speakers elsewhere) enjoyed by the early 1890s, the first decade when we can sensibly talk of a press as a polyphonic, non-official presence, the first decade to witness periodical publication in provincial cities, that is, outside of Cairo and Alexandria. In late 1895 *al-Hilāl* noted,

> The number of newspapers published in Arabic, in all regions of the world, exceeds 200, ranging from political to scientific, literary, humorous, medical, and other; nearly fifty appeared just in the past three years. Their number continues to increase, especially since they have been given such free rein in Egypt that one no longer has any sense of a boundary where they will stop.[18]

'Newspaper' (*jarīda*) included what would later be considered *majallāt*, magazines;[19] just as fluid as the rubrics were contents, layouts, page size and occasionally colour, divisions and prioritising of topics.

One subsector of this press was that of the colloquial-satirical press, presaged by Sanua's *Abū Nazzāra Zarqā'* and political activist, orator, poet and essayist 'Abdallah Nadim's (1844–1896) *al-Tankīt wa'l-tabkīt* (1881–1882). Others followed in the 1890s. Almost invariably such magazines and broadsheets labelled themselves as serious didactic presences; they did not exist just for fun. Their combinations of generic ingredients and linguistic flavours diverged, as did their level of politeness and longevity, though most were short lived for political or

---

[16] Brummett, *Image and Imperialism*, 27–28, mentions discussions in the Ottoman press following the constitutional revolution (1908) of the 'unbridled license' of periodicals both in Teheran and Istanbul, and the anxiety that the double-edged presence of press freedom might engender.

[17] "Bāb al-maqālāt: al-jarā'id wa-wājibātuhā wa-adābuhā," *al-Hilāl* 4, no. 1, 1 September 1895, 9–17. The essay begins by noting that in the journal's first issue it had addressed the history of the Arabic press, and that it also discussed general newspaper history in 3, no. 23. This notice announces and describes the recent publication *al-Kharā'id fī al-jarā'id*, by Hikmat Bek Sharīf, '*bāshkātib majlis baladiyat tarābulus al-shām*' (head clerk in the Municipal Council of the city of Tripoli, Syria), as a book about newspapers that also inscribes the local (regional) history of the press by listing newspapers and their dates of appearance. *Al-Hilāl* 4, no. 5, 1 November 1895, 200. 'Abduh, *Tatawwur*, 6–10, mentions other early studies. On the language of the press, sources are numerous; the most oft-cited turn-of-the-century commentary on this is al-Shaykh Ibrāhīm al-Yāzijī's *Lughat al-jarā'id*, a collection of essays first published in the magazine *al-Diyā'* (Cairo: Matba'at Matar, n.d.); al-Yāziji methodically criticises many examples of usage not conforming to the classical Arabic grammars and premodern literary usage. Ironically, those who supported a new language of the press did not always recognise language as dynamic by nature.

[18] "Bāb al-maqālāt," 12.

[19] A reader writing in refers to *al-Hilāl*, for example, as *jarīda*. "Bāb al-murāsalāt: al-shaykh ahmad fāris al-shidyāq wa-adīb bek ishaq: iqtirāh 'alā hadarāt al-udabā'," *al-Hilāl* 4, no. 5, November 1, 1895, 183.

financial reasons.[20] These pioneered the satiric-didactic vernacular dialogue, a genre in which Naggār excelled, while drawing on traditions of Arabic colloquial verse. The genealogy of forms here was a local (and regional) one, specific to the Arab literary and didactic heritage. At the same time, colloquial verse and dialogues are perhaps ubiquitous as effective satires that work in print and when read out loud: among its proliferation of satiric modes, the British *Punch* relies heavily on both genres. Like *al-Arghūl*, *Punch* deploys verbal caricature, often in verse form, and exploits linguistic variation as a marker of hierarchised social identities and class and regional differences. But *al-Arghūl* and its satiric sisters did not enjoy the financial and technological flexibility of *Punch*, which was by the 1890s a publishing and marketing empire in itself, with a highly developed marketing apparatus, as Brian Maidment reminds us in this volume. *Al-Arghūl* and its like were generally produced by one person and printed on cheap paper at small, hand printing presses. *Punch* and *al-Arghūl* drew on very different technological apparatuses in widely disparate technological and commercial settings. For 1890s Egypt, we must bear in mind the financial and technological challenges of producing anything but straight-forward printed matter. There were very few visual images anywhere in the late nineteenth-century Arabic press: advertisements on a few back pages of some dailies and magazines (more toward the end of the 1890s than at its start), occasional sketches in mainstream magazines whose editors had access to major presses or more income. Printed books were rarely illustrated or visually embellished beyond simple border and title page designs. Notwithstanding the lone example of Sanua's *Abū Nazzara Zarqa'*, there was as yet no visual culture of mass-produced media in Egypt or other Arabophone societies. That Naggār, like many other newspaper producers-editors of the time, appeals constantly for subscribers to pay up suggests that there were no extra funds to be had for printing costs (let alone wood-block printing or engraving). At the end of his magazine's first year, he suggests a link between maintaining the necessary support for the magazine and its outlook, while also implicitly noting that (unlike some other periodicals) the venture remained independent:

> An entire year has passed for this pleasure-making, homegrown flute, which began in the blessed month of Rabīʿ I 1312, a month in which the one on whom God's praises be was born [...] It spent this blessed year proceeding along its route of moral and literary merit, following its path of instruction and refinement, marking out its moderate line in which it did not get into any off-key blasting with anyone, and so our Egyptian brothers from all directions converged on it and supported it with subscriptions from all over.[21]

Most magazines and newspapers of the time declared reform of society as among their leading raisons d'être. Relatively few deployed sustained satire to further reformist agendas. The colloquial-satirical journals that took on this role were also an outgrowth of miscellanies that had their roots in premodern pre-print

---

[20] On this subgenre see Booth, "Colloquial Arabic Poetry".

[21] [Muhammad al-Najjār], "Khātimat al-sana al-ūlā min jarīdat al-arghūl," *al-Arghūl* 1, no. 22, end of Safar 1313, 367–68; 367–68.

anthologies of oral entertainment genres, textualised echoes of the *sahra* or *jalsa*; evening gatherings of friends and wits who traded stories and bested each other's elaborate word-play-laced concoctions. Several existed in print in the 1890s, the best known being Shaykh Hasan al-Alati's *Kitāb tarwīh al-nufūs wa-mudahhik al-'ubūs* (the book of diverting selves and making stern souls laugh, 1889), a print enactment of such sessions that mocked social pretensions and carried colloquial usage to exuberant, mock-serious heights.[22] It may be significant that this volume was published at the printing house owned by a periodical, *al-Mahrūsa*; and journals such as *al-Arghūl* carried the 'sessional' nature of such works into real-time serial existence.

The colloquial-satiric journals existed in dialogue with each other, with works such as al-Alati's and the still existing oral sociality that they enacted, and with the mainstream press. But they did not convey world headlines as the major dailies did. They tended to be insistently local in references and targets, language and genres; there is no sign of dialogue even with European-language publications in Egypt, including local Greek-language satirical journals.[23] If 'local' could be cosmopolitan—after all, Cairo's and especially Alexandria's populations included a Mediterranean miscellany as well as various Western Europeans—it did not necessarily mean that these co-existing linguistic and cultural communities spoke to each other in print, though they certainly did represent each other. 'Cosmopolitan' was processed in the local rhythms and tones of Egypt's existing traditions of satire and sociability. If local Greeks were part of Naggār's satiric representations, the intimacy of this represented lifeworld was not necessarily sketched as communal or positive. In this, *al-Arghūl* perhaps paralleled *Punch* in the latter's satiric take-offs on scenes and dialogues that placed upper-middling Britain at the social centre, with Empire as a penumbra of collective identities to be kept at some distance, even as readers might be sought in those dispersed spaces. For *al-Arghūl,* though, Empire was inescapably local. Readers of *Punch*, if they could not wholly avoid the effects of Empire, were more able than were *al-Arghūl*'s readers to ignore them.

Genres of Instruction and Invective

Al-Arghūl's first issue was dated 1 Rabī' I 1312 AH, or 1 September 1894 CE. It lasted at least until late 1901.[24] Throughout, it featured intersecting genres that buttressed each other thematically. The 'scientific' or 'learning-focused' section, editorials dressed up as articles, came first; next, there were colloquial dialogues;

---

[22] Al-Shaykh Hasan al-Ālātī, *Kitāb tarwīh al-nufūs wa-mudahhik al-'ubūs* (Cairo: Jarīdat al-Mahrūsa, 1889).

[23] I am grateful to my colleague Tony Gorman for mentioning the presence of these in late nineteenth-century Egypt.

[24] The last few issues I have seen are dated only with the year, 1319 AH (1900/01 CE).

third, strophic colloquial poems (*azjāl*) by the editor, always labelled as '*zajal al-Arghūl* on such and such', and announcing the journal's editorial position through verse 'editorials', akin to an editorial or signature political cartoon in a visual journal. Fourth came *azjāl* by letters from readers; and finally, occasional essays by contributors, riddles, and other filler material.

Colloquial strophic poetry (*zajal*) in colloquial-satirical journals drew on Arabic colloquial verse's long history (first emerging among poets of medieval Andalusia) of provocation to the authorities and critical social dissection in a language that could assert an a priori distance from the political and cultural centre, even when its users were associated with that dominant social group. *Zajal* was not 'folk poetry' in the sense of being an orally composed collectively attributed art form.[25] Though it was (and is) often orally composed, extempore *zajal* has comprised a distinct set of highly formalised compositional and linguistic patterns and practices (which are not always those of everyday spoken colloquial Arabics) and is regarded as a distinct art by practitioners and listeners, one associated with, if not constrained by, the written word. Yet *zajal* operates in a context of diglossia where the existence of many overlapping levels of language in practice has been glossed ideologically as a binary situation of vernacular vs. classical (including modern standard) Arabic, and thus, where the vernacular by virtue of its very existence can take on a binarised oppositional or at least critical role, a linguistically signalled distance from institutions and social tranches associated with the formally trained practice of the classical language (in its own varieties).[26]

To make matters more complicated, though, poetry in *al-Arghūl* did not bespeak socio-political distance from learned spaces or the elite establishment. To the contrary, as Naggār and his collaborators practiced it, poetry in vernacular Arabic was a product of the old elite social and educational space that they occupied and sought to preserve. Although their poems drew upon a vernacular genre associated with cultural margins, they sought to use colloquial Arabic, instrumentally and didactically, in service to an imagined polity where 'proper Arabic' would prevail—it was hoped by some language reformers of the time—over both colloquial Arabic and the invasion of European tongues. At a time when the use of colloquial Arabic as a mode of national/ist expression in the press, in schools and in literature was a hotly debated issue, made especially sensitive by the fact that

---

[25] The two compositional arenas are often confused; the ease of doing so is heightened by the fact that in some Arab societies, the term *shiʻr shaʻbī* ('people's poetry') may refer to either or both. See Marilyn Booth, *Bayram al-Tunisi's Egypt: Social Criticism and Narrative Strategies*, St. Antony's Middle East Monographs, 22 (Exeter: Ithaca, 1990).

[26] For more on this with regards to poetry, see Booth, *Bayram al-Tunisi's Egypt* and "Colloquial Arabic Poetry"; further sources on diglossia are listed there. In "The Cartoon in Egypt", Marsot misdefines *zajal* as rhymed prose (5) and suggests a more dichotomised oral-written compositional context, but I agree with her emphasis on the existence of indigenous antecedents for the cartoon—though I think it is important also to consider the importance of editors' and artists' growing familiarity with European forms, possibly indirectly. Afaf Lutfi al-Sayyid Marsot, "The Cartoon in Egypt," *Comparative Studies in Society and History* 13, no. 1 (January 1971): 2–15; 5.

certain British colonial officials advocated its use in lieu of classical Arabic, Naggār and his cohort deployed a carefully cleaned-up colloquial in the service of their didactic mission of conservative reform. A politics of language use the structured periodical's outlook: colloquial to assert a local and critical presence, and to educate the uneducated, but ultimately in the service of a nation of speakers of the classical tongue (in its rapidly-evolving modern version).

Some colloquial poems of the time echo the formal organisation of the classical Arabic *qasīda*, especially in moving from one theme to another and occasionally even preserving monorhyme. But they also have their own internal logic. Generally, *zajal*s in *al-Arghūl* blend overtly didactic frame commentary with narrative, creating an anecdotal vignette of a caricatured individual through physical description and narrated action. The poem concludes with a moral and—if by a contributor— calls on 'the Shaykh Joiner' to persevere in his repair of society. Thus, the narrative persona of the editor hovers over the entire journal—poetry by contributors, as well as those signed by the editor, and the dialogues in which this persona appears.

Poetry and prose in *al-Arghūl* voiced sustained critique of *fin de siècle* Egyptian society, picturing urban Egypt as caught in whirlwinds of Europeanist longings, thus vulnerable to the political and cultural asymmetries of European imperialism, represented as stripping the local populace of its collective and individual status as morally sober subjects. Caricature and satire produced these striking verbal images. But satire was often embedded in *shakwā*, 'plaint', a prevalent tonal pattern in oral traditions of verse and song composition, particularly the *mawwāl*, and taken on by *zajal* as a motif that could easily turn political. The very terminology of *zajal* gave it critical satirical purchase. The word *himl* (cargo, load, burden) was used conventionally in titles: *himl zajal*, a load of *zajal*. Introducing a poem sent in by an army officer, the editor comments, 'It's a burden like the counsel it bears, resting lightly on souls and weighing heavily on ignorant scowlers'.[27]

Like others, Naggār not only published *azjāl* in his own periodical and held *zajal*-salons in a café, but also published a collection of his poems, announced in the magazine and offered to subscribers, comprising poems previously published in the magazine. This concentrated *al-Arghūl*'s satirical critical presence in one slim volume.[28] It thus created an 'instant archive' distilling Naggār's social repair work for a longer-term audience—as *Punch* did with its republished volumes, albeit in a much more ambitious and longer-lasting marketing presence, as Maidment notes.

---

[27] 'Abd al-Majīd, officer in the camel corp [*zābit bi'l-hajjāna*], [Untitled *zajal*], *al-Arghūl* 1, no. 8, 1 Rajab 1312/28 December 1894, 138–40; 138.

[28] In traditional form, rather than a title as such, the title page says: 'This is the collection of *azjāl* composed by he who is ample in merits, and wondrous as exemplar, the fine professor and excellent human being, possessor of honour and respect, Shaykh Muhammad Naggār, may God gratify the days with his presence and not prohibit people from enjoying his merit and generosity'. (Cairo: The Literary Press, Old Greens Market, 1318 AH/1898/99 CE). First signature of the *azjāl* collection.

A study of caricature in select British and American periodicals (including *Punch*) suggests that '[c]aricature [is] [...] a representation of type that stands alone. Once grouped with like figures arranged in intercourse with one another, this tableau is transformed into a cartoon situation. Cartoons consist of caricatures inserted into socially layered relationships'.[29] *Zajal*s in *al-Arghūl* are akin to cartoons but with a temporal-narrative aspect, embedding representations of human types in narrated relationships of encounter and conflict that articulate the sociopolitical and economic as well as cultural asymmetries of the society in which they emerge, while retaining the concentrated imagery of caricature.

Voices of Satire: *Zajal* as Editorial and as Reader Contribution

Juxtaposing appearances and characteristic speech patterns of caricatured population groups, *zajal* in *al-Arghūl* underscores the perceived emergence of a young and local, would-be elite, aligning itself with European presences broadly represented as exploitative of local society and the economy through an apparatus of mutually sustaining economic and cultural aggrandisement. Later in the poem quoted at this chapter's start, the narrative voice invokes the *fallāh* (peasant), the romanticised symbol of Egypt's long and vital history as an agricultural society, in contrast to unrooted urban youth.

> *Ma'lishi*, a peasant and not *mōda*
>   He's so poor, he lives in one room
> While you, Moda, are in Roda
>   The fare? You get a shave, you trim it.[30]

An especially informal variant of the apologetic-sympathetic vernacular expression *ma'lish* ('never mind') contrasts the peasant's space with a derisive reference to the fashionable urban watering-hole of the hapless young, and to Moda, Fashion Personified, who stands in for Naggār's target. That *mōda*, derived from Italian, intensifies the juxtaposition. There is an interesting gender inversion here: Moda is feminine, and so literally the line reads: 'You, girl, Moda, are in Roda'; and yet the word play in the next hemistich suggests a masculine subject, alluding to shaving off the beard as the price of appearing in the Euro-entertainment zone.[31] And there are layers of word play here: the shaving (and consequent erasure of adult male Muslim identity); the notion of 'getting nicked' or financially ripped off; and also perhaps a notion of getting hurt. Through colloquial usages, a complex image of

---

[29] Martha Banta, *Barbaric Intercourse: Caricature and the Culture of Conduct, 1841–1936* (Chicago: University of Chicago Press, 2003), 4.
[30] [al-Najjār], "Al-qism al-adabī: himl zajal al-arghūl fī'l-moda," 43.
[31] Grammatically, the *sukūn* over the verbs here suggest masculine gender (*bti'liq* rather than *bti'liqi*).

the hapless, beardless (vulnerable, seducible) youth—and perhaps the young woman of fashion—is posed, rootlessly inhabiting fashionable Roda, while the 'real Egyptian'—the peasant—moves between his soil and his single room. Typically, the narrator is the straight man (always male), the editor-reformer, woeful and angry at his society, yet perhaps open to temptation, for he is both repentant and self-righteous:

> O my Lord! Guide me to the useful
> > I've returned from my lower self's longings
> I study my books and review
> > I've got love for my homeland and reverence.[32]

The minor note of self-mockery here hints at the narrating persona's stance and social location as both distanced from and perilously intimate with the targets he lambastes. In this, he echoes a long-attested picaresque structure in Arabic letters: the trickster figure and his shadow or semi-double, the narrator who bemoans and yet shares in the trickster's world (a structure under revival in the 1890s for social critical purposes).[33] In a sense, the persona in these poems (and the dialogues) parallels Mr Punch, both inside the text as observer and interlocutor and yet directly addressing and scrutinising the reader (as Prabhat Kumar mentions, too, in this volume)—and thereby suggesting the convergence of reader and satirised target.

*Zajal*s in *al-Arghūl* almost invariably focus on human types, offering a narrative of longing and dissipation emerging from associations across social boundaries that the magazine's narrating persona would rather preserve:

> Misfortunes start when Shaykh So-and-so chums
> > With the guy on the street or natty efendi
> The first pity's when he teaches him pronto
> > To imbibe cigs and fine drinks.[34]

This stanza highlights the punning capabilities of verbal caricature. *Sharāb* (beverage) can also be read as *shurrāb*, 'tassel' (on the fez) or 'stockings' (with *nidīf* in its basic meaning as 'clean' as well as one colloquial extension as 'fine' or 'high class'), whereby the image doubly satirises the Europeanised efendi as a figure of surface appearance as well as morally suspect behaviour. The poor shaykh, trying to participate in this fast urban life, becomes a caricature of the dignified cultural role that his title ought to encapsulate—a reversal signalled by the repeated use of the verb 'to teach', which ought to be reserved for the shaykh's traditional role. Of course, here the shaykh is the taught rather than the teacher, not subject but rather object of the new ways invading Egypt's culture.

> He'll teach him jokes and they'll do racy rhymed banter
> > The shaykh's now an oh-so-fine scoffer

---

[32] [al-Najjār], "Al-qism al-adabī: himl zajal al-arghūl fī'l-moda," 43.

[33] See Booth, *Bayram al-Tunisi's Egypt,* on the satirical *maqāma* and its trickster figure.

[34] [Muhammad al-Najjār], "Al-qism al-adabī: zajal al-arghūl fī al-sarmāha," *Al-Arghūl* 1, no. 3, 1 Rabīʿ al-thānī 1312/1 October 1894, 61–63; 61.

In the parlours of punning his turban's soiled,
    Amongst them his beard's splattered with spittle.[35]

The poet-narrator now turns to the nouveau-riche country boy, continuing to bemoan spendthrift ways as morally repugnant (money spent on wine, hashish, cigarettes, and sex) and as a loss of national income to 'Iliya' and 'Girgis'—stereotypical names referring to comprador populations from around the Mediterranean, non-Muslims who were often—and were perceived by locals to be—holders of legal and financial privileges accruing from association with European consulates, and who might enmesh locals in high-interest loans.

Europeanised Egyptian dandies—and young Europeanised women—performed their sought identities publicly through intense attention to physical appearance and language. Thus, it was comically effective to describe bodily surfaces by juxtaposing vernacular indigenous idioms and European terminology—and of course, colloquial genres were particularly apt vehicles for setting these linguistic clashes in play, as they incorporated the earthy vocabulary of lived experience in transition. Use of dialect could both establish a local authenticity and also mock pretensions of the 'non-authentic' westernising elite (or would-be elite) that mixed European lexica into its street language. Let's consider a narrative poem by an anonymous contributor: 'We happened upon this *zajal* by one of the fine poets and *rijāl al-harīdī*', says the editor. 'We published it for its beneficial counsels and because it accords with the journal's outlook'.[36] As is traditional for this strophic verse, the 12 stanza poem has a *matla'*, an opening couplet. When recited out loud, every stanza should be followed by the second two hemistiches of the *matla'*:

How ugly, to find lovely ugly kinds of imitation
    The guy who says, My freedom's European
In his chic style how much he subtracts and he adds
    And if you ask him, Why this? he'll say, Freedom!

How much he subtracts and he adds: alternatively, how much he lacks (or needs) and how excessive he is. The next stanza's pun depends on colloquial usage for its effect.

He told me, It's time, lad get some civilizin'!
    Leave off those antiques from olden days
Hum a new song, the new moda, do —
    Drink *mudām* with Madame and make alliance.

The very classical word *mudām* (wine) references what is insinuated here as a European import, though the word and image are frequently attested in premodern Arabic poetry of *ghazal* (love poetry) and Sufi devotion, and thus there is an element of travesty here. *Mudām* is juxtaposed with *madām*. Written Arabic typically shows no short vowels, and so the reader fills in cultural-linguistic blanks

---

[35] Ibid.
[36] [Untitled *zajal*], *al-Arghūl* 1, no. 18, 15 Dhū al-hujja 1312/8 June 1895, 313–16; 313. *rijāl al-harīdī:* see note 4.

while recognising the double-entendre couched in the language of uneven international diplomacy. The vocabulary is recognisable enough that hearers would not require much sophistication to appreciate the intertextual, intercultural satiric effect, exploiting asymmetric political and economic relations between Egypt, Britain and France, in the seductive figure of the European woman in the bar.

The poem goes on to satirise eating inappropriate foods with knife and fork, and learning civilisation by reading a little French, while remarking that 'Civilisation in Europe was absent/when over flourishing Egypt it first had charge'. Bodily habits are at the base of behavioural change: learning to urinate standing up becomes a (false) mark of sophistication, as is refusing to get circumcised so that one can pass as European, and wearing a European suit. That garb causes further restrictions:

> I woke up with civilisation—her clothes are amazing!
>   I went off at a run with my money to Muski
> I got a coat with trousers embroidered,
>   A waistcoat and two shirts Cossack-like
> I got myself a bow-tie, shoes and tarbush [...]³⁷

> But if I wanted to wash and worship my Lord
>   Or enter the mosque to do duty in prayer
> My tight long trousers bound me, my friends
>   I'm so caught, my honour's gone walking
> How can I take them off when this has been my goal? [...]³⁸

Going on to a hotel (*lōkanda*, Ital. *locanda*) for supper, this unfortunate finds himself among Europeans feeding their dogs by hand. Disgusted by this indication of uncleanliness, for an Egyptian, he reflects on the 'sullying' presence of Europeans and their practices in Egypt, declares that their *alafranka* way is irretrievably Other, and returns to the fold, wrapping up the saga with a flourish to the magazine:

> The door to civ'lisin' and right conduct is revelation
>   If you want its key you need Naggār/The Carpenter-Joiner.³⁹

Is the magazine intent on constructing an absolute divide between European Other and the Egyptian Self, a divide represented by the forlorn figure of the hapless 'civilised' shaykh? There is—as in much Arabic intellectual discourse at the time—an ambivalent or equivocal attitude toward European societies. In one area of cultural practice—the production and consumption of newspapers and treatment of newspapermen—Naggar advises his readers to take European practice as a model. Fiercely against the encroachment of European languages into Egyptian

---

[37] Ibid., 314. The meaning of *khās-kī* is unclear: 'Cossack' is a guess. The next lines mention 'a pair of high stockings [or tassels] with a royal *qūfī* [?]/and two *ildīwān*s one in each hand/and I said, who's up to me in reaching his hope?'

[38] Ibid., 315.

[39] Ibid., 316.

public and private conversation, he admires and advocates the protection of national languages that Europeans have implemented.

If moral and political aims are at the core of satire, *al-Arghūl*'s verse caricatures of human behaviours and aspirations answer that goal. Most satire in the journal takes the form of caricature, albeit verbal rather than visual, exaggerating physical, sartorial and behavioural characteristics of represented types. Targeting human behaviour as the focus of criticism, and doing so by constructing caricatured portraits of *folly and vice*—those twin poles between which some of the world's best-known satirists have declared themselves to operate[40]—these portraits move between invective and irony, activated by colloquial wordplay that yokes disparate semantic items into a common field of unacceptable, morally and politically dangerous, behaviours (*mudām/madām*). Verse monologue allows verbalisation of this irony through the speaking character's own word choices. This is most effective when the speaker is at the centre of the story, a persona who creates a comic self-caricature, as in the young man whose new European *bantalūn* trip him up at the mosque. Narrative movement occurs as the caricatured speaker learns his or her (usually his) lesson and returns to the moral compass of the Muslim *umma* and the guidance of the Shaykh Joiner.

Social Locations of Satire: Shaykh Naggār and Mr Punch

The ironising resonances in the monologue-poems of *al-Arghūl* allow readers or listeners to form their own ideas about the speaker's outlook, actively constructing the moral irony underlying it. Yet, the message is not ultimately left to audience participation; rather, it is imposed or at least clarified by the closing text. Perhaps this interpretive closure was dictated less by the traditional formal didactic cast of *zajal* than by Naggār's fears of not being taken seriously. As it elaborated its own sense of purpose and reiterated the difficult conditions of maintaining critical presence in the rough world of 1890s Egyptian journalism, *al-Arghūl* had much to say about audiences and the press—even as it published the congratulatory verses of contributors.

> Glad tidings for us come with you, O *Reed-Pipe*
>   This is how a newspaper should be
> And just as ably, I can say
>   The valley of the Nile needs your like.[41]

---

[40] See quotations from famous practitioners within the English satirical tradition, in Jane Ogborn and Peter Buckroyd, *Satire*, Cambridge Contexts in Literature (Cambridge: Cambridge University Press, 2001), 11–12.

[41] ʿAbd al-Majīd, officer in the camel corp [*zābit bi'l-hajjāna*], [Untitled *zajal*], *al-Arghūl* 1, no. 8, 1 Rajab 1312/28 December 1894, 138–40; 138–39.

Such were the words of one ʿAbd al-Magid, camel corps officer and colloquial poet. Press etiquette faintly echoed the practice of *madīh,* or formal praise poem, a convergence that poets exploited. Repeatedly, poems invoke Naggār by name or metaphorical association as a reformer and social model. Naggār was also representative of the religious establishment, as a trained religious scholar (*ʿālim,* pl. *ʿulamāʾ*) associated with al-Azhar, the state-funded university and mosque located in the medieval city (architectural and social antithesis of Roda). As we have seen, *al-Arghūl* was a forum for Naggār's own compositions as well as those of readers and colleagues writing in. It was a determinedly indigenous and indeed local voice on a publishing scene generated by transnational subjects (Ottoman Turkish, Syrian, European), as well as Egyptians of various ethnic and faith-community origins. As an Azhar-trained shaykh who held coffee-house sessions to educate other men into the etiquette of colloquial poetry composition, and as an editor and poet, Naggār positioned himself as an earnestly reforming member of a traditional professional class—the *ʿulamāʾ*, religious scholars and teachers—which he represents as vital to the national and faith community's future Yet, he simultaneously portrays the shaykhly sector of society as a liminal presence; for it is an elite in question. Once, and still ideally guarding the community's moral boundaries, the *ʿulamāʾ* that Naggār's verbal caricatures sketch enact the erosion of those moral boundaries, threatened as they appear to be by incursions of new lifeways, new languages, and new educational opportunities (the secular and missionary schools). As we have seen, these lifeways are comically yet darkly distilled as verbalised images of shaykhs in the *bīra*s, or drinking holes; young men prancing through the streets in their *zikitta*s and cravats; and women baring their faces as they promenade before crowded cafés.

Thus, Naggār's persona represented an indigenous and actively pious Muslim identity that poems in *al-Arghūl* bemoan as threatened or even near-extinct; if the ultimate villain is London, this persona castigates his local targets as playing an active role in their own demise. As a 'wearer of the turban' his persona within the text stands in for all that is *not* characteristic of the (caricatured) new status group of young men in *bantalūn, cravata, zikitta,* and *tarbush*.

In an essay published in 'al-Qism al-ʿilmī' (scientific section, or section on learned topics), the magazine's usual first feature, on 15 October 1894, the author (presumably Naggār) gave a stark warning in his title: 'In the fall of the *ʿālim* (scholar) lies the fall of the *ʿālam* (world)'.[42] The essay asserts the direct link between the status and role of the *ʿālim* and processes of governmentality:

> There is no doubt that in the fall of the *ʿālim* lies the fall of the world. For in his hands the *ʿālim* holds religion, which is what binds individuals together and comprises the soundness and righteousness of the community [*salāh al-umma*] which is preserved through preserving its religion. Religion is what gave foundation to its structure, what constructed its bases and pillars [...]. Indulgence or negligence [*al-tasāhul*] in [religion] is among the greatest causes of reversal and upheaval[43] to have impact on people; it alters the state of things, as is clearly

---

[42] [Muhammad al-Najjār], "Al-qism al-ʿilmī: fī suqūti al-ʿālim suqūtu al-ʿālam," *al-Arghūl* 1, no. 4, 15 Rabīʿ al-thānī 1312/15 October 1894, 65–67.

[43] *Inqilāb,* connoting radical if not necessarily permanent transformation; almost violent action.

shown by the news we hear, by what we witness, and by [our own] experience. [...] Not a single community [or nation: *umma*] lost its sovereignty nor did a single kingdom lose its glory nor did a single government [*dawla*] lose its honour but by going too easy [*al-tasāhul*] in the matter of its religion.[44]

As heirs to the prophets and messengers, the '*ulamā*' are those to whom 'the ruler is obliged to listen'. And finally, 'proper '*ulamā*' detest the new civilising process [*al-tamaddun al-jadīd*] whose purport amounts to nothing more than the abandonment of the sacred sources of law [*al-shar'*]'.[45] Naggār is asserting the '*ālim*'s role of moral watchdog and mediator between government and people—and by extension, the '*ālim*'s magazine's role.

In the next issue, Naggār expands on this role, noting that the '*ālim sharʿī* (scholar in religious law) has the most important (and 'most august') of positions. His responsibilities include writing 'useful books' on religion and the world (*dīn* and *dunyā*), void of mythologies or superstitions (*khurāfāt*), and furthermore, working to circulate these writings among individuals in the *umma*. The '*ālim* is to urge the importance of founding more schools and reducing criminality; the '*ālim* gets his audience to understand that increased knowledge will decrease 'the committing of that which requires punishment'. He provides ample texts to guide them in *tarbiya*, the proper raising and training of children, and helps them to exert exemplarity by acting as a role model.[46] The magazine's caricatures buttress the educational, exhortatory role of the '*ālim* in the images they propagate and in the moralising, didactic frame that reminds the audience of Naggār's presiding authority (the periodical as the new pulpit).

Yet Naggār's reminders are laced with a sense of threat.[47] His persona within the text—as poet-narrator, dialogue participant, and didactic essayist—is that of distanced critic and moral mentor, yet it is also, uneasily, part of the lifeworld of the target-victim shaykh. And it is an interesting moment when we learn that Naggār's son is an English teacher! (He publishes a *zajal* by his son to, as he puts it, 'encourage him'; it is not a very good *zajal*.) The transformations of society the narrating persona bemoans are invading his very family. His critique seems to aim for a nostalgic return to a status quo ante more than for positive change. Does the

---

[44] [al-Najjār], "Al-qism al-ʿilmī: fī suqūti al-ʿālim suqūtu al-ʿālam," 66–67.

[45] Ibid., 66, 67.

[46] [Muhammad al-Najjār], "Al-qism al-ʿilmī: sughāru qawmin kibāru ākharīn," *al-Arghūl* 1, no. 5, 1 Jumāda al-awwal 1312/15 November 1894, 81–85.

[47] In a *zajal* by a contributor, the rather straightforwardly sermonising language bemoans a loss of religion and suggests (unhappily) the '*ulamā*''s irrelevance. "Kathura al-fasād fī'l-barr wa'l-bahr bimā kasabat ayday al-nās," *al-Arghūl* 1, no. 20, 15 Muharram 1313/8 July, 1895, 330–33. This poem follows an editorial treatise—"A Reminder to Certain 'Ulamā'"—that directly addresses and censures those '*ulamā*' whom the magazine views as turning away from proper behaviour, as we have seen represented in poetic caricature. [Muhammad al-Najjār], "Tadhkārun li-baʿd al-ʿulamāʾ," *al-Arghūl* 1, no. 20, 15 Muharram 1313/8 July 1895, 325–27; seemingly attached to the opening editorial: [Muhammad al-Najjār], "Al-qism al-ʿilmī: madāris al-ʿarab wa'l-jāmiʿ al-azhar al-anwar," *al-Arghūl* 1, no. 20, 15 Muharram 1313/8 July, 1895, 321–25.

social location of the satiric voice suggest a parallel with *Punch*—at least in its late Victorian rendering? To address this question, I want to consider briefly *Punch*'s attention to Empire—and specifically to Egypt—late in the century. This provides a narrow focus: by no means do I aspire to analyse *Punch*'s temporally and spatially complex presence. The point is simply to suggest that one point of entry into *Punch*'s worldliness—and to the asymmetries within transnational circulations of culture and politics—is actually its imperial provinciality, a localness that ironically parallels *al-Arghūl*'s outlook. No doubt, grounding in the local is necessary for effective satire. But this need in itself cannot define the particular vision that local grounding effects would have.

If we turn to *Punch* in the early 1890s, when Naggār is castigating the permeation of European power—political and especially cultural and economic—into and through Egypt's urban scene, we find that Egypt is mostly absent from its pages and India hardly more noticeable. (The imperium closer to home, issues of local power in Wales and Scotland, and more so, troubles in Ireland, are more consistently present.) The 'distant' Empire is but an occasional touchstone for satirising political rivalries, a lack of interest, and downright ignorance among politicians and polity in London. To the contrary, in the early 1880s, following Britain's invasion and occupation of Egypt in 1882, Egypt had invaded *Punch*'s pages now and then. On 27 January 1883, a small cartoon shows a bent-over Egyptian, his hands out in supplication to 'Dr Dufferin', the epitome of a sleek London physician. This is not any Egyptian; it is a peasant. As in *al-Arghūl,* the *fallāh* (peasant) is Egypt downtrodden, though for *al-Arghūl,* the *fallāh* is also Egypt rooted in its cultural heritage—the reed-pipe player on the Nile bank. The good doctor, leaning slightly toward the *fallāh*, hands 'his Egyptian Patient' a slim walking stick labelled 'Financial Adviser', the euphemistic new title of the highest British official in Egypt's Ministry of Finance. On the ground are the pair of crutches labelled 'Dual Control', referring to the earlier British-French attempt to seize control of Egypt's debt-ridden finances. The figures, if upright, would be the same height; the Egyptian peasant might be slightly the taller if he were not clearly on the point of collapse.[48] This seems emblematic of *Punch*'s approach to Egypt and Egyptians: quietly sympathetic, recognising the dignity of colonised peoples (or at least some of them), while skewering the British paternalistic discourse that hardly concealed imperial ambition. In a 'private letter' from Lord Dufferin (D-ff-r-n) to the Khedive Tawfiq (Tewfik), the writer refers to the

> intense gratitude of the Egyptian 'Fellaheen' for the unexampled blessings which they now enjoy, which include the payment of the Bondholders and of an indemnity of somewhere about a million sterling [. . .]. As for those Fellaheen, who are still inconsiderate enough to

---

[48] "Much Better!" Cartoon signed H. F. *Punch, or the London Charivari* 84, 27 January 1883, 45. On the same page, "Hints from the Hindoo" pokes fun both at a provincial-colonised perspective on London and at the Londoners who cheat them and in general show no interest or hospitality toward them.

complain of oppression, the knowledge that the use of the 'kourbash' has been declared illegal should surely console them for any actual floggings they must have undergone [...].[49]

Less sympathetic (to anyone) is a mock-epic poem published a week later that re-enacts the September 1882 battle of Tel el-Kebir, the standoff between Egyptian military officer Ahmad Urabi and British (and Indian) troops that ended organised military resistance to the British. 'How Bull-Apis went up against Tel-el-Kebir: Fragments of an Epic from Modern Egypt' is illustrated by a small, mock-Pharoanic visual of Gladstone-Ra, 'Grandolman' in his enormous wing collar, pointing a hapless British centurion with frayed Union Jack toward battle against 'the SLY ONE of Egypt' and his troops 'from the wilds, and the slums, and the prisons'. The Egyptians melt away (as at the battle itself: by the time of Tel el-Kebir, the forces were largely spent), 'Grandolman' calls for the death of 'A-rab-i', and (John) Bull-Apis spouts the imperial line: 'I *must* have my trade-ways unblocked, but good Fellahs from me need not fear/King Bull-Apis fights not for booty; he means only kindness and good/[...] I mean to clear out, I assure you—as soon as I've set things all straight'.[50] Bull-Apis comes 'with hymn-book in hand': *Punch* notes the multiple ideological and institutional sources of imperial rule. Elsewhere, *Punch* mocks the official discourse that insists Britain's presence in Egypt is temporary; derides government attempts to keep imperial adventures out of the limelight; exposes euphemisms of British control; and hints at the possibly less than altruistic service of high British officials such as Lieutenant General Garnet Wolseley, who had commanded British troops against 'Urabi, or Sir Henry Drummond-Wolff, briefly High Commissioner in Egypt (1885–1887) after his diplomatic mission to the Porte and Cairo.[51] 'The Khedive's Pocket-Book

---

[49] "The Complete Letter-Writer on the Nile (a 'private' letter from D-ff-r-n to Tewfik [sic])," *Punch, or the London Charivari* 84, 19 May 1883, 233.

[50] "How Bull-Apis went up against Tel-el-Kebir: Fragments of an Epic From Modern Egypt," *Punch, or the London Charivari* 84, 3 February 1883, 53. Visual signed H. F.

[51] See, for example, "Essence of Parliament, Extracted From the Diary of Toby, M.P.," *Punch, or the London Charivari* 84, 17 February 1883, 76, and *Punch, or the London Charivari* 84, 10 March 1883, 112; "Essence ...," *Punch, or the London Charivari* 84, 28 April, 1883, 204; "Annexation Made Easy: A Page From the Future Journal of the House of Lords," *Punch, or the London Charivari* 84, 5 May 1883, 207; "Tiddy Fol Lol," *Punch, or the London Charivari* 84, 2 June 1883, 255; "Essence ...," *Punch, or the London Charivari* 84, 23 June 1883, 298; "Essence ...," *Punch, or the London Charivari* 85, 21 July 1883, 29, on how the war in Egypt has decreased stationery expenditure in London since 'when war going on no time for useless correspondence', says Sir George Balfour. See also "Something Like a Fellah!" *Punch, or the London Charivari* 85, 6 October 1883, 158; "Interviewing a la Mode: A Chat With the Prime Minister," *Punch, or the London Charivari* 92, 5 February 1887, 69; "Essence ...," *Punch, or the London Charivari* 92, 12 February 1887, 84; "Essence ...," *Punch, or the London Charivari* 92, 19 March 1887, 143–44 (on the cost of Drummond-Wolff's mission); "Wanted!—the Institute!" *Punch, or the London Charivari* 92, 4 June 1887, 274; and a single-line pun, "THE LATEST CRY OF 'WOLFF! —The Evacuation of Egypt," *Punch, or the London Charivari* 92, 21 May 1887, 245. Drummond-Wolff's mission comes in for considerable attention: see, e.g., "A la Porte!" and "Clear as Crystal; Or, All About

(A Leaf anticipatory of the Immediate Future)' exposes British pieties concerning an 'Egyptian Constitution' and the 'advisory' role of British officials, as Financial Councillor Sir Auckland Colvin tries to rein in a Khedive who has the odd idea of asserting real authority over a spectacle of parliamentary rule, but is quite content in the end with *baksheesh*.[52]

Punch's allusions to the complicating presence of the Ottoman Sultan in London's Egyptian ambitions—and the way they are entangled with French ventures, such as the Suez Canal project of Ferdinand de Lesseps—recognise both the restraining hand on London that these may exert and the powerlessness of the Egyptians, in the end, against combined if competing forces. On 28 July 1883, a Mr Punch-like figure appears in a fez on the bank of the Canal, as the gleeful 'Irrepressible One' (the Sultan) who exults in his (British-backed) power to curtail de Lesseps' privileges.[53] But perhaps from the bitterly satirising perspective of Shaykh Naggār, such distinctions and machinations were irrelevant.

Certainly, these invasions are one-way. Ultimately, in *Punch*, Egyptian usages invade London as (ineffective) markers of coercion—the kourbash (whip) and bastinado just brought as specimens from Cairo are to be used in Parliament as more effective 'Whips'.[54] Or, Egypt appears in the form of improbable dramatic productions laced with Orientalist suppositions, as in the play by Augustus Harris and G. F. Rowe called 'Freedom' which *Punch* viciously reviews for its vision of 'Modern Egyptian History', as well as its 'harlequinade-quartet' of characters.[55] In *Punch*, the Egyptian territory of Empire most often comes 'home' through local preoccupations: the occasional, gently lambasting focus on politicians' self-interested peregrinations, euphemisms, and silences. A colonial periphery that provides income and careers to young politicians, in *Punch* Egypt is but a mirror reflecting the self-interested preoccupations of those at the centre—as the magazine sardonically seems to recognise. Mr Punch, that avuncular observer hovering on the scene, does not need to dwell on or even recognise his own participation in the colonial project, in the way that Shaykh Naggār must, as an object of Britain's ambitions in Egypt and the broader European economic incursions there.

It," *Punch, or the London Charivari* 93, 23 July 1887, 29; "An Epitaph to the Memory of the Egyptian Convention," *Punch, or the London Charivari* 93, 30 July 1887, 40; "The Conventional Missionary Who Couldn't Convert the Sultan," *Punch, or the London Charivari* 93, 30 July 1887, 45; "Convention-al Politeness," *Punch, or the London Charivari* 93, 5 November 1887, 210–11.

[52] "The Khedive's Pocket-Book (A Leaf anticipatory of the Immediate Future)," *Punch, or the London Charivari* 84, 17 March 1883, 132.

[53] "The Friend,—in Need!," poem and cartoon, *Punch, or the London Charivari* 85, July 28, 1883, 42–43. See also "Approbation from Sir Hubert Stanley, &c.," *Punch, or the London Charivari* 85, August 4, 1883, 53, and the cartoon on p.55, "An Isthmian Game".

[54] "A New 'Whip'," *Punch, or the London Charivari* 84, March 10, 1883, 114.

[55] "Free and Easy-dom at Drury Lane," *Punch, or the London Charivari* 85, 18 August 1883, 76–77.

With time—as the memory of 1882 recedes—references to Egypt in *Punch* become rarer.[56] If *Punch*'s near-silence on Egypt in the early 1890s is hardly surprising, given its focus on the London scene and its shifting personae, this focus does pinpoint a provinciality of view made possible by power asymmetries which strongly structure *al-Arghūl* as well, though they are not entirely reducible to Empire. These are the uneven forces dictating that the *'ālim* is no longer centre of the *'ālam* (world); the *'ālim* who most acutely represents shifts locally and transnationally across the uneven terrain of Empire-fuelled modernity that subjects Egyptians, like so many others, to particular visions of the social that must exclude other ways of being in the world.

Punch and *al-Arghūl* are similar in that both take on a sweeping social landscape and yet their targets are socially located in the rather narrow territories of class and outlook. Perhaps both also question the reach, or the value, of their own satirical-critical presence. In a travesty of an interview with the prime minister, Mr Punch's anxious enquiry as to whether 'the Marquis of Salisbury' is too busy to speak is met with a genial response: 'Not at all [...] I was only knocking off a little thing in Egypt, settling some bother about the Afghan frontier, and reading a dispatch that had just been received from BISMARCK'.[57] The real targets of the text—aside from the government's first minister himself—are the government's face-saving use of secrecy, the cult of personality and public apathy to world events, reading habits and the profit-motive aims of the publishing business itself. The journalist has taken down a notebook-full of state secrets; but of course we are never privileged to share them. The meeting—and the article—are travesties. *Punch* in effect satirises its own efficacy as an engine of social critique—as does *al-Arghūl*. But they are positioned very differently in a global circuit of communications and power, and one indication of this is the much greater anxiety that *al-Arghūl* evinces toward the reach of its own voice. For *al-Arghūl* this is no joke.

The Plight of the Newspaper Publisher

Anxiety over the identities and efficacy of the *'ulamā'*, which I've already noted, punctuates *al-Arghūl*'s running metacommentary on the state of the press in Egypt. In the spring of 1900, *al-Arghūl*'s fifth year of publication, a prose colloquial

---

[56] I have not carried out a comprehensive survey, but the volumes of *Punch* for 1890–1992 suggest this, as do those for 1906–1908. Ritu Khanduri, in her study of *Punch* in colonial India, suggests that market ambitions may have tempered or reshaped representations of the Empire in this period, as the magazine's editors sought audiences in the subcontinent. However, it seems to me that this could have had varying effects, depending on just whom the publishers hoped to attract. Ritu G. Khanduri, "Vernacular Punches: Cartoons and Politics in Colonial India," *History and Anthropology* 20, no. 4 (December 2009): 459–86, as well as in this volume.

[57] "Interviewing a la Mode: A Chat With the Prime Minister," 69.

dialogue satirises this state of affairs. In this 'Dialogue between 'Ismat and Tawfīq about Opening a Newspaper', 'Ismat asks Tawfīq why he spends all his time in cafés arguing, rather than working as a craftsman or labourer. There is no work to be had, Tawfīq tells him.

Says 'Ismat: 'So, this wide world has narrowed in your face, all its doors have closed, and there's no longer even the eye of a needle through which work could reach you [...] by God if you open a *gurnāl* [journal] you'll be the victor'.[58] Tawfīq expresses doubt.

> Why not? [says 'Ismat]. You were originally a student, after all. You lost [or wasted] most of your life being a student—then, what's the use of the years you spent in the schools? And the money that was spent on you—every day, going where? Going to school. And coming from where? Coming from school. Your dad frittering all this money on books and clothes and other stuff till you left him clean broke.[59]

'So an education's no use unless a guy starts a newspaper?' asks his credulous friend. 'Ismat has a further rejoinder. 'So far you haven't been any use in government service or found anything for yourself where you'd earn. So this is all that's left, since these days it's what's closest and easiest. The wall [around it] is low, everyone can jump over it [and in]'.[60]

At least Tawfīq knows what a newspaper should be (and of course, this acts as didactic intervention with readers). One must know politics and history, and be able to compare the rulers of old to their contemporary likes, he protests. It isn't easy work after all. His friend has another suggestion:

> 'Ismat: *Balāsh*! Okay, forget it, don't start a political *gurnāl*, start a scientific one.
> Tawfīq: This is even stranger. No, you think a scientific journal is something less than the political journal, but editing a scientific journal is more fatiguing than the political, a hundred times more. It requires someone who is well read and writes on every subject [...].[61]

Tawfīq knows recent local intellectual history, reciting a list of luminaries who wrote for the earlier and famous *Rawdat al-madāris al-misriyya*. In exasperation,

---

[58] There's a double meaning here: the verb *ghalaba*, to conquer or be victorious, has a range of meanings: to wrest away or rob or plunder, to gain ascendancy; in the vernacular, by extension, to profit. (And a related adjectival form, also used as a noun, in Egyptian colloquial, *ghalabāwī*, means 'garrulous' and refers dismissively to a windbag.)

[Muhammad al-Najjār], "Muhāwara bayna 'ismat wa-tawfīq fī fath jarīdatin," *al-Arghūl* 5, no. 9, 1318, 137–41. 5, no. 9 is simply dated 1318, and is the first issue to be labelled with this year. If it were following in sequence, it would have come out in 1317, perhaps on 1 Dhū al-qaʿda 1317 (3 March 1900). If it really did come out in 1318, the magazine publication skipped at least 2 months, to Muharram, the first *hijrī* month; 1/1/1318 would be 1 May 1900. Early 1318 publication is likely since the next issue is also dated 1318; thus, this was probably not a typographical error.

[59] [al-Najjār], "Muhāwara bayna 'ismat wa-tawfīq fī fath jarīdatin," 137–38.
[60] Ibid.; 138.
[61] Ibid.

'Ismat gives him a blueprint for this proposed line of work which becomes a parody of the very journal in which the dialogue appears.

> The point is, you just bring out a newspaper under your name, and you write on the cover that it is a *jarīda siyāsiyya 'ilmiyya adabiyya tahdhībiyya fukāhiyya zirā'iyya tijāriyya tārīkhiyya* [Newspaper of politics, learning, literature, refined training, humour, agriculture, trade and history]. Then you fill up two signatures-worth of paper with talk however it comes to you, and you stuff into every issue a dialogue between two women or two men, or a *zajal*, or a eulogy poem on so-and-so, or a criticism of someone else. Then you call out to a few of those guys who sell newspapers, you make the price of a copy one *millīm*, and at the end of the day God won't leave you without income. The whole point is the morsel that stops up your belly and the bits of clothing you use to cover up your privates and the place you sleep in, even if it comes out a real donkey.[62]

A proper newspaper entrepreneur can put together an income very nicely indeed, 'Ismat suggests:

> Look, in every issue, you *do* talk about current politics, always with words that don't rise above and don't fall beneath. Like, if it was right now when there's the war of the English with the Transvaal, you read the Reuters and Havas telegraphs. If you see that the English are falling behind and the Boers are ahead, you write a bit saying how such a small group prevailed over such a huge one with God's leave. If you see that the English are victorious and the Boers are broken you say, well, it's the zeppelins [...] or that numbers beat out courage, and so it goes with this stuff—are you really so vacant you don't know? And then, for your *'ilmī* talk, you write up a few matters about filth and how people fall short in their ablutions. For the lit part, you go to someone and get him to write you a *qasīda* or make a *zajal* or dialogue—after all, 'everything can be got for a penny'. For the refinement bit, here you have these sons of Egypt [*awlād Misr*] who are committing everything, so you slam drunkenness and say gambling is reprehensible and awful, and you curse out the hash smokers [...]. And if you want your newspaper to become famous and make more money, have a go at some *gurnālgī* [newspaper hack] with a few ridiculous words and goad him a little with a few choice rebukes [...] so he will respond, and then people know to buy your paper so they can see exactly how you've insulted him, and whether you know how to swear as you should or whether he is better at it—it's all about making a living and it's a big fat joke anyway.[63]

When Tawfīq worries about a possible court case for libel, and 'Ismat shrugs it off saying it'll be no more than a fine, Tawfīq finally recoils in horror. 'No way, bro, I'm not starting a newspaper, even if they string me up [for refusing], because the aim of newspapers is to refine morals and discipline selves, not to teach people how to insult and swear at others, and how to act brazen'.[64]

This satirical picture may be quite pointed: it is hard not to wonder whether naming the would-be journalist 'Tawfīq' and the reference to the newspaper possibly 'coming out a donkey' was a reference to the invective-laden satirical journal *Himarat munyati*, founded in 1898 by Muhammad Tawfīq (who did face court cases)—although the fictional Tawfīq of this satirical dialogue apparently will

---

[62] Ibid., 139–40.
[63] Ibid., 140–41.
[64] Ibid., 141.

not follow in his footsteps. Yet, the dialogue acts as a self-mockery of the entire field of journalism in Egypt, and seems to put in question the possibility of a truly efficacious satirical-didactic organ.

Concern about this possibility weaves through the journal from its inception. What makes caricature, or satire, potentially effective? Naggār's opening editorial, in *al-Arghūl*'s first issue, draws on the rhymed prose of learned discourse of the time to call for the production and circulation of 'newspapers of benefit' [*nashr al-jarā'id dhāt al-fawā'id*], as one of humanity's 'most important tasks in this era' concerning *tarbiya* (training, upbringing) and *khidmat al-watan* (service to the homeland/nation). As a religiously trained pedagogue, that Naggār likens newspapers to 'the position of *khutba* orators in the mosque' underlines the seriousness with which he regards this area of production.[65]

In his 'Presentation of the Newspaper to the Masters of Learning, to Those Endowed with Knowledge, and the Possessors of Authority', Naggār declares his role 'non-political'; some may have embarked on newspaper publication out of love of self and money, he says, and all will be requited for what they do. He attacks those who, 'out of envying us, enjoy impeding [or interrupting, suspending] our newspaper, for it is rooted in their minds that to advance a nation via newspapers is a European summons'.[66] In his first colloquial dialogue, Naggār/the Carpenter-Joiner and his office boy/carpenter's apprentice converse about newspapers. Calling Naggār *yā mu'allim*, the youth refers to him as both [literary] master craftsman and teacher, a constructed identity in the newspaper which echoes through many of its texts, as we have seen. Says Naggār, 'That's a *gurnāl*, lad [...] it delights the folks who know how to listen'.[67] Through this dialogue, Naggār instructs the boy on the importance of the press as a means to create patriotic national subjects, reform behaviour, and advocate proper training. The boy asks Naggār whether he wants articles in 'colloquial talk like what you're saying now, or with the words like we see in scientific newspapers?'[68] Naggār responds that he wants them to be in learned Arabic so that readers will learn how to write. Yet the actual diction of the newspaper through its 5 years belies that aim.

'If they're so good', protests the lad, 'why do people not want to read them, and why do they say "*Dī harām* (these are forbidden), because the folks who write them mention verses in the *Qur'ān* and *hadīth*s and then people throw the papers on the ground or put things like dates and cheese in them, or paper over their windows and

---

[65] [Muhammad al-Najjār], [Untitled opening], *al-Arghūl* 1, no. 1, 1 Rabī' al-awwal 1312/1 September 1894, 1–2. Comparing newspaper oratory to that of mosque sermons, Naggār contrasts this to *sūq al-'Ukkāz*, the famous marketplace in the Hijaz in pre-Islamic Arabia where poets declaimed and posted their poems, a virtual clearing house of information but one which Naggār appears to see as too 'popular'.

[66] [al-Najjār], "Taqdīm al-jarīda," 3.

[67] [Muhammad al-Najjār], "Muhāwara bayna naggār wa sabiyhi," *al-Arghūl* 1, no. 1, 1 Rabī' al-awwal 1312/1 September 1894, 9–13; 9.

[68] Ibid., 12.

block holes?"' 'Amazing!' responds Naggār. 'Are there still people like this? It's because we have not got an education in how to behave properly. Why don't they look to the people who subscribe to newspapers, preserve them, bind them, and make them into volumes like books?'[69] This vernacular introduction to the proper handling and appreciation of newspapers parallels the earlier 'Presentation' addressed to the elite, leaders of the nation, and written in classical Arabic. Naggār reaches out for the broadest possible audience, even as he criticises the reception of newspapers in Egypt.

A contributor reiterates the same point. Referring to Egypt's prosperous class, he says, 'I see many, if they're sent a newspaper, whether literary or political, returning it even though by God they need it as the thirsty need water, and even though the cost of subscribing is miniscule. It is what they would spend on a single hour of pleasure which portends bad behaviour and may have bad consequences'.[70] Another elaborates on the impossible situation of the newspaper proprietor before an indifferent or scornful public.[71]

In a dialogue 'with a subscriber' in *al-Arghūl*'s fifth year Naggār brings together the newspaperman's plight and the question of audience. In an essay preceding the dialogue, Naggār calls attention to his periodical's positioning: it drew notice especially for its 'indigenous subjects' (*baladī*) and use of the colloquial, which 'dressed seriousness in the garb of comedy'.[72] Yet, 'what averted the eyes of certain stupid people from it was that it was not from Europe and neither was its proprietor'.[73] Highlighting the issue of cultural asymmetry as played out locally—the preference given by members of Egypt's elite to European cultural forms and products—Naggār signals ambivalence; 'if its proprietor *were* from Europe [...] and played on the likes of this reed-pipe amongst its people, they would single him out and value him, and make him a lantern [leading them] to prosperity and happiness, putting him as a crown at the head of the heads—consider Aesop'.[74]

The issue's colloquial dialogue with an anonymous subscriber complicates the question of competition amongst cultural flows, artefacts and representatives. 'We have not heard the reed-pipe's voice for a while, may its sound be sound!'[75] remarks the subscriber, and *al-Arghūl* responds:

---

[69] Ibid., 10.

[70] Muhammad Tawfīq, [Untitled Essay], *al-Arghūl* 1, no. 7, 15 Jumāda al-thānī 1312/13 December 1894, 117–20; 118. (According to conversion calendars, the corresponding date should be 14 December.) This is unlikely to be the Muhammad Tawfīq who founded *Himārat munyatī*, but it could be. This would have been 3 years before the first issue of that periodical, in Shawwāl 1315 (beginning 23 February 1898).

[71] Hikmat Sharīf, "Bāb al-murāsalāt: Lā salāmata min al-khalq," *al-Arghūl* 1, no. 16, 15 Dhū al-qaʿda 1312/10 May 1895, 262–64; 262.

[72] [Muhammad al-Najjār], "Iftitāh al-sana al-khāmisa," *al-Arghūl* 5, no. 1 Rabīʿ al-awwal 1317, 1–4; 3. (1 Rabīʿ al-awwal 1317 = 10 July 1899.)

[73] Ibid., 3.

[74] Ibid.

[75] [Muhammad al-Najjār], "Muhāwara bayna *al-Arghūl* wa-mushtarik," *al-Arghūl* 5, no. 1, Rabīʿ al-awwal 1317, 7–11; 7.

[...] It hasn't been coming out this last little while because we've needed to call in some texts our brothers were late with, these fellows who act the loyal nationalist ['āmilīn wataniyyīn] and [announce] that they're all about helping the newspapers, especially *The Reed-Pipe*, because, well supposedly, it is about knowledge and it is local/nationalist/ patriotic [wataniyya] and the guy who runs it is a Muslim[76] and a shaykh with turban who's from al-Azhar, when most folks have it in their heads that newspapers are only churned out by an efendi in tarbush or a guy from Syria who learned in Catholic schools.[77]

The subscriber remarks that 'the wealthy have no zeal for aiding newspapers' and *al-Arghūl* responds that they do so only when they fear the proprietor's tongue. The economy of periodical circulation in Egypt is described as a circulation of favours, a nepotistic and profit-driven sector wherein the timorous rich are blackmailed into garnering subscriptions by preying on the ignorant.

The dialogue presents an image of press readership that Naggār's use of colloquial would have suited. It also raises interesting questions of partial literacies: for presumably those who could not read classical Arabic could not read the colloquial tongue in writing either.

They [the wealthy] might force people to subscribe against their will, like getting the village headman who doesn't know an alif [ا, *first* letter of the alphabet] from a minaret to subscribe. They tell him, 'You'll learn how to figure out handwriting by looking, by a lot of peering at it, like So-and so who learned the prices of grain like beans and wheat from a *gurnāl* he subscribed to'. This is why the *gurnālgī* [journalist] stretches out the word *fūl* [broadbeans] and the expression *qamh* [wheat] and *sha'īr* [straw] and *qutn* [cotton] and writes these for him in huge, wide letters [...] and writes the numbers out large. So when he memorises the shape of the letter *fā'* he starts saying FŪL and the letter *qāf*, he [will always] say QAMH, and the *tā'*, he says QUTN [...]. He'll say to [his mates], 'I read in the *kazīta* [gazette, with *fallāhī* pronunciation!] the prices of grain. *Fūl* today is such-and-such, and wheat...', and so it goes.[78]

If this is terribly condescending to readers in the countryside, another point is being made here. Unsuccessful newspapers, suggests the subscriber, are focused on personalities and profit from blackmail; *al-Arghūl* adds, though, that 'there were newspapers that were good' but the 'sons of the *karafatta* [cravat] gave them no help', a jab at the westernised elite for refusing to subscribe to Arabic newspapers. The same fellow 'would spend the subscription amount a 100 times over in [the nightclub] Alf Layla wa Layla, the Luxembourg [bar] [...].' Those who do look at Arabic newspapers do so only in passing, saying to others, 'There's nothing'. In fact, says *al-Arghūl* to this subscriber, 'It has become *mōda* to say, I don't read newspapers, in fact I no longer read anything'. *Awlād al-balad* (non-elite though not poor; not westernised) who read newspapers 'are those whose fathers put them in school long ago and then opened a shop up for them; or maybe the boy went to a *kuttāb* and got a little knowledge, these are the ones who love to read. Amongst

---

[76] This could mean 'regular guy', as well as literally, Muslim.
[77] [al-Najjār], "Muhāwara bayna al-arghūl wa-mushtarik," 7.
[78] Ibid., 8.

them are some who see *al-Arghūl* and things like it, they love reading it, they say; they love to laugh at the talk it has, like the *zajal*s and dialogues'.[79]

Naggār and his contributors write an audience into existence that circulates *al-Arghūl* orally. By reporting on circuits of readers and listeners, he evokes an audience larger than those who could buy the paper. There are exchanges with readers outside of Cairo begging Naggār for free issues; for one, the village headman who had 'arranged a newspaper for us [...] whose best material I perfected [i.e. memorised]' had died; some time later, a young man had told them a tale 'that mesmerised us, and I asked, Where's the book? He said, That's a book called *al-Arghūl*'. But this *efendi* didn't possess the issues; he had 'begged them off some fellow'.[80] The story here is one of oral circulation, of avid groups of young men in the villages searching for a copy to share, one that might bring them closer to the city alleys around Naggār's beloved Azhar.

How can we use these commentaries to ponder interlaced issues of desired or constructed audience, newspaper success, the tasks of satire, and the interactions (or not) of *Punch* with local audiences around the globe? Studying satirical journals in Britain and the US, Martha Banta characterises *Life* (in its first life) as having 'never wavered in its appeal to "the best people", identified in occult ways with conduct that displayed the values shared by good American democrats [...] *Life* made it clear enough that it distrusted "floaters": people of any class, gender, race, or religion who did not fit in with the cultural fabric by which it defined civilized behaviour [...]'.[81] But if the readership really is (or aspires to be) an ideal audience constituted according to the magazine's notion of 'civilised behaviour', then why produce satire, as a mode that combines humour with critique? If its targets do not at least partially overlap with its imagined audience, what's the point? For Naggār, would the sharpest targets of his satire by definition not pick up his magazine? Is not his attack directed at those who would find it too local, too mundane, too distant from the flashy *mōda* habits they were trying to perform (and who might read *Punch* instead, as part of that performance)? After all, *al-Arghūl* would only use French expressions as markers of the satirised subject. Representing a marginalised cultural elite in Egypt (one unlikely to ever make it into the pages of *Punch*), *al-Arghūl* remains within its own very limited and monophonic sphere. Ironically, this insularity parallels the focus on *Punch;* indeed, in a sense, *al-Arghūl* is more worldly in that it has no choice but to articulate, however monophonically, the intensive, invasive, ever-present Empire. *Al-Arghūl* is emphatically not an appropriation or re-contextualisation of *Punch*: thematically, it is perhaps an outgrowth—though one with deep and entangled indigenous roots—of the asymmetric world forces that *Punch* addresses with gingerly focus on its own local world. *Punch* takes on the relations of Empire as they inform and shape local,

---

[79] Ibid., 9–10.
[80] [Untitled *zajal*], *al-Arghūl* 1, no. 17, 1 Dhū al-hujja 1312/25 May 1895, 281–84.
[81] Banta, *Barbaric Intercourse*, 3.

British-dominated interactions, dissecting the ways Empire socially shapes individual self-images. Implicitly, one of *al-Arghūl*'s duties is to remind an audience constantly of the local impacts of global events and flows, by representing their embodiment in the everyday shapes of Egyptian subjects. Perhaps *al-Arghūl* and its peers amongst satirical-colloquial print journals of the 1890s inspired the next generation of critical satirical journalists—those who would found the visually resonant periodicals of 1907–1908, as popular indignation at continued British occupation flared, at least temporarily—periodicals such as *HāHāHā/Khayāl al-zill* and *al-Siyāsa al-musawwara/The Cairo Punch*.

The Reed-Pipe and *Punch* both focus satirically on transgressions of 'rites of cultural decorum', to use Banta's phrase.[82] But *The Reed-Pipe* marks those transgressions as more than decorum—indeed, as the border infiltrations that Empire effects, bringing together politico-economic incursion with local adoptions of new cultural lifeways. *Punch*'s satirical targets are (partly) those at the top of the political pyramid who set in motion the forces that are creating changes in Egypt. These are changes *The Reed-Pipe* is loath to see but anxious to witness (in the sense of providing evidence) as a critical observer-reformer. If Mr Punch and Shaykh Joiner are not speaking to each other, they are in a sense speaking *at* each other in tracing local manifestations of the uneven yoking of their two social settings (among them, the very different circulations of their magazines). For *Punch* this means dissecting the pretensions of imperial power, but only on the level of individual performance: this is not a critique of the institution of Empire itself. But nor does *al-Arghūl* attempt that: it focuses on the pretensions—and the consequences—of attempting in irrevocably asymmetrical conditions to take on the identity of the dominant Other.

'Repair work' seems an apt metaphor for *al-Arghūl*'s vision: not reformist in the sense of forward-looking change, but rather the work of a skilled joiner in putting back together that which has snapped apart, perhaps by adding a few new pieces of wood, while realising that the whole edifice may not last much longer. Naggār as narrator is not a traveller: this magazine does not partake of cosmopolitanism in its critique of the manifestations of imperial power locally. There is indeed almost a claustrophobic space created in *al-Arghūl*. Naggār's satirical poems and dialogues—and contributions he approves of enough to publish—sketch out a world of cultural asymmetries that is recuperable, these texts suggest, only by the *ʿālim* in his vernacular robes, eschewing *bantalūn* and mounting a rearguard action against *mōda* in all of its forms—against the world represented and lampooned in *Punch*, but also against the marginalisation of the Egyptian populace in cultural discourses of the imperial centre. Naggār's commentary on journalistic efficacy recognises the unevenness of cultural 'flows' and the interruptions that define them: Will anyone but the thirsty young men in the village listen to his plaintive cry?

---

[82] Ibid., 2.

Abū Nazzāra's Journey from Victorious Egypt to Splendorous Paris: The Making of an Arabic *Punch*

Eliane Ursula Ettmueller

Among the Egyptian periodicals published at the end of the nineteenth century, there was no such thing as an Arabic *Punch*. It was only in 1907, decades after the period at stake in this chapter, that a '*Punch* proper', the *al-Siyāsa al-Musawwara* or *The Cairo Punch*, made its appearance[1] and was eventually followed, in the 1920s, by a massive flow of satirical magazines.[2] The absence of an Egyptian *Punch* version before the onset of the twentieth century, however, does not mean that there was no satirical press in Egypt, nor does it preclude an awareness of *Punch* and other European satirical periodicals in this country. The present chapter focuses on the late nineteenth century and reconstructs the somewhat complex and multi-layered story of how the Egyptian satirical press came into being. It deals, more specifically, with the first satirical journal in Egypt, Yaʿqūb Sannūʿ alias James Sanua's *Abū Nazzāra Zarqā* (1878–1911).[3] Sanua was essentially a dramatist, and tracing this history requires indeed close attention to the nineteenth century Egyptian theatre in order to capture, as this chapter will, the accommodation of drama in satirical journalism. The question of the British *Punch*'s (in this case mostly tacit) presence shall also be heeded and will be taken up summarily in the conclusion.

---

[1] For this *Cairo Punch*, see the contribution by Marilyn Booth, chapter What's in a Name? Branding *Punch* in Cairo, 1908 in this volume.

[2] Such as *Rūz al-Yūsuf*, *al-Kashkūl* and *Khayāl az-Zill*; all of these were illustrated with the most colourful caricatures.

[3] In order to make the reading more fluent, the name's transcription offered by Sannūʿ himself— namely 'James Sanua'—is used in the following. The same applies to all Arabic authors' names who published in English or in French.

E.U. Ettmueller (✉)
PhD in Islamic Studies, Associate Member of the Cluster Asia and Europe in a Global Context, Arabic Speaking Delegate for the ICRC, presently at Amman Delegation
e-mail: eliane.ettmueller@googlemail.com

Introduction

The Khedive Ismāʿīl (1863–1879), who attempted to Europeanise Egypt, temporarily provided the necessary freedom for the appearance of a variety of politically interested newspapers. One of these was *Abū Nazzāra Zarqā*[4] (the man with the blue glasses), a satirical journal, founded on 25 March 1878 (*Rabīʿ al-awwal* 1295) by James Sanua. After the fifteenth issue, published on 8 May 1978 (twelfth of *Jumāda al-ūla*, 1295), the newspaper was closed down by the ruling authorities and its editor was forced into exile. However, only 5 weeks after leaving his homeland, the author was able to continue the publication of his weekly journal. Not only did he carry on the mission he had set for himself—namely to instruct and inform his fellow countrymen—but he improved the layout of his four-page satirical magazine by adding caricatures and explanatory drawings to the cover-pages. James Sanua continued to publish his satirical journals under a variety of names, of which the main label was to remain *Abou Naddara*[5] (the man with the glasses') for 33 years.

In the first issue of his magazine, *Abū Nazzāra Zarqā*, published on the 25 March 1878, in Khawāgā Firdīnāndū Kūmbuzū's printing house at the Azbakiyya square in Cairo, Sanua, explicitly refers to the British *Punch*. He begins his first article with a description of the goals of his newspaper and of the means by which they are to be achieved. Written in classical Arabic, this prelude of Sanua's journalistic career eloquently displays the author's aim for progress. Sanua solemnly announces that he has decided to publish a newspaper which informs and removes the misery that ignorance has imposed on the souls of his countrymen. He makes a call for the (re)activation of their minds and, at the same time, speaks up for the union of all people who shall become like organs of one and the same body.

As far as the means for the achievement of his goals are concerned, Sanua praises the importance of humour (*fukāha*) for awareness-raising. He states that a satirical journal can be an important tool for the transmission of historical events and current affairs. Humour, as a consequence, must be considered the main tool but not the final aim of his publications. He insists that there has been a long tradition in Europe for people to subscribe at the same time to both 'serious' newspapers and satirical magazines. In England, he says, the audience of the *Times* also reads *Punch*; in France, the same happens with the *République* and the *Charivari* and, in Italy, with the *Nazione* and the *Fanfulla*.[6]

Here, through Sanua's own words, it becomes obvious that he had not only been acquainted with the most famous European satirical magazines of his times, but that he also tried to use their format for the propagation of his political and social message in his own specific cultural context.

---

[4] The transliteration is kept as near as possible to Sanua's original text in Egyptian colloquial Arabic (*ʿammiyya*).

[5] When referring to the journal, Sanua's French transliteration for the title is used.

[6] *Abū Nazzāra Zarqā*, 21 Rabīʿ al-awwal 1295/25 March 1878, 1–4.

Viewed in this light, Sanua's publications most certainly share at least four of the main characteristics of the *Punch,* as discussed by Brian Maidment[7]:

- Firstly, there is a continuous use of caricature. In the aforementioned first edition of the Cairene *Abū Nazzāra Zarqā,* Sanua already points out that he plans to introduce pictures *(taswīr)* into his magazine, that in Egypt there are very talented people who might draw those and that only the lack of money is an obstacle to their contributions.[8] James Sanua, as soon as he reached Paris and had the opportunity to draw and publish pictures, fulfilled this promise to his readers. From then onwards, he experimented extensively with the caricaturist genre for the illustration of his drama-like articles and thereby enabled the propagation of his political message to illiterate people. The caricature can also be seen as a substitution of the live stage of which James Sanua, the founding father of the Egyptian theatre, had been deprived.
- Secondly, from the very first issue of the Paris-based publications onwards, the option of purchasing a collection of these publications is mentioned. Nevertheless, providing his readership with a yearly collection, offering colourful and embellished reprints, seems to have turned into a habit only by the end of the year 1890. This first compilation, which unites 2 years (1889 and 1890) of the *Abou Naddara* journals, is introduced by its editor as being an answer to the loss of many journals and the eagerness of collecting them by the readership. From 1899, the yearly coloured publication got its final layout as an 'album' *(Album des Journaux d'Abou Naddara).*
- Thirdly, *Abou Naddara* had one single editor, James Sanua who drew on the help of a very small number of other contributors.
- And fourthly, like Mr Punch, the title figure of Abou Naddara, was the prominent voice and personification of the magazine.

But this list should not lead us to facile conclusions. For although there certainly was an impact of Western models for all kinds of newspapers of the Arabic-speaking intellectual elite of the time, the importance of the autochthonous elements must also not be underrated. *Abou Naddara,* as will be shown, is an excellent example of a transcultural literary format combining both.

The 30 issues of James Sanua's satirical newspaper which he first edited in exile, starting from 7 August 1878 until 13 March 1879, were collected under the title *Rihlat Abī Nazzāra min Misr al-Qāhira ilā Pārīz al-Fākhira* (Abū Nazzāra's journey from the victorious Egypt to the splendorous Paris')[9] and, therefore, presented as a personal travelogue in sequels. This is the reason why the 30 issues of *Abū Nazzāra's Journey* (*Rihla*) are analysed in this chapter as parts of one integral work.

---

[7] See chapter The Presence of *Punch* in the Nineteenth Century in this volume.

[8] Ibid.

[9] The titles of the handwritten lithographs varied slightly. The common element from the first to the last issue is: 'Abū Nazzāra's Journey from Egypt to Paris'. The adjectives attributed to both places and Sanua's professions or self-definitions changed over time. Starting from the eighth issue, the title included its number (out of 30), the price and the form of payment. Hereafter we refer to 'Abū Nazzāra's Journey' as the *Rihla* (journey).

The debut of this Arabic, and later Arabic-French, satirical magazine must be understood as the modelling of a new literary genre for political and social propaganda. When the origins of this new form, which Sanua provided for the Arabic *littérature engagée*, are traced, his efforts for the establishment of an Egyptian theatre must not be forgotten. Sanua's creations as a playwright were clearly the literary outcome of the fusion of different cultures and the point of departure for his much broader career as a journalist. Therefore, a somewhat extensive digression into the development of Arabic theatre especially during the nineteenth century is necessary to be able to position Sanua's satirical journalism.

The Transcultural Nature of Egyptian Theater

In theatre, the first important impact which was to shape Egypt's literary development in communication with the European tradition was the Napoleonic invasion of Egypt in 1798. After his victories over the occupying forces and their retreat, the new ruler, Muhammad ʿAli (r. 1805–1848), supported a massive import of French culture. One of his delegates, the religious scholar Rifaʿa Rafiʿ at-Tahtawi (1801–1873), who had travelled on the first educational mission to Paris in 1826, was to become one of Egypt's most important reformers. He describes the theatrical institutions of Paris in the travelogue *Takhlīs al-ibrīz fī talkhīs bārīz* (the refinement of gold in the summary of Paris).[10] Rifaʿa Rafiʿ at-Tahtawi portrays the French theatre as a pedagogical institution for general moral education. He made the first intellectual approach to modern theatre and opened up the minds of his contemporaries for French drama.

Three decades later, Muhammad ʿAli's grandson, the Khedive Ismāʿil, built the necessary infrastructure for the performance of theatre plays and modern musical productions. The Khedive was haunted by the ambition of Europeanising his country at all costs and did not hesitate to lead his homeland to complete financial ruin in order to achieve this goal. For the sumptuous opening celebration of the Suez Canal, he had built the wooden *Théâtre de la Comédie,* a circus and an opera house. After this historic event, European theatre and Italian opera turned into a common entertainment for the Egyptian ruling class.[11] Short Arabic handouts of the plays were distributed on the night of the performances or printed in advance by the official newspaper *al-Waqāʾiʿ al-Misriyya* (the Egyptian happenings).

This translation work for the audiences' understanding of the summary of the plot, as well as of entire plays and their adaptation to the Arabic culture, was a

---

[10] First published in Cairo in 1834. Louca's French translation: Rifâʿa At-tahtâwî, *L'or de Paris*, trans. Anouar Louca (Paris: Sindbad, 1988).

[11] As only a scarce number of Pashas were enthusiastic and regular theater-goers, the Khedive made it obligatory for some of his dignitaries to purchase seasonal tickets. See Philip C. Sadgrove, *The Egyptian Theatre in the Nineteenth Century 1799–1882* (Cairo: The American University in Cairo Press, 2007).

common starting point for the careers of the early modern Arab playwrights. As a matter of fact, the first theatre play to be written in Arabic and performed at the adapter's house in Beirut in 1848, was *al-Bakhīl*, an adaptation of Molière's *L'Avare* (*The Miser*) to the local context. The creator of this play, Marun an-Naqqash (1817–1855), was a Maronite who had studied in Italy. He is usually remembered as a pioneer of Arabic theatre. Other writers were to follow in his footsteps, such as his brother Niqula (1825–1894), his nephew Salim (1850–1884), and the journalist Adib Ishaq (1856–1885). All of them subsequently wrote and translated other plays, first in Beirut and then, starting from 1876, in Cairo.[12]

The first play to be published in an Arabic magazine in 1871 was an adaptation of Molière's *Le Médecin Malgré Lui* (*The Doctor in Spite of Himself*). Its Arabic title was *al-Fakhkh al-Mansūb li'l-Hakīm al-Maghsūb* (the trap for the coerced doctor) and it was published in three sequels in the fortnightly magazine, *Rawdat al-Madāris al-Misriyya* (the Egyptian schools), edited by al-Tahtawi. Its author was Muhammad 'Uthman Jalal (1829–1898), a former pupil of al-Tahtawi's school of languages. He translated and adapted various plays by Molière and Racine into colloquial Egyptian rhyme prose (*zajal*). At the same time, two more people were busy translating and adapting Molière in Cairo: the editor of the independent Arabic newspaper, *Wādī an-Nīl* (the Nile valley), 'Abd Allah Abu's-Su'ud, and his son Muhammad al-Unsi.[13] Mahmoud Manzalaoui clearly recognises the transcultural value of the early Arabic drama and highlights two important features of that genre:

> One is that the imported genre, from its earliest years, seeks to indigenise itself, and is at its most successful when it does so: notably, it only achieves the depth and breadth which make universal art when it becomes least derivative and most indigenised. The second is that, by contrast with the phenomenon of arrested development, modern Arabic drama, between 1848 and the present day, has run through manifold stages of development, adapted itself to changing conditions and new concepts, and assimilated new styles, in a speeded-up process even more striking than is the case with modern Arabic prose fiction.[14]

Even what one would consider to be autochthonous elements incorporated into the adapted European drama had a long history of cultural exchange. For example, the origin of the shadow play (*khayāl az-zill*)—which Landau[15] claims to be the direct predecessor of the modern Arabic theatre—is not yet clearly traced and is disputed between China and India.

---

[12] Landau disputes that, with the forced emigration of many of the Syrian actors and playwrights to Egypt, the drama culture in Beirut had come to an uneasy interruption, and quotes different travellers and chroniclers who have reported the continuity of the development of drama in that town. See Jacob M. Landau et al., *Études sur le théâtre et le cinéma arabes* (Paris: G.-P. Maisonneuve et Larose, 1965), 63–65.

[13] Sadgrove, *Egyptian Theatre*, 97.

[14] Mahmoud Manzalaoui, ed., *Arabic Writing Today 2: Drama*, American Research Center in Egypt, Cairo, 1977, 20.

[15] Landau, *Études sur le théâtre*.

Three plots of Egyptian shadow plays of the second half of the thirteenth century, which contain an important testimony to the Egyptian drama culture before the French invasion, have been preserved. Their author was Muhammad Ibn Daniyal (ca. 1248–1311), an Egyptian physician. The main feature of the texts are the comic-satirical elements—such as wordplays that focus on ambiguousness, dialects and accents—which are later to be found in Sanua's plays.

The Egyptian shadow play was so entertaining that it made its way to the Ottoman capital: The Egyptian chronicler Ibn Iyas (1448–1522) quotes in his *Tārīkh Misr* (the history of Egypt) an incident where the Ottoman Sultan Salim I (ca. 1465–1520), after having conquered Egypt in 1517, was so delighted with the local shadow plays that he took a company of performers with him back to Istanbul. The Ottomans integrated and refined at least one famous name with Egyptian origins in their shadow theatre: *Qarāqūsh*. Known as Karagöz (the black eye) in Turkish, he was a historically important soldier and statesman of Salāh ad-Dīn (Saladin, 1137 or 1138–1193), who was later ridiculed by hostile writings which, over time, became more numerous and more fantastic. At the beginning of the nineteenth century, however, Edward William Lane seems to have been rather disgusted by the Karagöz performance in Egypt as he states:

> The puppet-show of *Ckar'a Gyoo'z* (Qarāqūsh) has been introduced into Egypt by Turks, in whose language the puppets are made to speak. Their performances, which are, in general extremely indecent, occasionally amuse the Turks residing in Cairo; but, of course, are not very attractive to those who do not understand the Turkish language. They are conducted in the manner of the 'Chinese shadows', and therefore only exhibited at night.[16]

During the second half of the nineteenth century, shadow plays were reanimated through the efforts made by the puppet master Hasan al-Qashshash who had in Menzela discovered a manuscript, which was a compilation of different plots of shadow plays that seem to have been collected by another master of his art, Dawud al-Munadi or al-Manawi, about two centuries earlier. The former began to reproduce these plays in Cairo and introduced Syrian puppets into his shows. These puppets were made of very thin, parched and coloured leather, and were eventually found objectionable by some religious authorities because of their figurative attire. Landau comments that this is the reason why the puppet players pierced holes into the body of their puppets in order to clarify that they were only inanimate objects.[17]

Nonetheless, in Egypt, Karagöz and Hacivat did not experience the promotion that Theodor Kasab provided for them through his satirical newspaper *al-Khayāl*, published in Istanbul, in which he turned them into an Ottoman *Punch and Judy*, as Elif Elmas shows in her chapter, Teodor Kasab's Ottoman Adaptation of the Ottoman Shadow Theatre *Karagöz*, of this volume.[18] The anonymous author of the article 'An Arabic *Punch*' of the *Saturday Review*, published on 26 July 1879, states that,

---

[16] Edward W. Lane, *An Account of the Manners and Customs of the Modern Egyptians: The Definitive 1860 Edition* (Cairo: The American University in Cairo Press, 2003), 390.

[17] Landau, *Études sur le théâtre*, 36–37.

[18] See chapter Teodor Kasab's Ottoman Adaptation of the Ottoman Shadow Theatre *Karagöz* in this volume.

[m]ost visitors to Cairo, or indeed any town in the Levant, have seen a ludicrous exhibition of rude jests, bear-fighting, and un-seemly gestures carried on by two fantastically dressed personages known as Cáracús and Iwás, the Turkish equivalents for Punch and Judy, and this exhibition dates from remote antiquity, and has been supposed to represent the Fescennine games. But though the East has thus its Punch and its Charivari, it has hitherto had no literary representative of the hero of the cudgel, and satire has still now been a weapon almost exclusively wielded by poets and generally couched in the most classical language.[19]

Sanua, therefore, was the first to provide a modern (colloquial) literary framework for the satirical folk tradition of theatre—such as the shadow plays—through the establishment of the Egyptian stage, in the first place, and the foundation of *Abou Naddara*, in the second. By expressing the critique of the Egyptian-Arabic traditional folk satire through the means of European theatre and satirical journalism, Sanua visually created a fusion between 'Eastern' and 'Western' satire.

James Sanua, the 'Egyptian Molière' and the 'Man with Glasses'

Sanua himself was a polyglot and a transcultural individual. Born in Cairo in the month of April 1839,[20] he was the son of an Egyptian Jew with Spanish Sephardic roots. First, he studied the books of the three monotheistic religions and, at the same time, Hebrew, Arabic, English and Italian, under the supervision of his father Rafa'il. Impressed by the precocity of the young talent, Ahmad Yakan Basha,[21] his father's employer, granted him a scholarship, which made it possible for the 13 year old James to complete his studies in Italy. He arrived in Livorno in 1853 where he acquainted himself with Italian drama and the ideas of Mazzini's Young Italy movement. In 1855, he returned to Egypt, where, as a consequence of the deaths of his father and his wealthy protector, he found himself financially alone. He subsequently became a private teacher and worked his way up through rich Egyptian families until he attained a position at the *École Polytechnique* (*al-Muhandiskhana*), where he taught from 1868 to 1871. At the same time, he was employed as an examiner at governmental schools. In 1870, when Sanua was still busy teaching at the *École Polytechnique*, he decided to found his own Arabic theatre. Sanua was inspired by the performance of an open-air café-concert in the summer of 1870; he then started to translate and adapt European plays before attempting to write his own.

---

[19] "An Arabic *Punch*," *The Saturday Review*, July 26, 1879, 112.

[20] This date is the one quoted in his *Ma vie en vers et mon théâtre en prose*. There he writes that he was born in April 1939, maybe also due to a *Reimzwang*, in order to make it rhyme with 'Nil'. James Sanua, *Ma vie en prose et mon théâtre en vers* (Paris: Imprimérie Montgeronnaise, n.d.)) His biographers insist on the ninth of December as his true date of birth. See Irene L. Gendzier, *The Practical Visions of Ya'qub Sanu'*, publ. Centre for Middle Eastern Studies (Cambridge: Harvard University Press, 1966); Ibrāhīm 'Abduh, *Abū Nazzāra* (Cairo, 1953).

[21] Khedive Isma'il's brother.

> My theatre was born on the stage of a big open-air café-concert in our nice Azbakiyya Gardens. At this time, in 1870, a French troupe of musicians, singers and actors and a friendly Italian drama group enchanted the European colonies in Cairo. [...] The farces, comedies, operettas and dramas performed on this stage are what gave me the idea to create my own Arabic theatre, and God helped me to do it. But before the undertaking of the creation of my modest theatre, I seriously studied the European playwrights, especially Goldoni, Molière and Sheridan, in their respective languages.[22]

After his initial success, Sanua applied to the Khedive for a regular income for his troupe, just like the European theatre companies were usually paid. He was invited by the Khedive to perform at his palace Qasr an-Nīl after only 3 months of theatrical activities. On this occasion, his troupe performed three comedies, *Anīsa ālā Mūda* (demoiselle à la mode), *Ghandūr Misr* (the Egyptian dandy) and *ad-Darratayn* (the two co-wives). Sanua reports that after the first two plays had finished, the Khedive was so delighted that he came up to him on the stage and said: 'You are truly the founder of our national theatre, you are our Egyptian Molière'.[23] Nevertheless, the third play's harsh criticism of polygamy created problems. After witnessing the struggles of the main character Ahmad with his two co-wives, the Khedive was furious and told Sanua that if he was not man enough to satisfy two wives, he should at least leave alone the ones who were able to do so.[24] The plot and text of Sanua's play against polygamy certainly was offensive for the Egyptian Khedive. The language used among the characters, while they are fighting, is very vulgar and unpleasant and is not meant so much to portray Egyptian low society as to state how deep one can sink under the emotionally overloaded circumstances that the marriage of a second wife, and her introduction into the household, might entail.

Nevertheless, it seems unlikely that the Khedive would have closed Sanua's theatre because of his anger about this play only. Another possible reason for the forced abolishment of his theatre in 1871, which Sanua himself exposes in his unpublished *Memoires*, is that the British representatives felt offended by his sketch *As-sawwāh wa al-Hammār* (the tourist and the 'donkey-boy') and therefore put pressure on the Khedive to dismiss the playwright. However, the ultimate motive that made the Khedive censure the theatrical activities of his late protégé remains somewhat unclear.

As soon as Sanua was deprived of his theatrical occupations, he got more deeply involved with Freemasonry and founded two secret societies himself, which were closed immediately after their first reunions. In 1878, Sanua founded a satirical newspaper in order to raise national and political consciousness among the Egyptian people. His first, *Abou Naddara* (the man with glasses), was to last for only 2 months before being forbidden by the Khedive.

On 30 June 1878, after two failed attacks against his life, instigated by the ruler of Egypt, Sanua finally was forced to leave his beloved homeland and go into

---

[22] Jacques Chelley, "Le Molière Egyptien," *Abou Naddara* 6, 1 August 1906 (my translation).

[23] James Sanua, "Mémoires" [unpublished], courtesy of Mrs Eva Milhaud.

[24] Ibid.

exile.[25] Not even 2 months after his departure from Egypt, Sanua continued to publish his newspaper, of which the first 31 issues are analysed below. As we move into the investigation of the various textual genres he employed in his periodical, it will become clear how substantial the use of theatrical modes was to his satire.

The Genres and Characters of the *Rihla*

Abū Nazzāra's travelogue—the *Rihla*—is composed of 30 issues of 4 pages which contain 30 cover pages of caricatures (*rusūm*), 27 dialogues (*muhāwarāt*), 7 sketches (*al'āb*), 3 sessions (*jalsāt*), 11 sequels of Shaykh Yūsuf Efendī ash-Shaf'āwī's letter, several quotations of letters and articles from different magazines, and 4 'calls for papers', which were labelled "advertising" (*i'lān*) and intended to procure content. However, as will be shown, the genres are not always clearly labelled by Sanua himself. They have to be considered ideal types useful for the analysis. In order to deepen the understanding of the dialogue genre, I found it necessary to establish two categories which were not defined as such by Sanua. Nevertheless, there seem to be two kinds of literary compositions, different with regard to their structure and content, both of which are labelled as *muhāwarāt* (dialogues). This is the reason why I considered it important to distinguish between the 'ordinary' and the 'extraordinary' type of dialogue. The drawings or caricatures, which mostly depict scenes that are commented on in the text, are very simple. Sanua often uses elements of deformation in order to visualise injustice, such as the growing belly of the ruler in comparison to the starving figure of the oppressed subject.

The Drawing (rism): Even though James Sanua's drawing activities began at the same time as his exile and seem to have been the outcome of a generally autodidactic method,[26] he is mostly remembered as the founding father of the Egyptian caricature, which was to become a very important tool for propaganda and transmission of all kinds of socio-political messages starting from the beginning of the twentieth century.[27]

---

[25] Sanua reports his leaving Egypt as a personal decision for the sake of his physical integrity. Aboard the steamboat 'Freicynet', he spent, according to the seventh issue of the *Rihla*, his time among the passengers of the first and the second class, playing the flute for the ladies. See *Rihla* 7, 22. September (Aylūl) 1878. A very different picture of a journey into exile, is depicted 40 years later by the journalist Baīram at-Tūninsī who was squeezed into the fourth class by the French Consul in Alexandria. See Marilyn Booth, *Bayram al-Tunisi's Egypt, Social Criticism and Narrative Strategies* (Exeter: Ithaca Press, 1990).

[26] Where James Sanua studied drawing is not reported, but in the edition of the collected issues of his *Rihla* which features a 12 pages long annex in French, an article about *Abou-Naddarah* (here Sanua's pen-name) of the *L'Europe Diplomatique*, published on 8 June 1879, is quoted where the author mentions that Sanua used to teach drawing lessons to the Pashas' daughters in Egypt already. See *Rihla* 30, 13 March (Ādhār) 1879 (Paris: Imprimeuse Ragueneau), 6.

[27] Ahmad 'Abd an-Na'īm, *Hikāyāt fī al-fukāha wa al-kārikātīr* (Cairo: Dār al-'Ulūm, 2009).

Fig. 1 *Rihla* 9, 8 October (Tishrīn al-awwal) 1878. Paris: Imprimérie Ragueneau, 1878, 1

Forty-six drawings are displayed on the thirty cover pages of the *Rihla*. Four of them can undoubtedly be qualified as explanatory pictures because they show Mr Ragueneau's new manual print machine,[28] the port of Malta and Marseille[29] and the World Exhibition in Paris.[30]

How are the other 42 drawings to be defined? Are all of them caricatures? The first doubts about the nature of some of the pictures displayed in the *Rihla* arise from the fact that they are clearly not funny. Nevertheless, the ability to make the reader smile—mostly in a sarcastic way—is not the *sine qua non* of a drawing for being a caricature. Franz Schneider points out that from a philological point of view, if one bears in mind the Italian root of 'caricature', which is the verb *'caricare'* (to load, to charge), its substantive must be something related to an 'overload'.

> Caricature is therefore a depiction in which the natural balance is consciously disturbed by the overloading of certain parts. When it is transposed to the graphic field, 'overload' becomes 'exaggeration'.[31]

---

[28] *Rihla* 6, 18 September (Aylūl) 1878, 1.

[29] *Rihla* 7, 22 September (Aylūl) 1878, 1.

[30] *Rihla* 11, 22 October (Tishrīn al-awwal) 1878, 1.

[31] Franz Schneider, *Die politische Karikatur* (München: C.H. Beck, 1988), 32 (my translation).

In some of Sanua's drawings this exaggeration is not clearly detectable at first but becomes obvious when the picture is linked to the text. For example, the scene of a fight between the peasant Shaykh ʿAmr Shahāma and the Khedive's tax collectors, published in issue number 9 of the *Rihla*, is depicted in a naturalistic manner.[32]

The figures are dressed normally, show correct human proportions and take a natural position. They are also correctly dressed according to their social strata: the peasant and the Arab secretary wear a turban and a *galabiyya*,[33] and the two fiscal officers a suit and a *fez*. The background looks like a possible interior of an office of the Ottoman provincial authorities. The walls are covered in sophisticated paintings and the floor seems to be either parquet or a mosaic. A chair lies on the floor in front of what seems to be a treasure chest (Fig. 1).

This picture, for its outstanding naturalness and apparent veracity, seems far from being a caricature. Nevertheless, if caricature is defined by an imbalance, set up deliberately in order to transfer a (political) message, the drawing of the furious peasant who menaces the tax collectors can be categorised as such. The change of the social asymmetries, which turns the oppressed into the powerful, clearly introduces an unexpected imbalance into the social composition of the picture. The text adds the comic element which is so customary (but, as we saw, not necessary) in caricatures: The tax collectors have passed out in a rather comical way under the punches of the brave peasant. The secretary throws water on his superiors' faces in order to bring them back to consciousness. As soon as they are able to think again, they become aware of how ridiculously their authority had been violated. The situation of a single peasant beating them and escaping has to be kept a secret. The scene is dramatically exaggerated: the peasant gets hold of the pistol, menaces the tax collectors, whom he strikes down with easy punches, and the Arab secretary trembles and fears for his life next to the fallen chair. This picture cannot be understood correctly without the text. It is only after considering the imbalance created in the description of the theatrical scene that the drawing of the events at the public office can be considered a caricature. The same applies to pictures of the public demonstrations in front of the palace which are shown in issues number 20, 21 and 28.[34] Their satirical content becomes obvious only when reading the corresponding texts.

Another two pictures, published in issues number 15 and 25 of the *Rihla*, are also difficult to understand as caricatures if they are not combined with the story they depict. Both of them are illustrations of sessions. The illustration in issue number 15

---

[32] *Rihla* 9, 8 October (Tishrīn al-awwal) 1878, 1.

[33] For typically Egyptian expressions and direct quotes of Sanua's newspapers the letter 'ج' (*jīm*) is transliterated as 'g' which is phonetically nearer to the Egyptian pronunciation.

[34] *Rihla* 20, 30 December (Kānūn ath-thānī) 1878, 1; *Rihla* 21, 8 January (Kānūn ath-thānī)1879, 1; *Rihla* 28, 21 February (Shubāt) 1879, 1.

Fig. 2 *Rihla* 15, 21 November (Tishrīn at-thānī) 1878. Paris: Imprimérie Ragueneau, 1878, 1

(see Fig. 2) displays a gathering of Abū Nazzāra's Secret Society.³⁵ In contrast to the text, which is rather serious, it is 'the picture in the picture' which, in this specific case, helps the observer to understand that this cannot be a scene drawn from reality. The painting on the wall shows the Khedive alias 'Shaykh al-hāra' smoking the pipe and contemplating the heads of his enemies which are exposed on sticks of different sizes in front of him.

At a second of these gatherings, a session in parliament is depicted that is clearly satirical in its accusations against the Shaykh al-harā, as well as in its use of alterego characters that stand for the real representatives such as Shaykh ʿAbd al-ʿĀl Abū gāmūs³⁶ (gāmūs means buffalo). Here, again, the 'overloading' of the picture that turns it into a caricature is made clear by the text.

The last series of pictures, that could raise doubt as to their classification as caricatures, are the ones which illustrate the 'officer's family tragedy'. The argument established above also applies to this sequence of three pictures which is to be found in issue number 27.³⁷ The content is dramatically exaggerated and therefore causes a visual imbalance that turns the drawings into caricatures.

Thus, apart from the 4 pictures presented at the beginning, the remaining 42 must be considered caricatures. Some of them can be categorised more easily than those discussed above—for example, the ones that work with dislocation, deformation, and other kinds of travesties.

---

³⁵ *Rihla* 15, 21 November (Tishrīn ath-thānī) 1878, 1.

³⁶ Written without *alif* in the Egyptian dialect. *Rihla* 25, 7 February (Shubāt) 1879, 1.

³⁷ Ibid., 1.

Abū Nazzāra's Journey from Victorious Egypt to Splendorous Paris   231

Fig. 3 *Rihla* 30, 13 March (Ādhār) 1879. Paris: Imprimérie Ragueneau, 1879, 6

The most important victim of these caricatures is the Shaykh al-hāra (the character who stands for the Khedive Ismāʿil in the *Rihla*), who is depicted in all manner of weird dress, poses and roles such as: kneeling in front of Abū Nazzāra,[38] facing the dead,[39] playing the tambourine and wearing a skirt[40] or disguised as a clown,[41] having horns like the devil,[42] metaphorically drinking Egypt's finances out of a wine barrel with a straw, using the domestic and foreign dignitaries as marionettes,[43] being transformed into a fox or a buffalo [44] and, last but not least, standing on the top of the ruins of the land he has previously destroyed (see Fig. 3).[45]

---

[38] *Rihla* 1, 7 August (Āb) 1878, 1.

[39] *Rihla* 2, 14 August (Āb) 1878, 1.

[40] *Rihla* 5, 8 September (Aylūl) 1878, 1.

[41] *Rihla* 10, October (Tishrīn at-thānī) 1878, 1.

[42] *Rihla* 13, 8 November (Tishrīn at-thānī) 1878, 1; *Rihla* 18, 15 December (Kānūn al-awwal) 1878, 1.

[43] *Rihla* 25, 7 February (Shubāt) 1879, 1.

[44] *Rihla* 8, 30 September (Aylūl) 1878, 1; *Rihla* 29, 2 March (Ādhār) 1879, 1.

[45] *Rihla* 30, 1.

The Letter (risāla): A special kind of letter to the editor, published in sequels, is Shaykh Yūsuf Efendī al-Shafʿāwī's contribution. The Skaykh's letter is formulated in classical Arabic and contains quotations from the *Qur'ān* and *hadīth*, which are used in order to prove the appropriateness of all accusations against the wicked Shaykh al-hāra. Al-Shafʿāwī expresses in issue number 4 that he considers it his duty as a good Muslim to make public the atrocities committed by the active ruler of Egypt.[46] For his constant company throughout the whole text of the travelogue, Al-Shafʿāwī must be considered Abū Nazzāra's most loyal correspondent.

Shaykh Yūsuf Efendī al-Shafʿāwī's letter is different in nature from the other contributions. The Shaykh's letter most obviously talks to the heart of every believing Muslim, if not already through the language used, then certainly at the moment the *Qur'ān* and *hadīth* are quoted. Sanua's intention is clear: He, as much as his contemporary al-Afghani, makes use of Islam in order to foment a political ideology of liberation. Through al-Shafʿāwī's voice, Sanua bestows God's blessings upon his claims for freedom and the fall of the Khedive. To provide a platform for Islam as the point of departure for a nationalist ideology is of course very unusual for the newspaper of a non-Muslim Egyptian.[47]

The other letters and articles that reach Paris are usually read out during a dialogue, discussed, turned into sketches or poems in colloquial verse (*zajal*) or published as a whole and contain, besides the information about the situation in Egypt, acknowledgments for Abū Nazzāra's work. The letters bestow an appearance of immediacy upon the magazine, and offer the exiled the possibility to participate in deliberations about Egypt's problems at that time. Abū Nazzāra converts himself into a father of the nation, a patron saint of the liberal movement, who, from a distance, observes the situation through his blue glasses.

His position has a twofold nature: On the one hand, through his observations from afar, he is able to give advice to his countrymen from a comparative point of view. He therefore constantly mentions the greatness of the French Republic, the Revolution and the freedom the French people have acquired. On the other hand, the main character of the *Rihla* never tires of crying bitter tears of nostalgia. Abū Nazzāra feels helpless due to his forced inertia at a moment where all the Egyptian people should unite.

The Dialogue (muhāwara): Although the letters reaching the 'splendorous Paris' from the 'victorious Egypt' are certainly vital for the formulation of the *Rihla*, the main literary genres it encompasses are the 27 dialogues (*muhāwarāt*) and the 6 sketches (*alʿāb*).

Abou Naddara's typical dialogue can be defined as a conversation mostly between two speakers (which is the case in 21 of the 27 dialogues), set in a public

---

[46] *Rihla* 4, 30 August (Āb) 1878, 3.

[47] Sanua gives a quite mystic explanation for his sympathy for Egypt's dominant religion in his *Memoires*: His mother, after losing four children and when pregnant with him, out of her fear to suffer another son's death, went to see a Shaykh. The religious sage recommended she devote her future son to the faith of Islam. Then he would live a long and prosperous life. This is the reason she made her son James learn all about, and deeply respect, Islam.

place (generally a coffee shop) in Cairo, Alexandria or Paris. The editor's alter ego (Abū Nazzāra) participates as a main actor in 18 of the 27 dialogues and is explicitly mentioned or even talked about as a main topic in another three conversations. The most important character giving life to these conversations is therefore Abū Nazzāra himself.

Abū Nazzāra—The Character: In the varying titles of the 30 issues, Sanua first defines his personage as *al-walī* (the saint).[48] Under this denomination, he proclaims himself a national hero. At the very beginning of his journey, Abū Shukr, one of his friends who commonly lament his departure, states that no one has done as much for the freedom of the country as Abū Nazzāra and gravely concludes that their exiled friend prefers to die rather than endure oppression.[49]

In the ninth issue, in the aforementioned play at the tax collector's office, the *fallāh* (peasant) who refuses to pay the newly introduced mud taxes states self-consciously that he and his fellow peasants had sworn by the beard of Abū Nazzāra, the *walī*, not to endure any more cruelty or injustice.[50] Abū Nazzāra here clearly becomes an allegory for the fight for liberation.

Eighteen issues later, Sanua adds the attribute of 'the saint' to the name of his secret society, which is consequently labelled as *Shirkat Abī Nazzāra zarqā al-walī* ('the holy man with the blue glasses' society).[51]

Sanua even goes as far as publishing, in number 29 of the *Rihla*, a letter from a friend who thanks Abū Nazzāra for his vital contribution to the creation of the national party *(ahl al-watan)*.[52] As a nationalist leader, Sanua defines himself as Halīm's[53] most important intellectual ally who leads the patriots' struggle with his pen.

The visual climax of this is in the drawing of the last issue: While Shaykh al-hāra stands on the top of the pile of debris, into which he has converted the country, his uncle Halīm ascends from the right in order to overthrow him. On the left foot of the ruins, wearing a suit and a *fez*, stands Abū Nazzāra. Even though his figure is

---

[48] Numbers 1–7.
[49] *Rihla* 1, 1–4.
[50] *Rihla* 9, 3.
[51] *Rihla* 28, 21 February (Shubāt) 1879, 2.
[52] *Rihla* 29, 4.
[53] According to Wilfrid Scawen Blunt, Isma'il had not manipulated his own accession to the Egyptian throne, as Sanua eagerly claimed, but was rather overwhelmed by it.

His succession to the Viceroyalty had been more or less a surprise to him, for until within a few months of Said's death he had not been the immediate heir, and his prospects had been only those of an opulent private person. It was perhaps this unexpected stroke of fortune that from the beginning of his reign led him to extravagance. By nature a speculator and inordinately greedy of wealth, he seems to have looked upon his inheritance and the absolute power now suddenly placed in his hands, not as a public trust, but as the means above all things else of aggrandising his private fortune. At the same time he was as inordinately vain and fond of pleasure, and his head was turned by his high position and the opportunity it gave him of figuring in the world as one of its most splendid princes. Blunt, W. S., *Secret History of the English Occupation of Egypt* (London: T. Fisher UNWIN Adelphi Terrace, 1907), 16.

uncommonly small, and nearly invisible, he holds himself upright and menacingly points at the fat Shaykh al-hāra.[54]

In an interview with Jehan Soudan, editor in chief of the *Courrier d'Egypte*, James Sanua informs that, during the last years of Ismaʿīl's despotic rule, the oppositional forces, followers of Halīm, replaced among them the habitual greeting of *Allah maʿak* (may God be with you) with the formula *Allāh karīm wa halīm* (God is magnificent and clement).[55] As a seemingly harmless religious wordplay, this secretly supports the propaganda slogan through the mere naming of *Halīm*.

Abū Nazzāra, the saint, the national hero, is a figure like Mr Punch who—with the help of satire—unmasks the absurdity of corrupt political rule and moral perversion. Nevertheless, he presents himself as uncommonly serious in his appearance. Because of his very gentleman-like dress code, he seems to have more in common with Daumier's (self-) portraits than with the carnevalesque Mr Punch. Abū Nazzāra continuously wears a suit and a top hat, which is replaced by a *fez* in the last issue. His identity is not completely set apart from that of his creator. Sanua expresses his experiences and ideas through the speech of Abū Nazzāra, who is very often addressed as 'Abu James' in the outline of the dialogues of the *Rihla*.

Abū Khalīl—Abū Nazzāra's Companion: The character second in importance for Sanua's dialogue genre is Abū Khalīl. He participates in 16 of the 27 conversations included in the *Rihla*, generally as Abū Nazzāra's counterpart. Only in three dialogues does he act alone.[56] We learn through issue number 7 of the *Rihla* that Abū Khalīl was exiled because of his oppositional writings on the same day as Abū Nazzāra, but that he reached Paris much earlier than him. Their first encounter takes place in the Café Riche on the Boulevard des Italiens on 10 July.[57]

Abū Khalīl addresses his friend with 2 lines of *zajal* and Abū Nazzāra answers with another 12 lines of verse which describe the Khedive's cruelty. He concludes that one day he will go back to his beloved country and that, even if he dies, his friends will carry on his struggle for freedom and justice.

After this official greeting of the two patriotic poets, the conversation continues on a more informal level. Abū Khalīl is neither fully at ease with the French language nor with the Parisian culture. He has to rely on the translation of newspaper articles by an acquaintance in order to keep himself up-to-date. Abū Nazzāra considers it his task to introduce his companion to the new environment by, for example, showing him where to enjoy a good meal at low cost.[58] He guides Abū Khalīl step by step until the latter reaches the maturity required for solemnly closing the *Rihla*.

Back in Egypt, Abū Khalīl meets Abū Shukr, who was among the ones to lament Abū Nazzāra's departure in the first issue of the travelogue. Abū Shukr has only one

---

[54] *Rihla* 30, 1.

[55] Paul de Baignières, *L'Egypte Satirique, Album d'Abū Nazzāra* (Paris: Imprimerie Lefebvre, 1886) 12.

[56] In issues number 1, 13 and 30.

[57] *Rihla* 7, 2–3.

[58] Ibid.

line to say in this conversation and asks Abū Khalīl where he is coming from. The latter, surprisingly, does not say anything about his stay in Paris and closes the *Rihla* with an extensive solemn monologue. He starts his account by answering the question of his friend. He had just witnessed the quarrel between soldiers and pilgrims at their feast (*al-mahmal ash-sharīf*). Therefore he expresses deep sadness and his hope for a just and religious ruler for his country and ends by praying to God that He may fulfil this wish of the nation's children.[59]

Abū Khalīl's presence is not only vital for the unfolding of the *Rihla* and its frame story, but he is the key character for Abū Nazzāra's pedagogical aims to enlighten his countrymen. He is, in Sanua's opinion, the ideal of what the modern Egyptian citizen should become. The chain of dialogues between Abū Nazzāra and Abū Khalīl form the 'invisible' frame story of the *Rihla*. Their conversation is never depicted by a drawing. The two friends are the narrators who introduce the different parts of the travelogue to the reader and even explain some of the drawings. They step into the role of the storytellers who narrate their *hikāya* (live acted story) to an eager public. At the same time, they fit into the tradition of European satiric magazines in which this kind of 'Socratic dialogue' can be found between Punch and Judy, for example.[60] The interplay between the puppet show and the satiric magazine was, therefore, a Western model which could be easily adopted by the East.

The Extraordinary Dialogue: The dialogues of the *Rihla*, due to their differences in structure and content, are divided into two categories for this analysis: the 'ordinary' and the 'extraordinary'. Even though Sanua himself simply called the two of them *muhāwarāt* (dialogues), there are two kinds of conversation which can easily be distinguished. The first is the former, which takes place between two and three participants who—fully faithful to the Arab tradition of male gatherings—sit in a coffee shop and talk about the issues of the day, their experiences, dreams and hopes. As this is the case for 22 of the *muhāwarāt*, it is reasonable to classify this dialogue genre as the 'ordinary' type.

The remaining five conversations of the *Rihla*, however, are quite different. They assemble at least three participants, take place in a purely fictional scenery, include the Khedive, called Shaykh al-hāra (shaykh of the alley) as a protagonist, and are usually illustrated with a caricature. This is the reason why I label them 'extraordinary dialogues'.

The *Rihla* begins with such an extraordinary dialogue in which Shaykh al-hāra awkwardly begs Abū Nazzāra on his knees to stop his oppositional writing, while the peasant Abū al-ghalab (lit. the one who will be victorious) orders Abū Nazzāra never to forgive him.[61]

Two issues later, the judgment of the treacherous Shaykh al-hāra is performed in an exaggerated theatrical scene. Additionally, the dramatic elements of the dialogue

---

[59] *Rihla* 30, 4.
[60] See Richard G.G. Price, *A History of Punch* (London: Collins, 1957).
[61] *Rihla* 1, 1.

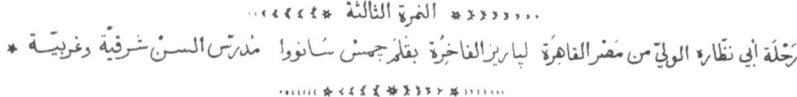

Fig. 4 *Rihla*, 3, 22 August (Āb) 1878. Paris: Imprimérie Ragueneau, 1878, 1–3

are highlighted by a drawing of the characters (see Fig. 4), theatrically placed, facing the audience, with a pompous curtain marking the background, and a Karagöz-like puppet figure (which is not mentioned in the text) hanging from the upper right corner into the picture.[62]

The title of the caricature defines it as a theatre play, whereas the text announces a dialogue. It lacks, however, a list of dramatis personae and scene structure (*manāzir*)—both important features of Sanua's plays.

---

[62] *Rihla* 3, 22 August (Āb) 1878, 1–3.

In the next issue there is a dialogue between the sick Khedive's mother, who fears for her son, Shaykh al-husarī, and Abū Nazzāra, in the role of the doctor. Abū Nazzāra explains to the helpless mother how badly her son has been behaving and the Shaykh adds his religious ratification. The deeply-moved mother promises them that she will guide her son to an honest life.[63]

The next 'extraordinary' dialogue is to be found as late as in issue 12 and is the only of this type which is not illustrated with a caricature. It is an imagined conversation between Shaykh al-hāra and four men of religion. The five discussants have a hypocritical conversation during which they openly praise each other while thinking the opposite.[64]

The last conversation of this type shows two particularities. It is held between two people only—Abū Nazzāra and Ghūbār Efend (Minister Nūbār's character in the *Rihla*)—and it is entirely written in *zajal*. It takes place in a dream in which Abū Nazzāra talks to the minister. The latter makes use of his Austrian ear trumpet. Abū Nazzāra warns Ghūbār Efendī of Shaykh al-hāra's treachery and advises him not to go to Upper Egypt—where he may disappear—or to drink the Khedive's (poisoned) coffee, as these are the two ways in which the tyrant commonly rids himself of his former servants. Ghūbār stays unmoved, boasts about his friendship with the British, exposes his unconditional love for money and concludes that the people take him for the *Mahdī*.[65]

These 'extraordinary' *muhāwarāt* are visually structured in a more dramatic way than their ordinary counterparts which form the frame narration. They bring together a fictional scene and a variety of 'over-dressed'—one could say 'masked'—characters who act one-dimensionally. By doing so, they embody the grotesque satirical content of the dialogue which moves the audience.

The Session (jalsa): Another quite dramatic genre Sanua uses in his *Rihla* is the session (*jalsa*). In total, there are three of them. They can be defined as meetings held by a secret (Masonic) organisation directed by a president who gives advice to his dervish members. The session usually includes a multiplicity of characters; however, Shaykh al-hāra and Abū Nazzāra are both absent.

The first is called *Jalsa Sirraiyya fī Jamʿiyyat at-Tarātīr al-Mashhūra bi-d-Dahk ʿalā Duqūn al-ʿĀlam* (a secret session at the union of the famous clowns for the parody of the world's powerful) and it appears in issue number 6 of the *Rihla*.[66] In the subtitle the text is introduced as a dialogue. Nevertheless, for not including the character of Shaykh al-hāra, and for depicting the meeting in the same manner as the other two sessions of secret (Masonic/Dervish) societies, it seems reasonable to classify the Secret Session at the Union of Clowns within this category. The session is a parody of the cabinet at the moment Ismaʿil's new Armenian Prime Minister

---

[63] *Rihla* 4, 1–3.
[64] *Rihla* 12, 30 October 1878, 2–3.
[65] Messianic savior. *Rihla* 17, 8 December (Kānūn al-awwal) 1878, 2.
[66] *Rihla* 6, 2–4.

Nubar arrives. The ministers are aware of their negligence and the greed of their ruler. They discuss that Egypt is menaced by England's navy and France's soldiers, and that even the Italian king—the son of yesterday who has not yet crawled out of his eggshells[67]—blames them for their financial mismanagement. Nevertheless, they are ordered to remain silent and to not ridicule the powerful of the world.

The second session is the meeting of Abū Nazzāra's own secret society. The Masonic character of this session is emphasised by the setting of the scene, which takes place next to the pyramids. Sanua founded two secret societies before being forced into exile. He was also received as a member of the Freemasons' Egyptian 'Lodge of Concordia' on the 25 February 1868.

The importance of Freemasonry is exposed as early as the second issue of the *Rihla*, in which the Khawāgā Yūsuf Ramla—introduced as a famous trader from Alexandria—and Abū Nazzāra praise the importance of the Freemasons' liberal thought and their effort to unite people of different religions.

The information provided by the *Rihla* about Abū Nazzāra's contacts in Egypt, as well as the sessions held by his secret society, are evidence for the continuation of the master's Masonic work in his homeland even after his exile.

In the first issue Abū al-'aynayn happily informs his friends Abū Khalīl and Abū Shukr, who deplore the disappearance of the satiric newspaper, and that a secret society has been founded named *Abū Nazzāra*. This association, he eagerly explains, will start a newspaper and call it *an-Nazzarāt al-Misriyya* (the Egyptian glasses)[68] which will fight against oppression and for the liberation of the fatherland.[69]

The third issue of the *Rihla* alludes to the existence of a group of Abū Nazzāra's followers by narrating of how one of them, 'the man with the white glasses' (Abū Nazzāra al-baydā), is searched by Shaykh al-hāra's hangmen at his house in Alexandria.[70]

Seven issues later Abū Khalīl tells Abū Nazzāra that their friends had gathered and founded another secret organisation which is working for freedom and progress.[71] In issue number 12 the main character of the *Rihla* explains that the information for the dialogue between Shaykh al-hāra and the religious dignitaries has been provided to him by one of these shaykhs, a member of a recently established Cairene secret society named *Abū Nazzara Zarqā*.[72]

For the setting of the session of this organisation, published in the fifteenth issue, James Sanua's alter-ego character seems to have undergone a threatening multiplication. The participants in the meeting are: Abū Nazzāra, the noble, the president of

---

[67] Ibid. (my translation).
[68] Which was to become the title of ten issues of Sanua's satirical magazine in the year 1880.
[69] *Rihla* 1, 2–4.
[70] *Rihla* 3, 3–4.
[71] *Rihla* 10, 2–4.
[72] *Rihla* 12, 2–4.

the society and members of the inner circle—here called dervishes—who are the secretary, the treasurer, the speaker and the poet—men with green, yellow, red and black glasses respectively. Abū Nazzāras' clones welcome a Frenchmen who, after a long speech about freedom, is accepted as a member. This eloquent exposition about liberties and civil rights allows the president of the society to prove to his adherents the rightfulness of his statement about the important contribution of the French people to the process of civilisation.[73]

The last of the three sessions is integrated into issue number 28 and displays another gathering of the *Shirkat Abī Nazzāra Zarqā al-Walī* (Abū Nazzāra Zarqā, the Holy's society). After the initial greetings by the president, the secretary introduces five of the greatest lovers of the homeland: Maksūr al-khātir (lit. 'the depressed'), a broke merchant; Shaykh Halkān, the peasant; Mughlis Efendī, the civil servant; Darghām Bīk, the soldier; and Zakī Bīk, the apprentice. Three of them explain their unpleasant stories to the members of the *Abū Nazzāra* society. As a kind of representative of their group of professionals, they share with the world, through the mouthpiece of the *Abou Naddara* newspaper, their individual cases of suffering inflicted upon them by the Khedive's despotic rule. The speaker of the present dervish calls out for union and resistance. He encourages the ones present in the session not to be afraid and to take the European's struggle for freedom as an example of how to patiently and constantly fight against oppression.[74]

The sessions become more and more frequent in the periodicals, which Sanua published after the termination of the *Rihla*. It is well known that not only Sanua but most of the influential intellectuals who were to engrave their names in the annals of Egyptian history of the end of the nineteenth century were Freemasons. Nevertheless, the openness in which Sanua documents their meetings is rather startling. Another surprising fact is that the lodges he is associated with, namely the *Kawkab ash-Sharq* (the Eastern star)[75] and the Concordia Lodge of Egypt respectively, observed the Scottish and English Masonic rites and therefore forbade the discussion of political and religious subjects. However, all sessions of Abū Nazzāra's secret society which Sanua documents are clearly of a political and even revolutionary nature.

Sanua shows the reader how the Egyptian secret societies learned from the French and afterwards proceeded to make use of the newly acquired knowledge and means for their own personal independence fight. Whereas in the first session held by Abū Nazzāra's secret society the members are taught the principles of freedom by a Frenchmen, during the unfolding of the second session, they listen carefully to the pleas against the Khedive's tyrannical actions brought before them by representatives of the three most important classes of the Egyptian people.

---

[73] *Rihla* 15, 2–4.

[74] *Rihla* 28, 2–4.

[75] Al-Afghani was the Grand Master of *Kawkab as-Sharq* while Sanua was busy publishing the *Rihla*.

Sanua's satirical magazines strongly aim to operate as a mouthpiece for 'Egyptian', or 'Egyptianised', Freemasonry. This feature of the *Rihla* and its successors distinguishes them from their British relative, *Punch*, which is far from being a Masonic propaganda sheet. The aforementioned prohibition for the lodges, which follow the English or Scottish rite to discuss politics, is perhaps one of the reasons why *Punch* cannot be directly linked to British Freemasonry.

In Egypt, Freemasonry, from al-Afghani's days as a Grand Master until President Nasser's forced abolition of the society in 1961, was neither strictly secret nor unpolitical. Starting with the Khedive Tawfīq in 1879, the Egyptian royal rulers were either made active or honorary Grand Masters of the Grand Orient National d'Egypte. The competition between the French and British rites virtually ended in a kind of transcultural fusion under al-Afghani's leadership. The latter, even though his lodge *Kawkab sh-Sharq* was under the patronage of the United Grand Lodge of England, ignored their instructions to end his talks about political Islam and hesitated briefly about whether or not to choose French guidance. This shift in patronage from English to French never officially happened, but al-Afghani and his followers combined the two rites as they pleased and made use of their lodges as platforms for all sorts of political activities.[76]

The Play (la'b): The third dramatic genre which Sanua uses in his *Rihla* is the sketch or play (*la'b*). It is difficult to establish a distinct line of separation between this form of play and the aforementioned 'extraordinary dialogue'. In some cases Sanua introduces a text as a 'dialogue', adds a list of characters, and structures the events into scenes. For these reasons, for example, the 'dialogue' of the nineteenth issue— discussed below—which, apart from being labelled dialogue, unites all features of a theatre play, should be classified as a sketch rather than a dialogue.[77] However, the most important points of distinction between the two theatrical forms—the dialogue and the sketch—are the following: Firstly, the play starts with a presentation of the *dramatis personae* in which the names of the characters, their professions and their functions or relations to one another are established. Secondly, the unfolding of the plot is structured into scenes (*manāzir*). Thirdly, the play is set with a sophisticated artificiality and solemnity in a scene—such as 'the highest of offices'—and, at a certain time, as 'in the dark ages' (*ayyām al-ghuz*).[78] Fourthly, the sketch is visualised

---

[76] Karim Wissa, "Freemasonry in Egypt: 1789–1921, A Study in Cultural and Political Encounters," *Bulletin (British Society for Middle Eastern Studies)* 16, no. 2 (1989): 143–161.

[77] *Rihla* 19, 21 December (Kānūn al-awwal) 1878, 3–4.

[78] The *Ghuz* were an ancient confederation of pagan Turkish tribes who founded nomad empires of vast extent in Central Asia from the sixth to the tenth century. See Charles Wendell, *The Evolution of the Egyptian National Image, From its Origins to Ahmad Lutfī al-Sayyid* (Berkeley: University of California Press, 1972), 109, fn. 66.

Jamal Mohamed Ahmed, when explaining the conflicts in Egyptian society after the retreat of the French, states that, '[t]he Mamelukes tried to restore the pre-Napoleonic supremacy; the Turks on the other hand wanted to put an end to them and re-impose their own rule. The people of Cairo hated them both; they referred to them disdainfully as "the Ghuzz"'. Jamal Mohammed Ahmed, *The Intellectual Origins of Egyptian Nationalism* (London: Oxford University Press, 1960), 6.

in a caricature which shows all of the characters. As far as the dialogues are concerned, their main topic is usually dealt with in a caricature also, but the discussants themselves are never depicted. In the entire *Rihla* there is not a single drawing which might hint at the physical appearance of Abū Khalīl. A final interesting feature of the sketch is Abū Nazzāra's absence from them.

The first play, which appears in issue number 9 of the *Rihla*, is not graphically separated from the previous dialogue between Abū Nazzāra and Abū Khalīl; it even derives directly from it. In it, Abū Nazzāra explains to his friend that he has received a letter from their friend Sa'īd from Egypt and has turned his funny story into a sketch. Then he starts to list the characters and to describe the scene. The plot of this play was already mentioned: A peasant attacks two officials who try to make him pay an unreasonable tax. The *fallāh* 'Amr Shahāma, after depriving Fara'ūn Aghā of his gun, slaps Ismā'īl Bīk Zulmi's face and soberly concludes that this was like 'the British Punch' (*al-būniyya al-inklīzī*). He leaves without touching the secretary, whom he friendly addresses as 'cousin' and 'friend of the peasants'. The secretary brings his masters back to consciousness by throwing water onto their faces and they finally agree not to tell anybody about these incidents in order to avoid public humiliation. This play, which is explicitly defined as such, is not structured into scenes but includes in brackets the characters' movements on the stage. The end is marked with a line which, unlike the beginning, graphically separates the plot from Abū Nazzāra and Abū Khalīl's concluding remarks.

The reader is introduced to the next play of the *Rihla* in a direct and visually clear manner. The title *Sultān al-Kanūz* (sultan of the treasures') is underlined and a subtitle even specifies that this is one of Abū Nazzāra's stories (*riwāyāt Abī Nazzāra*). The subsequent introduction places this theatre play (*la'iba tyātriyya*) in the 'western city of Zīrāb' and lists the characters' names. After another clear line of separation, the imaginary curtain opens on the first scene. The plot caricaturises in two acts the new loan from Lionel de Rothschild which was negotiated by Rivers Wilson, the British minister of finance, and Isma'il's Armenian prime minister Nubar. All names are changed. Rashīd, the Sultan of the treasures, represents Rothschild; Fānūs Kazandār stands for Nubar; the Pharaoh, king of Egypt, is the Khedive's alter-ego; and Mulsin, the minister of finance, personifies Rivers Wilson.

The third play, found in the sixteenth issue of the *Rihla*, is graphically shaped in the same way as the 'Sultan of the Treasures' and is split into four acts. The heading reads *Mal'ūb al-Hidiq* (the acting of the clever) and the play takes place during the dark ages (*ayyām al-ghuz*) in the entrance hall of a harem. The black Ottoman eunuch receives an officer who is forced to bring back the wife he had married from that establishment, and her servants, because he cannot afford keeping them. Shaykh al-hāra is said to be responsible for the husband's ruin, as he had permanently increased the taxes and refrained from paying the officers' salaries.[79] The next play may be understood as a continuation of the same plot: In issue number

---

[79] *Rihla* 16, 30 November (Tishrīn ath-thānī) 1878, 2–4.

19, separated by the small drawing of a crescent and a star, the sketch is preceded by a dialogue and then develops, in four acts, in a hall of the royal pharaonic chambers. Here a poor officer is forced to marry a princess from the royal harem because the pharaoh (the Khedive) cannot afford to maintain so many people any longer.[80]

The third play, which belongs to this succession what might be called the 'officers' families series', is contained in issue number 27. On this issue's cover page, three pictures chronologically portray the unfolding of this play, which is called *al-Jihādī* (the soldier). In the total absence of a list of characters, the drama fatefully starts in the officer's house: His children beg him for food and his wife sends him to request his salary, which is overdue, at the Ministry of War. The reader's suspicion is already raised by the Khedive kindly granting an audience to the officer. As soon as the coffee is served, the fatal ending is already more than obvious. The play reaches its climax when the officer, after reaching home, succumbs to the effects of the poison.[81]

It is important to recall the historical background of this play. It was written on 21 February 1879, 3 days after the officers' revolt that caused Prime Minster Nubar's fall. 2,500 officers had been released from the army and deprived of their pensions. The Khedive made use of their agitation in order to free himself from the foreign control of the 'mixed-cabinet'. At the same time, Ismaʿil turned his Prime Minister Nubar into a scapegoat for the general discontent of the people. Sanua supports the officers' revolt with his last play of the *Rihla*.

The plot of the three plays of the 'officers' families series', which display the increasing uneasiness among the Arab officers, culminates in the last one. The first two are of openly satirical nature and are meant to produce a sarcastic smile on their readers' faces: completely absurd incidents such as the forced return of a bride to her motherly harem, or the compulsory marriage of a princess to an officer due to the Khedive's lack of money, mockingly portray the precarious situation of the country. Nevertheless, the last play possesses an almost Shakespearian determinism which pushes the reader to assume from the outset that the cry of hunger from the officer's children and his wife's plea for justice can only lead to the destruction of the brave head of the family.

Conclusions

After analyzing the different genres which compose the 30 issues of Abū Nazzāra's *Rihla*, I wish to come back to the question initially raised, namely: how is *Abou Naddara* related to his European cousins, *Punch* and *Charivari*? Is the *Rihla* a

---

[80] *Rihla* 19, 21 December (Kānūn al-awwal) 1878, 3–4.

[81] *Rihla* 27, 21 February (Shubāt) 1879, 2–4.

prototype version of an Arabic *Punch* as the anonymous author of the aforementioned article 'An Arabic Punch' of *The Saturday Review* claims it to be?

Sanua, a polyglot who spoke eight languages and spent the time of his youth in Italy and half of his life in exile in France, where he claims to have actively participated in the most distinguished of intellectual circles, was acquainted, as it were, with the flourishing satirical press of his time. Still in Cairo, in the very first issue of *Abū Nazzāra Zarqā*, he had mentioned *Punch*, *Charivari* and the *Fanfulla* as traditional European magazines.[82]

Sanua therefore adapted the European journalistic satirical genre to his texts, as well as to his drawings. Unable to fulfil his wish of having his papers illustrated right from the start, Sanua drew his own lithographs as soon as he reached Paris in 1878.

The genre was, however, not the only link that Sanua established to his European models. While publishing the *Rihla*, he explicitly and implicitly sought the help of the European liberals and Freemasons in order to free his homeland from arbitrary tyranny. As far as his implicit search for support is concerned, he constantly alludes to the possibility of foreign aid, such as in the play about the *fallāh* who refuses to pay the taxes, where the main character fights his oppressors with an 'English Punch' (*al-būniyyat al-Inklīzī*).[83] This is the only line in the *Rihla* where a direct connection to *Punch* is established in order to satirically display the subversive qualities of European liberal thought.

At the same time, Sanua makes Abū Nazzāra frequently state that the whole world can gaze through his glasses now and has therefore become a witness of the cruelty without limits which is perpetrated on a daily basis by the Egyptian Khedive and his followers.[84] Abū Nazzāra also proudly gives details about his being an activist, especially in a secret (Masonic) society where he pleads for the freedom of Egypt almost every night.[85] At the same time he claims to propagate his message through the most important European newspapers.[86]

Apart from the help expected from outside, Sanua wanted his countrymen to become free-thinking citizens of a modern state. Abū Nazzāra, in the complex fusion between a Sufi-Shaykh, a master of the Freemasons and a modern *professeur*, teaches his friend Abū Khalīl, by the means of a travelogue, in the same manner that Egyptian students were taught at the schools founded by Muhammad 'Ali.

The pedagogical message of the dialogues between the master and his student is completely sober and lacks the burlesque character of the conversations between their Ottoman counterparts Hacivat and Karagöz. Abū Nazzāra's character as a master and teacher, which occupies the centrepiece of the *Rihla*, with his

---

[82] *Abū Nazzāra Zarqā* 1, 2.
[83] *Rihla*, 2–4.
[84] Ibid., 2–3.
[85] *Rihla* 21, 8 January (Kānūn ath-thānī) 1879, 2–3.
[86] *Rihla* 23, 23 January (Kānūn ath-thānī) 1879, 2–4.

exaggerated seriousness, reduces his satirical features. However, especially in the 'extraordinary dialogues', when Abū Nazzāra faces Shaykh al-hāra, the burlesque side of Mr Punch's Arabic cousin shines through. Despite his familial ties with Mr Punch, Abū Nazzāra is at the same time the grandson of the main character of the *maqāma*[87]—the traditional Arabic picaresque rhyme-prose oeuvres—and the storyteller of a *hikāya* (live acted story) or of a shadow play—specially when explaining the caricatures on the cover page.

Even while being plainly satirical, Abū Nazzāra, more than Mr Punch, concentrates his early efforts mostly on his political message—more so than on social habits. He therefore never tires of praising the republican ideals of the French Revolution.[88] This tribute to European modern political thought did not however seem to be an impediment for him to venerate the Sultan.[89] Sanua urges Abdülhamid II to substitute the Khedive Ismaʿil with his uncle Halīm. The continual mentioning of Halīm's name in all kinds of conversations, mostly as an attribute given to God, becomes an allegorical claim for the fall of the Egyptian regime as Daumier's *Poire* is for the French July Monarchy.

Sanua saw himself as a mediator who combines modern European achievements of a technical as well as humanistic nature with the traditional values of the Ottoman Empire. In content, as well as in style, *Abou Naddara*, as much as Sanua's theatre, must therefore be considered a transcultural product. Features of the European satirical tradition freely mingle with the Arabic heritage of the peasant satire, Karagöz elements and the traditional *maqāma*. *Abou Naddara*, an Arabic newspaper made in France, which became bilingual only 5 years after its founding, is not a mere adaptation of *Punch* or *Charivari* to the Egyptian context.

Mahmoud Manzalaoui's quote about the genesis of Arabic theatre perfectly fits the context of the satirical press; from the very beginning it indigenised itself, was very successful in doing so, and created something completely new that was the point of departure for the massive journalistic use of political satire and caricature at the beginning of the new century. Therefore, in summary, the *Rihla* is certainly not a self-proclaimed Arabic *Punch* version; but it can be considered as a prototype Arabic *Punch* if *Punch* is taken as the label of a specific genre of politically interested satirical magazines which are illustrated with caricatures.

---

[87] Traditional Arabic satirical and picaresque literary genre written in verse. For further reading, see Jaakko Hämeen-Anttila, *Maqama: A History of a Genre* (Wiesbaden: Harrassowitz, 2002).
[88] *Rihla* 11, 2–4.
[89] *Rihla* 4, 2–3.

Teodor Kassab's Adaption of the Ottoman Shadow Theatre *Karagöz*

Elif Elmas

This chapter focuses on the satirical journal *Hayal*, published by the Ottoman journalist and publisher Teodor Kassab who grew up in a Greek-speaking environment. I particularly emphasise Kassab's adaption of the so-called *Karagöz*, the traditional Ottoman shadow theatre, which has been a vehicle for oral social and political satire since the sixteenth century. Kassab made extensive use of this literary form in his satirical journal *Hayal*. He introduced the main protagonists of the shadow theatre, Hacivat and Karagöz, in the guise of 'journalists' into his satirical journal.

By the middle of the nineteenth century the *Karagöz* theatre had fallen out of favour among the Ottoman intellectuals. Teodor Kassab was the first of the Ottoman publishers who used these popular figures of the traditional shadow theatre as mascots in his satirical journals. This article shows how Kassab instrumentalises the characters of Hacivat and Karagöz to present the changes not only of social and political, but also of linguistic, literary and artistic life in the Ottoman Empire during the nineteenth century. Examples of how he equated his satirical journal with the traditional shadow theatre are also presented.

Introduction

Ottoman publishing is not directly comparable to the contemporaneous European press. Press and journalism first came to the Ottoman capital Istanbul in 1831 with the first Ottoman-language government gazette of Mahmud II, *Takvim-i vekayi*

E. Elmas (✉)
Doctoral Candidate at the Seminar for Languages and Cultures of the Near East at Heidelberg University, Heidelberg, Germany
e-mail: eflatun_ay@hotmail.com

(calendar of events).[1] Ottoman press history is a field that has been investigated only fragmentarily. In consequence, studies of subfields, such as the early satirical press before 1908, are very rare.[2]

The British weekly satirical journal *Punch* and the French *Charivari* circulated all over the world and inspired numerous satirical journals in countries such as Japan, China, India and Egypt during the nineteenth and the early twentieth century. In the second half of the nineteenth century, this new medium, the satirical press, also entered the Ottoman Empire. Especially during the Tanzimat era (1839–1876),[3] the Ottomans became increasingly familiar with European satirical journals and caricatures. Between 1870 and 1877, nearly 20 satirical journals appeared in the Ottoman Empire.[4] Most of them were short-lived and ceased after the first issue. However, the origins of the Ottoman press, in particular the satirical journals, are of a complex nature. In order to comprehend the development of Ottoman satirical journals, the following section of this chapter gives a brief overview about the genesis of satirical journals in the Ottoman Empire.

Initially, the Armenian community of Istanbul was the first to produce satirical journals.[5] The earliest of its kind was published in Armenian in 1852, 11 years after the famous British satirical weekly. It was called *Boşboğaz bir adem* (a chatty man) and edited by the Armenian author and government official Hovsep Vartanyan Pasha,[6] who also introduced caricatures in his satirical journal.[7] A second Armenian satirical journal, *Meğu* (the bee), published by Harutyun Sıvacıyan, followed in 1856.[8] *Meğu* also contained caricatures, drawn by the Armenian Harutyun Hekimyan.[9] In 1860, an unknown Armenian publisher began an Armenian *Punch*.[10] The existence of this satirical journal provides evidence that

---

[1] Orhan Koloğlu, *Takvimi Vekayi, Türk Basınında 150 Yıl (1831–1981)* (Ankara: Ankara Basım Sanayi, 1981), 1.

[2] See: Hamdi Özdiş, *Osmanlı Mizah Basınında Batılılaşma ve Siyaset (1870–1877)* (İstanbul: 2010); and Turgut Çeviker, *Gelişim Sürecinde Türk Karikatürü—I Tanzimat ve İstibdat Dönemi (1867–1878/1878–1909)* (Istanbul: Adam Yayıyınları, 1986).

[3] The Tanzimat (lit. reorganisation) era was a period of reformation that began in 1839 with the proclamation of the Hatt-ı Şerif of Gülhane and ended with the First Constitutional Era in 1876. See: Halil Inalcik, "Tanzimat Nedir?," in *Tanzimat, Değişim Sürecinde Osmanlı İmparatorluğu*, ed. Halil İnalcik (Istanbul: Phoenix Yayınevi, 2006), 13–35.

[4] Çeviker, *Gelişim*, 24.

[5] Johann Strauß, "Notes on the First Satirical Journals in the Ottoman Empire," in *Amtsblatt, vilayet gazetesi und unabhängiges Journal: Die Anfänge der Presse im Nahen Osten*, ed. Anja Pistor-Hatam, vol. 27 (Vienna: Lang, 2001), 121–138; 124.

[6] The transliteration of terms and names here is based primarily on *Redhouse Yeni Türkçe-İngilizce Sözlük* (Istanbul: Redhouse Press, 1968).

[7] The earliest caricature to evolve from a Muslim background was published in 1867 in the newspaper *İstanbul*. Çeviker, *Gelişim*, 17.

[8] *Meğu* appears from 1856 to 1874. Çeviker, *Gelişim*, 17.

[9] Çeviker, *Gelişim*, 35.

[10] Hıfzı Topuz, *II. Mahmut'tan Holdinglere Türk Basın Tarihi* (Istanbul: Remzi Kitabevi, 2003), 75.

the Armenian community of Istanbul in particular was also familiar with the famous British satirical journal.

The Jewish community of Istanbul followed in 1860 by publishing their own satirical journals. *Djoha i Djohayko* (Johā and little Johā) appeared as the first satirical edition in Judao-Spanish, a supplement of the weekly *Djurnal yisraelit*. Starting in the 1860s, the Bulgarian and Greek communities of the Ottoman Empire followed the Jews. However, much less is known about the Greek history of satirical press. Even now it is not clear when the first Greek satirical journal appeared, but the Greek chronicler Manuel Gedeon mentions one short-lived satirical journal called *Plaf-pluf* first published in 1863.[11] Similarly, the first Bulgarian satirical journal, *Gayda*, was founded by Petro R. Slaveykov in 1863 and included illustrations.

In May 1870, the first Turkish-language satirical journal called *Terakki* (progress) appeared, as a supplement of the newspaper of the same name. The latter was founded in 1868 by the journalists Ali Rashid and Filib Efendi, who had a Greek background.[12] On 24 November 1870,[13] a second Turkish-language satirical journal called *Diyojen* (Diogenes) appeared.[14] Initially, *Diyojen* appeared in French,[15] but as yet no definite evidence has been found confirming when exactly Kassab started publishing his journal in French, Greek and Armenian. Only the editorial to the first issue of the Turkish-language *Diyojen* mentions that the journal had appeared a few months before in French and Greek.[16] An editorial called *ihtar* (suggestion), which was published in the nineteenth issue of Kassab's first satirical journal, proves that an Armenian version of *Diyojen* also existed.[17] *Diyojen* was published by the Ottoman journalist Teodor Kassab (also: Theodoros Kassapis, Théodore Cassape), who had returned to Istanbul from France at the beginning of the year.[18] Although

---

[11] Strauß, "Notes," 124.

[12] M. Nuri İnuğur, *Basın ve Yayın Tarihi* (Istanbul: Çağlayan Kitabevi, 1982), 243. In this context it is important to emphasise the interaction of the different communities in the Ottoman Empire. That the Muslim and non-Muslim publishers cooperated with each other was a most common practice in Istanbul. Christoph Herzog, "Die Entwicklung der türkisch-muslimischen Presse im Osmanischen Reich bis ca. 1875," in *Amtsblatt, vilayet gazetesi und unabhängiges Journal: Die Anfänge der Presse im Nahen Osten*, ed. Anja Pistor-Hatam, vol. 27 (Vienna: Lang, 2001), 15–43; 20.

[13] *Diyojen* 1, 12 Teşrin-i sāni 1286/24 November, 1870.

[14] *Diyojen* was published in several languages such as French, Greek and Armenian. Strauß, "Notes," 132. *Diyojen* started as a weekly satirical journal; its popularity soared so quickly that he began to publish it twice and later on three times a week. İz, "Kasap," 681.

[15] Strauß, "Notes," 133.

[16] "Çand mah dan beru fransızca ve rumca olarak neşr olunmakda olub". *Diyojen* 1, 12 Teşrin-i sāni 1286/24 November 1870, 1.

[17] *Diyojen* 19, 13 Mayıs 1287/25 May 1871, 1.

[18] Biographical information on Ottoman journalists, with the exception of a few prominent ones, is often difficult to assemble. But there is some information about the founder of *Diyojen*. Teodor Kassab was a *Karamanlı* who was born in Kayseri in 1835 as the son of a Greek draper, Sarafim Kassaboğlu. Teodor Kassab was only 11 years old when he lost his father. He moved to his relatives in Istanbul (or to Izmir, according to İz), where he attended a Greek school. At the same time, he worked as an apprentice in a store run by a relative, where he met a French officer, a

Terakki is rightly recognised as the first Turkish-language satirical journal, it must be remembered that *Diyojen* was the first satirical journal to appear in its own right, and not as a supplement.

The satirical press was a new phenomenon for the Turkish-speaking audience. In this respect, Teodor Kassab seems to have been aware of the difficulties for Turkish-speaking readers to grasp the character of satirical journals. In the editorial (*ihtar*) of *Diyojen* number 19 he describes the character of satirical journals to his audience: 'Those who are familiar with the French language know that journals called "humoristique" always illustrate the truth jokingly'.[19] Later on, he explains why he had called his journal *Diyojen*: 'Diogenes, a Greek sage, was a perfect fool from Sinop, famous for living in a barrel. Since his temper and creed correspond to the mode of thinking of this journal, his has been considered a suitable name'.[20]

Publishing caricatures was not common in the first Turkish-language satirical journal such as *Terakki*, which had no caricatures[21] at all, and *Diyojen,* which had only three in 183 issues.[22]

Kassab's first satirical journal *Diyojen* quickly became a target for censorship[23] and was finally closed in January 1873 because it published satirical contributions that dealt with political and social issues.[24] A few months later, in April 1873, Kassab started publishing another satirical journal called *Çıngıraklı tatar*[25] (the courier with the bells). His second journal appeared only until July 1873 and was quickly suppressed, too.[26] But with *Çıngıraklı tatar*, Kassab established the caricature as an integral part of satirical journals. Every issue of *Çıngıraklı tatar* contains a caricature on its third page.

---

nephew of Alexandre Dumas (père), who was on his way back to France after the end of the Crimean War (1853–1856). Impressed by his intelligence, the French officer took Teodor Kassab with him and arranged for his further studies in Paris. Afterwards, Teodor started work as Dumas' private secretary and accompanied him on various journeys across Europe. However, there is a lack of information about Teodor Kassab's life and his journalistic activities in France. Because of the outbreak of the Franco-German War of 1870–1871, he had to leave France. After his return to Istanbul, he taught French at several schools. F. İz, "Kasap, Teodor," in *Encyclopedia of Islam, New Edition* (London: Brill, 1954), 681–82; 681. During his stay in Paris, he became acquainted with Namık Kemal (1840–1888), one of the most prominent Ottoman writers and poets of the nineteenth century. The latter was also a journalist and one of the early contributors to *Diyojen*. Çeviker, *Gelişim*, 99.

[19] *Diyojen* 19, 13 Mayıs 1287/25 May 1871, 1.

[20] Translation from Strauß, "Notes," 132.

[21] Çeviker, *Gelişim*, 119.

[22] Ibid., 22; and Mehmet Zeki Pakalın, *Sicil-i Osmanı Zeyli Son Devir Osmanlı Meşhurları Ansiklopedisi*, vol. 18 (Ankara: Türk Tarih Kurumu, 2009), 44–46.

[23] *Diyojen* was closed after the appearance of the third issue for the first time. See: İhsan Sungu, "Teodor Kassab," in Çeviker, *Gelişim*, 96.

[24] Ibid.

[25] *Çıngıraklı tatar* was also published in a French and Greek version. Strauß, "Notes," 134.

[26] Çeviker, *Gelişim*, 123.

Fig. 1 The header of *Çıngıraklı tatar*. *Çıngıraklı tatar* 8, 21 Nisan 1289/3 April 1873, 1

In October 1873, Kassab continued publishing his satirical essays and caricatures under a new name: *Hayal* (imagination, shade or shadow theatre), which was to be his longest running journal. He not only changed the name of his third satirical journal to a name his Ottoman readers were more familiar with, but also his mascots. For his earlier satirical journals *Diyojen* and *Çıngıraklı tatar*, Kassab had chosen mascots which were unfamiliar to the average Ottoman.[27] In his article "Notes on the First Satirical Journals in the Ottoman Empire" Johan Strauß comments that "'The Courier with the Bells' figuring on the title page (in the header of *Çıngıraklı tatar*) is very reminiscent of the Charivari, as presented in a famous cartoon by Grandville in the first issue of the Charivari on 1 December 1832' (Fig. 1).[28]

However, it seems that for his new journal, Kassab chose some well-known local characters. He also published a French (*Polichinelle*), Greek (*Mōmos*) and an Armeno-Turkish (*Kheyal*) edition of *Hayal*.[29] In contrast to *Diyojen* and *Çıngıraklı tatar*, Kassab used no illustrations for the header of *Hayal*.

Changing Formats: The Impact of British and French Satirical Journals on the Ottoman Satirical Press

The following section of this chapter gives a brief comparative overview of the influence of European satirical journals, such as *Charivari* and *Punch*, on the Turkish-language satirical journals that appeared 1870–1877. But the main focus

---

[27] Strauß, "Notes," 134.
[28] Ibid.
[29] Ibid.

of this article is not so much on the Western influence as on the development and introduction of local forms of satire. This text concentrates especially on *Hayal*, as a chief example of an Ottoman satirical journal, which involved local elements and formats of satire.

In the Ottoman Empire, the French *Charivari*[30] in particular must have left a deep impression on the mainly francophone Ottoman publishers. The name of this famous French satirical journal had become more or less synonymous with 'satirical journal' along with the Turkish terms *eğlence gazetesi* (entertainment journal) and *mizah gazetesi* (often translated as humour or joking or as satirical).[31] An Ottoman version of *Charivari*, in Turkish spelled *Şarivari*, was published in 1871 by the editor of the daily newspaper *İbret* (example).[32] In November 1874, a second Turkish-language *Şarivari* appeared as a supplement of the periodical *Medeniyyet* (civilisation).[33]

Later on, the British *Punch* also had an impact on the Ottoman satirical journals, published in Istanbul. In particular, the caricatures of this British weekly were a source of inspiration for most of the Ottoman caricaturists. In Turkish-language satirical journals such as *Kahkaha*[34] (laughter), *Letaif-i Āsār*[35] (monuments of jest) and *Çaylak*[36] (inexperienced) one can also find reprints (but without captions) or modified versions of *Punch* caricatures. Aside from that, there were many other caricatures that owed little or nothing to the styles published in the European gazettes. Furthermore, the Ottoman caricaturists merged these European influences with local satiric and artistic models available in cosmopolitan Istanbul.

Initially, the Ottoman publishers modelled their satirical journals on Western originals. The most important local element of Ottoman satire that was transferred to the satirical journal, were Karagöz and Hacivat, the main protagonists of the Ottoman shadow theatre. Kassab put these characters for the first time in leading articles and as caricatures in *Hayal*, just like the publishers of *Punch* used Mr Punch in the *London Charivari*.

There are some parallels between the British *Punch* and *Hayal*, too. One of the obvious similarities are their theatrical origins. The figure of Mr Punch is deeply

---

[30] The British *Punch* recognises itself as a kind of derivate of the French original because it also carries as a second title *The London Charivari*.

[31] *Terakki* 1, 10 Şaban 1287/5 November 1870, 1; *Letaif-i Āsār* 55, 22 Temmuz (July) 1872, 1; *Hayal* 72, 1 Haziran 1290/14 June 1874, 2; *Geveze* 1, 24 Temmuz 1291/5 August 1875, 1.

[32] *İbret* was founded by Aleksan Sarrafyan Efendi and first appeared under the name *Kevkeb-i Şarkī* in 27 *Şaban* 1286/1 December 1869. "İbret," in *Türk Dili Ve Edebiyatı Ansiklopedisi*, ed. Ramazan Acun (İstanbul: Dergah Yayınları, 1982), 332–336; 332. Çeviker, *Gelişim*, 123; and Strauß, "Notes," 130.

[33] *Hayal* 119, 13 Teşrin-i sāni 1290/25 November 1874, 2.

[34] In the fourth issue of *Kahkaha* there is a reprinted *Punch* caricature which appeared only a few months earlier in the *London Charivari*. Only the caption under the caricature differs from the original. *Punch*, 9 January 1875 and *Kahkaha* 4, 1 Nisan 1291/13 April 1875, 4.

[35] A caricature in the tenth issue of *Letaif-i Āsār* shows Mr Punch wearing the Ottoman fez. *Letaif-i Āsār* 10, 21 Kānun-i sāni 1290/2 February 1875, 83.

[36] *Çaylak* 117, Şubat 1292/24 April 1877, 4; and *Punch*, 2 December 1876.

rooted in the popular English glove puppet theatre, Punch and Judy Show, as much as the figures Hacivat and Karagöz are in the Ottoman shadow theatre. The connection between *Punch* and the Punch and Judy Show is clearly visualised on the cover page of the first issue of the *London Charivari*. Mark Lemon, the founder of *Punch*, explains why they decided to call their satirical journal *Punch*: 'We have considered him (Mr Punch) as a teacher of no mean pretentions, and have, therefore, adopted him as the sponsor for our weekly sheet of pleasant instruction'.[37]

There are other correlations between the satirical journals *London Charivari* and *Hayal*. Although *Punch* reflects English life in general on its pages, London always comes first. The same is true of *Hayal*, which is a mirror of Ottoman life, especially its capital, Istanbul. Moreover, the authors of both *Punch* and *Hayal* were closely connected with drama. The contribution of Teodor Kassab to Ottoman literary culture was not limited to his journalistic activities. Like his colleague Joseph Stirling Coyne, who belonged to the inner circle of *Punch* authors, Kassab also acted as a playwright.[38] Drama and its development in the Ottoman Empire were important topics in most of Kassab's contributions, such as articles, caricatures or editorials, and journals. He discussed and criticised the principles and techniques of the developing modern theatre in his articles, which were then published in his satirical journals.[39] More than other art forms drama was a symbol of social change in the Ottoman Empire. For upper-class Ottomans, the westernised theatre seemed to bear a special fascination. It was one of the art forms most readily and vigorously consumed by the westernising elites of Istanbul. This probably was the reason why Kassab also used his journals to promote Ottoman adaptations of European stage plays or to publish his own translations of famous French novels, such as *Le Comte de Monte-Cristo* (*The Count of Monte Cristo*) by Alexandre Dumas[40] and Molière's comedies *Sganarelle ou Le Cocu imaginaire* (*Işkilli memo*)[41] or *L'Avare* (*Pinti hamid*).[42] However, Kassab was aware of the specific civilisation out of which these plays arose, so he adapted his productions to the Ottoman environment. All the protagonists of his version of the French comedies bear Turkish names. Moreover, Kassab conceived his own adaptations as *Ortaoyun*.[43] He argued that the latter was the theatre of the Turks, which only needed a reform.[44]

---

[37] Marion H. Spielmann, *The History of 'Punch'* (London: Cassell & Co. Ltd., 1895), 2.

[38] Richard G. G. Price, *A History of Punch* (London: Collins, 1957), 27.

[39] Kassab published various contributions such as *Tiyatro terakki ediyor* (the theatre progresses), in *Diyojen* 76, no. 6, 12 Teşrin-i sāni 1287/24 November 1871, 2–3 or in *Hayal* 4, 31 Teşrin-i evvel 1289/12 January 1874, 1.

[40] See: *Diyojen* 98, 23 Şubat 1287/6 March 1872, 3–4.

[41] *Hayal* 58, 16 Nisan 1290/28 April 1874, 3–4.

[42] İz, "Kasap," 682.

[43] The Turkish *Ortaoyun* can be compared with the Italian *commedia dell' arte* but there are many more similarities to the *Karagöz* theatre. The main difference is that the *Ortaoyun* were performed by actors instead of puppets. Metin And, *Karagöz: Turkish Shadow Theatre* (Istanbul: Dost Yayınları, 1979), 12.

[44] *Diyojen* 168, 25 Teşrin-i sāni 1288/7 December 1872, 1–2; *Hayal* 85, 17 Temmuz 1290/29 July 1874, 1–3.

The Ottoman satirical press between 1870 and 1877 had a history of reporting on theatre productions and the theatrical scene. These journals, especially the publications of Teodor Kassab, criticised the newly established Ottoman theatre in a Western sense for bad acting, the use of artificial language, and the failure to adapt plays to Turkish society and Turkish cultural themes.[45] Additionally, Kassab published advertisements for the stage plays of Ali Beğ,[46] one of *Diyojen*'s authors, such as *Ayyar hamza*, an adaptation of Molière's *Les Fourberies de Scapin* or his other adaptation of Victor Bernard's *Madame est Couchée (Kokona yatıyor)*.[47] It was not only Kassab's journals that contained articles and caricatures referring to drama. Other contemporary satirical journals such as *Çaylak*[48] and *Meddah* (public storyteller)[49] also published contributions of this kind.

The Ottoman Shadow Theatre *Karagöz*

Satire, with its various styles and literary forms of expression, was quite familiar to people in the Ottoman Empire. Its population consisted of many different linguistic and religious groups, and accordingly, a plurality of forms of satire that would satisfy each of these existed for several centuries side by side. One of the most famous and popular forms of Ottoman satire, was the shadow theatre *Karagöz*.

In order to be able to make coherent statements about the transformation and the adaptation of the traditional Ottoman shadow theatre to a satirical journal format, it is necessary to know its origins and composition. The origins of the shadow theatre have not yet been precisely traced and vary between China, Java and India because they all had a shadow theatre. The German scholar Georg Jacob claims that Romanies, who emerged from northwest India and journeyed across Asia and Europe, most probably brought the Indian shadow theatre with them.[50]

The famous *Karagöz* expert Metin And notes in his monograph *Karagöz—Turkish Shadow Theatre* that the Ottoman shadow theatre comprises elements that confirm the Romani theory, such as the figure of Karagöz himself, who actually is Roman. He emphasises the fact that Karagöz occasionally appears as a blacksmith or as a seller of grills and tongs, which were some of the main trades of Romanies in the Ottoman Empire. But, he adds, there is not enough substantial proof in Jacob's thesis.[51]

---

[45] *Diyojen* 95, 12 Şubat 1287/24 Februar 1871, 4; *Diyojen* 161, 09 Teşrin-i sāni 1287/9 November 1871, 2. *Diyojen* 165, 23 Teşrin-i sāni 1288/5 December 1872, 3.
[46] Çeviker, *Gelişim*, 120.
[47] *Diyojen* 34, 1 Temmuz 1287/13 July 1871, 4.
[48] *Çaylak* 18, 20 Mart 1293/30 March 1877, 3.
[49] *Meddah* 31, 22 Receb 1292/25 August 1875, 4.
[50] And, *Karagöz*, 21.
[51] Ibid.

Another theory argues that the Ottoman shadow theatre has its origins in Egypt.[52] The Ottoman Sultan Selim I, who captured Egypt in 1517, watched a performance of a local shadow play and was so pleased with the performance that he took a troupe of players to his capital.[53] This event is documented in Ibn İyas' chronicle *History of Egypt* and is, according to And, a reliable source for the Ottoman adoption of the Egyptian shadow theatre.[54] Nevertheless, not only the Egyptian shadow theatre found its way to Istanbul; the preserved plots of Ibn Danyal also did.[55] Another theory claims that the name of the figure Karagöz is derived from the Egyptian vizier Bahaeddin Karakush, who was Saladin's confidant.[56]

According to the seventeenth century Ottoman traveller and author Evliya Çelebi, *Karagöz* was first performed during the reign of the Rum-Seldshuks.[57] Alternatively, various folk legends argue that Karagöz and Hacivat were actually real people. In one version of these stories they allegedly lived during the reign of Orhan Beğ in the early fourteenth century. Both were labourers during the construction of a mosque in Bursa. Hacivat was working there as a stonemason and Karagöz was a blacksmith. Nevertheless, the couple distracted other workers with their witty repartee so that building took much longer than expected, which very much upset Orhan Beğ, resulting in him ordering their execution. A person called Şeyh Küşteri created two-dimensional leather figures of Hacivat and Karagöz to comfort the sovereign who later regretted his order.[58] During the late sixteenth and seventeenth centuries the Ottoman shadow theatre established and further refined its structure by introducing new local characters. It became a popular feature of public and private festivities, taking place in public spaces, such as coffeehouses, and in private homes.

The Main Protagonists of *Karagöz*

The figures of Hacivat and Karagöz represent two extremes. Karagöz represents an uneducated person who is poor, coarse, cheeky, impulsive, always joking; he is eager to try out new ideas and always misbehaves. In contrast, Hacivat is educated and bound to the moral principles of the upper class. He is also a reflective

---

[52] But how the shadow theatre reached Egypt is also not well documented. Shadow theatre was present in Egypt from the eleventh century. And, *Karagöz*, 25.

[53] Ibid.

[54] Ibid., 26.

[55] Ibid.

[56] Ibid., 33.

[57] Cevdet Kudret, *Karagöz. I. Cilt*, (Istanbul, Yapı Kredi Yayınları, 2004), 21.

[58] Kudret, *Karagöz*, 12. This legend also shows similarities to the story of the genesis of the Chinese shadow theatre. See: Ibid, 9.

character. Hacivat usually offers useful advice to others and finds a new profession for Karagöz because the latter has no business and is usually unemployed.[59]

Generally, Karagöz does not understand Hacivat, or he pretends not to because the latter makes use of numerous Arabic and Persian words and speaks in exalted Ottoman, whereas Karagöz uses the vernacular language of ordinary people. Many of the misunderstandings, upon which the humour of the dialogues builds, originate from their different backgrounds. According to the plot of these plays, other characters, symbolising the different communities of the Ottoman Empire rooted in its capital, Istanbul, appear on the *Karagöz* screen.[60]

The Structure of a *Karagöz* Performance

The puppeteer, who had to be trained in different artistic forms of expression, was responsible for the organisation of a *Karagöz* performance. The *hayalbaz* (*Karagöz* puppeteer) had to merge various elements of Ottoman cultural and artistic life in a *Karagöz* performance, including poetry, music, and wordplays of oral literature. A *Karagöz* stage is separated from the audience by a screen which is white and translucent. The puppeteer stands behind the screen, holding the puppets up against it and using a lamp as a source of light from behind the screen.[61] The puppets of *Karagöz* characters are made usually of very thin leather, transparent and in colour.

A *Karagöz* performance consists of three parts, the *mukaddeme* (prologue), the *muhavere* (dialogue), and the *fasıl* (main plot), which ceases with a very short conclusion.[62] The plot and the texts of these plays were orally transmitted from one generation involved in the profession of a *hayalı* (professional shadow theatre puppet master) to another. In the *mukaddeme*, Hacivat enters the screen by singing a song in the form of a *semaı*.[63] Then he shouts *hay hakk!* (greetings to God) before he introduces himself by reciting a poem, called *perde gazeli* (curtain poem), and delivers a short speech to the spectators in which he mentions the impermanence of the world, and expresses his gratefulness to God and the sultan. After welcoming his spectators, he calls for his partner Karagöz, singing *yar bana bir eğlence* (some amusement for me, my dear).[64] Karagöz becomes very angry with Hacivat and his noisy disturbance and starts fighting with him.[65]

---

[59] And, *Karagöz*, 68.

[60] Ibid, 67.

[61] Kudret, *Karagöz*, 33.

[62] And, *Karagöz*, 44.

[63] A form used by minstrels in folk music. *Redhouse Yeni Türkçe-İngilizce Sözlük*, 997.

[64] Kudret, *Karagöz*, 15.

[65] Fighting and beating were also elements of the 'Punch and Judy show'. Mr Punch always had a reason for beating his wife. John McCormick and Benni Prastasik, *Popular Puppet Theatre in Europe 1800–1914* (Cambridge: Cambridge University Press, 1998), 140; and George Speaight, *The History of the English Puppet Theatre* (New York: John de Gaff, 1955), 184.

After Karagöz' anger abates, the characters proceed to the *muhavere*, the second part of the traditional play. The topic of the dialogue is not given and it has no relation to the play. The humour of the performances originates from the wordplays and misunderstandings. Basically, all dialogues have a similar structure: they show the contrast between Hacivat's formal, superior knowledge and Karagöz' common sense and occasional lack of understanding.[66] Subsequently the main plot (*fasıl*) follows, which involves different types of people who were living in the Ottoman Empire with their special kinds of clothes and dialects. Antagonisms, exaggerations, twists of meaning, wordplays, the mimicry of dialects and regional signs are the central elements in this traditional form of satire.

The satirical character of the *Karagöz's* performances was one of the main reasons they became a popular feature in the Ottoman coffeehouses. It was possible to display everything scorned on the *Karagöz's* screen.[67] On that account, *Karagöz* enjoyed the freedom to present extreme obscenity and perversion to his spectators. Several foreign visitors of the Ottoman Empire, who witnessed *Karagöz* performances, emphasised the vulgarity of some of them and noted in their records that Karagöz appears with a phallus.[68] Moreover, everything that actors could not act out on stage was presented in the shadow theatre by the figures. The interaction between man and woman was very limited or not feasible on stage, but it became possible on the *Karagöz* screen. Some *Karagöz* plays included raids on houses where adultery was being committed. Sexual intrigue, lesbianism and other such occurrences, too, played an important role.[69]

Joseph Pierre Agnes describes *Karagöz* as follows:

> Even the press in Europe is not so aggressive. Countries like America, England and France are much more restricted in political criticism than Turkey, which is a country ruled by an absolute monarch.
> Karagöz acts like some sort of unfettered press. Actually Karagöz dialogue is much more fearsome as it is improvised and not tied down to a written text. Apart from the person of the Sultan Abdülmecit, who is considered sacred, Karagöz makes no exception in his attacks. He lashed out at the British and the French Admirals in August 1854 for the way in which they slowed down their work. He criticised their manoeuvres and their lack of efficiency in manning their warships. Even the Grand Vizier appeared on the screen. He was seen to be tried in mock trial as if he were an infidel. The court, not finding his defence acceptable, sentenced him to a term in prison at Yedikule. If this should have happened in a different country, even a single showing of such seditious material would have been sufficient to promote the author's arrest and exile, where as nothing happened to Karagöz.[70]

---

[66] And, *Karagöz*, 45.
[67] Ahmet Yaşar, *Osmanlı Kahvehaneleri: Mekân, Sosyalleşme, İktidar* (Istanbul: Kitap Yayıyınevi, 2009), 42.
[68] Yaşar, *Osmanlı*, 42.
[69] And, *Karagöz*, 65.
[70] Ibid., 84.

Nevertheless, during the reign of Sultan Abdülaziz, the traditional shadow theatre had fallen out of favour[71] because the puppeteers had brought an important high official, Kıbrıslı Mehmed Pasha, to the *Karagöz* screen, and depicted the corruptness and disloyalty of his family, which proved too much for the official censor. As a result, political and social satire became strictly banned from the *Karagöz* plays.[72]

Kassab's Adaptation of *Karagöz*

Teodor Kassab was the first of the Ottoman publishers of satirical journals to provide a new context for the traditional Ottoman shadow theatre, *Karagöz* as well as the *Ortaoyun*, in a period when these forms of entertainment had already become unpopular among the contemporary Ottoman intellectuals.

As with *Karagöz,* Kassab's satirical journal *Hayal*, does not only deal with social and political, but also with linguistic, literary and artistic aspects of daily life in the Ottoman Empire, especially Istanbul. Ottoman satire and satirical journals targeted political activities of the European states and the political situation within the Ottoman Empire. In particular, social satire targeted certain transformations (and the impact of Europe) in language, literature, education, fashion (dress) and entertainment culture. Furthermore, satirists such as Kassab, outlined in their contributions and caricatures the westernisation of Istanbul society. The following part provides a glimpse at how Kassab transferred the satirical spirit of *Karagöz* to *Hayal*. Furthermore, it briefly demonstrates which subjects his satirical contributions, such as editorials, articles, caricatures and dialogues address.

Kassab referred not only to the *Karagöz* in *Hayal* but also in his political daily *İstikbal*, which appeared from August 1875 until September 1876, in which he published announcements for the performances of various *Karagöz* puppeteers across Istanbul.[73] However, other journalists such as Ayvazyan of the *Mamul* journal did not share Kassab's love for the *Karagöz*. Ayvazyan ridiculed the traditional Ottoman forms of entertainment such as *Ortaoyun*, *Meddah* and *Karagöz* in his articles. Consequently, Kassab answered him with his own satirical

---

[71] Namık Kemal, one of Kassab's close friends, intended to condemn *Karagöz* and the Ottoman improvisational theatre *Ortaoyun*. Kemal described these kinds of entertainments as 'schools of immorality' and 'schools of scandal.' One of the reasons for the upcoming unpopularity of *Karagöz* and *Ortaoyun* in the middle of the nineteenth century was also the developing Western style theatre. The Ottoman palace circles, state dignitaries and intellectuals, such as Namık Kemal, preferred the *tiyatro-i nevi* (the new theatre). The *Ortaoyun* is comparable with the shadow theatre *Karagöz*; one of the main differences is that the Ottoman improvisational theatre uses actors, and the shadow theatre utilises two-dimensional puppets. The *Ortaoyun* shared a similar fate as *Karagöz* in the nineteenth century and was transformed into a different kind of improvised theatre. And, *Karagöz*, 12.

[72] And, *Karagöz*, 85.

[73] *İstikbal* 195, 15 September 1876, 4.

commentary, published in the 161st issue of *Diyojen*, by postulating a reform of the *Karagöz* and *Ortaoyun*, which were, in his view, the original Ottoman theatre modes.[74] In his editorial to the second issue of *Hayal*, Kassab again stressed the importance and necessity of reforming the *Karagöz* and *Ortaoyun*. He emphasised that these theatrical performances had reached a new level of abomination and so they 'damage[ed] the good manners of the public', especially those of children who could visit these kinds of performances. For this reason, he claimed, there must be a reasonable regulation for performances in public spaces, which could be attended by everybody. If the *Karagöz* and *Ortaoyun* performances were regulated, Kassab thought they could be very useful for the good manners of the public.[75]

Ayvazyan was not the only Ottoman journalist to ridicule the *Karagöz*. Another journalist, of the newspaper *Hadika* also supported the opinions of Ayvazyan. As a result, Kassab also began disputing with him through his journal.[76] Kassab represented the position that traditional forms of entertainment such as the *Ortaoyun* and *Karagöz* were the authentic Ottoman performance arts. Presumably, these discussions between Kassab and his journalist colleagues were the source of inspiration for him to choose the characters of Hacivat and Karagöz for his satirical journal *Hayal*. Thus, Kassab composed his third satirical journal as a *Karagöz* screen. Through his new medium, *Hayal*, Kassab had the option to 'renew' the *Karagöz* and put it in a different context. Starting with the 58th issue of *Hayal*, Teodor Kassab also provided a new context for the *Ortaoyun*. As mentioned above, he published the sequels of his adaptation of Molière's stage play *Sganarelle ou Le Cocu imaginaire* (*İşkilli memo*) designed as an *Ortaoyun*. He presented his own adaptation as a possible model for how the European stage plays could be performed in the Ottoman Empire.[77]

The *Karagöz* Dialogues (*Muhavere*)

As mentioned above, the Ottoman shadow theatre *Karagöz* was a popular form of entertainment in the Ottoman Empire. Kassab adapted the *Karagöz* to the period and modified it to fit the format of a satiric dialogue (*muhavere*) by reducing the play only to this second formal element of the traditional *Karagöz* performance. Thus, the *muhavere* became the main plot (*fasıl*) and was adapted by Kassab as a standard feature of nearly every issue of *Hayal* with a variety of social, cultural and political themes.

Only in the first issue of *Hayal* does Kassab keep the traditional structure of the play. He starts his editorial with the traditional outcry *hay hakk!*, and omits the

---

[74] *Diyojen* 161, 9 Teşrin-i sāni 1288/21 November 1872, 2.
[75] *Hayal* 2, 14 Teşrin-i evvel 1289/26 October 1873, 1.
[76] *Diyojen* 164, 15 Teşrin-i sāni 1288/27 November 1872, 1–2.
[77] *Hayal* 58, 16 Nisan 1290/28 April 1874, 3–4.

semaı part, which the *Karagöz* performances usually started with.[78] Then, Hacivat continues with his prologue, as in the theatrical *Karagöz* presentation, with a reference to Şeyh Küşteri.[79] According to the tradition, Hacivat calls for his intimate friend Karagöz, and they start their dialogue. From the traditional set of characters, Kassab maintained only the two principal ones for these plays, Hacivat and Karagöz.

Kassab renounced a common style of *mukaddeme* (editorial) which usually opened all newspapers and journals in the Ottoman Empire. He used Hacivat and Karagöz as his mouthpiece and located his editorial and his reason for publishing *Hayal* in this first *muhavere*. In their first *muhavere*, published in the first issue of *Hayal*, Karagöz tells his friend Hacivat that he has now taken the profession of a journalist. Already in the first *muhavere*, Kassab uses the figure of Karagöz as his personal mouthpiece. In this dialogue, he says to his friend Hacivat that he was first turned into 'Diogenes in the barrel' before he took on the role of the 'messenger with the bells'. Kassab adds to his comments that he is still the same and still practicing his profession as a journalist, only his appearance has changed (*ben yine ben, yine san'at gazetecilik yalnız kılık başka*). But Karagöz's profession was not restricted to journalist. In the caricatures he appeared in different professional guises, like in the original shadow theatre.

Beginning with the first issue, journalism became a repeated topic and one of the main elements of their dialogues. Hacivat and Karagöz read and discussed different news and articles found in foreign and local periodicals which were published in the Ottoman Empire. Kassab placed his criticism of journalist colleagues into the mouths of Hacivat and Karagöz. The humour of Teodor Kassab's composition in these *Karagöz* dialogues stemmed from wordplays and misunderstandings which is why he would not eliminate the sharp contrast between Hacivat and Karagöz. They kept their respective characters and followed the traditions of the Ottoman shadow theatre. In Teodor Kassab's adaptation, Karagöz is multilingual; he speaks French, Greek, Armenian and Bulgarian.[80]

Moreover, Kassab presents Karagöz as a Roma, who speaks his native language and appears also as a blacksmith in caricatures.[81] Kassab's Karagöz is interested in exploring new things such as visiting a museum, theatre or opera performances that are taking place in the Ottoman capital. Although Karagöz retains his lack of understanding, he has his friend Hacivat who instructs him.

Kassab uses the freedom of the *Karagöz*'s traditional structure to set his 'plays' in different locations such as the Gedikpaşa theatre. In a dialogue that takes place

---

[78] Kudret, *Karagöz*, 47.

[79] "This screen is a keepsake (*yādigār*) of Küşteri". *Hayal* 1, 18 Teşrin-i evvel 1289/30 October 1873, 1.

[80] *Hayal* 1, 18 Teşrin-i evvel 1289/30 October 1873, 3.

[81] Ibid.

there, Hacivat explains to Karagöz the difference between a shadow theatre performance and the so-called 'theatre performance with curtains', meaning theatrical performance in the Western sense. Both visit the theatre regularly and discuss the viewed plays afterwards. Kassab uses the dialogues between Hacivat and Karagöz not only for describing the Western theatre, but also for promoting the plays of contemporary playwrights such as Namık Kemal.[82] The majority of these dialogues are probably not only created for the amusement of the readership. They also have some pedagogical intentions as with the *muhavere* in the Gedikpaşa theatre.[83]

Letters Addressed to Karagöz and the *Karagöz Telegraf Şirketi* (The Karagöz Telegraph Company)

Starting with the 71st issue, Kassab, alias Karagöz, also begins to communicate with his readers directly through letters.[84] The letters are addressed to Karagöz and also answered by him.[85] Previously, readers' letters were addressed to and answered by the editorial team of *Hayal*, but there is no evidence suggesting that the letters were sent out by readers because they bear no signature.[86] Only some of them feature pseudonyms or initials. They relate to the various articles, reports and caricatures of *Hayal*. For example, some of them describe interesting observations in the Gedikpaşa theatre.

Not only letters were addressed to Karagöz; he also received telegrams from different districts of Istanbul.[87] In the 103rd issue, *Hayal* introduced another instrument of communication—the Karagöz telegram company. *Hayal* was now able to receive fictive telegrams from Europe and the various districts of Istanbul at its own 'telegram company'. *Hayal* capitalised upon the idea of the telegraph and the opportunities for knowledge it provided by including humorous 'telegraph news'.

In 1870, the first news services Reuter and Havas opened offices in Istanbul. The first telegraph lines in the Ottoman Empire were laid out by the British and French

---

[82] On another occasion for example, in the seventeenth issue of *Hayal*, Hacivat and Karagöz have a conversation about Namık Kemal's theatre play *Zavallı Çocuk* (poor child). In this dialogue Hacivat, who has seen the stage play in the theatre, describes the plot to Karagöz in their typical manner. *Hayal* 17, 19 Kānun-i evvel 1289/31 December 1873, 1.

[83] *Hayal* 4, 31 Teşrin-i evvel 1289/12 November 1873, 2–3.

[84] *Hayal* 71, 29 Mayıs 1290/10 June 1874, 2.

[85] Hacivat's appearance is limited to the dialogues and the caricatures.

[86] There is evidence that the authors of *Hayal* were the writers of some of these letters to the editor. They are probably using this literary style to express their critique and at the same time to avoid punishment from the office of censorship. *Hayal* 222, 18 Teşrin-i sāni 1291/30 November 1875, 1–2.

[87] *Hayal* 97, 28 Ağustos 1290/9 September 1874, 3.

ـ وای! غرنه‌جی اولدك ها ! طوغری‌بی الکه اباغكه باقیشورىا؟ دوبه قرازاق.
ـ بکنه‌مدکی؟ بن کیدن اشانی قالیرم • کالی اغوب افندی ترکه اوکر، نوب پردهلی اورته او یونه ماصال بازدقدن صکره بن غرنه‌جی اولسه‌م چوقی؟...

Fig. 2 Karagöz (*right*) and Hacivat (*left*). *Hayal* 6, 07 Teşrin-i evvel 1289/18 October 1873, 4

during the Crimean War.[88] As a result, telegram news became a standard feature of the Ottoman gazettes[89] and also of *Hayal*, which satirises newspapers.

Hacivat and Karagöz in the Caricatures of *Hayal*

Caricatures were a common feature of nearly every issue of *Hayal* but the sophistication of the art work varied considerably. Firstly, Kassab commissioned the Armenian publisher and caricaturist Nişan Berberian to draw the caricatures for *Hayal*.[90] Berberian was the first caricaturist who transferred the shadow theatre puppets of Hacivat and Karagöz to caricature. Their shapes already looked like caricatures, so Berberian could easily transfer them to their caricature forms for the journal format. In the first caricature of Hacivat and Karagöz, which appears in the sixth issue, he presents them in their traditional format—as they appeared in the shadow theatre—for the first and last time: the thick arm of Karagöz was a symbol for a phallus and was later no longer presented because Kassab banished all obscene elements from his adaptation of the *Karagöz*. In his further caricatures, he thus kept the shapes of these figures, except for the thick arm (Fig. 2).

---

[88] Bernhard Lewis, *The Emergence of Modern Turkey* (London: Oxford University Press, 1961), 181.

[89] Christoph Herzog, "Die Entwicklung der türkisch-muslimischen Presse im Osmanischen Reich bis ca. 1875," in *Aneignung und Selbstbehauptung: Antworten auf die europäische Expansion*, ed. Dietmar Rothermund, (Munich: R. Oldenburg Verlag, 1999), 15–44; 35.

[90] Nişan Berberian, who was one of the most productive caricaturists during the period 1870–1877, worked as a caricaturist for several satirical journals in the Ottoman Empire. But very little is known about his life. See: Çeviker, *Gelişim*, 110.

The caption under the picture reads:

Hacivat: 'Wow, you are journalists now! Truly, it suits you[91] like the profession of a silk manufacturer suits a camel'.
Karagöz: 'You do not like it? Why can't I be a journalist?[92] Is it impossible for me? Güllü Agob Efendi also learned Turkish and started writing stage plays in the Turkish language'.[93]

This dialogue makes references to the Armenian playwright Güllü Agob who was also the director of the Gedikpaşa theatre. In 1870 Agob obtained a concession from the Sublime Port which guaranteed him a 10-year monopoly on the performances of all Turkish-language stage plays in Istanbul.[94] Kassab nurtured a profound aversion to Agob. He observed him precisely in order to pass judgment on him in his journal. From the time that Kassab started publishing satirical journals, he not only criticised Agob personally but he also targeted very harshly[95] his theatre—including its actors and his work as a whole. Nearly every issue of his journal features an article against Agob. Furthermore, Kassab accused Agob of communicating French and Armenian values and customs through the translated plays to his audience, without particularly reflecting on their compatibility with the cultural habits of Ottoman society.[96] Teodor Kassab noted the actors' bad Turkish pronunciations and ridiculed his target Agob, not only in articles but also in dialogues (*muhavere*) between Hacivat and Karagöz, as in the example given above.

In the context of modern Ottoman drama, there was an important discussion between the Armenian Agob and the Ottoman-minded Greek Teodor Kassab. Agob aimed to replace the *Ortaoyun* and *Kargaöz* with theatre in the Western sense.

---

[91] Literally: 'It fits to your hands and feet'.

[92] Literally: 'I'm down from whom?'.

[93] Hacivat: '*Vay! Gazeteci olduk ha! Doğrusu eline ayağına yakışır ya! Deveye kazzazlık*'. Karagöz: '*Beğenmedin mi? Ben kimden aşağı kalırım? Güllü Agob Efendi türkce öğrenib perdeli ortaoyuna masal yazdıkdan sonra ben gazeteci olsam çok mu?*' See *Hayal* 6, 7 Teşrin-i evvel 1289/18 October 1873, 4. This *muhavere* of Hacivat and Karagöz found its way to Budapest. It was probably a source of inspiration for *Karagöz* puppeteers around 1886, who performed a play called *Gazeteci* (Journalist) which is based on the dialogical editorial of *Hayal* and the further caricatures of the 6th issue. Kudret, *Karagöz III*, 1183–1888.

[94] In the 58th issue of Kassab is a reference to Agob's concession. *Hayal* 58, 16 Nisan 1290/28 April 1874, 1–2.

[95] In his first satirical journal, *Diyojen*, there are also numerous articles teasing Agob and his theatre, for example, in *Diyojen* 70, 13 Teşrin-i sāni 1287/25 November 1871, 2–3. Kassab continues using his satirical journal to ridicule his popular target Agob. In the twelfth issue of *Hayal* there is a very short contribution about some people who claim that Agob can wiggle his ears but he cannot believe this gossip. *Hayal* 12, 1 Kānun-i evvel 1289/13 December 1873, 4.

[96] *Hayal* 90, 3 Ağustos 1290/15 August 1874, 1–2; *Hayal* 9, 2 Teşrin-i sāni 1289/14 November 1873, 3.

Fig. 3 Kassab (*left*) and Agob (*right*). *Hayal* 87, 24 Temmuz 1290/5 August 1874, 4

A caricature in the 83rd issue of *Hayal* shows Kassab and Agob in front of a *Karagöz* screen (Fig. 3).

The caption of the caricature includes the following dialogue:

> Kassab: 'Oh, I want to see you, Agob'. (In the sense of 'show your skills, Agob!')
> Agob answers: 'That screen has to be burned down and destroyed'.
> Kassab: 'Do not feel sorrow about that baron Agob. I know how I have to show them their right place'.[97]

This caricature correlates with Kassab's articles about the reformation of the Ottoman shadow theatre.[98] Mostly, the caricatures that the caricaturists drew for *Hayal* are closely related to the editorials and articles.

Kassab's other principal targets included the foreign and local press of the Ottoman Empire. He harshly criticised their poorly investigated articles, accused them of spreading fictitious announcements and of copying articles from other newspapers.[99] A caricature in the eighteenth issue of *Hayal* presents Karagöz as a blacksmith who summons his apprentice to use current newspapers to light a fire, with the following comment: 'There are no cheaper combustibles available now, do not hesitate in using them' (Fig. 4).

---

[97] All translations by the author.

[98] *Diyojen* 168, 25. Teşrin-i sāni 1288/7 December 1872, 1–2; *Hayal* 85, 17 Temmuz 1290/29 July 1874, 1–3.

[99] *Hayal* 90, 3 Ağustos 1290/15 August 1874, 2.

شمدى ونلر ن اوجوز معدن قالدى چكنه، آت چكنه آت

Fig. 4 *Hayal* 18, 22 Kānun-i evvel 1289/3 January 1874, 4. ('*Şimdi bunlardan ucuz maden kalmadı, çekinme at, çekinme at!*')

Another example of how Kassab ridicules his rivals is printed in the 88th issue of *Hayal* in which Karagöz appears as a salesman of meat products. Here Kassab was not afraid to picture his colleagues as foul, stinking meat (Fig. 5).

— عوشت به ! لكن بو صجاقده بونلرده قوقدى قالدى ؟ بوندن بشقه ده مشترى يوق ! بونكده پاره سى يوق !

Fig. 5 *Hayal* 88, 27 Temmuz 1290/8 August 1874, 4

This caricature carries the following caption:

Karagöz: 'Go away! However, they are stinking now because of the hot weather. But there is nobody else who is interested besides him! And he has no money!' ('*Oşt be!* [cry used to drive away a dog] *Lakin bu sıcakda bunlarda kokdı. Bundan başkada müşteri yok. Bununda parası yok!*').

On the 'meat' there are the names of newspapers or journals which were published in the Ottoman Empire, such as *Şark* (the east), *Neologos*[100] (with three heads),

---

[100] Greek Newspaper.

Terakki, Menino (as a rabbit), *Mecmua-i maarif* (journal of knowledge), *Levant Times* and *Basiret* (discernment). An interesting detail in this caricature is Berberian hanging the publisher and owner of the daily newspaper, *Basiret*, who is known as Basiretci Ali, by his neck. One of the main reasons for making Ali one of his favourite targets is the fact that he supported the theatre of the Armenian Güllü Agob with his newspaper.[101] This caricature is only one example of Kassab's numerous contributions, such as articles, dialogues and caricatures, about Ottoman journalism.

Fig. 6 *Hayal* 330, 8 Mart 1292/22 March 1876, 4. (Karagöz: '*Beni sevmeyenlere!*')

---

[101] In the 103rd issue of *Hayal*, Kassab publishes a contribution with the title *müdafaa*, which means defence. *Basiret* claims in his 1,326th issue, that the negative publicity of *Hayal* regarding the bad condition of Agob's theatre building is not true. But Kassab argues that *Basiret* itself also writes about the bad situation of the theatre building. *Hayal* 103, 18 Eylül 1290/30 September 1874, 1–3.

His favourite target, Ali Efendi, started publishing his own satirical journal, *Kahkaha*, in March 1875. But his journal was not very prosperous. Just a few months later, in September 1875, *Kahkaha* disappeared. Only 20 issues of *Kahkaha* were published between March and September 1875.[102]

Kassab ridiculed Ali Efendi and his other targets in nearly every issue of his satirical journal. In numerous articles, short notices, *muhaveres* and other caricatures, he portrayed them as drunkards. The Ottoman journalists were mostly well informed. They read the publications of their colleagues. Kassab answered the counterreactions of his targets with a caricature of Karagöz, who offers a black hand to his castigators. The caricature carries a message: 'For those who dislike me!' *Hayal*'s caricatures are distinguishing and visualise Kassab's position very clearly (Fig. 6). Through the black hands of Karagöz, Kassab wants to 'blacken' his aggressors.

In the following caricature Kassab takes the position of Karagöz. It shows his rival Güllü Agob (depicted on the right) and his companion with a huge saw, with which they try to cut out the tongue of Karagöz alias, Kassab (Fig. 7).

The caption of this caricature reads: '*Nafile çabalıyorsunuz ayol! Ne kadar kesersekiz o kadar uzar! Kökü bundadır bunda.*' (Your efforts are useless! The more you cut off of it [the tongue], the longer it grows! The source [meaning the reason for his own satire] is with him [pointing to the man on the right]).

Fig. 7 *Hayal* 332, 28 Şubat 1292/12 March 1877, 4

---

[102] Çeviker, *Karikatür*, 130.

۔ اوغلان! بولری نیچون چپقاردك ؟
— ای حاجیواد نه چاره د زمانه ـ که او عزایسه اوی زمانه ـ ق ه یورلمشدر ؟

Fig. 8 *Hayal* 129, 18 Kānun-i evvel 1290/30 December 1874, 4

Another important issue of *Hayal* was fashion satire. Since the middle of the nineteenth century, the Ottoman upper-class women had been wearing garments imported from Paris.[103] The satire mocked the 'westernisation' of Ottoman society that imitated[104] Europe, especially France, as the embodiment of so-called progress. Fashion satire became a vehicle for passing judgment on cultural transformation. The targets of fashion satire were men as well as women. Another caricature (not reproduced here) is a good illustration of how *Hayal* ridicules changing fashions, which also represented the increasing establishment of European culture. Here we see Karagöz wearing westernised clothes that obviously do not fit him properly. In this case, Karagöz symbolises the 'modern', willing to abandon his traditional culture for Western fashion, and Hacivat represents the 'traditional'.[105] In addition, *Hayal* satirised changing fashion in the text.[106] However, the caricatures proved to be a more effective and pointed vehicle. For example, in the 130th issue there is a *muhavere* which belongs to a caricature of Hacivat and Karagöz (Fig. 8).

---

[103] Fanny Davis, *Osmanlı Hanımı: 1718'den 1918'e Bir Toplumsal Tarih* (Istanbul: Yapı Kredi Yayıynları, 2009), 216.

[104] Kassab especially mocked imitation, not only in fashion but also in theatre and journalism. *Hayal* 1, 18 Teşrin-i evvel 1289/30 October 1873, 4.

[105] In the background of this caricature a chair is also pictured, which symbolises Western goods which were adopted in the Ottoman households.

[106] *Hayal* 130, 21 Kānun-i evvel 1290/2 January 1875, 2.

Hacivat: 'Oh! Why did you change your old way of dressing?'
Karagöz: 'Oh Hacivat, there is no way out, it is said if the time doesn't fit you so you must fit in your time!' (Hacivat: *'Oğlan, bunları niçün çıkardın?'* Karagöz: *'Ey, Hacivat ne çare: zaman sana uymaz ise uy zamana sen, buyrulmışdır'*).

The next caricature is an example of the changing use of language, the introduction of foreign terms into Turkish in particular (Fig. 9):

Fig. 9 *Hayal* 130, 21 Kānun-i evvel 1290/2 January 1875, 4. (Karagöz: *'Efendim bizim bacı hanım, cariyeniz [...] takdim ederim. Hacivat: Ne halt etdin? Karagöz: Yani prezante yaparım. Şıklık o efendim'*)

In this caricature we can see Karagöz as *alafranga* Efendi, dressed in Western style, wearing glasses (symbolising imported Western goods)[107] and introducing his sister, who is dressed in traditional Muslim women's clothes, by using the term *takdim ederim* (let me introduce). Then he corrects himself and addresses Hacivat by using the loanword 'presente' ederim. It was during the nineteenth century that

---

[107] Bernard Lewis, *The Muslim Discovery of Europe* (London: Weidenfeld and Nicolson, 1982), 234.

some sections of the Ottoman bourgeoisie began using foreign terms, especially French ones. Formerly, the Ottoman loanwords originated largely from Italian.[108]

Both caricatures above mock the *alafranga* Efendi, who represents someone who has adopted Western style and manners. According to the definition of *Hayal*, the *alafranga* Efendi is a weird mixture of East and West. He wears European clothes in combination with the Ottoman headgear, a Fez, and also tries to speak French.[109]

Hayal was not afraid to ridicule the multiple relationships emerging between Europe and the Ottoman Empire, as well as local political events, such as the deposition of Sultan Abdülaziz in May 1876.[110]

A good example of how *Hayal* poked fun at different clauses of the promulgation of the First Constitution appeared on 23 December 1876. In this caricature, *Hayal* specifically criticises the twelfth clause of this constitution which restricted the freedom of press (Fig. 10):

Fig. 10 *Hayal* 319, 8 Şubat 1292/20 February 1877, 4

---

[108] Ibid., 84.
[109] *Hayal* 130, 21 Kānun-i evvel 1290/2 January 1875, 2.
[110] *Hayal* 252, 22 Mayıs 1292/3 June 1876, 2.

Hacivat: 'What happens to you Karagöz?'
Karagöz: 'This is the freedom given by the authorities (kanun dairesi [Law Office])'.
(Hacivat: *'Nedir bu hal Karagöz? Karagöz: Kanun dairesinde sebesiti Hacivat!'*).

The hands and feet of Karagöz are in chains, symbolising the 'freedom of press'. Teodor Kassab was not tired of fighting against the censorship through his journal, *Hayal*. He continued writing editorials and articles such as in the 278th issue, in which he placed his critique of suppression in the *muhavere* of Hacivat and Karagöz.[111] *Hayal* was constantly observed by Ottoman officials, especially because of its caricatures and other contributions with political content. After one such publication, Kassab was put in court and condemned to 3 years imprisonment.[112] Starting with the 341st issue, his representatives continued publishing *Hayal* until 30 June 1877, when the last issue appeared.[113] After a few months in prison, Kassab successfully escaped to Europe. A few years later, Sultan Abdülhamid pardoned him, so he could return to Istanbul, where he worked at the Imperial Library of the palace until his death in 1905.[114]

Conclusion

The Armenian and Jewish communities of the Ottoman Empire were the first to introduce the 'satirical press' to their communities. Because of their worldwide trade activities, they were familiar enough with Europe and were more receptive to new ideas from there. Their publications targeted specific linguistic communities. The Ottoman journalist Teodor Kassab was the most successful publisher of satirical journals such as *Diyojen*, *Çıngıraklı tatar* and *Hayal* between 1870 and 1877. He was an outstanding figure and the only one who succeeded in releasing a continuous publication of multi-lingual satirical journals in the Ottoman Empire. He also had the confidence to provide a reform for the traditional forms of Ottoman entertainment performances, such as the *Ortaoyun*, during a period when these traditional spectacles were in danger of disappearing.

As shown above, *Punch* and *Karagöz* had similar roots in popular theatre which was a source of inspiration for the creation of characters for satirical journals because of their extreme popularity in British and Ottoman societies. Kassab conveyed the spirit of *Karagöz* in his satirical journal *Hayal*. Berberian, the caricaturist of *Hayal*, transferred the shadow theatre figures Hacivat and Karagöz to caricatures. Their messages, though, depended mostly on the caricatures' captions.

---

[111] *Hayal* 278, 9 Ağustos 1292/21 August 1876, 1.

[112] Orhan Koloğlu, *Türk Karikatrü Tarihi* (Istanbul: Bileşim, 2005), 36.

[113] *Hayal* 368, 18 Haziran 1293/30 June 1877.

[114] İz, "Kasap," 681. The date of Kassab's death has not been determined exactly. Pakalın claims that Kassab died in 1905. Pakalın, *Sicil-i Osmanī*, 46.

Teodor Kassab used *Karagöz* as his personal instrument of satire to poke fun at his targets. He placed dialogic criticisms pertaining to social, cultural and political issues in the mouths of Hacivat and Karagöz. Kassab succeeded in creating a fusion between 'Eastern' and 'Western' satire in his satirical journals, of which *Hayal* was the most successful. The Ottoman caricatures synthesised a variety of both Ottoman and European satirical styles.

As demonstrated by the selection of the title *Hayal*, Kassab equated the Ottoman shadow theatre with the Ottoman satirical press. *Hayal* was also a kind of 'pedagogical institution' which aimed at instructing its readership about new developments and institutions such as theatres and museums. The pages of *Hayal* were Kassab's screen of the Ottoman shadow theatre, which provoked the reader to discern the 'truth'. Thus, a famous curtain poem of Hacivat appropriately fits here to describe the ambiguous character of the satirical journal *Hayal*:

> To the eye of the uninitiated this curtain produces only images
> But to him who knows the signs, it symbolises the genuine truth ...
> Şeyh Küşteri models this screen like the world ...
> It amuses those who are looking for entertainment
> Look to the meanings which are hidden in this play
> It is a show of subtlety intended for the experts to understand its subtle points ...[115]

---

[115] Kudret, *Karagöz*, 47. Translated by the author.

What's in a Name? Branding *Punch* in Cairo, 1908

Marilyn Booth

In February 1908, a double-page colour cartoon appeared in the new Cairo-based journal *al-Siyāsa al-musawwara* (politics illustrated, founded December 1907). Reflecting on the 'press wars' in Cairo at the time, the cartoon features men in fezzes and coats (and one in a turban and *abāya*) representing editors of leading nationalist and anti-London newspapers—*al-Liwā'* (founded 1890, Mustafa Kamil), *al-Mu'ayyad* (founded 1889, 'Ali Yusuf), and *al-Minbār* (founded 1906, Hafiz 'Awad).[1] Marching in procession, each bears a banner on which the title of his newspaper is stamped in Arabic and English. They head in the direction indicated by a sign saying 'To the Way of Independence [sic] and Lyberty [sic]' (in both English and Arabic). To the right, a beast with cloven hooves and three human heads (ears pointed) carries three flags with small Union Jacks on them. The heads face in three directions, straining against each other. One faces a sign saying 'To the way of protection'—in Arabic, *himāya,* meaning also the 'Protectorate'. This was the fiction by which London named its occupation of Egypt, which had lasted for a quarter century. One of the triple Union Jack flags bears the name AL MOKATTAM (*al-Muqattam*)—a newspaper slammed in the nationalist press as funded by and supportive of the British occupation.

This cartoon exemplifies several consistent, strongly marked features of a journal that was visually and thematically a culmination of the earliest period of political caricature in Arab media culture. The cartoon suggests, first, fierce interest in the nascent Egyptian Arabophone press as a player in national and nationalist politics, able to shape the outlooks of a rising constituency called the nation. Second, it locates its own critical power within that activist press in vivid graphic satire. Third, it manifests a strongly anti-imperialist nationalist stance. Fourth, it

---

[1] *Al-Minbār* was co-founded by Muhammad Mas'ūd, but the better known 'Awad is likely to be the editor portrayed.

M. Booth (✉)
Professor of Arabic and Islamic Studies at the University of Edinburgh, United Kingdom
e-mail: M.Booth@ed.ac.uk

offers visual markers of a collective Egyptian belonging that embraces portions of a westernising intelligentsia and a more locally oriented one—signalled in different clothing styles—while also demarcating a national 'us' and a varied 'them' predicated on international and local politics. The beast with three heads satirises the three Syrian publishers-editors of *al-Muqattam* (founded 1889), Faris Nimr, Yaʿqub Sarruf and Shahin Makaryus, representing them as both subhuman and evil, turning one face toward Egypt and the other toward England. Finally, though, the cartoon and the journal imagine a broader circuit of visual satiric politics in the use of a non-Egyptian brand name, the multilingual play of labels and captions, and an evocation of transcultural recognition.

From its very beginnings in the winter of 1907, the journal showed its nationalist colours. In successive cartoons it lampooned the Egyptian elite's collusion with the British, the European powers' eagerness to carve up West Asia and North Africa, the usefulness of colonial possessions as dumping grounds for unemployed European subjects, the ready adoption by an emerging Arab bourgeoisie of practices labelled as Western, and vagaries of local politics. None of these topics were unusual for the time or unique to this publication, but the newspaper's art was something new, as local observers remarked. Through its indebtedness to European visual satirical traditions and its deployment of three languages within and around its caricatures, *al-Siyāsa al-musawwara* seemed to signify the transnational circulation of a visual language of political satire, emanating outward from Cairo, including Arabophone audiences elsewhere whilst gesturing to readers of French and English.

How appropriate, then, that the journal had a second name: *The Cairo Punch*. This title appeared in English letters on every masthead and above every issue's double-page cartoon. Yet the linkage between *Punch* of the imperial capital and *Punch* of the Egyptian capital seems tenuous, a mere gesture via a title that fronts a journal written almost entirely in Arabic but with French and English hovering in and around its caricatures. While the visual satire of the two journals exhibits a similar level of complexity, albeit in one cartoon per issue in Cairo rather than the virtual bombardment of images (cartoons, illustrations, page décor) in London's paper, their association appears notional rather than genetic. This association inheres in the idea of visual caricature in service to political and social critical goals, and in the use of certain common visual tropes and strategies, rather than in any direct or traceable borrowing of genres or images. However, we do find in *al-Siyāsa al-musawwara* a notion that visual and written genres and registers work together to produce particular kinds of humour and social commentary. As in *Punch*, I will argue, it is not simply the visual but the interplay of visual images and verbal satire produced by juxtaposing different 'local' registers (including English and French) that constructs the satire. Finally, though, *Punch*'s 'self-conscious business practices', as Brian Maidment calls them in his study of the London magazine in this volume, may have inspired *The Cairo Punch*'s more modest but continually self-promoting presence: and surely appropriation of the title was itself a branding move, a signal to readers that this journal's producers intended a lavish cosmopolitan abundance of image and text, albeit one with local vision. The marketing *in* and marketing of Cairo's *Punch* seem to both signal its slightly peculiar or perhaps ambivalent location within Egyptian politics and media practices, and to remind us how multivalent and cosmopolitan *the local* can be.

I will first illustrate the interplay of the visual and the textual with reference to the cartoon described above. Next, I will consider the local context of *The Cairo Punch* within a short history of visual satire in Egypt. There then follows an analysis of the periodical's and founder-cartoonist's sense of mission, in conjunction with what we know of his trajectory and then of the journal's circulation beyond Egypt. I will address the controversy the journal's editor courted (with apparent relish), and link this to its discourse of self-advertisement. I will return to its cartoons, briefly setting out their presentational strategy. I will consider the way national and imperial politics are linked in cartoons and articles focused on the Egyptian street and end with some observations on the circulation of visual tropes.

This chapter introduces a satirical and heavily visual periodical that has fallen out of sight in histories of the Arabic press. Based on the first 37 issues, my characterisation of this paper must remain suggestive rather than comprehensive. If, in some form, *al-Siyāsa al-musawwara/The Cairo Punch* continued publication into the next decade, this is a story that demands further research.[2]

Local Scenes and Linguistic Manoeuvres

When *al-Siyāsa al-musawwara/The Cairo Punch/Politics Illustrated* appeared on the public scene at the very end of 1907, apparently it quickly drew notice for these double-page colour caricatures, one in every issue, more elaborate, larger and more vivid than anything that had appeared in the Arabic press, to my knowledge, including the cartoons of Jacob Sanua's (Yaʿqūb Sannūʿ's) *Abū Naddāra* (the man with glasses) series a couple of decades before. These forceful panoramic cartoons

---

[2] The 37 issues I have studied are held in the Hoover Institution Library, Stanford University, Stanford, California, USA. I thank the staff, particularly Paul H. Thomas, Librarian, for help, efficiency and generosity in providing me with material, which I reproduce here with the Library's knowledge. The copyright holders of this publication are untraceable. The US Library of Congress holds posters/covers from later years, as late as 1913. I am grateful to Yasemin Gencer for this information and to Eliane Ettmüller for putting me in contact with her, as well as alerting me to the mention of this journal that set me off on this detective spree. I am indebted as well to colleagues who have helped me with far-flung references or read a version of the chapter: Tony Gorman, Hans Harder, Sonja Hotwagner, Brian Maidment, Barbara Mittler, and I-Wei Wu. I am grateful to Anne Moßner for her careful editing.

In references, when an authorial name appears in brackets, it is because within the essay there are textual clues that this is the author, but the text is unsigned. For unsigned articles without unequivocal textual clues as to authorship, I omit any authorial name; for *al-Siyāsa al-musawwara* most, however, were very likely from the pens of either Zaki or his collaborator, the poet Hafiz Ibrahim. In this essay, I do not always use both titles to refer to the journal; but *al-Siyāsa al-musawwara/The Cairo Punch* are invariably the same journal.

Fig. 1 Untitled cartoon from *al-Siyāsa al-musawwara* 1, no. 8, 14 February 1908, 2–3

focused mostly on internal Egyptian politics and the British occupation, while also addressing European imperialism and global politics more generally.[3] Aligning itself with the nationalist opposition to British rule, the newspaper featured short texts by the renowned poet Hafiz Ibrahim, declaring that it would eschew the detailed political commentary of other journals—although, as the year went on, it offered just such lengthier commentary. Only four pages in total, half the fortnightly publication was occupied by its large, colour, double-page narrative cartoon.

Let us return to the cartoon with which we started. What immediately confronts us is a play of voices in three languages and two scripts, yet voices that are parallel rather than in dialogue, offering puns that work only in one tongue as well as unevenly trenchant commentary on Britain's presence in Egypt (Fig. 1).

---

[3] In the first 37 issues (15 December 1907–1914 December 1908), of 37 visual images, 19 focus centrally on the British in Egypt, six on British imperialism in the broader European context, three on local politics in Egypt (but with the overlay of foreign interference), three on the Ottoman Empire and European designs on it, three on European imperialism elsewhere in the Arab world, and one on international politics more generally. The remaining two are the only images that do not fall in to the category of cartoon or caricature: they are representations of the Egyptian Khedive and of Ottoman power following the 1908 Ottoman constitution, of which *al-Siyāsa al-musawwara* clearly approved.

A dog with bared teeth sporting the Union Jack faces the marchers, while amongst the marchers' legs run other dogs. In English, they are labelled 'AL MOKATTAM dogs' and in Arabic, with a wordplay, *adhnāb wa-kilāb al-Muqattam* 'Tails/appendages [i.e., followers] of *al-Muqattam* [newspaper]'. In the upper left-hand corner, pyramids frame a Sphinx pointing a finger and saying in English, 'Go ahead bravely my dear sons'. (A close translation of the Arabic would be: 'Walk with courage on this road my dear sons'.) Beneath the cartoon, a caption appears in Arabic (centre), English (left) and French (right). Although they are 'translations' of each other, the timbre of each one differs. In Arabic:

> Egypt addresses her sons: Persevere with patience—do not be sparing with the wages [or price, *ajr*]—and provision yourselves on hope—and avoid failure. For the hard journey is a long one and supplies are sparse—and the enemy [is procured] by ambush, and heed [comes] by watching.
>
> The Occupation addresses *al-Muqattam* [not, it seems, included in Egypt's 'sons']: Beware of them arriving, for in the Muqattam [Hills, above Cairo] are boulder upon boulder. So set your dogs on them, and let loose upon them your tails/followers.

In English, the Sphinx (as Egypt, but also as the double of the cartoonist-editor) is the speaker, saying simply, 'Continue on in the way to Independence and Liberty and by your united efforts you are bound to succeed'. *Al-Muqattam*, speaking, plays on the Arabic pun in the cartoon: 'I shall always hinder and dog your steps, and purpose to keep my colours, ever pursuing on in the path of protection'. In French, 'John Bull' speaks to 'the monsieur with three faces', saying, 'Leave these men tranquil for I see that your pack of dogs [*meute*] and your ways of sowing discord among them will finally bring them together in agreement'.[4]

The caricature's multilingual frame suggests multiple audiences. The overall message is unequivocally nationalist and anti-colonialist, slamming both the British as occupiers and the Arabophone editors of a newspaper that was a British mouthpiece, funded by the occupation. (That *al-Muqattam*'s editors were Syrian Christians who had immigrated to Egypt added fuel to a broader resentment against this group of Arab immigrants in the country.) Yet the different audiences appear subject to diverging messages. The Arabic caption and the double meaning of *dhanab* emphasise the mercenary aspects of supposedly local (provided by Ottoman Syrian residents) propaganda for the British and the difference in 'provisioning' between Egyptian nationalist organs and the occupation's mouthpiece, suggesting the unevenness of the contest. Moreover, double meanings intensify the message: *i'tasimū*, plural imperative for 'persevere', also means 'stage a strike/sit-in'. *Mashhad* suggests a viewing or watching but also can refer to a funeral cortege or a place of sacred sacrifice or martyrdom.

---

[4] [Untitled cartoon], *al-Siyāsa al-musawwara* 1, no. 8, 14 February 1908, 2–3. Image signed 'A. H. Zaki'. All translations from Arabic and French in this essay are mine. When a text appeared in English or in French in the journal, that is clearly indicated, otherwise it can be assumed that all quotations are my translations from the Arabic.

The French version, on the contrary, suggests that *al-Muqattam*'s political work will backfire, as will British attempts at a divide-and-rule policy which depend partly on fostering minorities as clients. The French text intimates the ultimate unity of those in the forefront of the nationalist cause. The English caption lacks these nuances. That the speaking characters are slightly different from one language to the next adds another layer of complication, suggesting perhaps that 'translation' changes the voice of the narrator itself.[5]

The Cairo Punch in Local Context

Al-Siyāsa al-musawwara's trilingual captions might have been influenced by locally produced newspapers, those put out by minority and multi-ethnic political groupings in Egypt at this time, whether Greek, Italian or French. Or they might hark back to Sanua's journal, which did carry Arabic and French captions, albeit ones that did not precisely mirror each other in meaning, as Eliane Ettmüller has shown.[6] At the same time, although satirical newspapers had been appearing in Egypt for some time, *al-Siyāsa al-musawwara* was one of the first since Sanua's to display visual satire. The political moment was significant. As this journal appeared in December 1907, nationalist, anti-colonial politics in Egypt were visibly emerging and beginning to take embryonic institutionalised form. Indeed, 1907 witnessed the founding of political parties and of several satirical newspapers, partly as a result of political events in 1906 that galvanised popular anger. Now the satirical commentary of café repartée, oral poetry and song, already taken up in print in 1890s journals such as *al-Arghūl*, saw a few attempts at visual portrayal, most flamboyantly in *al-Siyāsa al-musawwara*.

A few months before the appearance of this local *Punch* there had appeared the journal *HāHāHā* (March 1907), founded by the pair who had started the nationalist newspaper *al-Minbār* the year before. *HāHāHā* soon took on a more resonantly indigenous title, *Khayāl al-zill* (shadow theatre). Because the art it espoused was new on the scene (with the exception of Sanua's efforts earlier, as detailed in Eliane Ettmüller's chapter, Abū Nazzāra's Journey from Victorious Egypt to Splendorous Paris: The Making of an Arabic *Punch*),[7] the editors attempted to explain the power of visual caricature even as they acknowledged that to explain visual content would deaden the impact.[8] *HāHāHā*'s editors bemoaned that none of what they labelled

---

[5] This point about translation will also be seen at work in I-Wei Wu, chapter Participating in Global Affairs: The Chinese Cartoon Monthly Shanghai Puck in this volume.

[6] Eliane Ursula Ettmüller, 'The Construction of the National-Self through the Definition of its Enemy in James Sanua's Early Satirical Writings', PhD diss. [Inauguraldissertation], Universität Heidelberg, 2011, 215, 285–86.

[7] Chapter Insistent Localism in a Satiric World: Shaykh Naggār's 'Reed-Pipe' in the 1890s Cairene Press in this volume.

[8] Ahmad al-Maghāzī, *Al-Siḥāfa al-fanniyya fī Misr*, vol. 1, *Nash'atuhā wa-tatawwuruhā min al-hamla al-faransawiyya 1798 ilā Misr al-dustūriyya 1924* (Cairo: GEBO, 1978), 167–68.

the 'geniuses' of this art seemed to inhabit Egypt. Yet, they assured readers that as an art requiring 'skill, intelligence and practice', the practice of visual caricature could be acquired. Clearly aware that most of their readers would be unfamiliar with the art, they *explained* the meanings these drawings elicited—as even the better known and longer lasting periodical *al-Kashkūl*, a decade and a half later, would do for its earliest caricatures. At the same time, they declared, 'If there is among the readers anyone who needs explanation of these images, their likes are not the ones for whom this periodical is issued [...] the sharp-witted one will understand'.[9]

Like *al-Siyāsa al-musawwara,* this journal did not explicitly recognise Sanua as a precedent; unlike the former, it did not signal any link to European visual traditions by displaying a necessarily borrowed title, choosing one that could be seen as either borrowed or local.[10] Yet, these writers and artists did acknowledge inspiration from Europe, and specifically from Britain. The editor of *HāHāHā* was energised by an essay of Carlyle's on 'the philosophy of laughter'; the goal of his newspaper, he said, was 'to portray events and personalities in political issues through images that leave lasting impact on souls. For images fix in the mind or on the network of the eye, as they say in medicine, which articles do not do'.[11] Likewise, the editor of *al-Siyāsa al-musawwara* reminded readers that satirical newspapers were part of public discourse in 'civilised countries' and noted that its own editor-cartoonist had studied the art there, as we shall see. Yet, those who have studied Egyptian satire and the political cartoon in Egypt have neglected *al-Siyāsa al-musawwara/The Cairo Punch.*[12]

---

[9] "Rusūmunā," *HāHāHā* 1, no. 1, 8 March 1907, 7, quoted in al-Maghāzī, *Al-Sihāfa,* 171; my translation.

[10] The verb *ha'ha'* in Arabic signifies 'to laugh', though it is certainly not the most literary or classical choice. Deleting the glottal stop in a noun form associated with the verb further emphasises the colloquial and possibly foreign stamp of the title. A quadrilateral verb, *ha'ha'* could be of foreign provenance, but is also similar to other onomatopoeiac verbs in Arabic in using this form.

[11] Muhammad Masʿūd and Hāfiz ʿAwad [the editors], "al-Muqaddima al-ūlā," *HāHāHā* 1, no. 1, 8 March 1907; quoted in al-Maghāzī, *Al-Sihāfa,* 168; my translation. Al-Maghazi notes that they did not indicate Sanua's 'pioneering role' even though his newspapers had been widely distributed in Egypt and indeed were printed there for the first 2 years (see Ettmüller in this volume).

[12] Afaf Lutfi Al-Sayyid Marsot, for example, says that 'the graphic cartoon was not used in the period between 1880 and 1920', while noting that 'Lord Cromer, Kitchener and all the other personalities embroiled in Egyptian public life would have made marvellous subjects for graphic cartoons'—as is demonstrated in Zaki's cartoons from this allegedly cartoonless period. Afaf Lutfi Al-Sayyid Marsot, "The Cartoon in Egypt," *Comparative Studies in Society and History* 13, no. 1 (January 1971): 2–15; 12. No doubt the journal has not been widely available to researchers. Al-Maghazi does not mention it either.

In the various bibliographic and survey sources on the Arabic/Egyptian press, the journal is noted by its Arabic title, never by *'The Cairo Punch'*. See: Filīb dī [Philippe de] Tarrāzī, *Tārīkh al-sihāfa al-ʿarabiyya,* 4 vols. (Beirut: al-Matbaʿa al-adabiyya, 1913–1914), vol. 4, 189, 280, 370–71; *Mudawwanat al-sihāfa al-ʿarabiyya,* eds. Yūsuf Q. Khūrī and ʿAlī Dhū al-Faqqār Shākir (Beirut: Maʿhad al-inmā' al-ʿarabī, 1985), vol. 1, 228; Qustakī ʿAttāra, *Tārīkh takwīn al-suhuf al-misriyya* (Alexandria: Matbaʿat al-taqaddum, 1928), 305; Ibrāhīm ʿAbduh, *Tatawwur al-sihāfa al-Misriyya*

Unlike the editors of *HāHāHā,* the editor/artist of 'politics illustrated' does not instruct readers on how to read its graphic caricatures, other than internal guidance offered through use of Arabic and English within the drawing itself and in captions. Unlike other satirical newspapers and magazines in Egypt (whether contemporaries like *Khayāl al-zill,* earlier publications such as *al-Arghūl,* or later ones) this paper does not depend on colloquial poetry or other texts in vernacular Arabic.[13] The few dialogues in *al-Siyāsa al-musawwara/The Cairo Punch* are composed in standard formal Arabic, though they do constitute verbal caricature, for example, characterising recognisable men of Egypt's cabinet in conversation.[14] Although since their emergence cartoons in the Arab world have tended to be associated with colloquial Arabic forms, and to offer colloquial captions, this newspaper used a simplified, straightforward but 'literary' idiom, derived from classical Arabic that was becoming increasingly popular in news organs of the time.[15]

'Politics illustrated'/*The Cairo Punch* was praised by peer journals soon after its appearance—laudatory words that (somewhat unusually) the editor reproduced assiduously in his own paper. In these notices, the journal was always referred to by its Arabic title—never as *The Cairo Punch,* presumably because the Arabic title was more salient to local readers, and also perhaps because the London magazine did not serve as a recognised reference point for local audiences, whereas of course it may have served as just such a sign of familiarity for English- and French-language readers. These congratulatory words addressed the journal's strengths, as we shall see. But more indicative of the journal's immediate popularity and wide circulation is its description, a few years later, by the doyen of Arabic press history, Filib di Tarrazi, who commented in his 1913 book on the Arabic press that *al-Siyāsa al-musawwara* was

> ...the most excellent illustrated newspaper appearing in Egypt and giving visual portrayals of Egypt's circumstances. Its splendour and renown were enhanced by its front-page effusions from the pen of Hafiz Ibrahim, the poet of the Nile Valley. In its third year, it moved to the city of Bologna in Italy, and its founder-publisher limited himself to issuing one large-format page representing political conditions in the countries of the East (*bilād*

1798–1951 (Cairo: Maktabat al-Adab, 1944), 298; and the discussion of contemporary practice below.

[13] Except for a single *zajal* (colloquial Arabic strophic poem), a verbal caricature of a westernised Copt. "al-Qird yitburnat," *al-Siyāsa al-musawwara* 1, no. 33, 25 October 1908, 4.

[14] See, for example, a conversation between ministers on the train to Fayyum, where they will attend dedication of a new school. "Muhādathat al-nuzzār," *al-Siyāsa al-musawwara* 1, no. 14, 3 April 1908, 1.

[15] Thus Marsot suggests that amidst the serious nationalist journalism of the twentieth century's first decade, colloquial humour would have been out of place; and this is one reason why she places the emergence of the cartoon (with the exception of Sanua) later in the century (Marsot, "The Cartoon," 12–13). However, this view errs on two counts: there were satirical periodicals drawing wholly or partly on colloquial Arabic throughout this period (from the 1890s on); and, at least in *al-Siyāsa al-musawwara,* graphic cartoons did not necessitate the use of the vernacular.

al-Sharq) devoid of articles. Despite the great losses he incurred for its sake, it circulated more widely throughout the kingdoms of the East than any previous Arabic newspaper had done. Its drawings were beautifully printed and vied with its peers in Europe. Every illustration alluded to serious meanings geared to strike every politics maven and man of letters with wonder.[16]

A Mission and a Title (or Two)

The first issue of *al-Siyāsa al-musawwara/The Cairo Punch* was dated 15 December 1907 and datelined Cairo; the editorial office was described as located opposite the Egyptian [Khedivial] Bourse on Shāriʿ al-Maghribī.[17] In his opening salvo, the founder-editor made no mention of the existence of other Arabophone journals of this sort. Indeed, ʿAbd al-Hamid Zaki launched his newspaper with the following declaration:

> In journalism I noticed an empty space and so I occupied it; and in politics I saw a lack so I made it up. God chose that I would publish a newspaper silent of tongue but expressive of inner feelings, in which inference spares you explication; symbols and gestures make it unnecessary to communicate with proclamations and shouts; and just enough suggestion [replaces] the elaborate treatise.[18]

As he clears a space in public discourse for his non-verbal newspaper, Zaki implicates his readers as competent decoders of his art and technique. His stated aims are three: to insist on remembrance of events that people forget, to enliven a beautiful art, and to serve 'the sons [or children] of the East'.[19] Visual art, he declares, had been one of the three arts of 'the East'—poetry, painting and drawing, and music. Cradled and nurtured there, these arts had 'emigrated' to the West in its ascendant phase.[20] Art and the West had triumphed. Thus, Zaki defines his political project as a question partly of cultural reclamation. But this cultural politics of recuperation and revival is above all *political:* it yields a running commentary on transnational state politics. With his emphasis on indigenous creative forms—and given the journal's clearly anti-imperial stance—the borrowed Anglophone title,

---

[16] Tarrāzī, *Tārīkh al-sihāfa al-ʿarabiyya*, vol. 4, 188–89, n. 3.

[17] The few sources that mention this periodical differ on its launch date and its move to Bologna. Tarrāzī, *Tārīkh al-sihāfa al-ʿarabiyya*, gives 1 January 1908 as its appearance in Bologna (370–71) but it was still in Cairo at that time. Khūrī and Shākir, *Mudawwanat al-sihāfa al-ʿarabiyya*, vol. 1, 228, lists it as starting in Nov 1907. ʿAttāra, *Tārīkh takwīn*, 305, lists it for 1908 rather than 1907, noting that the first issue appears 'at the start of January'. ʿAbduh, *Tatawwur*, 298, lists it as the last newspaper appearing in Egypt in 1907.

[18] ʿAbd al-Hamīd Zakī, "al-Muqaddima", *al-Siyāsa al-musawwara* 1, no. 1, 15 December 1907, 1.

[19] Ibid.

[20] Ibid.

Fig. 2 Masthead, *al-Siyāsa al-musawwara* 1, no. 1, 15 Dec. 1907, 1

always printed in Latin characters on the masthead and in a font that shadows that of its London namesake, seems a curious choice (Fig. 2).

Indeed, an intriguing fact about *The Cairo Punch* is that its English-language name bears no semantic or situational connection to its Arabic title, *al-Siyāsa al-musawwara*, which as noted simply means 'politics illustrated'. Even more intriguing is the total silence (throughout the journal's first and probably only year) concerning this choice of a dual title with its reference to a famous London publication. While the editor-proprietor, who also signs the cartoons, notes that he has spent time in Europe to learn the art of caricature,[21] he never makes any reference to London's *Punch* and only once, late in the year, to a related publication, from Asia rather than from Europe: 'the Japanese *Tokyo Puck* took one drawing from us and praised the founding of such a paper as ours in the East'.[22] Neither Zaki nor the editors of other satirical newspapers, to my knowledge, ever mention that the London *Punch* might have been available in Egypt. It seems likely that colonial officials and their families subscribed or brought issues or volumes with them from Britain, but no doubt these circulated only amongst small circles, mostly European residents.[23] In 1902, as the publishers of *Punch* tested the

---

[21] Ibid.

[22] ['Abd al-Hamīd Zakī], "Maqām al-jarīda fī 'alam al-siyāsa," *al-Siyāsa al-musawwara* 1, no. 17, 1 May 1908, 1.

[23] Khanduri's archival work on *Punch* as a commodity amongst British army personnel in India notes its popularity there and the journal's 'patriotic' provision of free copies and occasional permission to reprint images. As she notes, this was also a savvy marketing strategy. Ritu G. Khanduri, "Vernacular Punches: Cartoons and Politics in Colonial India," *History and Anthropology* 20, no. 4 (Dec. 2009): 459–86; 463–64, as well as in this volume.

potential of a marketing campaign in the colonies, their business partner who travelled to India for this purpose stopped off in Egypt.[24] But amongst Egyptian newspaper proprietors, to my knowledge, familiarity with *Punch* was only obliquely present in their publications. Moreover, that familiarity was an aspect of the journey westward in search of new knowledge, which had already become part of the experience of male Egyptians with some education and resources, either through their own travels to Europe or as readers of the genre of travel memoir, fictional or not.[25] Could someone such as Zaki have been familiar with Urdu productions of *Punch*-like periodicals in North India? The young founder of *Sar Punch* (1909) had briefly been a professor of Arabic and Persian.[26] Is it possible that these graphic journalists learned of each other's work through the supposedly peripheral circulations of imperialized subjects in the empire?

Indeed, why does Zaki need *Punch* at all? Does he borrow the title and craft a masthead suggestive of the famous London paper for marketing purposes? To signal a political presence as a savvy cosmopolitan satiric voice? To acknowledge a personal indebtedness to its mode and artists? To insert himself into a transnational circulation of satiric graphic journals? He gives readers no clue. We do not know how many Arabophone readers in Egypt, or elsewhere in the Arab world (for the journal did travel, as Tarrazi notes), would have recognised the *Punch* on the masthead as an intertextual gesture, perhaps a resonant sign of hoped-for circulation across linguistic and cultural boundaries, a sly notation of the cosmopolitan purchase of visual satire. Might the lack of explicit reference to the London journal within the pages of *al-Siyāsa al-musawwara* signal ambivalence about possibly being considered a colonial imitator, a derivative of the metropolitan centre of empire?[27] Such recognitions did not entail the sort of critical evaluation of the journal that Ritu Khanduri finds operating in the late-nineteenth-century Indian context, wherein editors of other local newspapers interrogated the originality of the cartoon mode, wondering if it was merely a suspect sign of the mimicry (in Homi Bhabha's formulation) of the colonial subject—and not a very productive mimicry at that.[28]

Curiously, although the masthead prominently displays both borrowed finery and local belonging by calling itself in English *The Cairo Punch* (repeated at the top left of the double-spread cartoon), as far as I could tell, no cartoon nor any other feature is directly borrowed, though the fictional dialogues amongst Egyptian

---

[24] Letters were sent by this partner in early 1902 from Cairo and Port Said back to his offices in London. Khanduri, "Vernacular Punches," 465.

[25] This topic is beyond the scope of this chapter, but at the turn of the twentieth century a number of such works in Arabic were available in print.

[26] Khanduri, "Vernacular Punches," 476.

[27] On this in the Indian context, see Khanduri, "Vernacular Punches". However, it is not clear where Khanduri locates the colonial audience(s) for either the London journal or its vernacular incarnations, amongst the several possible readerships in colonial India.

[28] Khanduri, "Vernacular Punches," 459–61.

Cabinet members might echo *Punch*'s dialogues, even offer a whiff of its long-running 'Essence of Parliament' series.[29] In English, the Cairo newspaper advertises itself as 'The Only Oriental weekly Political Coloured Caricatured Journal', with a parallel, though more idiomatically correct, label in Arabic.[30] At first, the journal experiments with translating articles into English and French (for example, Hafiz Ibrahim's essay in the second issue, 'The Englishman according to himself', on English condescension and Egyptian self-abasement). But the translations are crude and by the third issue, the text is solely in Arabic, with the exception of the cartoon captions which continue throughout to be trilingual, in addition to labels within the cartoon in Arabic and English.

A Curious Figure and a Transnational Trajectory

'I relied on my own hands for drawing, and on the talent of my friend Hafiz Ibrahim for writing', explains the editor-artist in the first issue.[31] 'I travelled to the European lands to draw up and drink the water from its source. I came back with fertile seed, well-sown in what my hand could do with this art, and what my mind might absorb'.[32] Zaki announced his newspaper's slogan as 'The East for Easterners', echoing the Egyptian proto-nationalist slogan of the 1880s, 'Egypt for the Egyptians', popularised by another periodical publisher, 'Abdallah Nadim. Would this slogan and this echo—have highlighted an irony in his silent use of the *Punch* label for readers at the time? The editor sets his publication apart from others locally, as he links it to the caricature tradition in Europe, though not by naming any particular source.

> It is not our magazine's remit to delve into comic topics written in the language of the common folk, nor to institute long political articles; both [genres] have periodicals dedicated to them. Our newspaper was founded on the example of the greatest political caricature newspapers in the West, which give lasting representation to truths; thus we hope readers will not demand from us anything other than the short fragments that we write to elevate morals and customs.—[signed] 'Abd al-Hamid Zaki.[33]

---

[29] I examined all issues of *Punch* (the London original) for 1906, 1907 and 1908 (minus three issues for 1908) and found no borrowing of images between the two magazines, nor any references to *The Cairo Punch*.

[30] It is actually not weekly but rather comes out every fortnight.

[31] In the first few issues, Hafiz Ibrahim is clearly the author of the short and often satirical texts. Later in the first volume, longer and more specifically political articles appear, and are unsigned. A few poems by Hafiz Ibrahim—known in Arabic letters as a major neoclassical poet of the time—appear in later issues. It is unclear what role Ibrahim played in the journal after the first few issues.

[32] 'Abd al-Hamīd Zakī, "al-Muqaddima," *al-Siyāsa al-musawwara* 1, no. 1, 15 December 1907, 1.

[33] 'Abd al-Hamīd Zakī, "Bayān wa-tawdīh," *al-Siyāsa al-musawwara* 1, no. 4, 15 January 1908, 1.

Who is this individual, apparently producing high-quality sophisticated caricatures in a publication context where this practice set him apart from other newspaper proprietors? All we learn about ʿAbd al-Hamid Zaki's personal identity in the periodical derives from the reproduced praise of his peers. He is a former army officer, they tell us, and an efendi (that is, a white-collar worker with some education).[34] We know from the later newspaper or poster masthead and from Tarrazi, quoted above, that the newspaper moved to Bologna, Italy, apparently in its second year,[35] though the masthead also suggests that Zaki retained a post office box in Cairo. Thus Zaki echoed Sanua in moving his journal to Europe, but we have no information on the reasons, no indication that he and his newspaper were chased out of Egypt for political reasons (as Sanua had been). From the sparse information to hand, it seems likely that he was part of an economically middling, tenuously established nationalist oriented professional sector whose opposition to British rule was both political and economic, ideologically motivated but also entangled with questions of career and opportunity. These journalist-activists were not outside the system they critiqued, though they were by and large outside the large landowning families that had generally formed the ruling elite of the nineteenth century. We can even speculate that Zaki was a member of the ʿUrabi group, a collection of army officers who challenged this socio-political formation as well as the intensifying European presence just before the British occupation of 1882 (and indeed their revolt stimulated the occupation). Zaki's journal, therefore, was a product of specific and local political forces and events, unlike its English namesake.

The newspaper, in whatever form it regrouped in Europe, maintained a sharp anti-colonial commentary. In 1911, historian Christopher Harrison tells us,

> several caseloads of engravings depicting the Ottoman fleet outside Constantinople were seized in Dakar and Conakry. The engravings were printed on the presses of the Cairo Punch in Bologna and so the Colonial Ministry wrote to the Foreign Ministry asking for information about the paper. The Foreign Ministry asked the French plenipotentiary in Cairo to investigate and his findings were duly communicated to Dakar.[36] [Unfortunately, Harrison does not tell us what those findings were.]

---

[34] "Istiqbāl al-jarīda wa-numūww al-shuʿūr al-waṭanī," *al-Siyāsa al-musawwara* 1, no. 2, 27 December 1907, 4.

[35] I have one later image from this periodical, 4, no. 85 (dated simply 1911/1329), where a small masthead in Arabic and even smaller-type reference to *The Cairo Punch* also conveys the information that the head office is in Bologna, Italy. A. H. Zaki remains director and proprietor. On an image from the sixth year (no. 151, 1913), the same Cairo P.O. Box is given as we find in the first year. I am grateful to Yasemin Gencer and Eliane Ettmueller for providing me with this image.

Tarrazi says that in its third year the journal moved, but in his list of Arabic-language periodicals published in Europe, he has *al-Siyāsa al-musawwara* listed as published in Bologna from 1 January 1908. In fact it appears to have remained in Cairo for at least the first year, until the end of 1908. (Tarrāzī, *Tārīkh al-sihāfa al-ʿarabiyya*, vol. 4, 370–71).

[36] Christopher Harrison, *France and Islam in West Africa, 1860–1960* (Cambridge: Cambridge University Press, 1988), 52.

These fragments of information suggest that Zaki might have been not only an energetic young nationalist but also perhaps one of the late Ottoman-period Arab activists who moved amongst Mediterranean locations, as well as further afield. These peripatetic activists attempted to shape political sentiments and rouse awareness at least about European states' imperialising activities in the eastern Mediterranean and places further east. Facing and evading attempted censorship and control on the part of various colonial authorities, they often published short-lived periodicals or changed the titles of their publications to avoid trouble. In Zaki's case, both Tarrazi's description and the engravings in Dakar suggest that after leaving Cairo, he abandoned the printed word entirely in favour of visual commentary.

Clearly, Zaki did seek and value international recognition, just as he relished local notoriety. In addition to the welcome appreciation of his publication by its Tokyo cousin, a 'famous English' periodical, *The Review of Reviews* (called in Arabic *Majallat al-majallāt*), 'has begun to reproduce from our newspaper the political images that please it; not a single issue of it comes out but that it is adorned with one of our drawings'.[37] Further west, the *New York Times* (said Zaki) featured an illustration from *The Cairo Punch* and 'wrote a piece on [our newspaper's] political line and its fine illustration of political events, which measures up to its peers in Europe and America'. In sum, remarked Zaki,

> even though it is so recently founded, our newspaper has come to occupy a high position in the world of politics, and our work has been received in the press of East and West in a way that encourages our energy in continuing down this road, guaranteeing success by God's leave as long as we are accomplishing the duty required of us toward the nation and its noble children.[38]

Were these moments of self-congratulatory celebration accurate? The 'famous English newspaper' referred to the journal founded in January 1890 by the reform journalist William T. Stead (1849–1912) and Sir George Newnes who ran the miscellany *Tit-Bits,* and then run by Stead until his death. In the *Review of Reviews,* the monthly feature 'Current History in Caricature' is virtually a mapping of the world of caricature, moving from reproduced cartoons from British and continental periodicals, to those in the United States, Australia, and finally, Asia.[39] In 1908–1909 it was featuring cartoons from *Punch* (always with permission, as is never mentioned for any other publication except New York *Life*), other local publications (*Westminster Gazette*); various European purveyors of visual satire (*Ulk*/Berlin, *Nebelspalter*/Zurich, *Le Rire*/Paris, *Kladderadatsch*/Berlin, *Silhouette*/Paris, *Lepracaun*/Dublin, *Il Papagallo*/Turin and then Bologna, *Pasquino*/Turin, *Simplicissimus*/Munich, and others); a few North American ones (*International*

---

[37] ['Abd al-Hamīd Zakī], "Maqām al-jarīda fī 'alam al-siyāsa," *al-Siyāsa al-musawwara* 1, no. 17, 1 May 1908, 1.

[38] Ibid.

[39] This feature deserves a study in itself, which I cannot do more than suggest in this context. One fascinating issue is when and how the editor decides to explain caricature(s).

Syndicate/Baltimore, *Minneapolis Journal*) and some members of the international and colonial/imperial *Punch* and *Puck* clans: *Melbourne Punch, Sydney Bulletin, Tokyo Puck, Hindi Punch*/Bombay, *Kalem*/Istanbul.[40]

And there, in the February 1908 issue, is *The Cairo Punch*'s own second cartoon, reproducing the English dialogue-caption of the original but with neither its French nor its Arabic versions (which in any case are not translations in the sense of being close renderings, and we have no clear original text here) and with all of the Arabic inside the cartoon erased.[41] In *Review of Reviews*, the caricature production of the Cairo periodical has become monolingual, tailored to an Anglophone audience, with no unreadable clues retained. It is further distanced from its origin, and exoticised by the new title, 'A Curious Egyptian View of International Politics'. (It is also much smaller, the double page of the Cairo journal reduced to slightly more than a quarter page of the *Review*, and in black and white.) Zaki's signature—admittedly small and rather hard to see in the original—is completely absent in this version, which also does not retain the finer grading of greys that would be a more accurate black and white reproduction of the original colours. (In fairness, this is true of European caricatures as well: these are all reduced to monophonic tones, except for *Hindi Punch* which retains at least the shapes of Devanagari script.) *Review of Reviews* reduces caricature to fit its own linguistic, social and physical space; yet, giving space to caricatures from far-flung publications fascinatingly it suggests a supra-national visual conversation, a meeting of different visual styles as well as political messages (governed, of course, by Stead's reformist and even radical views).

In this caricature, an enormous John Bull in top hat, sporting a cane, and smoking a cigar bears a pair of equally enormous wings. Beneath them, tiny figures represent nations of Europe to the left; on the right, the 'British colonies' (labelled as such) are represented not by humans but by insects. In the top left- and right-hand sectors, the USA and Japan shout at each other, bypassing these various older worlds. But it seems that in the *Review*'s reproduction, the only colonies whose names can be read are Australia and India. Thus, the only identifiable site of *The Cairo Punch*'s transnational reach (to my knowledge, thus far) reduces the Egypt-based and Arabophone cartoon and journal to having a monolingual, English-language presence and naming a white settler colony as well as Britain's largest colony. There is no sign in *Review of Reviews* of any recognition that *The Cairo Punch* had Arabophone readers and viewers—or even that it bore an Arabic title. Unlike in the original, there is no sign of Egypt as a named and perhaps even

---

[40] I have not seen any other journals from India, Turkey, or Japan featured in this period in the *Review*.

[41] "A Curious Egyptian View of International Politics," in "Current History in Caricature," *Review of Reviews* 37, no. 218 (February 1908), 155. The original appears in *al-Siyāsa al-musawwara* 1, no. 2, 27 December 1907, 2–3. I have not been able to look at *Review of Reviews* for December 1907 but presumably the journal could not have printed a caricature from the Egyptian magazine so quickly (and there is none in January 1908)—unless of course these prints were being circulated pre-publication, and I have no evidence for that.

threatening presence: after all, the tiny be-fezzed scorpion is about to claw John Bull's foot. Is there perhaps a suggestion that Egypt, before any other occupied territory, will claw its way to some form of independence, even though John Bull is unaware of what is occurring around his feet?

The second *Cairo Punch* cartoon featured in *Review of Reviews* (April 1908) is likewise distanced by its (new) caption: 'A Curious View of European Politics'.[42] Like much commentary in *Review of Reviews*, this features the Moroccan situation and anxiety over (in this case) the German Kaiser's role (perhaps 'curious' because it was at odds with local anxieties, enacted in the *Review*, over France's bid to control Morocco). The editor of the *Review*, W. T. Stead, was critical of Britain's imperial adventures and of events in Egypt.[43] But, while he did reproduce a few of Zaki's caricatures, this was by no means a case of a caricature in every issue as Zaki implied. Indeed, by the time Zaki wrote his article on his periodical's alleged global reach, only two of his cartoons had appeared in this London digest. Moreover, the cartoons that Stead's *Review* chose to reproduce (or saw? or was sent?) have to do more with Britain and Europe as imperial masters than with the impact of this within Egypt or, certainly, internal politics; the final two are in line with the *Review of Reviews*'s heavy concentration on the aftermath of the constitutional 'revolution' in Turkey. From February 1908 through April 1909, *Review* published six cartoons attributed to *The Cairo Punch* (five of which appear in the issues I have seen), and then nothing through December 1909.[44]

I have found no indication that the London *Punch* ever recognised its Cairo cognate, though the London magazine did acknowledge a Turkish cousin:

> BARON MARSCHALL VON BIEBERSTEIN, the German Ambassador at Constantinople, has complained to the Porte of an article in the *Kalem*, the Turkish *Punch*, disparaging the German Emperor, and has demanded that legal proceedings be instituted against the editor. How fortunate that the English *Kalem* has been uniformly respectful to His Imperial Majesty![45]

---

[42] "Current History in Caricature," *Review of Reviews* 37, no. 220 (April 1908), 355. The original appears in *al-Siyāsa al-musawwara* 1, no. 10, March 6, 1908, 2–3. Unlike the first caricature reproduced from this journal, this one has an edited version of the English caption though not one identifiably edited for content or political line.

[43] See, for example, "Lord Cromer's 'Modern Egypt'. Various Views by Diverse Critics. A Writer of Half Truths," *Review of Reviews* 37, no. 220 (April 1908): 359–60.

[44] I examined the following issues of *Review of Reviews*: January-December 1908, January-December 1909, I went through the contents of each issue and examined in every issue the two features 'The Progress of the World' (which often included caricatures) and 'Current History in Caricature', plus any other feature with a cartoon and any articles on Egypt, Morocco or Turkey. I did not examine untitled features in the journal not labelled in the online contents as cartoon/caricature. My source for this publication is the database 'British Periodicals'.

[45] "Charivaria," *Punch, or the London Charivari* 135, 28 October 1908, 315. In this same issue in which appears a full-page cartoon showing the Emperor as a hunter with dog, running after a hare in a fez, and reassuring him: 'Dear old chap, you mustn't think I'm hunting you. I'm just running beside my friend here, to save him from feeling lonely!' Cartoon by Bernard Partridge, "Keeping

Of the cartooning styles I have seen represented in (for instance) the *Review of Reviews*, that of Zaki is closest in style and format to the Italian journal *Il Papagallo*, some of whose cartoons the *Review* also labels as 'curious'. Noticing this in their juxtaposed cartoons in *Review of Reviews*, I then observed that (as of September 1908) *Il Papagallo* is sited by the *Review* as Bologna-based, whereas previously it was published from Turin. That is, this journal was based in the city to which Zaki took his journal, apparently, after its first year.[46] Moreover, unlike the British *Punch*, the Italian *Papagallo* appears to have been known to Egyptian audiences. One local periodical that announced *al-Siyāsa al-musawwara*'s appearance on the scene remarked, 'It is in the manner of the famous newspaper *al-Bābāghallū*'.[47] Perhaps, indeed, that is the name Zaki would have chosen to borrow if he could have. But it had already been taken: in 1903, one ʿAbd al-Majid Kamil founded *The Egyptian Papagallo* (*al-Bābāghallū al-Misrī*). Could this have been an inspiration or a model for Zaki? Was there any link between it and the Italian journal of this name? *Il Papagallo* (1873–1915) was apparently a leader in the use of colour as an element of humour, and was one of the best-known of the late nineteenth-century crop of Italian satirical journals reviving lithography techniques made popular earlier in the century by the great artists of visual social commentary.[48]

This possible linkage complicates the story of the newspaper and its proprietor, when set against the cosmopolitan composition of urban Egypt in this period. Amongst the Mediterranean populations resident in Cairo and Alexandria were an entrepreneurial as well as politically active Italian populace. According to the 1907 Egyptian census, 34,926 Italian nationals were resident in Egypt that year, 38.1 % of them in Cairo.[49] Amongst Italians working in Egypt, there were a number of printers, and the International Printers League of Cairo had been started by Italian anarcho-syndicalists.[50] I suspect that there may be a connection here that would explain both the physical journeys of the journal and of Zaki and also its atypical

---

in with the hare," *Punch, or the London Charivari* 135, 28 October 1908, 309. The dog represents the British PM Asquith.

[46] A disclaimer here: I am not a historian of the European satirical/visual press. But I would venture to suggest that my lack of expertise perhaps makes more striking my immediate sense of the close visual correlation between these two journals.

[47] "Istiqbāl al-jarīda: taqārīz al-jarā'id," *al-Siyāsa al-musawwara* 1, no. 9, 28 February 1908, 4. This periodical is *al-Miusawwar*, the title suggesting a visually focused publication, but I have not seen it. The famous journal by this name was founded in 19.

[48] Michel Melot, "Social Comment and Criticism," in *Lithography: 200 Years of Art, History and Technique*, ed. Domenico Porzio, trans. Geoffrey Culverwell (London: Bracken Books, 1983), 207–21; 219–20.

[49] I thank my colleague Tony Gorman for this information.

[50] Anthony Gorman, "'Diverse in Race, Religion and Nationality [...] but United in Aspirations of Civil Progress': The Anarchist Movement in Egypt 1860–1940," in *Anarchism and Syndicalism in the Colonial and Post-Colonial World, 1880–1940*, eds. Steven Hirsch and Lucien van der Walt (Leiden: Brill, 2010), 3–31; 25.

technical sophistication. It might well have been produced by or with an Italian printer who might also have been involved in Zaki's earlier visit and possible later move to Europe. In this era, the art of caricature and its deployment in the press were sophisticated in Italy. Locally, Zaki may have participated in some of the radical Mediterranean-orientated political circles that produced journals. Such a connection may also explain, at least partly, the combination of politics and commerce that underlay the journal's self-advertisement, to which I now turn.

Courting Notoriety

Early in July 1908, the newspaper offers those subscribers who have paid fully for their subscriptions a special issue 'In Memorium: Dinshaway', featuring that infamous incident in late 1906 and also another frequent topic of *al-Siyāsa al-musawwara*'s caricatures, Morocco under European sway. The issue, announced Zaki, 'will demonstrate British scandals in the former and French ones in the latter'.[51] Apparently the issue was 'scandalous' indeed, for the editor reports a week later on its reception, in an article worth quoting at length, for it inscribes both the particular critical power of visual satire and the politics of colonial double standards within which the Egyptian press had to operate.

> We and the Foreigners
>
> The Egyptian's good attributes are bad ones in the foreigner's eyes, no matter how moderate the former is or how firmly he supports his views with sound proofs [...]. We thought we would remind the occupying nation of the deeds it has done here, so we portrayed Dinshaway—and the English justice entailed in it is clear for all to see. Next to it we showed Casablanca—and the French justice there is clear. No sooner did human hands pass this image around than the newspapers we thought were run by people of sound mind, who care about love of the homeland and understand the meaning of freedom, were up in arms [...] They do not know or recognise such things [i.e., love of homeland, the meaning of freedom] when it comes to Islamic countries. No one will deny what we have to say about this.
>
> The French newspaper *al-Nawfal* [*Les Nouvelles*] said beneath the headline 'Illustrated Newspapers in Egypt': 'Publishing the likes of this newspaper in an eastern country incites the emotions of the locals, whose gaze is forcibly turned to it, eyes wide. There is no doubt that these images carry the intent of stirring up nationalist ideas against the Europeans and getting the populace to hate them. They [the images] are worse than the articles of [the nationalist daily] *al-Liwā'* in this sense, because what *al-Liwā'* writes to promulgate partisan passion (*al-ta'assub*) are read by a group of educated people who have some knowledge, but the art of *al-Siyāsa al-musawwara* is tendered to everyone with a pair of eyes, so it can disseminate envy and anger in the breast of anyone who looks at it, whether he be an illiterate peasant or a bureaucrat with official diplomas.

---

[51] ['Abd al-Hamīd Zakī], "Dhikrā dinshawāy," *al-Siyāsa al-musawwara* 1, no. 24, 9 July 1908, 1. I have not been able to locate this special issue.

'Were we in any other country, we would let *al-Siyāsa al-musawwara*'s illustrations pass with an unconcerned shrug of the shoulders. But the conditions of the East do not permit us such unconcern, for people tend to believe what is sketched or written for them taking a partisan or fanatical line [...]'.

And from *The Egyptian Gazette*: 'The first error Lord Cromer fell into during his time in Egypt was giving freedom to the Egyptian press. The nearest indication at hand that we can present to readers is the newspaper *al-Siyāsa al-musawwara*, which has taken upon itself to combat the English occupation with drawings that represent our politics in Egypt in the worst way. Proof of this is the special number on Dinshaway published recently. With the superb quality of its images, it bored into the minds of the simple people in Egypt'.

Such are the rightly guided words, lofty sentiments and judgments we hear every day—indeed, every hour—issuing from the mouths of the masters [*murshidīn*] among the foreign writers [...] Those newspapers want us to bow before the occupiers and kiss their hands whenever they walk along in front of us [...] They say the Egyptian is a fanatic or partisan (*muta'assib*)—well, yes he is; he is a partisan of his religion and homeland [...] There is one further thing to say: Would the English like for the French to occupy their country? If so, then we will be content with this wrong and tyranny. Otherwise, though, we hate the English and we will despise them from our hearts as long as they occupy our country.[52]

The very existence of *al-Siyāsa al-musawwara* and certainly the reactions against it by European onlookers nearby—as well as, perhaps, the plaudits it drew from afar—display and even enact the asymmetries inherent in public discourse in a colonial situation. Taking its cues from British political graphic satire—and implicitly acknowledging its debt to this by adopting the title *The Cairo Punch*—the journal could not deploy visual satire to communicate its political stance without drawing the patronising ire of journals that opposed Egyptian nationalist goals. Like journal editors in colonised India, Zaki was not slow to point out the paradox of European-language periodicals claiming the benefits of liberal discourse for themselves but denying it to others.[53] He did not hesitate to name his adversaries, such as the local French-language *Les Nouvelles* which was known for its conservative outlook. It was owned by the French national M. Escoffier and edited by G. Dumani, probably a Syrian French protégé.[54] At the same time, these anti-nationalist organs cannot but admit both the skill of the journal's editor-artist and the potency of graphic satire. Slyly, Zaki turns the tables on his adversaries by quoting them. His images, they acknowledge, have power; even as they decry the 'conditions of the East' that make caricature dangerous in their eyes, they admit the fragility of the asymmetric structure that he both exploits and challenges in founding his newspaper and publishing his cartoons.

---

[52] "Nahnū wa'l-ajānib," *al-Siyāsa al-musawwara* 1, no. 25, 17 July, 1908, 1.

[53] Khandurī, "Vernacular Punches".

[54] I am indebted to my colleague Tony Gorman for this information.

Satirising London, Selling a Product

The Cairo Punch does echo its namesake in its methodically sardonic approach to British politics. If the original *Punch* criticised the scenes and outcomes—and especially the managers—of British imperialism more than it challenged the roots of said imperialism, *The Cairo Punch* took this satirical critique further, slamming the very presence of Britain in Egypt, associating itself with other fervently nationalist newspapers, and exhorting readers to become active nationalists. Hafiz Ibrahim's first article—titled 'The English' (*al-Inkilīz*)—was exhortatory rather than informative, as it drew a line in the political sands:

> They are a people of politicking and duplicity (*siyāsa, khatl*). [...] Their politics is like electricity: the eye comprehends what [this politics] does, while the mind does not take in where it comes from [...] their duplicity is like wine: weak in the glass, strong in the head. When they go into a village, they leave its mightiest person the weakest [or: lowest].[55]

Like its cartoons, the newspaper's articles and textual vignettes voice an insistently nationalist and indeed rather xenophobic outlook, albeit one that was set firmly within an anti-imperialist and anti-colonising discourse in the broadest sense. It rails not only against the British occupation and British imperialism in general but also against the growing presence of all non-Egyptians, or at least non-Arabs, in Egypt. In the third issue, the paper warns that the consequences of 'foreigners flooding in from everywhere [...] such that we have no air left to breathe' will be similar to 'what happened to the American Indian [...] all we lack is for their [the foreigners'] number to reach one million, whereupon they will demand formation of a new government'.[56] A short and often reproduced article found throughout the first year exhorts Egyptian readers to acquire an Egyptian flag and show it on national holidays, 'following the model of cultivated (*mutamaddina*) nations'—and then it notes that Egyptians can purchase their flags at the newspaper's office.[57]

In a number of ways, *The Cairo Punch* sells a brand of politics and sells itself and its by-products simultaneously. Indeed, the journal situates itself politically and centrally in the cause of generating nationalist activism and the development of a civic polity in Egypt by advertising itself and reproducing acknowledgments of its emergence printed in other periodicals—and, subtly or not, seeking financial support from readers.

> Among indications of the growth of nationalist sentiment is the nation's receptivity to the works of its every son who undertakes to serve it with sincerity and dedication. The circulation of our newspaper's first issue and its fine reception by all classes who have

---

[55] Hāfiz Ibrāhīm, "al-Inkilīz," *al-Siyāsa al-musawwara* 1, no. 1, 15 December 1907, 1. This is my translation from the Arabic; in this issue (alone), the article appears in English and French as well.

[56] Hāfiz Ibrāhīm, "Nahnu wa'l-ajānib: Mā lanā wa mā lahum," *al-Siyāsa al-musawwara* 1, no. 3, 3 January 1908, 1.

[57] "Al-rāya al-misriyya al-'uthmāniyya," *al-Siyāsa al-musawwara* 1, no. 5, 24 January 1907, 1.

taken it up offer indications that encourage us in our labour and lead us to spare no effort toward its improvement [...] as this [type of publication] is new in the East it requires enormous expenditure and with God's willing help we will firm up its support as a service to the nation and its sons [...] we hope for more support for this unique periodical in the East, the likes of which are numbered in the thousands in the West.[58]

From its second issue, the journal ran a regular column on the 'reception of the newspaper', reproducing the positive comments of other periodicals. It was a standard practice that periodicals would announce new members of the serial press community, generally with conventional praise.[59] What is different in *al-Siyāsa al-musawwara/ The Cairo Punch* is that it repeats these conventionally admiring announcements, across several issues (numbers 2, 4, 5, 8, 9, and 20), thereby accruing credit with the subscribers it so earnestly seeks. These notices also suggest the journal's transnational purchase, for praise comes not only from leading Egyptian periodicals (*al-Ahrām, al-Hilāl, al-Mu'ayyad, al-Liwā', al-Minbār*) but also from Arabic-language periodicals in Tunis and Brazil. Or at least this suggests the editor's aspirations, for it is implied that he sent copies to all the journalistic peers who then praised his newspaper. These editors variously recognise *al-Siyāsa al-musawwara*'s novelty and force; the nationalist daily *al-Mu'ayyad* calls it 'the first newspaper of its kind to be published in the [Arab] East, by its stellar proprietor 'Abd al-Hamid Efendi Zaki, former officer in the Egyptian army'. A nationalist compatriot (and sometime rival) *al-Liwā'* describes the first cartoon, noting that it 'demonstrates the fine taste and skill of its artist producer'.[60] The monthly miscellany *al-Hilāl* calls it 'the finest illustrated newspaper to appear in Egypt, depicting political sources [...] and its subscription price is paltry next to the expenses of drawing and printing that it requires'.[61] This is not the only journal to recognise the expense of such a venture; in the same issue, the satirical newspaper *al-Sā'iqa* lauds the editor's 'material sacrifice'.

That the editor also reproduces the more cautiously welcoming words of the generally recognised Arabic organ for the British occupation (and the newspaper attacked in the cartoon with which we began), the daily *al-Muqattam*, probably redounded to its credibility amongst nationalistically-oriented observers. Labelling the newspaper 'the tongue of the English occupation' (lest there be any doubt), *al-Siyāsa al-musawwara* describes *al-Muqattam* as commenting that the first caricature

---

[58] "Istiqbāl al-jarīda wa-numūww al-shu'ūr al-watanī," *al-Siyāsa al-musawwara* 1, no. 2, 27 December 1907, 4.

[59] I-Wei Wu shows a visual illustration of this practice, see chapter Participating in Global Affairs: The Chinese Cartoon Monthly Shanghai Puck in this volume.

[60] "Istiqbāl al-jarīda wa-numūww al-shu'ūr al-watanī," *al-Siyāsa al-musawwara* 1, no. 2, 27 December 1907, 4.

[61] "Taqārīz al-jarā'id," *al-Siyāsa al-musawwara* 1, no. 8, 14 February 1908, 4.

is intended as a complaint about the English in Egypt, as is the wont of the young people of this land (*qutr*). But it is a perfectly crafted image, and is witness to the artist's skill and superiority compared to similar images appearing in other Arabic pictorial newspapers. We wish success for its director and proprietor, and we hope it flourishes and spreads.[62]

From the start, the journal advertises itself most explicitly: with pleas for subscriptions, announcements (in early issues) of when the next issue will be out and what the upcoming cartoon will be ('an image representing the Englishman in the very sky of his arrogance and summit of his rank and power in the human world, in his view [...]').[63] It is not shy about self-advertisement, with large-font headlines announcing PUBLICATION OF THE FOURTH ISSUE: 'Number four will be out on Monday 13 January and will contain an important political drawing, and thus we draw [readers'] gaze to it in advance'.[64] Moreover, in its pages, *al-Siyāsa al-musawwara/The Cairo Punch* advertises adjunct services. Together with its frequent pleas to subscribers to pay up, and its offer of a photographic album on the Hijaz to those who pay up quickly, this suggests that money was indeed an issue.[65] This particular advertisement notes that the album's images are being printed in Europe; might this suggest that the newspaper itself was printed outside of Egypt? But elsewhere it is implied that the production is local. The management announces that the newspaper's press is prepared to draw and print colour images for merchants who desire them for marketing. In a notice appearing in almost every subsequent issue, '*al-Taswīr bi'l-zayt*' (oil portraiture/drawing), the potential customer base broadens:

> If you wish to adorn the reception hall of your home or make for yourself a memento to last a lifetime, simply send your photograph to the newspaper's management, who will make a perfect image in oils with colours matching the natural tones. [...] sized 73 cm × 59 cm, it is priced competitively low, at L.E. 8. It will be produced quickly and sent to the buyer in its perfection.[66]

Such advertisements imply that the journal had a local press capable of handling colour printing. Yet, in its welcome of this journal, *al-Manār* (eminently respectable organ of the religious scholar, populariser and reformer Rashid Rida) said its visuals 'were printed with utter skill in Europe'.[67] This certainly seems to magnify the mystery of this journal's production, but it may simply suggest mere assumptions about what could and could not be printed in Egypt at the time. Did *al-Manār*'s editor know that the periodical was published in Europe? Or, based on its stunning visuals—the like of which would not appear again in Egypt until the

---

[62] "Istiqbāl al-jarīda wa-numūww al-shuʿūr al-watanī," *al-Siyāsa al-musawwara* 1, no. 2, 27 December 1907, 4. I have not been able to access *al-Muqattam* to check whether it had additional things to say about the new journal.

[63] "I'lān," *al-Siyāsa al-musawwara* 1, no. 1, 15 December 1907, 1.

[64] "Sudūr al-ʿadad al-rābiʿ," *al-Siyāsa al-musawwara* 1, no. 3, 3 January 1908, 1.

[65] "Jā'iza li-mushtarikī al-jarīda," *al-Siyāsa al-musawwara* 1, no. 3, 3 January 1908, 4, appearing in many subsequent issues.

[66] "Al-Taswīr bi'l-zayt," *al-Siyāsa al-musawwara* 1, no. 13, March 27, 1908, 4.

[67] *al-Manār* 10, no. 12, February 1, 1908, 950. This is never said in 'politics illustrated' itself.

early 1920s—did he simply assume this? In any case, the journal did appear to follow its London namesake in attempted self-marketing—including an announcement, partway through its first year, that the journal's first volume had been reprinted and was available for purchase; the notice advertised 'twenty-three political illustrations alluding to myriad issues of Eastern politics' and included the special issues commemorating the late nationalist leader Mustafa Kamil and the Dinshawāy controversy.[68]

Visual Flair and Verbal Heterogeneity

The journal's cartoons are intricate and the images strong. In addition to captions in three languages (Arabic flagged by English and French), they carry text labels internal to the image, usually in Arabic and English. Each issue carries one double-page image, which in a sense overwhelms the text: at least in its first year, an issue comprises only four pages; the first page is fully text, beneath the bilingual masthead. There is a page of mostly advertisements and announcements, and the two-page visual.

That the Arabic within the visual is generally more profuse and more explanative than the English suggests a primary audience of Arabophone readers. The English words serve rather as part of the visual, a facet of the representation itself, a recognition of the imposition of Anglophone terminologies on Egypt as part and parcel of its imperial presence, for a majority of these cartoons comment on Egyptian-British relations and more broadly on Arab and 'Eastern' states' condition vis-à-vis Europe and the United States.

The first cartoon, for example, is titled (in the cartoon, and not over the captions, unlike later ones), '*Misr tahta al-'amaliyya*': 'Egypt operated on' (or, more metaphorically, Egypt under the knife). A doubled meaning operates both in Arabic and in English, Egypt under the procedure/process of British rule: a project of British operations. Egypt is a troubled, young, possibly emaciated, woman. On her body is stamped EGYPT in English as well as the Arabic equivalent, but also—only in Arabic, *al-Sūdān* (Sudan), *al-sharakāt al-ajnabiyya bi-Misr* (the foreign companies in Egypt), *al-dayn al-misrī* (the Egyptian national debt), *al-imtiyāzāt* (the privileges given to foreigners) and *jahl al-umma* (ignorance of the nation [as people]).[69] These are her chronic sores, but they are invisible to those who do not read or speak Arabic. And one of her breasts appears more like a wound, perhaps suggesting a loss of ability to nourish her young (Fig. 3).

---

[68] "Al-Mujallad al-awwal," *al-Siyāsa al-musawwara* 1, no. 24, July 9, 1908, 1. This is the issue following the one in which the Dinshawāy memorial issue is announced, suggesting a desire to immediately capitalise on its notoriety.

[69] [Untitled cartoon], *al-Siyāsa al-musawwara* 1, no. 1, December 15, 1907, 2–3. Image signed 'A. H. Zaki'.

Fig. 3 Untitled cartoon from *al-Siyāsa al-musawwara* 1, no. 1, 15 December 1907, 2–3

Egypt's hand is held out in weak supplication. Over her stands 'Dr. John Bull' (in English), labelled only as *Ingiltera* (England) in (Egyptian) Arabic. The cartoonist again seems to speak to two audiences: one that knows British caricature and political diction, and one that is more locally orientated, who might not know the figure of John Bull and thus must directly read the portly doctor-figure as *Ingiltera*. In other words, the local audience is recipient of a literal signalling while those who read English (including members of the Egyptian elite, though they were likelier to read French) are expected to read the figural signposts of British satirical political discourse and draw appropriate inferences.

'Dr. John Bull' has a kindly face in profile, but holds a pair of surgeon's scissors close as he earnestly leans over 'Egypt's' prone body. In the corner, 'The Egyptian' (written in English) is a bowed, seated, bearded father-figure in a headdress and gown, more a peasant than a religious figure, certainly a representation of a non-elite, non-westernised subject. Positioned to the side, he is marginal; stooped and weary, he is helpless. The eye travels downward from the turban—where the English letters sit—to the gown, where, in smaller Arabic, rests an elaborated characterisation: *al-Miṣrī yabkī ḥāl Miṣr*. The Egyptian weeps for Egypt's condition: but only the Arabophone viewer can read this.[70]

---

[70] One 'reading' of the cartoon comes from the nationalist newspaper *al-Liwā'*, describing the surgeon's scissors metaphorically: 'Before her [the ailing Egypt] stands an Englishman who

The mapping of Egypt/Sudan on the woman's body, beneath John Bull's 'weapon', as the bearded, turbaned (male) Egyptian sits powerless, 'lamenting Egypt's condition', reminds us graphically of the ubiquity of the gendering of nationalist imagery as female/land and male/national (emasculated) subject. But the Egypt that is under the British knife is more complicated in Arabic than it is in English: the geography is uneven and the resonances are many for the cartoonist-editor and presumably for his intended audience, while for an Anglophone onlooker they are reduced to the simplified—or simplistic—binary of Dr. John Bull and the ailing young woman, Egypt.

Do the expanded linguistic signs within the cartoon signify an intimate address to a like-minded audience, an invitation to conversation with local readers, a desire to emphasise the urgency of the national/ist cause, a recognition of local outlooks on these issues and a dismissal of Anglophone interpretations? Or are the fuller Arabic presences in the cartoon a sign that the editor-artist feels it necessary to spell things out for a local audience unaccustomed to caricature as a mode of political commentary?

Turning to the trilingual captions beneath the cartoon, we find that again, in each language the implication is slightly different. Signalling that the author does sense a need to explain English usages (but then why use them?), the Arabic begins the dialogue with 'John Bull (England)' while in English we find only 'John Bull' and in French, 'le docteur'. A quite direct translation of the Arabic text would read as follows:

> For a quarter century we have been treating you, trying various medicines, yet all that has been augmented in you is your relapse [or setback], young woman, and we have run out of tricks in treating surface [ills] so we have no recourse but to try the internal. We will start by extracting the heart, for in this lies swift recovery!
>
> [Egypt answers with a songlike couplet:]
> Truly my illness is long and drawn out   My illness will no doubt kill me
> But then, my doctor is in full accord   And he knows my mortal spots

In English, the caption is not so different but the diction is milder: 'my physician knows well how to hasten my end'.[71]

These cartoons are all signed (in Latin characters), A. H. Zaki. As I have noted, they show a high degree of skill in the art of caricature as well as a publishing capability that is admittedly startling for Cairo at that time even if we do not wish to assume it was impossible. As these cartoons show cosmopolitan awareness of the art of caricature and bear the imprint of European visual satire, they also move beyond Egypt and its own colonial situation thematically, placing Egypt in a

---

unsheathes his weapon to extract the heart; the drawing demonstrates the fine taste and skill of its artist producer'. "Istiqbāl al-jarīda wa-numūww al-shuʿūr al-waṭanī," *al-Siyāsa al-musawwara* 1, no. 2, 27 December 1907, 4.

[71] The French is different still.

Fig. 4 Untitled cartoon from *al-Siyāsa al-musawwara* 1, no. 2, 27 December 1907, 2–3

broader context of European colonialism and transnational relations. Several of the 37 cartoons in the first volume forthrightly attack the broader imperial context, though generally with specific reference to Great Britain's empire especially in its Egyptian incarnation. Let us return to the second issue's cartoon, that reproduced in *Review of Reviews*, displaying a cigar-smoking, top-hat wearing, bow-tie sporting 'John Bull' (in Arabic, simply *Ingiltera*) with angel wings—the vaunted and self-ascribed imperial civilising mission personified. He is flanked by figures representing European nations on one side and colonised nations on the other. John Bull is many times the size of the other human male figures, and in brighter clothes while they are in uniform. He is in a full frontal position, unlike the far smaller European nations who seem to be talking among themselves, disorganised. Showing himself conversant with conventions of caricature, the artist has given John Bull an exaggerated size commensurate with Britain's imperial role (and sense of self-importance), while the angel-wings, also conventionally, suggest an ironic vision of the self-justifications and self-presentation of the imperial master (Fig. 4).

The 'British settler colonies' *(al-musta'mirāt al-bārītāniya)* are insects: but Australia is a butterfly (lighter, prettier, able to fly, able to escape) and the Transvaal is a canny bat in a sunhat, while—below them—Sudan is a cockroach, Egypt a scorpion and India a fanged viper. Thus, a clear distinction is made between the white settler colony and other 'British' territories, which are represented as perhaps despicable, crawling or ready to slither—but also potentially lethal. Interestingly, the United States (Uncle Sam) and Japan are aligned significantly, Japan on the side of the 'insects' (though above them) and America on that of the 'men' (and above them).[72] The caption reads:

> John Bull (England): I am the one whose command orders all in the seas and the lands; I am the one who has put in servitude all those in the western lands and the eastern lands.
> Japan (speaking to America): May God have mercy on the bones of Washington, for if it were not for him, you would still, today, be amongst the subjugated and ludicrous insects.
> America: I ask God whose grace gave me freedom to seed beneath this tyrant in every land he treads, and every nation he rules, a Washington to lighten his heaviness and make faint his arrogance.

The English version offers the same meaning but with slightly less strong vocabulary. The Arabic, as well, has a footnote: 'Washington is the great hero and the immense leader who was liberator of America and its saviour from the rule of the English'.

National Politics and the State of the Street

The newspaper's focus was not exclusively on international politics and the British occupation, though its commentary, visual and written, on internal affairs generally linked imperialism and the local state of finance and morals, as measured by behaviour in the streets, especially that of women. Indeed, integral to its outlook on foreign presences is a gendered social critique that would have been familiar to press denizens at the time, and which was in turn related to an emerging discourse on gender, the allocation of social space, and the state of the family. Zaki, like many other editors of the time, expressed a sense of grievance and anxiety about shifting practices concerning time and space, which he articulated as a social unravelling that threatened to weaken the national fabric.

In the second issue, Hafiz Ibrahim chided his countrymen for their late-night sociability practices. That (male) Egyptians were spending time and money in bars and other sites of pleasure was a drain on national resources, mental and material.[73] This referred, of course, to practices that writers bemoaned as having arrived with European residents, visitors and entrepreneurs (as well as occupiers). Thus, it was a domestic issue with anti-colonial overtones. Ibrahim took up the topic again a

---

[72] [Untitled cartoon], *al-Siyāsa al-musawwara* 1, no. 2. 27 December 1907, 2–3. Image signed 'A. H. Zaki'.

[73] Hāfiz Ibrāhīm, "Kalima li-nābighat shuʿarāʾ al-mashriq hāfiz efendi ibrāhīm," *al-Siyāsa al-musawwara* 1, no. 2, 27 December 1907, 1.

fortnight later, enumerating the benefits of breaking such bad habits. The benefits (and present victims) would include

> domestic life whose disappearance has broken the bonds of family [...] brothers snub each other while neighbours turn their backs. Homes grow desolate, empty of convivial sociability, and people have become accustomed to sitting in clubs to the point where they get lonely in their homes because there are so few visitors. A person's presence in his home is more like absence, and he lives there like an emigrant, knowing it only as one distant does [...]
> Another [benefit] would be surmounting the obstacles that clubs and bars throw up in the way of people coming together. Egyptians, back in the era that people now call 'the age of darkness', gathered in homes and visited each other in palaces. The elite and those of means sat in their homes to socialise [...] when something had happened, they discussed it in detail and they came up with sound ideas and projects [...]. When someone behaved badly they kept after him, taking his hand to lead him out of it.[74]

This somewhat nostalgic look at the past as a time of social cohesion appears more obliquely in a later article that describes the writer's excursion to new Cairo (Heliopolis), which he dubs 'Cairo's [Bois de] Bologne':

> I saw women walking and riding who had rent [or dishonoured] the veil and thrown off all restraint, all pretence of shame, as though they had emerged from their houses only to snatch hearts and turn minds, and to expose on dishonour's stage the goods of wantonness [...] I saw them walking the streets in groups and alone, eyebrows painted and eyes flirtatious, transparent *burqu*'s and cloaks flapping open, and I said: What is this!

The onlooker decries the presence of mixed couples and notes that police there 'are rarer than pounds in the days of crisis. [...] I do not doubt that the Bois de Boulogne feels envy toward Cairo [...] These morals have without a doubt come to us from the Westerners' civilisation, and we craved them to the point where we flung away our customs'. The speaker blames the police for their neglect of public morals and the government for allowing a further influx of foreigners.[75] And indeed, in more than one caricature, police stand by as crimes are committed. 'Who is to say they are not as fine as those of other countries?'[76] In another one, Europeans beat up a weeping peasant as an urban Egyptian sits cowering at a café table and the policeman looks on as the peasant calls to him.[77] And in still another, ironically titled 'For the sake of progress' (*Fī sabīl al-taqaddum*), a lady whose face veil has slipped sits in a carriage accepting a bouquet from a young, Europeanised dandy, while nearby a 'Bar' is announced in English and Arabic, its patrons applauding a young woman in black (a traditional and appropriate colour for women to wear in public) but whose dress is flounced (neither traditional nor

---

[74] Hāfiz Ibrāhīm, "Tābiʿat kalimat hāfiz ibrāhīm (al-manshūra bi'l-ʿadad al-thānī)," *al-Siyāsa al-musawwara* 1, no. 3, 3 January 1908, 1.

[75] "Bulunyā misr, aw mahall jadīd lil-tahattuk," *al-Siyāsa al-musawwara* 1, no. 20, 5 June 1908, 1.

[76] "Kafaʾat al-būlīs al-Misrī!!!" [cartoon], *al-Siyāsa al-musawwara* 1, no. 30, 6 September 1908, 2–3. Image signed 'A. H. Zaki'.

[77] [Untitled cartoon], *al-Siyāsa al-musawwara* 1, no. 24, 9 July 1908, 2–3. Image signed 'A. H. Zaki'.

Fig. 5 '*Fī sabīl al-taqaddum!!!*' Cartoon from *al-Siyāsa al-musawwara* 1, no. 15, 17 April 1908, 2–3.

appropriate). She wears a face-veil but it is transparent, and her arms drip with jewellery. This is a visual caricature that reiterates and emphasises the 'Bois de Boulogne' article's thrust (Fig. 5).

Equally targeted for satire in this image are the young Egyptian efendi group in fezzes and a passively watching policeman. The efendis' shoes are fashionable, and slightly feminised. The women of course are veiled only in name. 'Truly', comments the Arabic caption, 'Egypt in this era lacks nothing that is found in the civilised nations. Just look at her youths with their flirting, her young women with their transgressions, her police with his satisfied, delighted gaze at it all. This, the apparatus of civilisation is made complete, and the conditions of progress amongst men and women are amply supplied [...]'.[78]

The efendis swarm through the centre of the image. Visually, with the use of colour, the couple in the middle stand out, appearing the most Europeanised (at least the male does). That the woman is at the very centre of the image conveys the centrality of gendered comportment and dress to nationalist politics. Other Egyptians (the peasant in the corner, the old shaykh in the other) are pushed to

---

[78] "Fī sabīl al-taqaddum!!!" [cartoon], *al-Siyāsa al-musawwara* 1, no. 15, 17 April 1908, 2–3. Image signed 'A. H. Zaki'.

the margins and only partly visible. They are behind, in back—the past. Their dress, not seen, no longer stands for Egypt. The politics of language, specifically the language of the urban street, conveys the same message. A cloud of very familiar vernacular expressions is interrupted by French near the centre. The humour inheres partially in the disjuncture between appearances (Europeanised) and colloquial expressions, echoing the misfit between caption below and title on the picture: 'For the sake of progress' versus 'the corruption of public morals in Egypt' (*fasād al-adāb al-'umumiyya fi Misr*). The linguistic play within the frame is part of the visual image of urban Egypt as both heterogeneous and dangerously fragmented. If such a scene might approach the combination of an urban gaze and humour of a whimsical sort that Maidment traces in *Punch, or the London Charivari,* it reaches beyond observation to pose a very pointed political critique of local social relations as reshaped, in the author's view, by globalising forces.[79]

Like the London parent, this Cairo offspring, or perhaps odd godchild, interleaved the local politics of the street with a broader and transnational context. And like *Punch, or the London Charivari,* it manifested a politics of location, an outlook grounded in a particular national collective identity that shaped a view of the world. A much smaller operation—basically, that of two men, as far as we know—it elaborated a concentrated rather than diffuse ideological perspective. Yet, *al-Siyāsa al-musawwara* was not local in the way that *al-Arghūl,* appearing just a few years earlier, had been. While *al-Arghūl* drew on indigenous art forms and colloquial, very local language—as its titular use of the reed-pipe, instrument of the Egyptian countryside, suggested—the later *al-Siyāsa al-musawwara/The Cairo Punch* eschewed both colloquial language (thereby making itself more marketable for Arab audiences outside Egypt) and vernacular expressive genres. It seemed consciously transnational in its recognition of an emerging circulation of critical images, the possibility of conversation amongst periodicals in various world sites, and the necessity for an anti-imperial politics of seeking alliances beyond the local. This is perhaps what its use of the *Punch* title was meant to communicate. At the same time, *al-Siyāsa al-musawwara* was similar to *al-Arghūl* and other colloquial-satirical journals in Egypt in that it offered a mode of reception other than reading. For *al-Arghūl,* this was the oral/aural communication of colloquial poetry and dialogue, read out loud. For *al-Siyāsa al-musawwara* it was the impact of the visual—as its adversaries so anxiously noted. Both made good use of the pun—not a form that Egyptians would have found new or unusual.[80]

---

[79] Moreover, the Cairo magazine exhibits no interest in parodying conventional genres, unlike the London journal. Such parodies would become important to Egyptian political satirical journals in the 1920s. On this, see Marilyn Booth, *Bayram al-Tunisi's Egypt: Social Criticism and Narrative Strategies,* St. Antony's Middle East Monographs, 22 (Exeter: Ithaca Press, 1990).

[80] Cf. Peter Duus's comments on Japanese receptivity to political cartoons around the turn of the twentieth century, in Peter Duus, "Presidential Address: Weapons of the Weak, Weapons of the Strong—The Development of the Japanese Political Cartoon," *The Journal of Asian Studies* 60, no. 4 (November 2001): 965–97.

The Circulation of Visual Tropes

While *al-Siyāsa al-musawwara* does not appear to borrow directly from the English *Punch*, the presence of tropes common to other satirical visual periodicals both in Europe and Asia is notable. Do these arise from a common language visualising international politics at the time, or were these tropes embedded in earlier and local modes of expression? While it is impossible to fully explore this question in the space of one chapter, it is possible at least to suggest some broad outlines.

Parallel to its eschewal of Egyptian vernacular art forms, *al-Siyāsa al-musawwara* does not rely heavily on local visual tropes that would have been obscure to non-Egyptian audiences. Even its fine satirical use of Pharaonic imagery might not have differed markedly from a European magazine's use of the same to represent Egypt—and indeed, is not fundamentally unlike *Punch*'s use of this imagery in the 1880s to represent the moment of British takeover.[81] However, it was distinctive in deploying the Sphinx as an implied narrator-figure, the artist in disguise, uttering directives and offering a decidedly non-Sphinx-like set of facial emotions usually from the upper left-hand corner of the cartoon, alternately scolding his compatriots and screaming in horror, and countering the bulk of John Bull. Would this localised and only intermittently present narrator-figure have corresponded, for the journal's more cosmopolitan readers, to Mr Punch? Unlike the vernacular *Punch* versions in colonised India before and around this time, and some of the *Puck* and *Punch* versions in East Asia, Cairo's version did not directly appropriate the English journal's narrator-figure.[82] Moreover, there was nothing comic about the Sphinx as hovering narrator-figure—though in one cartoon, he moves to central stage, kicking former High Commissioner Lord Cromer, then just departed, in the backside, catapulting him from the throne of the Pharoahs into the sea.[83]

Other local visual clues in these cartoons included dress and would become hallmarks of later caricature in magazines of the 1920s, notably *al-Kashkūl*: the fez of the government bureaucrat or other middling to high professional; the transparent face-veil of the elite woman with aspirations to Europeanise; the ragged gown and sandals of the peasant; the turban and caftan of the religious scholar. The use of these images is transparent in the sense that non-Egyptian viewers would have likely picked up the visual clues, though perhaps not resemblances to prominent individuals. It would be difficult to argue that there are significant concealed

---

[81] See Marilyn Booth, "Insistent Localism," chapter *Punch* in India: Another History of Colonial Politics? in this volume.

[82] On this appropriation see Khanduri, "Vernacular Punches," 469. She notes that this entailed a 'fusion' of the British figure with local mythical figures.

[83] [Untitled cartoon], *al-Siyāsa al-musawwara* 1, no. 11, 13 March 1908, 2–3. Image signed 'A. H. Zaki'. Unusually, this cartoon narrates the subject in two frames, the first titled 'Cromer on the throne of the Pharoahs' and the second, 'His exit from Egypt'. Of the first 13 cartoons, only 3 carry titles, in Arabic, above the Arabic caption. With no. 14, cartoons come to regularly carry titles, though a very few do not.

meanings in the visuals here, though we may elicit a sense of national belonging in the narratorial use of the Sphinx. As discussed earlier, the concealed meanings inhere rather in the differential sense and weight of the three languages deployed in and around cartoons.

The journal's artist also utilises tropes of wider circulation to the extent of being visual clichés (including representation of the nation as a woman—particularly emphatic, though, with connotations of vulnerability and sexual impurity as a colonised nation).[84] For example, Egypt is represented as a fowl on a platter, with European nations as national-stereotypical male figures arranged around a dining table and England about to carve, while Egyptian peasants in caps and gowns crouch on the floor, gnawing the bones handed to them.[85] Combining local imagery and a circulating transnational language of visual political satire, using the Sphinx as implied narrator/master of the gaze—perhaps as a local Mr Punch—the graphics of *al-Siyāsa al-musawwara* are truly arresting in the punch they deliver.

Citing *Punch* in Arabic, Siting *Punch* in Cairo: A Conclusion

I have already suggested that *The Cairo Punch* combined sternly local political vision (though one that embraced other colonised elites on the southern Mediterranean) with awareness that transnational circulations of satirical meaning were possible. After all, that periodicals in Tokyo and England could reproduce this Cairene journal's images as meaningful to their own local audiences must have signalled the itinerant political potential of cartoons etched in Cairo. Are there further meanings to *al-Siyāsa al-musawwara*'s citing of *Punch* graphically, and regularly by placing it on every fortnightly masthead in a *Punch*-like font, while localising it by incorporating the name and brand into an Egyptian context as *The Cairo Punch*—and even more by using this English title to head a largely Arabic-language periodical with a very clear anti-Empire political stance? *Al-Siyāsa al-musawwara* does not appear to imitate or derive direct guidance from the London *Punch*'s specific attributes: as Brian Maidment notes in this volume, and unlike some other Asian incarnations of *Punch*, the Cairo version was clearly not directed primarily at expatriates, though the language enframing its visual satire invited multilingual readings from readers positioned differently in

---

[84] In addition to the example mentioned earlier, Egypt is represented as an abject young woman in rags and chains crawling toward a devilish figure, over a sea of faces: the British Parliament (*al-Siyāsa al-musawwara* 1, no. 4, 15 January 1908, 2–3); as a young crowned haloed female figure mounted above a procession of nationalist newspaper editors (*al-Siyāsa al-musawwara* 1, no. 5, 24 January 1907, 2–3); and as a young Pharaonic queen held down by balls and chain (*al-Siyāsa al-musawwara* 1, no. 6, 31 January 1907, 2–3).

[85] "Misr bayna makhālīb al-ajānib" [cartoon], *al-Siyāsa al-musawwara* 1, no. 14, 3 April 1908, 2–3. Image signed 'A. H. Zaki'. Similar depictions of China as a melon or cake to be eaten are discussed by I-Wei Wu.

terms both of culture and political outlook: Arabic was literally central, but those who read English and French were also summoned to partake, though generally the captions that spoke to them were couched in slightly gentler language than was the Arabic. But this Egyptian publication differs from the London *Punch* above all in its tone: it is bitter critique rather than the whimsy that Maidment finds key to London *Punch*'s recipe (at least after its first few more radical years). *Al-Siyāsa al-musawwara/The Cairo Punch* sought direct political impact on its readers, sketching a situation of urgent political crisis, and its critics were probably not wrong to ascribe activist, indeed confrontational, motives to its cartooning.

Though, as noted above, *al-Siyāsa al-musawwara* exhibits visual tropes found in satirical journalism elsewhere, it seems more to be the idea of *Punch* than the London journal's specific internal patterning of visuals and text, its narrative personae, or its critical but not partisan view of national and international politics that *The Cairo Punch* emulated with its dual title. Using single-plate cartoons unaccompanied by a multitude of smaller illustrations; not directly linking cartoons and text, though all bore the same political outlook; relying on only one or two textual genres of expression, and eschewing representation of vernacular speech: formally, Cairo's *Punch* diverged from London's, while maintaining the feature that *Punch*'s English imitators saw as crucial, according to Maidment: 'the centrality of spectacular large-scale topical cartoons'. From the editor's intense investment (to judge by column inches) in publicity, ancillary activities that might bring in income, and validation and recognition by other journals, local and afar, it may well be that *Punch*'s venerable fame and its successful self-marketing were also attractive. Perhaps the use of the *Punch* label, suggestive of a brand allegiance with the use of a recognisable decorative English font on the Cairo masthead, was a hopeful gesture to desired circulation figures and geographic and social reach. Or perhaps 'Abd al-Hamid Zaki exploited the rubric to suggest that the imperial metropolis' institutions were not immune to cultural-political invasion or inversion, and certainly not to radical localisation. *Punch*—that most English of inventions—could be made to speak with the (multilingual) tongue of Egyptian anti-imperial nationalism. But did this very aspiration to exploit and perhaps to re-voice *Punch* compromise its editor-cartoonist's adamant stance against the feared Europeanisation, as he saw it, of his beloved homeland?

Part IV
Punch in East Asia

'Punch Pictures': Localising Punch in Meiji Japan

Peter Duus

The Discovery of the 'Punch Picture'

The earliest Japanese term for political cartoon—'Punch picture' (*Ponchi-e* ポンチ絵)—was invented in 1868 by a Japanese language news journal, the *Kōko shinbun* 江湖新聞 (the public news) published in the treaty port of Yokohama. The word endured until the early 1900s when it was slowly supplanted by the more familiar *manga* (cartoon), a broader term that came to mean not only single panel political cartoons but also four panel cartoons, comic strips, comic magazines and eventually animated cartoons.

'Punch pictures', the journal observed, were 'comical drawings with secret meanings'.[1] It astutely likened them to *hanjimono*: rebus puzzles sold in print shops and often designed by well-known woodblock print artists. Like Western rebus puzzles *hanjimono* were visual puns, pictures that mingled sounds and objects to represent words or phrases. In a comical *hanjimono* guide to the city of Edo, for example, a man with an arrow (*ya*) struck through his tongue (*shita*) indicated the Shitaya neighbourhood; and in a *hanjimono* map of the country Buzen province was represented by farting buttocks (making a *bu* sound) and a small tray table (*zen*). The pleasure of reading a *hanjimono*, like the pleasure of reading a political cartoon, was the satisfying Eureka moment when the puzzle was solved.

Political cartoons are visually more complicated than rebuses but easier to read. They are intended not to hide meaning so much as to convey it obliquely but suddenly. The Japanese had no difficulty recognising this essential element of the cartoon's humour. Interestingly enough, the recognition was mutual. Rutherford Alcock, the

---

[1] Ono Hideo, *Yokohama mochigusa shinbun. Kōko shinbun* (Tōkyō: Meiji bunka kenkyūkai, 1926), 10–11.

P. Duus (✉)
William H. Bonsall Professor of Japanese History, Emeritus, at Stanford University, United States
e-mail: pduus@stanford.edu

Fig. 1 Anonymous, *Seiyō no giga Ponchi no zu* 西洋の戯画ポンチえ圖 (a Western comic drawing/Punch picture). *Kōko shinbun*, 4 April 1868

first British minister to Japan, described a book of *hanjimono* that he had bought as 'a series of illustrated charades and rebuses, such as Charivari delights in'.[2] In other words he found it as easy to see the affinities between the *hanjimono* and 'Punch pictures'. This shock of recognition suggests how easy it is to link *Punch, or the London Charivari* to the development of modern Japanese visual satire.

The example of a 'Punch picture' published in the *Kōko shinbun*, however, presents a puzzle of its own (Fig. 1). One cannot find any remotely similar cartoon in the pages of the London *Punch*. The drawing style suggests that it came from another source—*Japan Punch,* a comic magazine that began publication in Yokohama in 1862 launched by Charles Wirgman, a draftsman of no exceptional talent, whose drawings are often closer to Edmund Lear's whimsical nonsense sketches than John Tenniel's polished caricatures in *Punch*. But the puzzle deepens because one can find no similar cartoons there either. There are only fragments from other *Japan Punch* cartoons: the looming figure in the drawing resembles Wirgman's caricatures of Sir Harry Parkes, the British minister to Japan from 1865 to 1883; and the tiny figures at the bottom appear to have come from an entirely unrelated cartoon. In effect the example of a 'Punch picture' presented by the news journal was not a London *Punch* cartoon but a pastiche of fragments from cartoons in an English language magazine that borrowed the *Punch* name but neither its format nor its content.

---

[2] Rutherford Alcock, *The Capital of the Tycoon: A Narrative of Three Years' Residence in Japan*, vol. 2 (London: Harper and Brothers, 1863), 289.

The puzzle of the *Kōko shinbun*'s 'Punch picture' illustrates the difficulties of tracing the influence of *Punch* on the development of visual satire in Meiji Japan— or perhaps any other non-Western country. The quick adoption of 'Punch pictures' as a generic name for political cartoons confirms that the British magazine had an impact but it does not illuminate what that impact was. In fact, the genealogy of the modern Japanese cartoon was far more complex than simple transmission, emulation and replication of a British model. Like so many cultural products in Meiji Japan, from fiction through music to painting and architecture, the political cartoon emerged from a mingling of influences, indigenous and exogenous, typical of colonial or semi-colonial societies seeking to catch up with the 'civilised countries'.

The localising of *Punch* involved adaptation and assimilation as well as importation. The complexities of the process may be illuminated by examples of three Meiji period illustrated humour magazines: *Japan Punch* (1862–1887); *Nipponchi* 日ポン地 ("Japan land" or "Japan Punch" (pun)) (1874); and *Marumaru chinbun* 團團珍聞 (blue pencil news) (1877–1907).

Visual Satire in the Edo Period

Although 'Punch pictures' were new to Japan, visual satire was not. It had long been produced by a robust indigenous print capitalism. By the middle of the nineteenth century there were perhaps 900 or so publishers in Edo as well as an elaborate network for the distribution and selling of books and prints. Best selling works of fiction might sell as many as 10,000 copies, and even sales of 3,000–4,000 copies were not unusual. Readership was much wider because commercial lending libraries dispatched delivery men, lugging bookcases on their backs, to deliver and pick up borrowed books. What made this mass market possible was growing literacy, especially in urban centres like Edo, the shogun's capital, where even women from samurai and merchant households could read.[3]

In contrast to *Punch*'s England where publishers were often printers, in Japan they were usually bookstore owners who relied on a technology quite different from their Western counterparts.[4] Although the Japanese had experimented briefly with movable type in the early seventeenth century, they soon shifted back to the use of woodblock printing instead.[5] Skilled artisans prepared the wood blocks,

---

[3] For a brief history of the publishing industry in the Edo period, see Peter Kornicki, *The Book in Japan: A Cultural History from the Beginning to the Nineteenth Century* (Leiden: Brill, 1998), Chap. 5.

[4] For the publishing industry in eighteenth-century England see Michael Twyman, *Printing 1770–1970: An Illustrated History of Its Development and Uses in England* (London: The British Library, 1998) Chap. 1.

[5] The Chinese, often noted as the inventors of movable type, also relied primarily on woodblock technology in publishing. Cf. Joseph P. McDermott, *A Social History of the Chinese Book: Books and Literati in Late Imperial China* (Hong Kong: Hong Kong University Press, 2006), Chap. 1.

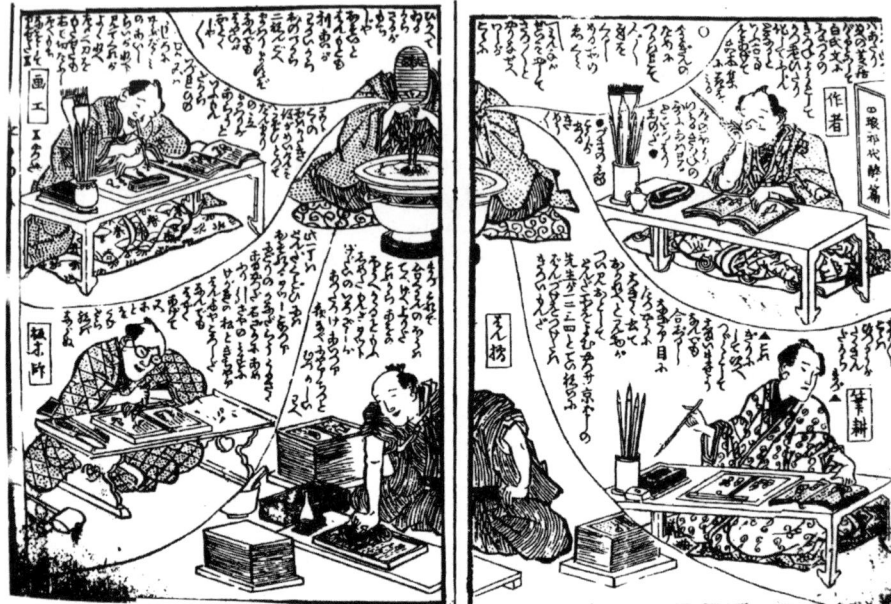

Fig. 2 A schematic view of Edo period publishing. Clockwise from the *upper right corner* are an author, a calligrapher, a printer, a block carver, an illustrator, and a publisher. The publisher, depicted with a gold piece for a head, provided the capital. Tōri Sanjin (1818), *Takarabune kogane no hobashira*. From Adam Kern, *Manga From the Floating World: Comic Book Culture and the Kibyōshi of Edo Japan.* (Cambridge: Harvard University Press, 2006), 37

carved text and illustrations into the blocks, printed pages by rubbing a damp sheet of paper over the inked block with a utensil called a *baren*, aligned the pages, and then stitched them together into a bound book. Each stage in the production was in the hands of a separate set of specialised workers, a labour intensive system that required less equipment investment than a Western printing press operation and appears to have been more economical (Fig. 2).

One major reason for the persistence of woodblock printing was the peculiarity of the Japanese writing system, which mixed Chinese characters (*kanji*) with a phonetic script (*kana*). Philosophical or religious works were often published entirely in Chinese characters, but popular books, especially popular fiction, were written in a graceful cursive phonetic script (*hiragana*) that even the minimally literate could read. Much of the visual appeal of a book was the beauty of the calligrapher's idiosyncratic rendering of the written text. These idiosyncrasies, indeed the cursiveness of the script itself, were not reproducible by standardised movable type. As Peter Kornicki has suggested, printed books in pre-Meiji Japan were essentially direct reproductions of manuscripts. Each book, he points out, 'had a different personality, and one that was related to the calligraphy, the written hand', and was thus unique and unrepeatable.[6]

---

[6] Kornicki, *The Book in Japan*, 27.

The appeal of reading a book lay as much in the visual experience as in the linguistic, and that experience was reinforced by the lavish use of illustrations to amplify and/or clarify the meaning of the calligraphic words on the page. Woodblock technology made it easy to integrate illustrations into the written text on the page. In contrast to England, where the art of illustrations did not blossom until the nineteenth century, almost all Japanese books, including technical as well as literary works, included monochrome line illustrations that transferred the pictorial brush stroke to the page as easily as it transferred the calligraphic. Publishers knew that they could enhance sales of a book by cramming it with illustrations and putting the term *ehon* (picture book) or *eiri* (with illustrations) in its title. By the end of the eighteenth century dialogue, narrative exposition, and authorial asides—in short, the whole prose text—wound across the page through the artist's illustrations competing for the reader's attention (Fig. 2). The act of reading was not unlike reading a contemporary graphic novel or comic book; it required decoding visual signs and allusions, as well as making sense of the words.

In his brilliant work on the 'yellow books' (*kibyōshi*) published in the 1780s, Adam Kern shows how the wedding of text and image were brought to the service of social satire—and even low-key political satire.[7] Authors of *gesaku* (literally 'playful compositions') light fiction poked fun at the extravagant behaviour of nouveau riche merchants, the hapless gaucheries of dissolute sons of the wealthy, the deceptive ways of courtesans in the entertainment quarters, and the pranks of boorish travellers on the Tokaido (the main national highway.) The subtext of these stories was often social resentment at the disparities in wealth and power in commoner society. Not surprisingly *gesaku* authors were often deracinated members of the elite samurai class.

During the 1780s, a time of poor harvests, widespread famine, and peasant unrest, some 'yellow books' mocked the corruption of samurai officials or the incompetence of the shogun's ministers in dealing with the economic crisis. Official censorship regulations, however, prohibited not only pornography but also unorthodox philosophical ideas and any mention of political leaders or events. To circumvent the censorship system authors and illustrators relied on the technique of *mitate-e* (simile pictures), popular prints that transformed characters or episodes from classic literature into contemporary equivalents, such as a print likening a courtesan writing a love note to Lady Murasaki composing *The Tale of Genji* (*Genji monogatari* 源氏物語), a classic eleventh century novel. Satiric barbs were also couched in comical historical allegories that mocked a historical figure in order to criticise a contemporary one. They would also appear as *reductio ad absurdum* narratives that turned conventional wisdom or morality upside down.[8] But authors and artists were always careful not to step too far over the line, and their satire never reached the often vicious intensity of a Jonathan Swift or a James Gillray. Had they done so they would have provoked the wrath of the censors—and received certain punishment.

---

[7] Adam Kern, *Manga from the Floating World* (Cambridge: Harvard University Press, 2006).
[8] Kern, *Manga*, 197–224.

Fig. 3 This *Toba-e* (Toba picture) illustrates the simple slapstick humor associated with the genre. It shows an amateur fisherman catching the topknot of one of his companions. Anonymous, *Akubidome* あくびどめ (yawn stoppers) (1793) (Courtesy San Francisco Public Library)

While Kern argues that the *kibyōshi* constituted the first Japanese *manga* (comic books), they might be better called the first Japanese graphic novels. Japanese publishers also produced more purely visual comical works. By the 1780s, books of captionless comic drawings known as *Toba-ehon* 鳥羽絵本 (Toba picture books) enjoyed a wide audience. The name came from Toba Sojo, a twelfth century priest regarded as the putative artist of the famous 'bird and animal scroll' (*Giga chōjū* 戯画鳥獣), an enigmatic work thought to satirise the Buddhist clerical hierarchy and/or their aristocratic patrons as rabbits, frogs, and monkeys. *Toba-e* (Toba pictures) were basically single panel cartoons illustrating puns or showing people in various awkward or ridiculous situations, such a fisherman catching a friend's topknot on his hook or a drunken samurai staggering down the street mocked by neighbourhood children (Fig. 3). Sometimes *Toba-ehon* parodied a famous literary work like the Japanese *Tale of Heike* (*Heike monogatari* 平家物語) or the Chinese *Tale of Three Kingdoms* (*Sangokushi* 三国志) but usually there was no narrative continuity between pictures, all of which were essentially 'gag cartoons'. What defined the genre was a distinctive style of drawing in the manner of Toba Sojo, simple sketches in playful and fluid calligraphic line that seemed dashed off in haste and populated by human figures with long spindly arms and legs, round heads, tiny triangular pug noses, and dots for eyes. The humour of the *Toba-e* was even gentler and blander than that of the *kibyōshi*.[9]

Social unrest and economic instability provided new grist for the satirist's mill again during the 1830s, when another series of bad harvests brought hard times to city and countryside. Mockery of the ruling elite became more explicit, and the *mitate-e* style was used to criticise specific officials. One of the best known examples was an elaborate 1837 three panel print by the famous Ukiyo-e artist Kuniyoshi. It depicted a semi-historical figure, an ailing Fujiwara Raikō, under attack by an evil Earth Spider, and threatened by a parade of hideous monsters while his retainers heedlessly sipped tea and played *go* (a Japanese board game). Fujiwara, it was said, was meant to represent the incumbent shogun, the retainers his high advisors, and the parade of monsters economic and social ills besetting the country. More than half the most notorious publications mentioned in diary of the bookseller Fujioka Yoshizo during the years 1848–1854 were illicit works that bore no official censorship seal. Needless to say, they were published without official approval and were probably sold under the counter, just as pornographic prints were.

Despite official constraints on public political commentary, during the 1840s and 1850s illustrated *kawaraban* broadsheets that reported occasionally on sensational events like lovers' suicides, earthquakes, personal vendettas, urban fires and floods, volcanic eruptions, and natural anomalies such as sea monsters, beached mermen and pregnant 8-year-olds, began to report on political events too. The arrival of the Perry expedition in 1853–1854, for example, was reported in great if not always accurate detail. Increasingly *kawaraban* broadsheets, implicitly or explicitly, also offered ironic or satirical commentary. Some lampooned the puniness or duplicity of the foreigners, and others complained about the price inflation brought on by the opening of the country to foreign trade. On the eve of *Punch*'s arrival in Japan indigenous visual satire was not only robust but a sense of national crisis was eroding restraints on public discussion.[10]

Japan Punch: Expatriate Humour

It is no accident that 'Punch pictures' made their first appearance in Yokohama, the largest of the treaty ports created by agreements with the foreign powers, and the one most easily accessible to Edo (later renamed Tokyo.) It was a semi-colonial enclave occupied principally by foreigners and their Asian servants, and it lay beyond the reach of the shogun's writ. The foreign residents, protected by extraterritorial privilege, were exempt from Japanese laws, including the censorship regulations that stifled political satire and commentary. It was here, shortly after

---

[9] A brief description of *toba-e* prints can be found in Jack Hillier, *The Art of the Japanese Book* (London: Sotheby's Publications, 1887), 598–607.

[10] For examples of late Edo period *kawaraban* broadsheets see Kōsaburō Nishimaki, *Kawaban: Shinbun. Edo Meiji 300 nen jiken*, vol. 1 (Tōkyō: Heibonsha, 1978).

his arrival in 1862, that Charles Wirgman (1835–1891), a young Englishman, began publishing *Japan Punch*.[11]

Wirgman belonged to the legion of expatriate British globe-trotters and fortune-seekers who wandered the cultural frontiers between the colonising West and the rest of the world during the Victorian era. A former British army officer, in 1857 he became a 'Special Artist and Correspondent' for the *Illustrated London News*, reporting first from Malta, then travelling to the Philippines, and ultimately to China, where he covered the Anglo-French military expedition in North China during the second Opium War in 1859–1860. His experience in China probably led to his selection to dispatch reports from the newly opened ports in Japan in 1861. A largely self-taught draftsman who may or may not have had formal training, he sent sketches, sometimes made on the spot, sometime drawn from memory or sometimes based on photographs, back to London where they were transformed into realistic-looking wood engravings in the *News*. In a sense Wirgman was the Victorian version of a photo-journalist.

Fig. 4 Charles Wirgman, cover of the *Japan Punch* (1862)

---

[11] The best brief biography of Wirgman is the essay by John Clark, "Charles Wirgman 1835–1891," in *Britain and Japan 1859–1899*, eds. Hugh Cortazzi and Gordon Daniels (London: Routledge, 1992), 54–63. See also Ian Nish, *Britain & Japan: Biographical Portraits* (Folkestone: Japan Library, 1994), 20–32.

In 1862 Wirgman decided to return to Japan, a country that clearly fascinated him. His decision to stay there may well have been determined by his affair, then marriage to a young Japanese woman, who bore him a son. He went into partnership with the pioneering photographer, Felix Beato, selling his own drawings and Beato's hand-coloured photos and paintings to residents and visitors to Yokohama; and he occasionally served as an interpreter for the British legation. However he earned his living, he was soon a fixture in the Yokohama foreign community, a 'Japan hand' known for his wit and his hospitality to visiting foreign artists and illustrators. His sketches of Japanese life, for example, provided the basis for illustrations in works like Aime Humbert's popular 1870 travel account, *Le Japon Illustré*. As the only working Western artist in Yokohama, he also made ties with the Tokyo artistic community. He acted as a cultural intermediary during the early years of Japan's renewed contacts with the West, introducing foreign diplomats and traders to the work of Japanese artists and offering oil painting lessons to pioneer Western-style painters like Takahashi Yuichi.

In May 1862, using funds borrowed from a foreign trader in Yokohama, Wirgman established *Japan Punch* (Figs. 4 and 5), a magazine published intermittently until

Fig. 5 Charles Wirgman, cover of the *Japan Punch* (1866)

1873, then as a monthly publication until 1887.[12] The magazine acknowledged the London *Punch* as its inspiration and model. The early covers displayed a humpbacked Mr Punch in his clown suit shaking hands with an equally humpbacked Japanese samurai, armed with a sword and clad in formal kimono, whose nose was as long as his own. In the background the sun rises over Mount Fuji framed by pine branches and storks, traditional good luck symbols, perhaps to emphasise an auspicious meeting between East and West (Fig. 4). Although Mr Punch continued to appear either in clown suit or some other garb (or as Wirgman's self-caricature) in the magazine's cartoons, he eventually disappeared from the cover, leaving only the Punch look-alike samurai armed with quill pen instead of sword. Mr Punch, as it were, went native, becoming an expatriate like Wirgman himself (Fig. 5).

In format and appearance the *Japan Punch* bore a closer resemblance to a traditional Japanese imprint than a Western one. The technology that produced *Punch* in England—steam press, movable type and wood engraving illustrations—had yet to arrive in Japan. Wirgman had to rely on traditional methods of woodblock printing to publish his magazine. He hired Japanese craftsmen to carve his sketches, cartoons, caricatures and hand-written essays and verse into wooden blocks that were then inked and printed on Japanese paper. Only 200 or so copies were printed per issue, so the process was more than adequate—and far less expensive—than Western technology. Apparently it satisfied his audience, the tiny but growing expatriate community in Yokohama, who were amused by his ironic commentaries on life in the port. (In this respect the magazine was very much like the *China Punch* discussed in the essays by Christopher Rea and Barbara Mittler in this volume.)[13]

Wirgman announced in the first issue that his intent was to provide entertainment for foreign residents of the treaty port community, whose opportunities for amusement were otherwise limited to smoking clubs and licensed brothels. Most of his cartoons, essays and doggerel verses referred to happenings in the foreign community: sporting events from horse races to ice skating; banquets for visiting dignitaries; local theatrical productions; commercial disputes; legal cases in the consular courts; tiffs among foreign language newspaper editors; problems in dealing with Japanese servants and officials; capricious changes in the weather, and the like (Fig. 6). He also poked fun at the national differences, for example, comparing the British taste for roast beef and the American taste for pork and beans with the French taste for fine and elaborate cuisine. Only rarely did the magazine refer to the revolutionary events in Japan that he was covering for the *Illustrated London News*: the rising anti-foreign movement; attacks on foreigners and foreign

---

[12] A complete reproduction edition of *Japan Punch* was published by Yushodo in 1976 and reprinted in 1999. The introductory essays by Japanese scholars are quite useful. For a sampling of Wirgman's cartoons and essays see Jozef Rogala, *The Genius of Mr Punch: Life in Yokohama's Foreign Settlement: Charles Wirgman and the Japan Punch* (Yokohama: Yurindo, 2004).

[13] See chapters 'He'll Roast All Subjects That May Need the Roasting': Puck and Mr Punch in Nineteenth-Century China and Epilogue in this volume.

Fig. 6 This spoof of local sporting activity in Yokohama is typical of the cartoons in *Japan Punch*. The skaters are all easily identifiable caricatures of the local foreign community, and the prostrate figure at the *bottom* is a self-caricature of Charles Wirgman. Charles Wirgman, 'A Prospect of the Yokohama Skating Club', *Japan Punch* (1866)

legations; the foreign bombardments at Kagoshima and Shimonoseki, and the struggle of rebellious domains against the shogunate. The magazine's audience, after all, was all too familiar with these events, and they read *Japan Punch* for its humour not its news reporting.[14]

It is clear that Wirgman's peculiar magazine fascinated Japanese who lived in Yokohama or frequented the port. His 'Punch pictures' offered a novel way of hiding meaning in comical pictures. First of all, since the magazine was not subject to censorship, Wirgman's cartoons made no attempt to conceal the identity of those they lampooned, as *mitate-e* and other satirical woodblock prints did. His skilled caricatures were immediately identifiable to the expatriate community, and he did not hesitate to make fun of officials like Harry Parkes, the British minister, and other foreign diplomatic representatives. His publication was also timely. Unlike one-off traditional satirical prints, the magazine provided continuing commentary on current happenings. While this was common sense in England, where the public

---

[14] After the overthrow of the shogunate in 1868, and particularly in the 1870s, Wirgman commented occasionally on Japanese domestic politics, especially the government's controls of the press.

selling of information at regular intervals was well established, the practice was unfamiliar to the Japanese. Indeed, street hawkers of the first Japanese newspapers had to convince readers accustomed to occasional *kawaraban* broadsheets that today's newspaper was not the same as yesterday's.

To be sure, in the early 1860s Japanese officials had discovered how useful newspapers in the West were in disseminating information from or about the outside world. In 1868 the shogunate's translation bureau began circulating the *Nihon bōeki shinbun* 日本貿易新聞 (Japan commercial news), a compilation of translated articles from foreign newspapers. A few privately published news journals and gazettes, like the *Kokō shinbun*, began to appear in Edo as well as in Yokohama and other ports too. Published on a regular periodical schedule, they carried commercial information, translations from the foreign press, and reports on domestic events. Printed from woodblocks and bound with covers like traditional books, these publications were called *shinbushi* (news journals) but physically they resembled Western pamphlets or magazines rather than Western newspapers.[15]

The first Japanese-authored 'Punch picture' depicting a political event appeared in an 1864 issue of the *Nihon bōeki shinbun* (Japan commercial news). Its satirical comment was directed not at the shogun's government but at a domestic opponent, the rebellious domain of Chōshū, whose shore batteries had been bombarded by an allied fleet of foreign gunboats after they fired on foreign merchant ships. In a figurative sense, the domain had lost its head—and is so depicted in the cartoon. Private newspapers like the *Yokohama shinpō moshiogusa* 横浜新法もしお草 (seaweed: Yokohama news report), published by the pioneer journalist Kishida Ginko and backed by a swashbuckling American merchant, also carried occasional cartoons critical of foreign intrusions in Japan. Just what provided models for these cartoons is difficult to determine but clearly copies of the *Japan Punch* were more readily at hand to the publishers than copies of the London *Punch*.

In any case, Wirgman's 'Punch pictures' provided the first and most immediate model for a new genre of visual satire. Their meanings were 'hidden' but not as hidden as they had been in indigenous political satire, and their focus on political current events was novel. Since his magazine focused on the narrow concerns and pastimes of a small expatriate community, it was able to reach only a small Japanese audience, but that audience was significant for the development of the Japanese political cartoon.

---

[15] For a history of early Japanese newspapers see James L. Huffman, *Creating a Public: People and Press in Meiji Japan* (Honolulu: University of Hawai'i Press, 1997), Chaps. 1 and 2. Also useful is Gerald Groemer, "Singing the News: *Yomiuri* in Japan During the Edo and Meiji Periods," *Harvard Journal of Asian Studies* 54, no.1 (June 1994): 233–61.

Nipponchi: The *Toba-ehon* Modernised

After the overthrow of the shogunate in 1868, the new Meiji government instituted a system of censorship more rigorously enforced than the old one. This slowed the diffusion of the new comic art until the mid-1870s. The first Japanese periodical illustrated solely with 'Punch pictures' was the *E-shinbun nipponchi* 絵新聞日本地 (illustrated news: Japan Punch), published in 1874. To attract readers it called itself an 'illustrated newspaper' (*e-shinbun*), like the daily or weekly news gazettes (*nishiki-e shinbun*) with lurid front page illustrations that were popular with the reading public, but it was really Japan's first modern *manga* magazine. Its office was located in Yokohama, where it was sheltered from the reach of government control.[16]

The magazine was a product of collaboration between two well-known members of publishing world, both habitués of the city's demimonde and steeped in urban plebeian culture. Kanagaki Robun (1829–1894), the son of a fishmonger, was a popular *gesaku* author who had worked for Edo publishing houses writing comic fiction or texts for woodblock prints.[17] His partner was the popular painter and woodblock print artist Kawanabe Kyosai (1831–1889), the son of a rice merchant, who had been trained in the ateliers of the *Ukiyo-e* print artist Utagawa Kuniyoshi as well as the classical court painter Kano Tohaku.[18]

Collaboration between the two men stretched back nearly two decades when they worked together on a series of 'catfish pictures' (*namazu-e*), satirical prints commenting on the impact of the 1855 earthquake in Edo. (According to local legend, earthquakes were caused by the underground movements of a giant catfish that the prints showed as both the source of the calamity and the benefactor of the carpenters, masons and lumber merchants who profited from rebuilding the city.) The prints sold so well that the young Kawanabe decided to launch a career as a freelance commercial artist (*machieshi*) accepting commissions from all comers. During the 1860s his best-selling comical prints—what he called 'crazy pictures' (*kyōga*)—were often based on ideas suggested by Robun. Publishers valued Kyosai so highly as a woodblock print artist that they hired the best carvers and printers to work with him.

---

[16] For a more detailed discussion of *Nipponchi* see Peter Duus, "Japan's First Modern Manga Magazine," *Impressions* 21 (1999): 31–41.

[17] For a brief comment on Robun's work see Donald Keene, *Dawn to the West: Japanese Literature in the Modern Era*, vol. 1, Fiction (New York: Holt, Rinehart and Winston, 1984), 14–17.

[18] For an early discussion of Kyosai's work, see Josiah Conder, *Paintings and Studies by Kawanabe Kyosai* (Tokyo: Maruzen/Kelly and Walsh, 1911). For more biographical information and examples of Kyosai's art see Timothy Clark, *Demon of Painting: The Art of Kawanabe Kyosai* (London: British Museum Press, 1993). Other useful works on Kyosai are Shigeru Oikawa and Seiichi Yamaguchi, *Kawanabe Kyosai no giga* (Tokyo: Tokyo shoseki, 1992); and Seiichi Yamaguchi, *Meiji hankotsu to fushi* (Tōkyō: Kyōsai kinen bijutsukan, 1987).

As members of an older generation, Robun and Kyosai were deeply ambivalent toward the cultural and social confusion that followed the fall of the old regime. It had launched an era of 'civilisation and enlightenment' (*bunmei kaika*) when outside influences suddenly flooded into the country. Government leaders returned from a trip around the world in 1871–1872 determined to rebuild Japan as a 'civilised country' (*bunmeikoku*) with an up-to-date political and economic infrastructure, and hundreds of foreign advisers were hired to assist the effort. A new westernised intelligentsia, some educated abroad but all conversant with foreign languages, worked feverishly to dispel the darkness of the country's 'barbarism' by introducing its people to the mores, values and practices of the 'civilised' West. Among the best sellers of the time were Fukuzawa Yukichi's *Seiyō jijō* 西洋事情 (*Conditions in the West*), an encyclopaedic guide to Western culture and institutions; a translation of Samuel Smile's *Self-Help* entitled *Saikoku risshin hen* 西国立志編 (success stories from the West); and a translation of John Stuart Mill's *On Liberty*.

Robun and Kyosai were fascinated by the 'new knowledge' (*shin chishiki*) imported from the West. Kyosai, for example, drew illustrations for new science and geography textbooks, and he illustrated a Japanese translation of Aesop's *Fables* using John Tenniel's engravings as his model. And Robun, relying on Fukuzawa's *Seiyō jijō* as his guide, wrote a comic tale about a tour of the Western countries by Kita and Yaji, two fictional characters from an early nineteenth century

Fig. 7 This illustration shows a young man clad in semi-Western costume, sporting a Western-style haircut, and reading a newspaper, demonstrating his embrace of 'civilisation' by eating beef stew. From Kanagaki Robun, *Aguranabe* (sitting around the stew pot), 1871

gesaku comic novel made famous by their pratfalls on their travels along the Tokaido, the country's main highway.

The often incongruous juxtaposition of the old and the new as 'civilisation and enlightenment' penetrated the everyday life of a country isolated for two centuries and offered endless satirical possibilities. In the early 1870s, for example, Kyosai produced a brilliant series of prints about the intrusion of 'civilisation' into the supernatural world, where bewildered deities and their minions tried to accommodate themselves to Western customs and mores: demons at the King of Hell's court donned frock coats and chopped off their horns to accommodate top hats, and the Buddhist deity Fudō read a newspaper in the midst of his fiery aura while his attendants prepared him beef stew in defiance of traditional Buddhist taboos against eating meat.

In 1871 Robun and Kyosai collaborated on *Aguranabe* あぐら鍋 (sitting around the stew pot), a collection of stories that satirised the folly of intoxication with the new. All the characters are patrons of the new beef stew (*sukiyaki*) shops that were all the rage in Tokyo. The fatuousness of their embrace of everything Western is the theme that links the stories. The protagonist of the first story, for example, is a semi-westernised dandy—'a man fond of the West'—heavily doused with eau de cologne, dressed in an ill-fitting Western jacket with calico underwear peeking from underneath, and ostentatiously consulting a cheap watch (Fig. 7). 'We should really be grateful that even people like ourselves can now eat beef', he proclaims,

Fig. 8 The cover of *Nipponchi* centered on caricatures of its creators: Kawanabe Kyōsai on the *left*; and Kanagaki Robun on the *right*. The characters imprinted on the rising sun parody the official censors' stamp: it is a homophone for 'officially approved' that means 'officially disapproved'. Kawanabe Kyōsai, cover of *Nipponchi*, 1974

'thanks to the fact that Japan is steadily becoming a civilised country'.[19] 'Beef-eating' became a symbol of the absurdities entailed by an uncritical embrace of the new and the foreign.

The initial issue of the *Nipponchi* claimed three sources of inspiration: Aesop's *Fables*; the comical paintings of Toba Sojo; and Wirgman's *Punch*. The title *Nipponchi*, written with characters that might be translated as 'Japan, the land of *Punch*', phonetically superimposed the word for 'Japan' (*Nippon*) on the word 'Punch' (*Ponchi*). The reference to the *Fables* perhaps suggested the publication's Aesopian intent to conceal 'hidden meanings' behind innocent pictures, as the *Fables* hid them behind innocent stories. The debt to Wirgman was obvious from the magazine's front cover, which was modelled on Wirgman's magazine and not on the London *Punch*. It borrowed the symbol of the sun rising over Mount Fuji, but perched on its summit instead of Mr Punch and his Japanese look-alike were caricatures of Kyōsai clutching his painting brushes and Robun clutching his writing brush (Fig. 8).

Fig. 9 This *Nipponchi* cartoon contrasts a big-nosed foreign merchant on the right with the spindly-looking Japanese merchants depicted in the *Toba*-e style on the *left*. The foreigner's big nose was a standard element in caricatures of foreigners, but it also reminded Japanese readers of a *tengu*, a troublesome long-nosed mountain goblin. The cartoon comments on a drop in the foreign market for silkworm eggs after an Italian factory began cultivating its own silkworms. *Nipponch*i, June 1874

---

[19] A translation can be found can be found in Donald Keene, *Anthology of Japanese Literature: From 1868 to the Present Day* (New York: Grove Press, 1955), 31–33.

The reference to Toba Sojo, however, is the most telling. The format of the new publication was not so different from traditional illustrated humour books. It was printed on Japanese paper stock in monochrome black ink from wooden blocks, and its pages were bound with string stitches between soft covers. The cartoons bore no captions as the cartoons in the London *Punch* did, and the text was intertwined with illustrations as it was in traditional books. In short, as a physical artefact, *Nipponchi* resembled a *Toba-ehon* (Toba picture book) rather than the London *Punch* or Wirgman's *Punch*. The cartoons were drawn with the traditional sinuous calligraphic brush line, not the wire line characteristic of wood engravings, and were dashed off with spontaneity rather than careful draughtsmanship. Human figures in *Nipponchi* also resembled the awkward, spindly people who populated the 'Toba pictures' rather than the realistic ones who appeared in *Punch* cartoons (Fig. 9).

Neither did the magazine contain any written satire or humour, an essential feature of both Wirgman's magazine and the original *Punch*, where prose overwhelmed the picture on most pages. (See Brian Maidment's essay on the London *Punch*.)[20] This was not because Kanagaki Robun was unable to write humorous pieces; on the contrary, he was an astonishingly productive author of comic fiction and non-fiction. It seems that *Nipponchi* was not designed on the original *Punch* template at all, nor even on Wirgman's *Japan Punch* with its brief and epigrammatic prose commentary. Rather it was simply a 'Toba picture book'

Fig. 10 A self-caricature by Kawanabe Kyōsai. Frontispiece, *Nipponchi*, 1874

---

[20] Chapter The Presence of *Punch* in the Nineteenth Century in this volume.

wrapped in Western clothes, just as Kyosai's caricature self-portrait in the first issue wore shoes and a top hat (Fig. 10). Ironically the magazine was a cultural patchwork of the kind that was spoofed by the beef-eating stories in *Aguranabe*.

Like many new publishing ventures of the time, *Nipponchi* was short-lived. Only three issues appeared and copies of only two have survived. Clearly it was a commercial failure. Perhaps the two founders were just too busy to publish a periodical magazine—or maybe their other enterprises were more lucrative. But the scarcity of surviving copies suggests that it was unable to attract an audience, perhaps because potential readers attracted by the traditional format were puzzled by the content or unable to make the connection between the comical pictures and current events. It is significant that the final page of the second issue provided a brief explanation of each cartoon—in a sense, a kind of belated caption. This editorial precaution indicates that readers may not have been getting the joke or understanding non-traditional humorous allusions or symbols. But an equally likely explanation is that *Nipponchi*'s resemblance to traditional illustrated humour books offered readers nothing new in an era when novelty was a selling point, and a 'civilised' look attracted customers. In short, *Nipponchi* may have failed precisely because it did not follow the London *Punch* template.

Otoge-e Marumaru Chinbun: **Punch Localised**

Full localisation of the *Punch* template came only with the publication in 1877 of *Otoge-e marumaru chinbun* お伽絵團團珍聞 (comical blue pencil news), a weekly magazine closer in form and content to the original *Punch* than either Wirgman's *Japan Punch* or Kyosai and Robun's *Nipponchi*. It was an omnibus humour magazine that included not only 'Punch pictures' but also parody editorials, comic verses and puzzles, gossip from the brothel quarters, jokes and riddles, reports of strange or peculiar happenings around town, and light fiction in the popular *gesaku* tradition mentioned earlier. Visually it resembled the English original more closely than either *Japan Punch* or *Nipponchi*, and it was produced with up-to-date Western printing technology –movable type, printing press, and at first wood-engraved, then zinc plate photoengraved illustrations. Its cartoons bore English as well as Japanese captions, and in its early years it published bilingual jokes and comic dialogues[21] (Fig. 11).

---

[21] In the early 1980s a reprint edition of the *Marumaru chinbun* was published by Tokyo shohan: Yamazaki Eiyu, ed., *Marumaru chinbun* (Tōkyō: Tōkyō shohan, 1981–1986). The introductory essay is quite useful: Yamaguchi Junko, "Kaisetsu," in *Marumaru chinbun*, ed. Yamazaki Eiyu, vol. 1, 1–25. For an extended discussion of the Marumaru chinbun see Itaru Kimoto, *Marumaru chinbun/Kibidango ga yuku* (Tōkyō: Tōkyō Shohan, 1989). For an English introduction to the magazine see Peter Duus, "The Marumaru Chinbun and the Origins of the Modern Japanese Political Cartoon," *International Journal of Comic Art* 1, no.1 (Spring/Summer 1999): 42–55.

'Punch Pictures': Localising Punch in Meiji Japan 325

Fig. 11 Initial cover of the *Marumaru chinbun*. With its elaborate border the cover format resembles that of the London *Punch*. All the characters' faces have strong Western features—especially big noses. The deer and the horse at the top are a visual pun in Japanese: the *kanji* character for horse can be pronounced *ba* 馬 and the kanji character for deer can be read *ka* 鹿; together they become *baka*—variously translated as 'fool', 'idiot', 'stupid', or 'ass'. *Marumaru chinbun* 1, 14 March 1877

The founder of the magazine, Nomura Fumio (1836–1891), the son of a physician from the Hiroshima domain, belonged to the first generation of the new 'civilised' intellectual elite.[22] Like many bright and ambitious young samurai energised by growing contacts with the outside world during the final years of the old regime, he studied Dutch, then English, to gain access to Western learning. Like his contemporary, Fukuzawa Yukichi, the foremost member of the new westernised intelligentsia, he attended Ogata Korin's famous Tekijuku academy in Osaka, and in 1862 the Hiroshima domain sent him to Nagasaki to study navigation and arrange for the purchase of a Western vessel. He was full of schemes for modernising his domain but his real dream was to go abroad. In 1865, defying the shogunal ban on foreign travel, he smuggled himself out of the country with the help of an English merchant, Thomas B. Glover, and spent several years in Scotland before going home in 1868.

Upon his return, with his short hair, moustache and Western clothes, Nomura must have looked a bit like the 'beefeater' mentioned above in *Aguranabe*. His familiarity with Western 'civilisation' and his experience abroad had made him a much sought after 'foreign expert' (*yōgakusha*). In 1869 he published *Seiyō kenbunroku* 西洋見聞録 (a record of personal observations of the West), an encyclopaedic introduction to Western customs, institutions and culture that resembled Fukuzawa's *Seiyō jijō* (conditions in the West). The Hiroshima domain not only hired him to teach at the local Western studies academy but to act as the domain's representative to the new national council (*gijisho*). He soon attracted the attention of the central government in its search for foreign-trained talent, and in 1870 he was called to Tokyo to serve in the Public Works Ministry, then the Home Ministry, where he rose steadily in the bureaucratic hierarchy as a technocrat, publishing works on everything from weights and measures to constitutional politics.

As an outsider, a 'foreign expert' with no ties to the government's inner circle, Nomura realised that his future as an official was limited. In 1877 he resigned his government post. Several large real estate properties that he had bought in Tokyo doubtless helped him found his new publishing venture. It was an opportune time to enter the journalism business. The circulation of so-called 'small newspapers' had grown after 1874 when the new government lifted its ban on public political discussion. The importation of up-to-date print technology made it possible to reduce costs per issue and publish larger print runs, and the outbreak of an anti-government rebellion in 1877 boosted newspaper circulation dramatically. The first issue of the *Marumaru chinbun* was printed in 5,000 copies, 2,000 of which were sold and the rest distributed for free. By 1878 the magazine was selling 15,000 per issue, and by 1880 its circulation in the provinces exceeded its circulation in Tokyo.[23]

The magazine aimed at a wide but mixed audience. The first issue expressed the hope that it would attract students, and even some foreigners, by offering 'short discussions on political events in Japan and other countries at other times, short amusing stories, and English pastimes, such as enigmas, conundrums, &c.'

---

[22] For a short biographical essay on Nomura see Kimoto, *Marumaru*, 39–87. His obituary can be found in *Marumaru chinbun* 1000, 9 February 1895.

[23] Yamaguchi, *Meiji hankotsu to fushi*, 4–5.

bilingually in English and Japanese. The smattering of English-language content revealed the magazine's pedagogical ambition as a vehicle for spreading 'civilisation and enlightenment' (*bunmei kaika*). But the magazine sought readers not only among the westernising elite but also among the less educated urban commoner class—shopkeepers, apprentices, merchants, petty functionaries and skilled artisans. It attached *furigana* (phonetic symbols) to Chinese characters in the text so that 'even children will be able to understand it'. Much of the magazine's light fiction and humorous poetry was produced by former *gesaku* authors familiar with popular taste. In short, the magazine offered a mix of the serious and comical intended to appeal to both the man in the street and the new intelligentsia.[24]

A number of other humour magazines began publication around the same time but most did not last beyond two or three issues. The *Marumaru chinbun* carefully cultivated its readership. Like more serious periodicals it encouraged readers to send in their own literary contributions or their ideas for riddles, cartoons, and comic quizzes. The new postal system facilitated sales outside Tokyo, and the magazine soon established a network of dealers and agents around the country (and even in the foreign settlement district in Tokyo). Provincial readers, many of them aspiring writers or humorists, sometime formed local clubs or held local gatherings to discuss the magazine or their own contributions. Given the magazine's novel and unorthodox character it is no surprise that among its readers were future renegade journalists like Miyataki Gaikotsu, publisher of several satirical magazines, and Kotoku Shusui, a radical newspaper reporter and political activist ultimately executed for his role in an alleged assassination attempt on the emperor.

Much of the magazine's appeal had to do with its politics. Nomura was impressed by the English political system, which limited monarchical power and placed government in the hands of an elected parliament. These institutions, he wrote in his widely read *Seiyō kenbunroku* (a record of personal observations of the West), rested on the notion that 'the nation belonged to the people not to the ruler'. He understood that the English notion of 'freedom' and the liberal politics it nurtured were sustained by a press that played the role of critic and kept the public informed. 'There is nothing to compare with the (newspaper)', he wrote, 'to learn about the condition of the people, the merits and weakness of government, the state of military preparedness, the competence or incompetence of officials, and so forth.' 'But it is important that editorial opinions (*ronsetsu*) should be fair and unbiased (*kōhei*), and above all, expressed without apology'.[25] It was in the service of this adversarial spirit that he entered the new world of journalism.

In its early years the magazine stood firmly behind the 'popular rights' movement, a rising political opposition that demanded that the new government establish a constitution and a national representative assembly. 'The interests of the government and the people are completely different', said the magazine's first editorial

---

[24] *Marumaru chinbun* 1, 14 March 1877, 7–8.

[25] Nomura's *Seiyō kenbunroku* was republished in Yoshino Sakuzō, *Meiji bunka zenshū*, vol. 16. *Gaikokubunkahen* (Tōkyō: Nihon hyōronsha, 1928), 189–276. His observations on newspapers can be found in ibid. 234–237.

Fig. 12 After the imperial palace burned down in 1873 the government was slow to build a new one. In this cartoon, as two top government officials look at blueprints, one says to the other, 'But the secret is the building would cost such an awful lot of money, which it is much more sensible to spend on erecting fine palaces for ourselves, his faithful servants. The shed (at the background on the right) is quite good enough for the *kami* (god, i.e. the emperor.)'. *Marumaru chinbun* 73, 10 August 1878

(*chasetsu*). 'What one sees as an advantage, the other deplores as a disadvantage (...). Although ordinary people prefer republican government with a constitutional political structure, the government completely abhors it'.[26] During the early 1880s Nomura became a member of the Kaishinto, an anti-government party led by former government officials such as he, who called for an immediate adoption of the British parliamentary system. He even travelled to the provinces to speak at the party's local rallies.

Despite continuing official restraints on the press, the magazine mocked the Meiji leaders, at first gently, then more boldly. The '*Marumaru*' (literally 'round, round') in the magazine's title referred to the circle marks inserted in newspapers to indicate names or words blue-pencilled by the censors. The magazine was dogged in its criticism of government efforts to control public debate and stamp down public criticism. It often portrayed government leaders as corrupt and self-interested; as brutally and harshly oppressive; as self-serving, self-indulgent and unfaithful to their wives; and profligate in the use of public funds.

The cartoons used no real names but it was usually clear from caricatures or from verbal and visual puns who was being referred to. A 'big bear' (*ōkuma*) in a cartoon meant Okuma Shigenobu, a powerful figure in the finance ministry, and a 'black

---

[26] *Marumaru chinbun* 1, 14 March 1877, 2.

octopus' (*kuroi tako*) meant Kuroda Kiyotaka, the director of the Hokkaido Colonisation Office. The boldness of the magazine's satirical comment is astonishing if one remembers how tightly controlled public discussion had been under the old regime—and even during the early years of the new government. One 1878 cartoon even hinted that government leaders did not pay sufficient respect to the emperor (Fig. 12).

Although Nomura did not mention London *Punch* in his *Seiyō kenbunroku* he surely encountered it during his stay in England. His own magazine resembled *Punch* in many significant ways. Since the latest print technology was available, it was easy to adopt the *Punch* template. While neither Mr Punch nor his little dog appeared on its intricately drawn cover, Mr Dandan,[27] his Japanese avatar, was one of three comical men in Western clothes in the cover's centre (see Fig. 11). In parodic reference to the three monkeys at the Nikko Mausoleum, who see no evil, hear no evil and speak no evil, they proclaimed the magazine's intent to see all, hear all, and write all.

From the outset the magazine promoted its illustrations modelled on 'the wit of the well-known Western *Punch*'. In an early issue the editors noted, 'The "crazy pictures" in our magazine are not done in the style of India-ink landscapes (*sumi-e*) nor are they done in the style of satirical woodblock prints. They belong to an unclassifiable kind of eccentric picture in the so-called *Punch*-style (. . .). They are dashed off spontaneously with the scratch of a pen, and they must have hidden meanings (*gūi*)'.[28] The magazine's success no doubt owed much to the unique and novel character of its illustrations and cartoons. To be sure, readers could enjoy the challenge of decoding the 'hidden meanings' in the cartoons, rebuses and other illustrations in its pages, but they were probably also attracted by the magazine's Western style drawing techniques—wire line drawing done with a pen, using crosshatching to show light, shadow and depth. These techniques, of course, were better suited to the new zinc plate engraving technology than the sinuous strokes of traditional brush painting were. While *Marumaru chinbun* cartoons during its early years were never as polished as those in the London *Punch,* for a Japanese audience they must have represented a first-hand encounter with a novel artistic style.

The magazine's first illustrator and cartoonist was Honda Kinkichiro (1850–1921), who, like Nomura, came from a samurai family in Hiroshima.[29] As a teenager he was selected as one of the three young men chosen to study Western-style military arts under the tutelage of two Englishmen hired by the domain. When Nomura returned from England to teach Western studies, Honda became one of his students—and soon found himself promoted to the academy's assistant instructor. In 1874 he departed for Tokyo to study English at Fukuzawa Yukichi's Keio Academy, and then became a student at the government's Surveying Office, at the time headed by Nomura.

---

[27] The Chinese characters for 'Dandan' can also be read as 'Marumaru'.

[28] Kimoto, *Marumaru*, 73.

[29] For a brief biographical essay on Honda see Kimoto, *Marumaru*, 69–78. See also Fukushima, "Honda Kinkichirō," *Meiji bunka kenkyū* 29 (1929): 51–52.

Fig. 13 This *Marumaru chinbun* cartoon was based on an 1878 Punch cartoon depicting Bismarck trying to avoid a clash between England and Germany. In this cartoon Mr. Dandan hopes to avoid a clash between the Meiji government and its opposition. *Marumaru chinbun* 69, 13 July 1878

Impressed by a foreign instructor's drawing skills, he decided to become a Western-style artist. On Nomura's advice he began to study oil painting with a pioneer Japanese artist who had studied in England. He eventually founded his own private art school, training a younger generation of painters. When his mentor Nomura asked him, he agreed to draw illustrations for the *Marumaru chinbun*.

Fig. 14 The Western practice of taking a summer vacation was quickly adopted by government officials, shown here as catfish lazing at the beach entertained by a catfish geisha. This practice, which was not enjoyed by ordinary workers, is satirised in this cartoon. *Marumaru chinbun* 71, 27 July 1878

In designing his cartoons Honda occasionally borrowed from English examples. In 1878, for example, he cribbed a *Punch* cartoon about Bismarck's foreign policy to make a cartoon statement about the *Marumaru chinbun*'s role as arbiter in the national political debate (Fig. 13). The cartoon shows Mr Dandan, resembling the original Mr Punch more than the cover's version, standing at a railroad switch coolly considering whether to support 'slow' progress or 'full speed' toward the expansion of political rights, while two reactionary samurai crows sitting on the signal mutter that either choice is foolish. The English caption seems to suggest that since the government is steadily increasing its own power Mr Dandan will choose 'full speed'.

There was no need for Honda to rely on foreign examples. He could rely on a well-stocked storehouse of allusions, icons, and symbols from traditional popular culture, familiar folk tales, literary classics, and a vast pantheon of Buddhist and Shinto deities. The visual language of Honda's satire was almost entirely indigenous. Often he put old symbols to new use: a badger was a trickster; a huffing and puffing rain god was a wind for change or reform; Emma, the lord of hell, with his crew of ogres stood for an oppressive judiciary and police force; and a sumo match or a game of *go* was an obvious way to represent a conflict between political rivals or factions.

Taking his cue from the resurgence in traditional *gesaku* humour in the mid-1870s, Honda invented a new satirical vocabulary drawing on traditional culture. One of his most piquant inventions was the transformation of the giant catfish (Fig. 14), portrayed in the *namazu-e* comic woodblock prints as the cause of Edo's earthquakes, into a symbol for pompous government officials who, like catfish, sported long drooping long moustaches—and wielded powers as threatening and disruptive as an earthquake. Until the reading public acquired a more cosmopolitan cultural literacy, this hybrid language predominated in humorous visual satire.

In 1881 Honda left the magazine staff after incurring official wrath for a cartoon (inspired by a Gilray print) that showed the government as a timorous man teetering on a log bridge as he is menaced by monsters on four sides—among them economic difficulties, a loss of public confidence, and petitions for a national assembly. He was replaced as the magazine's principal illustrator by Kobayashi Kiyochika (1847–1914), an innovative artist who made his reputation with a series of woodblock prints of Tokyo's rapidly westernising cityscape. His 'sunshine prints' (kōsenga), which introduced conventions of Western realism such as shading, chiaroscuro and perspective into woodblock print art, sold so well that publishers sought Kiyochika as an illustrator. He may have attracted Nomura's attention with an 1881 series of single sheet comical prints about famous Tokyo sites entitled *Kiyochiku ponchi* 清親ポンチ (Kiyochika's Punch).

It is not clear how Kiyochika, the son of a former shogunal retainer, trained himself as an artist.[30] According to some accounts, he learned the rudiments of Western oil painting from Wirgman in Yokohama; others report that Wirgman threw him out for painting in too much detail; and still others report that Kiyochika was so overcome by the smell of oil paints that he abandoned interest immediately. Nor is it known whether he received any formal training in Japanese-style painting. His turn toward comic drawings may have been inspired by Kawanabe Kyosai, the popular artist who started *Nipponchi*, with whom some claim he studied. More to the point, Kiyochika was a tremendously versatile artist, comfortable with a variety of media, and willing to experiment with blending Japanese and Western styles of illustration. His arrival at *Marumaru chinbun* coincided with the magazine's adoption of yet another new print technology—lithography. Along with his brush and pen-and-ink drawings, he produced elaborate two-page centrefold lithographed cartoons, at first in monochrome, then in multi-colour. He was equally at ease working with all print technologies, indigenous or foreign.

Although the content of the *Marumaru chinbun* shifted from the polemical to the more humorous, it maintained an adversarial stance toward the government until the 1890s. Kiyochika, following suggestions made by the magazine's editors, carried on the tradition of political satire. His cartoons attacked the government's continuing efforts to contain the 'popular rights' movement and it lampooned politicians inside and outside the government. His main innovation was his skill as a caricaturist, which he had honed with a series of woodblock prints comically and realistically depicting faces showing strong emotions—sadness, fear, anger, happiness, angry, fearful. This was a radical break from the poker face renditions of

---

[30] An excellent brief biographical essay on Kiyochika can be found in Henry Smith, *Kiyochika: Artist of Meiji Japan* (Santa Barbara: Santa Barbara Museum of Art, 1988).

people in traditional prints. His cartoons depicted leading politicians were so recognisable that there was no need to label them.

The *Marumaru chinbun* represented not only the most complete attempt at localisation of the *Punch* template but also the last. With the introduction of lithography, and the shift of editorial policy away from political satire, the magazine changed character. Its cartoons became more reportorial and less editorial, more descriptive and less judgmental. When its founder Nomura died in 1892 the new editors declared their intention to devote the magazine more to entertainment than politics. 'Punch pictures' still commented on politics and other current events, but the magazine's circulation kept falling, and it eventually ceased publication as it faced competition from new publications like *Tokyo Puck*, a magazine that followed a template from America—the New York *Puck* rather than dowdy old London *Punch*. (The spread of the *Puck* model in East Asia is discussed in the essays by I-Wei Wu and Sonja Hotwagner in this volume.)[31]

Localisation and Cultural Hybridity

All humour is local—in time as well as space. That is why it is so difficult to translate a joke from one language to another or to decipher a cartoon from another century.[32]

The locality of humour, including satire, complicates any attempt to assess the impact of London *Punch* on the production of humour in the outside world. Certainly the title of a magazine provides little certain guidance. Just because a publication calls itself '*Punch*' does not mean that it will read, or look like, the London *Punch*. As we have seen, the *Japan Punch* and *Nipponchi* shared little with the original *Punch* except a name and logo (Mr Punch), and they bore only a tenuous resemblance to one another. It seems unlikely that neither resembled any of the other numerous *Punch* magazines that appeared in Asia and elsewhere.

During the nineteenth century, at least in the Anglophone world, including its colonial and semi-colonial appendages, *Punch* was clearly a brand name. It was a

---

[31] Chapters Participating in Global Affairs: The Chinese Cartoon Monthly *Shanghai Puck* and '*Punch*'s Heirs' Between the (Battle) Lines: Satirical Journalism in the Age of the Russo-Japanese War of 1904–1905 in this volume.

[32] The difficulty of deciphering of humour across temporal and cultural boundaries can be illustrated by the example of a bilingual riddle in an early issue of *Marumaru chinbun*: 'Why is Mr Punch on the frontispiece like a compass?' The answer: 'Because he is pointing nose (north).' The joke might seem to be about Mr Punch's pointed nose but the connection with the compass—aside from its pointed arrow—is obscure unless one understands that Japanese speakers have difficulty pronouncing the *th* sound. A Japanese speaker thus turns 'north' into 'nose' with a sibilant final *s*. The punch line of the riddle can only be understood if one is bilingual or bicultural. Certainly the *Marumaru chinbun* must have had such readers but to most of its audience this riddle would be puzzling at best; and to an English speaker with no knowledge of the Japanese it would have been incomprehensible, unless he lived in Yokohama, where he heard his language mispronounced everyday.

proper noun that became a simple noun. Just as the brand name 'Cellophane' later came to mean many transparent wrapping material, and the brand name 'Xerox' came to mean any copy machine, *'Punch'* appears to have become a generic term for 'humour magazine'. Foreign embrace of this brand name underlines the immense 'soft power' of nineteenth century British imperialism, its ability to colonise culture as well as territory. It would be interesting, however, to investigate whether the *Punch* brand name made any headway in Francophone colonies—was there a *Hanoi Punch* or a *Saigon Punch*? One can imagine, for example, that had the French rather than the British backed the winning side in the Meiji Restoration, a *Japon Charivari* might well have appeared in Japan. (Certainly the title, probably pronounced *Charibari*, offered more promising opportunities for word play than the *Punch* title: *chari* ちゃり means 'jest' or 'comic relief' and *bari* 罵詈 means 'vituperation'.)

More important than a brand name, what *Punch* offered to the outside world was a particular template for a humour magazine. As Brian Maidment has suggested in his essay, this template included the physical appearance of the magazine's page, the centrality of engraved line illustrations, the multi-faceted nature of its visual and textual humour, and commentary on social and political issues.[33]

If we want to assess the impact of *Punch*, then, we should look for templates not at titles. In Meiji Japan the *Marumaru chinbun* best fit this template. Its debt to the London publication was clear in its print technology, its page format, its drawing style, its cartoons, its politics and even its occasional bilingualism.

Although it may seem obvious, the *Punch* template was also the product of a particular kind of Western 'news culture'. The significance of that culture's diffusion to Japan and elsewhere should not be ignored. In pre-Meiji Japan the government had discouraged the dissemination of anything but commercial and other practical information. The notion that political information and commentary could be circulated publically, and on a periodic basis, was potentially revolutionary. It made possible what Foucault once called the 'democratic surveillance' of those in authority. As the founder of the *Marumaru chinbun* was well aware, his magazine contributed to the formation of a new public sphere, informed and critical, willing to challenge government leaders and policy. Just as the London *Punch* made its wry contributions to liberal politics in Victorian England so too the *Marumaru chinbun* lent its voice to the liberalisation of politics and the emergence of civil society in Meiji Japan.

In the end, however, there is no mistaking *Marumaru chinbun* for *Punch*. The magazines made many adaptations to the template. The cartoon captions in Japanese, for example, were embedded in the comical drawings just as text was embedded in illustrations in the *kibyōshi*; and the magazine's humour, with its addiction to outrageous word play and visual punning, was predominantly local, drawing on an older tradition of visual and verbal satire. In sum, like so much of Meiji culture, the *Marumaru chinbun*— and its 'Punch pictures'—were the product

---

[33] Chapter *Punch* and Indian Cartoons: The Reception of a Transnational Phenomenon in this volume.

Fig. 15 An example of a two-age centerfold lithograph cartoon by Kobayashi Kiyochika. The English title is: "the Japanese exposition of social customs and manners"; the Japanese title is "*Chanpon uchimaze* チャンポン打交 (a mixed-up mess)". *Marumaru chinbun* 518, 14 November 1885

of cultural hybridisation. In their pursuit of 'enlightenment' the new Meiji intelligentsia felt compelled to 'civilise' the way they painted pictures, composed music, wrote fiction, designed houses, and sculpted statues. Sometimes this meant simply reproducing what they found in the West, but at other times it produced what students of Meiji architecture called a *setchū* (eclectic) style.

The juxtaposition of the foreign and the indigenous often struck foreigners as ridiculous but the hybrid character of Meiji culture, too, was a source of amusement for the Japanese. The bifurcated cultural mix was a common theme in 'Punch pictures'. A good example is an 1885 *Marumaru chinbun* centrefold lithograph cartoon by Kiyochika entitled *Champon uchimaze* (roughly 'a mixed-up mix') (Fig. 15). Comical pairs of men and women contrast the pervasive cohabitation of the indigenous and the foreign: an army officer with sabre and a samurai fencing master with a bamboo sword; a samisen player and a mandolin player; a man reading a book with a kerosene lamp with another using an abacus by candle light; a minister giving a sermon and a priest chanting a sutra; a waltzing couple in Western clothes and a geisha in kimono performing a solo dance; a bushy-haired student reading a text in Chinese characters and one with combed and pomaded hair reading a foreign book; and so forth. 'It is so diverse and unsettled as to give a complete puzzle', reads the English language caption. And that, of course, made it a perfect subject for a 'Punch picture'.

'*Punch*'s Heirs' Between the (Battle) Lines: Satirical Journalism in the Age of the Russo-Japanese War of 1904–1905

Sonja Hotwagner

Roy A. Roberts (1887–1967), president of the American Society of Newspaper Editors during WWII and editor of the Kansas City Star once stated: 'Keeping the home front unbroken (...) is the newspapers' first function in war'.[1] For this veteran journalist 'to keep the home front unbroken' meant to mobilise and strengthen the civil community spirit during wartime. The newspaper as a mass medium bundles the thoughts of individuals, skilfully channelling them in the desired way. In times of military conflict it can create strong bonds among the population behind the lines of the battlefronts and solidarity with the soldiers by underlining the legitimacy of waging a war. Here, the cultivation of images, particularly satirical images, is crucial. Rune Ottosen has pointed out that journalism in 'times of high tension' seems almost impossible without the presentation of images of the enemy.[2] Similarly, Heikki Luostarinen has identified propagandistic mockery of the enemy as 'a reflection of the actual tension and conflict between states and as a way of creating unity in a state and legitimizing its rulers'.[3]

And still, while the role of newspapers and posters in war propaganda has been discussed frequently, the function of satire and cartoon images in particular has, at least in the Japanese case, not become the object of scientific enquiry until recently.[4]

---

[1] Frank Luther Mott, *Journalism in Wartime* (Westport: Greenwood Press, 1984), 10.

[2] Rune Ottosen, "Enemy Images and the Journalistic Process," *Journal of Peace Research* 32, no. 1 (1995): 97–112; 98.

[3] Heikki Luostarinen, "Finnish Russophobia: The Story of an Enemy Image," *Journal of Peace Research* 26, no. 2 (1989): 123–137.

[4] For Japanese satire during WWII, see Detlev Schauwecker, "Verbal Subversion and Satire in Japan, 1937–1945, as documented by the Special High Police," *Japan Review* 15 (2003), 127–151. For cartoons during the Russo-Japanese war, see various articles by Yulia Mikhailova.

S. Hotwagner (✉)
Doctoral Candidate at the Institute for Japanese Studies at Heidelberg University, Heidelberg, Germany
e-mail: sonjahotwagner@googlemail.com

The ugly propagandistic character of wartime cartoons may be a reason for this. How could satire, a genre characterised by its purist moral and ethical stance, eager to criticise the blemishes and faults of the world, lower itself to become war propaganda? The strength of satire lies in creating catchy statements that can effectively shape public opinion. It may function either as an instrument of power and a tool for political agitation,[5] or as a form of protest and a method of resistance. Thus, satire can serve either rulers or the ruled. Recent research has emphasised the use of satire as a tool of political resistance,[6] but neglects the role of satirical cartoons as instruments of propaganda. In the language typical of satire and cartoons, the experience of reality is simplified and crystallised into clichés and conventional symbols. Satire produced in times of 'cultural violence',[7] such as war, speaks a very special 'dialect' of this language in order to keep the battlefront unbroken.

This essay examines precisely this dialect and the role of Japanese satirical magazines during the Russo-Japanese War, 1904–1905, based on three prominent magazines: *Nipponchi* 日ポン地 ('Japan land' or 'Japan Punch' (pun)); *Kokkei shinbun* 滑稽新聞 (comic news), and *Tokyo Puck*. They will afford brief glimpses of how the contemporary satirical landscape fed the 'cultural violence' of wartime Japan. Central to the argument are the function of satire in wartime, and the question of whether and how satire took a critical stance towards the government or whether it was used as a tool of propaganda. We will show that the particular (dis-)use of the type of satire associated with the English *Punch*[8] format for satire is indicative of the production of satire in war times. The war in Japan necessitated the need for a unified national spirit. This, as we will see, ultimately caused an abandonment of the *Punch* format which had been predominant in the 1870s and 1880s (with established journals such as the *Marumaru chinbun* 團團珍聞 in the forefront) andheavily criticised by governmental authorities of that time In 1904/1905, the new 'dialect' of satirical writing was shaped by publications in more 'traditional' styles, such as *Nipponchi*, but also increasingly by the New York based *Puck* magazine, which dethroned the veteran *Punch* as the main influential model of

---

[5] See for instance Henri Bergson, *Laughter: An Essay on the Meaning of the Comic*, originally published in 1900 (Mineola: Dover, 2005).

[6] Humour as a form of resistance against hierarchy can be traced back to the theories of Mikhail Bakhtin (Mikhail Bakhtin, *Rabelais and his World*, originally published in 1952 (Bloomington: Midland-Indiana University Press, 1984). The German philosopher Joachim Ritter stated that the cause of laughter is the incongruity which deeply opposes every norm or order. His work was essential for further research on humour theory, at least in Germany (Joachim Ritter, "Über das Lachen," *Blätter für deutsche Philosophie* 14 (1940/1941): 1–21).

[7] In describing war satire from Japan, I use Johan Galtung's expression 'cultural violence' instead of 'propaganda'. He states: 'By "cultural violence" we mean those aspects of culture, the symbolic sphere of our existence—exemplified by religion and ideology, language and art (...) that can be used to justify or legitimize direct or structural violence'.

[8] The weekly satirical humour magazine *Punch*, subtitled *The London Charivari*, was founded on 17 July 1841 by Henry Mayhew and the engraver Ebenezer Landells. It was published from 1841 to 1992 and again from 1996 to 2002.

satirical writing in Japan. This latter re-orientation becomes evident on the pages of *Kokkei shinbun* and *Tokyo Puck*.

In a discussion of representative cover pages, this essay will, in a first part, probe into the character of war-time satirical journalism. In its second part, it will discuss *Punch*'s (in-)ability to serve the war situation. The approach and thematic focus chosen in this chapter differ from research by Yulia Mikhailova on Japanese and Russian cartoons in 1904/1905:[9] this chapter concentrates on the second generation of Western-influenced satirical journalism in Japan in order to rethink and re-examine the impact of *Punch*. In times of war, the *Punch* format, which had originally served to point out social problems or grievances with respective governments, was now becoming a useful tool for the government's own (imperialistic) aims. This chapter elaborates on the question to what extent and by what strategies this became possible.

A Short History of *Punch*-Related Satirical Magazines in Japan (1862–1900)

As becomes evident from the contributions to this book, an almost matchless story of success began when in 1841 *Punch, or the London Charivari*,[10] was founded. While satirical magazines and pamphlets were nothing new in Europe at that time,[11] the *Punch,* featuring a harmonious interplay of visual as well as textual puns and commentaries, asserted its influence all over the world, even in countries as geographically and culturally remote from Victorian Britain as Japan.

Although the tradition of visual satire in Japan is a long and rich one, political cartoons in our Western understanding did not appear until Japan's encounter with the West. During the Tokugawa Period (1603–1868), harsh censorship laws lead to the development of visual satire, highly refined parody, and travesty in woodblock prints.[12] However, it was not until the opening of the country to the outside world in 1854 and the consequent modernisation efforts, that the power of humoristic journalism was explored further. The first and most important stimulus for

---

[9] Yulia Mikhailova, "Japan and Russia: Mutual Images (1904–1939)," *The Japanese and Europe: Images and Perceptions* (2000): 152–171.

[10] The subtitle is a reference to the French satirical magazine *Charivari* published from 1832 to 1937 in Paris.

[11] See Monica Lehner, "Function Follows Form(at)? Notes on Transcultural Adaptability of a Medium", talk presented on 14 November 2009 in the course of the Workshop "The British Punch Magazine as a Transcultural Format of Satire and Caricature" in Heidelberg, 13–15 November, 2009.

[12] For a comprehensive database of satirical woodblock prints (*ukiyo-e*), see the database of the Department of East Asian Studies at the University of Vienna, which includes examples dating from 1842 to 1905 www.univie.ac.at/karikaturen/, accessed 12 September 2011.

Punch-style publications in Japan came with the magazine *Japan Punch* published by a British correspondent for the *Illustrated London News*, Charles Wirgman (1832–1891), and the French journal *Toba-e* published by Georges Ferdinand Bigot (1860–1927). Beginning in the 1860s, foreign artists exerted direct influence by publishing and teaching the art of biting caricatures. They were protected by their status of extraterritoriality in the foreign settlement in Yokohama.[13]

Soon, the Western-style concept of satirical magazines gained popularity among the Japanese audience and in 1874 the first Japanese publication, the *E-shinbun Nipponchi*[14] (the illustrated newspaper: Japan *Punch*) was published. In the politically vivid years of the 1870s and 1880s, another such journal, the *Marumaru chinbun* (the 'circle' newspaper; named after the censor's round marks), too, played an important role as an opinion leader; its satirical pictures and articles commented on and criticised the Meiji government[15] and acted as mouthpiece for the so-called 'Movement for Freedom and People's Rights' (*Jiyū minken undō*).[16] The template for all of these magazines was visible through the use of 'ponchi'—the Japanese pronunciation of the English word 'punch'—which became the predominant term for almost every kind of humorous picture and a brand name that clearly marked journals as satirical.

This essay does not intend to offer yet another account of the cultural adaptation of *Punch* and its use in Japan's colonial struggle. Instead, it examines the 'heirs' of these early satirical beginnings. The history of Japanese satirical journalism, influenced by the English model, was almost 30 years old when, in 1904, Japan had to face new challenges. After the surprising victory over its great neighbour, China, in 1895, and the subsequent humiliation at the hands of Western powers with the Treaty of Shimonoseki,[17] Japan had watched the advance of Russian troops in Manchuria with growing concern. Imperialistic tendencies on both sides made the

---

[13] The early years of satirical journalism in Japan have been discussed by many scholars, first and foremost by Shimizu Isao, a pioneer of research on cartoons in Japan. Other excellent work can be found by Yulia Mikhailova, Peter Duus and Kinko Ito.

[14] The word *Nipponchi* is a pun on the British *Punch*: *Nippon* means 'Japan', *ponchi* was the Japanese expression for 'punch'.

[15] During the 1870s the criticism against the politics of the Meiji Government reached its peak. After the Meiji Revolution in 1868 and the end of the Shogunate, the hope for changes had not been fulfilled and the reign of a small oligarchy gave reason to be unsatisfied.

[16] The Movement for Freedom and People's Rights, a political and social force during the 1870s and 1880s, claimed civil rights, as well as the formation of an elective legislature, and the revision of the so-called Unequal Treaties with America and European nations. Furthermore, it called for the reduction of the centralised taxation.

[17] The Treaty of Shimonoseki was signed between Japan and China as result of the Sino-Japanese War on April 1895. As a result China recognised the independence and autonomy of Korea, agreed to the payment of 200,000 Kuping *taels* of war indemnity, and ceded Taiwan, the Pescadores and the eastern part of the Liaodong Peninsula to Japan. After the Western triple intervention (Germany, Russia, France) 6 days after the signing of the Treaty, Japan withdrew its claim on the Liaodong Peninsula (Port Arthur) in return for an increased war indemnity. The Japanese population saw in the result a bowing to the interests of the Western powers and felt betrayed.

political situation increasingly tense. In February 1904, the Imperial Japanese Navy attacked Port Arthur, and only 3 h later war with Czarist Russia was declared.

Although the real battlefields were far away in Korea and Manchuria, the war and its implications soon pre-occupied the Japanese. Ten years earlier, during the war with China, the mass media had had their first trial run. Magazines and newspapers were quite unprepared, so most of the war information as well as political agitation had therefore been distributed on traditional single-sheet prints.

However, during the Russo-Japanese War, the situation had changed significantly. Technical progress had led to an increase in the circulation of many print media. At the same time, nationalist consciousness had been growing and modern print media thrived. They aimed to keep the home front unbroken and did so by reporting imagined victories, suppressing news about any losses, and by stirring up a hostile attitude toward the invisible enemy.

Since its beginnings in the 1870s, the *Punch* template had served its role in political criticism. Satirical magazines like the *Marumaru chinbun* were engaged in the Freedom and People's Rights Movement (*Jiyū minken undō* 自由民権運動) and poked fun at well-known personalities from the highest ranks of the imperial government. This type of public pressure turned out to be quite effective: In 1889, the Meiji government was prompted to establish a constitution and in the following year the National Diet was convened. *Punch* or 'ponchi' came to stand for a voice against the leadership and thus became subject to strict observation and distrust by the authorities who clearly feared the power of the (satirical) media.[18]

Yet, shifting the target of attack away from figures in Japan's government toward the national enemies was not so easy for the *Punch*-influenced media. Witty caricatures of individuals, so characteristic of the original *Punch* as well as its Japanese siblings, did not quite fit the new political situation; they were not catchy enough, not always easy to understand, and thus not so useful for the purposes of war propaganda. Furthermore, the sophisticated *Punch*-style, admired in Japan in the 1870s and 1880s, was too closely associated with the westernising policies of the *bunmei kaika* period (period of 'Civilisation and Enlightenment')[19] to be considered appropriate for supporting the kinds of nationalist feelings that were now expected.

There is agreement among scholars about the eminent role that the Russo-Japanese War played in instilling in the minds of the Japanese people a solid

---

[18] Although the freedom of opinion and press was considered an indispensable element of civilisation in Western thought, in Japan, authorities were fully aware of the power lurking in the funny pictures, and shied away from granting a free hand. It was due to the rising power of the satirical magazines, headed by the political force of the *Marumaru chinbun*, that the law on publishing was modified in 1880. The decision has to be read as an anxious reaction to a medium which was able to endanger the stability of the Meiji regime by ridicule and laughter. The violation of the official press regulation in Japan was punishable by a lengthy prison sentence, and the general atmosphere regarding censorship was tense.

[19] After the forced opening of the country in 1854, Japan faced a period of rapid modernisation and change, and took up the challenge to close the gap on Western industrialised countries.

national consciousness and identification with the state. Before the Meiji Restoration, peasants and citizens had paid taxes directly to their landlords; there had been no inducement to think in national categories. Everything outside one's own territory or daimyate[20] was 'outside' and therefore 'foreign'. As Peter Duus has shown, however, a sense of national unity and uniqueness was already in existence by the 1870s, and was frequently highlighted by Japanese caricaturists.[21] Newspapers such as the *Yokohama shinpō moshiogusa* 横浜新法もしお草 ran cartoons of foreigners meddling in Japanese politics by selling arms or gaining economic control by giving loans.[22] in other words, an imagined or tangible and real threat from outside was already palpable at this time and gave reason for ever new attempts to define 'the Self' in contrast to 'the Other'.

The euphoria which had accompanied the radical socio-political, technological, and economic changes after the opening of the country in 1854 had, by 1904, made room for deep-rooted feelings of disorientation. Increasingly, the Japanese realised that 'the West' was in fact no solid block but consisted of a great variety of nations. While translation, imitation, and transformation continued to be important, it was now necessary to consider, which model would best suit which occasion. This change is also visually reflected in a shift of caricature styles, which will be discussed in the following section.

Satirical Journalism in the Age of the Russo-Japanese War

Three major incidents characterise the late Meiji period and mark important stepping stones on Japan's path into the twentieth century: the proclamation of the constitution in 1889, the war with China 1894–1895, and the Russo-Japanese War in 1904–1905. Due to government reforms of the educational system, school enrolment had risen from 50 % in 1891 to 97 % in 1907. As print media now no longer relied on the troublesome technique of the woodblock print, circulation numbers rose quickly.[23] Print media became consumer goods. Accordingly, the powers of the press as an opinion maker increased considerably, too.[24]

---

[20] A domain or *han* led by a *daimyō* or landlord. During the Edo Period there were around 300 *Daimyates* in Japan. In 1871, 3 years after the Meiji period, the system was abolished.

[21] Peter Duus, "Presidential Address: Weapons of the Weak, Weapons of the Strong: The Development of the Japanese Political Cartoon," *Journal of Asian Studies* 60, no. 4 (2001): 965–997; 984.

[22] Duus, "Presidential Address," 983.

[23] Besides other technical inventions, in 1903 a new technology, the Marinoni-made rotary magazine printing machine was adopted, which supported the development of a mass-production system.

[24] Misako Shinozawa, *Mirion sera tanshō e! Meiji Taishō no zasshi media* (The birth of a million seller: Magazines as media in the Meiji-Taisho era) (Tōkyō: Insatsu hakubutsu-kan, 2008), 179–191.

Chart 1. Cartoons published in *Tōkyō* Mainichi shinbun from January 1904 until December 1905

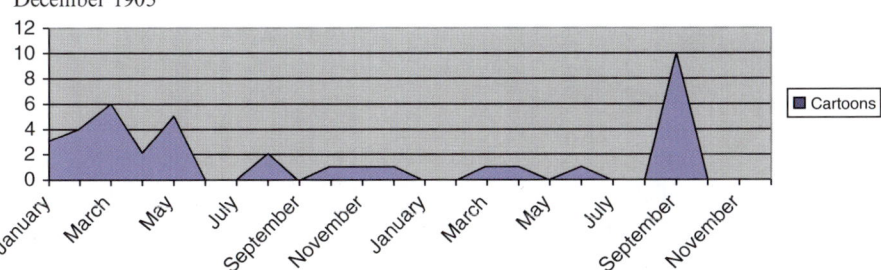

Source: Kijin Lee, "Shinbun ronhyō manga no shakaiteki kitai ni kan suru ikkō satsu (Considerations on the Social Function of the Editorial Cartoon : From Content Analysis of Editorial Cartoons during the Sino-Japanese War and Russo-Japanese War Periods)," *Masu Komyunikēshon kenkyū* (Studies on mass communication) 72 (2008): 117-113; 126.

The war with Russia in particular caused a boom of new magazines and a 'thirst for images' from the battlefront. Cartoons played a significant role: a multitude of almost textless *ponchi* magazines came into being. Caricatures of the Russian opponent and the latest news from the battlefield (only positive ones, of course) also gained prominent space in serious, text-dominated journals as the following chart illustrates. It shows the interconnection between current events and the publishing of cartoons in *Tōkyō Mainichi shinbun* 東京毎日新聞 (Tokyo daily news), a leading newspaper of the time. The declaration of war in February 1904 brought about an increase in satirical pictures; in September 1905, when peace between Russia and Japan was made and the Treaty of Portsmouth signed, the number of cartoons was at its peak.[25]

Nipponchi: The Renaissance of 'Tradition' in the Satirical Magazine
It might be no coincidence that popular wartime publications such as *Nipponchi* abandoned the 'modern' style of *Punch* and returned to the much more colourful visual language of 'traditional' woodblock prints: nationalist acts and ideas were required to motivate and mobilise the population, and accordingly, satirical magazines revived traditional Japanese motifs and styles.

Nipponchi (Japanese land/Japanese *Punch*) was founded in 1904 as one of the many publications which began to flourish in the rising pro-war atmosphere. Its first issue was published 7 September as a supplement to the magazine *Fūzoku gahō*

---

[25] Source: Kijin Lee, "*Shinbun ronhyō manga no shakaiteki kitai ni kan suru ikkō satsu* (Considerations on the social function of the editorial cartoon: From content analysis of editorial cartoons during the Sino-Japanese War and Russo-Japanese War periods)," *Masu komyunikęshon kenkyū* (Studies on mass communication) 72 (2008): 117–133; 126.

風俗画報 (illustrated customs of today), managed and edited by Yamashita Shigetami (1857–1941), a member of the Ministry of Finance.[26]

Yamashita was by training neither a political cartoonist nor an artist. His activities in the field of satirical journalism illustrate the level of interaction between government and media that was common at the time. This interaction explains the extremely nationalistic stance taken in many of these publications as well as their adherence to rigid self-censorship.[27] Yamashita, was an official who used the power of satirical journalism for nationalistic purposes, a fact unthinkable in the age of political power struggles between government and media some 20 years earlier.

The bi-monthly, small-format (B5), multicoloured magazine *Nipponchi* took advantage of the increased demand for publications that supported an anti-Russian attitude and as a matter of course recorded its peak in circulation during the war. *Nipponchi* ran until March 1906 and reached a total of 33 issues. Along with other supplements to the *Fūzoku gahō*, such as documentary photo magazines, it was responsible for providing entertaining war coverage.

By name, the journal refers back to Kanagaki Robun (1829–1894) and Kawanabe Kyosai's (1831–1889) satirical magazine *E-shinbun Nipponchi* (illustrated news of the land Japan).[28] *Nipponchi* is a compound that can be read in different ways: Firstly, as a word consisting of 'Nippon' as name for Japan and 'chi', meaning 'land' or 'territory' written in syllabic letters. A simple translation of this reading would be 'Land of Japan'. Another possibility would be to read it as *ni (chi)* (also symbolising Japan) and *ponchi* for '*Punch*-like funny drawing', i.e. 'Japanese *Punch*'.[29] Although the parallel is obvious, the later *Nipponchi* has to be seen as an independent publication with a very different thematic focus and artistic style than its short-lived precursor.

The periodical was located in Tokyo and gained popularity through its war-driving and propagandistic illustrations. Although the visual and literary quality of *Nipponchi* is surprisingly poor in parts, the men behind the magazine were well known, popular artistic personalities. Yamamoto Shokoku (1870–1965), originally

---

[26] Yulia Mikhailova, "Intellectuals, Cartoons, and Nationalism during the Russo-Japanese War," in *Japan's Visual Culture: Explorations in the World of Manga and Anime*, ed. Mark Wheeler MacWilliams (Armonk: M.E. Sharpe, 2008), 155–176; 164.

[27] As Okamoto Rei has shown in her dissertation on the Japanese political cartoon during World War I this relationship remained strong until 1920. It was due to this symbiotic coexistence that anti-war agitation was almost absent. Rei Okamoto, "Pictorial Propaganda in Japanese Comic Art, 1941–1945: Images of the Self and the Other in a Newspaper Strip. Single-Panel Cartoons, and Cartoon Leaflets" (PhD diss., Temple University, 1998), 67.

[28] *E-shinbun Nipponchi* was the first satirical magazine published by Japanese editors, or, to use Duus' words, the first 'modern Japanese Manga magazine'. It started in June 1874 but discontinued publication after only three issues. An article on the early *Nipponchi* can be found in Peter Duus, "'Japan's First Modern Manga Magazine," *Impressions: The Journal of the Ukiyo-e Society of America* 21 (1999): 30–41. See also his contribution in this volume.

[29] As mentioned before, the word was derived from the English word *Punch* which was used by Wirgman in his *Japan Punch*.

Fig. 1 Initial cover of the magazine Marumaru chinbun which, with its elaborate border resembles that of the London Punch. Marumaru chinbun 1, 14 March 1877

trained as a *nihonga* (paintings in Japanese style)[30] painter, and Nakashima Shuko were the artists responsible. The overall concept lay in the hands of Otei Kinsho (1868–1954). He was a writer by profession and contributed various sorts of short, popular songs or stories to the magazine. The number of illustrations related to Japanese traditions and customs in *Nipponchi* is significant: there are motifs derived from the Buddhist canon, Japanese daily life or traditional customs. The visual vocabulary is reminiscent of woodblock prints. Motifs from Kabuki theatre were introduced to appeal to readers' feelings of national belonging. The use of these familiar visual and semantic modes was crucial to the journal's success as propaganda, which always has to be easily comprehensible to a wide readership. Although magazines like *Nipponchi* continued to follow the tradition of European satirical journalism, they constitute a new style of Japanese satire. The allusion 'ponchi' included in the title suggests the importance of the European satirical model invoked but in style this publication has moved on and away from earlier *Punch*-inspired journalism such as the influential *Marumaru chinbun* (Fig. 1).

The illustration shows the cover page of its very first issue, published in 1877. The satirical vocabulary still followed the distinctive fine-shaded *Punch* style: Three men, dressed in Western style, serve as allegoric figures for the programmatic aim of the satirical magazine: Seeing, hearing and smelling all evil. In this earlier period, European satirical styles were popular, which explains why a magazine like *Jiji shinpō* 時事新報 (current news), for example, would, since the 1890s, frequently publish original European and American cartoons: a caricature of foreign policies after the Sino-Japanese War 1894/1895, first published in *American Life* magazine, appears in the Japanese *Jiji shinpō* on 8 February 1900. In order to help the audience understand the European symbols of bear, dragon, and rat that stood for Russia, China, and Japan they are labelled with small Japanese captions.

This style all but disappeared around the turn of the century and is replaced by *Nipponchi's* (re-)discovery of Japanese tradition. The magazine now never features English-language captions, while the iconography used in its cartoons is deeply rooted in Japanese tradition.

An analysis of the journal's 16 title pages published from 25 January until 20 September 1905 shows that only two examples lack a direct connection to Japanese religious or cultural aspects.[31] The legendary 'peach boy'

---

[30] *Nihonga* (paintings in Japanese style) is a term used in contrast to the *yōga* (paintings in Western style) during the Meiji period. It applies to paintings which are in accordance with traditional Japanese artistic conventions, sometimes with small adoptions of Western techniques such as shading. See, e.g., Takeuchi Seiho.

[31] The title page of April 5 with a globe-headed Western-style male figure carrying a Japanese flag emphasises Japan's attempt to become a new international superpower while the title page of 15 July shows a bull with a human couple. Traditional motifs are referred to through the depiction of the Seven Lucky Gods (25 January and 20 September) and a Shinto temple (2 February), the allusion to flower and bird painting (2 February), the depiction of the mythical Peach boy Kintarō (5 May) and a demon (*oni*) figure (6 June), octopuses and sea dweller cheering (3 March and 28 June), the fight of hyacinth (20 May) and the visual illustration of the saying 'neko mo shakushi mo' (an expression meaning 'everybody' or 'rag, tag and bobtail') as cat and spoon in kimono (8 August). Further a depiction of eagle and firefly on the moon (displacing the rabbit and

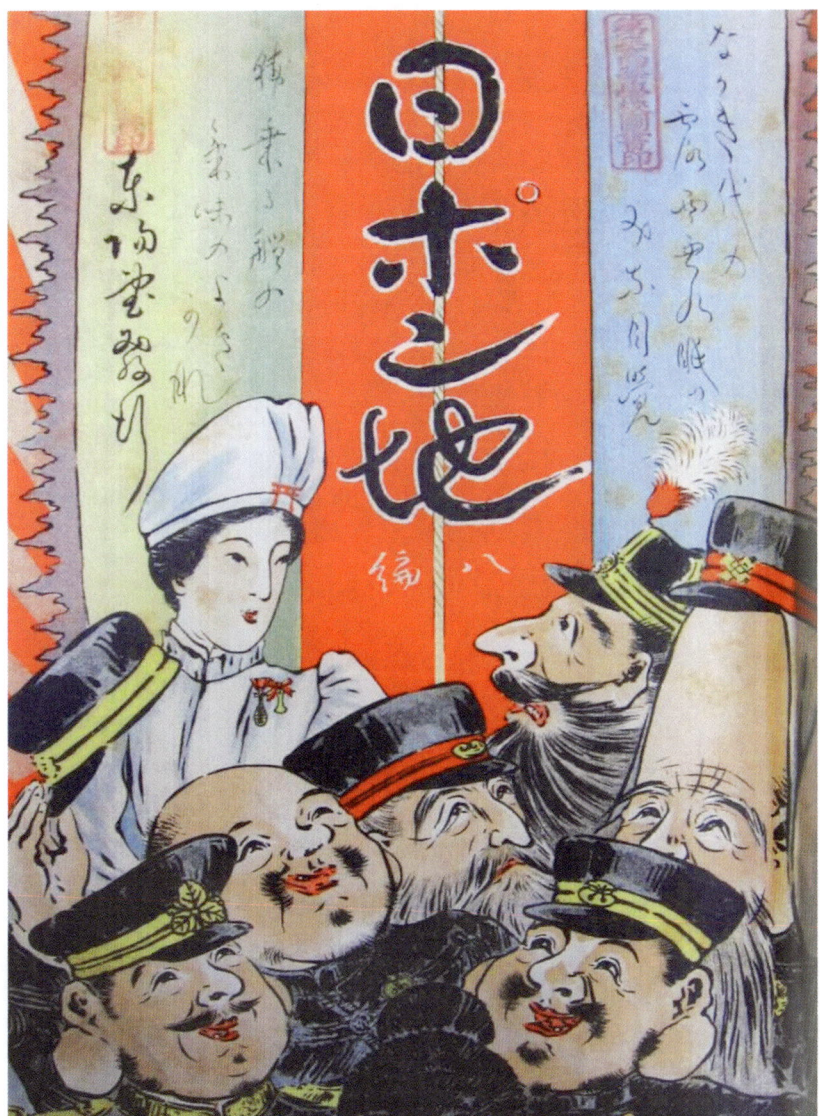

Fig. 2 Cover page of *Nipponchi* 8, 25 January 1904 (owned by The Kyoto International Manga Museum)

Momotarō,[32] for example, or traditional Japanese demon figures (*oni*) are used as motifs on *Nipponchi* cover pages.

---

symbolising Russia and Japan), a puppet player (20 April) and a battle of fishes in the tradition of woodblock prints (9 September).

[32] Momotarō is a popular figure from Japanese folklore. He is said to have been born out of a giant peach. Together with his three friends, a dog, a pheasant and a monkey, Momotarō fought against the demons on Onigashima (Demon Island).

This style is in sharp contrast to the *Marumaru chinbun*—where only two or three titles out of sixteen feature a connection with traditional motifs.[33] Clearly distinct from the *Punch*-oriented Western-style *Marumaru chinbun*, as well as the rather artistic *Kokkei shinbun*, the humorous illustrations published in *Nipponchi* were a new and, as we will see presently, very different, hybrid form of mockery based on old values.

The cover (Fig. 2) of *Nipponchi* 8, published in 1904[34] shows seven persons, six men in the foreground and one woman in the background. To a viewer with a Japanese cultural background the prominent forehead of the male figure to the far right, as well as the long earlobes suggest that these are Seven Lucky Gods (*shichifukujin*) celebrating Japan's victories in war. Since she is the only female in the exclusive club of gods, it is easy to identify Benzaiten 弁才天, the goddess of knowledge, fine arts and music. She is depicted as an elegant nurse in characteristic white dress on the left. The grey-bearded old man with the high forehead is Fukurokuju, the god of happiness, who is said to have the power to revive the dead.

The Seven Lucky Gods, guarantors of luck, prosperity and health in Japanese folk belief, have been a very popular topic in (non-satirical) traditional Japanese art for centuries. A print by Kawanabe Kyosai (1831–1889) (Fig. 3) documents this, but shows how different the styles and forms of depicting them has become with the arrival of *Nipponchi*: his undated, single sheet print shows the gods and the goddess as *tanukis* or raccoon dogs with exaggerated testicles.[35] The shapes of their testicles hint at their attributes, such as Fukurokuju's high forehead, mentioned before (see the dancing figure in the middle of the second panel). This disrespectful interpretation of the Seven Lucky Gods is countered by the *Nipponchi* cover, on which, in a reversal typical of wartime satire, the same gods are taken more literally as guarantors of luck, prosperity, and health: they are depicted as taking part in the current events of war and are appropriately dressed as soldiers and nurses. Traditional motifs and contemporary propaganda needs conflate in this image to legitimise the war effort. The necessity of war with Russia had been a controversial subject of discussion since the 1890s. In contrast to earlier iconoclastic and ironic takes on traditional motifs, the *Nipponchi* cover now takes these at face value and suggests that Japan's gods, as ultimate authorities, had given their blessings to the military measures.

The cover of *Nipponchi* 7 (Fig. 4) is a second example where Japan's cultural heritage is moved into the foreground to serve war propaganda. This cover uses another theme typical of woodblock prints: Kabuki theatre. Filling more than the right half and the centre of the image is a dangerous-looking, large Kabuki actor in

---

[33] The two covers addressed are the title pages with an oni figure (1 March) and a Japanese soldier in Samurai armament (19 April). The third is a cover page of figures with human bodies but objects instead of heads. This motif very often appears in woodblock prints, too.

[34] For another discussion on the topic of the Seven Gods of Luck (in this case an illustration), see Mikhailova, "Intellectuals, Cartoons, and Nationalism," 155–176.

[35] Particularly in the middle of the 1840s funny woodblock prints showing raccoon dogs with exaggerated testicles were extremely popular.

Fig. 3 'Raccoon Dogs as five of the Seven Gods of Good Fortune (*Tanuki no shichifukujin* 狸の七福神)'. Woodblock print (1844–1846) by Utagawa Kuniyoshi (1798–1861) (Source: International Research Center for Japanese Studies Library, Kyoto)

Fig. 4 Title page of *Nipponchi* 7, 15 January 1904 (owned by The Kyoto International Manga Museum)

characteristic *shibaraku* (Wait a moment!)[36] pose, which the hero of a Kabuki play assumes after he has walked down the stage and suddenly freezes in the moment of

---

[36] The *shibaraku* was invented by the prominent Kabuki actor Ichikawa Danjuro II (1688–1758) as part of the drama *Sankai Nagoya* in 1697 and became a speciality of the Danjuro-family style.

Fig. 5 'The actor Ichikawa Ebizo in a *shibaraku* role'. Woodblock print by Torii Kiyonaga, 1770 (Source: Steffi Schmidt, *Ostasiatische Holzschnitte I* (*East-Asian Woodblock Prints I*) (Berlin: Staatliche Museen Preußischer Kulturbesitz Berlin, 1976), 33)

highest excitement. He wears typical, colourful makeup and thus frightens a crowd of Russians dressed in suits, on the left. The square shape of his garment is pointing aggressively forward; the Russians, shocked as they appear to be, run the risk of getting smashed in the little left corner. Very clearly, Japanese tradition is put in the service of war propaganda: *shibaraku* plays are used in folk tradition as ritual plays of good repelling evil. The actor takes up precisely this position and the only confusing detail in his silhouette is the rather large nose, conventionally a marker of Westerners.

Again, satiric use of Japanese tradition as featured here has its precursors, but the meaning has shifted: The depiction of contemporary celebrities as Kabuki actors had long since been practiced in Japanese woodblock printing. Such portraits remained popular for centuries, but until 1904 there had rarely been a connection with the military. One such example, a woodblock print by Torii Kiyonaga (Fig. 5),

Fig. 6 'The pains of "frogfish" play' (*Kairo asobi sensō no hataraki* かいろ遊千艸の働) (Caricature by Kobayashi Kiyochika. *Marumaru chinbun* 585, 2 February 1887)

from around 1770, shows the actor Ichikawa Ebizo in his famous *shibaraku* role on stage. As with the figure on the *Nipponchi* title page, the depicted actor wears a brick-red garment with white *mon* emblems (representing a certain family or group) and stage makeup.

This erstwhile convention of depicting contemporaries as Kabuki actors was accompanied by a tendency—particularly strong during the Sino-Japanese War of 1894–1895—to represent Japanese heroes as 'modern' rather than 'traditional.' They were shown as wearing Western clothes, uniforms, and hairstyles that stood in sharp contrast contrasting with their apparently old-fashioned Chinese enemies. By 1904, the situation was different: faced with the 'Western' opponent Russia, satire had to find other methods of representation. Now it was a traditional figure, a Kabuki actor, who represented Japan. With the emblem of the sun on his garment and the Samurai sword (a detail not included in the 1770 example), he evokes the idea of Japan as the land of great warriors. By using the *shibaraku* play, *Nipponchi* thus stylises Japan's military conflict with Russia into a righteous war against evil forces. The satirical 'dialect' chosen here was one quite easily comprehensible to the audience.[37]

---

[37] Masakatsu Gunji, *The Kabuki Guide* (Tokyo: Kodan-sha, 1987), 122.

While traditional motifs are commonly used, cartoons modelled after Western prototypes, such as the works of Kobayashi Kiyochika, did not fare well in these times of virulent nationalist pride. They were not always easy to understand and they perhaps too strongly associated with the anti-governmental stance they had taken in former years. In times of war, people had to rally behind rather than against their country and their government, which meant that the language of satire had to change.

In the *Punch*-styled caricatures published in the 1870s and 1880s Kiyochika had often criticised the forced modernisation of Japan and the governmental policies associated with it. Figure 6 shows a well-known example: Frogs—animals common to Japanese satirical iconography—act as humans and are employed to poke fun at idealised 'modernity' and westernisation. In this case, there is a mismatch between the use of a European model with an English-language caption on the one hand and the critical stance taken against Western culture on the other. Such satirical pictures, as well as the characteristic portrait and the allegorical image in copperplate print, all of which had been favoured during the decades before the Russo-Japanese war, now became an outdated 'dialect'.

New Satirical Role Models: A Shift in Orientation

As we have seen, new types of satirical journalism came into being to help fight the new enemy successfully. Government-related magazines (such as *Nipponchi*) tended to reference traditional modes and iconography for propagandistic purposes. But pro-war agitation in 1904/1905 also appeared in other stylistic forms: one example is the magazine *Kokkei shinbun* 滑稽新聞 (comic news) which had a rather artistic approach to satirical journalism, modelling itself on newly rising global art movements such as Art Nouveau or Expressionism. *Tokyo Puck*, on the other hand, was a satirical magazine which not only in name relied heavily on the New York-based satirical journal *Puck* and thus marks a clear shift in orientation away from the *Punch* model.

The *Kokkei Shinbun*: Art Nouveau Meets Satire

The *Kokkei shinbun* (comic news) first appeared as a monthly, later bi-monthly, magazine founded 1901 in Osaka by Miyatake Gaikotsu. It abandoned the artistic conventions associated with *Punch* in favour of new forms of visual attraction. Fine shading, depth effects or detailed, realistic depictions as were characteristic of *Punch*'sstyle, all but disappeared. The highly graphic covers of *Kokkei shinbun* as well as its illustrations, on the other hand, were modelled on current global art movements like *Art Nouveau* or *Jugendstil*. In this new style, portraits are rare; the political message is cast into reduced symbols which also satisfy the particular aesthetics associated with these and other modernist artistic styles.

In changing the language of satire, these journals were in step with global trends: Similar tendencies can be found in many other places in the world, notably the Ottoman Empire.[38] What is more, artistic interaction was no one-way street. Not only did the World's Fairs, for example the exhibition in Paris in 1900, serve as platforms for international art; artists were also increasingly mobile. Artistic movements such as Impressionism in the nineteenth century and *Jugendstil* at the *fin de siècle* relied heavily on Japanese and other (East-) Asian aesthetics. Now this hybridized style in turn became influential in Japan.

If one compares the illustrations in *Kokkei shinbun* (e.g. 8 March 1905) and the influential German satirical magazine *Simplicissimus*[39] from the same year, one finds that both are colour lithographs and designed in a similarly abstract style. In both examples, the space is divided into two panels and the motifs refer to the Russo-Japanese war.

The cover page of *Simplicissimus* (April 1904) is similar in structure and almost the same size as the Japanese example. As in the case of *Kokkei shinbun*, allegorical emblems and fine shaded figures, as seen on earlier covers (see for instance Fig. 1), are abandoned in favour of a 'minimalist' style. Not unlike the Japanese page, the German page, with the magazine's name *Simplicissimus* at the top, features a split cartoon. The German caricature is entitled 'The Russian Snowman' (Der russische Schneemann). It ridicules the Russian Empire which is symbolised by a giant snowman figure with the sword. The image consists of two segments with a temporal connection. In the panel on the left, the snowman stands in front of a starry sky while small monarchs adore him in the foreground. In the panel on the right, the situation has changed. A sun (anthropomorphised by a face), with its shafts of sunlight, reminiscent of the Japanese naval flag, i.e., an emblem of the successful Japanese nation, gives the snowman serious trouble. He is about to melt and lose his power because of the heat.

Similar in style, the Japanese cover page of *Kokkei shinbun* appears only slightly more abstract: A Japanese flag on the left is contrasted with a white flag, which appears on Russian territory on the right. As the caption informs us, this symbolises what the enemy deserves: the white flag of surrender. To attract the audience and to satisfy its demands for novelties, these two panels can actually be detached from the journal proper to be used as postcards.[40]

---

[38] Tobias Heinzelmann, "Imitating, Adapting and Citing Cartoons—Ottoman References to European Satirical Gazettes, 1867–1918" (Talk on 14 November, 2009 in the course of the Workshop "The British Punch Magazine as a Transcultural Format of Satire and Caricature" in Heidelberg, 13–15 November, 2009).

[39] The *Simplicissimus* (named after the main protagonist of Grimmelshausen's novel *Der Abenteuerliche Simplicissimus Teutsch*) was a weekly magazine, after 1964 a bi-weekly, which was published from 1896 until 1967 in Munich. Due to the biting criticism of the clergy and Prussian military figures it was a thorn in the side of government authorities and repeatedly condemned.

[40] Whether the context could be grasped or not when receiving a plain white card, might be a matter of consideration, but is not relevant to our topic here.

The editor of the *Kokkei shinbun*, Miyatake Gaikotsu, was not unknown among officials. Before founding his magazine in Osaka, he had been responsible for the monthly magazines *Tonchi to kokkei* 頓智と滑稽 (wit and humour), as well as *Tonchi kyōkai zasshi* 頓智協会雑誌 (wit-club magazine) for which he was arrested, convicted and sent to prison for 3 years. His later *Kokkei shinbun* was equally widely known for its criticism of the Meiji government. During the war, however, it changed its position, became an ally and helped to keep the 'home front unbroken'. Nevertheless, this support was ambivalent: While mocking the Russians and celebrating Japan's victories on the cover page, as well as in small cartoons, the paper did not hold back its indirect criticism of the authorities and the governmental press policy regarding the outcome of the war, either.

One such example is the article published in *Kokkei shinbun* on 20 July 1905. It takes the form of a letter of complaint to the abandoned household of the vice admiral Kamimura.[41] Due to his current failures the military leader is vilified as rather useless, a rather direct accusation against a military leader in charge of national troops. Apparently, the periodical had not completely buried its hatchet with the Meiji government.

The *Tokyo Puck*: An American-Oriented Satirical Format

As the examples of *Nipponchi* and *Kokkei shinbun* show, there was no longer *one* model of satirical journalism to be found in Japan around the turn of the twentieth century but a variety of styles. Whether they employed traditional motifs or were orientated toward Art Nouveau, the majority of publications were united by their pro-war stance. This can also be said for the third magazine under scrutiny here, the *Tokyo Puck*. With the advent of the Russo-Japanese War the influence of American style publications on the Japanese publishing industry increased. This holds true particularly for the satirical field, where it even replaced former English models. The most successful and influential American satirical publication was *Puck*, a weekly publication founded in St. Louis in 1871 by the Austrian Joseph Ferdinand Keppler (1838–1894). The title derives from the character of *Puck* in Shakespeare's *A Midsummer Night's Dream*. A typical issue of the American magazine consisted of 32 pages containing colour cartoons on the front and back cover, often political in nature, a double-page centrefold, and anecdotes illustrated with caricatures in black and white. The most striking invention was the attractive technique of full-colour lithographs, which *Puck* was the first to adopt for a weekly publication.

During the Russo-Japanese War, Japan apparently discovered the gaudy appeal of magazines like this one: upon publication, *Tokyo Puck* immediately became a bestseller. The magazine was founded on 15 April 1905, in the last months of the war. Kitazawa Rakuten (1876–1955), the publisher and artist in charge, had studied Japanese painting as well as Western cartoons and intended to make his paper a

---

[41] "Yowaimono ijime no bankō," *Kokkei shinbun* 7, 20 July 1937.

piece of 'modern journalism'. Not only does the title *Tokyo Puck* refer to the American model, the visual composition in general, as well as the cartoons in particular, owe much to its intercontinental counterpart: *Tokyo Puck* adopted a large format[42] and included big colourful illustrations and *Puck*-style caricature. These similarities are perhaps less surprising if one considers that Kitazawa himself had been working for the American magazine *Box of Curio(u)s* in Yokohama.

As a 19-year-old, Kitazawa had been the assistant of Frank Nankivell (1869–1959), an Australian cartoonist who possessed a big collection of *Puck* magazines and introduced his Japanese colleague to the 'American way' of caricature before leaving Japan. When Nankivell moved to the United States and worked in the editorial office of the original *Puck* in New York, Kitazawa inherited his position at *Box of Curious*. Before setting up his own business with the *Tokyo Puck*, he later joined Fukuzawa Yukichi's daily newspaper *Jiji shinpō* and became responsible for the special cartoon page on Sunday entitled '*Jiji manga*', which started in 1902.[43] Through his contact with Western models, Kitazawa was convinced that it was necessary to launch a new type of satirical cartoon in Japan. In his view, the established *Punch*-influenced magazines were outdated. Small in format and printed in black and white, they could no longer compete with the fancy colourful print media which had begun to be published in the West.[44] His new magazine was part of a wider trend which featured a clear emphasis on the visual and abandoned the long textual passages that had been a crucial element in the older (*Punch*-style) formats. Around 1904/1905, the satirical magazine was thus stripped off its last connections to the newspaper and became a distinct print medium.

To adopt the American model of the 'yellow pages' (with which Kitazawa had become acquainted while working on *Jiji shinpō*), as well as the design of the American *Puck* (as presented to him by Frank Nankivell) as a new model, was not a subtle change, however. Already the name *Tokyo Puck* was a conscious and bold statement by an ambitious artist. Kitazawa insisted vehemently on keeping this name and the direct reference to *Puck*, in spite of protests from his financial supporter who had suggested an alternative, 'Tanuki' (raccoon dog), which he considered more suitable as a name for a Japanese satirical paper.

From the beginning, the *Tokyo Puck* was globally conceived. It was the first Japanese magazine which also sold in Taiwan, Korea and China. The first issues included short captions in Japanese and English (a practice that was not totally new as the *Marumaru chinbun*, founded in 1877, had included English captions from the beginning), and in later issues Chinese captions were also added. Kitazawa's fashionable journal, however, was much pricier: it cost 12 *sen* per issue, more than twice the price of one issue of *Marumaru chinbun* at 5 *sen*.

---

[42] *Tokyo Puck*'s size is the B4 format, which is about 25.7×36.4 cm. The American *Puck* magazine measured 25.5×33 cm.

[43] Isao Shimizu, *Manga no rekishi* (*A History of Japanese Cartoons*) (Tōkyō: Iwanami Shoten, 1991).

[44] Okamoto, "Pictorial Propaganda in Japanese Comic Art".

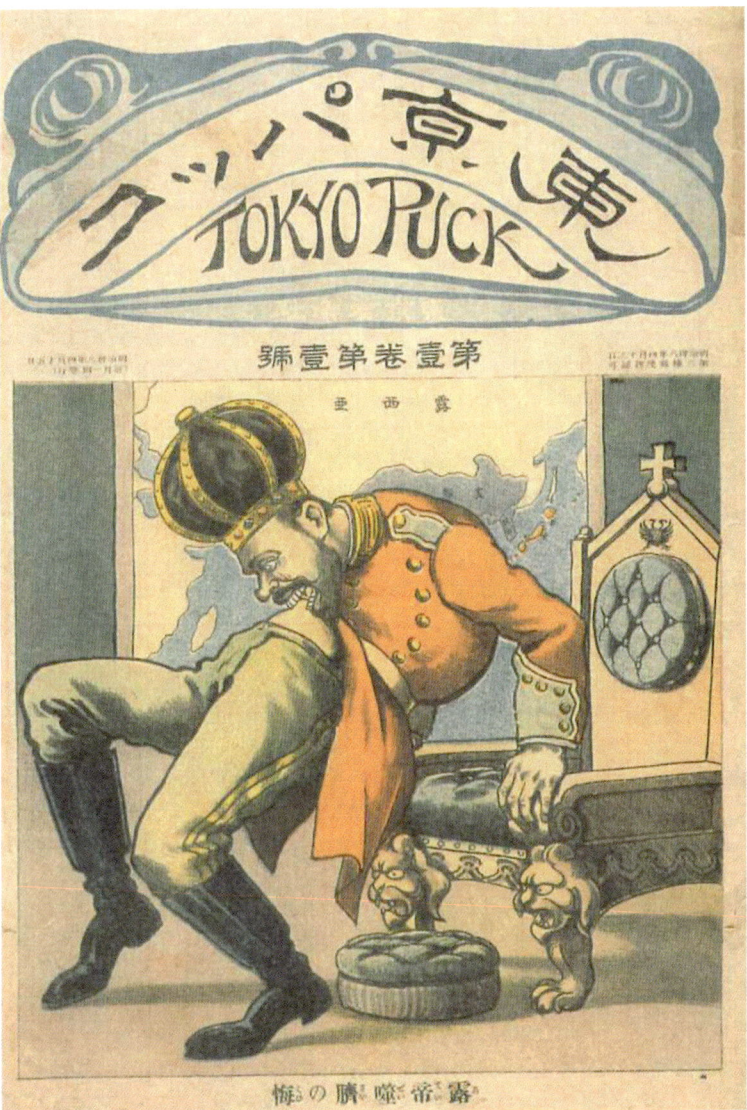

Fig. 7 Title page by Kitazawa Rakuten. *Tokyo Puck* 1, 15 April 1905

The first cover page of *Tokyo Puck* in April 1905 (Fig. 7) shows a caricature of the Russian Czar Nicholas II by Kitazawa. The picture entitled 'The Belly-biting Repentance of the Russian Czar' (*rotei zeisai no kui*) shows the monarch, a giant male figure dressed in military uniform with a bulky crown on his head, grotesquely contorted: He desperately tries to bite into his own navel. In front of a giant map of Russia, China, and Japan stands a throne decorated with the emblem of the double-headed Russian eagle on the back rest and small footrest. The cartoon with its voluminous realistic figure, the colourful design and the fine shading shows the influence of the *Puck* style, yet a specific cultural background is needed to decode the depicted scene. The Japanese saying 'to bite into one's own navel' (*hozo o kamu*) is an expression of deep regret. In this depiction, Czar Nicholas II, feeling remorseful because of his failed ambitious plans, takes the allegory literally. The caricature is related to the great military losses Czarist Russia had to face in 1905: the capture of Port Arthur by Japan and the subsequent Russian losses in Mukden.

With the *Tokyo Puck* a shift in readers' interests is evident. In the first generation of *Punch*-related Japanese satirical magazines, which featured columned texts and cartoons in simple black and white, the boundary between satirical magazines and conventional newspapers was not always entirely clear. In contrast, *Puck* mainly consists of pictures and hardly contains any texts. While *Nipponchi* shared the same emphasis on the visual, its contents are slightly different. Kitazawa Rakuten widened the horizon of caricature. In his work the war is no longer a matter of two opponents but rather a performance on the international stage. Before the *Tokyo Puck*, the repertoire of satirical characters in cartoons during the war had been limited to the 'brave Japanese' confronted with the 'weak Russian'. In Rakuten's *Tokyo Puck* figures representing other national identities, like John Bull or the Prussian general, are used increasingly, showing the journal's international orientation.

The abandonment of the *Punch* format was accompanied by a thematic reorientation in Japan's satirical media: in *Tokyo Puck*'s famous double-page caricatures, decorative and apolitical comical elements outweighed satirical comments with a political message. The journal depicted a new political future and also contained much positive commentary on Japanese society.

With the end of the war with Russia, and after almost 30 years of satirical journalism in Japan, it may have appeared that neither the satirical picture fighting for democratic rights (as seen in the case of the Movement for Freedom and Peoples' Rights) nor the propaganda cartoon were required any longer. And yet, during the following years, satirical 'entertainment' magazines continued to boom. The political concerns of the 1870s and 1880s, such as the establishment of the constitution and the setting up of a parliament, had been successful. Now that the war had come to an end, there was no concrete need for satire to support the government. Nevertheless, Kitazawa's *Puck* continued what the original *Punch* had begun more than 60 years earlier: celebrating a fanciful kind of humour combined with witty puns on politics and society, without becoming pedantic or overtly striving for betterment. Thus, the follies of mankind continued to amuse the readerships of these magazines,

Not unlike the *Marumaru chinbun*, which became the (*Punch*-inspired) archetype for a number of satirical papers within Japan, Kitazawa Rakuten's *Tokyo Puck*, also had a legacy of magazines with 'puckish' references, such as *Osaka Puck* or *Joto Puck*. The *Tokyo Puck* also became the model for satirical magazines in other Asian countries, too: China also had its *Puck*, the *Shanghai Puck*, discussed in I-Wei Wu's chapter, Participating in Global Affairs: The Chinese Cartoon Monthly *Shanghai Puck*, in this volume.

Voices Against the War: Satirical Anti-war Agitation

It is not easy to evaluate the importance of satirical journalism in the years 1904–1905. Official documents by the Home Ministry do not differentiate between newspapers and magazines,[45] nor do they give information about the number of satirical formats available. Moreover, the records only report periodicals that start with a set minimum circulation; data about even smaller pamphlets and magazines cannot be found at all.

According to the lists published by the Home Ministry, the *Dai-nihon teikoku naimushō tōkei hōkoku* 大日本帝國內務省統計報告 (record of the Home Ministry), the number of periodicals was about 1,590 in the year 1904 (Meiji 37), nearly twice the number listed 4 years earlier. The listed cases of governmental censorship and punishment of newspapers and magazines are also surprising: for 1904, the sales of only seven journal or newspaper issues were stopped; they were confiscated and ceased. One was banned from publishing for a while, but no single paper was completely closed down. The situation was almost identical in the second year of the war, 1905. Had the war and the need to 'keep the home front unbroken' taken the sting out of satirical journalism?

Censorship regulations intimate governmental perceptions of the satirical press. On 28 June 1875, the responsible ministries issued a special regulation for newspapers and magazines (*shinbun-shi jōrei*). The law can be considered a governmental reaction to the threatening activities by the Movement for Freedom and the abovementioned People's Rights, which had been supported by many harshly critical cartoons in different satire magazines.[46] During the Russo-Japanese War, again, press censorship was rigid. Shortly after the outbreak of war, on 10 February 1904, the army issued a set of 'rules for war correspondents' (*jōgun kasha kokoroe*) and supported a policy of keeping vulnerability 'completely secret so as not to undermine the people's spirit'.[47] But in contrast to earlier decades, especially the 1870s and 1880s, governmental control in the field of satirical journalism had in fact become unnecessary.[48] The larger part of the print media in fact frenetically supported the war effort, without being forced to do so.

---

[45] They are summarised under the subject of the *shinbun-shi kyū zasshi*.

[46] Although relying on control mechanisms from the Tokugawa period, such as requiring prior approval, this comprehensive law was the first regulating the news-media. Main changes included the need to declare the name of the editor and the printer at the end of every issue as well as to disclose the identities of the authors.. The list of punishments entailed in the law was striking. For a comprehensive analysis of Meiji journalism and censorship, see James L. Huffman, *Creating a Public. People and Press in Meiji Japan* (Honolulu: University of Hawai'i Press, 1997).

[47] Shōho Tokutomi, cited in Huffman, *Creating a Public*, 288.

[48] Most of the fines and penalties for print media were actually recorded shortly after the end of the war when the outcome of the peace negotiations became public and the discontent of the population cumulated in a riot called the Hibiya Incendiary Incident.

One reason for this support might have been intrinsic: in times of war, journalists would have wanted to fulfil their patriotic duty. On the other hand, editors also made themselves liable to prosecution if they printed critical material. It appears that they only accepted cartoons which were in line with state policies. While pressure by governmental authorities was great, the self-imposed moral pressure to be a good citizen and serve the community may have played a significant role. Strict self-censorship as well as the government's penalty policy created a situation in which satirical magazines that raised their voice against the war were very rare. They could be found only in socialist publications such as the *Heimin shinbun* 平民新聞 (commoners news) or in obscure papers like *Jiji manga hibijutsu gahō* 時事漫画非美術画報 (non-artistic magazine of current events). *Jiji manga hibijutsu gahō*, a Kyoto-based magazine was founded, like *Nipponchi,* shortly after the outbreak of war. The magazine included cartoons drawn by the artist Kanokogi Takeshiro (1874–1941) who had specialised in mocking portraits of leading war figures.

Perhaps the harshest criticism on the rising war euphoria came from the ranks of the political opposition such as the pro-Russian minded 'Socialist Democratic Party' (*Shakai minshutō*). Here is an example of a cartoon published in the socialist newspaper *Heimin shinbun*[49] during wartime.

The illustration (Fig. 8) shows two soldiers, a Russian on the right and a Japanese on the left. Captions label them as workers, but in arms, they apparently play another role. With their rifles aimed at each other, they seem to serve in war, but the cartoon reveals the reality: These two soldiers are quite clearly only puppets in the hands of their regimes. Illustrations like these circulated internationally. Not only socialist papers frequently exchanged their cartoons. The newspaper *Miyako shinbun* 都新聞 (news of the capital), likewise featured a special column with cartoons borrowed from English, American, or even Russian sources. These would adhere to a common international visual language which made them comprehensible without prior and specific cultural knowledge.

The Japanese socialist *Heimin shinbun* with its strong political backing and a circulation of 4,500 copies cannot be considered to have loomed large in the generally more jingoistic mood of the press.[50] But its extremely critical perspective immediately caused the issue of a banning order (*hakkō kinshi*) by the alarmed authorities.[51] Editor Sakai was sentenced to 3 months in jail. Even after the ban was overturned by the Higher Court and the fine reduced, pressure on the journal remained high. On the other hand, anti-war papers were clearly not in demand:

---

[49] The weekly periodical was published from 29 May 1903 until 29 January 1905; one of its editors was Kotoku Shusui (Denjiro, 1871–1911). *Heimin shinbun* was the leading socialist publication; throughout its publication history, many issues had been banned by the authorities for offending the Meiji government.

[50] Many satirical illustrations were published in newspapers and satirical magazines like *Nipponchi*, served as supplements to those. This is why the chapter speaks of satire media in the context of the press more generally.

[51] Huffman, *Creating a Public*, 276.

Fig. 8 'Soldiers as string puppets'. *Heimin shinbun* 21, 3 April 1905, 2

after the outbreak of war, circulation dropped to only 1,700 copies.[52] The final prohibition by the Home Ministry in November 1904 turned out to be more of a symbolic act.

Another example for a publication that offered pacifist overtones is the rather obscure *Jiji manga hibijutsu gahō* (non-artistic magazine of current events) already mentioned above. This thin journal was penned by Kanokogi Takeshiro (Futo, 1874–1941),[53] a well-known and established artist who had been influenced by European art, especially French oil painting, during his studies abroad. The magazine was published after Kanokogi's return to Japan, where he settled in Kyoto and

---

[52] Nobuya Bamba and John F. Howes, *Pacifism in Japan: The Christian and Socialist Tradition* (Vancouver: UBC Press, 1978), 139, quoted in Huffman, *Creating a Public*, 297.

[53] Kanokogi was born 1874 in Okayama. After training under the supervision of Koyama Shotaro, he went abroad to study and reached Paris in 1901 after short stays in America and London. Here he was influenced by the painter and sculptor Jean Paul Laurens, a representative of the French Academic style. In April 1904, the war with Russia caused Kanokogi to return to Japan and set up his magazine *Hibijutsu gahō* in Kyoto. Together with Asai Chu he acted at the Kansai Art Center.

Fig. 9 'Commander-in-chief Togo' (*Tōgō rengō kantai shirei chōkan* 東郷連合艦隊司令長官) (Cartoon by Kanokogi Takeshiro. *Jiji manga hibijutsu gahō* 1, 10 May 1904, 1 (owned by The Kyoto International Manga Museum))

taught at the School for Applied Art for 11 years.[54] In a cartoon published on 10 May 1904 (Fig. 9), he portrayed Admiral Togo Heihachiro (1848–1934), one of the most significant figures of the war, in a highly caricatured way. In this depiction, the popular and esteemed admiral is shrunk to the size of a stocky dwarf. Due to the exaggerated head his proportions resemble those of a child. With his deformed legs and clumsy fingers he looks rather amusing, wearing a uniform and holding his sword. Around Togo's head the Japanese fleet, recognisable by the small Japanese flags, gathers, forming almost a halo for its leader.

As commander-in-chief of the Imperial Japanese Navy, Togo played a crucial role in the Russo-Japanese war. Thanks to his contribution, the Russian Baltic Fleet

---

[54] Mie Prefectural Art Museum, ed., *Takeshiro Kanokogi 1874–1941* (Kyoto: Museum of Modern Art Kyoto, 1990).

was destroyed almost completely in the battle of Tsushima only about 2 weeks after this caricature was published (27 May). However, the picture which the artist Kanokogi drew of him is a different one. He shows Togo as a fanatic militarist, who is completely absorbed by matters of war. In this caricature the commander-in-chief is not at all a figure of identification. In addition to his wretched, deformed body, he seems to assimilate the subjects of his profession. His eyes are reminiscent of gun muzzles, his hair and beard resemble area marks on a military map. This depiction, thus uncovers the 'real face' of 'patriotic duty': Togo is no longer human. He has become a lifeless tool.

Here, satire evidently does not only not support militarism in Japan, but criticises what was called 'patriotic duty' instead. Evidently, the fever of war had added fuel to the flames of propagandistic cartoons (as the booming numbers of satirical magazines, such as *Nipponchi*, show). Did it stimulate the production of pacifistic cartoons? It did not: although the *Jiji hibijutsu gahō* as a whole, and Kanokogi as an individual, remained unmolested by governmental censorship, Kanokogi had to recognise the limits of his time: the lack of a market for magazines in Kyoto forced the journal to quit publishing after three issues.[55] One could conjecture that this was due not only to the fact that Kyoto was disadvantageous as a location, but also because of the magazine's critical attitude, which was evidently considered unsuitable for wartime.

Like the *Heimin Shinbun*, *Jiji hibijutsu gahō* was an exceptional phenomenon. Even though there is no evidence as to the number of copies in circulation, it is most unlikely that a significant number of issues found their way to a receptive audience. Even today, the thin publication is virtually unavailable. Another reason might have been that the journal did not portray men, such as Admiral Togo or Oyama Iwao, who was commander-in-chief of the Japanese armies in Manchuria, patriotically enough. To see these heroes of the nation criticised and caricatured in such an unflattering way must have discomforted the war-euphoric audience.

Conclusion

In Japanese satirical journalism covering the Russo-Japanese war of 1904/1905, an overwhelming number of cartoons and caricatures attempted to legitimate military action and poked fun at the Russian enemy. The main function of satire in 1904/1905 was to act as a tool for the political aims of the government. This can be explained by 'external' influences such as governmental censorship and economic 'realities', on the one hand and on the other by 'internal' influences, such as self-censorship and a feeling that the satirist too must serve the good of his nation by 'keeping the home front unbroken'. Only very few journals used satire to decry

---

[55] Shimizu Isao, *Meiji mangakan* (*Cartoon-Collection from the Meiji Period*) (Tōkyō: Kōdansha, 1979). 134.

militarism and the war. Small in circulation and short-lived, they did not exert a lasting influence on the shaping of Japanese public opinion.

During the tension-filled months of 1904/1905, most Japanese cartoonists responded to the war euphoria and supported the government by using the power of the mass media. In the last instance, it was the Japanese audience's which actively participated in shaping the satirical landscape by either buying or ignoring particular satirical journals—and with them, their inherent political stance. Most satirists accommodated their readership by creating cartoons that followed rather than made public opinion. Claiming the rights of the people, satire temporarily stopped criticising the political class and thus served governmental aims.

The transformation of satirical magazines into tools of propaganda in 1904/1905 was accompanied by a change in style and the decline of the established *Punch*-inspired magazine. There can be no doubt that *Punch* as a 'brand' (to use Brian Maidment's term) exerted an important influence all over the world, including Japan. Yet magazines which became popular during the Russo-Japanese War clearly abandoned the 'old' style of *Punch*. The veteran *Punch* format was no longer the only option and, as shown, not the most conducive for pro-nationalist agitation. By the beginning of the twentieth century Japanese editors had new possibilities available to them. They used other international satirical formats, such as the colourful American *Puck* magazine, or employed traditional visual vocabulary. The choice of a particular satirical format depended on current tastes, ideological backgrounds, accessibility and influences, as well as the desired audience. At the turn of the century visual satire in Japan spoke many different languages and dialects, *Punch* remained one of them, but one used less and less frequently.

Participating in Global Affairs: The Chinese Cartoon Monthly *Shanghai Puck*

I-Wei Wu

To situate *Punch* and the Asian versions of *Punch* in relation to each other serves to illustrate not only the multidirectional movement of images between Europe and Asia but also the asymmetrical realities and imaginaries of international politics reflected in these images and even, as Ritu Khanduri has put it, the 'affective registers [...] generated by seeing the images'.[1] A detailed study of these images thus opens new ways of seeing and understanding international interactions at the times of the colonies. In previous chapters we have observed how both in Europe and in Asia, satirical journals followed a model of, in the words of Brian Maidment, outspoken 'denunciation of social evils or political chicanery', as was considered typical of *Punch*'s satire which, 'both recognised and cathartically laughed away the fears and anxieties of its readers, reducing perceived dangers and threats to manageable proportions through the construction of a comic world turned upside down'.[2] The aim of this chapter is to examine the adaptation of '*Punch*-like' publications in early twentieth century China and to discuss how the Western genre satirical cartoon magazine in fact participated in the Chinese public sphere, wielding power over public issues, which derived largely from China's peculiar 'semi-colonised' status. This chapter concentrates principally on 'Shanghai Puck', a cartoon monthly first published in 1918, which, as will be demonstrated below, is a typical product of multidirectional transcultural exchange. In exploring the visual world of 'Shanghai Puck' and its 'models', the chapter will deliberate the following questions: How did 'Shanghai Puck' relate to foreign satirical cartoon magazines?

---

[1] The citation is taken from the conclusion to Khanduri, chapter *Punch* in India: Another History of Colonial Politics? in this volume.

[2] Brian Maidment "Why was *Punch* so influential?", chapter The Presence of *Punch* in the Nineteenth Century in this volume.

I.-W. Wu (✉)
Doctoral Candidate at the Institute for Chinese Studies at Heidelberg University,
Heidelberg, Germany
e-mail: iwai.wu@gmail.com

Here, the focus will not only be on the London *Punch* but the American *Puck* as a possible template as well. This chapter also investigates 'Shanghai Puck's' global agency: What does the intervisuality observed on the pages of Chinese, Japanese and foreign satire magazines and pictorials tell us about the anxieties of the respective journals' readers and the emotions triggered by such images? How were China and the Chinese, as well as foreigners, portrayed and transformed pictorially on the pages of the 'Shanghai Puck'? What strategies did 'Shanghai Puck' apply when it came to raising China's global position?

'Shanghai Puck' (上海潑克) and Shen Bochen (沈泊塵)

'Shanghai Puck' (上海潑克) is the earliest cartoon monthly in China, published in 1918 by Shen Bochen (沈泊塵, 1889–1919). It was also called *Bochen huaji huabao* 泊塵滑稽畫報 (Bochen's comic pictorial). Shen was born in 1889. He was educated as a traditional painter, but was also known as one of the most influential cartoonists of the so-called 'May Fourth Movement', a cultural and political crusade, which had originally grown out of student demonstrations in Beijing on 4 May 1919, and protested the Chinese government's weak performance in the negotiations over the Treaty of Versailles, and especially their inability to ensure the return of the German colony Shandong to China—it was passed on to Japan. The demonstrations sparked a wave of national protests and an upsurge in nationalist thinking. More than 1,000 of Shen's cartoons were published in *Shenbao* 申報 (Shanghai daily), *Shenzhou huabao* 神州畫報 (Shenzhou pictorial), *Minquan huabao* 民權畫報 (civil rights pictorial), *Da gonghe ribao* 大共和日報 (great republic daily), *Shishi xinbao* 時事新報 (current news) and other Shanghai newspapers and pictorials during the 1910s.[3]

After a short visit to Japan and Beijing in 1917, Shen established the 'Shanghai Puck' cartoon monthly. He and other painters such as Chen Baoyi and Wang Dun'gen contributed their caricatures to the magazine. *Shenbao* (Shanghai daily) reported that more than 10,000 copies of the first bilingual monthly issue had been distributed in the lower Yangzi River region. Because it was published in the May Fourth period, most of the cartoons were directly related to political issues current. However, the magazine published only four issues and then stopped when Shen Bochen died in 1919.[4]

---

[3] Shen Kuiyi, "Lianhuanhua and Manhua—Picture Books and Comics in Old Shanghai," in *Illustrating Asia: Comics, Humor Magazines, and Picture Books*, ed. John A. Lent (Honolulu: University of Hawai'i Press, 2001), 109.

[4] Shen, "Lianhuanhua and Manhua," 109–10.

The Web of *Punch*, *Puck*, and 'Shanghai Puck'

In his first issue, Shen introduces Puck as a famous character from William Shakespeare's play *A Midsummer Night's Dream*. Shen describes him as a clever and mischievous elf, a trickster and wise knave. Then Shen explains (slightly skewing the genealogy, see Table 1) that an English cartoon magazine bearing the elf's name as its title, had already been published. It had amused large numbers of readers, had educated people, and had thus helped to improve society. Shen describes how this English *Punch* had soon become hugely popular, while similarly successful magazines had begun to appear in St. Louis and New York in the USA, and Tokyo and Osaka in Japan.[5]

The appearance of 'Shanghai Puck' can be seen as the beginning of China's satirical cartoon magazine history. While it is clear that 'Shanghai Puck' based itself on available models and templates from elsewhere, the chronology of its particular genealogy is not entirely clear: a number of Japanese scholars and cartoonists contend that since Shen had published 'Shanghai Puck' soon after coming back from Japan, *Tokyo Puck* must have been the immediate model.[6] The fact that in the inaugural issue of his magazine Shen refers to the English *Punch* rather than the American *Puck* as the 'original', may make one wonder whether he had seen much of the American *Puck*, but pictorial evidence (as discussed below) shows that in later editions, the intervisual and intertextual connections between the American *Puck* and the 'Shanghai Puck' are quite obvious.

A number of Chinese scholars and cartoonists contend that neither the Japanese nor the English or American *Puck* had been decisive in the conception of the 'Shanghai Puck', but that it was instead influenced most decisively by the London *Punch*.[7] This chapter will show that there are indeed important connections between *Puck* and *Punch*. They become particularly obvious when we explore the visual aspects of the 'Shanghai Puck' publications. However, I will argue that by referencing *Punch* and *Puck*, 'Shanghai Puck' in fact positioned itself neither as a direct descendant of *Punch* nor of *Puck*, although both were acknowledged as important models. Instead, the journal, in its self-fashioning, presents itself as a member of a much larger network of satirical cartoon magazines around the world, in a way quite similar to how satirical magazines had done it for decades.

---

[5] Shen Bochen 沈泊塵, "Poke 潑克 (Puck)," *Shanghai poke* 上海潑克 (Shanghai Puck) 1, September, 1918.

[6] Ishiko Jun 石子順, *Nihon no shinryaku chûgoku no teikô manga ni miru ni nitchû sensô jidai* 日本の侵略 中国の抵抗 漫画に見るに日中戦争時代 (Japanese invasion, Chinese resistance: the period of Japan-China war presented in comic books) (Tokyo: Oshiki, 1995), 10–11.

[7] Chu Chi-Shuan (Qiu Zhixuan) 邱稚亘, "Liudong de jiangjie: yi manhua wei li kan minchu Shanghai gaoji yu tongsu meishu de fenlei yu jiexian wenti 流動的疆界:以漫畫為例看民初上海高階與通俗美術的分類與界線問題 (flowing boundaries: on categorisation and barriers of high and popular art in the early republic era of China Shanghai)" (MA thesis, National Central University, Taiwan, 2004), 80–85.

Table 1 *Puck* and *Punch* genealogies[8]

Publication	Place	Author(s)	Term	Frequency
Punch	London, UK	Henry Mayhew and Ebenezer Landells	1841–2002	Weekly
Puck	St. Louis and New York, USA	Joseph Ferdinand Keppler	1871–1918	Weekly (1871–1917) Semi-weekly (July, 1917–Jan, 1918); weekly (Feb–Sept, 1918)
Puck[9]	London	William Mecham	1889–1890	Weekly
東京パック (*Tokyo Puck*)	Tokyo, Japan	北沢楽天(Kitazawa Rakuten)	1905–1912 1919–1923	Weekly
大阪パック (Osaka Puck)	Osaka, Japan	赤松麟作 (Akamatsu Rinsaku)	1908	Semi-monthly
上海潑克 (Shanghai Puck)	Shanghai, China	沈泊塵 (Shen Bochen)	1918	Monthly

The cover of what originally was a German-language *Puck* (founded in St. Louis in 1871), first published in New York in 1876, shows this quite clearly (Fig. 1). Joseph Ferdinand Keppler, one of the journal's founders, an Austrian immigrant illustrator, depicted Puck as an elf standing on a stage passing out subscriptions to audience members—some of them delighted, some appalled. From these sheets of papers, which are scattered around and flying all over the place, the reader can make out drawings which illustrate the features and other practical information about the *Puck* magazine, including its price, the illustrator's name and a number of portraits that suggest the variety of its contents.

This information is presented to a large crowd and among them, on one of the balconies on the right, right above Puck, we see a cheering crowd of mascots representing notable satire magazines of nineteenth-century Europe. On the left is a man with a cock's head who portrays the *Kikeriki* magazine (Cock-a-doodle-doo) in Vienna. Next to him is Mr Punch from the English magazine *Punch*. The

---

[8] In mind: in June 1871, an English cartoon magazine *Puck, or the Shanghai Charivari* was published in Shanghai. The title seems to be a mixture of *Puck* and *Punch, or the London Charivari*. The publisher was a British company based in Shanghai, F. & C. WALSH, which dealt with the wholesale and retail of stationers and printers. This magazine was published every three months from June 1871 to November 1872, i.e., a total of seven issues. It can be referred to as the first *Punch*-like magazine appearing in mainland China. However, this chapter focuses on the magazines repeatedly mentioned by Shen in 'Shanghai Puck', so *Puck, or the Shanghai Charivari* will not be discussed in this chapter.

[9] In July 1890, *Puck* (London), as an important notice on the front page declared, changed its title to *Ariel, or the London Puck* in order to 'prevent the prevalent confusion with the American *Puck*, with which the *London Puck* has no connection'. Therefore, the London *Puck* seemed to have no official and administrative relation with the American *Puck*.

Participating in Global Affairs: The Chinese Cartoon Monthly *Shanghai Puck* 369

Fig. 1 Cover of the first New York edition of the American *Puck*. Cartoon by Joseph Ferdinand Keppler. *Puck*, 27 September 1876 (Richard Samuel West, *Satire on Stone: The Political Cartoons of Joseph Keppler* (Illinois: University of Illinois, 1988), 693)

grinning boy with a finger pointing downwards is representative of the German magazine *Kladderadatsch* (Crash) and the two men, with moustaches and wearing bandanas, are the French *Figaro* magazine.[10] *Charivari*, a traditional French satirical magazine, is also present, standing behind everyone, dressed as a clown.

It is not surprising that Keppler, when facing the absurdity and distortion of American politics, would have come up with the idea of expressing his opinions by means of caricature and satirical pictures:[11] he had contributed many caricatures to *Kikeriki* in Vienna.[12] For Keppler to present his magazine as taking its place among

---

[10] For the importance of these magazines, see Monika Lehner, *Der Chinadiskurs in der satirisch-humoristischen Publizistik Österreich-Ungarns 1894–1917* (forthcoming).

[11] West, *Satire on Stone*, 14–15.

[12] Ibid., 6–7.

Fig. 2 London *Puck*, 12 January 1889

similar satire magazines, such as *Punch*, *Figaro* and *Kladderadatsch,* was probably a matter of course. The front cover of this first edition thus signifies the magazine's legacy: the European tradition of satirical papers. The figure of Puck is central in this depiction, standing and receiving praise from all his predecessors, with *Charivari* cheering, *Kladderadatsch* smiling, and *Punch* applauding; it is clearly a relationship of closeness and intimacy that is suggested. And indeed, this relationship was indeed quite close: *Punch*, for one, did not miss any of *Puck*'s debuts, no matter if in the USA or in London, reporting and praising the new sister journals to come. And this type of self-fashioning was obviously quite in order, as the first issue of the London *Puck* in 1889 also carries a similar image (Fig. 2). Here, Puck is depicted as a lissome figure, cap in hand, arriving in London and standing before an assembly of London and provincial newspapers,[13] with Mr Punch right in front. Accompanying the image is a report written in fairy-tale fashion, which records the dialogue between them. The other newspapers have assembled to 'inspect' Puck as a new 'wannabe' member by testing and questioning him. In the end, and after quite some argument, and, as the text reads, 'amid a whirlwind of applause, Puck was ensconced on a throne, relieved of his overcoat as well as five guineas as an entrance subscription, and elected, without opposition, a Full Member of Journalistic Guild'.[14]

In these self-depictions, then, it is never a question of *Puck* or *Punch*. Instead, every new satirical journal is depicted to become part of a larger field of (not just satirical) journalism. Instead of neatly categorising satirical journals into *Puck* or *Punch* types, they are all considered part of a tightly knit community of (satirical) journals and, as the London *Puck* image also insinuates, also associated with the larger world of journalism. Here, *Puck* not only faces *Punch* and *Judy*, but also many other papers such as *The Star*, *The World*, *The Daily Telegraph*, or *The Morning News*.

---

[13] London *Puck* 1, 12 January 1889, 2 (a description of the illustration).
[14] Ibid.

Fig. 3 'Ever-lasting memory to our late contemporaries' (Cartoon by Shen Bochen. 'Shanghai Puck', 1 September 1918)

This process of inscribing oneself into the larger picture of journalism as a whole is even more obviously reflected in another similar picture, which appeared in the first issue of 'Shanghai Puck', entitled 'Ever-lasting memory to our late contemporaries' (Fig. 3). Here, Puck appears as a man in Western suit. The other papers, his 'contemporaries' are no longer able to act as inquisitors, however: they are all dead; all we see is their gravestones in the cemetery. *Shanghai Puck* takes a bow, giving his regards to them, among whom are some of the more famous cases of late Qing newspaper censorship, such as the *Subao* 蘇報 (Jiangsu gazette, censored in 1903) and Yu Youren's 于右任 (1879–1964) abortive 'People's trio' from 1909/1910, the last of which was the *Minlibao* 民立報 (people's paper). An editorial, entitled 'Responsibilities of This Paper' provides an explanation of the image: here it is said that 'nowadays newspapers which maintain justice cannot be found very often' and that they are not strong enough to sustain themselves. As a consequence, 'Shanghai Puck' had 'made its start', to make the unfulfilled wishes of his contemporaries come true after all[15] *Puck* thus confirms an uncompromising attitude, as a medium of the public opinion and political criticism. 'Shanghai Puck' was thus used in precisely the way that Keppler had originally prescribed for his *Puck* as well.

---

[15] Shen Bochen 沈泊塵, "Benbao de zeren 本報的責任 (the responsibilities of this paper)," *Shanghai poke* 上海潑克 (Shanghai Puck) 1, September 1918, 6.

Fig. 4 A page of 'Shanghai Puck' (Cartoon by Shen Bochen. 'Shanghai Puck', 1 November 1918)

Transplanting New Visual Worlds

In its later editions, 'Shanghai Puck', as just one participant in a rather complex web of *Pucks* and *Punch* versions, and other such journals, continued to incorporate ideas from caricature magazines all over the world. Time and again, we find concrete pictorial evidence illustrating how 'Shanghai Puck' was an integral part of global trends and circulations of satirical journalism. From the publishing format to the types of satirical pictures and caricatures it carried, 'Shanghai Puck's' visual appearance draws on a variety of different sources. Shen Bochen produced many original pen-and-ink drawings in a style similar to Western drawings from both *Punch* and *Puck*. 'Shanghai Puck' shares with *Punch* one feature in its layout: the page containing a picture in the middle with a text surrounding it[16] (see Fig. 4, from 'Shanghai Puck', and Fig. 5, from the London *Punch*) *Puck* and *Tokyo Puck*, on the other hand, do not often feature this particular page arrangement.

---

[16] Chu, "Liudong de jiangjie," 84–86.

Participating in Global Affairs: The Chinese Cartoon Monthly *Shanghai Puck* 373

Fig. 5 A page of *Punch*, vol. 151, 9 August 1916

Caricatures, as well as caricature styles, were often exchanged between magazines from the *Punch* and *Puck* family. 'Shanghai Puck's' visual language borrows visual vocabulary, such as the use of huge heads for figures to be ridiculed (e.g. from *Punch*, see Figs. 6 and 7)—In one edition of 'Shanghai Puck', for example, the German Kaiser is ridiculed in such a way for his belief in militarism. The bandaged earth appearing in the third issue of 'Shanghai Puck' in 1918, on the other hand, is a direct 'visual quote' from the American *Puck* (Figs. 8 and 9).

Clearly, then, *Punch* was not the only brand to influence satirical production all over the world, but several satirical journals became transcultural brands, so to speak. While *Punch* may thus have been one of the interlocutors for 'Shanghai Puck', it is the American *Puck* that 'Shanghai Puck' appears to respond to most directly in these pictorial quotations. As we have just seen, Shen would take images from the American *Puck* and adapt them to current Chinese events by making minor alterations in the overall set, while leaving the principal elements intact. Figure 10, for example, is an illustration in the American *Puck* issue, from 17 June 1916. It depicts Russia and Germany as two children. On the left, the Russian bear is

Fig. 6 Cartoon by Shen Bochen. 'Shanghai Puck', 1 November 1918

holding a stick; on the right, the German is dressed in military uniform, likewise holding a stick. They are standing on a giant figure garbed as a traditional Turk, obviously meant to represent Turkey. This picture mocks World War One as a

Fig. 7 A page from *Punch Almanack*, 1918

Participating in Global Affairs: The Chinese Cartoon Monthly *Shanghai Puck*

Fig. 8 Cartoon by Merle Johnson. American *Puck*, 1917 (no exact date given)

children's game; it ridicules by exaggeration. Furthermore, it derides Turkey's situation—the country had promised to join the war by accepting financial support from Germany. By having done so, the image insinuates, Turkey has no means to keep the fighting children away from its own territory.

Figure 11, on the other hand, is an illustration from the first issue of 'Shanghai Puck'. There is no doubt that the two pictures are intervisually connected: here, two

Fig. 9 Cartoon by Shen Bochen. 'Shanghai Puck', 1 November 1918

Fig. 10 Cartoon by Merle Johnson. American *Puck*, 17 June 1916

small persons are fighting on top of another figure in almost exactly the same posture as in the American *Puck*. Again, the original image is re-contextualised to satirise the political situation in 1918 China. The Russian and German children have turned into two warlord leaders of the northern and southern governments, which we are able to recognise from their facial features: the left one marked 'South' is Tang Jiyao (唐繼堯) and the right one marked 'North' is Duan Qirui (段祺瑞). Shen considered these warlords' behaviour a very serious problem. Rather than giving the 'kids' in his image sticks to brandish, he substitutes them with swords. There are further variations to be considered: the Turkish man in Fig. 10 was by no means considered an innocent bystander and had only himself to blame for where he lay, but the Chinese man labelled "the People", who substitutes for Turkey in Shen's depiction, represents China's commoners who are too innocent and helpless to alter their predicament.

Fig. 11 Cartoon by Shen Bochen. 'Shanghai Puck', 1 September 1918

Multilingualisms: Asymmetrical Reversals

These images suggest that the visual language used in 'Shanghai Puck' is quite international. But linguistically, too, publications like the 'Shanghai Puck' reach out to the world: 'Shanghai Puck' as well as the American *Puck* and the *Tokyo Puck* have a multilingual background. As mentioned above, *Puck* had originally been published in German in St. Louis in 1871, targeted primarily at Germans in the United States of America. Many years later, and with successful sales, *Puck* had moved to New York and begun issuing both English and German language editions. *Tokyo Puck*, rather than publishing several editions in different languages, carried texts in several languages and provided each picture with multi-language captions: Japanese, English, and later also Chinese (Fig. 12). The editor was apparently aware of readers outside Japan and attempted to internationalise his magazine. 'Shanghai Puck' also assimilated this feature by using two languages, English and Chinese, in both captions and texts.

This multilingual format creates two very different linguistic but also visual worlds in 'Shanghai Puck': the customarily vertical print of Chinese texts, which are read from right to left, and the horizontal print of English texts, which are read in exactly the opposite way, cross in interesting fashions. There are no separate sections for print in either language, so the two worlds frequently blend into each other. According to the inaugural statement, the magazine had three goals: firstly, to give advice and warnings to the governments of the north and the south, and to spur them on to work in a concerted effort to create a unified government; secondly, to help Westerners understand Chinese culture and customs, and thus raise China's position in the world; and thirdly, to promote new morals and practices and discard the old. The second aim apparently necessitates bilingualism. Undoubtedly, English texts would be helpful to foreigners trying to understand Chinese culture, thus helping to bridge different worlds.[17] And with regard to the third goal of promoting a new morality while discarding the old, multilingualism could also serve to highlight distinctions between diverse standpoints. 'Shanghai Puck' was published during a period which saw Western culture and customs often described as new and novel, while Chinese traditions were considered old and outdated. The different languages on the pages of 'Shanghai Puck' could also be used to represent different ideologies; appearing in the fourth issue, the fashion page, for example, attempted to draw public attention to the outdated fashions of Chinese women by displaying pictures of Western women's dresses. While the theme was clearly aimed at Chinese readers the main text was written in English so as to underline the novelty of Western clothing.

This use of English in a Chinese satire magazine might look slightly asymmetrical, but in fact it was one method of trying to minimise asymmetries between the two worlds by associating Chinese public opinion with that of the world, thus presenting a China vying for equality and respect. In terms of quantity, the number of English

---

[17] Shen Bochen, "Benbao de zeren," 6.

Fig. 12 Cover of *Tokyo Puck*, 1911 (no exact date given)

texts increases over time, thus making the situation appear even more asymmetrical: There are 7 English and 26 Chinese articles in the first issue; in the second issue the number of Chinese texts is reduced to 18. This trend continues in the third and the fourth issue where the number decreases to 11, while the number of English texts gradually increases. In the second and third issues, 9 English articles appear; in the fourth issue this number grows to 14, thus exceeding the number of Chinese texts by 3.

However, if one looks at the contents of these texts, an acknowledgement of a power asymmetry is clearly not the point; indeed, the choice of language serves as a method of empowerment: English texts are used to voice some of the more critical subjects, the use of English rather than Chinese therefore appears as a safety device. Generally speaking, English texts deal with both domestic and international themes such as 'The Opium Tragedy', 'An Editorial: China as a Participator in the Coming Peace Conference', 'The League of Nations', 'Chinese Women and Dresses'; while Chinese texts focus mainly on domestic issues, such as governmental policies and opium issues. In the first issue, Chinese still serves as the primary channel; however, the second issue already begins to carry English texts and editorials that address sensitive subjects such as the new president, freedom of speech and the question of selling opium as a medicine. Increasingly, they are used to discuss domestic concerns. The third issue presents bilingual content in a closely connected way by translating, and publishing a series of criticisms against the governmental policy of selling opium as medicine. In the fourth issue, the significance of English texts rises dramatically because of the shift of concern from internal to external affairs. Critical issues such as the Versailles Peace Conference are discussed mostly in English, which now becomes the principal and primary voice to express disapproving and critical Chinese opinion.

Participating in Global Affairs

Since imperialism and colonialism reached China in the nineteenth century, Chinese illustrated newspapers had produced many kinds of images of foreigners. Those with satirical implication tend to stress the asymmetry between the respective sides. One 'Allegory Painting' (Fig. 13) from *Tuhua ribao* 圖畫日報 (pictorial daily), dating back to 1910, is a good example. In this picture, a Westerner and a Chinese man are looking at each other through binoculars; curiously, the Westerner is holding his binoculars backwards. From the Chinese man's point of view, then, the image of the Westerner would be large and close-up; from the Westerner's point of view, on the other hand, the image of the Chinese man would appear tiny and far away. This picture thus illustrates their unequal relationship. While the Westerner is only implicitly ridiculed for holding the binoculars the wrong way, this act can also be interpreted as anything *but* innocent: it quite literally 'belittles' the Chinese.

Fig. 13 'Allegory painting'. *Tuhua ribao*, 1910 (no exact date given)

Pictures such as this one, of which China's periodical press abounds at the time, highlight the power asymmetry between China and the foreign Powers—China's position is 'obviously' inferior. In another 'Allegory Painting' from the daily *Shishibao* 時事報 (current news) of 1907 (Fig. 14), this idea is addressed again: a Chinese governmental officer is depicted as a toy played with by an oversized Westerner. Each figure's size conveys their power; the Chinese is quite obviously unable to do anything against the foreigner. In this sense, even a Chinese governmental officer is just a toy to foreigners, let alone the ordinary people. The picture 'Can't you see the hegemony in the world' (Fig. 15), published in *Tuhua Ribao* 圖畫日報 in 1910, shows exactly this situation again; a foreigner who sees only himself in a large mirror is standing on a group of Chinese people who serve as his stepping stone.

This type of imagery of weakness and victimisation is repeated again and again, effectively becoming the fuel for caricatures. China's newspapers and magazines spared no effort uncovering and attacking unfairness and injustice by emphasising the victimisation of the Chinese people (and were thus censored time and again by their own government). In 'Foreigners divide up China among themselves' (Fig. 16), published in *Minhu ribao* 民呼日報 (people's call pictorial), one of Yu Youren's 'People's Trio' dating from 1909, the Chinese territory is even portrayed as pork which is served at a table of Westerners, who are discussing how to share China with each other. What is ironic is that a Chinese governmental officer serves different types of drinks, symbolising (which is clear from the labels) the Chinese mineral and railway businesses dominated by Westerners (Fig. 16). Similarly, in 'A Game of Division' (Fig. 17), published in 'civil right pictorial' in 1910, Westerners

Fig. 14 Cartoon in *Shishibao*, 1907 (no exact date given)

Participating in Global Affairs: The Chinese Cartoon Monthly *Shanghai Puck* 381

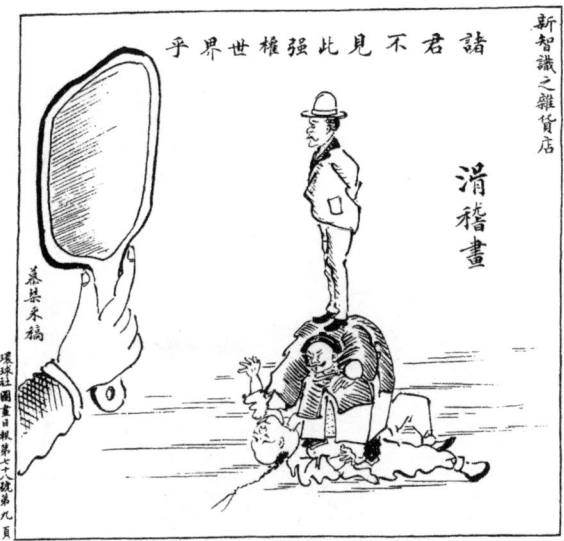

Fig. 15 'Can't you see the hegemony in the world?'. *Tuhua Ribao*, 1910 (no exact date given)

clutching a giant knife, try to cut a melon into pieces. The melon symbolises China, prepared for partition.

'*Shanghai Puck*' caricatures are somewhat different from these: they convey a slightly more hopeful attitude with regard to raising China onto the global stage. 'Mr Earth's weary party after the war' (Fig. 9), for example, depicts the Peace Conference as a feast in a hall with rows of national flags hanging overhead, highlighting internationalism. The bandaged earth is the host, inviting people from different countries to a main course of pork, in a depiction very similar to Fig. 16. Yet, in 'Shanghai Puck', a Chinese man has come to join the feast as well, even if he is small in size and held back by a huge Japanese hand right next to him.[18] Moreover, Fig. 18 also has some semblance with Fig. 17, because at the Peace Conference, an American is preparing to divide a melon with a knife aptly called 'Democracy'. We can see a Chinese man sitting among the onlookers as a participant.

The all but slight yet significant changes in these depictions clearly suggest China's rising status and her growing concern for international issues. In earlier depictions satire focused strongly on what happened within China, not outside her borders. This was a residue of the past when China had thought of herself as the

---

[18] This image, in spite of its attempt to raise China's position in the global context, simultaneously reveals the real situation China is in: small in size and obstructed by a huge Japanese hand beside it. This image caricatures the Paris Peace Conference in 1919 after World War One, in which most of the Chinese proposals were rejected, such as a call for an end to imperialist institutions, including extraterritoriality, legation guards, and foreign leaseholds. The conference even approved the transfer of German concessions in Shandong in China to Japan rather than return sovereign authority to China, which resulted in the Chinese delegation being the only one not to sign the Treaty of Versailles.

Fig. 16 'Foreigners divide up China among themselves'. *Minhu ribao,* 1909 (no exact date given)

centre of the world. In 'Shanghai Puck', however, the world has come to its readers. International inequalities still exist, but China is starting to get involved internationally. The tenor of these satirical images now is 'we face the same problems as others'; instead of the earlier 'we have problems with others'.

Moreover, the visual juxtaposition of particular symbols also prepares, metaphorically, for a new world order. From the third issue on, the editorial page and the last page of 'Shanghai Puck' were often decorated with the countries' national flags, either in the form of an angel holding flags or as a simple 'exhibition of flags'. This was done intentionally in order to introduce an image of internationality. The caricature entitled 'The question of Tsingtao' (Fig. 19), for example, is concerned with the Japanese intention to take on what once were German profits in Shandong. In the caricature, a Chinese man and a Japanese man sit next to each other as equals; neither is inferior to the other. However, the English caption reads sarcastically 'Drink up the beer and return the bottle generously' while in the Chinese translation

Participating in Global Affairs: The Chinese Cartoon Monthly *Shanghai Puck*   383

Fig. 17 'A game of division'. *Minquan ribao* 1910 (no exact date given).[19]

an addition is made at the end which openly expresses Chinese indignation: 'That is asking too much' (*weimian qirentaishen* 未免欺人太甚).

The idea of participating as an equal on a global level can be seen in the changing ways that foreigners (and their interactions with Chinese) were depicted.

Fig. 18 Cartoon by Shen Bochen. 'Shanghai Puck', 1 November 1918

---

[19] For a discussion of this image, see Rudolf G. Wagner, "China 'Asleep' and 'Awakening'. A Study in Conceptualizing Asymmetry and Coping With It", *Transcultural Studies* 1 (2011): 4–135).

Many pictures implicitly or explicitly criticise militarism (see Figs. 9 and 19). In one of these, for example, we see the German Kaiser jumping over the shoulders of Crown Prince Friedrich Wilhelm. The caption, 'Making it easy for him', indicates that the Crown Prince is responsible for assisting German militarism (*Shanghai Puck*, 1 November 1918). In an early issue of the 'Shanghai Puck', a one-page English essay is published which satirises the prince as the 'hand-shaker', a figure even more sinister than the Kaiser. His evilness is camouflaged by his image, that of a good-looking, kind and tender man. However, in truth, he is a proud, cruel and unsympathetic militarist. The picture is no doubt meant to serve as a complement to the essay ("The Hand-Shaker." Shanghai Puck, October 1918). Figure 6, too, demonstrates the kind of anti-militarism typical of the 'Shanghai Puck'. The ridiculously oversized head depicted there becomes a perfect target for the cannon of public opinion, which is believed to be capable of defeating militarism.

'Shanghai Puck' even satirises foreigners' images by imitating caricatures from foreign magazines. In 1906, *Tokyo Puck* carries a picture in which President Roosevelt is caricatured as a hugely obese, greasy king sat at a table (Fig. 20). He wears a belt displaying Pan-Americanism; the figure shows that the US has obviously found a better way to satisfy her own interest and strengthening her power by abandoning the former treaty and burning the Monroe Doctrine that is represented as a towel. Originally meant to stop European powers from influencing the US, the Monroe Doctrine was later interpreted as a way of interfering with US politics.

Fig. 19 'The question of Tsingtoa [*sic!*] (Tsingtao)'. Cartoon by Shen Bochen. 'Shanghai Puck', 1 December 1918

Fig. 20 'Pan-American Trust'. *Tokyo Puck*, 15 October 1906

Because of Pan-Americanism, the Americans would undertake many actions from which they profited. As this caricature insinuates King US has just eaten two courses, whose labelled remains are on the table: Cuba and the Philippines. And yet, these have not yet satisfied American greed. The world map on the wall behind fat King US indicates that he is now searching for his next 'meal'.

This caricature was meant as a smear campaign against the US, who advocated Pan-Americanism and put it into practice. The fat and clumsy body illustrates foolishness and rapacity; however, it also sends the message to Japanese society that the US may soon stretch out its claws to Japan, wield huge influence on her, and accomplish the King's conspiracy to bring the entire globe to his table.

Japan, in turn, adopted a similar strategy. Pan-Asianism/Great Asianism, proposed by Japan in the early twentieth century, urged the ideology that Asia should fight as one against Western imperialism by uniting in solidarity and creating a continental identity to perpetuate hegemony. Gradually, Pan-Asianism became the excuse to justify Japanese invasion, for example, in China. Therefore, from the Chinese perspective, Pan-Asianism served as a rationalisation for Japanese military aggression and political absorption. Under the cover of solidarity and cooperation, Japan attempted to assert control over China and the rest of East-Asia.

In the first issue of 'Shanghai Puck', Shen caricatured a similarly obese man, incapable of maintaining a proper posture due to his hugely oversized belly (Fig. 21). Two symbols reveal his national identity: the traditional kimono and slippers, which he wears, and Mount Fuji, in the background. Furthermore, he has a 'Pan-Asianism' sash wrapped around his extraordinary girth, likened to a huge balloon which seems about to burst. The caricature makes a clear visual declaration that it would be impossible for Japan to keep expanding without limitation under the camouflage of Pan-Asianism.

The Chinese caption satirises Japan with a parody of an ancient Chinese proverb, which is changed from 'The sun goes down after midday; the moon is eclipsed after a full moon' (*rizhong ze ze, yueying ze shi* 日中則昃, 月盈則食) to 'The sun goes

Fig. 21 Cartoon by Shen Bochen. 'Shanghai Puck', 1 September 1918

down after midday; the belly explodes after being sated' (*rizhong ze ze, fuman ze lie* 日中則昃, 腹滿則裂), i.e., Shen reversed the letter sun (*ri* 日) to literally and symbolically signify Japan (*riben* 日本) and the sun (*ri* 日) on the Japanese national flag. He thus mocks Japan's future in the same way that *Tokyo Puck* had mocked the US. Again, we see a web of satirical exchanges; again we see how contents and apparent asymmetries may be reversed in this process. The changes in the selection, and modification of pictorial elements from satire magazines world wide, thus reveal changing views of the power of China and Chinese public opinion.

Conclusion

The aim of this chapter was to discuss how the Western genre of the satirical cartoon magazine made its inroads into the Chinese public sphere and began to wield power over public concerns which derived from China's peculiar 'semi-colonised' status. As one of the first Chinese satire and cartoon monthlies, 'Shanghai Puck' shows itself in constant engagement with satirical publications worldwide. The *Puck*s and versions of *Punch* from which it draws its visual material are seen to belong to one global community of critical journals to which the Chinese journals such as the 'Shanghai Puck' also belong. As such, 'Shanghai Puck' took up its responsibilities within and for Chinese society, in the same way that similar magazines in Europe and elsewhere did. It expended its efforts in drawing satirical portraits of current politics, denouncing social evils and political chicanery, criticising what was felt as unfair, and reflecting public opinion, fearlessly, often against its own government and officials which were increasingly under attack after the diplomatic disaster at the Versailles Peace Treaty Negotiations and the ensuing May Fourth demonstrations in 1919.

'Shanghai Puck's' attempt to advocate China's participation and acceptance in global affairs is of great significance. On the pages of the 'Shanghai Puck', one can see the urge to comment on international issues and the call for China's inclusion in the global community. In these images, and in the bilingual texts that accompany them, the Chinese, instead of assuming the role of weak victims, present themselves as forward-thinking participants in a global *imaginaire*, sitting at the table with others, sharing a drink and a meal (almost) as equals and expressing their (often controversial and aptly (mis-)translated) opinions. 'Shanghai Puck', by taking up the template of the satirical cartoon magazine, thus addressed the asymmetries that came with China's semi-colonial status and attempted to not only bring the world to China but to present China to the world as well.

'He'll Roast All Subjects That May Need the Roasting': Puck and Mr Punch in Nineteenth-Century China

Christopher G. Rea

This chapter examines two *Punch*-inspired English-language periodicals published in colonial enclaves in nineteenth-century China: *The China Punch* (1867–1868, 1872–1876) and *Puck, or the Shanghai Charivari* (April 1871-November 1872).[1] The former was a subsidiary publication of the newspaper *The China Mail*, which since its inception in 1845 had been the 'Official Organ of all Government Notifications' in the British colony of Hong Kong; the latter was issued quarterly by a printing and stationary company in treaty-port Shanghai.[2] Both periodicals featured staples akin to London's *Punch* (1841–1992) such as whole-page caricatures, comedic verses, wry commentaries on local society and politics, filler jokes, and editorials written in the voice of their namesake trickster. Each struggled to solicit contributions from its small Anglophone community and ultimately ceased publication upon the abrupt departure of a proprietor.

Despite their short life spans and sometimes amateurish execution, these little-examined magazines are milestones in the history of the cartoon in China, not because of their influence on Chinese cartoonists, but as the earliest known examples of how foreigners brought literary humour and pictorial satire to bear on colonial society in China. Like the earlier Yokohama-based *Japan Punch* (1862–1887), each appears to have been the first humour magazine in its respective foreign enclave; both, I argue, thus constitute an important part of the colonial

---

[1] My thanks to Andrew Rodekohr at Harvard and Michel Hockx and Joshua Mostow (visiting) at SOAS for helping me obtain these two periodicals. Thanks also to Hans Harder for inviting me to Heidelberg and to workshop participants for several days of stimulating presentations and discussions.

[2] The terms 'colony' and 'treaty port' denote a basic legal distinction between these two locales. My use of the term 'colonial' throughout this chapter posits a 'colonial mindset' or 'colonial attitude', which, in my reading of these and other primary materials, were common to British inhabitants of both locations.

C.G. Rea (✉)
The University of British Columbia, Vancouver, BC, Canada
e-mail: chris.rea@ubc.ca

history of the entertainment press and the cartoon in China, having been published around the time Chinese print culture began to diversify in the 1870s.[3] The case of *Puck* is particularly interesting both because of its location in Shanghai, which was to dominate China's publishing market in ensuing decades,[4] and because evidence suggests that it had a readership overseas.

Indeed, these magazines are part of a global history of the dissemination of the visual grammars of cartoon and caricature during the age of colonialism. Both *The China Punch* (hereafter *China Punch*) and *Puck, or the Shanghai Charivari* (hereafter, *Puck*) were directly inspired by *Punch,* though, as Barbara Mittler and I-wei Wu also show in this volume, *Punch* progeny had already appeared elsewhere in East Asia, as well as in South Asia and other parts of the world. The foreign-language print milieu in which these humour publications appeared included both local and international periodicals, from commerce-focused colonial newspapers, that included dispatches and digests from other parts of the world, to popular periodicals from England, including *Punch* and *The Illustrated London News* (est. 1842).

Both periodicals made extensive use of satirical caricature in a mimetic idiom, in which distorted representations of officials and society types presume correspondence to a 'real' referent. This chapter, however, highlights *whimsy*—a partiality to fantastical and farcical conceits—as an essential part of their overarching comedic rubric. In particular, the titular comic personae of Mr Punch and Puck were invoked both as a license to be funny and as cosmic figures presiding over an otherworldly domain. In verse, prose, and cartoons alike, *China Punch*'s Hong Kong appears as a

---

[3] In Shanghai, for instance, *Puck* ceased publication in 1872, the same year that Ernest Major founded the more enduring *Shenbao*, from which later emerged the influential pictorial, *Dianshizhai huabao* (1884–1898). To note just a few historical studies that focus on print culture in later periods: Barbara Mittler's *A Newspaper for China? Power, Identity, and Change in Shanghai's News Media, 1872–1912* (Cambridge: Harvard University Asia Center, 2004) begins with the founding of *Shenbao* in 1872; Christopher A. Reed's *Gutenberg in Shanghai: Chinese Print Capitalism, 1876–1937* (Vancouver: University of British Columbia Press, 2004) begins with the introduction of lithography to China in 1876 by Jesuit missionaries; Catherine Vance Yeh's studies of the Shanghai entertainment press focus on *Youxi bao* 遊戲報 (founded in 1897) and its contemporaries, though they also extend earlier. See her "Shanghai Leisure, Print Entertainment, and the Tabloids, *xiaobao* 小報," in *Joining the Global Public: Word, Image, and City in Early Chinese Newspapers*, ed. Rudolf G. Wagner (Albany: State University of New York Press, 2007), 201–33; and *Shanghai Love: Courtesans, Intellectuals, & Entertainment Culture, 1850–1910* (Seattle: University of Washington Press, 2006). Robert E. Hegel's *Reading Illustrated Fiction in Late Imperial China* (Stanford: Stanford University Press, 1998) briefly discusses Western-style cartoons in a comparative, rather than genealogical, context. Jonathan Hay has noted that the illustrated magazine *The Far East* (1876–1878) helped introduce photographs to Shanghai print culture, transforming illustration style. See: "Notes on Chinese Photography and Advertising in Late Nineteenth-Century Shanghai," in *Visual Culture in Shanghai, 1850s–1930s*, ed. Jason C. Kuo (Washington, DC: New Academia Publishing, 2007), 95–119.

[4] According to one estimate, Shanghai accounted for 86 % of books published in China between the 1880s and 1937. See: Alexander Des Forges, *Mediasphere Shanghai: The Aesthetics of Cultural Production* (Honolulu: University of Hawai'i Press, 2007), 17.

dream world, and *Puck*'s Shanghai as a fairyland. Both also make frequent references to Shakespeare, a consummate symbol of English culture, and in particular *A Midsummer Night's Dream*, the *locus classicus* of the Puck character. I argue that Shakespeare, who appears frequently in London's *Punch* as the 'national dramatist', and whose works '[w]ithin Victorian culture at large [...] served as a kind of literary and moral touchstone',[5] had special meaning in the colonial context. In light of their laments about diplomatic isolation and the insularity of local society, the whimsical use of Shakespearean motifs reveal self-consciousness about the theatrical nature of colonial life, and signify the periphery's longing for a cultural 'home'. Innocuous though it may seem, whimsy's imaginative openness helps us identify comedic agendas not detectable in satire's more restricted focus on representation.

The humour in these monolingual magazines offered their readers 'a vacation from thinking', to borrow the Chinese intellectual Qian Zhongshu's 錢鍾書 (1910–1998) phrase, in indulging their prejudices.[6] I show that while many of the cultural prejudices we see in these magazines are typical of colonial contact zones, others are unexpected. If we would expect to see stock caricatures of Chinese people, equal space is given to caricatures of Irish...fellow colonials. Combined with their presumption of reader familiarity with a wide array of other periodicals from Asia and Europe, they exhibit an orientation that is simultaneously provincial (in indulging pre-existing prejudices) and cosmopolitan (in reading habits). While these two magazines apparently had no lasting influence on Chinese print culture, I argue that they offer revelations about the imaginative life of British colonists in mid-nineteenth century Asia.

'Print Comedy' and the Press in Early Modern China

The colonial perspective offers new insights into the history of what I will call 'print comedy'—comedic modes (satire, farce, whimsy, etc.) and comedic forms (cartoons, caricature, parodic verse, etc.) in print culture—in China. China-related print comedy studies to date have focused primarily on Chinese-language publications during and after the Shanghai periodical boom of the 1890s, especially the 'golden age' of Chinese cartooning in the 1930s, and WWII.[7] Mainland Chinese

---

[5] Alan R. Young, *Punch and Shakespeare in the Victorian Era* (Bern: Peter Lang, 2007), 11. On *Punch* and 'Shakespeareanity', see Young's Chap. 2, esp. 69–70 on *Punch*'s famous reverse caricature of Shakespeare as Chinese, inspired by an 1842 London exhibition of Chinese artefacts.

[6] See: "A Prejudice" [1939], in Qian Zhongshu, *Human, Beasts, and Ghosts: Stories and Essays*, ed. Christopher G. Rea (New York: Columbia University Press, 2011), 62–65.

[7] See, for example: Hongying Liu-Lengyel, "Chinese Cartoons: History and Present Status" (PhD diss., Temple University, 1993); John A. Lent, "Comic Art," in *Handbook of Chinese Popular Culture*, ed. Wu Dingbo and Patrick D. Murphy (Westport: Greenwood Press, 1994), 279–306;

scholarship has historically treated cartoon periodicals, many of which had bilingual captioning, as if they were purely 'Chinese' publications, and dismissed foreign-language periodicals in general as the 'mouthpieces of imperialists'.[8] As Rudolf Wagner has repeatedly pointed out,[9] however, such nationalistic moralising has severely distorted our picture of nineteenth- and early twentieth-century China's print culture and public sphere.

Studies of cartoons,[10] for instance, have to date concentrated on Chinese-language publications and periodicals run by Chinese proprietors. Bi Keguan 畢克官 and Huang Yuanlin's 黃遠林 pioneering study, *Zhongguo manhua shi* 中國漫畫史 (a history of cartoons in China, 1986) traces a genealogy back to such pre-modern proto-cartoons as stone etchings (*shike* 石刻) from the Eastern Han dynasty (25–220 CE) and humorous brush paintings from the Ming dynasty (1368–1644). Foreign language and foreign-owned periodicals in Qing dynasty and Republican China are virtually absent from this history, despite the testimony of Chinese cartoonists that they read them and in some cases worked for them.[11]

Chang-Tai Hung, "The Fuming Image: Cartoons and Public Opinion in Late Republican China, 1945 to 1949," *Comparative Studies in Society and History* 36, no.1 (1994): 122–45. Of these, Lent's 'Comic Art,' a historical overview, has the most to say about the nineteenth century, albeit from a bird's-eye view.

[8] For a representative example of this rhetoric, see Fang Hanqi 方漢奇, *Zhongguo jindai baokanshi* 中國近代報刊史 (a history of late Qing and early Republican periodicals) (Taiyuan: Shanxi Educational Press, 1996), 31–38 *passim*, which appears under the heading, 'wei zhiminzhuyi yaoqi nahan de waiwen baozhi 為殖民主義搖旗吶喊的外文報紙 (Foreign-language newspapers waving the flag and shouting the slogans of colonialism)'. The only book to date focused on foreign-language periodicals in early modern Shanghai is Shen Shuang's *Cosmopolitan Publics: Anglophone Print Culture in Semi-Colonial Shanghai* (Camden: Rutgers University Press, 2009), which is concerned primarily with configurations of cosmopolitanism from the 1920s to the 1940s.

[9] See, for example: Rudolf G. Wagner, "The Role of the Foreign Community in the Chinese Public Sphere," *China Quarterly* 142, no. 6 (1995): 423–43; Wagner, *Joining the Global Public*; and Wagner, "Don't Mind the Gap! The Foreign-language Press in Late-Qing and Republican China," *China Heritage Quarterly* 30/31 (June/Sept. 2012): http://www.chinaheritagequarterly.org/features.php?searchterm=030_wagner.inc&issue=030 (accessed 15 March 2013).

[10] Various Chinese terms for cartoon, comic, and caricature have held currency at different points in time since the nineteenth century. The current umbrella term is *manhua* 漫畫, from the Japanese *manga* 漫畫, whose popularisation in China beginning in the 1920s is generally credited to the famed Chinese *manhua* artist Feng Zikai 豐子愷 (1898–1975), the subject of the monograph: Geremie Barmé, *An Artistic Exile: A Life of Feng Zikai (1898–1975)* (Berkeley: University of California Press, 2002). *Fengcihua* 諷刺話 (satirical drawing, caricature) and *lianhuanhua* 連環畫 (comic strip, cartoon storybook) are just two of many subcategories. While scholars have differing opinions about the exact scope of *manhua*, in practice it is used to denote a wide range of pictorial humour and satire. In the pages of *China Punch* and *Puck*, the terms that appear are 'cartoon', 'caricature', and 'drawing'.

[11] Cartoonist Ye Qianyu 葉淺予 (1907–1996), for example, was an enthusiastic reader of *The China Press* (aka *Ta-lu bao* 大陸報, 1911–1941, 1945–1949), an English-language newspaper founded by three Americans, which serialised John McManus's comic strip *Bringing Up Father* (1913–2000), which in turn inspired Ye's hit comic strip 'Mr Wang'. See: Ye Qianyu 葉淺予, *Ye*

A case in point is Bi and Huang's cursory treatment of *Dianshizhai huabao* 點石齋畫報 (1884–1898), which the authors admit was 'the most influential' pictorial of the late Qing period. The periodical is relegated to a footnote on the grounds that its visual style was not cartoon-like enough to warrant discussion.[12] This aesthetic distinction seems arbitrary, however, given the inclusion of the above-mentioned cartoon antecedents, and further overlooks *Dianshizhai*'s measurable influence on humorous images in pictorials such as 'pictorial daily' (*Tuhua ribao* 圖畫日報, 1909–1910).[13] A more likely, unstated reason for the omission is that it was founded by a foreigner, Ernest Major (1841–1908), the proprietor of the major newspaper *Shenbao* 申報 (1872–1949), and was therefore insufficiently 'Chinese'.[14]

Adopting a 'functional as opposed to a moral treatment'[15] of colonial print comedy in Hong Kong and Shanghai enables us to identify a sensibility at work in these magazines: *whimsy*. Whimsy—namely, an inclination towards or

---

Qianyu zizhuan: Xixu cangsang ji liunian 葉淺予自傳:細敍滄桑記流年 (*The Autobiography of Ye Qianyu: Carefully Narrating the Changes of the Ages, Recording the Passing Years*) (Beijing: Shehui kexue chubanshe, 2006), 64. (Ye mistakenly gives the English title of the newspaper as *China Daily*.)

[12] Bi and Huang state unconvincingly that 'Although its timely reflections on society and current events bear some resemblance to cartoons of current events (*shishi manhua* 時事漫畫), they diverge in the specific manner of their conception and execution. Thus, we believe that the earlier denotation of this periodical as "China's first cartoon periodical" is inappropriate'. See: Bi Keguan 畢克官 and Huang Yuanlin 黃遠林, *Zhongguo manhua shi* 中國漫畫史 (a history of cartoons in China) (Beijing: Wenhua yishu chubanshe, 1986), 16–17, esp. 16, note 2.

[13] See: Lei Qinfeng 雷勤風 (Christopher G. Rea), "Jietan xiangyu de ciyuanxue: Lun Qingmo Minchu de Shanghai suyu tushuo 街談巷語的辭源學—論清末民初的上海俗語圖說 (alleyway etymology: illustrated dictionaries of Shanghai slang, 1900s–1940s)," in *Zhongguo jinxiandai baokan yu wenhua yanjiu: diba jie guoji qingnian xuezhe hanxue huiyi lunwenji* 中國近現代報刊與文化研究:第八屆國際青年學者漢學會議論文集 (Early Modern Print Culture in China: Papers from the Eighth International Junior Scholars Conference on Sinology), ed. Cheng Wen-huei 鄭文惠 (Taipei: Huayi chubanshe, forthcoming).

[14] *Dianshizhai huabao* has subsequently been recognised as a catalyst for the incorporation of images in the Chinese print media. See, for example: Wagner, "Foreign Community"; Christopher A. Reed, "Re/Collecting the Sources: Shanghai *Dianshizhai* Pictorial and Its Place in Historical Memories, 1884–1949," *Modern Chinese Literature and Culture* 12, no. 2 (2000): 44–72; Ye Xiaoqing, *The* Dianshizhai *Pictorial: Shanghai Urban Life, 1884–1898* (Ann Arbor: The University of Michigan Centre for Chinese Studies, 2003); and Rudolf G. Wagner, "Joining the Global Imaginaire: The Shanghai Illustrated Newspaper *Dianshizhai huabao*," in Wagner, *Joining the Global Public*, 105–73. Rudolf Wagner, for example, has credited Major with 'pioneer[ing] the use of the image in the new mass media', adding that, '[t]he *Dianshizhai huabao*, which he published from 1882, established the illustrated paper in the style of the *Illustrated London News*, *Harpers* [*New Monthly Magazine*, est. 1850] or *The Graphic* [est. 1869] among the Chinese media'. See: Wagner, "Foreign Community," 440. On the adaptation of foreign images and news items into the *Dianshizhai*, see: Julia Henningsmeier, "The Foreign Sources of *Dianshizhai Huabao* 點石齋畫報, a Nineteenth Century Shanghai Illustrated Magazine," *Ming Qing Yanjiu* (1998), 59–91.

[15] Wagner, "Foreign Community," 426.

indulgence in extravagant fancies—is a familiar part of the *Punch* idiom,[16] but one that rarely enters into discussions of comedy in China. Whimsy underlies the comic conceits of *China Punch* and *Puck* and informs much of their content, both literary and pictorial. More than just an editorial or readerly disposition towards the frivolous, it shapes the overarching comedic logic of the magazines. We see this first in the figure of each publication's titular trickster, a leitmotif who provides the fictional or imaginary context for the humour therein. Whereas Mr Punch is lord of his domain—a mock colonial administrator—Puck is a pixie with supernatural powers of transformation. Second, Shakespearean language is repeatedly used to 'stage' China in a British idiom. Finally, we see whimsy in both magazines' idiosyncratic mix of caricatures, verses, 'filler' jokes, puns, and other, even more miscellaneous content. These three features are related: by establishing a loose thematic framework, the editors grant themselves broad comic license and can follow their fancies in populating its pages. Whimsy, in this sense, is closely related to farce, whose scope of vision is totalising or 'cosmic,' rather than strictly mimetic. Satire, the descriptor most commonly applied to *Punch*-style cartoons and magazines, in contrast, presumes a one-to-one correspondence between real individuals or classes and a degraded representation.[17] As I show below, however, satire was but one part of the comic appeal of *Punch*'s colonial progeny.

Hong Kong as a Dream World

The China Punch (1867–1868, 1872–1876) appeared about a quarter century into Hong Kong's colonial history. Hong Kong Island had been a crown colony since 1842, when the Treaty of Nanking formalised the end of the First Opium War (1839–1942), though it had been occupied by British forces since 1841. As a part of the British Empire, Hong Kong served as a military and economic base for protecting British interests in the region, especially mainland China. Following the Second Opium War (1856–1858), Britain expanded the territory of the colony by annexing the Kowloon peninsula and Stonecutter's Island. Up to 1898, when Britain

---

[16] Richard Altick, for example, distinguishes *Punch* from one of its important predecessors by noting: 'Also absent from *Figaro in London* [est. 1831], also, were the social satire and whimsy that characterized the writings and pictures of the two men who most influenced the direction the new weekly was to take by showing how it was possible to avoid the gamy flavor that had permeated the humorous journalism of the 1830s'. See: Richard D. Altick, *Punch: The Lively Youth of a British Institution 1841–1851* (Columbus: Ohio State University Press, 1997), 3.

[17] For an in-depth discussion of the distinction between the totalising vision of farce and the mimetic or 'significative' practice of satire, see: Edith Kern, *The Absolute Comic* (New York: Columbia University Press, 1980).

signed a 99-year lease on the New Territories, then, 'British living in Hong Kong had strong reason to believe that Hong Kong was theirs'[18] and always would be.

China Punch was a subsidiary publication of *The China Mail* (est. 1845)—which it dubbed *The China Snail*—one of the three main English-language newspapers that catered to Hong Kong's Anglophone population.[19] In addition to government and commercial notices, classified advertisements, and local news, the newspaper also carried digests of news from papers in Europe, Australia, and elsewhere in Asia.[20] *China Punch*'s potential local readership was in the low thousands. According to G.B. Endacott's *A History of Hong Kong*, in 1865 Hong Kong had a total estimated population of 125,504, of which 2,034 were Europeans and 1,645 'coloured' people. After dipping slightly to 121,985 in 1872, the population of the colony grew to 138,144 by 1876, and accelerated in the following decades.

The British community in nineteenth-century Hong Kong included merchants, civil servants, military personnel, missionaries, journalists, bankers, tradesmen, sailors, and various types of drifters. Anecdotal evidence suggests that the white-collar class, British assistants in merchant firms, had ample time for leisure reading. Gillian Bickley cites the observations of a British entertainer who visited Hong Kong in 1858 that '[t]he young men in the different large houses have a sad mind-mouldering time of it [...]. They loaf about the balconies of their houses, or lie in long bamboo chairs; smoke a great deal; play billiards at the club, where the click of the ball never ceases, from earliest morning; and glance vacantly over their local papers'.[21] Even if Hong Kong was to be Britain's for good, it still felt like a transient place where 'only the temporary was permanent'.[22] This was a community in search of diversion.

---

[18] Gillian Bickley, "Early Beginnings of the British Community (1841–1898)," in *Foreign Communities in Hong Kong, 1840s–1950s*, ed. Cindy Yik-yi Chu (New York: Palgrave Macmillan, 2005), 17–39; 18.

[19] The other two were: *Hong Kong Daily Press* (1857–1941) and *The Daily Advertiser* (1871–1873), which later became *The Hong Kong Times: Daily Advertiser and Shipping Gazette*, (1873–1876). Another major English newspaper, *The Friend of China and Hongkong Gazette* (est. 1842) had recently closed, in 1859. Since 1858 *The China Mail* had also published a Chinese edition. See: Lin Yutang, *A History of the Press and Public Opinion in China* (Chicago: The University of Chicago Press, 1936), 80–81. Lin notes an 'interesting point was the fact that the earliest Chinese dailies started in the 1860's as Chinese editions or issues of some foreign daily papers' (87) including *The China Mail*, suggesting that *China Punch* should have been known to some Chinese readers. For a bibliography of Hong Kong newspapers up to 1979 (which does not list *China Punch*), see: Kan Lai-bing and Grace H. L. Chu, *Newspapers of Hong Kong, 1841–1979* (Hong Kong: Chinese University of Hong Kong, 1981).

[20] A typical issue might feature digests from, for example, the *Manchester Guardian*, *Liverpool Times*, *Hallowell Gazette*, *South Australian Register*, the *Canton Register*, and 'our overland edition'.

[21] Bickley, "British Community," 26. Bickley later makes the point that there existed 'no single British community, but several communities' (33).

[22] Quoted in N.J. Giradot, *The Victorian Translation of China: James Legge's Oriental Pilgrimage* (Berkeley: University of California Press, 2002), 69.

Fig. 1 Original cover illustration of *The China Punch*. *The China Punch* 1, no.1, 28 May 1867

The first order of business for *China Punch*, as later for *Puck*, was to define its comic domain—China—and to assert its authority over it. For *China Punch*'s editors, China came with a ready-made set of associations. The original cover illustration, for instance, features Mr Punch—recognisable by his large nose—in the stereotyped guise of a Qing official, complete with cap, pigtail, robe decorated with a dragon and tigers, and long fingernails (Fig. 1). He stands on a book with 'his arms open to welcome the reader', his head and a Chinese landscape framed within a 'symmetrical design of dragons holding a circular plate'[23] topped with a pagoda, all circumscribed within a rectangular bamboo frame. More subtly, Mr Punch hints his irreverence by winking at the reader, while the two dragons appear to be thumbing their noses at each other.

A revised cover appeared when *China Punch* resumed publication in November 1872 (Fig. 2). The new version featured a similar array of pseudo-Chinese imagery surrounding the central figure of Mr Punch, again clad in the Qing mantle of authority. He sits in the middle of the page underneath the magazine title: a bamboo 'CHINA' being hammered into the wall by a coolie standing on a bamboo rod, from which hang dragons that spell out 'PUNCH'. Mr Punch has his foot on a book, and

---

[23] The original cover was used for 16 issues, from 28 May 1867 to 9 January 1868. Quotations from: Wendy Siuyi Wong, *Hong Kong Comics: A History of Manhua* (New York: Princeton Architectural Press, 2002), 31.

Fig. 2 Cover illustration of the revived *China Punch* 2, no. 2, December 1872

sits opposite a stone lion, which rests its paw on a globe. As Barbara Mittler points out in the epilogue, the lion may be a local substitute for Toby, Mr Punch's dog in London, here projecting less canine companionship than imperial domination. Mr Punch's comedic authority in the new cover is symbolised by his grotesque nose and the big books of 'Hoax'[24] and 'Wit' that lean against the back of his chair.

Amidst this Chinoiserie, several textual allusions to Shakespeare entreat the reader to view the theatre of wit within its pages with a sympathetic heart. Mr Punch gestures with his hand and eyes towards a hanging scroll that reads: 'Take our Good Morning, for our judgment sits / Five times in that ere once in our five wits',[25] a line spoken by Mercutio in *Romeo and Juliet* (I, iv, 46–47). A vertical scroll on the left reads: 'We beseech thee take it not amiss', an adaptation of Gloucester's line from *Richard III* (III, vii, 209): 'I do beseech you, take it not

---

[24] One *Punch* historian notes that 'In the first part of the nineteenth century the hoax was a favourite kind of practical joke [...]. The jester's mask that was an emblem of [*Punch*'s] trade enabled it to keep a straight face, thus lending plausibility to its fictions'. See: Altick, *Punch*, xxi.

[25] Some scholars interpret 'Five wits' as meaning 'five senses'.

amiss'. To the right is a vertical scroll which is unrolled enough to read 'If we offend, it is. . .'—the beginning of Quince's Prologue to 'Pyramus and Thisbe', the play-within-a-play in *A Midsummer Night's Dream* (V, 1, 116): 'If we offend, it is with our goodwill'. This last line is an ironic choice, since in *Midsummer Night's Dream* Quince's convoluted appeal inspires only mockery from his audience of nobles. Whether or not the specific allusions were recognisable to readers of the day, their subject and rhyme establish a theme of well-intentioned wit—a pre-emptive self defence by a humour publication wary of offending its readership.

Mr Punch, a puppet whose comedy originally consisted of mimicry and the well-timed wallop, would of course need little introduction to Britons abroad in the 1870s. In the first issue of the revived *China Punch*, however, Mr Punch makes his narrative return to Hong Kong in a peculiar way: by slipping into a dream

> MR PUNCH lay, in his arm-chair, asleep; he had just returned from Pekin, having been present at the Emperor of China's wedding. Ah! favoured mortal; but then, *Punch*, all over the wide world, wherever Britons dwell, reigns as King. *Punch* is always—*Punch!*[26]

Mr Punch dreams of being visited by an old man, a representative of Commerce, who grumbles about bureaucratic red-tape. '"Peace!" said *Mr Punch*, "I will see to this"'. A sword hanging on the wall then laments to Mr Punch that Hong Kong's inhabitants 'live alone for gold and gain' and 'have no ambitions above figures', disdaining valour. Impatiently dismissed by Mr Punch, the sword is followed by representatives of various social activities of the colony, such as boating, ballet, horse racing, theatre, cricket, and rowing, whom Mr Punch greets more amiably: 'I know ye all: fear not, I will be your friend'. Finally, Mr Punch is met by a 'dear little woman' who asks him to put a fashion column in the next issue of his magazine.

Through this dream reception, Mr Punch promises (through his new publication) to remonstrate with colonial administrators, exhort citizens to pursue higher ideals, and contribute to the entertainment options in the colony. Indeed, throughout *China Punch*'s run, Mr Punch acts as benevolent lord of misrule over these constituencies—commerce, leisure, and the (rare) fair sex—considering petitions, entertaining requests, presiding at court, and giving all those under him just enough print space to make fools of themselves before cutting them short. In his topsy-turvy world, government officials can do no right, gender norms are suspended (if not inverted), and Europeans are often at the mercy of their supposed inferiors, the Chinese.

China Punch's Hong Kong is quickly revealed to be a city of dreamers, and Mr Punch tasks himself with puncturing their delusions. He takes an interest not only in the surreal official proceedings of the colonial government (discussed below), but also in the fantasies that the Oriental dream world engenders among Europeans.

---

[26] *The China Punch* 2, no.1, November 1872 (no date given), 3. This is Mr Punch's first, but not last, China dream. One later caricature (*The China Punch* 2, no. 5, 20 February 1873, 6) has Mr Punch reclining on a couch, a copy of *The China Mail* and an opium pipe by his side, dreaming of aspects of contemporary Hong Kong life, such as late steamers and horse racing.

A recurring theme is the ever-renewing crop of Western fortune-seekers arriving in the colony. Adopting the jaded voice of experience, *China Punch* takes these young lads to task for their naïveté, while lamenting the siren song of the East, as in the following poem:

Six Simpletons.
Three Youths they resolv'd to sail out to the East,
Away to the East, call'd the Far Cathay;
Each thought that of riches he'd soon have a feast—
Their friends seemed quite happy to get them away!
    For sons must work, if their fathers be poor,
    And better to leave for abroad, I'm sure,
        That [*sic*] at home be in poverty moaning.
Three maidens grand castles built high in the air,
And deck'd them with thoughts of a speedy return;
How, with well-to-do husbands, in marriage they'd pair—
And then all their poorer relations they'd spurn!
    Thus, while men did work, the women in sleep
    Laid up for themselves cruel waking to reap
        Accompanied soon with sad moaning.—
Three Clerks are a-toiling away in the East,
Away in the East, call'd the Far Cathay;
But their purse hasn't swollen with golden yeast—
And it's difficult sometimes their chits to pay!
    Alas! they must work to the end of their lives,
    But they never can make these girls their wives—
        For China with poverty's moaning![27]

In the poem, The East, or 'Far Cathay', is a dream world to those in Europe but a land of fruitless toil for those on the ground. While striking a rueful tone about how China makes Westerners 'moan', it is quite ambivalent about the young dreamers themselves, whose poverty might inspire sympathy, but whose friends 'seemed quite happy to get them away!' and whose fiancées relish the prospect of looking down on poor relations.

A Page in the Life

The regular fare of *China Punch* includes caricatures of colonial government officials and their Chinese counterparts, roundups of fictitious social events, parodic telegrams and letters to the editor, witty rhymes on financial, political, commercial, and social topics, and copious one-off puns. A sense of its heterogenous content literary can be gained from a sample page from an early number (*China Punch* 2, no. 1, November 1872, 7), which includes four features, a joke, and a call for submissions.

'At the Opera' is a snapshot depicting a chattering audience during a fictional Anglo social event: an amateur opera performance of *Macbeth* at the German Club. Audience 'types' take turns voicing their opinions on the performance, though

---

[27] *The China Punch* 2, no. 17, 25 May 1874, 12.

most, we are told, 'have come to drink'. Visitors from Shanghai and Yokohama allude to the superiority of the 'German performances' in their own colonial enclaves to an American visitor, who replies only 'let's liquor'. An 'Ancient and loyal Briton' huffs about a play in a British colony being performed in German, to which a German replies that his is the language of the future. The sole Hong Kong Resident, meanwhile, is not allowed to get a word in edgewise. Filling in the bottom of the left column is a brief call for submissions, and above it a joke: 'An elegant friend of ours, a passionate admirer of the fair sex generally, has been understood to state the only woman he was not partial to was Carry—Cature'.

The right column contains three features. 'Latest Telegrams' consists of five enthusiastic responses of fictitious *China Punch* readers ('Should Punch really come out, I will leave for Hongkong by next mail certain'. 'Charter P.&O. Steamer, to carry copies to meet demand. Intense excitement old China residents'). Below is 'The Queen of Cathay', a rhyme in pidgin by 'Alfred Tenis Enlister' (Tennyson?). Written in the voice of a Chinese woman, the vulgar vernacular clashes with the speaker's aristocratic pretensions. The third and final stanza gives a sense of the tone:

> My go sleep litte tim to-nightee, Amah, to-mollow you show my chop chop,
> Must fixee that hair tea-pot fashion, gala, and puttee that flower on top,
> Must paintee my facee and wear handsome clothesee, that chair soon come take my away,
>   For my belong Queen of Cathay, Amah, my belong Queen of Cathay.

The third section contains four 'Hongkong Nursery Rhymes', along the following lines:

> Stickery stickery stock
> (Trash, according to Jock);
> Investors fall on
> And buy till its gone—
> Stickery stickery stock.

In one page, then, we see a variety of comedic modes, including satirical mimicry (opera), parody (nursery rhyme), travesty (Cathay), and puns, as well as topics such as society, commerce, uppity natives, vain women, and the magazine itself (Carry-Cature). Uniting them is a veneer of whimsy, most strongly expressed in the infantile language of the verses and the self-indulgent tone of the pun. I will now briefly introduce *China Punch*'s contemporary, *Puck*, before turning to an examination of both periodicals' comedic treatment of race, gender, politics, and social life.

Shanghai as a Fairyland

The inaugural issue of *Puck, or the Shanghai Charivari* (1871–1872), issued by the Shanghai printer and stationer F&C Walsh, appeared on April Fools' Day, 1871. The timing is notable not just because of the joke date but because it occurred less than a month after the first issue of the better-known American *Puck* was published in St. Louis, Missouri.[28] Given that mail service between London and Hong Kong took 6 weeks,[29] however, it seems improbable that *Puck* was the inspiration for its Shanghai cousin, though the coincidence is highly suggestive. Only seven issues of the Walsh's *Puck* are extant. Issue six (1 July 1872) announces the death of C. Walsh, but no cessation notice appears in the last issue, dated 15 November 1872.

Shanghai was then one of five Chinese seaports (the others being Guangzhou [Canton], Xiamen [Amoy], Fuzhou, and Ningbo) where foreigners had been allowed to live since the signing of the Treaty of Nanking. In 1842, the Chinese population had been concentrated in a walled city while foreigners established 'settlements' bordering Shanghai's main waterway, the Huangpu River. In the years leading up to *Puck*'s founding, treaty port Shanghai was in the throes of change. The Taiping rebellion (1851–1864) had led to an economic boom in Shanghai as half a million refugees flowed into the foreign settlements from the provinces. When the rebellion was crushed, these refugees left in droves, leaving the city's economy gutted. In the British Settlement, for example, the Chinese population 'fell from over 500,000 to just 77,000 in less than a year (1864–1865) and to just 51,421 by 1870'.[30] That year the total foreign population of Shanghai numbered 1,666—down from 2,297 in 1865, but thrice the 1860 population. British residents accounted for over half this total,[31] and, as in Hong Kong, women were a small minority.

Given this population base, *Puck*'s potential local European readership during the early 1980s was likely in the hundreds. According to the census, Shanghai in 1870 had 1,149 residents from English-speaking countries (predominantly from Great Britain and the United States). Assuming that some other foreign nationals could read English, and that *Puck* had some distribution in other treaty ports in the region, its readership could have been as high as the low thousands. *Puck* did have some Chinese readers, as we shall see, but its content seems clearly designed to appeal to Westerners.

---

[28] *Puck* (1871–1918) was to become the United States' first successful humour magazine featuring cartoons and caricatures, publishing both English and German editions, both of which gained wide popularity for their timely political satire and creative illustrations. The magazine soon moved its operations to New York City (the German edition in 1876, the English edition in 1877).

[29] Bickley, "British Attitudes," 47. The telegraph first reached Shanghai (from Hong Kong, via underwater cable) the same month that *Puck, or the Shanghai Charivari* first appeared (April 1871), so it is highly unlikely that its creators would have even heard of the St. Louis *Puck*, much less been able to peruse its layout, in advance of their first issue. On China's nineteenth-century communications infrastructure, see: Erik Baark, *Lightning Wires: The Telegraph and China's Technological Modernization, 1860–1890* (Westport: Greenwood Press, 1997), 82. For a history of the telegraph in Hong Kong, see: Austin Coates, *Quick Tidings of Hong Kong* (Hong Kong: Oxford University Press, 1990).

[30] Edward Denison and Guang Yu Ren *Building Shanghai: The Story of China's Gateway* (Chichester: Wiley-Academy Press, 2006), 66.

[31] Ibid, 251–52. The total foreign population of Shanghai remained under 5,000 until 1895, when it began a rapid rise that continued until the outbreak of war with Japan in 1937.

Major changes were afoot in Shanghai's media environment. Like Hong Kong, Shanghai had several English-language newspapers in the 1870s, the largest being *The North-China Daily Herald and News*, which had been founded by a Canadian in 1850.[32] The *Evening Express* (est. 1867) and *The Shanghai Evening Courier* (est. 1868),[33] both new arrivals, are mentioned in the pages of *Puck*. More importantly, telegraph service officially opened in Shanghai from Hong Kong in April 1971—the same month that *Puck* first appeared—a major step in linking the region to the outside world, and which helped to spur the growth of the local media, notably the influential Chinese-language newspaper *Shenbao*, which was founded in 1872.

If *China Punch*'s Hong Kong was a dream world, *Puck* transports the reader into an East–west fantasy realm through its use of Shakespearean motifs from *A Midsummer Night's Dream* (Fig. 3). Its cover illustration is dominated by the word PUCK in lettering that resembles tree roots (perhaps symbolising the Athenian forest), upon which clamber tiny, pigtailed Chinese men, underneath which is a large image of a winged Puck 'put[ting] a girdle round about the earth' (*Midsummer*, II.i.178–179), while looking left toward a giant mosquito. The image is flanked by two ladders overflowing with Chinese (left) and drunken foreigners (right). At the top, five bowing foreigners face five bowing Chinese with a pagoda in the middle.[34]

At the bottom of the page, the words 'A Midsummer Night's Dream' stand out above detail of lounging foreigners being served drinks by Chinese as jumbo insects hover overhead. This last detail presents the 'midsummer night's dream' of Shanghailanders as one of Western leisure and Chinese servitude. Later, the Shanghai dream is shown to be at risk of turning into a nightmare. In the fifth issue of *Puck*, a full-page cartoon shows a dreaming Puck having 'A Vision of the Future' (Fig. 4) in which the power relationship is inverted, and Europeans have become nannies, attendants, and coolies of Chinese.

Like the enchanted wood in *A Midsummer Night's Dream*, *Puck*'s Shanghai wreaks changes on how outsiders see, dress, think, behave, and speak. Complementing

---

[32] It changed its name from *The North-China Herald* in 1864. Like *The China Mail*, it also published a Chinese edition, *Shanghai Xinbao* 上海新報 (1863–1866), which attracted readers with news about the Taipings. A new Chinese edition, *Hubao* 滬報, was founded in 1882 and headed by Sinologist Frederic Henry Balfour. See: Roswell S. Britton, *The Chinese Periodical Press, 1800–1912* [Shanghai: Kelly & Walsh,1933], reprint. ed. (Taipei: Ch'eng-wen Publishing Company, 1966), 49. On *The North-China Herald* as a 'globalising' force in Shanghai, see: Jeffrey N. Wasserstrom, *Global Shanghai, 1850–2010: A History in Fragments* (New York: Routledge, 2009), 21–33.

[33] A weekly edition, *Shanghai Budget and Weekly Courier*, was issued beginning 1871. Another major English-language paper, *The Celestial Empire* (1874–1929), was founded a few years later. Three short-lived French papers were reportedly published between 1870 and 1873. See the entry on "Press, European" in Samuel Couling, *The Encyclopaedia Sinica* (London: Oxford University Press, 1917).

[34] Like its American cousin, the Walshes' *Puck* in its pages invokes its namesake's famous exclamation, 'What fools these mortals be!' though not on its cover, where we simply *see* the clambering and tumbling fools.

Fig. 3 *Puck* cover illustration showing Chinese and foreigners bowing to each other (*top*), falling drunkards (*sides*), and relaxing foreigners being served drinks by Chinese while gigantic bugs circle overhead (*bottom*). *Puck, or the Shanghai Charivari* 1, 1 April 1871

the trope of the naïve and bewildered new arrival, lamented in the *China Punch* poem 'Six Simpletons', is the long-time sojourner who has unwittingly gone native. In one pair of cartoons, a 'New Arrival in China' misunderstands the pidgin phrase 'chop chop catchie dinner' (i.e., Hurry up and prepare dinner) to mean that his servant is going to have to go hunting, while a repatriated 'China Hand' astonishes his British servant by asking her 'What side have puttee that chow-chow?' (i.e., Where's my dinner?).[35] The two cartoons present a compressed arc of the Shanghailander experience, in which

---

[35] The cartoons are preceded by a full-page caricature of an extremely tall gentleman whose height puns on him having been 'Too Long in China!' See: *Puck, or the Shanghai Charivari* 4, 1 January 1872, 52–53.

Fig. 4 Puck envisions the future of Sino-British relations as a reversed hierarchy of servitude. *Puck, or the Shanghai Charivari* 5, 1 May 1872, 70

prolonged contact with the Chinese turns a man, Bottom-like, into an ass without his realising it.³⁶

Puck Arrives in Shanghai

The fairyland theme is introduced in the first issue in a long poem describing Puck's arrival in Shanghai. The narrative voice is ethereal and lyrical. Oberon, 'reclining on a bank of fairy flowers' with his queen Titania by his side, laments the devolution of man since they last 'dwelt in the sylvan shades of yon far earth'. Titania proposes that they revisit the 'dull world' of mortals, so they ride a fairy cloud past the battlefields of the West towards the East. When their fairy chariot stops, Oberon asks Puck where they have landed.

> Puck took the chart—'We've passed the Rhone and Rhine, ah!'
> 'That river's the Wang-poo: this must be China.'

Puck suggests that they continue on past 'the land that never knows a change', since they've been there before, but they then hear the sound of foreign voices singing and howling, and Oberon remarks:

> 'I recollect it now, this is Shanghai,
> 'A world within a world, within another,
> 'I wonder what they do from home so far.
> 'Go down there, Puck, and see what means that bother,
> 'And bring me a report of what they are.'

Puck's perspective is cosmic; his errand, to investigate the petty goings on of a thrice-isolated ('world within a world ...') community of sojourners. Sliding down a beam of sunlight he follows the crowd straight to the Club, where he pinches copies of the Shanghai daily papers for Oberon. His lord is initially delighted, until he finds in the leader 'a mixture of fact and drivelling poesy'. 'What a pity!' he exclaims, 'That people should read this, and call it witty.' Puck, at the poem's end, is thereupon dispatched a second time with a new mission: to 'teach them to be funny' (and, in doing so, perhaps 'make money').

> And Puck has come, no more of idle boasting,
> Written below behold his guarantee;
> He'll roast all subjects that may need the roasting,—

---

³⁶ The dreaming British expatriate is something of a complement to nineteenth-century European representations of China as the 'sleeping dragon', which Eric Reinders calls a 'pervasive metaphor consistent with other metaphors of mindlessness' such as opium-drugged, mentally deficient, diseased, and atrophied. (See: Eric Robert Reinders, *Borrowed Gods and Foreign Bodies: Christian Missionaries Imagine Chinese Religion* (Berkeley: University of California Press, 2004), 52.) The inaugural issue of *Puck*, 1 April 1871, 7, playfully alludes to the 'China wakes' cliché in a self-advertising cartoon showing a personified 'China' past (sleeping), present (waking), and future (grinning while reading *Puck*)—that is, China awakening to humour For the China Awakening Trope ee Rudolf G. Wagner, "China 'Asleep' and 'Awakening'. A Study in Conceptualizing Asymmetry and Coping With It", Transcultural Studies 1 (2011): 4–135.

Henceforth he'll rule the roast. So mote it be.[37]

Puck thus arrives not only to save Shanghailanders from the local press, but also as a fortune-seeker. While the 'subjects' for roasting ostensibly refer to the topics or targets of *Puck*'s humour, given that Puck is a fairy servant on business to minister to British 'subjects' on the margins of empire, the line carries colonial undertones.

In the following section, 'A Word to the Wise', the narrative voice switches from that of the lyrical poet to the brisk, authoritative tone of a government proclamation:

> We have this day established ourselves as General Supervisors of all Public affairs in China and Japan, and anywhere else we may hereafter think fit. We have also taken charge of the Legations at Pekin, and all Governments, Municipal and otherwise, in all Foreign Settlements.
>
> To this Censorship we have added the profession of General Punsters, Riddle Manufacturers, Wits, Critics, and Public Autocrats. N.B.—Dramatic and Musical critiques written to order, and Free Tickets (to include dinner) accepted for all performances.—No bribery.
> (signed) PUCK
> Hong Name: Heä-wi-ah.

Puck thus arrogates sweeping authority for *Puck* as the head of its editorial collective, whose scope of vision extends from the regional (Japan) down to the local (performances). Puck himself goes local by adopting a Chinese business (hong) name: Heä-wi-ah (i.e. Here we are).

Cultural Stereotypes

So how did *Puck* and *China Punch* go about their 'business'? One common feature is that they presume, tolerate, and promote reader prejudices—even as they make fun of them. Prejudices are a type of subjective truth (based on opinion or emotion), but their comedic expression implies an objective truth about society and the world. In addressing key areas of concern, such as Britain's standing in Asia, these magazines turned time and again to cultural stereotypes.

Some of these are predictable. As may be expected of nineteenth-century colonial publications, *Puck* and *China Punch* take a generally condescending attitude towards Chinese people. On the whole, both treat British and Chinese more or less as different species, even though they were equals under the law.[38] Some British Shanghailanders may have 'felt ambivalent about or were openly critical of the structure of foreign privilege that made Chinese residents of the

---

[37] *Puck, or the Shanghai Charivari* 1, 1 April 1871, 1–2. All excerpts keep to original punctuation.

[38] As early as 1858 the Hong Kong Colonial Office announced it would abolish racial preference from legislation, a pledge renewed by Governor Richard Graves MacDonnell in 1866. See: Gillian Bickley, "British Attitudes Toward Hong Kong in the Nineteenth Century," in *Foreign Communities in Hongkong 1840s–1950s*, ed. Cindy Yik-yi Chu (New York : Palgrave Macmillan, 2005), 39–61; 45.

(Settlements) feel like second-class citizens',[39] as Jeffrey Wasserstrom claims, but little such ambivalence is reflected in these periodicals. Many of the Chinese stereotypes proffered are unoriginal, even by the standards of the era: thieving servants ('Wong-Ah-Chizzle'), indolent opium smokers, deceitful mandarins, plus the other China tropes found on their covers.[40]

More surprising is the degree to which their stereotypes of the Chinese are relative to those of other cultures and nationalities. This relativity, indeed, was part of a broader Anglophone phenomenon. James Parton's *Caricature and Other Comic Art in All Times and Many Lands* (1877), for instance, opines that although Westerners are 'apt to think of the Chinese as a grave people' they are in fact (borrowing a quip) 'the *French* of Asia—"a nation of cooks, a nation of actors"'.[41] Parton's remark encapsulates the striking tendency of these magazines to combine British prejudices about different nationalities, treating the Chinese—however tongue-in-cheek—as comparable to other Europeans. Wendy Siuyi Wong's claim that '*The China Punch*'s content often maligned Chinese customs while praising the superiority of British culture',[42] is thus misleading, not just because praise for the British in its pages is in fact rare, but also because its cultural representations are by no means dualistic.

Consider, for instance, the similarities in how Chinese and European nationals are represented through distorted speech and distorted bodies. Bodies, as Eric Reinders has pointed out, were extremely important in nineteenth-century Western representations of the Chinese population. 'New arrivals could not understand what was being *said*, and knew it; but they could write about what they *saw* of the Chinese people, and what they saw was bodies'.[43] In *Puck*, Chinese bodies are used for visual puns, as in a pair of cartoons depicting 'A run on the bank' and

---

[39] Wasserstrom, *Global Shanghai*, 24.

[40] Such pervasive bias in the Western-language press provoked biliterate Chinese such as Wang Tao 王韜 (1828–1897) to advocate the establishment of Chinese-run Western-language newspapers to counter Western misrepresentations of the Chinese. Britton cites Wang as arguing that 'The Chinese should establish foreign-language newspapers to convert the foreigners. The foreigners have established daily papers at the treaty ports. [...] Their general tendency is to praise the foreigners and to belittle the Chinese, to the extent of utter falsification, representing black as white, and confusing right and wrong. The Western readers generally know only their own foreign languages, and receive as true whatever their papers say. In international issues, the words that first reach the ears exert the greatest influence. The readers are biased from the beginning, and so it is difficult for China to argue. If we were in a position to guide opinion, and could set forth carefully the history of each particular issue, then the rights of the case might be manifested. Then how could the foreigners play their tricks?' See: Britton, *The Chinese Periodical Press*, 44–45.

[41] James Parton, *Caricature and Other Comic Art in All Times and Many Lands* (New York: Harper & Bros., 1877), 191. Referring to Punch and Judy style street puppetry, Parton likens the Chinese Empire to 'an immense fair' and speculates that '[t]he Orient knew Punch perhaps ages before England saw him'.

[42] Wong, *Manhua*, 31.

[43] Reinders, *Borrowed Gods*, 39.

Fig. 5 Chinese bodies, English puns. *Puck, or the Shanghai Charivari* 5, 1 May 1872, 63

'Depositing an amount at the bank' (Fig. 5). In *China Punch*, a recurring visual feature that exemplifies the textual ubiquity and subordination of Chinese people is their use as letters at the beginning of columns and other written features (Fig. 6). Chinese bodies in ethnic garb are twisted into English letters, literally bent to serve the foreign culture. In the text of every issue, then, the natives are domesticated and made useful to a British narrative.

Then again, so are Western bodies (Fig. 7). During the run of *China Punch*, two Irishmen, Sir Richard Graves MacDonnell (1866–1872) and Sir Arthur Kennedy (1872–1877), served successively as Governor of Hong Kong, and also as fodder for Irish caricature in that magazine. Germans are also regularly made fun of for

Fig. 6 Chinese bodies and English letters in *The China Punch*

Fig. 7 Western bodies and English letters in *The China Punch*

their outlandish dress and heavy accents.[44] One *China Punch* caricature (Fig. 8) depicts the Portuguese in neighbouring Macau as effeminate fops in high-heeled shoes, reacting to a sniping editorial comment in the *Gazette of Macao & Timor* (1 April 1873) that 'We, the Portuguese, have far too honourable traditions not to have the just pride to regard ourselves as occupying an exalted place in the aristocracy of nations. We did not rise yesterday, in the midst of lucky commercial speculations, carving out our dominions with a foreign sword'.[45] Britain's perceived rivals in the region were thus not just the Chinese.

As for language, the British were simultaneously fascinated, amused, and repelled by 'pidgin English'. British residents of China found pidgin English to be indispensable but irretrievably vulgar. The introduction to *Pidgin-English Sing-Song Rhymes* (1876), a British anthology, calls it 'a very rude jargon, in which English words, strangely distorted, owing to the difficulty of representing their sounds in Chinese writing, are set forth according to the principles of Chinese grammar'.[46] Britons thus attributed the vulgarity of pidgin to the inferiority of Chinese language, rather than their own unwillingness to learn Chinese, and they only condescended to use it to converse with the natives out of necessity. A simple

---

[44] See, for example, the caricature above 'Never seed the dawg your Vurship' (*The China Punch* 2, no. 19, 16 October 1874, 13) and 'I gif you my vord of honour' (*The China Punch* 3, no. 7, 22 November 1876, 2). Ricardo K. S. Mak notes that, early on, Hong Kong's small German community tried to hide their German identity and assimilate into British society. With the establishment of the German Empire under Otto von Bismark in 1871, however, German national identity consciousness led to increased tensions with the British. See: Ricardo K. S. Mak, "Nineteenth-Century German Community," in *Foreign Communities in Hong Kong, 1840s–1950s*, ed. Cindy Yik-yi Chu (New York: Palgrave Macmillan, 2005), 61–85; 68, 75.

[45] *The China Punch* 2, no. 7, 24 April 1974, 6. Much fodder for both magazines' humour was drawn from news reports in other periodicals. China at the time had foreign-language publications in English, Japanese, Portuguese, French, German and Russian. See: Fang, *Zhongguo jindai baokanshi*, 31.

[46] Charles G. Leland, *Pidgin-English Sing-Song* (London: Trübner, & Co. Ltd, 1876), 1.

Fig. 8 Effeminate Portuguese (note high heel-like shoes). *The China Punch* 2, no.7, 24 April 1873, 6

vernacular, it was claimed to 'present no difficulty to any one who can understand negro minstrelsy or baby talk'.[47]

We also see foreign examples of linguistic travesty akin to pidgin. The *Puck* staple with the greatest word count is the series 'Intercepted Letters', an occasional

---

[47] Ibid, 9.

commentary on social life in the Far East, written in the voice of Miss Juliana Giggles, a middle-aged British lady. Her letters are tours-de-force of linguistic carnival. Recounting her trip to Hong Kong, for instance, she complains about a 'Trewly Coarse indiwiddle', tells how her mama cursed someone as a 'hipperpotermus' (later 'hippanbottomuppermus'), and butchers French ('Garçong!').[48] In another entry she talks about how much she enjoyed a horse ride in the country: 'I fancied myself a—what was it those strange Animals were called that used to live in the history of Greece ever so many years ago—Dear, dear! Something like a Mirmaid, only instead of a Fish it was a Horse—Oh I know! A Centipede—yes, that's the word'.[49]

In short, Chinese people play a conspicuous but 'supporting' role in the humour of these magazines, which are more particularly concerned with Anglo society. This is not to trivialise offensive representations of Chinese found in their pages, but rather to point out that their exploitation of cultural prejudices for comedic purposes was more democratic.

Political and Social Satire

Politics and society were the bread and butter of both publications. *Puck* establishes this thematic purview up front by making bureaucrats part of their editorial staff and promising: 'The Foreign Representatives at Pekin will do for us what they have done so well for foreigners generally, nothing'.[50] *China Punch*, for its part, keeps up a steady drumbeat of mockery aimed at the colonial administration's ineptitude, insensitivity, and obstructionism. 'The Salt Junk Inspector's report', for instance, mocks tax officials' sloth and stupidity with a graph of snails crawling over an ass (Fig. 9). Colonial officials in *China Punch*, when not appearing with their Chinese counterparts, are emasculated in caricatures by carrying enormous phallic swords. 'Shaksperian [sic] Illustration' (Fig. 10), for example, depicts the colonial government's cowardly reaction to the catastrophic typhoon of 1874, which took over 2,000 lives and caused enormous property damage in Hong Kong, Macau, and the South China Sea.[51] Other *China Punch* caricatures frame administrators in stained glass in an ironic hagiography that seems to wish their subjects dead (a prerequisite to being sainted).

Incompetent officials also appear in parodic advertisements. One mock theatre advertisement in *China Punch* employs the breathless, 'roll-up! roll-up!' style of a carnival barker to attract attention to government inefficiency, promising, among other things (Fig. 11):

---

[48] *Puck, or the Shanghai Charivari* 5, 1 May 1872, 62–63.

[49] *Puck, or the Shanghai Charivari* 2, 1 July 1871, 21.

[50] *Puck, or the Shanghai Charivari* 1, 1 April 1871, 2.

[51] *The China Punch* 2, no.19, 16 October 1874, 15. 'On horror's head horrors accumulate' (*Othello* III, iii, 370).

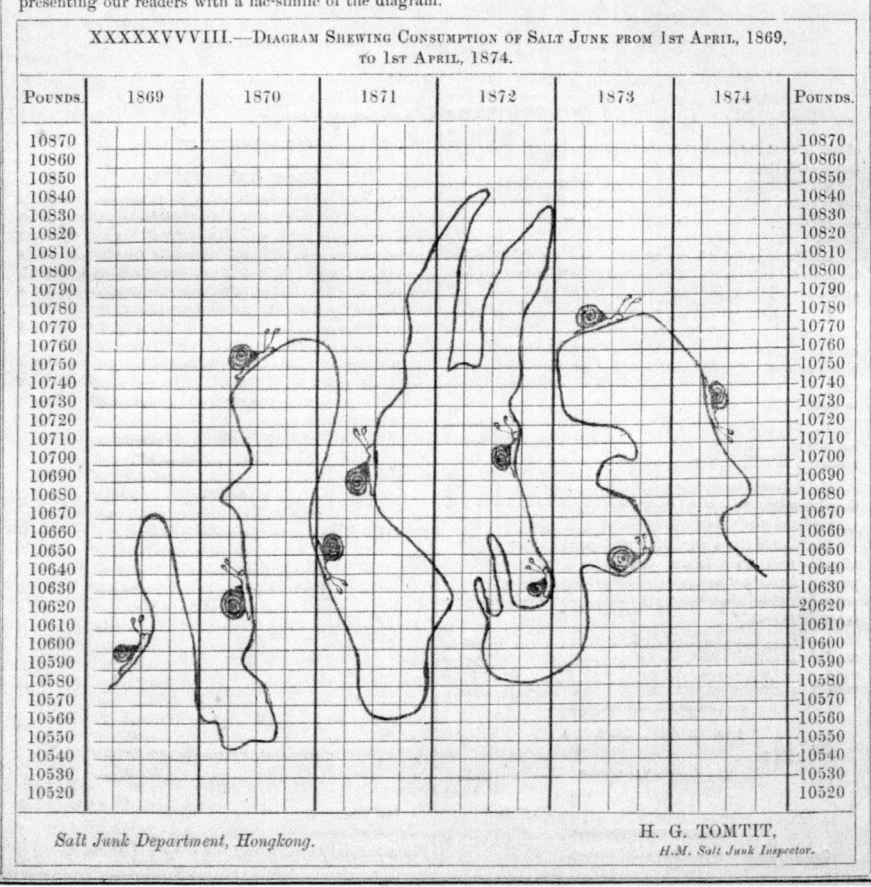

Fig. 9 Mocking tax officials' sloth and stupidity: the Salt Junk Inspector's report as snails crawling over an ass. *The China Punch* 2, no.15, 11 April 1874, 12

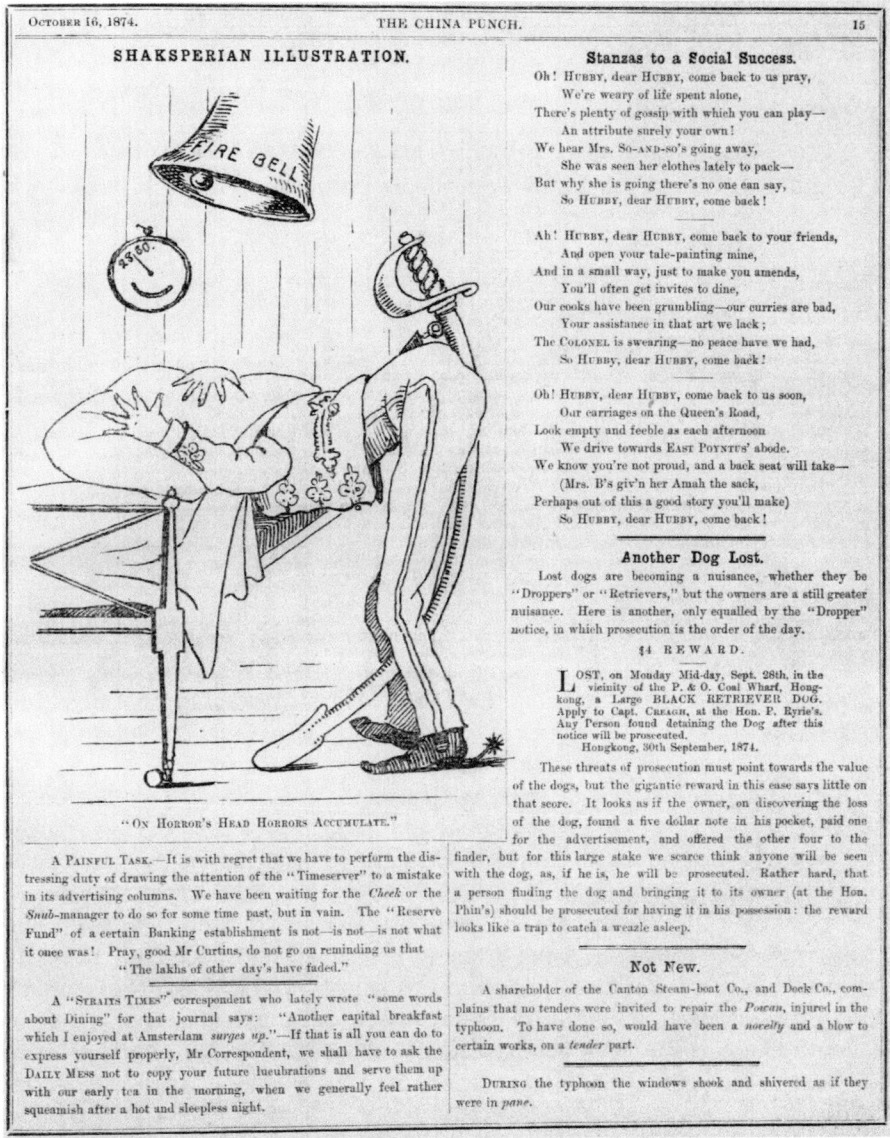

Fig. 10 A 'Shaksperian [sic] Illustration' of the colonial government's response to the 1874 typhoon. *The China Punch* China Punch 2, no.19, 16 October 1874, 15

EXTRAORDINARY EXCITEMENT.
MORE NOVELTIES.
FUN STILL INCREASING!
...
PROFESSOR PUNCH,
...
ON THIS OCCASION HE WILL HAVE THE HONOUR OF EXPOSING
A SERIES OF NOVEL EXPEDIENTS,
As performed at the Government Offices and establishments, differing entirely from any elsewhere than in Hwang Kwang.
...
PART II.
THAT GRAND AND ANGELIC SCENE
OFFICIAL SUSTENTION.
Wherein, by Mysterious Powers of Reasoning, the most Incapable officers will be retained in positions, causing them to be suspended, as it were, between *Heaven* and *the other place*. A most trying and wonderful exhibition of patience on the part of the Public.[52]

An inside front cover of *Puck*,[53] meanwhile, touts:

Dr. STOUT'S
Superior, Unapproachable, Patent Self-sticking
GUNPOWDER PASTE,
FOR
MENDING CRACKED CHINA.

below which appear opinions on the product from Foreign Ministers of the gunboat diplomacy era such as 'T.F. W—de' [Sir Thomas Francis Wade, British Ambassador to China], along the lines of: 'My China's so awfully broken, your Paste is no use', and 'I should like very much to use your Paste; but I've no China to mend'.[54]

Diplomatic relationships are routinely gendered. If gendered representations of the Orient typically feminised the Orient and masculinised the Occident,[55] these humour periodicals offered a couple of twists. Most intriguing is the sprite Puck, who, while nominally male ('Robin Goodfellow'), is a relatively gender-neutral representative of the West; little, however, is made of his androgyny within the pages of *Puck*. More noticeably, Chinese-British relations, particularly in the diplomatic sphere, are frequently depicted as gender inversion. Satirical cartoons in both periodicals portray the Chinese as sexually aggressive, implicitly chiding the European male for being hen-pecked, put upon, or otherwise subordinated by the Chinese, and implying that he has relinquished his rightful authority. One image

---

[52] Excerpted from: *The China Punch* 2, no.19, 16 October 1874, 2.

[53] *Puck, or the Shanghai Charivari* 1, 1 April 1871, inside cover.

[54] Metaphors of China being broken or in pieces (or carved up like a melon, as seen in I-Wei Wu's chapter, Participating in Global Affairs: The Chinese Cartoon Monthly *Shanghai Puck*) were to become even more common in the early twentieth century, after the collapse of the Qing dynasty.

[55] The literature on this topic is vast, with much attention paid to canonical texts such as Giacomo Puccini's *Madama Butterfly* (1904). For a theoretical introduction to gender and Orientalism, see: Meyda Yeğenoğlu, *Colonial Fantasies: Towards a Feminist Reading of Orientalism* (Cambridge: Cambridge University Press, 1998).

Fig. 11 Professor Punch presents the inept colonial government through a parodic theater advertisement. *The China Punch* 19, 14 October 1874, 2

in *China Punch*, 'The Return of the Prodigal' (Fig. 12), shows a British gentleman with his hands in front of him to ward off the affectionate embrace of a fat, pigtailed Chinaman. The caption picks up a quote from a British diplomat's letter to the London *Times* that 'The feeling of the Chinese, so far from being hostile, is of the most cordial description.'

Both magazines also stage the theatre of officialdom as mock meetings and court cases. The first feature in *China Punch* (2, no. 2) transforms the story of 'Aladdin

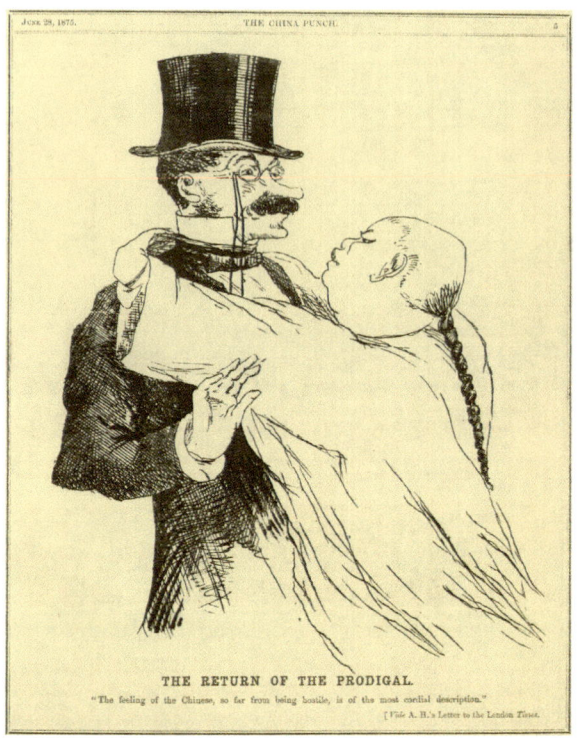

Fig. 12 Gendering Sino-British diplomacy: the put-upon British gentleman and the (sexually) aggressive Chinese. *The China Punch* 3, no.4, 28 June 1875, 5

and the Lamp' into 'The Trial of Aladdin the Wonderful Scamp',[56] a parable about Chinese servants 'chiselling' their masters by overcharging them when making purchases and pocketing the difference. The court case is presided over by A——g C——f J——e (Acting Chief Justice) Pounce, witnessed by jurors such as J. G. T. Billiard Cue, T. Chetah, and Verdant Green, and involving the participation of Captain O'Grady (Irish), witness Chun A Kee (Chinese), and Audit Office clerk J. A. da Silva (Portuguese). In sorting out whether or not Aladdin defrauded his employer by charging him $6 for a $3.50 lamp, the court concerns itself with such issues as how many d's there are in 'Aladdin'. The defence attorney, Mr Drumstick, dismisses the case as frivolous on the grounds that his client is an 'orderly', and therefore not disorderly, and that 'We all know that it is not considered dishonest in this Colony to buy things at one price and to charge them to your employer at another'. He further notes that the A——g C——l S——y (Acting Colonial Secretary) had been drawing the A——g A——r G——l (Acting Auditor General)'s pay: 'the *gold* which ought to have gone to *Silva*'. Aladdin is nevertheless convicted.

---

[56] In a much later cross-cultural roundabout, the bilingual intellectual Lin Yutang 林語 (1895–1976) promoted the scamp as the centrepiece of his 'wise and merry' humanistic philosophy. See: Lin Yutang, *The Importance of Living* (New York: The John Day Company, 1937), 11–14.

A trial with a strikingly similar premise appears in the inaugural issue of *Puck*. Plaintiff Mr Ebeneezer Jollipaunch accuses his former Chinese servant, Sah-si-djo, of being a bad cook and having stolen 500 Havana cigars. This being Shanghai's 'mixed court' (est. 1863) with joint Chinese and British jurisdiction, the case is presided over by two judges: the sleepy and 'self-complacent' Chen and the near-deaf Georgy, who mishears the defendant's name as 'Saucy Joe' and 'seesaw'. (After stalled proceedings, the justices suggest that the case be settled out of court.)

These protracted jokes illustrate several shared characteristics of the two magazines' political humour, particularly their fondness for parody of official ritual and bureaucratic procedure. The *China Punch* case, though most critical towards the Chinese, employs as props several of colony's many coexisting nationalities, interspersed as silly joke names. Most eye-catching at a visual level is the use of blanks for official titles—transparent roman à clef digs at members of the colonial government, a libel-avoidance practice that is also used liberally in *Puck* (though not in this example). The *China Punch* piece also carries a running joke about the revolving door of civil service in Hong Kong (5-year terms were standard): all colonial administrators are 'Acting'

The Chinese Versions of *Punch* That Almost Were

The final page of *China Punch* 3, no. 7 (22 November 1876) announces: 'In consequence of the departure of Mr W. N. Middleton, the registered proprietor of this spasmodic periodical, its publication will cease with the issue of the present number'. The announcement goes on to commend the Hong Kong community for its support, and claim that the lack of discord therein caused *China Punch* to

> languish for want of material. He could no more
> 'Shoot folly as it flies,
> And catch the manners living as they rise'

What influence did these two periodicals have in their day? Evidence suggests that it was limited. Wendy Siuyi Wong notes that *China Punch* 'introduced Hong Kong to humorous and satirical cartoons as a genre'.[57] To date, however, we have no clear indication that *China Punch* directly inspired nineteenth-century Chinese cartoonists, Chinese-language humour periodicals, or even other colonial periodicals.

With *Puck*, we do know that it was read by inhabitants of other treaty ports in Asia and that news of its existence reached a North American readership. James Parton's 1877 history of caricature devotes much of his chapter on China to an anecdote from the British press in 1874 about the supposed awe of the British ambassador to China, Thomas Francis Wade (1818–1895), upon meeting the Chinese Emperor. Parton quotes a revelation by a reporter for the London literary magazine *Athenaeum* (1828–1921) about the remarkably circuitous route of this news item:

---

[57] Wong, *Manhua*, 12–13.

It now turns out that the imaginary narrative first appeared in the columns of *Puck*, a comic paper (in English), published in Shanghai; that it was translated into Chinese by some native wag, who palmed it off on his countrymen as a truthful account of the behaviour of the English barbarian on this occasion; and that some inquiring foreigner, ignorant of the source from whence it came, retranslated it into English, and held it up as another instance of the way in which the Chinese pamphleteers were attempting to undermine our influence in China by covering our minister with contempt![58]

Whether or not the particulars are true, the account confirms both that *Puck* reached Chinese readers and that its reputation extended overseas to England and the Americas. Despite its editors' complaints about Peking and London's neglect of Shanghai, *Puck*'s voice was heard back home, if indirectly. The context of this anecdote also reveals the British continued fascination with how they were perceived by the Chinese, a relationship that humour periodicals like *Puck* helped mediate.[59]

Evidence from overseas also suggests that *Puck* might have inspired an encore. *The Japan Gazette*, a fortnightly English-language newspaper published in the treaty port of Yokohama mentions a *Shanghai Charivari* in its 8 July 1881 issue. Given that this was 6 years after the last extant issue of *Puck*, the review raises the tantalising possibility that *Puck* was revived in the 1880s. The review, which confirms the continued relevance of *Punch* among Anglophone communities in Asia, and whose biting sarcasm evinces a spirit of regional competition between colonial publications, is worth quoting in full:

> Our ancient friend *Punch* continues to hold his own amidst a heap of cheap, servile imitators, scarcely any of whom can compare in genuine wit and humour with the jovial old soul.
>
> We are induced to make these remarks because such so-called comic publications are beginning to crop up in this part of the world. We have received the first number of *Quis, The Shanghai Charivari*, a paper of the class above referred to, printed and published, for the proprietors, at the *Shanghai Mercury* office. We regret our inability to compliment the promoters of the venture upon either its style or 'get up.' The cartoons are indifferently executed, utterly pointless, and very far fetched. The letter-press consists almost entirely of wretched, doggerel rhymes which the writers probably call poetry and intend to be witty. These Homeric strains might perhaps be intelligible to the Poet Laureate, whose last poem passed all comprehension, but to ordinary mortals, like ourselves, they are simply *vox et proetera nihil* [voiced but not carried out]. As for wit, all we can say is, that we fail to discover any. We would advise *Quis* in future to supplement his effusions by a series of foot-notes indicating to his readers what passages are to be considered as funny, and what as serious.
>
> If *Quis* intends favouring the Shanghai public with any more poetry of the same sort as that contained in his first issue, as friends—that is, if he will consider us as such—we would strongly recommend him, before doing so, to diligently peruse *Punch*'s advice to those

---

[58] Parton, *Caricature*, 196–1997. This account of Chinese misreading of Western humour (albeit with Western agency) recalls the 2002 case of the *Beijing Evening News* publishing a freelance journalist's plagiarism/translation of a parodic item from *The Onion* humour magazine about the U.S. Congress threatening to relocate to the south unless the Capitol dome is rebuilt with a retractable roof. See: http://www.wired.com/culture/lifestyle/news/2002/06/53048, accessed 21 April 2010.

[59] See, for instance, *Punch*'s satirical reaction to an 1842 Chinese exhibition in London shortly after the First Opium War, as described in Altick, *Punch*, 615–16. For a detailed analysis of how the periodical *Dianshizhai huabao* helped mediate Chinese perceptions of foreigners during the late nineteenth century, see Henningsmeier, "Foreign Sources".

about to marry and to be guided by the same. For the paper itself, the best wish we can offer is, that it may have a safe and speedy passage 'over to the great majority' wither so many of its kindred have already gone.[60]

Quis, unfortunately, is not mentioned in any histories of the press in China and appears to be no longer extant. The allegations of 'indifferently executed' cartoons and failed wit, however, deserve to be taken seriously as possible factors contributing to *Puck*'s and *China Punch*'s obscurity.[61] Judging from the middling quality of many of the illustrations, a far cry from the best of *Punch*, neither periodical was able to have a professional illustrator on staff. This should not have condemned either of them, however, given the abundance of 'sophomoric humour' found in the early years of *Punch* itself. Richard Altick writes that some *Punch* cartoons were 'so unskilled that they would seem not to have justified the cost of engraving them [...]. Wit that we may consider to be almost beneath contempt was welcomed as a genuine expression of the comic spirit'.[62] The same may be said for its progenies' liberal sprinkling of groaning puns, textual and pictorial, all over the world.

I have found no evidence of influence on Chinese cartoons or humour periodicals. Indeed, Tse Tsan-tai's 謝鑽泰 collage-style illustration 'the situation in the far east' (*Shiju tu* 時局圖), frequently cited as the first cartoon by a Chinese artist,[63] did not appear until 1899—and in Japan. Meanwhile, Ernest Major's *Yinghuan huabao* (1877–1880) and *Dianshizhai huabao* are entirely dissimilar from *China Punch* and *Puck* in layout, content, and visual composition. *Punch*-style illustrations appear in the missionary publication *Huatu xinbao* (1880–1921, retitled several times), discussed in Barbara Mittler's epilogue. In 1896, Kelly & Walsh, the successor of F.&C. Walsh, published an encore of *Puck* entitled *The Rattle* (1896-1903), an illustrated humour magazine, which closely follows *Puck*'s layout. *Shanghai Puck* (*Shanghai poke* 上海潑克, 1918), discussed in the preceding chapter, is another concerted revival of the distinctive *Punch* cartoon style.[64] 'Shanghai Puck' shares

---

[60] *The Japan Gazette* 28, no. 1, 8 July 1881, 105.

[61] *The China Punch* once felt compelled to answer criticisms even from its parent publication: 'CHINA SNAIL—We are obliged to you for your handsome tribute to our humble efforts. So you think that "some of our contributions are indifferent, and some—well worse", do you? No, Sir, nothing that appears in our columns is "indifferent or—well, worse". There may be some articles, the wit of which is so transcendent and the satire so keen that it is beyond your appreciation. A "China Snail" is after all a thing that crawls along but slowly. We are far too fast for a Snail'. (*The China Punch* 2, no.5, 20 February 1873, 3).

[62] Altick, *Punch*, xxii.

[63] See: Wong, *Manhua*, 31; Bi and Huang, *Manhua shi*, 17. The cartoon appears on p. 6 of the illustration insert in Bi and Huang's book, reproduced from a 1903 Shanghai reprint. The authors' comment that the illustration 'shows that the rise of China's early modern print cartoons had begun at least by 1903' (17) is misleading in that it excludes both colonial Hong Kong and cartoons drawn and published by foreigners in China.

[64] *Punch*-style cartoons also appear in a book published earlier that decade: 'VALDAR' and others, *Yiqian jiubai ershi nian Zhongguo lishi chahua wushi'er fu* 一千九百十二年中國歷史插畫伍拾弍幅 (the history of China for 1912 in 52 cartoons) (Shanghai: The National Review, 1912).

with the Walshes' *Puck* both a name and the fate of its lifespan being cut short by the untimely death of its founder. In style, however, 'Shanghai Puck' was markedly different from its predecessor, not least in that it actively courted multiple readerships with cartoon captions and articles in both Chinese and English.[65]

Punch influenced later Chinese cartoonists too. Ye Qianyu 葉淺予 (1907–1995), the creator of Shanghai's most famous comic strip of the 1930s, 'Mr Wang' (*Wang xiansheng* 王先生), for instance, recounts in his memoirs that while working for the cartoon periodical *Shanghai Sketch* (*Shanghai manhua* 上海漫畫, 1928–1934) he bought every issue of *Punch*, which was regular reading fare for Chinese cartoonists in the 1920s and 1930s:

> *Punch*, an old-style humour magazine which often published social satire caricatures, was well-known to Chinese cartoonists [...]. In Shanghai, Master Shen [Bochen, 1889–1919] founded the cartoon periodical 'Shanghai Puck', which showed a clear *Punch* influence. This demonstrates that Chinese cartoon art undeniably was stimulated by foreign culture. That said, influence and stimulation notwithstanding, Chinese cartoon artists' creative brilliance and wisdom was deeply rooted in the fertile soil of indigenous culture [*minzu wenhua*]. [Cartoons by] Shen Bochen [...], Zhang Guangyu, Huang Wennong, and Hua Junwu are a few examples of this, as is, I believe, my 'Mr Wang'.[66]

In contrast to Japan, where *Punch* and its progeny had a lasting influence on domestic cartooning as early the 1860s,[67] the influence of the *Punch* cartoon in China appears to have skipped a generation or two, from the 1870s to the 1910s. *The China Punch* and *Puck* may be considered part of the pre-history of modern Chinese pictorial satire and humour magazines because they appeared before the attitude towards the West of Chinese intellectuals in China's print capital 'changed from hostility to curiosity and finally acceptance,'[68] reflected in their new receptivity towards *Punch* and other Western illustration styles.

Conclusion

China Punch and *Puck* represent some of the earliest known examples of pictorial satire drawn by foreigners living in China. As the foreign populations of Shanghai, Hong Kong, Guangzhou (Canton), Beijing, and other Chinese cities grew between the 1860s and the 1940s, so too did cartooning for foreign-language periodicals in

---

[65] This multilingualism was inspired by *Tokyo Puck* (est. 1905), which published captions in Japanese, Chinese and English, and *Shanghai Puck*, which focused on contemporary politics, and whose founder had visited Japan in 1917. *Tokyo Puck*, whose circulation reached 100,000, was sold in China, Taiwan, and Korea as well as in Japan.

[66] Ye, *Ye Qianyu zizhuan*, 112.

[67] See: Peter Duus, "Presidential Address: Weapons of the Weak, Weapons of the Strong—The Development of the Japanese Political Cartoon," *The Journal of Asian Studies* 60, no. 4 (November 2001): 965–97; esp., 974.

[68] Catherine Vance Yeh, "The Life-style of Four *Wenren* in Late Qing Shanghai," *Harvard Journal of Asiatic Studies* 57, no.2 (December 1997): 419–70; 420.

China, the history of which remains yet to be written. Cartoons and comic strips began appearing in foreign language periodicals with some regularity in the early 1900s and had become a standard feature of many newspapers and magazines by the 1930s. Georgii Sapojnikoff (d. 1949), a white Russian refugee to Shanghai, for instance, for 15 years drew cartoons for *The North-China Daily News* under the *nom de plume* Sapajou.[69] In terms of volume, however, serialised cartoons from abroad (sometimes with translated captions) always outnumbered cartoons published in the local press by foreigners living in China, a fact which makes the expatriate viewpoints of *China Punch* and *Puck* all the more valuable.

These magazines are ephemera of the British colonial enterprise in Greater China. Each lasted for only a few years, publishing on a monthly or less frequent schedule, and expired upon the departure of a proprietor.[70] While drawing contributions from English-speaking colonists in Hong Kong and Shanghai, both publications come across as personal enthusiasms, hobby-like undertakings meant to enliven a small colonial society. It should be pointed out, however, that the same may be said for many other nineteenth and early twentieth-century periodicals in the region, including *Shanghai Puck*. In the case of these two, their lack of continuity indicates that, unlike *Punch*, neither succeeded in becoming a cultural institution in its particular locality, much less at a regional or global level. Both nevertheless confirm Rudolf Wagner's observation from the Heidelberg *Punch* conference that humour and pictorial satire flourish not just in 'high temperature' times of war and conflict, but also in 'low temperature' environments, such as a colonial outpost during an economic slump.

Stylistically, both *China Punch* and *Puck* were clearly inspired by *Punch*, but they did not fully adhere to its layout, comic motifs, or pictorial style. In terms of subject matter, both publications are more preoccupied with the Anglo colonial experience than they are with China per se. And while unflattering and stereotypical depictions of the local population are to be found with regularity throughout their runs, 'the Chinese' are in some ways most notable for their absence.[71] Ethnic caricatures are often of other colonials, including such perennial butts of British humour as the Irish, the Scots, and the Portuguese. In tapping pre-existing prejudices, these periodicals exhibit a conservative strain. Combined with their intolerant treatment of other Anglo colonials, their laments about the stifling

---

[69] 'Sapajou' is a double pun on Sapojnikoff's last name and the French word for a species of monkey. Some of his cartoons have been republished as: Sapajou with R.T. Payton-Griffin, *Shanghai's Schemozzle: Volumes 1 and 2 Together* (Shanghai: Earnshaw Books, 2007). Others appear in *Five Months of War* (1938) and Carl Crow's *Four Hundred Million Customers* (1937). One version of a Richard Rigby essay on Sapajou is available online at: http://www.chinaheritagequarterly.org/features.php?searchterm=022_sapajou.inc&issue=022, accessed August 20, 2010.

[70] *China Punch*'s demise also coincided with the merger of its parent publication, *The China Mail*, with *The Evening Mail and Shipping List* in 1876, suggesting that business considerations may have also contributed to its termination.

[71] See the contribution by Barbara Mittler, the epilogue, in this volume.

atmosphere of colonial society, compared to back home, ironically convey the editors' own cultural myopia. At the same time, these periodicals were self-consciously part of a broader periodical matrix, and they presumed reader familiarity with both the British press and the Western-language colonial press in other parts of Asia. They are thus best understood as nodes within regional and international circuits, rather than as purely local publications.

The humorous ethos of these periodicals contained a good deal of satire, especially in the forms of pictorial caricature of colonial administrators and local social types. As this chapter has emphasised, however, whimsy was also important in establishing the overarching thematic rubric of each publication and the tone of its discourse. Mr Punch and Puck, symbolic rulers of a cosmic order, signify a license to be satirical but, to put a fine point on it, they are not themselves satirical. Puck's boast that he will 'put a girdle round about the earth, in forty minutes' (as seen put into practice in some I-Wei Wu's illustrations) takes on a new meaning in this colonial context: he is now a representative of an imperialist global order. He is a twist on the discourse of China as the ultimate Other—China, a fairyland, is presided over by a Western fairy. In contrast, in *China Punch*, colonial Hong Kong is depicted as a realm of fools, filled with social rejects, slippery mercantile characters, and starry-eyed youths hoping to make their fortunes.

British colonialists' ambivalence about the colonial life is reflected in, among other things, their numerous references to Shakespeare, which suggest the need of those residing on the margins of empire to invoke a cultural authority—something quintessentially British. Stereotypical representations of Irishmen and Scots themselves provide an unchallenging form of comfort for the British reader. The turn to farce and whimsy, especially play with cultural selves (Shakespeare) and others (foreigners), thus betrays fundamental anxieties of the British abroad.

This chapter opens the door for a comparative study of whimsy in Chinese-language and bilingual periodicals in late imperial and modern China. Allegorical satire was a dominant mode during the late Qing period cartoons, as seen in publications such as *Tuhua ribao*, but not all modern Chinese comedic modes were purely representational and corrective. Catherine Yeh has noted that late Qing literati gave themselves license to engage in various types of tomfoolery by constructing an image of Shanghai as a 'big playground' (*da youxichang* 大遊戲場).[72] I have also written about the farcical 'funny' (*huaji* 滑稽) sensibility that was especially popular in the 1920s.[73] In both cases, the comedic agenda was more about sustaining a gay mood rather than delivering the singular 'punch' of satire. The present chapter thus hopes to provoke further exploration of how self-imaginaries of place are formed through comedy, both during and after the colonial era.

---

[72] Yeh, "Shanghai Leisure," 204.

[73] See: Christopher G. Rea, "Comedy and Cultural Entrepreneurship in Xu Zhuodai's *Huaji* Shanghai," *Modern Chinese Literature and Culture* 20, no. 2 (Fall 2008): 40–91.

Epilogue

Ten Thousand *Puck*s and *Punch*es: Satirical Themes and Variations Seen Transculturally

Barbara Mittler

> There is an imitation of Punch regularly published at Turin. There is to be a Punch, also, in St. Petersburgh. The latter at all events will be a novelty, though we can hardly understand "Wit dancing a hornpipe in fetters". Our vanity will not allow us to believe that Punch will be any the better for being "bound in Russia", and for having clasps put by the Censorship to each volume. However the two facts above are highly promising. As the world grows more civilized, we shall next hear of Punch appearing, as second Pasquin at Rome, or at Naples, perhaps; and who knows but we may yet see a Punch in Paris.[1]

China's illustrated magazines, which came into being in the mid-1880s, quickly became part of a community of illustrated papers from all over the world. These publications knew of each other, they would reprint each other's illustrations and they would quote each other's articles as a way to improve and authenticate their global coverage. Magazines like the *Dianshizhai huabao* 點石齋畫報 (1884–1898), the *Illustrated London News*, the *Leipziger Illustrierte* and the *Graphic* all worked from a similar set of pictorial modules. As the Chinese *Dianshizhai huabao* copied pictures from foreign magazines (something which occasionally also happened the other way round), its readers became part of an

---

[1] *Punch*, 5 December 1857, page 236.

B. Mittler (✉)
Professor of Chinese Studies at Heidelberg University, Heidelberg, Germany
e-mail: barbara.mittler@zo.uni-heidelberg.de

evolving world community of readers being educated and shaped by a homogenous, or what may be called a 'transcultural',[2] journalistic code.[3]

Members of this community of readers in Shanghai, London, Leipzig, and New York, were apparently all familiar with the same events and able to understand the same visual messages about them. *Dianshizhai huabao* thus can be said to have linked up with illustrated magazines elsewhere and to have integrated China into a worldwide aesthetic agenda.[4] By spreading a common visual code, pictorial journals thus created a set of (visual) terms of reference across the globe.

In the words of Partha Mitter and following Benedict Anderson, print culture created the conditions for a globally 'imagined community', which gave rise to a form of what one could call 'virtual cosmopolitanism' that brought the centre and the periphery closer in a 'free circulation of ideas'.[5] According to Anderson, print culture was thus able to overcome local and regional differences.[6] Illustrated papers are one example to show the development of a global *imaginaire* in which images, perspectives, scenes, plot lines, and readers' attitudes were increasingly shared between virtual equals in Leipzig, London, New York, and Shanghai. In this context, asymmetrical conceptions of centre and periphery seem to have lost at least some of their epistemological force.

The aim of this book has been to consider whether similar things can be said for satirical journalism as well. We have studied the ways in which the London-based weekly journal *Punch* (1842–2002), which by calling itself also the *London Charivari* pointed to the French prototype it decided to follow, served the nineteenth and early twentieth century world of satirical journalism as an 'inspiration', a 'model', a 'mould', an 'interlocutor', or a 'legitimating force'. Ever new versions of *Punch*

---

[2] To speak of phenomena from the perspective of transculturality allows us to explain a degree of intermixing of particular styles on the one hand and to observe the emergence of ever new stylistic variations on the other. A transcultural method looks beyond notions of 'cultural origins' as such because 'origins' are convoluted and difficult to uncover. Instead, it focuses on issues of creative translation or transformation by acknowledging and tracing the importance of cultural flows. My use of 'transcultural' follows ideas formulated in: Wolfgang Welsch, "Transculturality—The Puzzling Form of Cultures Today," in *Spaces of Culture: City, Nation, World*, eds. Mike Featherstone and Scott Lash (London: Sage, 1999), 194–213; Hans-Jörg Sandkühler and Hong-Bin Lim, eds., *Transculturality: Epistomology, Ethics and Politics* (Frankfurt: Peter Lang, 2004); Nicholas Mirzoeff, *An Introduction to Visual Culture* (London: Routledge, 1999), Chap. 4.

[3] Julia Henningsmeier, "The Foreign Sources of *Dianshizhai huabao* 點石齋畫報, a Nineteenth Century Shanghai Illustrated Magazine," *Ming Qing Yanjiu* (1998): 59–91. This article includes a large number of illustrations from Western magazines with their respective copies in China.

[4] Rudolf G. Wagner, "Joining the Global Imaginaire: The Shanghai Illustrated Newspaper *Dianshizhai huabao*," in *Joining the Global Public*, ed. Rudolf G. Wagner (Albany: State University of New York University Press, 2006), 105–73; 156.

[5] See Partha Mitter, chapter *Punch* and Indian Cartoons: The Reception of a Transnational Phenomenon in this volume.

[6] See Mitter in this volume.

appeared in societies both geographically and culturally far removed from British Victorian culture.[7] Even though the 1857 *Punch* vision quoted in the epigraph above that 'as the world grows more civilized [...] we may yet see a *Punch* in Paris'—a statement which appears a little ironic in view of *Punch*'s own stated connection to the Paris *Charivari*—never materialized, *Punch* did find its way to places as far away as Asia.

To what extent, we have been asking, did *Punch* and other such satirical publications from all over the world, serve the creation of a global satirical *imaginaire*? This book has illustrated that we are able to see obvious visual traces of the *Punch* legacy—or brand—in many Asian publications. We have also observed that the legacy is not one of *Punch* alone: there are several prototypes, *Charivari* and *Puck* featuring prominently among them, all of which helped to create a satirical style for which 'Punch' simply became shorthand.[8] From its beginnings, and by describing itself as the *London Charivari*, *Punch*—and the satirical legacy named after it not only for the purposes of this book—is both the perpetuator and the product of cultural flows. Its national or historical fixations are but contingent. The *Punch* phenomenon is determined by border-crossings, and one of its main *raisons-d'être* is confluence rather than influence. As such, *Punch* becomes the shorthand for a global *imaginaire* of satirical image and text which travels, flows and zigzags across the globe. This volume attempted to follow a few of its traces.

One of the earliest and rather long-lived Chinese-language satirical magazines was published between 1880 and 1921 by an American Presbyterian missionary, John Marshall Willoughby Farnham (1829–1917), or Fan Yuehan 范约翰, who worked in Shanghai between 1860 until his death in 1917. The journal had changing names, the first being *Huatu xinbao* 花图新报 (new pictorial paper).[9] The many Chinese stories it featured were critical of both Chinese and foreigners and employed both Chinese and foreign modes of depiction. For example: the below series of humorous images, drawn in simple and non-

---

[7] For *Punch*'s legacy see especially Brian Maidment, chapter The Presence of *Punch* in the Nineteenth Century, and Ritu G. Khanduri, chapter *Punch* in India: Another History of Colonial Politics? in this volume.

[8] For the many *Charivari*s and *Puck*s, see Khanduri and Mitter, as well as Elif Elmas, chapter Teodor Kasab's Ottoman Adaptation of the Ottoman Shadow Theatre *Karagöz*, I-Wei Wu, chapter Participating in Global Affairs: The Chinese Cartoon Monthly *Shanghai Puck*, Christopher Rea, chapter 'He'll Roast All Subjects That May Need the Roasting': Puck and Mr Punch in Nineteenth Century China in this volume; and Monika Lehner's *Der Chinadiskurs in der satirisch-humoristischen Publizistik Österreich-Ungarns 1894–1917* (forthcoming).

[9] The name changed as follows: 1880 花图新报, 1881 画图新报, 1914–1921 新民报, cf. Zhu Junzhou *Unpublished Lecture Notes*, Heidelberg: Cluster of Excellence "Asia and Europe in a Global Context" 2009:5–8.

Fig. 1 Chinese story in *Huatu xinbao*, vol. 1 1880

distinctive style, show a Chinese man who cannot ride a bike and therefore falls into the water (Fig. 1).

But the journal also featured English-language captions and contained images reminiscent in iconography and style of the *Punch* tradition as described in this

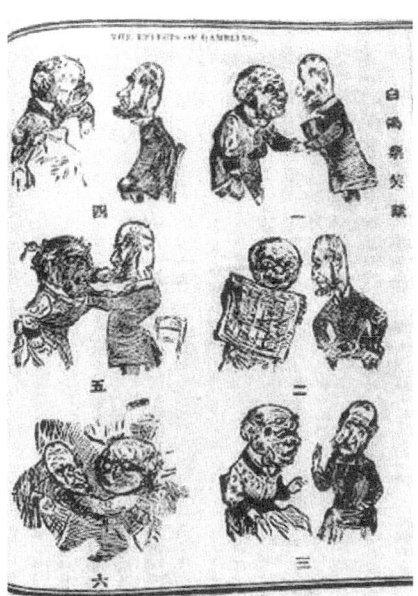

Fig. 2 *Punch*–style illustration in *Huatu xinbao*, vol. 1 1880

book. One set of caricatures, for example, ridicules the transmutation of two perfectly good (gentle)men into monsters through the effects of gambling. It is rendered in typical *Punch* style, focussing on the metamorphoses of these two men's enormous heads (Fig. 2), a characteristic of *Punch* style which refers back to Regency obsessions with body shape.

This book offers first forays into analysing the precise relationship between some of the 'older brothers' of satirical journalism and their younger 'siblings'—or 'cousins all over the world'[10] as Mr Punch himself would call them.[11] What we begin to see throughout this volume is the fact that the *Punch* legacy is clearly in the backs of the minds of those producing (and presumably also those consuming) these magazines. As in the case of illustrated magazines, we can therefore speak of a truly transcultural phenomenon, a globally imagined satirical community of sorts.

It is the purpose of this epilogue, to take stock of some of the answers given throughout this volume to the questions raised in the prologue by Hans Harder, and to point to some of the themes and variations in the development of satirical journalism that played out transculturally throughout this volume. The epilogue will take its point of departure from a discussion of the Hong Kong *China Punch*

---

[10] *Fifth Album of Cartoons* (Bombay: Hindi Punch Office, 1904).

[11] See especially the essays which trace direct flows, e.g. Wu, Khanduri, Elmas and Hotwagner, chapter '*Punch*'s Heirs' Between the (Battle) Lines: Satirical Journalism in the Age of the Russo-Japanese War of 1904–1905 in this volume.

and its very literal use of the *Punch* tradition which made it an immediate success among the colonisers, but a failure in the larger Chinese context. As Brian Maidment points out, *Punch* constantly re-asserted a particular type of bourgeois respectability (which itself was subject to constant *Punch* mockery) as the norm to which the whole of society aspired. However harshly it ridiculed the absurdities and compulsions of genteel conduct, *Punch* nonetheless, as he argues, maintained a firm alliance with its (genteel) readers. As Maidment put it '*Punch* lost much of its radical energy in its later history, but remained a broad-based repository of social and political commentary'.[12] Accordingly, the voice of *Punch*'s original satire was never quite the voice of the 'less privileged'. Yet, in their attempts to be heard, these 'less privileged' voices all over the world (faced with the asymmetrical power relations imposed by (semi-) colonialism) often made use of none other than the *Punch* tradition to reply to the world.[13] Accordingly, the second section of this epilogue, will briefly deliberate the powers of the shorthand label *Punch,* and discuss the myriad formats it takes through its Asian 'cousins'. We will end with a discussion of questions about translating laughter and the transcultural world of journalism in the late nineteenth and early twentieth century.

Punch in Chinese Gown: Picturing the *Other*

There were many satirical magazines in China. Some of them, such as the 1898 Hong Kong *Shijutu* 时局图 (present conditions illustrated) (Fig. 3),[14] or the 1907 *Zhongguo xinbao* 中国新报 (China's new magazine) adopted the visual language of *Punch*.[15] To depict foreign imperialist aspirations in China, both used gestures and symbols (such as the Russian bear, the British lion, the American eagle) that can also be found in contemporary *Punch* editions, but also many other satirical magazines of the time, as Sonja Hotwagner, I-Wei Wu, Ritu Khanduri, and others in this volume show.[16]

The *Minxu ribao* 民吁日报 (people's outcry daily) of 24 September 1909 (Fig. 4) and the *Minli huabao* 民立画报 (*people's pictorial*) of 1911, also uses one set of familiar visual markers—large heads, for example—which, as we have seen above, can be traced back to famous *Punch* caricatures. *Shanghai Puck*, which

---

[12] See Maidment in this volume.

[13] For some of the reversals between colonisers and colonised see, for example, Prabhat Kumar, chapter From *Punch* to *Matʻvālā*: Transcultural Lives of a Literary Format, and Chaiti Basu, chapter The *Punch* Tradition in Late Nineteenth Century Bengal: From Pulcinella to Basantak and Pãcu as well as Wu and Hotwagner in this volume.

[14] Zhu, *Unpublished Lecture Notes*, 9.

[15] Ibid., 11.

[16] Cf. ibid., 13, Rudolf G. Wagner, "China 'Asleep' and 'Awakening'. A Study in Conceptualizing Asymmetry and Coping With It", *Transcultural Studies* 1 (2011): 4–135, Lehner, *Der Chinadiskurs*.

Epilogue

Fig. 3 One of China's earliest satirical magazines, the Hong Kong *Shijutu*, 1898

first appeared in 1918, also continues to make frequent and direct references to *Punch* as its source of inspiration.[17]

Many of the satirical magazines mentioned in this book, including those appearing in Europe, were marginal phenomena in the thriving world of publishing. Only *Punch*

Fig. 4 *Punch*–style illustrations in *Minxu ribao*, 24 September 1909

---

[17] See evidence in Wu's contribution in this volume.

and very few others may have been an exception.[18] Nevertheless, the almost Sisyphean acts (in face of suppression and censorship,) of producing ever new satirical magazines all over the world speak to their transcultural significance, regardless of how shortlived each of them may have been. They engaged globally in a satirical voice-over which often went unheard, or unanswered, but remained an ambient noise which only at certain times became audible enough so that it was heeded.

Brian Maidment points to many reasons why *Punch* did not remain marginal and became so successful in Britain. Some of these reasons have been used to explain its legacy beyond Britain throughout this volume. Yet, even those publications using exactly the same recipe as *Punch*, were not always equally fortuitous elsewhere. The China copy of *Punch*, called *China Punch*, published intermittently in Hong Kong in the 1860s and 1870s, and discussed by Christopher Rea, is a case in point: In studying the peculiar nature of *China Punch*, this epilogue argues that *China Punch* could not find a larger Chinese readership and thus could not be sustained in China. In this regard, *China Punch* was unlike some of the other satirical magazines discussed in this volume which took great pains—more or less successfully—to please their readers' minds and tastes and not to offend their conventions and assumptions by changing, adapting, and translating the *Punch* template.[19] *China Punch*, on the other hand, while donning a Chinese gown, never considered adapting to Chinese realities: in spite of the availability of a substantial Chinese readership capable of reading English-language copy, *China Punch* remained, throughout, a colonial endeavour.

Can *China Punch* nevertheless be considered to be the beginning of satirical media in China? Can [*China Punch*] be understood as a catalyst for the production of later Chinese-language satire magazines in China...? (and as is similarly argued by Peter Duus for a parallel development, the *Japan Punch*)? It has been the aim of this volume to start thinking about such asymmetries *within* cultural flows of (popular?) graphic satirical material and the asymmetries created *by* cultural flows of such material between Asia and Europe. *China Punch*, to which we will now turn again, constitutes a particularly attractive example to scrutinize these points.

Its cover relates very closely to the original *Punch* cover (see Paranjape, this volume, Fig. 3), which had remained unaltered for some 107 years, since Richard Doyle had first designed it in 1849. On the original cover, Mr Punch sits at a desk with a quill in his hand painting the British lion, the symbol of the British Kingdom. Toby, his pug dog, with ruff and huntsman's hat, sits somewhat haughtily on a pile of *Punch* volumes. There is a scroll with the number, the volume and date of publication of each issue. The image is framed by several elves, acrobats and jesters

---

[18] Cf. the presentation given at the *Punch* conference to be published in Lehner, *Der Chinadiskurs*.

[19] See Basu, Swarali Paranjape, chapter Crossing the Boundaries: *Punch* and the Marathi Weekly *Hindu Pañca* (1870–1909) and Marilyn Booth, chapters Insistent Localism in a Satiric World: Shaykh Naggār's 'Reed-Pipe' in the 1890s Cairene Press and What's in a Name? Branding *Punch* in Cairo, 1908 in this volume, for example.

who come gushing forth from two cornucopia on the bottom left and right which makes for a graceful appearance.[20]

The cover page of *China Punch* (see Rea, this volume, Fig. 2), when it resumed publication in November of 1872, not unlike that of the first edition, used throughout 1867–1868 (and discussed by Christopher Rea), offers interesting elements of 'sinification' to this template: Mr Punch, clearly marked by his ridiculously large nose, is seated on the left. He does not wear his characteristic striped outfit with jelly bag cap. Instead he sports a Chinese style gown and scholar's hat. Sitting across from him, as Toby does in the original, is a British (or Chinese?) lion,[21] looking somewhat like a crossbreed with a dragon. While the lion could be interpreted as a sign of British imperialism, in China he is the guardian of official halls and temples. And indeed, this lion is equipped with the 'ball' (here, a globe) that he plays with in Chinese iconography to calm his nerves.[22] The entire scene is framed, as was the original *Punch* cover. Yet here, the frame is not created by two cornucopias releasing an 'elastic band' of elves, acrobats and jesters, but, quite the contrary, by firm and sturdy bamboo scaffolding. The whole set-up with the bamboo poles looks like a stage for hand puppets and thus can be taken to allude to the theatrical origins of the *Punch* figure.

Suspended from the scaffolding is a rope on which a tiny Chinese worker in short-legged trousers, with a queue, and bare upper body is standing. His back is turned to the viewer, as he finishes hammering at the bamboo letters to make up the word 'CHINA' on the wall. The letters for 'PUNCH', on the other hand, are already suspended from the same rope below him. They are made up of one dragon for each letter, hanging down from the tightrope to form the word in a manner somewhat reminiscent of the original *Punch* cover in which a number of figures protruding from the cornucopia are playing around the letters making up the title word. However, unlike Toby, his Chinese-style substitute, the lion, is not sat on top of several volumes of *Punch*. Instead, Mr Punch rests one of his feet on one fat volume. At the back of his chair there are two large books containing his tricks of trade: one is titled *Wit*, the other *Hoax*. To the left and right there are two corresponding hanging scrolls, in the form of a Chinese traditional *duilian* 对联. A third scroll is put up horizontally in the middle. It parallels the painting of the British lion in the original *Punch* cover. The scrolls contain not Chinese writing, but Shakespearian quotes. Two of them, on the right and in the middle, are rolled up a bit to cover some of the writing, which, is vertically arranged to imitate Chinese practice. Yet, the writing on the scroll on the left proceeds from bottom to top in a

---

[20] Cf. the description by Ursula E. Koch, "*Le Charivari* (Paris), *Punch* (London) und *Kladderadatsch* (Berlin): Drei Satire-Journale zwischen Kunst und Journalismus," in *Europäische Karikaturen im Vor- und Nachmärz*, ed. Hubertus Fischer (Bielefeld: Aisthesis Verlag, 2006); 17–61; 50–51.

[21] Khanduri in this volume remarks on Dickens' vision of a similar change of animal (to Indian monkey) to indigenize Punch there.

[22] For the lion in Chinese thought, see Wolfram Eberhard, *Chinese Symbols* (London: Routledge, 1983), 164.

manner no Chinese text would ever be written. It reads: 'We do beseech thee, take it not amiss'. On the right, vertically, the text reads: 'If we offend, it is ... (with our goodwill)'.[23] The scroll in the middle reads:

> Take our good meaning, for judgement sits
> Five times in that, ere once in our five wits.

The theme of well-meant satire, which is played out in these texts, is well taken in view of the many cases of censorship that satirical journals were submitted to in China (and elsewhere).[24] It also points to the precarious situation of *Punch* in China, one that we will return to shortly.

As a whole, the page thus dons a Chinese gown. Yet, this superficial 'sinification' of the cover page picks up on nothing but stereotypes common in *Punch*'s visual repertoire: the bamboo scaffolding, the scrolls and vertical script, the plumed hat, the queue, the fierce-looking lion; they all are parts of a visual code signifying China, as it is familiar to European readers of the nineteenth century. Would such a cover page be inviting to a contemporary Chinese reader? We do not know. What it shows very clearly, however, are some of the asymmetrical relations between colonial subject and object. The colonised are seen as subordinate (as the man on the scaffolding) if potentially fierce and dangerous (as the tamed and ambiguous, British or Chinese lion).

This type of depiction, which shows at once condescension and respect (or fear), is even more pronounced in some of the discussions and depictions inside *China Punch*. Either in text or image, they deprive the Chinese of any refinement and honour. Yet at the same time, they never stop poking fun at the boisterous racism so obvious in such remarks. The position of the Hong Kong colonial government versus the home government, too, is one that is ambiguously represented. This makes one think that the 'colonial subject' is quite obviously involved in an equally asymmetrical relationship vis-à-vis his government as the colonial object vis-à-vis the colonisers. This fact puts colonial superiority into question at all times. Obviously, superiority is with those who are at home and at the British court, not those who are in the outports, such as Hong Kong. One image demonstrates this particularly clearly. It ridicules the very pompous behaviour that accompanies such 'superiority:' a man 'dressing for court' as the caption discloses, is seen bowing quite ridiculously in front of a mirror, thinking: 'What would they say in Hong Kong and Macao, if they should see me now?' (Fig. 5).

What Brian Maidment argues for *Punch* is true for *China Punch* as well: while it could be outspoken in its 'denunciation of social evils or political chicanery' its satire was often 'more defensive than confrontational', its humour 'both recognised and cathartically laughed away the fears and anxieties of its readers, reducing

---

[23] For the Shakespearian origins and sources of the quotes and a discussion of their significance, see Rea in this volume.

[24] On the question of censorship of these Chinese journals, see the contribution by WuI-wei in this volume.

Epilogue 433

Fig. 5 *China Punch*, 2 December 1872, 5–6

perceived dangers and threats to manageable proportions through the construction of a comic world turned upside down.'[25]

In spite of the fact that in this instance ridicule is dished out to both sides, the ultimate order of asymmetries remains clearly fixed. This is true of representations of the Chinese vis-à-vis their colonial 'superiors' as well. One image of two well-behaved Chinamen (see Fig. 6 in Rea's contribution to this volume) accompanies an article which reports a session of the legislative council in which it is discussed whether or not to admit Chinese members. The article entitled 'Our New Legislators' begins in characteristic manner:

> His Excellency said there was a matter—one of much interest—which he wished to lay before honorable members. The subject had been a good deal ventilated in the newspapers lately, and he might therefore at once say that he proposed shortly, with the approval of Her Majesty's Secretary of State for the Colonies, to introduce a few Chinese gentlemen upon the Council.
> Honorable Richard Go-it: Your Excellency said Chinese gentlemen, I think!
> Honorable Funnyas Riley wished to know where his Excellency was going to find them.
> His Excellency said he had made the acquaintance of a great many Chinese since he had been here, and he had formed a very favourable opinion of their characters.

The members of the council then acknowledge that in character the Chinese 'might be good enough but their habits were objectionable', and that it was 'not

---

[25] The citation appears in Maidment's chapter in this volume.

Fig. 6 *Punch*, vol. 62, 9 November 1872

pleasant to have a man sit next to you in the Council who once cleaned your shoes [...]'. The session comes to a close with a discussion about whether one should at least admit compradores, as they could be called 'refined' Chinese. This, however, also appears to be no solution, as one member points out: 'Well, really it is a Portuguese word and means House Steward'. The session finally ends in a great hubbub which mocks the conservative positions voiced by the majority against their own governor (and the home government): the council retires in quite some confusion, which is clear from the fact that not even the time of its adjournment is noted by the scribe (*China Punch*, 2 August 1873, p. 4). The accompanying image of the two extremely clean and demure Chinamen holding hands in a somewhat naive and innocent manner, provides a powerful visual counterpoint to the marked disorder among their 'superiors' as described in the text.

While the problem discussed and played out here can be made out to be a specific Hong Kong problem, and one of race, it comes down to the essential question of whether or not those who are considered to come from the lower echelons of society should be allowed to rise. And this question is discussed perennially in contemporary editions of the London *Punch* as well. There, one would find numerous examples of housewives and heads of household complaining that their servants are really just getting too independent and that helpers are no longer helpers as they should be, but have risen to unforeseen heights, or so they would think. In a first image, which may serve to illustrate this trend, the butler is asked by his master why he serves the same humble pie every day, to which the butler answers that, indeed, it is *not* the same: 1 day, it may be 'Geneva Humble Pie' and 'Berlin Humble Pie' the next (Fig. 6).

In the second image that illustrates this tendency of low outdoing high, the text explains: 'Latest from Dundee' (Where, readers will be happy to know, the Maid's Rebellion has revived in great force.) Mistress: 'I did not ring, Mary!' Mary: 'I know that, Mum; but as I was moping in the kitchen, I thought, I'd come and sit a bit with you!' (Fig. 7). Quite obviously, shifting asymmetries between high and low were troubling Britain's *haute société*, too.

But let us get back to China: similarly ambiguous in its message as the case just discussed, is a second example from the China Punch, (Fig. 8) which shows an extremely ugly Chinese presenting a roast pig to two rather fat but stylish wannabe British gentlemen. The text reads: 'The Major keeps his Birthday. Colonel: Come now, Major, send that infernal thing away, or I'm hanged if I don't place you under arrest. Major: Get along with you, Colonel. It's a Birthday Present from Bertie, and I tell you I'm going to eat it'. What 'That infernal thing' referred to by the Colonel is supposed to be, is not quite clearly defined. It could be the pig or the Chinese man carrying the pig on a platter. After all, he is very, very ugly. Yet, the two British men are not drawn in a very flattering manner either: they are extremely fat, for example, and thus constitute the typically deformed bodies so well-known from the pages of *Punch*.

There are many more elements which make *China Punch* a perfect offspring in the *Punch* family tradition: in studying perceptions of the 'Other' in *Punch* and its China copy, in terms of race, class and gender, it can be argued that it is indeed asymmetries of a very similar kind which are driving the satirical mode in both publications. Moreover, it is the ambiguities that these asymmetries leave with the reader that form the dynamic power of the satirical mode. Not unlike the original *Punch*, the *China Punch* also offers perspectives on a range of socio-cultural issues—for example, the effete posturing of fin-de-siècle intellectuals, the presumptuousness of the working classes, or the absurdity of the aspirations of women to public life. All of these remained as accessible as they were popular in *China Punch*

Fig. 7 *Punch*, vol. 62, 16 November 1872

(and other *Punch* versions).[26] After an early interest in inherited elements of Regency caricature, *Punch* apparently replaced the grotesquerie of eighteenth and early nineteenth century satire with a more fanciful kind of humour that delighted in parodying the pomposity and overstatement of public discourses of all kinds.

---

[26] See, for instance Chaiti Basu, Prabhat Kumar, and Eliane Ettmueller, chapter Abū Nazzaāra's Journey from Victorious Egypt to Splendorous Paris: The Making of an Arabic *Punch* in this volume.

Epilogue

Fig. 8 *China Punch*, 31 March 1872

As for another asymmetry just mentioned—that between men and women—both *Punch* and *China Punch* are dominated by discussions of the celebrated, notorious and newsworthy men of the day, thus making *Punch* and *China Punch* periodicals written largely by men about men and for a predominantly male audience.[27] In Hong Kong, this is almost a given, too: depictions of women were a rarity, as one *China Punch* image clearly illustrates: It shows a 'painful domestic incident' in which 'the unfortunate Charles will begin 'well, dear, if you will wear...'. She then interrupts him and says 'Oh, nonsense' (which it is). *China Punch* thus satirizes the same issue as *Punch* would, where women and their perennial interest in fashion are made fun of constantly. To give but one example, *Punch* publishes the following text under the title 'Astounding Intelligence':

---

[27] Cf. Richard Noakes, "Punch and comic journalism in mid-Victorian Britain," in *Science in the Nineteenth Century Periodical*, eds. Geoffrey Cantor et al. (Cambridge: Cambridge University Press, 2004), 91–122; 101. On the 'male' qualities of *Punch* generally, see also Maidment in this volume. Cf. also Laurel Brake and Marysa Demoor, eds., *The Dictionary of Nineteenth Century Journalism* (London: British Library, 2008), 327–328.

> Are we in Wonderland? We rub our mental eyes, and wildly stare and fancy that we must be dreaming. Still, here it is in actual print, like the ballad of the Jabberwock: Bonnets are still worn much the same in shape as those of last month. 'Can this really be true? Is it possible that ladies can consent for two whole months to wear their bonnets much the same in shape?' Variatio et mutabile semper in most affairs of life, the fair sex in none is more so than in fashionable matters. We shall be tempted to believe in the strong-mindedness of women, when we find them wearing bonnets of the same shape for a month or two together.[28]

Such satirical remarks about the 'fair sex' in London can be directly translated into those about the 'fair sex' in colonial Hong Kong. Indeed, Frank Hugget writes in a manner about the relationship between *Punch* and London of its time which could immediately be used to describe the situation for *China Punch* and Hong Kong (and *Hayal* and Istanbul as Elif Elmas suggests in her chapter, Teodor Kasab's Ottoman Adaptation of the Ottoman Shadow Theatre *Karagöz*): 'Nothing gives a better impression of what it was like to be living in London at that time than *Punch*. *Punch* alone, week after week, reproduces the feeling of the middle classes who lived in that age with all its current irritations, anxieties and absurdities. People do not live only at the peaks of history, though these are all registered in the pages; they live far more in the general trends of the immediate times, which can throb like some dull, depressing ache, or, in more open and expansive periods, can flow swiftly and clearly like an unimpeded stream. But people's transitory impressions of great events are always intermingled in daily life with an equivalent consciousness of the foibles, fads and fashions of the age. Life is experienced at many different levels simultaneously. To open any volume and to turn the pages, is to be transported back into those vanished times'.[29]

In spite of the cover page that might suggest so, and the fact that even as an English-language magazine it would have had a sizable Chinese readership, *China Punch* does not, in the end really 'go native'. This sets it apart from, for example, missionary publications, such as the *Shijutu*, which, as we have seen, would have done so (see Fig. 1), while also adhering to the *Punch* model (see Fig. 2). Thus, *China Punch* led only a marginal existence, regardless of the many implicitly positive, or at least ironical messages it conveys about China and the Chinese, and the many different levels of life in colonial Hong Kong which it recounts to the reader. While making fun of foreign residents in China as well as of Chinese, the magazine played out the asymmetries between colonial subject and colonial object as well as those between colony and home. Clearly, the asymmetries imposed upon the 'colonial object' in the pages of *China Punch* paralleled some of the dependencies between colonial subject (in China) and colonial power (in Britain) in historical experience. *China Punch*, therefore, is a transcultural product, but in half-gear, so-to-speak: as a very close English-language China copy of the original *Punch*, it features some of the rather more paradoxical shifts to be observed in the asymmetrical relations between the 'colonial subjects' speaking in *China Punch* and the 'colonial objects' it depicts.

---

[28] "Astounding Intelligence," *Punch* 62, 13 November 1872.

[29] Frank E. Hugget, *Victorian England as seen by Punch* (London: Sidgwick & Jackson, 1978), 50.

The colonised Chinese, on the other hand, do not strike back immediately with satire, but with some delay, when they themselves take up the *Punch* tradition around the turn of the century (see, I-Wei Wu's and Christopher Rea's chapters, Participating in Global Affairs: The Chinese Cartoon Monthly *Shanghai Puck* and 'He'll Roast All Subjects That May Need the Roasting': Puck and Mr Punch in Nineteenth Century China, in this volume). With regard to the asymmetries inherent in and caused by cultural flows, the *Punch* legacy in China illustrates that some of these particular power relations may at first be reified while being slowly undermined at the same time. Satire in the *Punch* tradition has helped this process enormously. Self-critical imagery and ambiguous argumentation in which text and image often say different, even contradictory things, further supports this phenomenon: in the hands of numerous younger 'cousins', the *Punch* tradition thus displayed its inherently transcultural nature.

Citing *Punch*: The Powers of Branding

Punch was a success: there is no doubting the centrality of *Punch* in shaping satirical journalism all over the world in the nineteenth century. In Peter Duus's formulation, for Japan, for example, 'the quick adoption of "*Punch* pictures" as a generic name for political cartoons confirms that the British magazine had an impact'.[30] Similar observations can be made for the other cases considered in this book. Yet, it was not the original *Punch* itself that was the global success. While it was 'available' almost everywhere, *Punch* the original, failed to establish a significant market in most of the countries under scrutiny here.[31] Instead, *Punch*, the template, became a branded and thus authoritative form for imagining asymmetries in local (as well as global) power politics.[32] *Punch*'s application was 'notional rather than genetic' as Marilyn Booth puts it.[33]

Punch became the label for a genre of politically interested satirical magazines, that distinctively engaged with contemporary attitudes and included ample illustrations. Not unlike the original, local *Punch* versions in Asia incorporated a branded satirical persona that served as the 'voice' or collective identity of the periodical and its contributors. Not unlike the original, Asian *Punch* versions displayed a mix of satire, travesty, invective and whimsy. They posed an internally focused critique of society but always within an internationalist, even cosmopolitan framework.[34] More often than not, they constructed an East-West or Oriental-Occidental dichotomy as they critiqued the imitation and acceptance of European

---

[30] See Peter Duus, chapter 'Punch Pictures': Localising *Punch* in Meiji Japan in this volume and passim.

[31] See the contributions by Khanduri, Booth and Wu.

[32] See Khanduri, chapter *Punch* in India: Another History of Colonial Politics? in this volume and, for availability, Kumar and others.

[33] See Booth, chapter What's in a Name? Branding *Punch* in Cairo, 1908 in this volume.

[34] See Duus, Wu, Hotwagner, Booth and others in this volume.

lifestyles in Asia; they highlighted the behaviour of girls and women and sustained a meta-commentary on problems of language, communication, reform, and the media: on newspapers, readerships, circulations, the economy of the print sector, and the viability of a (free and open) public sphere.[35] To use the label of *Punch*, then, was to engage a particular notion of solidarity with a broader community that went beyond class, gender, culture, and language: it stood for a particular type of critical journalism.

While most of the publications under scrutiny here question the actual reach, or the value, of their own satirical and critical presence, they, like the original *Punch*, are seen as the stock-in-trade for opposition: In a play discussed by Eliane Ettmueller, for example, the main character fights his oppressors with an 'English Punch' (*al-būnīyat al-Inklīzī*).[36] This political use of the original *Punch* is, as we have discussed above, at least to some extent, a projection: the Asian *Punch* versions analysed in this volume tend to be much more radically political and much less conservative than the original.[37] Accordingly, many of these could include images such as that from the *Shanghai Puck*, as discussed in I-Wei Wu's contribution, which depicts a cemetery for satirical (and other) papers that had been censored in preceding years.[38] Most of the histories of the *Punch* versions we have told here have involved issues of censorship and restriction, by either local or colonial governments. Still, for them to use the *Punch* style or the *Punch* label was a roundabout way of saying (radical) things that would otherwise—using a different (local) genre and format—be easily censored.

To use satire and label it *Punch* was one way of evading censorship, albeit not always successfully.[39] In Ritu Khanduri's words: 'The indigenous proprietors' insistence on being imitators of *Punch* added a new dimension for understanding the place of cultural forms, such as the cartoon, which was neither absolutely hard nor soft. Appropriating *Punch*, whether in the newspaper's title or its cartoon style implied a kinship that tested colonial officials' tools for critiquing a persuasive copy: It was a close call'[40] The use of *Punch* as a label seems to have offered the involved editors and journalists a possibility: power asymmetries might shift, after

---

[35] For these aspects see the chapters Participating in Global Affairs: The Chinese Cartoon Monthly *Shanghai Puck*, Insistent Localism in a Satiric World: Shaykh Naggār's 'Reed-Pipe' in the 1890s Cairene Press, Teodor Kasab's Ottoman Adaptation of the Ottoman Shadow Theatre Karagöz, and 'Punch's Heirs' between the (Battle) Lines—Satirical Journalism in the Age of the Russo-Japanese War of 1904–1905 by Wu, Booth, Elmas and Hotwagner in this volume.

[36] J. Sanua, *Rihla* 7, 2–4. For the political uses of *Punch* in India, see also Mitter, chapter *Punch* and Indian Cartoons: The Reception 2 of a Transnational Phenomenon in this volume.

[37] See especially Ettmueller and Hotwagner in this volume.

[38] See Wu, chapter Participating in Global Affairs: The Chinese Cartoon Monthly *Shanghai Puck* this volume, Fig. 3 (page 5 please adjust after typesetting).

[39] See contributions by Wu, Elmas, Ettmueller, Booth, Duus, Khanduri among others.

[40] See Khanduri, chapter *Punch* in India: Another History of Colonial Politics? in this volume. Addressing the proliferation of *Punch* versions in India she states (ibid.): 'This of course, led to intense official surveillance of comic newspapers and created an administrative need to detect embedded insurgency in comic newspapers. The vernacular cartoon became suspect; it still is as

all (even though, power does come less into its own in the 'virtual cosmopolis' than in actual encounters, as Partha Mitter reminds us).[41] And thus, the Asian *Punch* version was, almost literally, also imagined to write its critical audience into existence. It did so, in an extremely moralist and didactic tone (to ensure that, in the words of the original *Punch*, 'the world grows more civilized').[42]

Last but not least among the reasons for adopting the *Punch* label and engaging with the *Punch* legacy, using *Punch* also signalled the editors' aspirations: it constituted, at least in part, a hopeful gesture for desired success, both in terms of circulation figures and of geographic and social reach.[43] The original *Punch* reflects English life in general in its pages, but London always comes first. In the very same way, Hong Kong and China, Istanbul and the Ottoman Empire are linked globally and privileged locally on the pages of the Asian *Punch* versions, thus suggesting translocal, transnational, and transcultural connections of a special kind.[44] In other words: to use the *Punch* label was a branding move, signalling to readers that the particular journal's producers intended to include considerations that were rooted in the local but would go far beyond it. Asian *Punch* versions thus promised to present a lavish cosmopolitan abundance of image and text, albeit with local vision:[45] The use of the *Punch* label was convenient as it was on the one hand so adaptable and yet on the other clearly fixated in contemporary local *imaginaries*.

Translating Laughter: The Transcultural Wor(l)d(s) of Journalism

> We shall always play PUNCH, for we consider it best to be merry and wise—
> 'And laugh at all things, for we wish to know,
> What, after all, are all things but a show!'—*Byron*.[46]

This book was conceived because reading ten thousand *Puck*s and *Punch*es transculturally means dissecting and rewriting the pretensions of European power—a task that, as the above quote from Lord Byron's inaugural editorial

---

cultural historical material, hence its eclipsed history. While the British could appreciate *Punch* humour, the cartoons of the vernacular *Punch* versions did not seem to them a laughing matter'.

[41] See Mitter, chapter *Punch* and Indian Cartoons: The Reception 2 of a Transnational Phenomenon in this volume. For the question of whether or not virtual cosmopolitanism is, as Mitter argues, indeed not as dangerous as real, see Barbara Mittler, *A Newspaper for China? Power, Identity and Change in Shanghai's News-Media, 1872–1912* (Cambridge: Harvard University Press, 2004). I argue that the news media are powerful less by nature than by default: their perceived powers may make them powerful in spite of the fact that a 'virtual cosmopolis' can never *actually* throw a bomb or start a revolution.

[42] The citation is taken from the motto at the beginning of this *Epilogue*.

[43] Booth makes these observations for the *Cairo Punch*, but they are equally valid for many of the other publications discussed in this volume.

[44] See Elmas and Booth in this volume.

[45] See Wu, Hotwagner, Duus, Kandhuri, Mitter and Booth on the *Cairo Punch* in this volume.

[46] "The Moral of Punch", inaugural editorial, *Punch*, 17 July 17, 1841.

illustrates, *Punch* itself engaged in—or at least, pretended to. The story of satirical journalism or *Punch* in Asia has not been told in detail before and this volume is a first and modest attempt to address the 'eclipsed history' of the Asian *Punch* versions', as Ritu Khanduri calls it. Their neglect has been caused in part by an asymmetrical perception of the *Punch* phenomenon at large: if one's philosophical position is that imitation is but limitation, the publications under discussion here cannot fare well. What this volume attempts to show, however, is that Asia's *Punch* versions were in fact neither limited, nor 'mere imitations.'

The idea that there could have been some 'pure' or 'authentic' model of a genre (such as the satirical journal in the *Punch* tradition), available in Europe, that was then imported to the colony or elsewhere, is deeply flawed as this volume attempted to show. Each such genre must be examined, as Francesca Orsini suggests, 'so as to explain the particular social and cultural mediation it performs and the dialectical relationship it has with other genres at any given point in history'.[47] Taking a 'transcultural' perspective—which forfeits the notion of authenticity, or origin and copy—it is obvious that while *Punch* served as an inspiration and a legitimating force for satirical magazines published outside of Britain, it was considered an interlocutor, and a significant partner in a global satirical *imaginaire* which consisted not just of *Punch* (and *Puck*) but a thousand *Puck*s and *Punch*es that were in (intermittent) dialogue, exchange, even negotiation with each other.

Moreover, not only do the *Punch* versions react to *Punch* the London 'cousin', by borrowing its texts, images and styles, but *Punch* also responds to the *Punch* versions, even if it does so in a slightly condescending tone, which Marilyn Booth describes as 'speaking *at*', rather than 'speaking to.'[48] This is evident, for example, when *Punch* acknowledges the arrival of one of his 'cousins', the *Hindi Punch*:

> The Baron begs to acknowledge the fourth edition of Hindi Punch, just received from Bombay. Mr Punch, who traces his own origin back to prehistoric times when the pharaohs and such like moderns were neither born nor thought of, when all the world was young, as Mr Punch himself ever remains, is delighted to find his family so well represented and so highly popular in India as from this volume of Hindi Punch is evidently the case.[49]

Such interlocution suggests that it may be important to study the traffic in satirical journalism as more than a one-way process: not only was Asia appropriating *Punch*, Asia's *Punch* versions were not only acknowledged but occasionally also provided a pool of images and a topic of discourse in European

---

[47] Francesca Orsini, *Print and Pleasure: Popular Literature and Entertaining Fictions in Colonial North India* (Ranikhet: Permanent Black, 2009), 164.

[48] See Booth's contribution on 'the reed-pipe', chapter Insistent Localism in a Satiric World: Shaykh Naggār's 'Reed-Pipe' in the 1890s Cairene Press in this volume, 'If Mr Punch and Shaykh Joiner are not speaking to each other, they are in a sense speaking *at* each other in tracing local manifestations of the uneven yoking of their two social settings (among them, the very different circulations of their magazines)'.

[49] *Fifth Album of Cartoons* (Bombay: Hindi Punch Office, 1904).

satire magazines.[50] Even more significantly and as this volume has shown, the various *Punch* versions also speak to each other: the founder of 'Sar Punch' (*sarpanc*) (1909), for example, had briefly been a professor of Arabic and Persian in North India, and may have been directly inspired by the *Punch* versions he encountered there.[51] It is likely that *Punch* journalists all over the world, as Marilyn Booth suggests, 'learned of each other's work through the "peripheral" circulations of empire'.[52] And evidently, many of the journals under consideration in this book were not copying from the 'home front' at all. The *Tokyo Puck* would, for example, take drawings from the *Cairo Punch* rather than the London Punch.[53] The crisscrossing exchange of visuals and texts was far more complex than simple derivative models of original and copy would allow for.

Yet, in this complex networking we continually see signs of asymmetries. The practice of giving space to caricatures from a myriad of far-flung publications may suggest a meeting of different visual styles as well as political messages on equal terms. However, the cultural capital that went along with *Punch* the brand was reason enough for editors of the *Hindi Punch*, for example, to hold up with pride their much remoter relationship with the London *Punch* and eclipse their indebtedness to the Marathi *Hindu pañca*, which quite evidently seems to have been their immediate model.[54]

This book was also written to show why, ultimately, *Punch* the journal, as an imperial cultural product (or products like *China Punch* as its near equivalent) turned out to be unmarketable in Asia.[55] Its legacy could only develop when *Punch* traditions were adapted to particular regional and vernacular contexts and produced by local proprietors: and some, if not all of these vernacular *Punch* versions did find a market. The proliferation of multiple *Punch* versions, as we have argued, and their regional distribution shows that creative agency is to be found in what can no longer be called simply 'peripheral cultural space'.[56] It also shows that *Punch* itself is but a first among (almost) equals. By translating laughter, by creating satirical magazines for imaginary markets in several languages at the same time, bilingual, trilingual and more,[57] thus signifying the transcultural circulation of a visuality and a

---

[50] See, e.g. Lehner, *Der Chinadiskurs*.

[51] This is suggested by Booth in her chapter, What's in a Name? Branding *Punch* in Cairo, 1908, on the *Cairo Punch*. She follows Ritu G. Khanduri, "Vernacular Punches: Cartoons and Politics in Colonial India," *History and Anthropology* 20, no. 4 (December 2009): 459–86; 476.

[52] Booth on the *Cairo Punch*, chapter What's in a Name? Branding *Punch* in Cairo, 1908, 8 please adjust after typesetting.

[53] For this instance, see Booth on the *Cairo Punch*, chapter What's in a Name? Branding *Punch* in Cairo, 1908. A history of these many crisscrossing references is yet to be told.

[54] See Paranjape in this volume.

[55] See Booth and Khanduri in this volume.

[56] See Khanduri in this volume.

[57] See the contributions by Alok Rai, chapter The Possibility of Satire: Reading Pratap Narain Misra's **Brāhmaṇ**, 1883-1890, and Booth, Wu, and Hotwagner among others.

language of social and political satire; by playing with particular linguistic codes and registers, the *Punch* versions discussed in this book are deeply involved in the establishment and acknowledgement (if not the creation) of 'satirical universals' such as the Russian bear, the English lion, the militarist's fat belly, the divided globe, or simply the hugely blown up head. These symbols are therefore much more than simply traces of a singular London *Punch* legacy; they serve, in fact, the creation of a global satirical visual *imaginaire*. This is obvious from the possibility of using these elements in satire magazines all over the world and knowing with confidence that the audience will not only enjoy the play but, most importantly, grasp its serious polemical intent. In the end, it is a case of chicken or egg: while without *Punch*, its legacy—this global satirical *imaginaire*—may have looked rather different; without the *Punch* versions, the *Punch* legacy would never have attained global dimensions.

Thus to situate *Punch*, and the Asian *Punch* versions relationally, and emphasize their vertical, interconnected rather than their horizontal, hierarchical relations is to be able to perceive what would otherwise remain invisible: issues of agency in historical production, the interconnectedness of cultural spaces that are geographically far removed, and the affective as well as the effective and creative dimensions of coping with asymmetrical power relations.

Printed by Printforce, the Netherlands